The Principles of
Learning and Behavior

The Principles of
Learning and Behavior

MICHAEL DOMJAN

University of Texas at Austin

BARBARA BURKHARD

*State University of New York
at Stony Brook*

Brooks/Cole Publishing Company

Monterey, California

Brooks/Cole Publishing Company
A Division of Wadsworth, Inc.

Printed in the United States of America

10 9 8 7 6 5 4 3

Library of Congress Cataloging in Publication Data

Domjan, Michael, 1947–
    The principles of learning and behavior.

    Bibliography: p.
    Includes index.
    1. Learning, Psychology of.   2. Conditioned
response.   3. Behaviorism.   I. Burkhard,
Barbara, 1947–   . II. Title.
BF319.D65   150.19′43   81-10205
ISBN 0-8185-0466-8   AACR2

Subject Editor: *C. Deborah Laughton*
Manuscript Editor: *Rephah Berg*
Production Editor: *Fiorella Ljunggren*
Interior and Cover Design: *Victoria A. Van Deventer*
Illustrations: *Barbara Hack*
Typesetting: *Interactive Composition Corporation, Pleasant Hill, California*

To Paul,
Hannah,
and Jacob

Preface

From the early 20th century to the mid-1960s, the study of learning constituted the foundation of the study of psychology in North America. Prominent investigators of learning, such as Hull, Spence, Mowrer, Tolman, Miller, and Skinner, were considered prominent in the field of psychology as a whole rather than just major figures in a subspecialty. The thrust of the effort during this period was devoted to developing a general theory of behavior based on extensive laboratory investigation of a few specialized experimental situations. The findings derived from these investigations were used to construct theories of learning and behavior that were assumed to be applicable to a variety of species and situations. The concepts and findings were also used to construct models of abnormal behavior, personality, and the acquisition of special skills, such as language use. Students training in psychology were first taught the principles of learning and behavior even if they ended up specializing in some other area.

The field of psychology has changed dramatically during the last 15–20 years with the growth of such subdisciplines as cognitive psychology, psycholinguistics, physiological psychology, behavior genetics, and developmental psychology. The study of learning and behavior no longer has the dominant position it once had. Nevertheless, it remains a vital area of investigation addressed to certain fundamental aspects of how behavior is governed by environmental events. The contemporary study of learning and behavior is enriched by numerous new findings and new ways of thinking. Our basic ideas about the mechanisms of classical and instrumental conditioning have gone through profound changes during the past 15 years. In addition, the study of conditioning and learning is becoming better integrated with related investigations of the biological bases of behavior and studies of cognitive processes.

The purpose of our book is to introduce students to contemporary investigations of learning and behavior. We endeavor to emphasize the development of ideas rather than familiarize the student with all the relevant research and technical issues concerned with the design and conduct of experiments. The historical antecedents of ideas are presented insofar as they are important to the understanding of contemporary issues. However, we did not write a detailed historical account. Given the major changes that are taking place in the field, not all contemporary ideas about learning and behavior can be fully integrated with earlier findings. Nevertheless, we try to provide an integrated approach wherever possible. For example, recent information on biological constraints on learning is interwoven into the fabric of the presentation rather than discussed in a separate chapter divorced from the basic phenomena of conditioning.

To assist the student, we provide numerous examples of the major points in the text and include a glossary of key terms. Most of the research examples are drawn from animal experimentation. However, we frequently point out the potential relevance of the findings and concepts to the analysis of human behavior. In addition, we have felt free to rehearse certain ideas by pointing out analogous human situations. These extensions to human behavior should be treated as food for thought rather than as the outcome of definitive scientific reasoning.

The book is organized in a hierarchical fashion, with early chapters providing the foundation for information presented later. However, concepts are repeated as they come up in later chapters so that all the preceding chapters do not necessarily have to be read. The book begins with a statement of the basic elements of the behavioral approach to the study of psychology. Chapter 2 is devoted to a discussion of the structure of innate behavior. Information on innate behavior is presented early in the book because learning procedures are always superimposed on innate predispositions. Chapter 3 is devoted to a discussion of habituation and sensitization. These are the simplest and perhaps most pervasive phenomena involving behavior change and are also relevant to what happens in more-complex conditioning experiments. Chapters 4 and 5 discuss some old and many contemporary issues in classical conditioning. The basic concepts and theoretical foundations of the study of instrumental conditioning are presented in Chapter 6. Chapter 7 is devoted to a description of schedules of reinforcement, and theoretical issues concerning the mechanisms of reinforcement are discussed in Chapter 8. Chapters 9, 10, and 11 present, in order

of increasing complexity, procedures and phenomena that have been analyzed in terms of the interaction of classical and instrumental conditioning processes. Chapter 9 is devoted to a discussion of stimulus control and secondary reinforcement. Avoidance and punishment are discussed in Chapter 10, and Chapter 11 treats in a more general fashion theoretical and empirical issues concerned with the interaction of classical and instrumental conditioning processes. The last chapter, Chapter 12, describes recent and somewhat controversial research on cognitive processes in animal learning and behavior.

We are grateful to the many specialists who generously studied earlier drafts of the manuscript and offered invaluable suggestions for improvements. They include James V. Devine of the University of Texas at El Paso, Douglas S. Grant of the University of Alberta, Stewart H. Hulse of Johns Hopkins University, Steven F. Maier of the University of Colorado, Jack Marr of Georgia Institute of Technology, Susan Mineka of the University of Wisconsin, Michael E. Rashotte of Florida State University, J. E. R. Staddon of Duke University, and Harry Strub of the University of Winnipeg. Our revisions were also guided by helpful comments from classes at the University of Texas at Austin that used earlier drafts of the book. We would like to thank C. Deborah Laughton and others on the staff of Brooks/Cole Publishing Company for their encouragement and assistance in all phases of the project and Patty Ardies for typing most of the original manuscript as well as the seemingly endless revisions. We are also indebted to our families, friends, and students who stood by patiently while we concentrated on completing the book. Finally, we owe a special thanks to D. W. Tyler and Neil D. Kent, who started us in psychology, and Shepard Siegel, Howard Rachlin, Fredric Levine, and others who taught and advised us during our formative years in the field.

Michael Domjan
Barbara Burkhard

Credits

This page constitutes an extension of the copyright page.

Brief Contents

CHAPTER

ONE   **Introduction**   1

TWO   **The Organization of Innate Behavior**   21

THREE   **Habituation and Sensitization**   35

FOUR   **Classical Conditioning: Basic Concepts**   55

FIVE   **Classical Conditioning: Mechanisms**   86

SIX   **Instrumental Behavior: Foundations**   116

SEVEN   **Instrumental Behavior: Experimental Analysis**   143

EIGHT   **Reinforcement: Theories and Experimental Analysis**   168

NINE   **Signal Value in Instrumental Conditioning: Stimulus Control and Secondary Reinforcement**   195

TEN   **Aversive Control: Avoidance and Punishment**   237

ELEVEN   **Interactions of Classical and Instrumental Conditioning**   273

TWELVE   **Cognitive Aspects of Animal Behavior**   303

Glossary   337

References   352

Name Index   375

Subject Index   380

Contents

CHAPTER ONE

Introduction 1

Informal reflections about behavior 1
Disadvantages of informal reflections
about behavior 2
The behavioral approach to the study
of psychology 3
Historical antecedents of the behavioral
approach 6
    Cartesian dualism 6
    Historical developments in the study of the mind 7
    Historical developments in the study of reflexes 9
    Charles Darwin and the concept of evolution 10
    The behavioral approach viewed
    in historical context 11
Learning and the study of behavior 12
    The definition of *learning* 12
    Distinction between learning and other sources
    of behavior change 13
Use of animals in research on learning 14
    Practical advantages in the use of animals 14
    Conceptual advantages in the use of animals 15
    Laboratory animals and normal behavior 15
Significance of research on animal learning
for human behavior 16
    Analysis of nonlinguistic and emotional behavior 16
    Development of models of behavior 16
The behavioral approach and other aspects
of psychology 17
Behaviorism and you: The problem
of free will 18

Incompatibility of determinism and free will 19
Free will and the frame of reference 19
Determinism and social responsibility 19

CHAPTER TWO

The Organization of Innate Behavior 21

The concept of the reflex 22
The nature of response-eliciting stimuli 25
    Relational sign stimuli 26
    Supernormal sign stimuli 26
The role of feedback in elicited behavior 27
    Elicited behavior independent of feedback
    stimuli 27
    Presence or absence of the eliciting stimulus
    as feedback 28
    Responses elicited and guided by different
    stimuli 29
Elicited behavior and internal state 30
Elicited behavior and complex response
sequences 31
Concluding comments 34

CHAPTER THREE

Habituation and Sensitization 35

Effects of repeated stimulation:
Three examples 35

Sucking in human infants   35
Startle response in rats   36
Mobbing in chaffinches   37
The concepts of habituation and sensitization   38
Adaptiveness and pervasiveness of habituation
and sensitization   38
Neural analysis of habituation and sensitization   39
Other experimental situations   42
Characteristics of habituation and sensitization   45
Time course of habituation and sensitization   45
Stimulus specificity of habituation and
sensitization   47
Effects of strong extraneous stimuli   48
Effects of stimulus intensity and frequency   48
Changes in complex emotional responses   49
The opponent-process theory of motivation   49
Mechanisms of the opponent-process theory   50
Examples of opponent processes   51
Concluding comments   53

CHAPTER FOUR

**Classical Conditioning: Basic
Concepts   55**

Pavlov and the early years of classical
conditioning   56
The classical-conditioning paradigm   58
Experimental situations   59
Eyeblink conditioning in rabbits   59
Fear conditioning   60
Sign tracking   62
Taste-aversion learning   64
Possible excitatory conditioning procedures   65
Measurement of the conditioned response   66
Effectiveness of the excitatory conditioning
procedures   67
Control procedures in classical conditioning   68
Classical conditioning and the signal relation
between CS and US   69
Examples of signal relations   69
CS-US contingency   70
Inhibitory conditioning   71
Procedures for inhibitory conditioning   72
Measuring conditioned inhibition   74
Extinction   77
Extinction and habituation   78
What is learned in extinction   79
Classical conditioning outside the laboratory   80
Digestion   80
The milk-letdown reflex   81

Learning of emotional responses   82
Psychotherapy   83
Concluding comments   84

CHAPTER FIVE

Classical Conditioning: Mechanisms   86

How to choose conditioned and unconditioned
stimuli   86
Initial response to the stimuli   86
The concept of biological strength   87
Novelty of conditioned and unconditioned
stimuli   89
CS and US intensity   90
CS-US relevance, or belongingness   90
How conditioned and unconditioned stimuli
become associated   94
Two views of the acquisition process   94
The blocking effect   95
The Rescorla/Wagner model of conditioning   97
What is learned in classical conditioning?   103
The stimulus-substitution model   104
The preparatory-response model   108
The compensatory-response model   109
The conditioned stimulus and the form of the
conditioned response   111
The conditioned response as an indicator of learned
associations   113
The conditioned response as an interaction between
conditioned and innate behavioral processes   114
Concluding comments   115

CHAPTER SIX

**Instrumental Behavior:
Foundations   116**

Definition and types of instrumental
contingencies   117
The instrumental contingency   117
Types of instrumental contingencies   117
Instrumental behavior in the laboratory: Problems
and approaches   121
Preliminary problems   121
Thorndike and the law of effect   122
Instrumental behavior and the study of
learning   123
Operant behavior   127
Experimental analysis of instrumental behavior:

Preliminary considerations   131
    Subject variables   132
    Response variables   137
    Reinforcer variables   140
Concluding comments   141

CHAPTER SEVEN

**Instrumental Behavior:
Experimental Analysis   143**

Delay of reinforcement   144
Simple schedules of intermittent
reinforcement   145
    Ratio schedules   146
    Interval schedules   147
    Comparison of ratio and interval schedules   150
Response-rate schedules of reinforcement   151
Concurrent schedules: The study of response
choice   152
    Measures of response choice   154
    The matching law   154
    Matching and maximizing rates of
    reinforcement   157
Concurrent chained schedules: The study of
complex choice   159
Extinction   163
    Effects of extinction procedures   163
    Determinants of extinction effects   164
    Mechanisms of the partial-reinforcement extinction
    effect   165
Concluding comments   167

CHAPTER EIGHT

**Reinforcement: Theories and
Experimental Analysis   168**

What is the effective feature of
instrumental-conditioning procedures?   169
    Correlation and contiguity   169
    Cause and effect as an epistemological problem   172
What makes reinforcers reinforce?   175
    Theories involving biological motivating forces   176
    Biological homeostasis and drive reduction   176
    Reinforcement and the sources of motivation   177
    Brain stimulation: Reinforcement and
    motivation   178
    Theories involving behavioral homeostasis   181

Premack's theory of reinforcement   181
    The deprivation hypothesis   186
    Parameters of time allocation   187
    Multiple-response approaches   188
Reinforcement as response selection   191
    Staddon and Simmelhag's superstition
    experiment   191
    The evolutionary model of behavior   192
Concluding comments   194

CHAPTER NINE

**Signal Value in Instrumental
Conditioning: Stimulus Control and
Secondary Reinforcement   195**

Stimulus control of instrumental behavior   197
    Differential responding and stimulus
    discrimination   197
    Stimulus generalization   199
    Classical conditioning and instrumental behavior:
    The pairing hypothesis   202
    The environment as viewed from the subject's
    perspective   203
    Effects of past experience on stimulus control   205
    What is learned in discrimination training?   212
    Effects of intradimensional discrimination
    training   216
    Control by elements of a compound stimulus   221
    Applications of stimulus control: Self-control   226
Secondary reinforcement   227
    Three functions of secondary reinforcers   227
    Laboratory analyses of secondary
    reinforcement   228
    Applications of secondary reinforcement: Token
    economies   235
Concluding comments   235

CHAPTER TEN

**Aversive Control: Avoidance and
Punishment   237**

Avoidance behavior   237
    Origins of the study of avoidance behavior   238
    Two-process theory of avoidance   241
    Experimental analysis of avoidance behavior   242
    Alternative theoretical accounts of avoidance
    behavior   253
    The avoidance puzzle: Concluding comments   258

Punishment   258
   Experimental analysis of punishment   259
   Theories of punishment   266
   Use of punishment outside the laboratory   270

CHAPTER ELEVEN

**Interactions of Classical and
Instrumental Conditioning   273**

Role of instrumental reinforcement in
classical-conditioning procedures   274
   The omission control procedure   274
   Conditioned-response modifications of the US   276
Role of classical conditioning in
instrumental-conditioning procedures   278
   The r_g-s_g mechanism   278
   Concurrent measurement of instrumental behavior
   and classically conditioned responses   284
   Modern two-process theory   288
   Role of response interactions in the effects of
   classically conditioned stimuli on instrumental
   behavior   292
   Discriminative-stimulus properties of classically
   conditioned states   297
Concluding comments   302

CHAPTER TWELVE

**Cognitive Aspects of Animal
Behavior   303**

Cognitive aspects of classical conditioning   305
   S-R versus S-S learning   305
   Evidence for S-S learning from conditioning with
   lights and tones   306
   The US representation as a determinant of the
   conditioned response   307
Memory mechanisms in animal behavior   308
   Short-term, or working, memory   309
   Disruption and facilitation of memory   317
   Interrelations of learning and memory   323
Complex cognitive processes in animals   326
   Serial-pattern learning   326
   Concept formation in animals   330
   Teaching language to chimpanzees   332
Concluding comments   336

Glossary   337

References   352

Name Index   375

Subject Index   380

The Principles of
Learning and Behavior

CHAPTER ONE

Introduction

The goal of Chapter 1 is to introduce students to the study of learning and behavior and the method of investigation used in this field. Modern experiments on learning are based on the behavioral approach to the study of psychology. The chapter describes the behavioral approach and its historical antecedents and contrasts the behavioral approach to other strategies used in the study of psychology. Because numerous experiments on learning have been performed with animal subjects, the chapter also discusses the rationale for using animals in research. Finally, the relevance of the behavioral approach and animal research to human behavior is discussed.

People have always been interested in understanding their own and others' behavior. This interest is much more than idle curiosity. Because we live in a complex society, many aspects of our lives are governed by the actions of others. How much you get paid in your work depends on what your boss decides to give you. Whether your home life is pleasant or unpleasant depends on how accommodating or hostile your housemates are. Whether you get admitted to college depends on the decision of an admissions officer. Whether you get to school on time depends on traffic and how well your car was repaired the last time you had it in the shop.

Because we depend a great deal on other people in nearly every aspect of our lives, it is important for us to be able to predict how others will behave. Life would be unbearable if you could not predict when your mother was about to scold you, when your classes were to be held, and when the bus would arrive and how long it would take to get you home or if the grocery checker were as likely to hit you as to ring up your groceries. Much of our interest in behavior is motivated by a desire to better predict the actions of others.

Informal reflections about behavior

There are many possible approaches to understanding and predicting behavior, ranging from the reading of tea leaves to scientific observation. Everyone probably adopts certain unique strategies in figuring out why others act as they do. However, informal reflections about behavior often share certain common features. First, in the absence of specific training in psychology, people who try to figure out what makes someone do certain things are likely to think about how they themselves would act in similar situations. That is, by reflecting on one's own reasons for doing something, one tries to gain insight into the reasons others act as they do. This method of reaching understanding about behavior is called **introspection.*** For most of human history, introspection provided the primary means of gaining information about behavior. However, informal introspection is no longer used in systematic investigations of behavior. Many areas of psychology have abandoned the use of introspection altogether. In other areas, introspection is used only under highly restricted and controlled circumstances. For example, a subject may be asked to respond to a carefully worded questionnaire item or to make a judgment about a stimulus presented in a laboratory situation.

In addition to using informal introspection as their primary method for obtaining insights into behavior, people not trained in psychology are likely to attribute actions to forces within the actors. That is, behavior is assumed to be caused by internal factors, such as the person's free will or wishes. If we see someone running toward a bus stop, we are likely to explain this by assuming that the person wants to catch the bus. If one of our friends spends a great deal of time studying, we interpret this by concluding that he or she wants to get A's in school. Internal motivation is also frequently used to explain the behavior of animals. If a dog stands facing the door, we are likely to explain this by saying that it wants to go out. If a cat jumps on the kitchen counter when dinner is being prepared, we are likely to conclude that it wants to steal pieces of food.

A third common characteristic of informal reflections about behavior is that they are stated in terms of large and complex units of behavior. For example, when we say that someone is in

love or is angry, we are referring to a great many activities. Being in love may involve making frequent phone calls to the loved one, not paying close attention to other people, eagerly anticipating meetings with the loved one, buying gifts, being much more careful than usual about one's grooming, and other behaviors. Similarly, many responses are involved in being angry. An angry person may shout, threaten people, throw things, drive too fast, or engage in physical aggression.

Disadvantages of informal reflections about behavior

Informal reflections have not contributed much to the understanding of behavior, because of their reliance on unsystematic introspection, their focus on internal causes, and their consideration of large and complex units of behavior. Each of these aspects of the informal approach has certain shortcomings.

Unsystematic introspection is often not very useful in furthering the understanding of behavior because people are generally not very skillful at accurately interpreting their own behavior. In addition, introspective contemplation may distract people from focusing on the behavior that actually occurs. People are often self-serving in the analysis of their own behavior. An overweight person may report not eating frequent snacks although he or she often eats between meals. A husband with marital difficulties may regard himself as a model spouse who is being ignored by his wife, when in fact he rarely compliments her or pays attention to her. Parents may think of themselves as very much interested in what their teenagers are doing, even though they may inquire about these activities but once or twice a week. Often the task of a therapist is to get past such self-serving introspective accounts of behavior and teach people to pay closer attention to what they actually do. For example, the overweight per-

---

*Terms printed in **boldface** type are defined in the Glossary, which follows Chapter 12.

son may be asked to make a note in a diary each time he or she eats something.

The focus on internal sources of motivation in the informal approach to the study of behavior has two disadvantages. First, the internal cause of an act is often merely inferred from the behavior we are trying to explain, so that the "explanation" tells us nothing new. For example, suppose that you see a stranger running toward a bus stop. If you say that he is running because he wants to catch the bus, you are inferring the cause of the behavior (wanting to catch the bus) from the behavior you are trying to explain (running). There may be no evidence that the person is trying to catch the bus independent of his running. Therefore, we do not gain any further insight into the behavior from saying that it occurs because he is trying to catch the bus. An explanation of this type is called a **circular explanation.** The only evidence for circular explanations is the event being explained.

The second shortcoming of focusing solely on internal causes of behavior is that in experimental attempts to prove the existence of such internal motives, the assumption that internal causes exist may become unnecessary. Consider the example of the man running toward the bus stop. For us to prove that he is running because he wants to catch the bus, we would have to somehow manipulate his wish to do so. We could do this in several ways. One simple way would be to tell him that we would give him $100 if he caught the bus. This would presumably create the appropriate internal motivation, and he would run toward the bus stop. However, the best explanation of his running would then be that we were paying him. To add that he wanted to catch the bus would not provide us with any further insights into his behavior. The postulation of internal motives or processes is often important in scientific analyses of behavior. However, internal processes used in scientific analyses are much more precisely defined than those used in informal reflections

about behavior. Furthermore, they are related to observable events in ways that increase our understanding of behavior rather than just restate the obvious.

The third characteristic of informal analyses of behavior, the focus on large, complex behavioral units, sometimes also hampers understanding of behavioral processes. Human experiences such as love (broadly defined) are very complex and are likely to be determined by a multiplicity of factors. Before one can gain much insight into such complicated psychological processes, one has to define and analyze their components. Simple behavior patterns are presumably governed by less complicated mechanisms, which should be easier to discover. The knowledge gained from the investigation of elementary responses can then be used to guide the study of more complex behavioral systems.

The behavioral approach to the study of psychology

As we have seen, the overall problem with informal reflections about behavior is that in actuality they rarely lead to meaningful insights. The approach to the study of behavior to be described in this book differs from informal reflections in several important respects. It does not rely on introspection, does not attribute actions solely to internal sources of motivation, and focuses on small rather than large and complex units of behavior. We characterize this approach as *behavioral* to emphasize that the primary object of the study is the behavior of organisms.

The method of investigation that provides the foundation of behavioral studies is the same as that used in natural sciences, such as biology, chemistry, and physics. Basically, behavioral studies are concerned with only those aspects of behavior that can be publicly observed so that the observations can be verified by anyone who wishes to do so. To aid in the collection of data, experiments are often done with automated recording devices, such as movie or videotape cameras or microswitches that record every time an animal moves some aspect of its environment. One common experimental situation, for example, is shown in Figure 1.1. The apparatus shown is used to study the pecking behavior of pigeons and other birds. Each time the bird pecks at the response key, it displaces the key slightly, and the displacement is automatically recorded on counters, chart paper, or some other device.

In the interest of studying only those aspects of psychology that can be observed in a publicly verifiable fashion, behavioral investigations have often been limited to observable responses. Many experiments have involved measuring the actions and movements of animals. Other responses that can be objectively measured are more physiological in nature. Some experiments have involved, for example, measuring salivation, blood sugar level, brain electrical activity, or heart rate. Behavioral experiments traditionally have not addressed such topics as thinking. We will not be concerned with how people come up with ideas, how they abstract information from printed letters, how

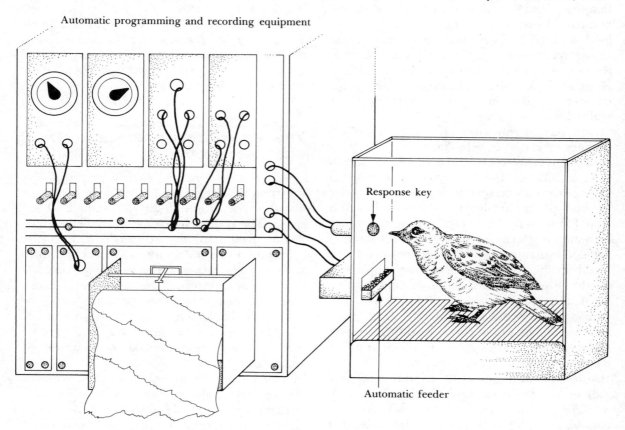

Automatic programming and recording equipment

Response key

Automatic feeder

Figure 1.1. Apparatus for the study of key pecking in pigeons and other birds. The subject is placed in a small enclosure with a response key. Each time the bird pecks at the response key, it displaces the key slightly, and the displacement is automatically recorded on counters, chart paper, or some other device.

they remember things, or how they reason and figure out solutions to problems. Rather, the behavioral approach focuses on the causes of motor and emotional responses: how we learn to get around in our environment, how we learn proper table manners, and why we like certain experiences, such as playing baseball. This book will not discuss, for example, what your thought processes are in solving a math problem. However, it will discuss why you study your math assignments, why you attend math classes, and why you may dislike mathematics.

A second important difference between behavioral investigations and informal reflections about behavior is that the behavioral approach does not look for causes of behavior solely inside the organism. Instead, a fundamental assumption is that organisms adjust their behavior to meet the demands of the environment. How they go about doing this often depends on motivation and other internal processes. However, internal processes are viewed as making the individual more (or less) responsive to certain external stimuli, not as being the sole cause of a particular behavior. Thus, animals are more responsive to food-related stimuli when they are hungry and are more sensitive to members of the opposite sex when their hormonal state makes them sexually receptive. This focus on the external environment as a cause of behavior makes explanations of behavior easy to prove or disprove experimentally. For example, if we decide that the reason someone is running toward a bus stop may be that the bus is quickly approaching, we can easily test this idea by looking to see what the person does when the bus is removed from the situation or made to turn away.

Some people believe that if you study only actions that are controlled by the external environment, you are limiting yourself to rather uninteresting aspects of behavior. According to this idea, behavior that occurs in response to external stimuli is reflexive, and reflexes are viewed as simple, automatic, and invariant reac-

tions to specific eliciting stimuli. Thus, it is assumed that a behavioral analysis cannot consider the unpredictability, flexibility, and complexity of more interesting aspects of human and animal behavior. This view is unjustified for two reasons. First, studying only responses that are controlled by the external environment does not limit the investigations to reflexive behavior. We will also be concerned with goal-directed behavior, such as searching for food. Goal-directed behavior is not an invariant, reflexive response to a specific eliciting stimulus. Rather, it is more importantly governed by stimuli signaling the nature and location of the sought-after goal (such as food). Second, reflexive behavior is not necessarily simple, automatic, and invariant. The complex emotional reactions you experience when you listen to a moving piece of music or watch a good movie are reflexive, but they are very different from simple reflexes such as jerking of the leg when the knee is tapped or constriction of the pupil in bright light. Further, many reflexes do not occur every time the appropriate eliciting stimulus is presented, and one can learn to make reflexive responses to new stimuli. One of the goals of this book is to illustrate the richness, complexity, and variability of behavior that occurs in response to external environmental events.

Finally, unlike informal reflections, the behavioral approach is typically concerned with small units of behavior. In fact, many behaviorally oriented investigations of complex psychological processes begin with the definition of a restricted class of responses that is to be considered indicative of the processes of interest. For example, food gathering in rats may be defined in terms of how often they press a lever for a food reward. Aggression may be defined in terms of how often monkeys bite a hose when aversively stimulated, and fear may be defined in terms of how fast rats run to avoid shock. The scientific study of behavior, of course, can be applied to more complex forms of behavior as well. However, the bulk of the research has not been of this sort.

Historical antecedents of the behavioral approach

Cartesian dualism

The behavioral approach to the study of psychology can be traced to the French philosopher René Descartes (1596–1650). Before Descartes, the common belief was that human behavior was entirely determined by conscious intent and free will. People's actions were not thought to be controlled by external stimuli or mechanistic natural laws. What someone did was presumed to be the result of his or her deliberate intention. Descartes took exception to this view of human nature because he recognized that many things people do are in fact automatic reactions to external stimuli. However, he was not prepared to abandon altogether the idea of free will and conscious control of one's own actions. He therefore formulated a dualistic view of human behavior known as Cartesian **dualism.** According to this view, there are two aspects of human behavior. One set of actions are involuntary and occur in response to external stimuli. These actions are called **reflexes.** Another aspect of human behavior involves voluntary actions which do not have to be triggered by external stimuli and

which occur because of the person's conscious choice to act in a certain way.

The details of Descartes' dualistic view of human behavior are diagramed in Figure 1.2. Let us first consider the mechanisms of involuntary behavior. Stimuli in the environment are detected by the person's sense organs. The sensory information is then relayed to the brain through nerves. From the brain, the impetus for action is sent through nerves to the muscles that create the involuntary response. Several aspects of this system are noteworthy. Stimuli in the external environment are seen as the cause of all involuntary behavior. These stimuli produce involuntary responses by way of a neural circuit that includes the brain. However, only one set of nerves is involved. Descartes assumed that the same nerves transmitted information from the sense organs to the brain and from the brain down to the muscles. This circuit, he believed, permitted rapid reactions to external stimuli, as when you quickly withdraw your finger from a hot stove.

Descartes assumed that the involuntary mechanism of behavior was the only one available to animals. According to this view, all of animal behavior occurs as reflex responses to external stimuli. Descartes did not believe that animals had free will or were capable of voluntary, conscious actions. Free will and voluntary behavior were considered to be uniquely human attributes. This superiority of humans over animals existed because only human be-

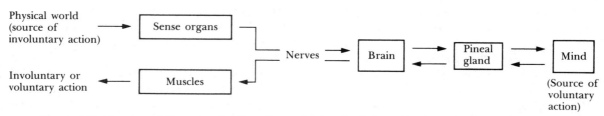

Figure 1.2. Diagram of Cartesian dualism. Events in the physical world are detected by sense organs. From here the information is passed along to the brain. The brain is connected to the mind by way of the pineal gland. Involuntary action is produced by a reflex arc that involves messages sent first from the sense organs to the brain and then from the brain to the muscles. Voluntary action is initiated by the mind, with messages sent to the brain and then the muscles.

ings were thought to have a mind, or soul. The mind was assumed to be a nonphysical entity. However, if the mind, or soul, is not physical, how can it generate the physical movements involved in voluntary behavior? Descartes believed that the mind was connected to the physical body by way of the pineal gland in the brain. Because of its connection to the brain, the mind could be aware of and keep track of involuntary behavior. Through this mechanism the mind could also initiate voluntary actions. Because voluntary behavior was initiated in the mind, its occurrence could be independent of external stimulation.

The mind/body dualism introduced by Descartes was followed by two intellectual traditions. One of these involved discussions about what is in the mind and how the mind works. Because the mind is not considered a physical entity, one cannot discover where the mind is located or any of its characteristics by dissecting the body or conducting some other kind of careful physical investigation. Therefore, the study of the mind was carried out by the method of introspection. The thinkers involved were philosophers rather than experimental scientists. Nevertheless, some of their ideas were important to the foundation of a scientific study of human behavior. The second intellectual tradition has been concerned with the mechanisms of reflexive behavior. Because reflexes are produced entirely by external stimuli acting on body organs, the study of reflexes has been conducted using the methods of direct observation and experimentation.

Historical developments in the study of the mind

As we noted above, one set of issues that concerned philosophers involved questions about what is in the mind and how the mind works. Descartes had some things to say about both these questions. Because Descartes thought the mind was connected to the brain by way of the pineal gland, he believed that some of what is in

the mind came from sense experiences. However, he also believed that some of the contents of the mind were innate and existed in all human beings independent of worldly experience. He believed that all human beings were born with certain ideas, including the concept of God, the concept of self, and certain fundamental axioms of geometry (such as the fact that the shortest distance between two points is a straight line). The philosophical approach that assumes we are born with innate ideas about certain things is called **nativism.**

Some philosophers after Descartes took issue with the nativist position. The British philosopher John Locke (1632–1704), for example, believed that all the ideas people had were acquired directly or indirectly through experiences after birth. He believed that human beings were born totally innocent of any preconceptions about the world. The mind was considered to start out as a clean slate (*tabula rasa*, in Latin), to be gradually filled with ideas and information as the person had various sense experiences. This philosophical approach to the question of what the mind contains is called **empiricism.** Empiricism was accepted by a group of British philosophers who lived from the 17th to the 19th century and who came to be known as the British empiricists.

The nativist and empiricist philosophies differed not only on what the mind was assumed to contain but also on how the mind was assumed to operate. Descartes believed that the mind did not function in a predictable and orderly manner according to discoverable rules or laws. One of the first to propose an alternative to this view was the British philosopher Thomas Hobbes (1588–1679). Hobbes accepted the distinction between voluntary and involuntary behavior stated by Descartes and also accepted the notion that voluntary behavior was controlled by the mind. However, unlike Descartes, he believed that the mind operated just as predictably and lawfully as reflex mechanisms. More specifically, he proposed that voluntary behavior was governed by the pursuit of pleasure and the avoidance of pain. Thus, functions of the mind were not determined by reason but by a principle of hedonism. Whether or not the pursuit of pleasure and the avoidance of pain were laudable or desirable was not an issue for Hobbes. Hedonism was simply a fact of life. As we shall see, this conception of behavior has remained with us in one form or another to the present day.

According to the British empiricists, another important aspect of how the mind works involved the concept of associations. Recall that empiricism assumes that all ideas originate from sense experiences. But how do our experiences of various colors, shapes, odors, and sounds allow us to arrive at more complex ideas? Consider, for example, the concept of a car. If someone says the word *car,* you have an idea what the thing may look like, what it is used for, and how you might feel if you sat in it. Where do all these ideas come from just given the sound of the letters *c, a,* and *r*? The British empiricists proposed that simple sensations were combined into more complex ideas by associations. Because you have heard the word *car* when you saw a car, considered using one to get to work, or sat in one, associations may have become established between the word *car* and various aspects of cars. The British empiricists considered such associations to be very important in their explanation of how the mind works. Therefore, they devoted considerable effort to detailing the rules of associations.

The British empiricists accepted two sets of rules for the establishment of associations, one primary and the other secondary. The primary rules were originally set forth by the ancient Greek philosopher Aristotle. He proposed three principles for the establishment of associations—contiguity, similarity, and contrast. Of these, the contiguity principle had been the most prominent in considerations of associations. It states that if two events repeatedly occur together, they will become associated. Once this association has been established,

the occurrence of one of the events will evoke a memory of the other event. The similarity and contrast principles state that two things will become associated if they are similar in some respect or have some contrasting characteristics (one might be strikingly tall and the other strikingly short, for example). The various secondary laws of associations were set forth by the empiricist philosophers. Thomas Brown (1778–1820), for example, proposed that a number of factors influence the formation of associations, including the intensity of the sensations and the frequency and recency of their pairing. In addition, whether one event becomes associated with another was considered to depend on the number of other associations in which each event was already involved and the similarity of these past associations to the current one being formed.

The British empiricists discussed rules of associations as a part of their philosophical discourse. They did not perform experiments to determine which rules were correct and which ones were incorrect or the circumstances in which one rule was more important than another. Empirical investigation of the mechanisms of associations did not begin until the pioneering work of the 19th-century German psychologist Hermann Ebbinghaus (1850–1909). Ebbinghaus invented **nonsense syllables** to use in his experiments. The nonsense syllables were meaningless three-letter combinations (a consonant followed by a vowel and another consonant) so that their meaning could not influence how they were learned. Ebbinghaus presented lists of these nonsense syllables to himself and measured his ability to remember the syllables under various experimental conditions. With this general method he was able to answer experimentally such questions as how the strength of an association improves with increased training, whether syllables that appear close together in a list are associated more strongly with one another than syllables that are farther apart, and whether a syllable becomes more strongly associated with the next one on the list than with the preceding one.

Historical developments in the study of reflexes

The concept of reflex action, introduced by Descartes, greatly advanced our understanding of behavior. However, Descartes was mistaken in his assumptions about how reflexes are produced. He believed that sensory messages going to the brain and motor messages going to the muscles traveled along the same nerves. The nerves were considered to be hollow tubes. The pineal gland was thought to release a substance called "animal spirits," which flowed down the tubes and entered the muscles, causing them to swell and create a movement. Finally, Descartes considered all reflexive movements to be innate and to be fixed by the anatomy of the organism.

Experimental observations after Descartes showed that he was wrong about the anatomy of the reflex arc and the mechanism of neural conduction. Later research also indicated that not all reflex responses are innate. The anatomy of the reflex arc was established in experiments performed by Charles Bell (1774–1842) in England and François Magendie (1783–1855) in France. They discovered that separate nerves are used to transmit sensory information from sense organs to the central nervous system and motor information from the central nervous system to muscles. If a sensory nerve is cut, the animal remains capable of muscle movements, and if a motor nerve is cut, the animal remains capable of registering sensory information. Establishing the mechanisms of neural conduction involved much more extensive experimentation. The idea that animal spirits were involved in neural transmission was disproved soon after the death of Descartes. In 1669 Swammerdam (1637–1680) showed that mechanical irritation of a nerve is sufficient to produce a muscle contraction. Thus, infusion of animal spirits from

the pineal gland was not necessary. In other studies Francis Glisson (1597–1677) demonstrated that muscle contractions are not produced by a swelling of the muscle by the infusion of some fluid, as Descartes thought. Glisson had people submerge one arm in water and observed that the water level did not change when they were asked to make a muscle contraction. Such experiments indicated that neural conduction did not occur by the mechanisms Descartes proposed. However, positive evidence of what was involved in neural conduction had to await the great advances that occurred in the understanding of electricity and chemistry in the 19th century. According to contemporary thinking, neural conduction involves a combination of chemical and electrical events.

Better understanding in the 19th century of the physiological processes responsible for reflexive behavior was accompanied by a liberalization of the restricted role of reflexes in the explanation of behavior. Descartes and most philosophers after him assumed that reflexes were responsible only for simple reactions to stimuli. The energy in a stimulus was thought to be translated directly into the energy of the elicited response by the neural connections. The more intense the stimulus, the more vigorous the resulting response. This view of reflexes is consistent with many casual observations. If you touch a stove, the hotter the stove is, the more quickly you withdraw your finger. However, reflexes can also be more complicated.

Two Russian physiologists, Sechenov (1829–1905) and Pavlov (1849–1936), were primarily responsible for extending the concept of reflexes to explain more complex behaviors. Sechenov proposed that in some cases the effect of a stimulus is not to elicit a reflex response directly. Rather, a stimulus may release a response from inhibition. Sexual responses, for example, are suppressed in most social situations. These responses may be released between lovers by the stimuli of their private bedroom. With this type of mechanism the intensity of a stimulus does not necessarily become translated into the intensity of the elicited response. In our example, it is not the vividness of the stimuli in one's bedroom that determines the vigor of the sexual behavior. The sexual behavior is simply released from inhibition by the bedroom cues, and how passionate the behavior is depends on other factors, such as how long it has been since the lovers were together. If the intensity of a stimulus does not determine the vigor of the elicited response in every case, it is possible for a very faint stimulus to produce a large response. Sechenov took advantage of this type of mechanism to provide a reflex analysis of voluntary behavior. He suggested that complex forms of behavior (actions or thoughts) that occur in the absence of an obvious eliciting stimulus are in fact reflexive responses. It is simply that in these cases the eliciting stimuli are so faint that we do not notice them. Thus, according to Sechenov, voluntary behavior and thoughts are actually elicited by inconspicuous, faint stimuli.

Sechenov's ideas about voluntary behavior represent a major extension of the use of reflex mechanisms to explain a variety of aspects of behavior. However, his proposition was a philosophical extrapolation from the actual research results he obtained. In addition, Sechenov did not address the question of how reflex mechanisms can explain the fact that the behavior of animals and people is constantly changing, depending on their experiences. From Descartes through Sechenov, reflex responses were considered to be innate and to be fixed by the anatomy of the organism's nervous system. They were thought to depend on a prewired neural connection between sense organs and the relevant muscles. According to this view, a given stimulus is expected to elicit the same response throughout the organism's life. Although this is true in some cases, there are also many examples in which the response to a stimulus changes. Explanation of such cases by reflex processes had to await the experimental and theoretical work of Ivan Pavlov. Pavlov showed experimentally that not all reflexes are innate. New reflexes can be established to stimuli through the mechanisms of association. Pavlov's role in the history of the study of reflexes is comparable to the role of Ebbinghaus in the study of the mind. Both were concerned with establishing the laws of associations through empirical research.

Charles Darwin and the concept of evolution

Another very important historical antecedent of the type of study of behavior we will describe is the work of the 19th-century British biologist Charles Darwin (1809–1882). Darwin was concerned with figuring out why different species and subspecies have different physical characteristics. On the basis of extensive observation of various types of animals, he formulated his theory of evolution. He recognized that each member of a species is slightly different from other members. These individual variations, he thought, occurred randomly through unspecified processes. Some rabbits, for example, can run slightly faster than others, and some birds have slightly better eyesight than others. These features may make it more likely for these individuals to survive in nature than individuals without these characteristics. The ability to run fast helps rabbits escape from predators, and exceptionally good eyesight enables birds to detect food from a distance. Individuals whose skills best match the challenges to survival posed by the environment will be most likely to survive and pass on these characteristics to their offspring. This process is repeated over and over again across generations, with the result that more and more members of a group of animals will have the particular traits that promote survival in their environment. The process is called **evolution through natural selection.**

Through the process of evolution, one set of organisms can have descendants after many generations that bear little resemblance to their ancestors. Darwin proposed that evolution was responsible for the appearance of new species and saw no reason that unique human characteristics could not have developed from other types of organisms in the same way. He believed in a continuity of species that included human beings. No species was considered fundamentally different from any other. One species may simply be further along in the course of evolution than another. The belief in a continuity of species provides a strong rationale for the study of animals as a way to gain insights into human beings. If human beings in fact evolved from other animal forms, then information gained about animals could very well provide important information about human nature.

All of Darwin's scientific observations were concerned with the physical traits of animals. However, he did not restrict his theory of evolution to explaining physical characteristics. He also believed that behavioral characteristics, emotional expressions, and intelligence can evolve in the same way that physical traits evolve. If this assumption is true, then the detailed investigation of animal behavior should be very relevant to the understanding of human behavior.

The behavioral approach viewed in historical context

The behavioral approach to the study of psychology may be viewed as the modern extension of the study of reflexes started by Descartes. The behavioral approach uses the methods of scientific observation, focuses on aspects of behavior that are caused by environmental events, and is devoted to the study of small units of behavior before the investigation of complex psychological processes. However, the behavioral approach is not rooted entirely in the reflexology tradition. Some aspects of it can be traced to earlier philosophical debates about the nature of the mind. The nativism/empiricism controversy, for example, has had its counter-

part in the development of behavioral psychology in the 20th century. The first and most vigorous advocate of the behavioral approach was the American psychologist John B. Watson (1878–1958), who believed that behavior was almost infinitely malleable by experience. In a famous statement, he once said:

> Give me a dozen healthy infants, well-formed, and my own specified world to bring them up in and I'll guarantee to take anyone at random and train him to become any type of specialist I might select—doctor, lawyer, artist, merchant-chief and, yes, even beggar-man and thief, regardless of his talents, penchants, tendencies, abilities, vocations, and race of his ancestors [Watson, 1924, p. 104].

Watson acknowledged that this statement was an exaggeration. However, the view that behavior is highly malleable may be considered analogous to the empiricism advocated by Locke in the 17th century. As we shall see in the following chapters, contemporary investigations of behavior are much more respectful of the fact that organisms are born with strong innate tendencies. It is now widely accepted that what organisms can learn through experience is limited by inherited behavioral characteristics. Thus, contemporary investigations of behavior have more of a nativist flavor.

Other respects in which the behavioral approach may be traced to earlier philosophical discussions about the mind include the concept of hedonism and the great importance placed on associations in the explanation of behavior. Hobbes proposed in the 17th century that the mind works by way of the pursuit of pleasure and the avoidance of pain. Many contemporary investigations may be viewed as an experimental analysis of the role of pleasure and pain in the control of behavior (see Chapters 6–11). The concept of associations has been an even more pervasive influence in behavioral investigations. Most experiments conducted within the framework of the behavioral approach have been concerned in one way or another with the role of associations in the control of behavior.

Finally, the behavioral approach was greatly influenced by the ideas of Charles Darwin and the concept of evolution. Much of the research conducted in the behavioral tradition has been performed with animal subjects. Many of these experiments would not have been done if the investigators had not believed that the study of animal behavior can provide important insights into human behavior. This view is not as fervently held today as it was before about 1970. However, many animal experiments are still conducted with the intent of developing models and theories that are also applicable to human behavior. The concept of evolution is also important because it has made investigators sensitive to the fact that behavior in a given situation is determined not only by the stimuli animals encounter there but also by their inherited behavioral tendencies.

Learning and the study of behavior

The behavioral approach has been applied to the study of a variety of aspects of psychology, including abnormal behavior, speech, and personality. However, it has been used most extensively in the study of learning and conditioning mechanisms, and this aspect of the behavioral approach will provide the focus of our book.

Learning is one of the biological processes that are crucial for the survival of many forms of animal life. There are numerous threats to the well-being of organisms. Animals have to take in nutrients, eliminate metabolic wastes, and otherwise maintain proper balance in internal functions. Through evolution, a variety of biological systems have emerged to cope with these challenges to survival. Many of them are primarily physiological, such as systems involved in respiration, digestion, excretion, and the like. However, finely tuned internal physiological processes are often not enough to maintain the integrity of life. The environment is constantly changing because of climatic and

other factors. Adverse effects of these changes often have to be minimized by behavioral adjustments. Animals have to know, for example, how to find and obtain food as food sources change, avoid predators as new ones enter their territory, and find new shelter when storms destroy their old homes. Accomplishing these tasks obviously requires motor movements, such as walking and manipulating objects. These tasks also require the ability to predict important events in the environment, such as the availability of food in a particular location and at a particular time. Aquisition of new motor behavior and new anticipatory reactions involves learning. Thus, animals learn to go to a new water hole when the old one dries up and learn new anticipatory reactions when a new predator enters their territory. These learned adjustments to the environment are no less important for survival than internal physiological processes such as respiration and digestion.

The definition of *learning*

No entirely satisfactory definition of *learning* exists. However, one fairly useful way to look at **learning** is as an *enduring change in the neural mechanisms of behavior that results from experience with environmental events.* Although learning involves a change in the neural mechanisms of behavior, we typically do not observe the critical neural processes directly. Rather, we infer from the subject's behavior that learning has taken place. However, behavior provides only an indirect assessment of the existence of learning. The behavior of organisms does not always reflect what they have learned. Sometimes evidence of learning cannot be obtained until special test procedures are set up. Children, for example, learn a great deal about driving a car just by watching others drive. However, this learning may not be apparent until the child is permitted behind the steering wheel. In other cases, a change in behavior is readily observed but cannot be attributed to learning either because it is not sufficiently long-lasting or because it does not result from experience with environmental events. The imprecise correspondence between learning and behavior requires us to distinguish between learning and performance. **Performance** refers to an organism's actions at a particular time. To conclude that a subject has learned something, we must see a change in its performance. However, the learning-related change in performance may be evident only in special test situations. Furthermore, not all changes in performance reflect prior learning.

Most people automatically associate learning with the acquisition of new behavior. That is, learning is identified by the gradual appearance of a new response in the organism's repertoire. This is the case when people learn to read, ride a bicycle, or play a musical instrument. However, the behavior change involved in learning can just as well consist in the decrease or loss of some behavior in the organism's repertoire. A child, for example, may learn not to cross the street when the traffic light is red, not to grab food from someone else's plate, and not to yell and scream when someone is trying to take a nap. Learning to withhold responses is just as important as learning to make responses, if not more so.

Distinction between learning and other sources of behavior change

Evaluating various situations in terms of the abstract definition of *learning* stated above may be difficult because some aspects of the definition are rather imprecise. It is not specified exactly how long behavioral changes have to last to be considered instances of learning. It is also sometimes hard to decide what constitutes sufficient experience with environmental events to classify something as an instance of learning. Therefore, it is useful to distinguish learning from other known mechanisms that can produce changes in behavior.

Several mechanisms produce changes in behavior that are too short-lasting to be considered instances of learning. One such process is **fatigue.** Physical exertion may result in a gradual weakening in the vigor of a response because the subject becomes tired or fatigued. This type of change is produced by experience. However, it is not considered an instance of learning, because the decline in responding disappears if the subject is allowed to rest and recover. Behavior may also be temporarily altered by a *change in stimulus conditions*. If birds that have been housed in a small cage are suddenly set free, for example, their behavior will change dramatically. However, this is not an instance of learning, because the birds are likely to return to their old style of responding when returned to their cage. Another source of temporary changes in behavior that is not considered learning is *alterations in the physiological or motivational state* of the organism. Hunger and thirst induce responses that are not observed at other times. Changes in the level of sex hormones will cause temporary changes in responsiveness to members of the opposite sex. Short-lasting behavioral effects may also accompany the administration of psychoactive drugs.

Other mechanisms produce persistent changes in behavior but without the type of experience with environmental events that satisfies the definition of *learning*. The most obvious process of this type is **maturation.** A child will be unable to reach a high shelf until he or she grows tall enough. However, this change would not be considered an instance of learning, because it occurs with the mere passage of time. One does not have to be trained to reach high places as one becomes taller. Maturation can also result in a loss of certain responses. For example, shortly after birth, touching an infant's feet results in foot movements that resemble walking, and stroking the bottom of the foot causes the toes to fan out. Both these reflex reactions are lost as the infant gets older.

Generally, the distinction between learning and maturation is based on the importance of special experiences in producing the change in behavior. However, the distinction has become blurred in instances in which experience has been found to be necessary for developmental changes that originally were thought to involve only maturation. For example, the visual system of cats will not develop sufficiently for them to be able to see horizontal lines unless they are exposed to such stimuli early in life (see, for example, Blakemore & Cooper, 1970). The appearance of sexual behavior at puberty was originally also thought to depend on maturation. However, experiments suggest that successful sexual behavior may require social contact early in life (for example, Harlow, 1969).

So far we have discussed mechanisms that create changes in behavior during the lifetime of the organism. Changes in behavior may also occur across generations through *evolutionary adaptation*. Individuals possessing genetic characteristics that promote their reproduction are more likely to pass these characteristics on to future generations. Adaptation and evolutionary change produced by differential reproductive success can lead to changes in behavior just as they lead to changes in the physical characteristics of species. Evolutionary changes are similar to learning in that they are also related to environmental influences. The characteristics of individuals that promote their reproductive success depend on the environment in which they live. However, evolutionary changes occur only across generations and are therefore distinguished from learning.

Although learning can be distinguished from maturation and evolution, it is not independent of these other sources of behavioral change. Whether a particular learning process occurs or how it operates depends on the subject's maturational level and evolutionary history. The dependence of learning on maturation is obvious in certain aspects of child rearing. For example, no amount of toilet training will be effective in a child until the nerves and muscles have developed sufficiently to make bladder control possible. The dependence of learning

on evolutionary history can be seen by comparing learning processes in various types of animals. For example, fish and turtles appear to learn differently than rats and monkeys in instrumental-conditioning situations (Bitterman, 1975). We will have more to say about the interaction of evolutionary history and learning processes in later chapters.

Use of animals in research on learning

The study of learning can be conducted by investigating the behavior of either human beings or other animals. The scientific study of behavior is not restricted to any part of the phylogenetic scale. Nevertheless, most of the experiments we will be considering have been conducted with nonhuman animals. A variety of animals have been used, including rats, mice, rabbits, fish, pigeons, and monkeys.

Practical advantages in the use of animals

Use of animals rather than humans in research on learning has several important advantages, many of which involve practical problems encountered in research. It is much easier to control the past experience of animals than that of people. Ethical considerations, for example, preclude raising human beings in totally controlled environments. There are also important ethical restrictions on the conduct of animal research, and laboratory animals are generally much better cared for than animals in the wild. Without imposing the kind of hardship that animals have to live with in the wild, one can easily design laboratory environments in which many of the things animals experience are highly regulated.

Another practical advantage afforded by the study of animals in laboratory settings is that the genetic history of the subjects can be regulated, making it much easier to evaluate the contribution of genetic factors to behavior than with human beings. Use of animals also makes it easier to control the experimental situation. Experimental chambers can be smaller and do not need as many costly comforts, such as carpeting and furniture. Animals can also be subjected to such procedures as food or water deprivation with much less trouble than would be involved with human subjects. Finally, because animals rarely have a choice in whether they will participate in an experiment, investigations are not limited to those individuals who volunteer. This makes it more likely that subjects in animal experiments will be representative of their species. Ethical considerations often limit human research to those individuals who choose to participate in the experiment. For some kinds of studies (for example, those that involve a great deal of time and effort or include some kind of aversive stimulation), people who volunteer may not be representative of all humans.

Conceptual advantages in the use of animals

In addition to practical considerations, use of animals in the study of behavior has possible conceptual advantages. There is the hope that processes of learning may be simpler in animals reared in controlled laboratory situations than in people, whose backgrounds are much more varied. One cannot tell at present all the respects in which learning in animals is simpler than in humans. However, it is agreed that most animal behavior is not complicated by the linguistic processes that have a prominent role in certain kinds of human behavior. One of the most exciting contemporary areas of research is the study of linguistic abilities in primates (see Chapter 12). However, there is no evidence that learning processes of the sort we will discuss in most of this book involve linguistic functions.

Another important advantage of using animals is that one does not have to be concerned with the demand characteristics of the experiment. In many forms of research with people,

one has to make sure their actions are not governed by their efforts to please (or displease) the experimenter. People serving in experiments often try to figure out what the purpose of the study is and what they are "supposed" to do. Whether or not they identify the purpose of the experiment correctly, their actions may be motivated by their wish to "do well" in the experiment rather than by the stimuli and the experimental conditions that were set up. Consequently, a person may react to circumstances in the laboratory very differently than he or she would respond to the same circumstances outside the laboratory. Such problems are not likely to arise in research with animals such as rats and pigeons. There is no reason to suspect that the actions of rats and pigeons in the laboratory are determined by their desire to please the experimenter or to do well in the experiment to avoid embarrassment.

Laboratory animals and normal behavior

Some have suggested that domesticated laboratory strains of animals may not provide useful information because such animals have degenerated in various ways as a result of many generations of inbreeding and long periods of captivity (for example, Lockard, 1968). However, this idea is probably false. In an interesting test, Boice (1977) took five male and five female albino rats of a highly inbred laboratory stock and housed them in an outdoor pen in Missouri without artificial shelters. All ten rats survived the first winter with temperatures as low as $-22°$ F. The animals reproduced normally and reached a stable population of about 50 members. Only three of the rats died before showing signs of old age during the 2-year period. Given the extreme climatic conditions, this level of success in living outdoors is remarkable. Furthermore, the behavior of these domesticated rats in the outdoors was very similar to the behavior of wild rats observed in similar circumstances.

The vigor of inbred laboratory rats in outdoor living conditions indicates that they are not inferior to their wild counterparts. Domesticated rats act similarly to wild rats in other tests as well, and there is some indication that they perform better than wild rats in learning experiments (Boice, 1973). Therefore, one should not dismiss the results we will be describing in this book simply because many of the experiments were conducted with domesticated animals. In fact, it may be suggested that laboratory animals are preferable in research to their wild counterparts. Human beings in civilized society are raised and live in somewhat contrived environments. Therefore, research with animals may prove most relevant to the human case if the animals are domesticated and live in artificial laboratory situations. As Boice (1973, p. 227) has commented, "The domesticated rat may be a good model for domestic man."

Significance of research on animal learning for human behavior

Even granting that domesticated laboratory animals have not degenerated, one might still wonder what research on learning using animals has to do with human behavior. Human beings are obviously very different from laboratory animals in many ways. Why should we accept any findings of animal experiments as being relevant to people? There may not be any logical reason for doing so. However, research has shown that animals and humans have many things in common. The physiological systems of lower mammals are very similar to those of humans. This correspondence provides the rationale for conducting most exploratory medical research with animals. Similarities between animal and human behavior are harder to prove than similarities in physiological function because it is difficult to identify human test situations that are comparable to animal test environments, and vice versa. Nevertheless, research on animal behavior has provided important insights into human behavior in several ways.

Analysis of nonlinguistic and emotional behavior

Research of the sort described in this book provides a good account of nonlinguistic and emotional aspects of human behavior. It tells us about aspects of human behavior that are not rationally and consciously motivated. We do many things that are irrational and contrary to our best intentions. The research to be described provides important insights into these aspects of behavior. It tells us why we get scared when we know very well that we will not suffer harm. It tells us why we get nervous before taking tests even though we know that nervousness does not help in answering the questions. It tells us why we eagerly anticipate meeting good friends and approach with foreboding a meeting with someone unpleasant. It suggests why we tend to put off studying until just before a test even though we know it is better to study regularly throughout a course. It suggests why some people like dogs and others do not. It suggests why some people are neat and others are messy.

Development of models of behavior

The insight into human behavior provided by animal research usually does not come from a direct application of animal results to the human case. There are too many differences in the motor movements, life histories, and environments of animals and humans to make such a direct application of animal research possible. Instead, animal research is used to develop models and theories of behavior that are then generalized to human beings. For example, animal experiments have allowed scientists to construct a model of how goal-directed behavior is motivated by reward and punishment. This model can then be used to understand certain aspects of human behavior. Thus, the inference from animal to human behavior is somewhat indirect and involves formulation of a general model of behavior that is then assumed to be applicable to a variety of species.

Models of behavior developed from the results of animal experimentation often provide explanations of human behavior that are good enough to satisfy one's nonscientific curiosity. For example, experiments have shown that animals become aroused and excited when they are exposed to a stimulus, such as a noise or an odor, that reliably signals that they are to be fed. (This kind of behavior can be easily observed in zoos at feeding time.) Research has also shown that the arousal of animals in response to signals for food is governed by conditioning mechanisms. Similar behavioral effects are evident in people. It is not uncommon, for example, for children and young adults who have been away from home for a long time to become very excited on smelling their mother's cooking when they return. Experiments have not been done specifically on what makes the smell of mother's cooking exciting and whether the same conditioning processes are involved as in the behavior of animals close to feeding time. However, it is a good bet that the same processes are involved, and most people would be sufficiently satisfied by the analysis not to demand that experiments be conducted with humans to prove the point.

Extrapolation from animal experiments to human behavior is often interesting and fun and can satisfy one's idle curiosity about human behavior. However, the results of animal research are sometimes used for more serious purposes, such as the design of procedures for psychotherapy or special training programs. In such cases, it is important to verify the applicability of animal behavior processes to people by conducting experiments with human subjects. Historically, one of the important functions of animal research has been to provide a framework and model for certain types of research with human beings. This has been particularly true in attempts to use the results of animal

research to alleviate human problems. Much of the current work on biofeedback, for example, developed from experiments designed to teach animals to control their heart rate and other physiological functions. Another prominent example is the application of reinforcement principles to classroom behavior problems and the training of mentally retarded people. The methodology and theoretical framework for these techniques were first developed in research with animals. However, before the principles were put into practice with human beings, the techniques were extensively evaluated with human subjects as well.

The behavioral approach and other aspects of psychology

There are probably few aspects of nature more complicated and difficult to study than behavior. One result of this complexity is that it is difficult to decide how to go about the investigation. Scientists do not agree on how to define the subject matter, what kinds of behavior to study first, and how long to pursue one approach before proceeding to the next stage of analysis. The absence of obvious answers to such questions has created a great deal of diversity in the way psychologists pursue their work. Some areas of psychology can be obviously differentiated from others by what aspect of behavior is being investigated. Sensory psychologists, for example, investigate the processes involved in sensation and perception, cognitive psychologists are interested in the processes of thinking and information processing, and clinical psychologists are interested in abnormal behavior. Another way to categorize various approaches to the study of behavior is by the complexity of the behavior under investigation. Psychologists interested in personality and intelligence, for example, study very complex behavioral systems. They do not investigate individual responses but rather response styles and aggregates of behavior that are organized in complex ways. A high score on a test of intelligence or a test of masculinity, for example, does not refer to a particular response. Rather, such scores identify a complex constellation of response tendencies of varying degrees of strength.

The behavioral approach may be distinguished from other approaches in psychology both by the aspect of behavior it focuses on and by the level of complexity of the behavior. As we have already noted, many experiments using this approach are concerned only with aspects of behavior that can be observed directly and involve discrete responses, small units of behavior instead of response styles and constellations of response tendencies. It is assumed that complex behavioral systems consist of the combined action of simpler responses. Therefore, the understanding of simple responses is viewed as a prerequisite for the study of complex psychological processes. The information gained from studying simpler responses is assumed to be useful in the design of studies of more complex systems.

The behavioral approach is part of a comprehensive position in psychology identified as behaviorism. Many diverse ideas are subsumed under this philosophical position. Some have argued, for example, that the behavioral approach is the only one that is likely to be fruitful in the study of psychology (Watson, 1913). Such a radical behavioristic position is not advocated in this book. Given the complexity of behavior and given that there is no way to know at this point what is the best way to study it, the variety of approaches used in contemporary psychology is justified. The study of behavior can be profitably conducted at several levels of complexity simultaneously. Information gained in the various approaches can then be exchanged back and forth in the development of a complete description of behavior. Each level of analysis plays an integral role in such a multifaceted and integrated study. Thus, studies of physiological bases of behavior, simple responses, and complex response systems (as in personality

variables) all make important contributions to a complete understanding of behavior. Our purpose in advocating this integrated approach is not to denigrate the importance of the behavioral approach but to allow the reader to better relate the information provided by this text to information about behavior presented in other discussions of psychology.

Behaviorism and you: The problem of free will

Behaviorism focuses on aspects of behavior that are stimulated by the external environment, and in its strongest version, it assumes that all behavior is caused by environmental events in one way or another. This assumption makes behaviorism a form of **determinism.** According to the determinist position, no aspect of behavior is capricious and unpredictable. Every aspect is assumed to follow natural laws. If we cannot predict some aspect of behavior, the determinist position is that either the relevant laws for the behavior have not been discovered yet or the aspect of the environment that controls the behavior has been overlooked.

The determinist position is difficult for many to accept as a proper description of their own behavior. People readily acknowledge that some aspects of their behavior are controlled by external factors, such as peer pressure, institutional rules, traffic regulations, or interpersonal obligations. However, most people feel that they also do some things solely because they feel like it. This experience is the basis for the notion that human beings have free will and are in control of their destiny in some sense. In fact, the quality of life is sometimes measured by the extent to which one can exercise free will. People take pride in achieving a status that permits them to do whatever they want, to take holidays whenever they like, to go to work whenever they like, and to work on whatever problems they choose. Having such freedom is often a goal in life. The higher one goes in an organization and the more reputable one becomes in a profession, the less likely are one's daily activities to be governed by what someone else dictates. The "boss" can come in late to work, can take extra time for lunch, and sets deadlines rather than having them imposed on him or her by someone else.

Incompatibility of determinism and free will

What should we make of the conflict between the determinist position and the concept of free will? One approach is to acknowledge the existence of free will on the evidence that most people strongly feel it at one time or another and simply to reject the determinist position. If we accept such a resolution, we would agree that some but not all behavior is governed by natural laws. Although this position may be personally satisfying, it is incompatible with the pursuit of a science of behavior. If we acknowledge that behavior can occur spontaneously, free of the constraints of natural laws, then we have to admit the possibility that such spontaneous behavior will occur on occasions as an intrusion into the lawful aspects of behavior. If such intrusions of free will are always possible, then no aspect of behavior will be predictable. However, a science of behavior cannot be built on the assumption that no aspect of behavior is predictable. For this reason, psychologists have rejected the notion that the concept of free will can remain in a science of behavior.

Free will and the frame of reference

A scientific approach to behavior has to accept the determinist position. However, a scientific approach also has to provide satisfactory explanations for all aspects of behavior, including the feelings of free will that most of us have. A resolution of this problem is provided by a careful look at the situations that give rise to feelings of free will and control. Such situations invariably involve our doing something we want. However, what we want and how we go about getting what we want are very much under the control of external factors. It is often said, for example, that the hallmark of effective leaders or administrators is to identify the motivations of the people who work under them and then to manipulate the work situation so that people will benefit the corporation or institution in the pursuit of their own individual desires. Are workers in such a situation exercising their free will? It depends on how you look at it. From their point of view, they are. They are doing what they want. However, from the boss's perspective, the workers are pursuing the interests of the institution.

Whether free will exists depends on the frame of reference. From a subjective, personal point of view, it does exist and is very important. From the view of external controlling forces, free will does not exist. This characteristic of free will was illustrated in a charming cartoon in *The Jester,* a Columbia University publication. As shown in Figure 1.3, rats that press a lever for a food reward may feel that they have free will and are in control of the situation. However, the experimenter who sets up the situation believes that free will does not exist, because the rats' behavior in this situation is perfectly lawful.

Determinism and social responsibility

If we assume that free will does not exist independently of one's frame of reference and that all behavior is controlled by external, environmental factors according to natural laws, then in a sense we are not responsible for our own actions. Does this mean that people should not be held responsible for what they do? Obviously, if we accept such a proposition, and if we all behave as if we were not responsible for our actions, society as we know it cannot function.

How is the concept of determinism to be reconciled with social responsibility? The answer comes from an analysis of what we mean by "to be held responsible" for one's actions.

*"Boy do I have this guy conditioned. Every time
I press the bar down he drops in a pellet of food."*

Figure 1.3. *(After a cartoon in* The Jester, *Columbia University.)*

Holding people responsible usually means punishing them in some way for doing something bad, by imposing a fine or a sentence. Holding someone responsible may also involve giving a reward for good behavior. For example, when Menachem Begin and Anwar Sadat were awarded the Nobel Peace Prize in 1978, the award was given in the belief that these gentlemen were responsible for progress toward peace between their countries.

Rewards and punishments are typically not as obvious and institutionalized as Nobel Prizes and jail terms. Nevertheless, they operate throughout society and play an integral part in holding the fabric of society together. The determinist position does not advocate abandoning this means of behavior control. Quite the contrary. Behavior theory has done more than any other aspect of psychology to uncover the mechanisms whereby rewards and punishments operate. Therefore, behavior theory can contribute to maintaining the integrity of social responsibility.

CHAPTER TWO

The Organization of Innate Behavior

Before embarking on a discussion of learning mechanisms, we must first consider aspects of behavior that are innate—that occur without special learning experiences. Often, what an animal learns and how it learns depend on its behavior in the absence of learning. We will describe several important concepts and phenomena concerning the organization of innate behavior. Our discussion begins with the concept of the reflex. We will then describe how elicited behavior is governed by the nature of the eliciting stimulus, feedback cues that are produced by the response, and the organism's internal state. Finally, we will describe how innate behavioral mechanisms can produce complex response sequences.

During the early years of research on learning, psychologists tended to think of learning as operating independently of other processes controlling behavior. It was assumed that any response could be changed or learned with the proper experience. Idealists suggested that everyone could be taught any skill or behavior. However, this has not turned out to be so. In reality, behavior is not infinitely malleable. Learning can produce changes in behavior only within the constraints of the organism's innate responses.

Learning mechanisms do not operate in a behavioral vacuum. Rather, the changes in responding that are produced by various experiences are superimposed on the organism's innate behavior repertoire. All animals engage in a variety of responses that are not the products of learning but are inborn, inherited responses or behavior tendencies. Learning may change these innate tendencies, teach animals to make the innate responses in new situations, or combine with innate behavior mechanisms to create new forms of behavior. A great deal is known about the nature of innate behavior. Much of this information has been obtained by investigators who have had only a passing interest in the study of learning. This chapter will not try to summarize all this research. Rather, our goal is to examine those aspects of innate behavior that are particularly important to the understanding of learning and to show that innate reactions to external stimuli can result in rather complex forms of behavior.

The concept of the reflex

It is a commonplace observation that organisms react to events in their environment. This is true for all animals, including human beings. If something moves in the periphery of your vision, for example, you are likely to turn your head in that direction. A particle of food in the mouth elicits salivation. A light puff of air directed at the cornea makes the eyes blink. A tap on a certain part of the knee causes the leg to kick. Irritation of the respiratory passages causes sneezing and coughing. Exposure to a bright light causes the pupils to constrict. The pain of touching a hot surface elicits a quick withdrawal response. These and numerous other responses are simple, unlearned reflexes.

The above examples illustrate that a reflex involves two closely related events. One is the *eliciting environmental stimulus;* the other is a *specific response.* The stimulus and response are closely linked in a special way: the occurrence of the stimulus generally leads to the occurrence of the response, and the response rarely occurs in the absence of the stimulus. Thus, salivation occurs when food is presented and rarely occurs in the absence of food.

The specificity of the relation between a par-

ticular type of stimulus and a particular reflex response reflects the organization of the nervous system. In vertebrates (including humans), simple reflexes are mediated by a minimum of three neurons. The neural organization of simple reflexes is shown in Figure 2.1. The environmental stimulus for a reflex activates a **sensory,** or **afferent, neuron,** which transmits the sensory message to the spinal cord. Here the neural impulses are relayed to the **motor,** or **efferent, neuron,** which creates the observed reflex response. However, sensory and motor neurons do not communicate directly. Rather, the impulses from one to the other are relayed through an **interneuron.** Interneurons are located in such a way that one set of sensory neurons is connected to only one set of motor neurons. Because of this restrictive connection between particular sensory and motor neurons, the reflex response is elicited only by a restricted set of stimuli. The afferent neuron, interneuron, and efferent neuron together constitute what is called the **reflex arc.**

The reflex arc in vertebrates represents the fewest neural connections that are necessary for reflex action. Additional neural structures are often involved in the elicitation of reflexes. The sensory messages are often also relayed to the

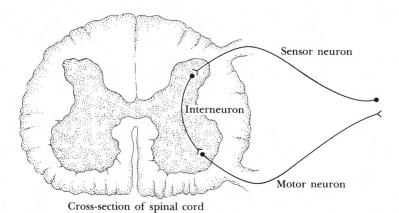

Cross-section of spinal cord

Figure 2.1. Neural organization of simple reflexes. The environmental stimulus for a reflex activates a sensory neuron, which transmits the sensory message to the spinal cord. Here the neural impulses are relayed to an interneuron, which in turn relays the impulses to the motor neuron. The motor neuron activates muscles involved in movement.

brain, which may influence the course of the reflex in various ways. For example, arousal mechanisms in the brain may influence the excitability of the interneurons. If you are highly aroused by a good horror movie, for example, you may startle more easily when someone taps you on the shoulder. The details of how this type of thing occurs are not essential to the present discussion. However, it is important to keep in mind that the occurrence of even simple reflexes can be influenced by higher nervous-system functions.

Reflexes have, no doubt, evolved to provide rapid behavioral adjustment to environmental events. Most reflexes promote the well-being of the organism in obvious ways. For example, in many animals painful stimulation of one limb causes withdrawal, or flexion, of that limb and extension of the opposite limb (Hart, 1973). Thus, if a dog stubs a toe while walking, it will automatically withdraw that leg and simultaneously extend the opposite leg. This combination of responses removes the first leg from the source of pain and at the same time allows the animal to maintain balance. The same sequence of reflex responses, however, would not benefit the two-toed sloth. The sloth is a primate that spends much of its time hanging upside down on branches. Consider what would happen if it responded to pain in the same way as the dog. If it flexed the injured limb and extended the opposite limb, it would end up putting most of its weight on the injured foot. As you might suspect, the sloth has evolved with a different sequence of responses. It extends the injured foot, thereby removing that foot from the branch it is on, and flexes the opposite foot, thereby putting more of its weight on that leg, as shown in Figure 2.2 (Esplin & Woodbury, 1961).

Innate reflexes constitute much of the behavioral repertoire of newborn infants. Because newborn infants have not had much time to learn how to respond to environmental events, they have to survive with mainly inborn reactions to stimuli. Some of these reflexes can be a

Figure 2.2. Painful stimulation of one leg of a dog causes withdrawal (flexion) of that leg and extension of the opposite leg. In contrast, painful stimulation of one leg of a sloth causes extension of that leg and flexion of the opposite leg. *(After Hart, 1973.)*

source of enjoyment for the parents. For example, newborn babies reflexively clench their fingers around anything that is placed in their hand. Another prominent reflex probably evolved to facilitate finding the nipple: if you touch an infant's cheek with your finger, the baby will reflexively turn his or her head in that direction, with the result that your finger will probably fall in the baby's mouth. When an object is in the infant's mouth, he or she will reflexively suck. The more closely the object resembles a nipple, the more vigorous the elicited sucking behavior.

Figure 2.3 Sucking is one of the prominent reflexes in infants.

Although reflex responses are usually beneficial to the organism, the organization of reflex behavior can also lead to unexpected difficulties. The head-turning and sucking reflexes make it easy for newborn babies to get fed. However, sometimes another important reflex, the respiratory occlusion reflex, gets in the way. The respiratory occlusion reflex is stimulated by a reduction of air flow to the baby, caused by, for example, a cloth covering the face or an accumulation of mucus in the respiratory passages. When confronted with a reduction of air flow, the baby's first reaction is to pull his or her head back. If this does not remove the eliciting stimulus, the baby will move his or her hands in a face-wiping motion. If this also fails to remove the eliciting stimulus, then the baby will begin to cry. Crying involves vigorous expulsion of air, which is often sufficient to remove whatever was obstructing the air passages. The respiratory occlusion reflex is obviously essential for survival. If the baby does not get enough air, he or she may suffocate. The problem arises when the respiratory occlusion reflex is triggered during nursing. While nursing, the baby can get air only through the nose. If the mother presses the baby too close to the breast during feeding so that the baby's nostrils get covered by the breast, the respiratory occlusion reflex will be stimulated. The baby will attempt to pull his or her head back from the nipple, may paw at his or her face to get released from the nipple, and may begin to cry. Thus, successful nursing requires a bit of experience. The mother and child have to adjust their positions so that nursing can progress smoothly without occurrence of the respiratory occlusion reflex.

The nature of response-eliciting stimuli

In each of the examples of reflexes described above, the eliciting stimulus is fairly obvious. However, this is not true of all reflexes. In many situations a response is elicited by a complex sequence of events or stimuli, and it is not easy to tell exactly which features of the situation are critical for the occurrence of the response. Consider, for example, the sequence of events during the feeding of herring-gull chicks. The chicks remain in the nest after hatching and are entirely dependent on food brought to them. When the parent returns from a feeding trip, the baby chicks peck at the tip of its bill (see Figure 2.4). This causes the adult to regurgitate. The parent then picks up some of the vomitus in its bill. As the chicks continue to peck at the bill, they manage to get some of the regur-

Figure 2.4. Feeding of herring-gull chicks. The chicks peck a red patch near the tip of the adult's bill, causing the adult to regurgitate food for the chicks.

gitated food, and this provides their nourishment.

One of the critical aspects of this feeding sequence is how the chicks peck at the parent's bill to stimulate the parent to regurgitate. This is an elicited innate behavior. However, from casual observation of the situation, one cannot easily identify the critical stimulus features for eliciting the pecking behavior. Herring gulls have a long, yellow bill with a striking red patch near the tip. Pecking in the chicks may be elicited by movements of the adult, the color, shape, or length of its bill, the noises the adult makes, or some other stimulus. To isolate which of these features are important for the pecking response, Tinbergen and Perdeck (1950) tested herring-gull chicks with various artificial models instead of live adult gulls. From this research they concluded that a model had to have several characteristics to strongly elicit pecking. It had to be a long, thin, moving object that was pointed downward and had a contrasting red patch near the tip. These experiments suggest that the yellow color of the adult's bill, the shape and coloration of its head, and the noises it makes are all unimportant for eliciting pecking in the gull chicks. The specific features that were found to be required to elicit the pecking behavior are called the **sign stimulus** or **releasing stimulus** for this behavior.

Various sign stimuli have been identified in investigations of elicited behavior. A classic example is provided by the stimuli that elicit aggression or courtship in the three-spined stickleback, a small fish that breeds during the spring. During the breeding season, the male stickleback establishes and defends a territory. If another male intrudes into its territory, the intruder is attacked. In contrast, if a female stickleback enters, it is courted. How does the occupant of the territory distinguish between fish it should attack and fish it should court? A male intruder has several stimulus characteristics—a particular movement pattern, pattern of coloration, size, shape, and so on. To isolate the critical stimulus features, male sticklebacks were tested with various cardboard models (Tinbergen, 1951). This research showed that to elicit aggression, the model had to have a red underside. Movement was also relevant. The model was more likely to be attacked if it was presented in a head-down posture similar to that of a threatening live fish. In contrast, the critical stimulus feature to avoid attack and possibly elicit courtship was a rounded, "swollen" underside similar to that of female sticklebacks holding many eggs.

Relational sign stimuli

In the examples noted above, the sign stimuli were specific stimulus features that could elicit the relevant response even if they appeared as a part of inanimate models. In other cases the sign stimulus may involve a relation between two discrete stimuli. A famous example is provided by an investigation (Tinbergen, 1951) of the gaping response of nestling thrushes (*Turdus merula*). Unlike the gull chicks that peck at the parent's bill, nestling thrushes open their mouths in a gaping response whenever the parent appears, starting several days after birth. Research with various inanimate models revealed that the gaping response is released by and guided by visual cues. Furthermore, the response is directed toward a portion of a model that is analogous to its head. But what makes a nestling respond to something as if it were the parent's head? Is it the absolute size of the protrusion, or is it the size of the protrusion relative to the rest of the model? Nestlings were tested with models that had two "heads" of different sizes. Figure 2.5 shows two of the models. Note that the heads on the two models are the same sizes. When tested with the smaller model (A), the nestlings gaped at the smaller of the two heads. If they were responding to the absolute size of this head stimulus, they would be expected to gape at the smaller head on the larger model (B) as well. However, when tested with model B, they gaped at the larger of the two

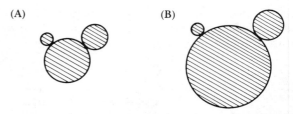

Figure 2.5. Diagram of models used to elicit the gaping response in nestling thrushes. Nestlings gaped at the smaller of the two heads on model A but the larger of the two heads on model B. *(After Tinbergen, 1951.)*

heads. The larger head was in the same proportion to the body of model B as the smaller head to model A. Therefore, this experiment shows that the relative stimulus characteristics of the shapes were the critical sign stimulus for eliciting the gaping response, rather than the absolute size of the head.

Supernormal sign stimuli

By definition, sign stimuli are cues that are especially effective in eliciting a particular innate response. In nature the range of intensities and sizes for such stimuli is limited. What would happen if the sign stimulus were artificially made much more vivid and intense than it would ever be in nature? Would the elicited response also increase correspondingly, or would the animal recognize that the stimulus was abnormal and therefore not make the usual elicited response? Research with models of sign stimuli has shown that the first of these alternatives is more likely. An artificially exaggerated sign stimulus will evoke an unusually strong innate response. A striking example is the brooding (incubating) response of the herring gull. The bigger the egg, the more vigorously the bird tries to brood it (Tinbergen, 1960). Furthermore, the gull will prefer to brood an artificially large egg instead of a real egg that is smaller. An artificially enlarged sign stimulus is called a **supernormal stimulus.** Research with supernormal stimuli has shown that innate response mechanisms can govern behavior even outside the range of normally encountered stimuli.

The role of feedback in elicited behavior

Responses usually produce specific stimulus consequences. This is true for all behavior, including responses elicited by environmental events. When your pupils constrict in bright light, for example, less light reaches the retina as a result. The salivation elicited by food in the mouth makes the food softer and less concentrated. Coughing and sneezing in response to irritation of the respiratory passages produce loud noises and rapid expulsion of air and usually remove the irritant. A specific stimulus that results from a particular response is called a **feedback stimulus** for that response. A consideration of the role of feedback stimuli provides important insights into behavior. The present section will consider the role of feedback in the control of innate elicited behavior. Later chapters will discuss the importance of feedback in the control of learned responses.

Feedback stimuli may arise from sources internal or external to the organism. Internal feedback cues are provided by sensory neurons that allow the animal to feel the muscle and joint movements involved in making the response. If someone tapped your knee in the appropriate place and elicited the knee-jerk reflex, you would feel your leg kick. You would know when you make the response even if you closed your eyes, because of sensations provided by sensory neurons in the leg muscles and knee joint. Such internal feedback cues are called **proprioceptive stimuli.** The movement of most skeletal muscles provides proprioceptive sensations. However, not all reflex responses are accompanied by proprioceptive cues. For example, constriction of the pupils creates few internal sensations. Rather, the feedback that results from pupillary constriction occurs because less light reaches the retina. This feedback changes the external stimuli to which the organism is exposed. We will discuss the role of only such external feedback cues in elicited behavior. Some response patterns are largely independent of external feedback cues. In other cases, the behavior is almost exclusively controlled by feedback.

Elicited behavior independent of feedback stimuli

Once some responses are initiated, they go to completion largely independent of the consequences of the behavior. Because of the fixed nature of such responses, they are called **fixed action patterns.** There are numerous instances of fixed action patterns in animal behavior. Some familiar examples may be observed in common pets. When eating, cats, for example, often take a bite, shake their heads slightly, and then proceed to chew and swallow. The shaking response is very useful when the cat is about to eat a live mouse because it helps to kill the mouse. This part of the fixed action pattern continues to occur even when the food does not have to be killed. Another commonly observed fixed action pattern in domestic cats is seen when they use the litter box. Elimination in cats ends with their scratching the dirt to cover up their waste. However, this scratching response is independent of its stimulus consequences. Cats scratch for a while after eliminating whether or not the dirt they scratch covers up their waste. In fact, sometimes they scratch on the side of the litter box and do not even move any dirt.

A dramatic example of a fixed action pattern is the cocoon-spinning behavior of the spider *Ciprennium salei* (see Eibl-Eibesfeldt, 1970). The spider begins by spinning the bottom of the cocoon; then it spins the sides. It lays its eggs inside the cocoon and then spins the top of the cocoon, thereby closing it. This response sequence is remarkable because it occurs in the specified order even if the usual outcome of the response is altered by an experimenter. For example, the spider will continue to spin the sides of the cocoon and lay the eggs even if the bottom of the cocoon is destroyed and the eggs fall through the cocoon. If the spider is placed on a partly completed cocoon, it will nevertheless begin the spinning response sequence as if it had to start an entirely new cocoon. Another remarkable aspect is that the spinning responses occur in much the same way even if the spider is unable to produce the material with which to construct the cocoon. Thus, although the spider appears to go through the spinning movements in order to have a place to lay its eggs, the consequences of the behavior do not control its occurrence.

Presence or absence of the eliciting stimulus as feedback

Fixed action patterns like those described above are generally elicited by discrete releasing stimuli. In other situations, responses are elicited by events that may be present for a long time. In some of these cases, the elicited response may either maintain the animal in contact with the eliciting stimulus or remove the animal from the stimulus. Which of these feedback events takes place strongly determines the future occurrence of the response. If the reflex response maintains the animal in contact with the eliciting stimulus, the response will persist. In contrast, if the behavior removes the animal from the eliciting stimulus, the response will cease.

We have already encountered reflex systems in which the response feedback is provided by the presence or absence of the eliciting stimulus. Consider, for example, the sucking reflex of newborn babies. When presented with a nipple, the baby begins to suck. This response serves to maintain contact between the baby and the nipple. The continued contact, in turn, elicits further sucking behavior. In other cases, the

outcome of the reflex response removes the eliciting stimulus. Reflexive sneezing and coughing, for example, usually result in removal of the irritation in the respiratory passages that originally elicited the behavior. When the irritation is removed, the sneezing and coughing cease.

Feedback involving the presence or absence of the eliciting stimulus is very important in controlling reflexive locomotor movement in many animals. In one type of reflexive locomotion, the eliciting stimulus produces a change in the speed of movement (or the speed of turning) irrespective of direction. Any such movement is called a **kinesis**. The behavior of woodlice provides a good example. The woodlouse (*Porcellio scaber*) is a small isopod usually found in damp areas, such as under rocks, boards, and leaves. From a casual observation of the places in which woodlice are found, one might be tempted to conclude that they move toward damp places because they prefer such areas. However, their tendency to congregate in damp places is a result of a kinesis. Low levels of humidity elicit locomotor movement in the lice. As long as the air is dry, the lice continue to move. When they reach more humid places, a higher proportion of them are found to be inactive. Thus, they tend to congregate in areas of high humidity not because they prefer such areas and "voluntarily" seek them out but because in damp places the stimulus for movement is absent (Fraenkel & Gunn, 1961).

Kinesis determines the resting location of other types of animals as well. In contrast to the woodlice, both adult and larval grasshoppers are more active in moist areas and quiescent in dry places (Riegert, 1959). This response increases the likelihood that they will remain in dry areas. In flatworms kinesis is controlled by illumination rather than humidity. Several types of flatworms are more likely to stop in dark than in well-lit places (Walter, 1907; Welsh, 1933). Another interesting kinesis controlled by light is found in the larvae of the brook lamprey (*Lampetra planeri*). When exposed to light, they wriggle around with the head pointed downward. The greater the illumination, the greater the activity. On a muddy substrate, the wriggling movement results in the animal's burrowing into the ground. The burrowing persists until the light receptors at the tip of the tail become covered up with mud (Jones, 1955).

Kinesis produces movements toward (or away from) particular stimuli as an indirect result of changes in the rate of movement triggered by the stimuli. In another type of reflexive locomotion process, the stimulus directly creates movements toward or away from it. This type of mechanism is called a **taxis** (plural, *taxes*). A taxis is identified by the nature of the eliciting stimulus and whether the movement is toward or away from the stimulus. Earthworms tend to turn away from bright light (Adams, 1903). This is an example of a negative phototaxis. The South American bloodsucker orients and goes toward warm bodies (Wigglesworth & Gillett, 1934). In the laboratory, for example, the bloodsucker will go toward a test tube of warm water. This is an example of a positive thermotaxis. The tree snail exhibits a negative geotaxis (Crozier & Navez, 1930). Pulling of the shell in one direction causes the snail to move in the opposite direction. In nature the result is that the snail climbs trees because gravity pulls its shell toward the ground. The direction of flight in many insects is controlled by taxes. Locusts, for example, have small tufts of hair on the front of the head. The animals always orient their flight in such a way that the hairs are bent straight back (Weiss-Fogh, 1949). Changes in flight orientation produce feedback in the form of changes in the hair tufts, and this feedback stimulates further changes in orientation that make the locust fly directly into the wind.

Taxes and kineses are remarkable because they illustrate how responses that appear to be goal-directed and volitional can be produced by relatively simple and mechanistic reflex processes. To explain the behavior of woodlice, for example, it is not necessary to postulate that they enjoy and seek out damp places. Similarly, it is not necessary to postulate that locusts seek to fly into the wind or enjoy doing so. Rather, these apparently goal-directed movements can be explained in terms of reflex responses controlled by feedback cues involving the presence or absence of the eliciting stimulus. The locomotor/orientation movement will persist as long as the response feedback involves continued contact with the eliciting stimulus and will cease when other types of feedback cues occur.

Responses elicited and guided by different stimuli

So far we have discussed elicited behavior that is largely independent of the feedback cues and elicited behavior that is controlled by feedback involving the presence or absence of the eliciting stimulus. There are also innate responses that are elicited by one stimulus and guided by feedback involving a second stimulus. A good example is provided by the mouth-breeding cichlid (*Tilapia mossambica*), a basslike fish that incubates its eggs in its mouth. After hatching, the young remain close to the mother for a number of days. The approach of a large object or turbulence in the water causes the young to swim toward the mother. More specifically, they approach her lower parts and dark areas. When they reach the mother, they push on the surface and penetrate into holes, and hence many of them end up in the mother's mouth. If the mother is replaced by a model, the young also approach its lower parts and dark patches and push against these areas (Baerends, 1957). The stimulus that elicits the entire response sequence is the approach of a large object or water turbulence. However, the behavior is guided by other cues—the lower side of the mother (or model) and dark patches.

Certain aspects of the egg-retrieval response of the greylag goose also illustrate how one stimulus may be responsible for eliciting a behavior and another involved in guiding it (Lorenz & Tinbergen, 1939). Whenever an egg rolls out of the nest, the goose reaches out and pulls the egg back with side-to-side movements of its beak. This behavior has two components. One involves extension of the body to reach the wayward egg and then movement of the beak back toward the nest. The other component is the side-to-side adjustments of the beak involved in rolling the egg. The first component is a pure fixed action pattern. Once elicited, it goes to completion regardless of the response feedback that occurs. After the goose has extended its body to reach the egg, it pulls its beak all the way back to the nest even if the egg rolls out from under the beak somewhere along the way. In contrast, the side-to-side movements of the beak occur only if the goose is pulling back a rounded, egg-shaped object. If a straight pipe is substituted that does not wobble, the side-to-side movements do not occur. These movements are closely governed by response feedback. If the egg wobbles in one direction, the goose will move its beak more to that side to support it. This movement may cause the egg to wobble in the other direction, producing another side-to-side adjustment. The sequence of responses guided by feedback continues until the goose has pulled its beak all the way back.

Elicited behavior and internal state

Simple reflexes such as the knee jerk and pupillary constriction can be elicited just about any time in healthy organisms. In fact, reflexes of this type are used to measure the integrity and proper functioning of the nervous system. Medical emergency personnel, for example, routinely check whether the pupils contract when a light is shone into the eyes as a preliminary assessment of neural damage in accident victims. In contrast to pupillary constriction, many more-complicated elicited response patterns occur only when the organism is in the proper physiological state or "mood." Eating

and drinking are obvious examples. Edibles are more likely to elicit eating or drinking when the animal is hungry or thirsty than at other times. Similarly, many fixed action patterns involved in aggression, courtship, sexual behavior, and parenting occur only when the organism is in the proper physiological state. The same stimulus may therefore elicit dramatically different responses, depending on the state of the organism. A striking example is the reactions of a female hamster to an approaching male. If she is in a sexually receptive state, the female will permit the male to come near. If she is not, she is likely to attack him (Payne & Swanson, 1970). In this example, as in many others, the physiological state that determines whether a stimulus will elicit a particular behavior is produced by the presence of various hormones in the body.

The reproductive behavior of the ring dove provides a good illustration of the role of hormones in elicited behavior (Lehrman, 1965). (The ring dove is evolutionarily related to the domestic pigeon but is slightly smaller. Its back is light gray, its underside is a creamy color, and it has a semicircular black ring on the back of its neck.) A highly predictable, stereotyped sequence of events occurs when a male and a female bird are placed together in a cage provided with nesting material and a shallow glass bowl. They begin to interact with a courtship routine during which the male struts around and makes a cooing sound. Several hours later, they select a nest site (invariably the glass bowl) by crouching at the site and making a distinctive coo sound. Then the doves begin to build the nest. The male usually brings the nesting material to the nest site, where the female constructs the nest. Nest building may take a week or more, during which time the doves also copulate. Toward the end of this period, the female becomes very attached to the nest. She rarely leaves it, and if she is picked up, she holds onto some of the nest material with her feet. This attachment to the nest indicates that the female is ready to lay her eggs. She usually lays her first egg around 9 A.M. and her second at 5 P.M. the second day after that. Only two eggs are laid in each reproductive cycle. When the eggs are laid, the doves take turns incubating them. The female usually spends about 18 hours a day sitting on the eggs, and the male incubates the eggs the rest of the time. After 14 days of incubation, the eggs hatch, and for 10 to 12 days the parents feed the young with a substance called "crop milk," which they regurgitate from the crop. The young leave the nest after that, and the parenting behavior gradually subsides.

During the normal sequence of events, the doves start incubating their eggs as soon as the eggs are present. The presence of the eggs elicits incubation behavior. However, this behavior does not always occur when a pair of doves is exposed to a nest with eggs. Rather, there are certain special preconditions for incubation. The doves have to remain in social contact with each other for five to seven days and be given a chance to build a nest. If they do not have sufficient contact or are not permitted to build a nest, incubation does not occur right away. The prolonged interaction between male and female and the nest-building behavior stimulate the release of an ovarian hormone, progesterone. This hormone must be present for eggs in a nest to elicit incubation behavior. Other aspects of the reproductive sequence also appear to be controlled by the presence of particular hormones. Estrogen is involved in elicitation of nest-building behavior, and prolactin, a hormone secreted by the pituitary gland, facilitates parental feeding behavior elicited by newly hatched young. Thus, the reproductive behavior of ring doves represents a sequence of hormone/behavior interactions. Lehrman (1965, p. 370) has described the events as follows:

> Participation in courtship appears to induce the secretion of hormones which facilitate the building of a nest; participation in nest building under these conditions contributes stimulation of the secretion of the hormone(s) which induce the birds to sit on eggs. Stimulation arising from the

act of sitting on the eggs induces the further secretion of a hormone which (a) induces the birds to continue incubation, and (b) helps bring the birds into a condition of readiness to feed the young when they hatch.

Box 2.1. Man and Bird "Dance" Together

On a recent springlike morning in the rolling farmlands among the foothills of the Baraboo (Wisconsin) range, a male researcher at the International Crane Foundation quietly approached a female whooping crane that was pacing, with stately strides, in its 25-foot-long enclosure. In step with her in a kind of informal ballet, he moved closer, and the five-foot-tall animal showed no fear.

At about eight feet from her, he stopped, first raised one arm high, then the other, then both, as he alternately crouched and stood upright in a kind of crude bobbing dance.

The crane responded by bowing her neck and head up and down, almost matching the man's rhythm, made movements that resembled a dance on stilts and then spread her wings apart [Webster, 1980, p. C1].

The "dance" is part of the procedure to induce Tex, a female whooping crane, to reproduce. Presumably because Tex has been raised in captivity without association with male cranes, the bird will not engage in courtship with other whooping cranes. However, she will court a human being, preferably a male Caucasian who wears glasses and does not have red hair. The courtship behavior is an integral part of initiating the reproductive cycle. The hope of the "dancers" at the International Crane Foundation is that the courtship dance will make Tex more receptive to artificial insemination, thus enhancing the chances that she will lay a viable egg.

Elicited behavior and complex response sequences

In our discussion of elicited behavior so far, we have been concerned mainly with how occurrences of individual responses are controlled by specific eliciting stimuli. However, elicited responses do not occur in a behavioral vacuum. Live animals are continually engaged in one activity or another, and elicited responses are part of this ongoing stream of behavior. Some elicited responses are not closely linked to the animal's other activities. Reflexive eye blinking, swallowing, and sneezing, for example, can occur just about anywhere in the organism's stream of activities. In contrast, other types of elicited behavior occur only as a part of rigid response sequences. Such responses always occur after certain specific activities and are followed by other specific actions. Rigid response sequences are observed if one response produces stimuli that elicit a second response, the second response produces stimuli that elicit a third response, and so forth. In such a sequence, the order of responses is fixed.

An interesting example of a fairly rigid response sequence resulting from a chain of elicited responses is the courtship and reproductive behavior of the three-spined stickleback fish (Tinbergen, 1952). After the male stickleback has staked out his territory at the beginning of the breeding season, he builds a nest. The male first digs a shallow pit about 2 in. square. He then collects a heap of weeds in the nest, coats the weeds with a sticky substance from his kidney, and makes a tunnel in the pile of weeds. The finished tunnel is slightly shorter than the length of an adult stickleback. During all this activity, the male's coloration changes. When not breeding, the male is an inconspicuous gray. By the time the nest is finished, the male's chin and belly have turned a bright reddish color, his back bluish white, and his eyes blue. In this state, the male is ready to begin courtship and reproduction.

While the male has been preparing the nest, the females have developed swollen bellies holding 50 to 100 eggs each. When a female comes near the nest area, the male begins to court her with a series of zigzag swimming motions (see Figure 2.6). He turns away from her and then turns toward her. After each zigzag advance toward the female, the male stops for a moment and then performs another zigzag movement. This distinctive swimming pattern causes the female to swim toward the male with her head up. When she begins to approach, the male swims toward the nest, and the female follows. At the nest, the male makes a series of rapid thrusts with his snout at the entrance of the tunnel while raising his dorsal spines. These actions stimulate the female to swim into the nest tunnel, her head sticking out at one end and her tail at the other. The male then prods the base of her tail, causing her to release the eggs. When the eggs are released, the female leaves the nest, and the male enters the tunnel and fertilizes the eggs. He then chases the female away. Remarkably, the entire response sequence from courtship to fertilization takes only about 1 min. A given male may entice three to five females to lay eggs in his nest. After this, his coloration becomes darker, and he becomes unresponsive to females swimming near his territory, sometimes even chasing away ones that get too close to the nest. Instead of courtship, the male becomes preoccupied with fanning the eggs to provide sufficient oxygen until they hatch.

Just as in other types of animals, reproductive behavior in the stickleback requires the presence of certain sex hormones. These hormones are produced in the early spring in response to lengthening of days. However, the specific sequence of responses that occurs in nestbuilding, courtship, and reproduction is governed by the presence of the proper eliciting stimuli in the proper order. Each response in the sequence creates the stimulus that elicits the next response. Thus, the male does not collect a pile of weeds until he has dug out a shallow nest site. If the nest somehow becomes filled with soil, the male will dig the nest out again before collecting the weeds. Courtship does not begin until the nest is complete. In the courtship routine, the male's zigzag movements elicit the ap-

Figure 2.6. Courtship and reproduction in the stickleback. (A) The male first swims toward the female with zigzag motions. (B) He then guides the female to the nest and makes a series of rapid thrusts with his snout at the tunnel entrance with his dorsal spines raised. (C) The female swims into the tunnel, and the male prods the base of her tail, causing her to release the eggs. (D) After fertilizing the eggs, the male fans them to provide sufficient oxygen until they hatch. *(After Tinbergen, 1952.)*

proach response in the female. The female's approach behavior, in turn, acts as a stimulus to make the male swim toward the nest. This behavior on the part of the male stimulates the female to follow. The male's thrusts at the entrance of the nest stimulate the female to enter the nest. This in turn stimulates the male to stroke the female's tail, which in turn stimulates the release of eggs, and so on. Because a given response of one of the animals constitutes the eliciting stimulus for the next response in the other animal, the responses always occur in the prescribed order. This mechanism serves to connect a series of elicited responses into a predictable sequence that takes place very rapidly. The behavior of the male and the female are thus coordinated so as to result in propagation of the species. It is rather remarkable that such a complex response sequence involving the social interaction of two organisms can be so precisely put together by merely linking a series of elicited responses.

Concluding comments

Even in the absence of learning, animals are capable of a great variety and richness of activities. Much of innate behavior occurs as reflex responses. Some reflexes are elicited by relatively simple types of stimuli, whereas others involve more-complicated sign stimuli. Once elicited, the responses are usually followed by feedback cues. Feedback may be provided by the presence or absence of the eliciting stimulus or by other events. In either case, feedback cues can have an important role in determining the future likelihood and direction of elicited responses, resulting in seemingly purposive activities, such as taxes and kineses. Another important source of control for innate behavior is the internal state of the organism. Internal physiological state may reflect the organism's level of arousal or the presence of circulating hormones. Certain innate responses (those involved in sexual behavior in most species, for example) will not occur unless the proper internal state exists. These innate behavioral mechanisms can result in complex response sequences and social behavior and provide the substrate on which learning mechanisms operate.

CHAPTER THREE

Habituation and Sensitization

Chapter 3 begins our discussion of learning by introducing two of the most elementary processes involved in changing behavior by providing particular types of experiences. In one of these processes, habituation, the organism's responsiveness to the eliciting stimulus decreases. In the other, sensitization, responsiveness increases. Repeated presentations of the eliciting stimulus may activate one or both of these processes. After describing several examples of habituation and sensitization, we describe both neurophysiological and behavioral investigations of habituation and sensitization. We then describe the role and mechanisms of habituation in situations that evoke complex emotional responses.

In the previous chapter we discussed various types of innate behavior that are elicited and/or controlled by environmental events. Some of the responses we described are relatively simple and are elicited by particular discrete stimuli. Others involve numerous response components and are triggered by more complex forms of stimulation. Nevertheless, all are reflexes in that they are caused by identifiable stimuli. Most people believe that reflexive behavior invariably occurs every time the required eliciting stimulus is presented. It is assumed that such behavior is not subject to modification. As it turns out, this belief is very far from the truth. Many of the chapters of this book are devoted to describing how elicited behavior can be changed. Some mechanisms of behavioral change involve com-

plex procedures and processes. In the present chapter, we begin the discussion of the flexibility of elicited behavior by considering a very simple question: How does elicited behavior change with repetitions of the eliciting stimulus?

Effects of repeated stimulation: Three examples

Sucking in human infants

One of the most important reflexes in the newborn is sucking. Infants will suck when something such as a nipple, finger, or pacifier is touched to the cheek or placed in the mouth. Does this response always occur in the same way when the eliciting stimulus is presented? This question has been studied by several investigators. In one experiment (Lipsitt & Kaye, 1965), reflexive sucking of a baby-bottle nipple was compared with sucking of a piece of 1/4-in. rubber tubing. The stimulus was repeatedly presented to newborn infants. Each stimulus presentation lasted 10 sec, and 30 sec elapsed between successive presentations. Tests with the tube and nipple were alternated so that the babies received five trials with one stimulus followed by five trials with the other, and so on. Figure 3.1 shows the number of sucking responses observed on each trial.

The results shown in Figure 3.1 have several noteworthy aspects. First, we see that the initial amount of sucking differed for the two stimuli. The babies sucked the nipple more than the rubber tube. This is not surprising, because the nipple no doubt more closely resembles the natural stimulus for sucking (the mother's nipple) than the tube. Second, there were systematic differences in the patterns of responses to repeated presentations of the two stimuli. Generally, as the nipple was repeatedly introduced, the babies sucked more and more vigorously. The overall level of sucking was higher in the

fifth series of five trials than in the first series. In addition, within each series of five nipple trials, the babies usually increased their sucking from the first to the fifth trial. The opposite trends occurred when the babies were tested with the tubing. Here, the overall level of sucking was lower during the fifth series of five trials than during the first, and the babies usually decreased their sucking from the first to the fifth trial within each series.

Startle response in rats

Variations in elicited behavior of the type that occur when a stimulus is repeatedly presented to elicit sucking can also be observed in many other response systems. The startle reaction of rats provides another illustration. The startle response is a sudden jump or tensing of the muscles when an unexpected stimulus is presented. You can be tremendously startled, for example, when a friend unexpectedly comes up behind you and taps you on the shoulder. In rats, the reaction can be measured by placing the animal in a stabilimeter chamber (see Figure 3.2). A stabilimeter is a small enclosure held in place by several springs. When startled, the animal jumps, producing a bouncing movement of the stabilimeter chamber. Sudden movements of the chamber can be precisely measured to indicate the vigor of the startle reaction.

The startle reaction can be elicited in rats by all sorts of stimuli, including brief tones and lights. In one experiment, Davis (1974) investigated the startle reaction of rats to presentations of a brief (90-millisecond) loud tone (110 decibels [dB], 4000 cycles per sec). Two groups of rats were tested. Each group received 100 successive tone trials separated by 30 sec. In addition, a noise generator provided background noise that sounded something like water running from a faucet. For one group, the background noise was relatively quiet (60 dB); for the other, the background noise was rather loud (80 dB).

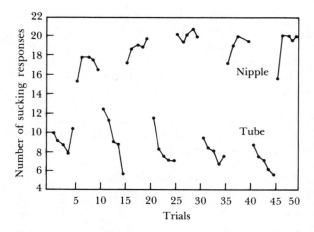

Figure 3.1. Number of sucking responses by human newborns during successive trials. A rubber nipple and a rubber tube served as stimuli in alternate 5-trial blocks. (*After Lipsitt & Kaye, 1965.*)

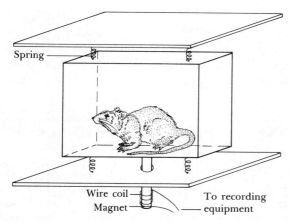

Figure 3.2. Stabilimeter apparatus to measure the startle response of rats. A small chamber is balanced on springs between two stationary platforms. A magnet, surrounded by a wire coil, is fixed to the bottom of the chamber. Sudden movements of the rat result in movements of the chamber that produce an electrical current in the wire coil. (*After Hoffman & Fleshler, 1964.*)

The results of the experiment are presented in Figure 3.3. As was true of the sucking reflex, repeated presentations of the eliciting stimulus (the 4000-cycles-per-sec tone) did not always produce the same startle response. For subjects tested in the presence of the soft background noise (60 dB), repetitions of the tone resulted in smaller and smaller startle reactions. This outcome is similar to what was observed when the rubber tube was repeatedly presented to elicit sucking in babies. In contrast, when the background noise was loud (80 dB), repetitions of the tone elicited progressively larger and more vigorous startle reactions. This outcome is comparable to what was observed when sucking was repeatedly elicited by the nipple. Thus, as with sucking, repeated elicitations of the startle reflex produced a decrease in the startle reaction in some circumstances and an increase in others.

Mobbing in chaffinches

In the examples described above, repeated presentations of the eliciting stimulus produced either a decline or an increase in the elicited response. There are many examples of such one-directional changes in responsiveness with repeated stimulation. However, in numerous other circumstances, a combination of these two types of changes occurs. Repeated stimulation may at first produce an increase in responsiveness, which is followed by a decrease. To illustrate the diversity of response systems in which such changes in responsivity occur, we shall describe the mobbing behavior of chaffinches.

Mobbing directed toward a potential predator occurs in a variety of small birds. When it is sufficiently vigorous, the mobbing behavior may cause the predator to leave the area. Chaffinches, for example, will mob a live owl or a stuffed model of an owl. When the owl first appears, the birds become agitated and begin to move their heads and then their bodies and tails. If the owl remains, the vigor of these movements increases, and the birds begin to make the "mobbing call." If there are enough chaffinches in the area, the mobbing call can become very loud and may scare the owl away.

In a classic experiment, Hinde (1954) mea-

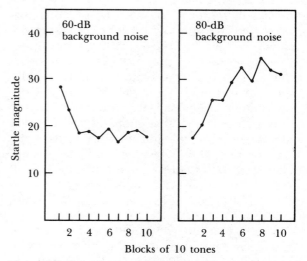

Figure 3.3. Magnitude of the startle response of rats to successive presentations of a tone with background noise of 60 and 80 dB. (*From Davis, 1974.*)

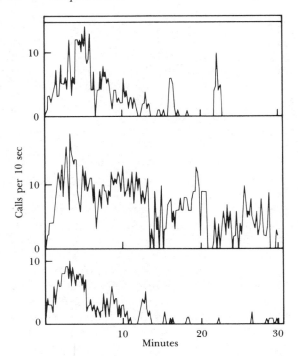

Figure 3.4. Mobbing calls of three individual chaffinches when exposed to a stuffed owl for 30 min. *(From Hinde, 1954.)*

sured the mobbing calls of individual chaffinches in response to a stuffed owl that was presented continuously for 30 min. Figure 3.4 shows the calls of three of the birds during the 30-min period. The presence of the stuffed owl initially resulted in a progressive increase in the intensity of the mobbing call. However, as the owl stimulus remained, the intensity of calling gradually declined. The mobbing call stopped almost entirely in the first and third birds by the end of the 30-min test period. The second chaffinch continued to make the mobbing call for 30 min. However, the intensity of its call also decreased with prolonged exposure to the stuffed owl.

The pattern of responding shown by the chaffinches is observed with a wide variety of species in a variety of situations (see Thompson, Groves, Teyler, & Roemer, 1973, for a review). Responding first increases and then declines

with repeated presentations (or one prolonged presentation) of the eliciting stimulus. The opposite type of bidirectional change in responsiveness, an initial decline in responding followed by an increase, does not occur.

The concepts of habituation and sensitization

The three studies described above show that both decreases and increases in responding occur with repeated (or continuous) presentation of an eliciting stimulus. Decreases in responsiveness produced by repeated stimulation are examples of **habituation.** Increases in responsiveness are examples of **sensitization.** Habituation and sensitization represent the most fundamental changes in behavior that result from experience.

Adaptiveness and pervasiveness of habituation and sensitization

At any moment, there are always many stimuli impinging on the organism. Habituation and sensitization processes help organize and focus behavior so that it can be effective in this sea of stimulation. Even such a simple situation as sitting at a desk involves a myriad of sensations. There are the color, texture, and brightness of the paint on the walls, sounds of the air-conditioning system, noises from the other room, the smell of the air, the color and texture of the table, the tactile sensations of the chair against your legs, seat, and back, and so on. If you were to respond to all the stimuli in the situation, your behavior would be disorganized and chaotic. Habituation and sensitization mechanisms help reduce reactivity to irrelevant stimuli and channel behavior into organized and directed actions in response to only some of the stimuli you experience.

Habituation and sensitization process are so fundamental to the adjustment of organisms to the environment that they occur in nearly all species and response systems. We have discussed three examples in some detail. There are also numerous instances of habituation and sensitization in common human experience. For example, most people who own a grandfather clock do not notice each time it chimes. They have completely habituated to the clock's sounds. In fact, they are more likely to notice when the clock misses a scheduled chime. In a sense, this is unfortunate, because they may have purchased the grandfather clock specifically for the beauty of its sound. Similarly, people who live on busy streets, near railroad tracks, or close to an airport may become entirely habituated to the noises that frequently intrude into their homes. In contrast, visitors are much more likely to respond to, and be bothered by, such sounds.

Driving a car involves exposure to a large array of complex visual and auditory stimuli. You may recall that the first time you drove a car for a few hours, you were probably very anxious and alert and found driving to be rather tiring. The fatigue probably occurs because naive drivers respond to many more stimuli in their environment than highly experienced drivers. As a person becomes an experienced driver, he or she habituates to the numerous stimuli that are irrelevant to driving, such as details of the color and texture of the road, what kind of telephone poles line the sides of the road, certain tactile sensations of the steering wheel, and certain sounds from the engine. Habituation to irrelevant cues is particularly prominent during long driving trips. If you are driving continuously for several hours, you are likely to become oblivious to all kinds of stimuli that are irrelevant to keeping the car on the road. If you then come across an accident or arrive in a new town, you are likely to "wake up" and again pay attention to various things that you had been ignoring. Passing a bad accident or coming to a new town is an arousing stimulus that changes your state and sensitizes various orientation responses that were previously habituated.

If you ever had a cat or dog that you brought home when it was young, chances are the animal was extremely agitated and cried a great deal during the first few days. This occurs because most of the stimuli in the animal's new environment are effective in eliciting responses. As the cat or dog gets used to its new home— that is, as it becomes habituated to many of the stimuli in the situation—it stops being agitated and becomes generally less active. Similar effects are experienced by people. If you visit a new place or encounter people you have never dealt with before, you are likely to pay attention to all sorts of stimuli that you ordinarily ignore. If you are in a new building, for example, you are likely to study every sign on the walls in an effort to find where you have to go. You fail to respond to such details in places that are highly familiar, so much so that you may not be able to describe certain salient features, such as the color of certain walls or the type of knob that is attached to a door you use every day.

Neural analysis of habituation and sensitization

Because habituation and sensitization involve the simplest types of modification of elicited behavior, these phenomena have attracted the attention of many investigators interested in the neural basis of learning. We will describe one of the prominent neurophysiological models of habituation and sensitization. However, before doing so, it is important to distinguish between habituation and other processes that can also decrease the likelihood that a stimulus will elicit a response.

Distinctions between habituation, sensory adaptation, and response fatigue. As noted above, in many situations the response initially elicited by a stimulus ceases to occur when the stimulus is frequently repeated. This decline in responding is one of the identifying characteristics of habituation. However, not all instances in which repetitions of a stimulus result in a decline in responding represent habituation. As discussed in Chapter 2, three types of events take place whenever a stimulus elicits a response. First, the stimulus activates one of the sense organs of the body, such as the eyes or ears. This process generates sensory neural impulses that are relayed to the central nervous system (the spinal cord and brain). Here the sensory messages are relayed to motor nerves. The neural impulses in motor nerves in turn activate the muscles that create the observed response. The elicited response will not be observed if for some reason the sense organs become temporarily insensitive to stimulation. You may be temporarily blinded by a bright light, for example, or suffer a temporary hearing loss because of repeated exposures to a loud noise. Such decreases in sensitivity are called **sensory adaptation.** The reflex response will also fail to occur if the muscles involved become incapacitated by fatigue. Sensory adaptation and response fatigue are impediments to the elicited response that are produced outside the nervous system, in sense organs and muscles.

The likelihood of a response will also be changed if the neural processes involved in the elicited behavior are altered. Transmission of neural impulses from sensory to motor neurons can be hindered or facilitated by various types of changes in the nervous system. Habituation and sensitization are assumed to involve such neurophysiological changes. Thus, habituation is different from sensory adaptation and response fatigue. In habituation, the subject ceases to respond to a stimulus even though it remains fully capable of sensing the stimulus and of making the muscle movements required for the response. The response fails to occur because for some reason the sensory neural impulses are not relayed to the motor neurons.

Dual-process theory of habituation and sensitization. Different types of underlying neural processes are assumed to be responsible for increases and decreases in responsiveness to stimulation. One category of changes in the nervous system involves reductions in the ability of a stimulus to elicit a response. Such a change is called a **habituation process.** Another category of changes in the nervous system produce increases in responsiveness. Such a change is called a **sensitization process.** Both types of processes may occur simultaneously in a given situation. The results observed will depend on which process is stronger. The left-hand graph in Figure 3.5 illustrates a hypothetical situation in which repetitions of a stimulus strengthen the habituation process more than the sensitization process. The net effect of these changes is a decline in the elicited response across trials (a habituation effect). The right-hand graph illustrates the opposite outcome: repetitions of a stimulus strengthen the sensitization process more than the habituation process, and the result is an increase in the elicited response across trials (a sensitization effect). Thus, the changes in the elicited behavior that actually occur in a particular situation represent the net effect of habituation and sensitization processes.

On the basis of neurophysiological research, Groves and Thompson (1970; see also Thompson et al., 1973) suggested that habituation and sensitization processes occur in different parts of the nervous system. Habituation processes are assumed to occur in what they call the **S-R system.** This system consists of the shortest neural path that connects the sense organs stimulated by the eliciting stimulus and the muscles involved in making the elicited response. (The S-R system may be viewed as the reflex arc.) In contrast, sensitization processes are assumed to occur in what is called the **state system.** This consists of other parts of the nervous system that determine the organism's general level of responsiveness, or readiness to respond. The state system is relatively quiescent during sleep, for example. Drugs such as stimulants or depressants may alter the functioning of the state system and thereby change responsiveness. The state system is also altered by emotional experi-

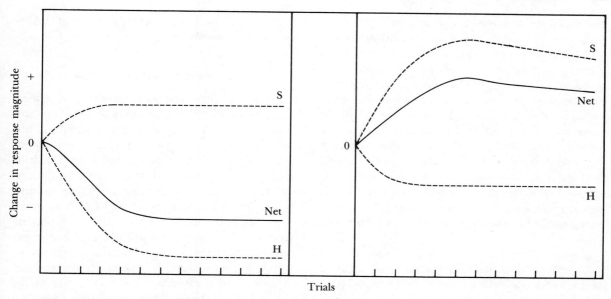

Figure 3.5. Hypothetical data illustrating the dual-process theory of habituation and sensitization. The dashed lines indicate the strength of the habituation (H) and sensitization (S) processes across trials. The solid line indicates the net effects of these two processes.

ences. The jumpiness that accompanies fear is caused by sensitization of the state system. The state system thus determines the animal's readiness to respond, whereas the S-R system enables the animal to make the specific responses elicited by the stimuli in the situation. The behavioral changes that are observed reflect the combined actions of these two systems.

The examples of habituation and sensitization described at the beginning of the chapter can be easily interpreted in terms of the dual-process theory. First consider the results with the sucking reflex (Figure 3.1). Repeated presentations of the 1/4-in. tubing produced a decrement in responding. This may be explained by assuming that the tube stimulus influenced only the S-R system and hence activated habituation processes. The interpretation of the results with the nipple stimulus is a bit more involved. The nipple was a much more powerful stimulus for the babies than the 1/4-in. tubing; it elicited much more vigorous

sucking even at the beginning of the experiment. The increases in sucking that occurred with repeated presentations of the nipple can be explained by assuming that the nipple stimulus not only involved the S-R system but also activated the state system. Because a nipple is a very significant stimulus for babies, presentations of the nipple increased the babies' alertness and readiness to respond, and this effect presumably produced the progressive increments in sucking. Such sensitization did not occur with the 1/4-in. tube; this stimulus evidently does not increase babies' alertness and arousal.

The dual-process theory is also consistent with the habituation and sensitization effects we noted in the startle reaction of rats (Figure 3.3). When subjects were tested with a relatively quiet background noise (60 dB), there was little in the situation to arouse them. Therefore, we can assume that the experimental procedures did not produce changes in the state system. Repeated presentations of the startle-eliciting tone merely activated the S-R system and resulted in habituation of the startle response. However, the opposite outcome occurred when the animals were tested in the presence of a loud background noise (80 dB). In this case increased startle reactions occurred to successive presentations of the tone. Because the identical tone was used to elicit the startle response for both groups, differences in the results cannot be attributed to the tone. Rather, one has to assume that the loud background noise increased arousal or readiness to respond. This sensitization of the state system was presumably responsible for the increase in the startle reaction.

Interpreting the changes in mobbing calls made by chaffinches to a stuffed owl requires the sensitization as well as the habituation process. The birds first increased and then decreased their mobbing calls. Apparently, the stuffed owl first increased the chaffinches' arousal or readiness to respond. However, the stuffed owl was not a strong enough stimulus to produce prolonged sensitization, and the mobbing calls habituated with continued exposure to the owl.

The above analyses of sucking, startle, and mobbing highlight several important features of the dual-process theory. As we have seen, the state and S-R systems are differently activated by repeated presentations of a stimulus. The S-R system is activated every time a stimulus elicits a response, because it is the neural circuit that conducts impulses from sensory input to response output. The state system becomes involved only in special circumstances. First, some extraneous event (such as an intense background noise) may increase the subject's alertness and sensitize the state system. Second, the state system may be sensitized by the repeated stimulus presentations if the stimulus is sufficiently intense or significant for the subject (a nipple as opposed to a rubber tube, for example). If the intense stimulus is presented often enough so that successive presentations occur while the subject remains sensitized from the preceding ones, progressive increases in the response will be observed.

Other experimental situations

The dual-process theory gives us a general framework for understanding habituation and sensitization. In addition, much research has been done to describe these phenomena in more detail. Research on this topic has involved numerous response systems, from contractions in earthworms to orienting responses in humans. We have already described three such experimental situations, involving sucking, the startle reflex, and mobbing. Several other experimental situations have played a prominent role in the understanding of habituation, sensitization, and elicited behavior in general. We will examine three other important response systems below.

The orienting response. A great deal of research on habituation and sensitization has concerned the orienting response in humans. Much of this work was performed by the Soviet psychologist Sokolov and his intellectual descendants (see Sokolov, 1963; Sokolov & Vinogradova, 1975). Many of the conclusions of the Soviet research have been confirmed by American scientists (for example, Zimney & Kienstra, 1967; Zimney & Miller, 1966; Zimney & Schwabe, 1965). The **orienting response** is defined as "an unspecified reflex or set of responses which is elicited by a novel stimulus (or a change in a familiar stimulus) and which habituates with repetitions of the eliciting event." The orienting response may include overt motor movements, such as turning toward the novel stimulus. However, in most experiments various physiological responses to novel events have been measured as indexes of orientation. Novel stimuli often elicit momentary changes in the electrical resistance of the skin (this is the galvanic skin response, or GSR), heart rate, and respiration rate and also result in a desynchronization of brain waves (recorded on the EEG) and a redistribution of blood (vaso-constriction in the fingers and vasodilation in the head). These physiological responses are considered to be part of the orienting response because they are elicited by novelty itself rather than by any particular features of the novel event. Thus, a common set of physiological responses occurs when novel lights, tones, or other stimuli are presented as well as when familiar stimuli of all sorts are changed.

Being interested in the effects of novelty on the organism's reactions, Sokolov conducted many experiments in which a stimulus was first repeatedly presented until the orienting response became habituated. The subjects were then tested with variations of the original stimulus. The common finding in these experiments was that the orienting response remained minimal if the test stimulus was very similar to the original habituated stimulus. However, various alterations of the original habituated stimulus resulted in recovery of the orienting response. Sokolov observed that many types of changes in the habituated simulus could produce response recovery. On the basis of such experiments, he formulated the *response-comparator model*. According to this model, repeated presentations of a stimulus result in the formation of a neuronal model of the stimulus in the cortex. The subject presumably compares all incoming stimuli with the neuronal model it has formed. When an incoming stimulus matches the neuronal model, the stimulus processing ends there, and no overt response occurs. In contrast, when an incoming stimulus does not match the neuronal model, neural impulses are sent to the reticular formation, and the orienting response occurs.

Contemporary theories of habituation have abandoned many of the physiological assumptions that Sokolov made, because experiments have shown that habituation can take place without an intact cortex. Thus, habituation does not depend on high-level neural processes. However, some current theorists retain the idea that some kind of comparison takes place between incoming stimuli and stimuli that are already somehow represented in the nervous system. We will describe one of these theories in Chapter 12 (Wagner, 1976, 1978, 1979).

Ingestional neophobia. Many species of animals avoid eating new foods or foods in a new container or a new place. This phenomenon is called **ingestional neophobia**—suppression of eating induced by a fear of novelty. Most things in the physical environment are inedible or poisonous. Ingestional neophobia ensures that animals will not eat much of unfamiliar substances and thereby provides protection from harmful materials. The phenomenon is well known to exterminators. It is very difficult, for example, to kill rats or mice in a barn by putting out poisoned bait, because the bait is likely to be unfamiliar and the animals will avoid eating it. Animals will similarly avoid unfamiliar traps. However, neophobia gradually habituates with repeated exposure to the novel food or trap.

Domjan (1976) investigated habituation of the initial aversion response to a novel taste solution. Two groups of water-deprived laboratory rats were tested. On each day of the experiment, group S received access to a 2.0% saccharin solution for 30 min, followed by access to tap water for 30 min. The controls, group W, received access to tap water only for 30 min daily. The amount of saccharin and water each group drank is shown in Figure 3.6. Group S drank very little saccharin the first time it encountered the solution but drank a substantial amount of water instead. With repeated exposure to the saccharin solution, saccharin intake gradually increased and water consumption gradually declined for group S. In contrast, group W drank approximately the same amount of water throughout the experiment. By the end of the study, group S was consuming as much saccharin solution as group W drank of water. Other research has shown that the habituation of ingestional neophobia is produced merely by exposure to the novel edible. It is not necessary

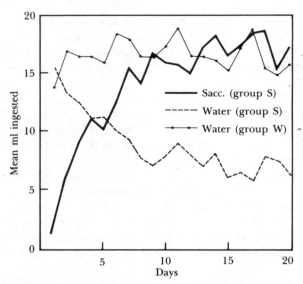

Figure 3.6. Habituation of ingestional neophobia. Group S was given access to a 2.0% saccharin solution for 30 min, followed by tap water for 30 min, each day. Group W received access to tap water for 30 min daily. Saccharin intake in group S gradually increased with repeated exposures to the solution. *(From Domjan, 1976.)*

for the animals to experience positive benefits from ingestion (such as satisfaction of hunger or thirst) in order for them to lose their neophobia (Domjan, 1976).

Neophobia for taste and other stimuli is also subject to sensitization. If an animal becomes sick, its wariness of eating new foods will be increased. This sensitization of ingestional neophobia occurs even if the sickness was produced by something other than food poisoning (Domjan, 1977). You may have experienced something like this when you were sick with the flu or another disease. People are much less inclined to try new foods when they are sick than when they are feeling fine.

Alarm and escape response in birds. Animals display aversion responses to a variety of novel stimuli in addition to novel foods. For example, this aversion to novelty appears to be the basis for the alarm reactions of birds to certain visual stimuli. Many birds make alarm calls

Box 3.1. Mere-Exposure Effects in Humans

Social psychologists have extensively studied the effects of repeated exposure on the acceptability of various types of stimuli for humans. The experiments are similar to the neophobia-habituation experiments conducted with animals. People are repeatedly exposed to a stimulus and are then asked to rate how much they like it. The common finding has been that repeated exposure increases the favorability rating. Such results have been obtained with all sorts of stimuli, including pictures of faces, nonsense words, Chineselike ideographs, and musical excerpts (for example, Heingartner & Hall, 1974; Zajonc, 1968). Although people say that they know what they like, it is often found that they like what they know!

Repeated exposure generally increases preference for various stimuli, but not always. Excessive exposure to a stimulus may result in a temporary decline in preference, as implied by the adage "Familiarity breeds contempt." It appears that repeated exposure to a stimulus produces both a relatively long-lasting increase in preference and a temporary decline in preference with extensive exposure (Hill, 1978).

and try to flee when they see a potential predator, such as a hawk, flying overhead. The alarm reaction can also be elicited by the silhouette of a hawklike model that is moved above the bird. Research by early European ethologists suggested that the model had to have certain critical hawklike features and had to be moved in the same way that a hawk would fly in order to elicit the alarm reaction (see Tinbergen, 1951). It was therefore suggested that the alarm reaction was the product of an evolutionary adaptation to respond to specific sign-stimulus characteristics of hawk predators. More recent experiments suggest an entirely different interpretation. Studies with quail (Martin & Melvin, 1964) and young turkeys (Schleidt, 1961a, 1961b) indicate that novelty is the critical feature for eliciting alarm and escape responses. Birds will become alarmed the first time they see even a circular or rectangular silhouette moving overhead. These alarm responses habituate if the subjects are repeatedly exposed to the eliciting stimulus. Habituation occurs both with hawklike models and with arbitrary circular and rectangular shapes. However, after subjects have become habituated to one stimulus, the response will reappear when another stimulus is presented. These results suggest a new explanation for alarm and escape responses in the natural environment. Hawks are seen much less often than other types of birds. Consequently, animals become habituated to the sight of other flying birds but not to the sight of hawks or hawklike figures. The frequency of hawks compared with other moving silhouettes appears to control the alarm response, rather than special sign-stimulus characteristics.

Characteristics of habituation and sensitization

Much research has been performed to determine how various factors influence habituation and sensitization processes. The characteristics of habituation and sensitization are not perfectly uniform across all species and response systems. However, there are many commonalities; we will describe some of the most important.

Time course of habituation and sensitization

Most of the types of learning we will describe in later chapters are retained for long periods of time (one or more years). In contrast, habituation and sensitization effects are not invariably long-lasting. In many cases, the procedures used strongly determine how long the effects persist.

Time course of sensitization. Sensitization processes generally have temporary effects. Al-

though in some instances sensitization persists for several weeks (for example, Kandel, 1976), in most situations the increased responsiveness is short-lived. In fact, the temporary nature of an increase in responding may be used to identify the phenomenon as a sensitization effect. Different sensitization effects may persist for different amounts of time. Davis (1974), for example, investigated the sensitizing effect of a 25-min exposure to a loud noise (80 dB) in rats. As expected, the loud noise sensitized the startle response to a tone. However, this increased reactivity persisted for only 10–15 min after the loud noise was turned off. In other response systems, sensitization dissipates much more rapidly. For example, sensitization of the spinal hindlimb-flexion reflex in cats persists for only about 3 sec (Groves & Thompson, 1970). However, in all response systems the duration of sensitization effects is determined by the intensity of the sensitizing stimulus. More intense stimuli produce larger increases in responsiveness, and the sensitization effects persist longer.

Time course of habituation. Habituation also persists for varying amounts of time. With sensitization, differences in the time course of the effect usually reflect only quantitative differences in the same underlying mechanism. In contrast, there appear to be two *qualitatively* different types of habituation effects. One type of habituation is similar to most cases of sensitization in that it dissipates relatively quickly, within seconds or minutes. The other type is much longer-lasting and may persist for many days. These two types of habituation were nicely illustrated in a recent experiment on the startle response of rats (Leaton, 1976). The test stimulus was a high-pitched, loud tone presented for 2 sec. The animals were first allowed to get used to the experimental chamber without any tone presentations. Each rat then received a single test trial with the tone stimulus once a day for 11 days. Because of the long (24-hour) interval between stimulus presentations, any decrements in responding produced by the stimulus presentations were assumed to exemplify the long-lasting habituation process. The transient (short-lasting) habituation process was activated in the next phase of the experiment by giving the subjects 300 closely spaced tone presentations (every 3 sec). Finally, the animals were given a single tone presentation 1, 2, and 3 days later, to measure recovery from the short-term habituation.

Figure 3.7 shows the results. The largest startle reaction was observed the first time the tone was presented. Progressively smaller reactions occurred during the next 10 days. Because the animals were tested only once every 24 hours in this phase, the progressive decrements in responding indicate that the habituating effects of the stimulus presentations persisted throughout the 11-day period. This long-lasting habituation process did not result in complete loss of the startle reflex. The animals still reacted a

little even on the 11th day. In contrast, startle reactions quickly ceased when the tone presentations occurred every 3 sec in the next phase of the experiment. However, this loss of responsiveness was only temporary. When the animals were tested with the tone 1, 2, and 3 days later, the startle response recovered to the level of the 11th day of the experiment. This recovery occurred simply because the tone was not presented for a long time (24 hours) and is called **spontaneous recovery.** Spontaneous recovery is the identifying characteristic of the short-term, or temporary, habituation effect.

Repeated presentations of a stimulus do not always result in both long-lasting and short-term habituation effects. With the spinal leg-flexion reflex in cats, for example, only the short-term habituation effect is observed (Thompson & Spencer, 1966). In such cases, spontaneous recovery completely restores the

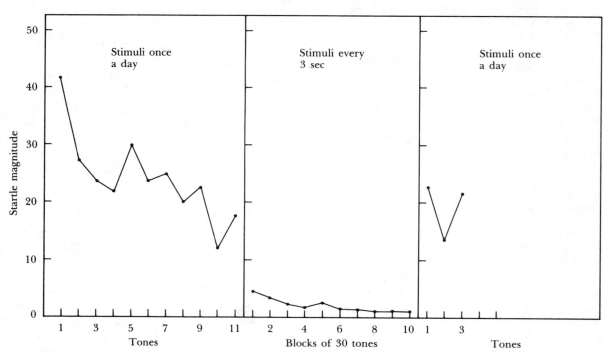

Figure 3.7. Startle response of rats to a tone presented once a day in Phase I, every 3 sec in Phase II, and once a day in Phase III. *(From Leaton, 1976.)*

animal's reaction to the eliciting stimulus if a long enough period of rest is permitted after habituation. In contrast, spontaneous recovery is never complete in situations that also involve long-term habituation effects, as in Leaton's experiment. As Figure 3.7 shows, the startle response was restored to some extent in the last phase of the experiment. However, even here the animals did not react as vigorously to the tone as they had the first time it was presented.

Few theories can explain the qualitative differences between the short- and long-term habituation effects. The dual-process theory described above was formulated primarily to account for only the temporary aspects of habituation and sensitization. Differences in the mechanisms of the short- and long-term habituation effects are detailed in a recent behavioral theory of information processing (Wagner, 1976, 1978, 1979). However, because this theory involves concepts in conditioning and memory, we will delay consideration of it until Chapter 12.

Stimulus specificity of habituation and sensitization

Habituation processes are assumed to be highly specific to the repeated stimulus. A response that has been habituated to one stimulus can be evoked in full strength by a new eliciting stimulus. We saw several instances in the examples of habituation described in the preceding section. The alarm reactions of small birds habituate when a particular shape (a circle, for example) is repeatedly passed overhead. However, the birds again show extreme alarm when a different shape (a rectangle, for example) is used as the eliciting stimulus. After complete habituation of the orienting response to one stimulus, the response occurs in its normal strength when a new stimulus is presented. Stimulus specificity characterizes all examples of habituation and has therefore been considered one of the defining characteristics of habituation (Thompson & Spencer, 1966).

Box 3.2. Sexual Responsiveness and Stimulus Change

Sexual intercourse is often followed by a temporary decrease in sexual responsiveness. Male rats and guinea pigs, for example, are not sexually aroused by a female after they have just mated with her. However, this decrease in responsiveness is specific to the female involved in the mating. If a new female is introduced, the male is again likely to engage in sexual activity. This effect is sometimes called the "Coolidge effect," after an anecdote involving President Coolidge and his wife. The story is that President and Mrs. Coolidge were taking a tour of an egg farm in separate parties. When Mrs. Coolidge saw one of the roosters, she asked her guide how many times the rooster mated each day. Impressed with the large number she was given, she asked one of her aides to make sure President Coolidge was told about this fact. When President Coolidge heard about the frequent sexual activity of the rooster, he asked whether the rooster always mated with the same female. He was told that of course it was often a different hen. Satisfied with the answer, the President asked that Mrs. Coolidge be also informed of this.

The fact that sexual responsiveness returns when a new female is introduced has applications in animal husbandry. For artificial insemination of cattle, for example, it is desirable to obtain large quantities of semen from bulls. The responsiveness of bulls declines if they are repeatedly presented with the same cow or cow model. Much more semen can be collected if several cows or models of cows are used (Hale & Almquist, 1960).

Although habituation effects are always stimulus-specific, some generalization of the effects may also occur. If birds have been habituated to a particular circle repeatedly passed overhead, they will also fail to respond to a new circle that is only slightly different from the old one. This phenomenon represents the **stimulus generalization** of habituation. As the new stimulus is made increasingly different from the habituated cue, the animals' reaction will increasingly resemble the response in the absence of habituation.

In contrast to the stimulus specificity observed with habituation processes, sensitization processes have traditionally been characterized by the absence of stimulus specificity. If the animal becomes aroused or sensitized for some reason, its reactivity to a variety of stimuli increases. Thus, if you have just become aroused by the sight of a bloody accident on the road, chances are you will become very sensitive and attentive to a wide variety of driving-related cues.

Effects of strong extraneous stimuli

As noted above, changing the nature of the eliciting stimulus can produce recovery of a habituated response. However, this is not the only way to quickly restore responding after habituation. The habituated response can be also restored by sensitizing the subject with exposure to a strong extraneous stimulus. This phenomenon is called **dishabituation.** The results of one dishabituation experiment are shown in Figure 3.8. The startle reaction of rats was repeatedly elicited by brief presentations of a tone. The animals' reaction to the tone at first increased and then habituated as the tone was repeatedly presented. (We saw a similar pattern of response changes in mobbing calls in chaffinches, Figure 3.4.) The process of habituation appeared to be finished by the 8th tone trial. Just before the 15th trial, half the rats were sensitized by exposure to a brief, bright flashing light, resulting in a substantial recovery of the habituated startle reaction. The animals responded much more to the tone on trial 15 than on the preceding trials. However, the sensitization effect was short-lasting. Responding to the tone returned to the habituated level on trials 16 and 17.

It is important to keep in mind that *dishabituation* refers to recovery in the response to the *previously* habituated stimulus. Figure 3.8 shows only the animals' reactions to repeated

presentations of the tone. Whatever responses the animals made to the dishabituating stimulus (the flashing light) are not of interest. The purpose of the experiment was to see how exposure to the dishabituating flashing light changed the animals' response to the original tone stimulus.

Effects of stimulus intensity and frequency

Habituation and sensitization effects are closely related to the intensity and frequency of the eliciting stimulus. (The frequency of a stimulus is the number of presentations in a given amount of time, such as a second.) Because of the importance of stimulus intensity and frequency for habituation and sensitization, many investigators have been concerned with these variables. Studies have provided a rather complex pattern of results. The outcomes observed depend on the response system investigated and the types of stimuli and test procedures used. Generally, an increase in responding (sensitization) is more likely if the repeatedly presented stimulis is very intense. Furthermore, with intense stimuli, more sensitization

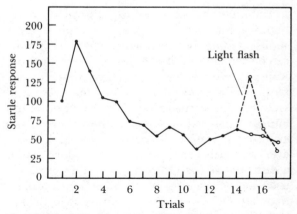

Figure 3.8. Dishabituation of the startle response to a tone. The response was first habituated by repeated presentations of the tone (trials 1–14). A brief flashing light was presented to half the subjects before the 15th tone trial, causing a temporary recovery of the startle reaction to the tone (see trial 15). (*From Groves & Thompson, 1970.*)

occurs as the frequency of the stimulus is increased (for example, Groves, Lee, & Thompson, 1969). In contrast, habituation effects predominate if the repeated stimulus is relatively weak. Furthermore, the rate of habituation increases as the frequency of the weak stimulus is increased, because more frequent presentations of the weak stimulus permit summation of the short-term habituation process (see Figure 3.7). Long-term habituation processes are not facilitated by increasing the frequency of stimulus presentations. In fact, there is some evidence that less long-term habituation occurs with more frequent stimulations (for example, Davis, 1970). Because repeated presentations of a stimulus can activate sensitization as well as short-term and long-term habituation processes, the effects of stimulus intensity and frequency in any given situation will depend on the combined effects of these various processes. For this reason, it is often difficult to predict what effects changes in stimulus intensity and frequency will have in any particular situation.

Changes in complex emotional responses

So far we have discussed how repetitions of an eliciting stimulus produce changes in relatively simple response systems. However, many stimuli produce much more complex effects on organisms than such responses as startling or orienting. A stimulus may evoke love, fear, euphoria, terror, satisfaction, uneasiness, or a combination of these emotions. In this section we will describe the pattern of reactions by organisms to complex emotion-arousing stimuli and how this pattern of emotional responses changes with repetitions of the stimulus. These issues have been most systematically addressed by the **opponent process** theory of motivation proposed by Solomon and his collaborators (Hoffman & Solomon, 1974; Solomon, 1977; Solomon & Corbit, 1973, 1974). We will describe the theory and its implications.

The opponent-process theory of motivation

What happens when an emotion-arousing stimulus is presented and then removed? Consider the reactions of a dog exposed to brief, painful electric shocks while restrained in a harness. Solomon and Corbit (1973, pp. 158–159) describe as follows what was observed in one experiment:

> During the first few shocks, the dog appeared to be terrified: it screeched, thrashed about, its pupils dilated, its eyes bulged, its hair stood on end, its ears lay back, its tail curled between its legs. . . . If the dog was removed from the harness suddenly . . . it moved slowly about the room, appeared to be stealthy, hesitant, and unfriendly. Its "state" had suddenly changed from terror to stealthiness.

Obviously, different emotion-arousing stimuli elicit different types of emotional responses. However, the patterns of the emotional changes appear to have certain common characteristics. Solomon and his associates have called these characteristics the **standard pattern of affective dynamics** (Solomon & Corbit, 1974). The key elements of the pattern are shown in Figure 3.9. The onset of the emotion-arousing stimulus,

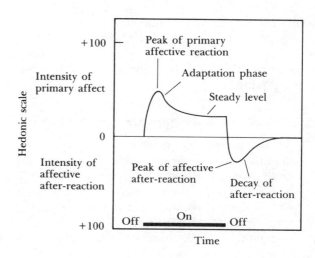

Figure 3.9. Standard pattern of affective dynamics. *(From Solomon & Corbit, 1974.)*

such as shock, elicits a strong emotional response that quickly reaches its *peak*. This peak reaction is followed by an *adaptation phase* during which the emotional response subsides until it reaches a *steady state*. When the stimulus ceases, the emotional state quickly changes to feelings that are opposite to those that occurred in the presence of the stimulus. This reversal of emotional state, called the **affective after-reaction,** gradually decays as the subject returns to its normal state.

How will dogs react to a painful electric shock if they have had extensive experience with shocks? As it turns out, their reactions are very different than in animals shocked for the first time. Solomon and Corbit (1973, p. 159) provide the following description:

> During shocks, the signs of terror disappeared. Instead, the dog appeared pained, annoyed, anxious. For example, it whined rather than shrieked, urination and defecation were absent, and struggling was gone. Furthermore, when released suddenly at the end of the session, the dog rushed about, jumping up on people, tail wagging, in what we called "a fit of joy."

Thus, the pattern of emotional changes to a habituated emotion-arousing stimulus is different from the standard pattern of affective dynamics. This habituated pattern is shown in Figure 3.10. The stimulus elicits only a slight emotional response. However, the affective after-reaction is much stronger than in the standard pattern.

Mechanisms of the opponent-process theory

What underlying mechanisms produce the standard pattern of affective dynamics and modifications in this pattern with habituation to the emotion-arousing stimulus? The opponent-process theory assumes that emotion-arousing stimuli elicit two opposing processes. The presence of the stimulus initially elicits what is called the **primary process,** or **"a" process,** which is responsible for the quality of the emotional state (happiness, for example) that occurs in the

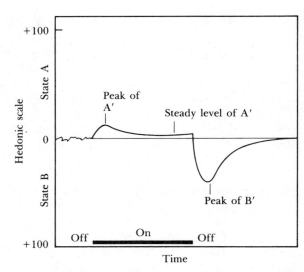

Figure 3.10. Pattern of affective changes to a habituated stimulus. *(After Solomon & Corbit, 1974.)*

presence of the stimulus. The primary, or *a*, process is assumed to elicit, in turn, an **opponent process,** or **"b" process,** that generates the opposite emotional reaction (unhappiness, for example). The emotional changes observed when a stimulus is presented and then removed are assumed to reflect the net result of the primary and opponent processes. The strength of the opponent process subtracts from the strength of the primary process to provide the emotions that actually occur.

Figure 3.11 shows how the primary and opponent processes determine the standard pattern of affective dynamics. When the stimulus is first presented, the *a* process occurs unopposed by the *b* process. The primary emotional reaction can therefore reach its peak quickly. The *b* process then becomes activated and begins to oppose the *a* process. The *b* process reduces the strength of the primary emotional response and is responsible for the adaptation phase of the standard pattern. The primary emotional response reaches a steady state when the *a* and *b* processes have each reached their maximum strength during the stimulus presentation. When the stimulus is withdrawn, the *a* process is quickly terminated, but the *b* process lingers

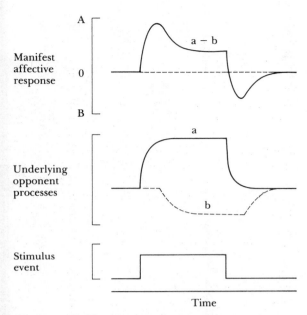

Figure 3.11. Opponent-process mechanism that produces the standard pattern of affective dynamics. *(From Solomon & Corbit, 1974.)*

for a while. Thus, the *b* process now has nothing ing to oppose. Therefore, the emotional responses characteristic of the opponent process become evident for the first time. These emotions are typically opposite to those observed during the presence of the stimulus.

The summation of primary and opponent processes provides a good explanation for the standard pattern of affective dynamics. How do these underlying processes change during the course of habituation to an emotion-arousing stimulus? As we saw in Figure 3.10, after extensive exposure to the emotion-arousing stimulus, the stimulus ceases to elicit strong emotional reactions, and the affective after-reaction becomes much stronger when the stimulus is terminated. The opponent-process theory explains this outcome by assuming simply that the *b* process becomes strengthened by repeated exexposures to the stimulus. The strengthening of the *b* process is reflected in several of its charcharacteristics. The *b* process becomes activated sooner after the onset of the stimulus, its max-

imum intensity becomes greater, and it becomes slower to decay when the stimulus ceases. In contrast, the *a* process is assumed to remain unchanged. Thus, after habituation, the primary emotional responses are more strongly opposed by the opponent process. This effect of habituation reduces the intensity of the observed primary emotional responses during presentation of the emotion-arousing stimulus. It also leads to the excessive affective after-reaction when the stimulus is withdrawn (see Figure 3.12).

Examples of opponent processes

Love and attachment. The reactions of a dog to repeated painful electrical shocks, described above, are just one example of opponent-process mechanisms. Corresponding changes may be experienced by human couples. Newlyweds are usually very excited about each other and are very affectionate whenever they are together. This primary emotional reaction habituates as years go by. Gradually, the couple settles into a comfortable mode of interaction that lacks the excitement of the honeymoon.

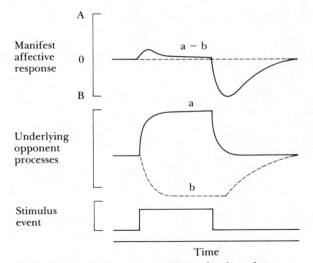

Figure 3.12. Opponent-process mechanism that produces the affective changes to a habituated stimulus. *(From Solomon & Corbit, 1974.)*

However, this habituation of the primary emotional reaction is accompanied by a strengthening of the affective after-reaction. The more time a couple have spent together, the more unhappy they become when separated for some reason, and this unhappiness lasts longer. ("Absence makes the heart grow fonder.") After a couple have been together for several decades, the death of one partner is likely to cause a very extensive grief reaction in the survivor. The intense grief may last several years and sometimes also hastens the death of the surviving partner. This strong affective after-reaction is remarkable, considering that by this stage in their relationship the couple may have entirely ceased to show any overt signs of affection.

Similar emotional effects occur between children and their parents. Many children who have lived with their parents for a long time cease to show much love or affection toward them. When older teenagers or young adults are ready to leave home, they are more likely to complain about their parents than to praise them. This emotional state represents habituation of the primary affective reaction. Despite their lack of overt affection for their parents, when the children move away, they are likely to become homesick. The parents will also miss the children. This state represents the affective after-reaction. For both children and parents, many years of living together serve to strengthen the affective after-reaction that accompanies a separation.

The predictions of the opponent-process theory for human love and attachment have not been tested experimentally. However, animal research provides strong support for the theory in the area of attachment and separation (see Hoffman & Solomon, 1974; Mineka, Suomi, & DeLizio, 1981; Starr, 1978).

Skydiving. Skydiving is an unusual sport intensely enjoyed by some people. Those who do not practice the sport are often puzzled about why others find it enjoyable. Indeed, there is little to enjoy in one's first jump. Inexperienced people are invariably terrified about jumping from an airplane. Studies have shown that they exhibit extreme physiological arousal, and their facial expressions indicate that they are terrified. This is the primary emotional reaction to jumping. With repeated jumps, the primary affective reaction habituates as the opponent process is strengthened. Since the primary emotional reaction is terror, the opponent response is elation. In highly experienced jumpers, the primary process is canceled out by the opponent process, and they are not terrified by the jump. The strengthened opponent reaction is also evident in their affective after-reaction when they reach the ground. Experienced jumpers are exuberant and exhilarated when they land, and this good feeling may last several hours. In fact, the affective after-reaction is much more pleasant than the jump itself and may constitute most of the pleasure derived from jumping (Epstein, 1967).

Drug addiction. Many drugs are taken mainly for their emotional effects. The emotional changes that result from initial and later drug administrations are accurately described by the opponent-process theory of motivation in many cases (Solomon, 1977). The opponent-process theory predicts that psychoactive drugs will produce a biphasic emotional effect the first few times they are taken. One set of emotional responses is experienced when the drug is active (the primary affective response), and the opposite emotions occur when the drug has worn off (the affective after-reaction). Such biphasic changes are evident with a variety of psychoactive drugs, including alcohol, opiates (such as heroin), amphetamine, and nicotine. The sequence of effects of alcohol is very familiar. Shortly after taking the drug the person becomes mellow and relaxed because the drug is basically a sedative. The opponent after-reaction is evident in headaches, nausea, and other symptoms of a hangover. With amphetamine, the presence of the drug creates feelings of euphoria, a sense of well-being, self-confidence, wakefulness, and a sense of control. After the drug has worn off, the person is likely to be fatigued, depressed, and drowsy.

The opponent-process theory predicts that with repeated frequent uses of a drug, the primary emotional response will weaken and the opponent after-reaction will strengthen. Habituation of the primary drug reactions is an example of **drug tolerance,** in which the effect of a drug declines with repeated doses. Habitual users of alcohol, nicotine, heroin, caffeine, or other drugs are not as greatly affected by the presence of the drug as naive drugtakers. An amount of alcohol that would make a casual drinker a bit tipsy is not likely to have any effect on a frequent drinker. Frequent drinkers have to consume much more alcohol to have the same reactions as a naive drinker. Because of this tolerance, habitual drug users sometimes do not enjoy taking the drug as much as naive users. People who smoke many cigarettes, for example, rarely derive much enjoyment from doing so. Accompanying this decline in the primary drug reaction is a growth in the opponent after-reaction. Therefore, habitual drug users experience much more severe "hangovers" on termination of the drug than naive users. Someone who stops smoking cigarettes, for example, will have headaches, become irritable, anxious, and tense, and will feel generally dissatisfied. When a heavy drinker stops taking alcohol, he or she is likely to experience hallucinations, memory loss, psychomotor agitation, delirium tremens, and other physiological disturbances. For a habitual user of amphetamine, the fatigue and depression that follow the primary effects of the drug may be so severe as to cause the person to commit suicide.

If the primary pleasurable effects of a psychoactive drug are gone for habitual users, why do they continue to take the drug? Why are they addicted? The opponent-process theory suggests that drug addiction is mainly an attempt to reduce the aversiveness of the affective after-reaction to the drugs—the bad hangovers, the

amphetamine "crashes," the irritability that comes from not having the usual cigarette. There are two ways to reduce the aversive opponent after-reactions of drugs. One is to simply wait long enough for them to dissipate. This is what is known as "cold turkey." For heavy drug users, cold turkey may take a long time and may be very painful. The opponent after-reaction can be much more quickly eliminated by taking the drug again. This will reactivate the primary process and stave off the agonies of withdrawal. Many addicts are not "trapped" by the pleasure they derive from the drug directly. Rather, they take the drug to reduce withdrawal pains.

Concluding comments

Studies of habituation and sensitization show that innate responses do not always occur in the same way following presentations of the appropriate eliciting stimulus. If a stimulus does not arouse the organism, repeated presentations of the stimulus will evoke progressively weaker responses. This pattern represents the phenomenon of habituation. If the eliciting stimulus is particularly intense or of great significance to the subject, repeated presentations will arouse the organism and lead to progressively stronger reactions. This pattern represents the phenomenon of sensitization.

Any environmental event will activate habituation and sensitization processes to varying degrees. The strength of the responses that are observed reflects the net effect of habituation and sensitization. Therefore, if one does not know the past experiences of the organism, it is impossible to predict how strong a reaction will be elicited by a particular stimulus presentation.

Repeated presentations of an eliciting stimulus produce changes in simple responses as well as in more complex emotional reactions. Organisms tend to minimize changes in emotional state caused by external stimuli. According to the opponent-process theory of motivation, emotional responses stimulated by an outside event are counteracted by an opposing process in the organism. This compensatory, or opponent, process is assumed to become stronger each time it is elicited, leading to a reduction of the primary emotional responses if the stimulus is frequently repeated. The strengthened opponent emotional state is evident when the stimulus is removed.

Habituation, sensitization, and changes in the strength of opponent processes are the simplest mechanisms whereby organisms adjust their reactions to environmental events on the basis of past experience.

CHAPTER FOUR

Classical Conditioning: Basic Concepts

The goal of Chapter 4 is to introduce the basic concepts and procedures involved in another basic form of learning, classical conditioning. Investigations of classical conditioning began with the work of Pavlov. Since then the research has been extended to a variety of organisms and response systems. We will describe several important procedures for studying classical conditioning and introduce the concept of a signal relation. Some classical-conditioning procedures result in the learning of new responses to a stimulus, whereas others result in learning to withhold, or inhibit, responses. We will describe both types of procedures and also discuss how the learning can be extinguished. Finally, we will discuss various examples of classical conditioning outside the laboratory.

We began our discussion of the principles of behavior by describing the ways external environmental events can control behavior in the absence of learning (Chapter 2). We then described how innate reactions to stimuli can be either reduced or increased through the processes of habituation and sensitization (Chapter 3). Given the various mechanisms of innate behavior and modifications of innate responses through habituation and sensitization, a great variety of responses to environmental challenges are possible. However, if organisms had only the mechanisms described in Chapters 2 and 3, they would remain rather limited in the kinds of things they could do. The could not, for example, learn to make entirely new responses to stimuli, responses that would never occur as innate reactions to these cues. They also could not learn about relations between stimuli in their environment.

Learning to make new responses to stimuli is obviously of great importance. The world is always changing in various ways, and innate response mechanisms are not sufficient to enable organisms to cope effectively with all the experiences they might have. Therefore, animals have to learn to respond in new ways as they encounter new stimuli or familiar stimuli in novel contexts. Being able to learn about relations between stimuli is equally important. Events in the world do not take place in isolation or randomly with respect to other events. Rather, stimuli occur in predictable sequences. One reason is that cause/effect relations determine whether physical events will occur. Your car engine does not make noises unless it is running; you cannot walk through a doorway until you have opened the door; it does not rain unless there are clouds. Even social institutions and customs result in predictable events. Classes are scheduled at predictable times; you can count on being allowed to pick out what you want to buy in a store before having to pay for it; you can predict whether someone will engage you in con-

versation by the way he or she greets you. Learning to predict events in the environment and learning to respond on the basis of such predictions constitute a very important aspect of behavioral adjustment to the environment. Imagine how much trouble you would have if you could never predict how long something would take to cook, when stores were open, or whether your car would start in the morning.

The simplest mechanism whereby organisms learn to make new responses to stimuli and learn about relations between stimuli is **classical conditioning.** Classical conditioning enables animals to take advantage of the orderly sequence of events in the environment and learn which stimuli tend to go with which other events. On the basis of this learning, animals come to make new responses to stimuli. For example, classical conditioning is the process whereby animals learn to approach signals for food and to salivate when they are about to be fed. It is also integrally involved in the learning of emotional reactions such as fear and pleasure to stimuli that initially do not elicit these emotions. Before discussing further the role of classical conditioning in animal and human behavior generally, we will first describe some of the kinds of detailed experimental investigations that have provided us with what we know about classical conditioning.

Box 4.1. I. P. Pavlov: Biographical Sketch

Born in 1849 into the family of a priest in Russia, Pavlov spent a life dedicated to scholarship and discovery. He received his early education in a local theological seminary and planned a career of religious service. However, his interests soon changed, and at 21 he entered the university in St. Petersburg, where his studies focused on chemistry and animal physiology. After obtaining the equivalent of a bachelor's degree, he entered the Imperial Medico-Surgical Academy in 1875 to further his education in physiology. Eight years later, he received his doctoral degree for his research on the efferent nerves of the heart and then began investigating various aspects of digestive physiology. In 1888 he discovered the nerves that stimulate the digestive secretions of the pancreas, and this finding initiated a series of experiments for which he was awarded the Nobel Prize for Physiology in 1904.

Pavlov did a great deal of original research while a graduate student as well as after obtaining his doctoral degree. However, he did not have a faculty position or his own laboratory until 1890, when he was appointed professor of pharmacology at the St. Petersburg Military Medical Academy. In 1895 he became professor of physiology at the same institution. Much of the research for which he is famous today was performed after he received the Nobel Prize. Thus, unlike many scientists, who have their most creative periods early in their career, Pavlov remained very active in the laboratory until close to his death in 1936.

Pavlov and the early years of classical conditioning

Even today, nearly 50 years after his death, classical conditioning is intimately associated with the name and work of Ivan P. Pavlov. Pavlov began his investigations in the late 19th century in Russia. The phenomenon of classical conditioning was also independently discovered by Edwin B. Twitmyer in 1902 in a Ph.D. dissertation submitted to the University of Pennsylvania (see Twitmyer, 1974). However, Twitmyer did not conduct an extensive research program, and his findings were ignored for many years. Although Pavlov's writings were widely disseminated in the United States, the most thorough scholarly criticism and tests of his ideas were first performed by Konorski and his associates in Poland (see Konorski, 1948). Vigorous research focused on classical conditioning did not begin in the United States until the 1960s.

Pavlov's investigations of classical conditioning were an extension of his research on the processes of digestion. Much of his work on conditioning involved the actions of the salivary glands. Most people associate digestion primarily with activities of the stomach and intestines. However, digestion begins in the mouth, where food is chewed and mixed with saliva. Thus, the salivary glands are the first digestive glands involved in the breakdown of foods. They are also large glands and have ducts that are close to the surface and can be easily observed. For example, the ducts of the submaxillary glands run along each side of the bottom of the mouth, coming together and releasing saliva near the lower front teeth. (You can readily see these ducts under your tongue with a mirror.) The submaxillary duct can be easily separated from the surrounding tissue, brought out through an incision in the bottom of the mouth, and secured with stitches to the outside skin surface. With this surgical modification, secretions of the gland can be collected, measured, and analyzed (see Figure 4.1).

Pavlov's initial interest in digestive functions was concerned with purely physiological matters. He was interested in the neural systems responsible for food-elicited salivation in dogs. However, he found that dogs that had served in several experiments did not wait to salivate until the experimenter presented the food; they began to salivate as soon as they entered the experimental situation or saw the experimenter. This anticipatory salivation made it difficult to study salivation in response to the food. If the dog was already salivating before the food was presented, one could not easily attribute its salivary secretion to the food presentation. Confronted with such a problem, scientists less astute than Pavlov might have restricted their investigation to animals that were more naive to the experimental situation and did not engage in anticipatory salivation. Instead, Pavlov rede-

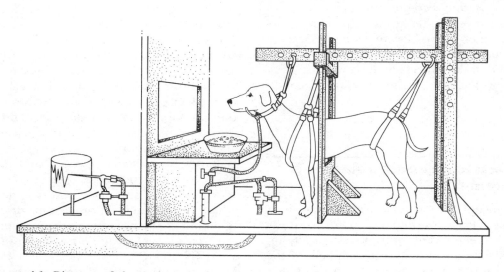

Figure 4.1. Diagram of the Pavlovian salivary conditioning preparation. A cannula attached to the animal's salivary duct conducts drops of saliva to a data-recording device. *(After Yerkes & Morgulis, 1909.)*

fined the goals of his research and began an extensive investigation of what controls anticipatory salivation (Pavlov, 1927).

The salivation that occurred in experienced dogs before the actual presentation of food was called **psychic secretion.** This phrase was meant to convey the notion that the dogs were salivating in response to the thought of food rather than the food itself. If this was so, what made the animals think about food? Pavlov's answer was that various stimuli that usually accompanied the presentation of food (such as the sight and odor of the experimenter) made the animal think of food because these cues had previously been paired with food presentation.

If one assumes that experienced dogs salivate in anticipation of food as a reaction to stimuli that have been paired with food presentation, then numerous experimental questions arise. What kinds of stimuli can come to elicit salivation; how do stimuli gain the ability to elicit salivation; do stimuli that become able to elicit psychic secretions ever lose this function; can animals learn to withhold salivation in response to a stimulus in the same way that they can learn to produce salivation; are the principles involved in psychic secretion similar to the principles that govern other kinds of "psychic" activity? The latter part of Pavlov's scientific career was devoted to answering questions such as these, and in the process he discovered a great deal about the mechanisms of classical conditioning.

The classical-conditioning paradigm

Most people are familiar with the type of procedure Pavlov eventually used to study psychic secretion. The procedure typically involved a stimulus such as a tone, a bell, or the turning on of a light. On its first presentation this stimulus might have elicited an orienting response, but it did not elicit salivation. The other stimulus in the situation was food or the taste of a sour solution placed in the mouth. In contrast to the first stimulus, this second one elicited not only orientation movements but also vigorous salivation, even the first time it was presented. Pavlov referred to the tone or light as the **conditional stimulus** because the ability of this stimulus to elicit salivation depended on (was conditional on) pairing it with food presentation several times. In contrast, the food or sour-taste stimulus was called the **unconditional stimulus** because its ability to elicit salivation was not dependent on any prior training of the subjects. The salivation that eventually came to be elicited by the tone or light was called the **conditional response,** and the salivation that was always elicited by the food or sour taste was called the **unconditional response.** Thus, stimuli and responses whose properties and occurrence did not depend on prior training were called "unconditional," and stimuli and responses whose properties and occurrence depended on special training were called "conditional."

In the first English translation of Pavlov's writings, the term *unconditional* was erroneously translated as *unconditioned*, and the term *conditional* was translated as *conditioned*. The -ed suffix was used exclusively in English writings for many years. However, the term *conditioned* does not capture Pavlov's original meaning of "dependent on" as well as the term *conditional* (Gantt, 1966). The words *conditional* and *unconditional* are more common in modern writings on classical conditioning and are now used interchangeably with *conditioned* and *unconditioned*. Because the terms *conditioned (unconditioned) stimulus* and *conditioned (unconditioned) response* are frequent in discussions of classical conditioning, they are often abbreviated. *Conditioned stimulus* and *conditioned response* are abbreviated **CS** and **CR,** respectively. *Unconditioned stimulus* and *unconditioned response* are abbreviated **US** and **UR**, respectively.

Experimental situations

Classical conditioning has been investigated in a large variety of situations involving a variety of species. Pavlov did most of his experiments with dogs using the salivary-cannula technique. However, this kind of research is rather costly. Therefore, most contemporary experiments on Pavlovian conditioning are carried out with domesticated rats, rabbits, and pigeons. Some of the more popular techniques are described below.

Eyeblink conditioning in rabbits

The rabbit eyeblink conditioning paradigm was developed by I. Gormezano (see Gor-

mezano, 1966). Large albino rabbits are typically used. Gormezano chose the eyeblink response to investigate because in the absence of special training, rabbits rarely blink their eyes. Therefore, if the animal is observed to blink after the presentation of a stimulus, one can be quite certain that the response occurred because of the stimulus and would not have occurred otherwise. In eyeblink conditioning experiments, a rabbit is placed in a plastic holder, as shown in Figure 4.2. The animal's head protrudes from the holder, and one end of a fine string is attached to the upper lid of one eye. The other end of the string is tied to a small potentiometer. Eyelid movements produce movements in the potentiometer, and these are translated into electrical signals that allow pre-

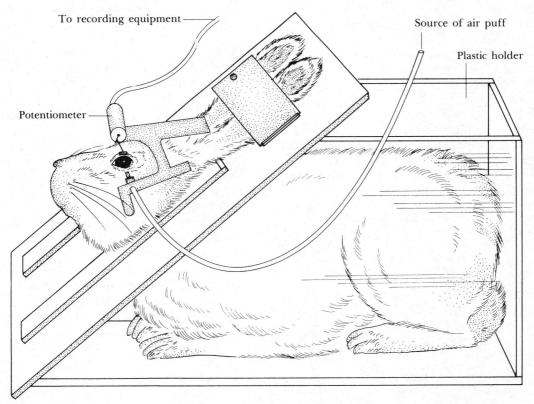

Figure 4.2. Diagram of the rabbit eyeblink conditioning preparation. A puff of air directed at the eye or a mild shock to the skin below the eye serves as the US. Eyeblinks are detected by a potentiometer.

cise recording of the eyelid responses. The unconditioned stimulus is either a puff of air to the surface of the eye or a brief shock (.1 sec, for example) to the skin below the eye. Animals rapidly blink in response to the US. Various stimuli have been used as conditioned stimuli, including lights, tones, or vibration of the animal's abdomen with a hand massager.

In the typical conditioning experiment, the conditioned stimulus is presented for 500 msec and ends in the delivery of the unconditioned stimulus. The unconditioned stimulus elicits a rapid and vigorous eyelid closure. As the CS is repeatedly paired with the US, the eyeblink response also comes to be made to the CS. In the usual procedure, investigators record whether an eyeblink occurs during the CS, before the US is presented, on each trial. The data are presented in terms of the percentage of trials on which a CR is observed in blocks of trials.

Eyelid conditioning is often a relatively slow process, and even with extensive training subjects do not make a conditioned response on every trial. Figure 4.3 shows a typical learning curve for eyelid conditioning. The animals received 82 conditioning trials each day. By the eighth day of training (656 trials), conditioned responses occurred on about 70% of trials. When the conditioned response was made, it occurred very soon after the start of the CS (within 525 msec). Control groups in such experiments, which do not receive the CS paired with the US, typically blink on fewer than 5% of trials.

Fear conditioning

The conditioning of fear is typically studied with the use of rats and sometimes dogs. In most experiments the aversive unconditioned stimulus is shock to the feet delivered through a metal grid floor. The level of shock is considerably more intense than that used in eyelid conditioning. The conditioned stimulus is often a tone or the turning on of a light, and conditioned fear is measured indirectly by measuring

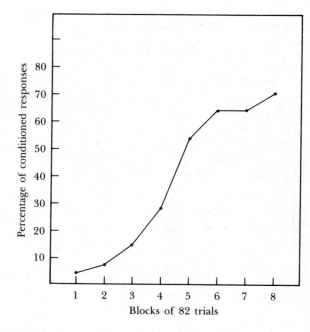

Figure 4.3. A typical learning curve for eyelid conditioning. *(From Schneiderman, Fuentes, & Gormezano, 1962.)*

how the conditioned fear stimulus alters the animal's ongoing activity.

One technique for indirect measurement of conditioned fear is called the **conditioned emotional response** (or **conditioned suppression**) procedure, abbreviated **CER.** This procedure, devised by Estes and Skinner (1941), has since been used extensively in the study of Pavlovian conditioning (Kamin, 1965). Rats are most often used in conditioned-suppression experiments. The animals are first trained to press a response lever for intermittent food reward in a small experimental chamber (see Figure 4.4). After sufficient lever-press training, they come to press the lever at a steady rate, earning a food reward every 2–3 min. The classical-conditioning phase of the experiment is instituted once the lever-press responding has been well established. The duration of the CS is usually longer than in rabbit eyelid conditioning (3 min, for example), and the shock US is typically also longer (.5 sec, for example). The typical condi-

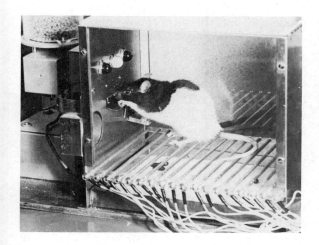

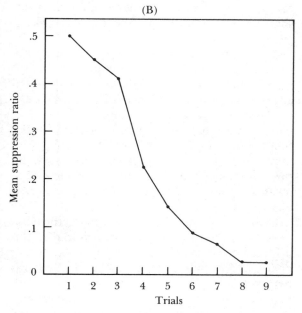

(B)

tioning procedure involves presentation of the shock US at the end of the conditioned stimulus. The intertrial interval is usually 15–30 min.

The progress of fear conditioning is evident from the disruption of the food-rewarded lever pressing by the conditioned stimulus. If subjects have never encountered the conditioned stimulus before, the first time it is presented, a slight disruption of lever pressing may occur. If the CS is not paired with shock, this initial slight response suppression habituates: within 3–4 trials the CS has no effect whatever on the rats' behavior. However, if the CS is paired with footshock, it soon becomes conditioned to the shock, and the animals suppress their lever-press response when the CS is presented. Within 3–5 conditioning trials with an effective shock intensity, the conditioned suppression of lever pressing can become complete (Kamin & Brimer, 1963). The animals may not press the lever at all when the CS is presented. The response suppression, however, is specific to the CS. Soon after the CS is turned off, the animals resume the food-rewarded behavior.

Freezing, or the interruption of activity, is one of the innate reactions of rats to fearful and aversive stimuli (Bolles, 1970). The CER procedure is designed to provide a sensitive measure of the response suppression induced by fear. Because the animals are first trained to press a response lever at a steady rate for a food reward, deviations from this baseline of responding can be easily measured. The quantitative measure of the degree of response suppression produced by the conditioned stimulus is usually calculated by dividing the number of lever-press responses the subject makes during the CS by the sum of the number of responses it makes during the CS and during an equally long period preceding presentation of the CS. The formula is

$$\text{Suppression ratio} = \frac{\text{CS response}}{\text{CS response} + \text{pre-CS response}}$$

This index has a value of zero if the subject

Figure 4.4. (A) A rat pressing a response lever for food reward in a conditioned-suppression experiment. (B) Sample results of a conditioned-suppression experiment with rats (from Domjan, unpublished). Three conditioning trials were conducted on each of three days of training. The CS was an audiovisual stimulus, and the US was a brief shock through the grid floor. A suppression ratio of .5 indicates that subjects did not suppress their lever pressing during the CS. A suppression ratio of 0 indicates total suppression of responding during the CS.

suppresses lever pressing completely during the CS, because the numerator of the ratio is zero. At the other extreme, if the rat does not alter its rate of lever pressing at all when the CS is presented, the index takes on the value of .5. You can confirm this by considering some hypothetical cases. For example, assume that the CS is presented for 3 min and that in a typical 3-min period the rat makes 45 responses. If the CS does not disrupt lever pressing, the animal will make 45 responses during the CS, so that the numerator of the ratio will be 45. The denominator will be 45 (CS responses) + 45 (pre-CS responses), or 90. Therefore, the ratio will be .5. Values of the ratio between 0 and .5 indicate various degrees of response suppression, or conditioned fear.

Figure 4.4 shows sample results of a conditioned-suppression experiment with rats. Three conditioning trials were conducted on each of three days of training. Very little response suppression occurred the first time the CS was presented, and not much acquisition of suppression was evident during the first day of training. However, a substantial increase in suppression occurred from the last trial on day 1 (trial 3) to the first trial on day 2 (trial 4). With continued training, responding gradually became more and more suppressed, until the animals hardly ever pressed the response lever when the CS was presented.

Sign tracking

Pavlov's research concentrated on response systems such as salivation that may be characterized as highly reflexive. In such systems a distinctive unconditioned response occurs invariably following presentations of the unconditioned stimulus and comes to be also elicited by the conditioned stimulus as the CS and US are repeatedly paired. Because of Pavlov's work, for many years it was believed that classical-conditioning procedures could produce learning only in highly reflexive systems. Stud-

ies of eyeblink conditioning exemplify this approach. In fact, because the eyeblink response occurs with shorter latencies and shows less variability than salivation, some considered this to be an even better paradigm for investigations of classical conditioning than salivary conditioning (Amsel, 1972). This restrictive attitude toward the applicability of classical-conditioning procedures is not characteristic of all contemporary approaches. The conditioned-suppression procedure, which was popularized as a technique for investigations of classical conditioning in the 1960s, is partly responsible for this trend. Another contemporary procedure for the study of classical conditioning that has greatly broadened our perspective of classical conditioning is called **sign tracking** or **autoshaping** (Hearst, 1975; Hearst & Jenkins, 1974).

Animals tend to approach and contact stimuli that signal the availability of food. In the natural environment, the availability of food is usually indicated by some aspect of the food itself. By approaching and contacting the food signals, animals in effect come in contact with the food. For a predator, for example, the sight, movements, odor, and perhaps noises of the prey are cues indicating the possibility of a meal. By tracking these stimuli, the predator is likely to catch its prey.

Sign tracking may be investigated in the laboratory by presenting a discrete, localized stimulus just before each delivery of a small amount of food. The first experiment of this sort was performed by Brown and Jenkins (1968) with pigeons. The animals were placed in an experimental chamber that had a small circular key which could be illuminated and which the pigeons could peck (see Figure 1.1). Periodically, the animals were given a small amount of food. The key light was illuminated for 8 sec immediately before each food delivery. The pigeons did not have to do anything for the food to be presented. The food was automatically delivered after each illumination of the response key no matter what the animals did. Since the animals were hungry, one might predict that when they saw the key illuminated, they would go to the food dish and wait for the forthcoming food presentation. Interestingly, however, that is not what happened. Instead of using the key light to find out when to go to the food dish, the pigeons started pecking the key itself. This behavior was remarkable because they were not required to peck the response key to get food at this point in the experiment.

Since its discovery, many experiments have been done on the sign-tracking phenomenon. We will describe some of these in later chapters. These experiments show that sign tracking is an instance of classical conditioning. The conditioned stimulus is illumination of the response key, and the unconditoned stimulus is presentation of food. As in other conditioning procedures, learning proceeds most rapidly when the CS is presented just before the US, and learning does not occur if the CS and US are presented at random times in relation to each other (Gamzu & Williams, 1971, 1973).

The tracking of signals for a food reward is dramatically illustrated by instances in which the signal is located far away from the food-delivery site. In one such experiment (see Hearst & Jenkins, 1974), pigeons were placed in a 6-ft (182-cm) alley that had a food dish in the middle (see Figure 4.5). Each end of the alley had a circular disk that could be illuminated. Presentation of food was always preceded by illumination of the disk at one end of the alley. The visual stimulus at the opposite end was uncorrelated with food. One other aspect of the experiment is important to point out. The food was available for only 4 sec each time it was presented. Therefore, if the animal did not walk to the food cup within 4 sec, it did not get any food on that trial.

After illuminations of the light at one end of the alley had been paired with delivery of food a number of times, the pigeons started doing a most remarkable thing. As soon as the light came on, they would run to that end of the alley, peck the illuminated disk, and then run to the center of the alley to get the food. Because the alley was very long, the pigeons did not always get back to the food dish in the middle before the food was removed. This sign-tracking behavior was amazing because it was entirely unnecessary. The animals did not have to peck the lighted disk to get the food reward. They could have sat in the middle of the alley and just waited for the food on each trial. The fact that they did not do this is evidence of the compelling attraction of classically conditioned signals for food reward. In contrast, the subjects did not consistently approach the light at the other end of the box, which was uncorrelated with food presentations.

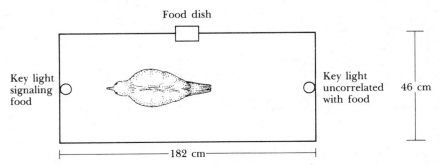

Figure 4.5. Top view of "long box" used in sign-tracking experiment with pigeons. The conditioned stimulus is illumination of the key light at one end of the experimental chamber, and food is delivered in the middle of the chamber. (*Based on Jenkins, 1980.*)

Taste-aversion learning

Another procedure for investigating classical conditioning involves taste-aversion learning. Although this learning phenomenon has been known for nearly 30 years (see Richter, 1953; Rzoska, 1953), it did not become a popular technique for the study of classical conditioning until the 1970s as the work of John Garcia, James Smith, Paul Rozin, Sam Revusky, and others became well known (see Barker, Best, & Domjan, 1977; Milgram, Krames, & Alloway, 1977). In the taste-aversion conditioning technique, animals are given a flavored solution to drink and are then made to feel sick by injection of a drug or exposure to aversive radiation. As a result of the experience of ill effects after the taste exposure, the animals acquire an aversion for the taste. Their preference for and voluntary ingestion of the taste solution are suppressed by the conditioning treatment.

Taste-aversion learning is a result of the pairing of the CS (in this case a taste) and the US (drug injection or radiation exposure) in much the same manner as in other examples of classical conditioning. When taste-aversion learning was not yet well understood, it was believed that this type of conditioning was governed by some unique laws of learning that did not apply to conditioning situations such as eyelid and salivary conditioning (see Rozin & Kalat, 1971, for example). Many of the reasons for maintaining this belief are not compelling in light of more recent research (see Domjan, 1980, for a review). However, taste-aversion learning differs from other conditioning situations in some important respects. First, strong taste aversions can be learned in one pairing of the flavor and illness. Although one-trial learning is also observed in fear conditioning, one-trial learning is rarely, if ever, observed in eyelid conditioning, salivary conditioning, or sign tracking. The second unique feature of taste-aversion learning is that learning is evident even if the animals do not get sick until several hours after exposure to the novel taste. The interval between the CS and the US in eyelid conditioning, for example, is usually less than 1 sec because very little, if any, conditioning occurs when longer delays separate the two events. In contrast to the short CS-US intervals that are necessary in salivary, fear, and sign-tracking conditioning situations, animals will learn an aversion to a flavored solution even if the unconditioned stimulus is not presented for several hours (Garcia, Ervin, & Koelling, 1966; Revusky & Garcia, 1970).

A dramatic example of long-delay taste-aversion learning in rats is provided by an experiment by Smith and Roll (1967). The animals were first adapted to a water-deprivation schedule so that they would readily drink when a water bottle was placed on their cage. One day when they were thirsty, the animals were allowed to drink a novel .1% saccharin solution for 20 min. At various times after the saccharin presentation ranging from 0 to 24 hours, independent groups of animals were exposed to radiation from an X-ray machine. Animals serving as controls were also taken to the X-ray machine but were not irradiated. They were called the sham-irradiated rats. Starting 24 hours after the radiation or sham treatment, each rat was given a choice of saccharin solution or plain water to drink for two days. The preference of each group of animals for the saccharin solution is shown in Figure 4.6. Animals exposed to radiation within 6 hours after tasting the saccharin solution showed a profound aversion to the saccharin flavor in the postconditioning test. They drank less than 20% of their total fluid intake from the saccharin drinking tube. Much less of an aversion was evident in animals irradiated 12 hours after the saccharin exposure, and hardly any aversion was observed in rats irradiated 24 hours after the taste exposure. In contrast to this gradient of saccharin avoidance observed in the irradiated rates, all the sham-irradiated groups highly preferred the saccharin solution. They drank more than 70% of their total fluid intake from the saccharin drinking tube.

Taste-aversion learning attracted a great deal of attention when it was first discovered

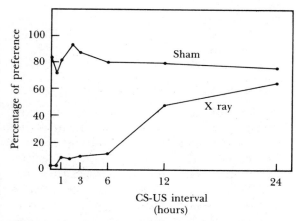

Figure 4.6. Mean percent preference for the CS flavor after pairings with X irradiation or sham irradiation with various CS-US intervals. Percent preference is the percentage of a subject's total fluid intake (saccharin solution plus water) that saccharin constituted. *(After Smith & Roll, 1967.)*

that the learning could occur in one trial with very long delays between CS and US. On further reflection, however, one would be more surprised if taste-aversion learning did not have these characteristics. Taste-aversion learning plays a critical role in food selection. If animals encounter and eat poisonous food, they become sick. By learning an aversion, they can avoid the poisonous food in subsequent meals. To provide much protection, however, this learning has to occur over long CS-US intervals. Toxic materials in food often do not have their bad effects until the food is digested, absorbed in the blood, and distributed to various body tissues. This process takes time. Therefore, if animals were not able to associate the taste of bad foods with delayed ill effects, they would not be able to learn to avoid eating toxic materials. Poison-avoidance learning is especially important for such animals as the rat. Rats eat a large variety of foods and are therefore highly likely to encounter toxic materials.

People are similar to rats in that their diet is diverse. Therefore, one would expect people to be just as able to learn taste aversions as rats. A survey of eating habits supported this predic-

tion (Garb & Stunkard, 1974). Of 696 subjects questioned, 38% reported having at least one strong food aversion. In most cases (87%) this aversion resulted from the pairing of the food with gastrointestinal upset. The aversions were often learned in one trial even though the malaise did not begin until several hours after the food was eaten, and some of the older subjects reported food aversions that they had learned in childhood about 50 years earlier. Another interesting finding in this survey was that people were more apt to learn food aversions between ages 6 and 12 than at any other time of life. The reasons are unclear at present. Taste-aversion learning is probably also involved in the loss of appetite commonly observed in patients receiving chemotherapy treatment for cancer. Chemotherapy often induces feelings of sickness and severe discomfort, and patients who eat something before chemotherapy learn an aversion to that food (Bernstein, 1978; Bernstein & Webster, 1980).

Possible excitatory conditioning procedures

One of the most important factors that determine the course of classical conditioning in each of the situations described above is the relative timing of the conditioned stimulus and the unconditioned stimulus. Seemingly small and trivial variations in how a CS is paired with a US can have profound effects on the rate and extent of classical conditioning that is observed. Five classical-conditioning procedures that have been frequently investigated are diagramed in Figure 4.7. The horizontal distance in each diagram represents the passage of time, and vertical displacements represent the onset and termination of a stimulus. Each configuration of CS and US represents a single presentation of each stimulus—that is, one **conditioning trial.** In the typical classical-conditioning experiment, numerous such trials may be presented in one or more training sessions. The interval between conditioning trials is called the **intertrial interval.** In contrast, the interval between the start of the CS and the start of the US within a conditioning trial is called the **interstimulus interval** or **CS-US interval.** The interstimulus interval is always much shorter than the intertrial interval. In many experiments the interstimulus interval is less than 1 min, whereas the intertrial interval may be more than 5 min.

1. *Simultaneous conditioning.* Perhaps the most obvious way to expose subjects to the CS paired with the US is to present the two stimuli at the same time. This procedure, called "simultaneous conditioning," is the first procedure depicted in Figure 4.7. The critical feature of this procedure is that the conditioned and unconditioned stimuli are presented concurrently.

2. *Short-delayed conditioning.* The CS can be be presented slightly before the US. This procedure, called "short-delayed conditioning," is the most frequently used technique. The critical feature of this procedure is that the onset of the CS precedes the onset of the US by a short period (less than 1 min), and the US is presented either during the CS or immediately afterward.

3. *Trace conditioning.* The trace-conditioning procedure is similar to the short-delayed procedure except that the US is not presented until after the CS has ended. The interval between the end of the CS and the beginning of the US is called the **trace interval.**

4. *Long-delayed conditioning.* This procedure is also similar to the short-delayed-conditioning procedure in that the CS precedes the US. However, in this case the CS remains present much longer (5–10 min) before the US is delivered.

5. *Backward conditioning.* The last procedure depicted in Figure 4.7 differs from the other procedures in that the CS is presented shortly *after,* rather than before, the US. This technique is called "backward conditioning."

Measurement of the conditioned response

Pavlov and others after him have conducted systematic investigations of procedures of the type depicted in Figure 4.7 to find out how the conditioning of the CS depends on the temporal relation between the CS and US presentations. To make comparisons of how learning proceeds with various procedures, one has to devise some method of measuring conditioning to the CS. Furthermore, this method should be equally applicable to all the procedures. One technique involves measuring how soon the conditioned response occurs after presentation of the conditioned stimulus. This measure of

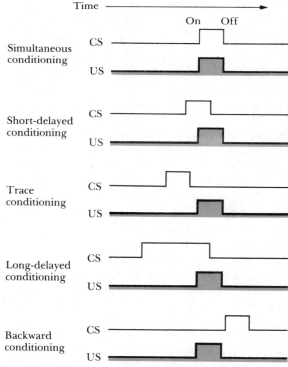

Figure 4.7. Five frequently investigated classical-conditioning procedures.

the strength of the response is called the **latency of the conditioned response.** Latency is the amount of time that elapses between presentation of the conditioned stimulus and the occurrence of the conditioned response.

Measurements of response latency can tell us what the course of conditioning is in the short-delayed, long-delayed, and trace-conditioning procedures because in all these cases the conditioned response can begin before the unconditioned stimulus is presented. However, the latency of the response in the simultaneous- and backward-conditioning procedures cannot be used as an index of conditioning. In these cases, the behavior observed during the CS is not clearly due just to the presence of the CS alone. This is particularly true for simultaneous conditioning. Any behavior observed during the CS in that procedure could have been elicited by the US rather than the CS, because the US is present at the same time. In backward conditioning, behavior observed during the CS may have been elicited by the US, which occurred before the CS. Measures of the latency of the response in the short-delayed, long-delayed, and trace-conditioning procedures similarly may not indicate what learning has taken place if the conditioned response happens to be delayed until after the unconditioned stimulus is presented.

One way to avoid the problems described above is to test for conditioning by presenting the CS by itself (without the US) periodically during training. Responses elicited by the CS can then be observed without contamination from responses elicited by the US. Such CS-alone trials introduced periodically to measure the extent of learning are called **test trials.** Test trials permit measurement of not only latency but also other aspects of the conditioned response. When studying salivation, for example, Pavlov often measured how many drops of saliva were elicited. Such measures of response strength are said to reflect the *magnitude* of the response.

Effectiveness of the excitatory conditioning procedures

Using test trials and measures of either the latency or magnitude of the conditioned response, one can compare the effectiveness of the various procedures depicted in Figure 4.7. Rarely have all five procedures been compared in the same experiment. Furthermore, the results of the comparisons that have been performed sometimes differ depending on the type of response that is conditioned. However, certain generalizations may be made on the basis of the available evidence.

Simultaneous conditioning. Presenting the CS at the same time as the US is not always effective in establishing the conditioned response. Some investigators have reported successful conditioning of fear after small numbers of simultaneous-conditioning trials (for example, Burkhardt & Ayres, 1978; Mahoney & Ayres, 1976). However, simultaneous conditioning is not as effective in conditioning fear as short-delayed conditioning (Heth & Rescorla, 1973). Furthermore, in other types of classical-conditioning experiments, simultaneous conditioning has been found entirely ineffective (for example, Bitterman, 1964; Smith, Coleman, & Gormezano, 1969).

Short-delayed and trace conditioning. In many situations the optimal procedure for classical conditioning is one in which the CS is presented shortly before the US. This can be accomplished with either the short-delayed or trace-conditioning procedure. As we noted earlier, the interval between the start of the CS and the start of the US is called the interstimulus or CS-US interval. Generally, conditioning improves up to a point as the CS-US interval is increased, beyond which progressively less conditioning occurs (for example, Ost & Lauer, 1965; Schneiderman & Gormezano, 1964). In the short-delayed procedure, the CS persists until the US is presented on each trial, whereas in the trace-conditioning procedure, the CS ends before the US occurs (see Figure 4.7). Whether there is a trace interval between the CS and US has a significant effect on the amount of conditioning observed. Trace conditioning is less effective than delayed conditioning (for example, Ellison, 1964; Kamin, 1965). However, trace conditioning is still preferable to simultaneous conditioning (Smith et al., 1969).

Long-delayed conditioning. With the short-delayed and trace-conditioning procedures, as training progresses, the magnitude of the conditioned response increases and its latency decreases. Interestingly, however, this does not happen if a longer CS-US interval is used. With long-delayed conditioning, as the animal begins to learn the conditioned response, the latency becomes shorter only up to a point. After extensive experience with the procedure, the animal appears to learn that the US is not presented for some time after the beginning of the CS, and it starts to delay its conditioned response until the presentation of the US. Pavlov referred to this withholding of the conditioned response at the start of the CS in long-delayed conditioning as *inhibition of delay.* Inhibition of delay has been observed in several response systems, including salivary and fear conditioning (for example, Pavlov, 1927; Rescorla, 1967a; Williams, 1965). However, it has not been investigated in some of the more recently developed classical-conditioning preparations, such as sign tracking and taste-aversion learning.

Backward conditioning. There are some isolated examples of conditioned responses acquired in backward-conditioning procedures (for example, Keith-Lucas & Guttman, 1975). However, the more common finding is that backward conditioning does not lead to the development of new responses to the CS. In fact, many experiments have reported that animals learn to suppress, or inhibit, their behavior through backward conditioning (for example, Maier, Rapaport, & Wheatley, 1976; Moscovitch & LoLordo, 1968; Siegel & Domjan, 1971). We will have much more to say about the conditioning of inhibitory response tendencies later in the chapter.

Control procedures in classical conditioning

All the procedures shown in Figure 4.7 involve exposing subjects to both the conditioned and the unconditioned stimulus. The fact that they produce learning at different rates indicates that classical conditioning does not result from mere exposure to the CS and US. Learning occurs only if there is a special arrangement of presentations of the conditioned and unconditioned stimuli, as in the short-delayed-conditioning procedure. Actual experiments on classical conditioning rarely include all the procedures described in Figure 4.7. Rather, the common practice is to choose just one procedure (usually short-delayed) that is sure to work. However, if learning takes place under these circumstances, one cannot be certain that it results from the *association* of the CS and US. It may be that the same outcome would have occurred if the animals had been repeatedly exposed to only the CS or only the US. Another possibility is that alternating trials with the CS alone and the US alone would have produced similar results. Control groups of subjects are usually tested to rule out these possibilities.

There has been a great deal of discussion about what constitutes proper control procedures in classical conditioning. One important control procedure involves repeatedly presenting subjects with both the conditioned and the unconditioned stimulus but arranging the schedule so that the two stimuli occur at random times with respect to each other (Rescorla, 1967b). This **random control procedure** appears to work well provided that there are numerous presentations of both the CS and the US. If only a few trials of each are given, there may be evidence of conditioning in the random control groups (Benedict & Ayres, 1972; Kremer & Kamin, 1971; Quinsey, 1971). In experiments calling for few trials, it is preferable to use control groups that receive only the CS, only the US, or both the CS and the US but never paired with each other. If resources prevent testing all three of these control procedures, the procedure involving unpaired presentations of the CS and US is recommended.

Classical conditioning and the signal relation between CS and US

Why is it that certain procedures are much more effective than others in producing classical conditioning? This question has preoccupied investigators for decades. We will discuss some of the details of this theoretical work in the next chapter. For now, it will suffice to think about classical-conditioning procedures as involving special signal relations between the conditioned and unconditioned stimuli. Generally, animals are most likely to learn to make the conditioned response to a CS if occurrences of the CS can be used as a signal of the forthcoming presentation of the US. Procedures in which the CS cannot be used as a basis for predicting the US often do not promote rapid acquisition of the conditioned response.

Examples of signal relations

One can easily assess how useful the conditioned stimulus is for predicting the unconditioned stimulus by thinking about real-world situations in which signals are used. There are many such situations. One involves sirens that ordinarily signal the approach of an emergency vehicle, such as an ambulance or fire truck. The purpose of the siren is to get people to make

way for the emergency vehicle. The siren is analogous to the conditioned stimulus, and the arrival of the emergency vehicle is analogous to the unconditioned stimulus. If you always heard the siren just before the ambulance arrived, you would quickly learn to get out of the way. In this case, you would be experiencing a short-delayed-conditioning procedure, in which the CS is a good predictor of the US. In contrast, if you never heard the siren until the ambulance was on the scene, there would be no reason for you to react to the siren. You could simply step aside when the ambulance arrived. This case is analogous to the simultaneous-conditioning procedure, in which the signal relation between the CS and the US is not very good. You would have even less reason to get out of the way when the siren sounded if you always heard the siren only after the ambulance had already left. This case is comparable to the backward-conditioning procedure. If you learned anything under these circumstances, it would be that the siren indicates the departure of the ambulance.

The analysis is a bit more complicated if the relation between the sounding of the siren and the presence of the ambulance is comparable to the trace-conditioning procedure. In this case, the siren would stop just before the ambulance arrived. Therefore, the end rather than the beginning of the siren would be the best predictor of when the ambulance would arrive. Under these circumstances you would be most likely to make way for the ambulance when the siren ended. If you experienced something comparable to the long-delayed-conditioning procedure, you would always hear the siren for a long time before the arrival of the ambulance. In this case, you would learn to ignore the siren when you first heard it, and you would worry about getting out of the way only after the siren had been on for a while. Most people's experience with sirens and emergency vehicles is closest to the long-delayed-conditioning procedure. Perhaps this is why people rarely respond immediately when they hear a siren while driving.

CS-US contingency

One can often figure out whether one stimulus (for example, the CS) serves as a good signal for the forthcoming presentation of another event (for example, the US) by reflecting on common experience. However, this decision can be made more precisely with the use of for-

---

Box 4.2. A local paper features the headline: MR. T KILLED AS TRAIN HITS CAR

An investigation of the accident revealed that the signal lights and bells at the crossing were working properly. Mr. T was said to be in fine physical and mental condition, and he had not been drinking. What happened? Why did Mr. T drive his car onto the tracks when the signals, both visual and auditory, clearly indicated the approach of a train? One possible explanation is that the warning signals were not arranged in a temporal relation with the coming of the train to make them effective. Often the warning bells and lights start going long before the train is at the crossing, and often they continue for some time after the train has left. Because of this ineffectual arrangement, if one arrives at a crossing when the warning signals are on, one cannot be sure whether a train is about to come or whether it has just passed. Therefore, drivers invariably approach the railroad tracks slowly when the warning signals are on, look both ways to see the train, and try to get off the track quickly if they see the train. Some of them do not make it in time, like Mr. T. A much more effective arrangement would be to have the warning signals start very shortly before the train was to reach the crossing and go off as soon as the train had passed. People could then be sure that the train would soon arrive when they saw the warning lights and bells, and they would not be tempted to take their lives in their hands by venturing onto the tracks to find out where the train is.

---

mal definitions. One highly influential treatment of signal relations in classical conditioning was presented by Robert Rescorla (1967b). His discussion was important not only because of its precision but also because he pointed out certain aspects of signal relations that had not been thought important for classical conditioning. One was the fact that the extent to which one stimulus signals another depends only in part on the specific way the two events are paired but also on the number of times each of the two events occurs by itself. In fact, the number of times the CS and US occur by themselves may be more important in determining the strength of conditioning than how the two are paired when they occur together. A second important idea that Rescorla emphasized is that signal relations need not always be positive: they can also be negative. That is, one stimulus can signal the absence of another stimulus, in much the same way that one stimulus can signal the forthcoming presence of another event.

Rescorla's ideas about signal relations were formally summarized in his concept of the **contingency between the conditioned and unconditioned stimuli.** If the US is more likely to occur when the CS is presented than without the CS, then one can predict occurrences of the US from the presence of the CS, and a **positive contingency** is said to exist between the two stimuli. Notice that the definition of a positive contingency does not require that the US be presented with *every* occurrence of the CS. All that is needed is that the US be presented more often with the CS than without it. Deer hunters, for example, make use of such positive contingencies when they predict the presence of deer from seeing deer droppings. One does not invariably see deer when deer droppings are found. However, there is a positive contingency between these two events because deer are more likely to be located in areas where there are droppings than in other places.

In contrast to the positive contingency, which allows for prediction of one event on the basis of the occurrence of another stimulus, such a prediction is not possible when the contingency between two stimuli is zero. A **zero contingency** between CS and US is said to exist if the US is just as likely to occur with the CS as without the CS. A zero contingency can exist even if on some occasions the conditioned and unconditioned stimuli occur together. For example, even though some warm days begin with a clear sky, one cannot predict that it will be warm just because it is clear in the morning. Some days that start out with clear skies turn out to be cold, and some warm days begin with cloudy skies. Thus, the occasional coincidence of warm days following clear mornings is not sufficient to associate clear skies with warm weather.

If the US is more likely to occur in the absence of the CS than in the presence of the CS, the contingency between CS and US is said to be negative. In cases of a **negative contingency,** the presence of the CS can be used as a signal for the *absence* of the US. A CS that is in a negative contingent relation with the US provides as much information about the US as a CS that is related to the US according to a positive contingency. The only difference is that a negative contingent CS signals the absence of the US, whereas a positive contingent CS signals the presence of the US. We have already seen an example of a negative contingency in backward-conditioning procedures. Here the US is presented before the CS on every trial, so that the CS comes to signal the absence of the US during the forthcoming intertrial interval (Moscovitch & LoLordo, 1968). There are also many instances of negative contingencies in common experience. For example, if you just had a test in a college course, that is a good indication that you will not have another test in that class for the next several class periods. Such symptoms as normal weight, normal blood pressure, and normal heart rate are used by doctors to predict the absence of illness because illness is much less likely in such people than in people whose weight, blood pressure, and heart rate are abnormal.

By specifying that learning depends on the contingency between CS and US, the contingency model emphasizes that the pairing of CS and US is not sufficient to produce classical conditioning. Furthermore, one cannot predict what the animal will learn, if anything, from being exposed to the CS paired with the US on a number of occasions. For example, suppose that a dog is presented with a tone 100 times, and a random 50 of these tone presentations are immediately followed by the presentation of food. On the basis of this information, we cannot predict what the dog will learn, because we do not know what its probability is of getting food in the experimental situation when the tone is absent. If the animal is never given food in the absence of the tone, a weak positive contingency will exist between the tone and food. Under these conditions the dog will learn to salivate to the tone. However, if the dog is fed as often in the absence of the tone as it is immediately after the tone, the contingency between CS and US will be zero. In this case the dog may learn not to do anything in response to the tone. Finally, if the dog is fed more often in the absence of the tone than it is immediately after the tone, there will be a negative contingency between CS and US, and the dog may learn to treat the tone as a weak signal for the absence of food.

Inhibitory conditioning

As noted above, stimuli can become conditioned to signal the forthcoming absence of the unconditioned stimulus just as well as to signal its forthcoming presence. Learning that a stimulus signals the absence of the US is called **inhibitory conditioning.** Although inhibitory conditioning was discovered by Pavlov along with excitatory conditioning, it did not command serious attention among American psychologists until the mid-1960s (Boakes & Halliday, 1972; Rescorla, 1969b). This relatively long neglect of inhibitory conditioning processes is puzzling. Conditioned inhibition teaches animals how to inhibit (hold back) responses. This is as important in the organization of behavior as the ability to make responses. Furthermore, signals that indicate what unconditioned stimuli will not occur provide as much information about the world as signals that tell organisms what will occur. We have noted briefly that inhibitory conditioning involves the learning of a negative signal relation between CS and US. We will now discuss some of the important procedures for producing conditioned inhibition. We will also discuss how animals react to conditioned inhibitory stimuli.

Procedures for inhibitory conditioning

An important prerequisite for conditioning a stimulus to signal the absence of some US is that the US be periodically presented in that situation. There are many signals for the absence of events in our daily lives. Signs such as "Closed," "Out of Order," and "No Entry" are all of this type. However, these signs provide meaningful information and influence what we do only if they indicate the absence of something we otherwise expect to see. For example, if we encounter the sign "Out of Gas" at a gas station, we may become frustrated and disappointed and will not enter the station. The sign "Out of Gas" provides important information here because we ordinarily expect service stations to have gas. However, the same sign does not tell us anything of interest if it is put up in front of a jewelry store, and it is not likely to discourage us from going into the store. This example illustrates the general rule that inhibitory conditioning and inhibitory control of behavior take

place in an excitatory context for the unconditioned stimulus in question (Wagner & Rescorla, 1972). This principle makes inhibitory conditioning very different from excitatory conditioning, which is not as dependent on a special context in the same way.

Standard procedure for conditioned inhibition. Pavlov recognized the importance of an excitatory context for the conditioning of inhibitory response tendencies and was careful to provide such a context in his standard procedure for conditioning inhibition (Pavlov, 1927). The technique, diagrammed in Figure 4.8, involves two conditioned stimuli and two kinds of conditioning trials repeated in random order. The unconditioned stimulus is presented on some of the trials. Whenever the US occurs, it is announced by one of the conditioned stimuli, the CS+. On the other type of trial, the CS+ is presented together with the second conditioned stimulus, the CS−. The US does not occur on these trials. As the animal receives repeated trials of CS+ followed by the US and CS+/CS− followed by no US, the CS− gradually becomes a signal for the absence of the US (for example, Marchant, Mis, & Moore, 1972). The trials in which the CS− and CS+ are presented without the US are the inhibitory conditioning trials. The excitatory context for this conditioning is provided by the presence of the CS+ on the inhibitory conditioning trials. Because the CS+ is paired with the US on some of the trials, the CS+ becomes conditioned to elicit an expectancy of the US. The absence of the US on the inhibitory conditioning trials therefore occurs in a context in which the sub-

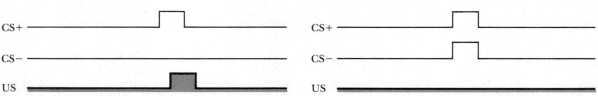

Figure 4.8. Standard procedure for conditioned inhibition. On some trials the CS+ is paired with the US. On other trials the CS+ is paired with the CS− and the US is not presented. The procedure is effective in conditioning inhibitory properties to the CS−.

ject expects the US. This expectancy makes the absence of the US an important event and results in inhibitory conditioning of CS−.

The standard conditioned-inhibition procedure is analogous to situations in which something is introduced that prevents an otherwise inevitable event. Old cars, for example, inevitably break down often. Thus, driving an old car can be considered a signal (CS+) for car trouble (US). However, breakdowns can be avoided if you are careful to perform preventive maintenance, such as tune-ups and lubrications (CS−). Frequent tune-ups and lubrications in an old car (CS+ with CS−) substantially reduce the chances of car problems.

Differential inhibition. Another frequently used procedure for conditioning inhibition is called **differential inhibition.** This procedure is very similar to the standard procedure described above. As in the standard procedure, the US is presented on some trials, and its occurrence is always announced by the presentation of the CS+. On other trials, the US is not presented, and animals experience only the CS−. Thus, the differential-inhibition procedure involves two types of trials, CS+ followed by the US and CS− followed by no US (see Figure 4.9). As in the standard procedure, the CS− becomes a conditioned inhibitory stimulus (for example, Rescorla & LoLordo, 1965).

The differential-inhibition procedure is analogous to having two cars, one old and one new. The old car (CS+) is prone to break down, and if you drive it, you are bound to have car trouble (US). In contrast, the brand-new car (CS−) is in excellent working order. If you

drive the new car, you can be entirely confident that you will not have car problems (no US).

It is not as obvious what provides the excitatory context for the conditioning of inhibition in the differential conditioning procedure as in the standard procedure. In the standard procedure, the presence of the CS+ leads to some expectation of the US on the initial inhibitory conditioning trials. The CS+ is not present on the inhibitory conditioning trials of the differential-conditioning procedure. In fact, this is the only important difference between the two procedures. However, there is another factor that may produce an excitatory context during the inhibitory conditioning trials (CS−, no US) in the differential-conditioning procedure. Because the US is periodically presented, the stimuli of the experimental situation may become conditioned by the US so that the animal has some expectation of the US whenever it is in this situation. (You can expect some car trouble whenever you are driving.) Thus, the contextual cues of the experimental situation may provide the excitatory context for the learning of inhibition in the differential-inhibition procedure.

Negative CS-US Contingency. Both the standard procedure and the differential procedure for producing conditioned inhibition involve a negative contingency between the conditioned inhibitory stimulus (CS−) and the unconditioned stimulus. In both procedures the probability of getting the US with or shortly after the presentation of the CS− is zero. The probability of getting the US when the CS− is not present is greater than zero. However, both

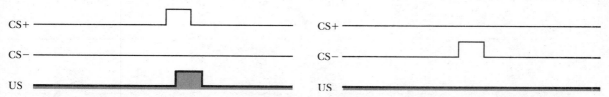

Figure 4.9. Procedure for differential inhibition. On some trials the CS+ is paired with the US. On other trials the CS− is presented alone. The procedure is effective in conditioning inhibitory properties to the CS−.

procedures also involve excitatory conditioning of the CS+. This aspect of the procedures is not absolutely necessary for the occurrence of conditioned inhibition. Subjects do not have to be exposed to an explicit CS+ paired with the US in order to acquire inhibitory tendencies to the CS−. The only thing that is critical is that there be a negative contingency between the inhibitory CS and occurrences of the US. Therefore, conditioned inhibition can also result from procedures in which there is only one explicit conditioned stimulus, provided that this CS is in a negative signal relation to the US. That is, the probability that the US will occur has to be greater in the absence of the CS than in the presence of the CS or immediately after the CS occurs. A sample arrangement that meets this requirement is diagrammed in Figure 4.10. The US is periodically presented by itself. However, each occurrence of the CS is followed by a predictable absence of the US.

Conditioned inhibition is reliably observed in procedures in which the only explicit conditioned stimulus is in a negative contingent relation to the US (Rescorla, 1969a). What provides the excitatory context for this inhibition? Since there is no explicit CS+ that predicts occurrences of the US in this procedure, the US is presented in the experimental situation without being signalled. The environmental cues of the experimental chamber therefore become conditioned to predict occurrences of the US. Thus, as in differential inhibition, the excitatory context for the inhibitory conditioning is provided by the contextual cues of the experimental situation (Dweck & Wagner, 1970).

Measuring conditioned inhibition

Once an animal learns that a stimulus signals the forthcoming absence of an unconditioned stimulus, what does it do with this information? How are conditioned inhibitory processes manifest in behavior? For conditioned excitation, the answer to the corresponding questions is straightforward. Stimuli that have become conditioned to predict the occurrence of a US usually come to elicit behaviors that were not evident in the presence of these stimuli before conditioning. Thus, conditioned excitatory stimuli come to elicit new responses such as salivation, approach, and eye blinking, depending on what the unconditioned stimulus is. One might expect that conditioned inhibitory stimuli would elicit the opposites of these reactions—namely, suppression of salivation, approach, and eye blinking. How are we to measure these response opposites?

Bidirectional response systems. Identification of opposing response tendencies is very easy with response systems that can change in opposite directions from baseline (normal) performance. This is characteristic of many physiological responses. Heart rate, respiration, and temperature, for example, can either increase or decrease from normal. Certain behavioral responses are also bidirectional. For example, animals can either approach or withdraw from a stimulus, and their rate of lever pressing for a food reward can either increase or decrease. In these cases, conditioned excitation results in a change in behavior in one direction, and conditioned inhibition results in a change in behavior

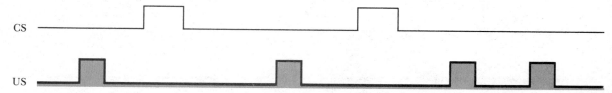

Figure 4.10. Negative CS-US contigency procedure for conditioning inhibitory properties to the CS.

Box 4.3. Conditioned Inhibition and Protection from Ulcers

Exposure to unpleasant and aversive situations can result in various physiological symptoms of stress, including stomach ulcers. One important factor that determines the severity of stress symptoms is the extent to which occurrences of the aversive stimulus are signaled and therefore predictable by the individual. In many cases stress symptoms are much less severe if aversive stimuli are signaled than if they are unpredictable (for example, Weiss, 1970). For example, rats exposed to signaled shock develop fewer and milder ulcers than rats exposed to unsignaled shock (Seligman, 1968; Weiss, 1971). In addition to the reduced gastric pathology, signaled shock produces less chronic fear or anxiety than unsignaled shock (for example, Seligman, 1968; Seligman & Meyer, 1970). An interesting explanation called the "safety-signal hypothesis" attributes these findings to conditioned inhibition (Seligman, 1968; Seligman & Binik, 1977). The presence of a shock signal obviously allows animals to predict when the aversive event will occur. The safety-signal hypothesis points out that shock signals also allow subjects to predict when shocks will not occur, because shocks never occur when the signal is absent. Therefore, the absence of the shock signal serves as a conditioned inhibitory stimulus and indicates periods of safety from shock. According to the safety-signal hypothesis, animals exposed to signaled shock develop fewer ulcers and have less anxiety because they experience such safe periods. Animals for which the shocks are not signaled can never be sure when the shock will or will not be presented and therefore never experience periods of safety. The research findings suggest that psychosomatic illnesses caused by exposure to aversive events can be substantially reduced by introducing conditioned inhibitory stimuli that signal safe periods and allow subjects to relax. The implication is that an executive bothered by ulcers does not necessarily have to quit his or her job. The symptoms of stress can be reduced if the person learns to relax periodically during a hectic day.

in the opposite direction. Although there has been little research on inhibitory conditioning using bidirectional response systems, the results generally support the prediction. That is, conditioned inhibitory stimuli produce responses that are opposite to those produced by conditioned excitatory stimuli. The sign-tracking procedure provides a good example. As noted earlier, pigeons will approach visual stimuli that signal the forthcoming presentation of food. If an inhibitory conditioning procedure is used instead, so that the visual stimulus becomes a signal for the absence of food, the pigeons will withdraw from the CS (Hearst & Franklin, 1977; Wasserman, Franklin, & Hearst, 1974). Similar results are obtained in the conditioned-suppression situation. As we saw, stimuli that have been conditioned to signal forthcoming shock suppress the rate of food-rewarded lever pressing in rats. In contrast, stimuli that have been conditioned to signal the forthcoming absence of shock increase the rate of food-rewarded lever pressing (Hammond, 1966). Another good example of bidirectionality involves taste preference. We noted that animals reduce their preference for a taste that has been paired with sickness. However, animals increase their preference for tastes that have been conditioned to predict the absence of sickness (Best, 1975).

It is important to note that the simple observation of a response opposite to the reaction to a conditioned excitatory stimulus is sometimes not sufficient to conclude that inhibitory conditioning is involved. One must make certain that the topography, or form, of the opposing response was due to the negative contingency between CS and US. Mere exposure to the CS sometimes results in a reaction to the CS that is opposite to what is typically observed with conditioned excitatory stimuli. This is true, for example, for taste preferences. As we noted in Chapter 3, mere exposure to a flavor often increases preference for it. Inhibitory conditioning with poisoning also increases taste preference (Best, 1975). Therefore, inhibitory conditioning has to produce higher taste preferences than are observed with mere taste exposure before one can be sure that conditioned inhibition is responsible for the outcome.

Retardation-of-acquisition test. Inhibitory conditioning can be investigated directly in bidirectional response systems. However, many responses cannot change in both directions. Eye blinking is a good example. In the absence of an eliciting stimulus, rabbits rarely blink. If a stimulus had been conditioned to inhibit the eyeblink response, we would not observe eyeblinks when this stimulus was presented. The problem is that the animal also would not blink when the stimulus was absent. Therefore, we could not be sure whether the lack of responding reflected an active suppression of blinking or merely the low level of this behavior in the absence of any stimulation. More sophisticated techniques have to be used before one can conclude that a stimulus actively inhibits blinking. The **retardation-of-acquisition test** is one such technique (for example, Hammond, 1968; Rescorla, 1969a).

The rationale for the retardation-of-acquisition test is straightforward: If a stimulus actively inhibits a particular response, then it should be unusually difficult to condition that stimulus to elicit the behavior. In other words, the rate of acquisition of a particular conditioned response should be retarded if the stimulus initially elicits an inhibition of the response. Different groups of animals are typically used to measure the extent of the retardation of acquisition. The conditioned-inhibition group initially receives inhibitory conditioning to the CS. During this first phase of the experiment, the comparison group either is not exposed to the CS and US or receives presentations of these stimuli in a random order with respect to each other. (With response systems such as eye blinking, there is no evidence of conditioning in either group of subjects during the first phase of the experiment.) Both groups then receive ex-

citatory conditioning with the CS. Their rates of acquisition of the conditioned response are compared. Because of the initial phase of inhibitory conditioning, the conditioned-inhibition group is slower to learn the conditioned response than the comparison group.

Figure 4.11 shows sample results of a fear-conditioning experiment using the retardation-of-acquisition test. The conditioned-inhibition group was first exposed to a procedure in which a tone signaled the absence of shock. For the comparison group, the tones and shocks were presented randomly with respect to each other during the first phase of the experiment. Then, presentations of the tone ended in shock for

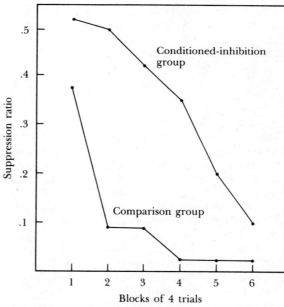

Figure 4.11. Retardation of acquisition of conditioned suppression in rats. The conditioned-inhibition group was first exposed to a procedure in which a tone signaled the absence of shock. For the comparison group, the tones and shocks were presented randomly with respect to each other during the first phase of the experiment. Then, presentations of the tone ended in shock for each group, and the development of conditioned suppression to the tone was plotted. The figure shows that the conditioned-inhibition group was slower to learn to suppress responding during tone presentations than the control group. (*After Rescorla, 1969a.*)

both groups. The conditioning of fear was measured in terms of the suppression of food-rewarded lever pressing. Figure 4.11 shows that the conditioned-inhibition group was slower to learn to suppress responding during tone presentations than the comparison group.

Compound-stimulus test. Another technique for assessing conditioned inhibition in cases that do not involve bidirectional response systems is the **compound-stimulus test.** This procedure was particularly popular with Pavlov (for example, Pavlov, 1927). As noted above, response inhibition is difficult to observe directly in such response systems as eye blinking because the extremely low baseline rate of the behavior makes it virtually impossible to observe suppression of the behavior below the baseline rate. This problem is solved in the compound-stimulus test by presenting an excitatory conditioned stimulus that elicits the conditioned response. Conditioned inhibition is then measured in terms of the suppression of this conditioned responding.

An experiment by Reberg and Black (1969) illustrates the use of the compound-stimulus test to evaluate inhibition in a conditioned-suppression experiment. Subjects in the conditioned-inhibition group received differential conditioning in which a CS+ was periodically presented ending in a brief shock and a CS− was periodically presented in the absence of shock. (Visual and auditory stimuli were used as CS+ and CS−.) The comparison group received only the CS+ paired with shock during this part of the experiment, so that for them the CS− did not become a signal for the absence of shock. Then, both groups received two types of test trials. During one test trial, only the CS+ was presented, to determine the degree of response suppression the animals learned to this stimulus. During the other test trial, the CS+ was presented simultaneously with the CS−. The results are summarized in Figure 4.12. For the conditioned-inhibition group less response suppression occurred when the CS− was

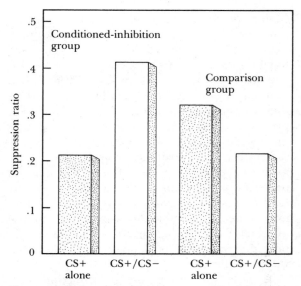

Figure 4.12. Compound-stimulus test of inhibition in a conditioned-suppression experiment. For the conditioned-inhibition group, the CS− was a predictor of the absence of shock. For the comparison group, the CS− was a novel stimulus. The CS− reduced the degree of response suppression produced by a shock-conditioned CS+ in the conditioned-inhibition group but not in the comparison group. *(After Reberg & Black, 1969.)*

presented simultaneously with the CS+ than when the CS+ was presented alone. This outcome occurred because the CS− had become a signal for the absence of shock. Thus, the CS− inhibited the response suppression produced by the CS+. Such an inhibition effect did not occur in the comparison group. For these subjects, the CS− had not been conditioned to signal the absence of shock. In fact, the CS− was presented for the first time during the test trials. Thus, the presence of the CS− did not inhibit the response suppression produced by the CS+.

Extinction

So far our discussion of classical conditioning has centered on various aspects of the acquisition of new responses to stimuli, be they excitatory or inhibitory. It would be maladaptive, however, if once stimuli became conditioned, the animal's response to these stimuli remained fixed for the rest of its life. Just as it is useful for animals to learn new responses to stimuli, it is also adaptive for them to lose this behavior once the circumstances no longer require it. One process whereby conditioned responses to stimuli are decreased is called **extinction.** The procedure for extinguishing a conditioned stimulus is to repeatedly present the CS without the unconditioned stimulus or in the absence of any kind of signal relation with the US. If the animal has been conditioned to salivate in response to a bell, for example, and the bell is then repeatedly presented in the absence of food, salivation to the bell will gradually decline.

A note on terminology: Extinction procedures are said to extinguish responses and/or conditioned stimuli, not organisms. Animals do not die when they are exposed to extinction procedures. Another important definitional comment about extinction is that the loss of the conditioned response that is produced by extinction is not the same as the loss of behavior that may occur because of **forgetting.** In extinction, the repeated presentations of the CS by itself are responsible for the gradual decline of the conditioned response. Forgetting, in contrast, is a decline in the strength of the conditioned response that may occur simply because of the passage of time. Extinction involves a particular experience with the conditioned stimulus. Forgetting occurs with prolonged absence of exposure to the conditioned stimulus.

Extinction and habituation

The procedure for extinction of conditioned stimuli is very similar to the procedures we discussed in Chapter 3 for producing habituation. Both extinction and habituation involve repeated presentation of a stimulus. The critical difference between them is that in extinction the stimulus involved was previously conditioned.

An earlier phase of conditioning is not required for habituation. Because of the similarity in the procedures for extinction and habituation, one might expect that there would also be similarities in the results observed. This is in fact the case.

One characteristic of habituation is that the response is observed to decline more rapidly with repeated presentations of the stimulus if the interval between successive stimulus presentations is short. A similar relation is observed in extinction. A response extinguishes more rapidly if the conditioned-stimulus presentations are massed than if they occur at longer intervals (Hilgard & Marquis, 1935; Pavlov, 1927). Massing of extinction trials may facilitate extinction because of the same kind of short-term inhibitory processes that are responsible for this kind of effect in habituation (see Chapter 3). However, this possibility has not been experimentally verified in extinction, as it has been in habituation.

Another important characteristic of habituation is that the habituated stimulus recovers its ability to evoke the response with the passage of time. This phenomenon is called the "spontaneous recovery" of habituation. A similar effect is observed with extinguished stimuli and/or responses. If, after a series of extinction trials, the animal is given a period of rest away from the experimental environment, **spontaneous recovery** of the extinguished response may occur (Pavlov, 1927). Less spontaneous recovery would be expected after successive series of extinction trials, as was true in habituation. Eventually, there would be no recovery after rest periods.

Habituation and extinction are also similar in the effects of novel stimuli on the loss of responsiveness. As we noted in Chapter 3, presentation of a novel stimulus often results in recovery of the response elicited by the habituated stimulus (dishabituation). A comparable effect occurs in extinction. If, after a series of extinction trials, a novel stimulus is presented, recovery may occur in the response to the extinguished CS (Pavlov, 1927). This recovery in the conditioned response produced by novelty is called **disinhibition.** It is important to differentiate disinhibition from spontaneous recovery. Even though both processes are forms of recovery in the conditioned response, in spontaneous recovery the recovery occurs simply because of the passage of time, and in disinhibition it occurs because of the presentation of a novel stimulus.

What is learned in extinction

The phenomenon of extinction fits our definition of *learning* in that it involves a change in behavior (loss of responsiveness to a stimulus) as a result of experience (repeated presentations of the CS). However, one may wonder what is actually learned. One obvious answer is that extinction does not involve the learning of something new but rather just the unlearning of the previously conditioned response tendency. According to this view, the gradual decline in the conditioned response in extinction simply reflects the loss of whatever was learned earlier. Rather than adopt this view of extinction, Pavlov (1927) suggested that during extinction animals learn to actively inhibit making the conditioned response in the presence of the CS. According to this interpretation, extinction of a conditioned response does not involve any loss of the original learning but rather the learning of a new antagonistic, or inhibitory, response tendency. This conditioned inhibition then prevents the appearance of the conditioned response.

The primary evidence for the conditioned-inhibition interpretation of extinction was provided by the phenomenon of disinhibition. Pavlov reasoned that if extinction involved learning to inhibit the conditioned response to the CS, then the response should recover if this inhibition was disrupted by some treatment. Presentation of a novel stimulus presumably disrupts the inhibition, thereby producing the recovery of the conditioned response in the disinhibition phenomenon.

The phenomenon of disinhibition provides some support for the idea that extinction involves the conditioning of inhibition to the CS. Extinction, however, does not appear to involve the same type of inhibition that animals learn from a negative contingency between CS and US (Rescorla, 1969b). As noted above, evidence of conditioned inhibition resulting from negative CS-US contingencies may be provided in three ways. One possibility is that responses elicited by the inhibitory CS will be opposite to those elicited by an excitatory conditioned stimulus in bidirectional response systems. Other types of evidence are provided by a retardation of excitatory conditioning with the inhibitory CS and attenuation of the conditioned responses elicited by excitatory conditioned stimuli in compound tests. According to each of these three types of evidence, an extinguished CS is not inhibitory. Extinguished conditioned stimuli have not been observed to elicit responses opposite to those elicited by excitatory conditioned stimuli in bidirectional response systems. In fact, after extinction the CS is not likely to elicit any change in behavior from the baseline conditions. An extinguished conditioned stimulus is also no more difficult to condition than a novel stimulus. Indeed, the opposite result is usually observed: conditioning proceeds more rapidly with previously extinguished conditioned stimuli than with novel stimuli (Konorski & Szwejkowska, 1950, 1952). Finally, an extinguished stimulus does not inhibit the conditioned responses elicited by an effective conditioned stimulus in a compound test. Rather, it is not unusual to observe some facilitation of responding when the extinguished CS is presented together with an effective CS (Reberg, 1972).

The evidence summarized above indicates that extinction does not produce the same kind of inhibition of behavior that is learned in conditioned-inhibition procedures. However, if extinction is not a type of conditioned inhibition, how are we to interpret the results of the disinhibition phenomenon? One possibility is to view extinction not as the learning of inhibition but simply as the gradual loss of the ability of the CS to elicit the conditioned response. However, we must assume that extinguished CSs always retain some residual capacity to elicit the CR. The phenomenon of disinhibition is then attributed to arousal created by the novel stimulus that sensitizes the nervous system so that the residual conditioned properties of the extinguished CS can elicit the CR. The notion that the CS always has some residual capacity to elicit the CR is also consistent with the observations, noted above, that an extinguished CS is easier to recondition than a novel stimulus and that an extinguished CS facilitates elicitation of the conditioned response by nonextinguished conditioned stimuli.

Classical conditioning outside the laboratory

Classical conditioning is typically investigated in artificial laboratory situations. However, one does not have to know much about classical conditioning to realize that it often occurs outside the laboratory. Classical conditioning is most likely to develop when one event reliably precedes another in a short-delayed CS-US pairing or in situations with a strong contingency. These conditions are met in nearly every aspect of life. As we mentioned at the beginning of the chapter, stimuli in the environment occur in an orderly temporal sequence. One reason is the physical constraints of causation: some events simply cannot happen before other events have taken place. Social institutions and customs are also usually arranged to make things happen in a predictable order. Because of these factors, in many situations certain stimuli reliably precede others, and whenever that is the case, classical

conditioning may take place. Therefore, classical conditioning is potentially operative in just about every aspect of life.

Digestion

One clear example of a temporal sequence of events necessitated by the physical arrangement of causes and effects is the digestive system. Food does not enter the mouth until the subject has seen it, approached it, smelled it, and put it in the mouth. Food is not swallowed until it is chewed, and it does not appear in the stomach until it has been swallowed. Similarly, it does not enter the small intestine until it has been in the stomach, and it does not enter the large intestine until it has been in the small intestine. This sequence of events makes the digestive system a prime candidate for the involvement of classical conditioning.

Although not all the conditioning processes involved in digestion have been experimentally verified, it is not difficult to speculate about the role of classical conditioning in digestion. We know that different types of food require secretion of different combinations of digestive juices into the alimentary canal. It takes certain combinations and amounts of stomach and intestinal secretions to digest a large, tasty steak, and it takes other combinations and amounts to digest scrambled eggs. Because food always passes through the alimentary canal in the same sequence (mouth to stomach to small intestine to large intestine), one may speculate that the stimuli involved in one stage of the process become signals for where the food will be and what will happen in the next stage. In this way, the relevant digestive juices can be secreted in each part of the alimentary tract in anticipation of the actual arrival of food there. Thus, the stomach can begin to secrete the relevant digestive materials when the food is in the mouth or when the subject first smells the food. Similarly, the small intestine can become prepared for the arrival of food on the basis of the stimuli provided by food in the mouth and stomach. If such anticipatory secretions occurred (and there is no reason to believe they do not), they would substantially speed up the digestive process.

Most people eat at regular times and eat regular meals. Furthermore, the variety in the foods eaten is ordinarily not very large. Considering the tremendously large range of edible foods in the world, most people have a highly restricted diet. This is particularly true with breakfast. If people eat breakfast at all, they typically restrict their choice to one of fewer than ten combinations of foods. The conditioning model suggests that this regularity of the timing and choice of foods, together with the orderly sequence of eating-related cues, allows for the occurrence of anticipatory digestive secretions throughout the alimentary tract.

If such anticipatory secretions occur and ordinarily play an important role in facilitating digestion, digestive disorders should be evident in their absence. Consistent with this prediction, most people feel a bit sick to their stomachs whenever they eat something they are not used to. For example, is you rarely eat steak, you will probably feel a heaviness in your abdomen after eating steak, and such a meal will make you more sluggish than your usual meal. These are symptoms of slow digestion. Similar digestive disorders are experienced when meals are eaten at unusual times, as on trips. If you are driving all night and stop to have a meal at 3:00 A.M. because you are hungry, chances are the meal will not taste and feel good.

Digestive disorders are often more common among older people. Although there could be a variety of explanations, this phenomenon is also predicted by the conditioning model. Each meal a person eats is an alimentary conditioning trial. This means that the older the person, the more strongly the entire digestive system will have become conditioned to a restricted set of stimuli. This strong attachment of anticipatory secretory responses to a restricted set of stimuli makes the person increasingly prone to digestive disorders when the cues present at a certain meal are not exactly the ones that the person is accustomed to having at meals.

One concrete example of a digestive conditioned response is the release of insulin in response to sweet tastes. Insulin is involved in the digestion of sugars. It is released by the pancreas as an unconditioned response to the presence of sugar in the digestive tract. The presence of sugar in the stomach and small intestine is always preceded by the taste of sugar in the mouth. Therefore, the taste of sugar can become conditioned to stimulate the release of insulin as an anticipatory conditioned response. After such conditioning, insulin may also be released as an anticipatory response when subjects taste artificial sweeteners, such as saccharin. If a real sugar is ingested (sucrose or glucose, for example), the released insulin is used up in the digestion of the sugar. However, if the subject ingests only saccharin, the released insulin is not used up, because there is no sugar to digest. Therefore, ingestion of saccharin results in excessive amounts of circulating insulin. This causes a drop in blood sugar level and is responsible for the "heady" feeling people sometimes get after having a diet drink on an empty stomach. Interestingly, the drop in blood sugar level elicited as a conditioned response by the taste of sweets can become extinguished if the subject receives extensive exposure to an artificial sweetener (Deutsch, 1974). Because insulin is not required for the digestion of saccharin, the release of insulin following ingestion of saccharin becomes extinguished. Perhaps this is why heavy consumers of diet drinks do not have the same reactions to artificially sweetened drinks as occasional users.

The milk-letdown reflex

One of the prominent physiological changes that occur in women after giving birth is the appearance of the milk-letdown reflex. Initially, the reflexive flow of milk from the breast occurs only in response to sucking by the infant. However, within a few days, the new mother may discover that she also uncontrollably secretes milk when the baby cries or after the usual period between feedings has elapsed. Later still, the milk-letdown reflex may occur when the mother thinks about feeding the child. All these stimuli (the baby's crying, the time of normal feedings, and thoughts about feeding the baby) always precede sucking by the infant. They therefore become conditioned by the sucking stimulation and come to elicit milk secretion as a conditioned response in the absence of sucking.

Learning of emotional responses

One of the areas of our lives in which classical conditioning has a prominent role is the control of emotional reactions. In fact, for some time it was believed that classical conditioning was involved exclusively in the conditioning of glandular and emotional responses. Recent research on such phenomena as sign tracking has disproved this restrictive belief. Nevertheless, classical conditioning remains the primary mechanism for the learning and modification of emotional behavior.

Learning is very important in emotional behavior. Perhaps the most obvious fact about emotions is that there are large individual differences. Some people like quiet blues and pinks; others like browns and yellows. Some people like rock and roll; others like opera. Some people enjoy being invited to parties; others dread such invitations. Some of these idiosyncratic emotional reactions may be the result of past conditioning experiences. If you usually have a good time at parties, you will learn to look forward to invitations. If you usually have a miserable time, you will hate to be invited. Long-time lovers often have a special sentimental attachment to certain pieces of music. ("They're playing our song, honey.") This attachment usually results from having heard the song during particularly romantic moments in their courtship.

Classical conditioning no doubt also has an important role in sexual and interpersonal attraction. You may favor tall people, short people, brunettes, or blonds because your previous experience with such people was particularly pleasant. You may seek out either talkative people or quiet ones for the same reason. Finding certain stimuli sexually arousing may also result in part from previous conditioning. Particular perfumes may acquire special significance for you because of the situations in which you encounter them.

The entire movie industry is based on the role of conditioned stimuli in the control of emotional behavior. Good movies evoke strong emotional experiences even though there are no unconditioned stimuli in the situation. An effective horror movie can make you very frightened even though you well know that you are in no physical danger during the show. A love scene performed well can put you in a romantic mood even if you are watching the movie by yourself, obviously without an appropriate unconditioned stimulus. The joy and the sorrow that you experience in movies are elicited by exposure to stimuli that have acquired a special significance for you because of your past experiences. Children often do not enjoy "adult" movies because they have not yet had the necessary conditioning experiences.

Although individuals have many unique emotional conditioning experiences, people who share a language and a culture also have certain common experiences. One example is provided by what we learn about words. Words are most obviously used to communicate information and ideas. However, many words also induce emotional experiences. Great writers are experts in the use of words to evoke special emotional reactions. Works by Shakespeare, Tolstoy, and Hawthorne, for example, would not be considered masterpieces if they did not stimulate strong emotional reactions.

The emotional effects of words are the result of conditioning experiences. If someone tells you that you are incompetent and a scoundrel, chances are you will feel bad. These words evoke an unpleasant emotional reaction because they are associated with other aversive events, such as the loss of a job. Conversely, such words as *good, intelligent,* and *beautiful* evoke pleasant emotions because they are usually associated with pleasant events.

Psychotherapy

We have seen that people can learn many relations among stimuli in their world by way of classical-conditioning experiences. In many cases the conditioning results in associations that help people adjust to their environment. In other cases the associations may result in maladaptive behavior. An accidentally learned taste aversion, for example, may lead to avoidance of a healthful food. Some clinical psychologists believe that conditioning may play an important role in the development of various behavior problems.

Phobias. One example of the influence of conditioning is the origin and treatment of **phobias.** Phobias are instances of fear for which there is generally no rational basis. A person may experience intense fear on seeing a caged snake. No real danger exists, but the sensation of fear may be as intense as in a truly threatening situation. Irrational fears can be extremely debilitating. Some people are so fearful of leaving their homes (agoraphobia) that they remain housebound for years.

Dr. Joseph Wolpe, a British clinical psychologist, cites one example of a phobia in which classical conditioning appears to have been involved (Wolpe, 1962). Mrs. C experienced intense fear in certain traffic situations. Dr. Wolpe describes how this developed:

> Briefly her story was that . . . while her husband was taking her to work by car, they entered an intersection on a green light. On the left side she noticed two girls standing at the curb . . . and then, suddenly, became aware of a large truck that had disregarded the red signal, bearing down upon the car. She remembered the moment of

impact, being flung out of the car, flying through the air, and then losing consciousness [p. 317].*

After recovering from the accident, Mrs. C began to experience anxiety in certain traffic situations. The fact that her fears were specific to certain types of situations provides evidence that the accident resulted in classical conditioning. Notice the similarity between the accident and the fear-provoking situations:

> While in a car, though relatively comfortable on the open road, she was always disturbed by seeing a car approach from either side, but not at all by vehicles straight ahead. Along city streets she had continuous anxiety which would, at the sight of a laterally approaching car less than half a block away, rise to panic. . . . Reactions were extraordinarily severe in relation to making a left turn in the face of approaching traffic on the highway. Execution of them, of course, momentarily placed the vehicle to the right of her car, and there was a considerable rise in tension even when the vehicle was a mile or more ahead. . . . Besides her reaction while in a car, she was anxious while walking across streets, even at intersections with the traffic light in her favor, and even if the nearest approaching car was more than a block away [p. 317].

The development of a phobia is usually not as clear as it was with Mrs. C. People often come to the psychologist with phobia symptoms but no clear history of conditioning. However, the assumption that behavior can be influenced by conditioning procedures gives the clinician tools to use even when the original learning of the maladaptive behavior is not clear. Various procedures based on conditioning principles are frequently successful.

One widely used method is **systematic desensitization.** Systematic desensitization is based on counterconditioning (described in

---

*From "Isolation of a Conditioning Procedure as the Crucial Psychotherapeutic Factor: A Case Study," by J. Wolpe. In *Journal of Nervous and Mental Disease,* 1962, *134,* 316–329. This and all other quotations from this source are reprinted by permission.

Chapter 5). The idea is to present the fear-eliciting stimuli when it is impossible for the subject to make any fear responses. Relaxation training is usually employed to prevent the occurrence of fear responses. The subject is initially given relaxation training. When he or she is able to maintain a state of deep relaxation, the fear-eliciting stimuli are presented. This is done in a hierarchical fashion. Stimuli that only slightly elicit fear are presented first, and the cues are repeated until the subject remains completely relaxed in their presence. Subsequently, more fearful stimuli are used. For example, to desensitize a person of a snake phobia, a stylized picture of a snake from a child's picture book is first presented until it does not elicit any fear. A more realistic picture of a small snake may be presented next. Then the size and vividness of the pictured snake may be increased. After the person has learned to relax with the picture stimuli, a live snake may be presented.

Clinicians using systematic desensitization have found that it is not always necessary to use realistic stimuli. The procedure also works with imagined stimuli. Mrs. C, for example, was successfully treated by having her envision a series of fear-provoking situations while relaxing. The effects of using imaginary stimuli seem to transfer well to the real world.

Although systematic desensitization is based on classical counterconditioning procedures, there are many differences between systematic desensitization and laboratory demonstrations of classical conditioning. Unlike the laboratory experimenter, the clinician does not have precise control of the stimuli involved. The clinician cannot precisely control the imaginary stimuli or the exact level of relaxation of the patient. Furthermore, the competing response, relaxation, is not a discrete response but an ill-defined, pervasive state. It may be that systematic desensitization works for reasons other than those suggested by classical-conditioning paradigms (see Bandura, 1969, for an extensive review of the clinical research on this topic). Whether or not the therapy works for the rea-

sons we suspect, classical conditioning has played a major role in its development.

Alcohol-aversion therapy. Another treatment procedure that evolved directly from classical-conditioning procedures is aversion therapy used in treatment of alcoholism. As early as 1934 Kantorovich (cited in Razran, 1934) attempted to treat alcoholics by pairing the sight, smell, and taste of alcohol with electrical shocks. Another more widely used approach was developed largely by Voegtlin and his associates (see Elkins, 1975, for a recent summary). These clinical researchers used drug-induced nausea and vomiting as an unconditioned stimulus. The patient in these procedures is given an injection of a drug such as emetine, which induces severe nausea. Just before the onset of the nausea, the patient is asked to smell and taste various alcoholic beverages. The procedure is repeated until the smell and taste of alcohol alone elicit aversion responses.

Various researchers have reported reasonably high success rates with aversion therapy (for example, Boland, Mellor, & Revusky, 1978). In some cases abstention from alcohol has lasted for several years after treatment. However, it must be understood that aversion therapy is not a panacea for treatment of alcoholism. Alcoholism is a highly complex phenomenon. It is often accompanied by various physical diseases and psychological disorders. All these problems have to be dealt with in addition to the excessive alcohol drinking. Aversion therapy is only one weapon in the clinician's armamentarium. Used carefully and in conjunction with other therapies, it can be very useful.

Concluding comments

As we have seen, classical-conditioning processes are involved in a wide variety of important aspects of behavior. Depending on the procedure used, the learning may occur quickly or slowly. With certain procedures, excitatory response tendencies are learned, whereas with other procedures subjects learn to inhibit a particular response in the presence of the conditioned stimulus. Both types of learning involve the signal relation between the conditioned and unconditioned stimuli. Organisms can learn that a CS signals the impending presentation of the US or the absence of the US for a while. Finally, if the CS is repeatedly presented without the US after conditioning, it will become extinguished and lose most of its conditioned properties.

CHAPTER FIVE

Classical Conditioning: Mechanisms

Chapter 5 is devoted to describing in greater detail the factors that influence the formation of an association between two stimuli. The discussion is organized in three parts. First we will describe what makes environmental events effective as conditioned and unconditioned stimuli. Then we will discuss how the conditioned and unconditioned stimuli become associated. Finally, we will discuss how the organism's behavior is influenced by the association between the CS and US.

How to choose conditioned and unconditioned stimuli

Perhaps the most basic question to ask about classical conditioning is what makes some stimuli effective as conditioned stimuli and what makes others effective as unconditioned stimuli. Traditionally, Western investigators have been concerned mainly with how classical conditioning is influenced by various temporal arrangements and signal relations between conditioned and unconditioned stimuli. The issue of what makes stimuli effective as CSs and USs was originally addressed by Pavlov and is also increasingly attracting the attention of contemporary researchers.

Initial response to the stimuli

Pavlov provided a partial answer to the question of what makes effective conditioned and unconditioned stimuli in his definitions of the terms *conditioned* and *unconditioned*. According to these definitions, the conditioned stimulus is one that does not elicit the conditioned response initially but begins to do so with training. In contrast, the unconditioned stimulus is one that is effective in eliciting the response in question without any special training experiences. It is important to note that these definitions are stated in terms of the elicitation of a particular response, the one to be conditioned. The conditioned stimulus is usually not entirely ineffective before conditioning. It elicits orientation and perhaps other responses as well. However, initially it does not elicit the response to be conditioned.

Because Pavlov defined conditioned and unconditioned stimuli in terms of the elicitation of a particular response, identifying potential CSs and USs involves comparing the responses elicited by each before conditioning. Such a comparison makes the identification of CSs and USs relative to the stimuli in question. Therefore, a given stimulus may serve as a US in some situations and as a CS in others. Consider, for example, a palatable saccharin solution for thirsty rats. This stimulus might serve as an unconditioned stimulus in a sign-tracking experiment. The conditioning trials might involve the illumination of a light for 15 seconds immediately preceding presentation of several drops of the saccharin solution. After a number of trials, the animals would begin to approach the light whenever it was illuminated. The saccharin solution might also serve as a conditioned stimulus in a taste-aversion experiment. If the animals were allowed to drink the solution before being injected with an aversive drug, they would learn an aversion to the saccharin. Thus, whether the saccharin solution is considered a US or a CS depends on its relation to other stimuli in the situation. In the sign-tracking experiment, the saccharin solution serves as the US because it elicits the response in question (approach) without conditioning. In the taste-aversion experiment, the saccharin solution serves as the CS because it elicits the conditioned response (withdrawal or aversion) only after pairings with sickness.

The concept of biological strength

If the definition of the conditioned stimulus were accepted without qualification, selecting stimuli would be simple. One would predict that any stimulus that did not initially elicit some behavior could become conditioned to do so, provided that it were paired with a stimulus (the US) that already elicited the response of interest. For example, we would predict that any stimulus could become conditioned to elicit salivation if the stimulus were repeatedly paired with food. Such an extreme belief in the power of conditioning mechanisms was seriously entertained when Pavlov's research was first discussed among Western psychologists. However, Pavlov did not himself advocate such a radical view. Instead, he suggested that for a stimulus to become conditioned, it had to be a weaker biological stimulus than the unconditioned stimulus with which it was to be paired (Pavlov, 1927). By "weaker biological stimulus," Pavlov meant one that elicited fewer and weaker responses at the start of training than the US. This second Pavlovian criterion for conditioned stimuli is not as well known as the first. However, it is true in most examples of classical conditioning. The familiar salivation in response to a bell is a good example. In this situation, the conditioned stimulus (bell) initially elicits only orientation movements. In contrast, the US (food) elicits vigorous approach, salivation, chewing, swallowing, and so on.

Higher-order conditioning. One implication of Pavlov's criteria for conditioned and unconditioned stimuli is that a stimulus may serve in the role of an unconditioned stimulus after it has become conditioned. Consider, for example, a tone that is repeatedly paired with food. After a sufficient number of trials, the tone will come to elicit salivation. Because of its association with food, the tone will also result in stronger biological reactions than novel tones or lights. It will elicit orientation movements and approach responses, and the animal will become generally aroused when the tone is presented. According to Pavlov, the tone should be effective in conditioning salivation to other stimuli that do not initially elicit salivation. Pairings of the previously conditioned tone with a novel light, for example, should gradually result in the conditioning of salivation to the light. This result is often observed and is called **higher-order conditioning.** Figure 5.1 diagrams the sequence of events that brings about higher-order conditioning.

As the term *higher-order conditioning* implies, conditioning may be considered to operate at different levels. In the example above, conditioning of the tone with food is considered first-order conditioning. Conditioning of the light with the previously conditioned tone is

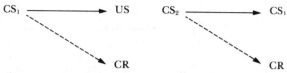

Figure 5.1. Procedure for higher-order conditioning. CS_1 is first paired with the US and comes to elicit the conditioned response. A new stimulus (CS_2) is then paired with CS_1 and also comes to elicit the conditioned response.

considered second-order conditioning. If the conditioned light were then used to condition yet another stimulus—say, an odor—that would be third-order conditioning. Although there is no doubt that second-order conditioning is a robust phenomenon (for example, Rescorla, 1980), little research has been done to evaluate the mechanisms of third and higher orders of conditioning. However, even the existence of second-order conditioning is of considerable significance because it greatly increases the range of situations in which classical conditioning can take place. With higher-order conditioning, classical conditioning can occur without a primary unconditioned stimulus. The only requirement is that a previously conditioned stimulus be available.

Sensory preconditioning. The phenomenon of higher-order conditioning supports Pavlov's criteria for identifying conditioned and unconditioned stimuli. However, there are other conditioning phenomena that are difficult to think about in terms of the Pavlovian criteria. One of these is **sensory preconditioning.** The sensory-preconditioning experiment involves a two-phase procedure (see Figure 5.2). In the first phase, animals repeatedly receive one weak biological stimulus (a tone, for example) followed by another one (a light, for example). No response conditioning is evident in this phase of training. Neither the tone nor the light comes to elicit new responses. Response conditioning takes place in the second phase of the experiment, in which the light is now paired with an unconditioned stimulus, such as shock

to the feet. Fear becomes conditioned to the light in this phase. However, when the animal is then tested with the tone, the conditioned fear reaction also occurs in response to the tone. Various experimental results indicate that this transfer of the conditioned response from the light to the tone occurs because of the pairings of the tone and the light in the first phase of the experiment. The initial pairings of tone and light produce conditioning that is not evident until the light is conditioned to elicit a new response.

The conditioning that occurs between the tone and the light in the sensory-preconditioning experiment appears to violate both of Pavlov's criteria for identifying conditioned and unconditioned stimuli. The tone and the light cannot be distinguished by the responses they elicit before conditioning begins (both elicit orientation movements and not much else), and they are of apparently comparable biological strength.

Counterconditioning. Another situation that appears to violate Pavlov's criteria for identifying conditioned and unconditioned stimuli involves some examples of **counterconditioning.** In counterconditioning, the response an animal makes to a stimulus is reversed through conditioning. For example, counterconditioning would be implicated if an animal is trained to approach a stimulus that initially elicits withdrawal. Some counterconditioning experiments have involved pairs of stimuli that are ordinarily

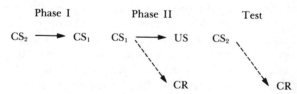

Figure 5.2. Procedure for sensory preconditioning. CS_2 is first paired with CS_1 without an unconditioned stimulus in the situation. CS_1 is then paired with a US and comes to elicit a conditioned response. In a later test session, CS_2 is also found to elicit the conditioned response, even though CS_2 was never paired with the US.

considered unconditioned. Sexual-aversion conditioning is often of this type. If a male rat is presented with a receptive female and is then shocked, it may learn an aversion to the female. Although a response is learned to the female, it is difficult to argue that this learning occurs because the biological strength of the shock is greater than the biological strength of the female rat. Both stimuli initially elicit very vigorous unconditioned responses. Furthermore, the responses elicited are very different (chasing, sniffing, and mounting for the female-rat stimulus and startle, jumping, and possibly aggression for the shock stimulus). Therefore, it is impossible to decide whether the initial responses to the female rat are stronger (or weaker) than the responses to the shock.

Although Pavlov was correct in rejecting the radical behaviorist view that any stimulus can become conditioned to elicit any response, his criterion that conditioned stimuli have to elicit weaker innate reactions than unconditioned stimuli has not turned out to be very useful. More recent research has identified other stimulus variables that influence the extent to which conditioned and unconditioned stimuli become associated. Some of these are described below.

Novelty of conditioned and unconditioned stimuli

One of the stimulus characteristics important in classical conditioning is the novelty of the conditioned and unconditioned stimuli. If either the conditioned stimulus or the unconditioned stimulus is highly familiar, learning will occur more slowly. Experiments that have demonstrated these effects typically involve two phases. In experiments that address the issue of CS novelty, for example, animals are first given repeated exposure to the stimulus that is later to be used as the CS. During this initial phase of the experiment, the CS-to-be is always presented by itself. After this stimulus familiarization, the CS is paired with an unconditioned stimulus using conventional classical-conditioning procedures. Animals that have received preconditioning exposures to the CS are usually slower to learn the conditioned response than animals for which the CS is novel. This phe-

---

Box 5.1 Counterconditioning and the Pain of Childbirth

Many expectant parents today are receiving training to deal with the discomforts of childbirth without the use of anesthesia. One popular technique was developed by a French physician, Dr. Lamaze, after observing the practice of Russian obstetricians. The Lamaze method, as it has come to be called, was developed by Russian physicians as an application of counterconditioning. Childbirth involves a series of uterine contractions that become stronger and stronger until the baby is born. Women in labor frequently become fearful, tense, and panicky in response to this increasing discomfort. The tension elicited by the contractions only makes the situation worse—the tension increases the discomfort. The Lamaze training technique is intended to countercondition the contraction sensations so that they will elicit a new response that is incompatible with tension. The woman is first given relaxation training. She then learns a set of breathing patterns to perform at the onset of each contraction. These breathing patterns require a good deal of concentration, which distracts the woman from the discomfort and thereby inhibits tension. Thus, instead of eliciting tension, the labor contractions elicit a complicated breathing pattern.

Although the Lamaze technique was originally based on the concept of counterconditioning, it is not entirely clear that the mechanisms responsible for the pain reduction are really those of counterconditioning. The technique varies from standard laboratory procedures in that the training is done almost entirely with mock contractions. Little direct conditioning with a true labor contraction is done. However, whether or not Lamaze training is a valid example of counterconditioning, it illustrates how laboratory principles can lead to beneficial applications. Many women today deliver their babies with less discomfort than before and avoid pain-killing drugs that may be harmful to the infant.

nomenon is called the **CS-preexposure** or **latent-inhibition effect** (Lubow & Moore, 1959). Experiments that address the issue of US novelty are conducted in a manner similar to the CS-preexposure experiments. In the first phase of the study, animals are given repeated exposures to the unconditioned stimulus presented alone. The US is then paired with a conditioned stimulus, and the progress of learning is monitored. Animals familiarized with an unconditioned stimulus are slower to associate the US with a conditioned stimulus than animals for which the US is novel during classical conditioning. This result is called the **US-preexposure effect.**

It is interesting to note that the CS- and US-preexposure effects are produced by the same procedure, repeated stimulus presentations, that results in habituation. In fact, these two effects are closely related to the phenomenon of habituation, discussed in Chapter 3, and demonstrate the interaction of habituation and conditioning processes. As discussed in Chapter 3, there are both short-term and long-term habituation effects. Similarly, there are two types of CS- and US-preexposure effects. A short-lasting, temporary reduction in CS effectiveness results from presentation of the CS shortly before the conditioning trial (for example, Best & Gemberling, 1977). A more durable interference with conditioning results from repeatedly presenting the CS-to-be in the same environment where the subsequent conditioning trials will be conducted (Lubow, 1973). Comparable short-lasting and long-lasting interference effects of US preexposure also occur (Domjan & Best, 1977, 1980; Randich & LoLordo, 1979; Terry, 1976). The CS- and US-preexposure effects are also similar to habituation in that manipulation of such variables as the intensity of the preexposed stimulus or the interval between stimulus presentations during preexposure has comparable effects in the two situations (for example, Lantz, 1973; Randich & LoLordo, 1979). Apparently, repeated preconditioning presentations of the CS and US in an unpaired arrangement result in the habituation of some reaction or process that is important for the normal functioning of conditioning mechanisms.

CS and US intensity

Another important stimulus variable for classical conditioning is the intensity of the conditioned and unconditioned stimuli. Most biological and physiological effects of stimulation are directly related to the intensity of the stimulus input. This is also true for conditioning. The association of a CS with a US occurs more rapidly, and the final amount of conditioning achieved is greater, when more intense stimuli are used (for example, Kamin & Brimer, 1963; Kamin & Schaub, 1963). This relation is observed over a broad range of stimulus intensities. However, if the CS or US intensity is too high, conditioning may be disrupted, probably because very intense stimuli elicit strong unconditioned reactions that may make it difficult for the animal to engage in the conditioned response. Experiments on classical conditioning rarely involve such extreme CS and US intensities.

The fact that conditioning is facilitated by increasing the intensity of the CS and US may be related to the novelty of the conditioned and unconditioned stimuli. Animals and people rarely encounter stimuli that are very intense. Therefore, high-intensity conditioned and unconditioned stimuli may be more novel than lower-intensity stimulation. Novelty may be at least partly responsible for the stimulus-intensity effects in classical conditioning (see Kalat, 1974).

CS-US relevance, or belongingness

Early in our discussion of stimulus variables in classical conditioning, we noted that the decision of what stimulus can serve as a CS often has to be made in relation to what stimulus is to serve as the US, and vice versa. The relation we discussed involved the initial responses to the CS and US and the biological strength of the stimuli. Another relation between the CS and US that governs the rate of classical conditioning is the relevance, or belongingness, between the CS and US. It seems that certain conditioned stimuli are more easily associated with certain types of unconditioned stimuli, whereas other types of CSs are more easily associated with other USs. Apparently, some CSs are more relevant to or belong better with certain USs.

Stimulus relevance in aversion conditioning. The phenomenon of CS-US relevance was first clearly demonstrated by Garcia and Koelling (1966) in what has come to be one of the classic experiments in conditioning. They used two types of CSs (tastes and audiovisual cues) and two types of USs (shock and sickness). The experiment, diagrammed in Figure 5.3, involved having rats drink from a drinking tube before administration of one of the unconditioned stimuli. The drinking tube was filled with water flavored either salty or sweet. In addition, each lick on the tube activated a brief audiovisual stimulus (the click of a relay and a flash of light). Thus, the conditioned stimulus was rather complex, involving both taste and audiovisual components. After exposure to this complex CS, the animals either received shock through the grid floor or were made sick with radiation exposure or drug injections.

Because all the unconditioned stimuli used were aversive, it was expected that the animals would learn some kind of aversion. The experimenters measured the response of the animals to the taste and audiovisual stimuli separately after conditioning. To measure the animals' reaction to the taste CS, the water was flavored as before, but now licks did not activate the audiovisual stimulus. To measure reaction to the audiovisual CS, the water was unflavored, and the audiovisual stimulus was briefly turned on whenever the animal drank. The degree of conditioned aversion to the taste or audiovisual CS was inferred from the amount of suppression of drinking.

The results of the experiment are summarized in Figure 5.4. Before this experiment was performed, there was no reason to expect that one of the unconditioned stimuli would be more effective than the other in conditioning an aversion to one aspect of the conditioned-stimulus complex. However, that is precisely what happened. Animals conditioned with shock subsequently suppressed their drinking much more when tested with the audiovisual stimulus than when tested with the taste CS.

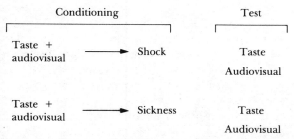

Figure 5.3 Diagram of Garcia and Koelling's (1966) experiment. A compound taste/audiovisual stimulus was first paired with either shock or sickness. The subjects were then tested with the taste and audiovisual stimuli separately.

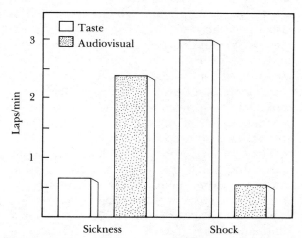

Figure 5.4 Results of Garcia and Koelling's (1966) experiment. Rats conditioned with sickness learned a stronger aversion to taste than to audiovisual cues. In contrast, rats conditioned with shock learned a stronger aversion to audiovisual than to taste cues.

The opposite result occurred when animals were conditioned with sickness induced by radiation or drug treatment. These rats suppressed their drinking much more when the taste CS was present than when drinking produced the audiovisual stimulus. Thus, stronger aversions were conditioned to audiovisual cues than to taste cues when the US was shock, and stronger aversions were conditioned to tastes than to audiovisual cues when the US was internal malaise.

Garcia and Koelling's experiment demonstrates the principle of CS-US relevance, or belongingness. Conditioning in this experiment was governed only by the combination of the CS and US involved in the association. For example, one cannot explain the results by saying that the audiovisual cue was more novel or intense than the taste stimulus. If that had been true, the audiovisual CS should have been better conditioned than the taste with both shock and illness. One also cannot explain the data by appealing to differences in the intensity or novelty of the unconditioned stimuli. For example, one cannot argue that shock was generally more effective than illness. If it had been, the shock should have been more effective than illness in conditioning an aversion to both the audiovisual and the taste CSs. The only way to explain the results Garcia and Koelling observed is to acknowledge that certain combinations of conditioned and unconditioned stimuli (tastes with illness, audiovisual cues with shock) are more easily associated than other combinations of conditioned and unconditioned stimuli (taste with shock, audiovisual cues with illness).

The CS-US relevance effect demonstrated by Garcia and Koelling has since been observed in numerous experiments. Some have suggested that the effect occurs only when subjects receive exposure to the taste and the audiovisual stimuli simultaneously before the US during conditioning trials. However, the phenomenon is apparent even if the animals are exposed to only one or the other CS, not both, during conditioning (for example, Domjan & Wilson, 1972).

Box 5.2. Food-Aversion Learning in Humans

Human food-aversion experiences often parallel laboratory findings (Garb & Stunkard, 1974). For example, if you eat a pleasant dinner at a restaurant and then get sick, you are likely to learn an aversion to one or more of the foods you ate. You will develop the aversion whether you became ill because of the food or because of some other cause, such as the flu. Furthermore, your aversion will be specific to food items. You will not learn an aversion to the color of the tablecloth, the candles, or the waiter's uniform even though you were exposed to each of these stimuli during the dinner. This example illustrates the phenomenon of stimulus relevance. CS and US novelty factors are also important in human food-aversion learning. You are not likely to learn an aversion to highly familiar foods, such as bread and butter. You are also less likely to learn an aversion if your illness started some time before the dinner and was therefore somewhat "familiar" before the meal.

The phenomenon also occurs in rats 1 day after birth (Gemberling & Domjan, in press). This last finding indicates that extensive experience with tastes, sickness, audiovisual cues, and peripheral pain is not necessary for the stimulus relevance effect. Rather, the phenomenon appears to reflect a genetic predisposition for the selective association of certain combinations of CSs and USs.

It is important to note that the CS-US relevance principle identified by Garcia and Koelling does not mean that associations between CSs and USs that are not relevant to each other are impossible. The Garcia/Koelling experiment and similar studies do not purport to show that rats cannot learn aversions to tastes paired with shock or to exteroceptive cues paired with sickness. In fact, both these types of associations have been demonstrated (for example, Best, Best, & Henggeler, 1977; Krane & Wagner, 1975; but see Hankins, Rusiniak, & Garcia,

1976). Rather, stimulus relevance and belongingness rest on the demonstration that associations are learned *more easily* between CSs and USs that are relevant to each other than between other CSs and USs.

Generality of stimulus relevance. For several years, the stimulus-relevance effect described above was the only known instance of CS-US relevance in classical conditioning. Consequently, some theorists suggested that the relevance of tastes to toxicosis and of audiovisual cues to foot shock in rats represented a unique learning mechanism (for example, Rozin & Kalat, 1971). However, recent research has uncovered other stimulus-relevance relations. For example, LoLordo and his associates found that pigeons associate visual cues with food much more easily than they associate auditory cues with food. In contrast, if the conditioning situation involves shock, auditory cues are more effective as the CS than visual cues. Thus, visual cues are relevant to food and auditory cues are relevant to shock for pigeons (see LoLordo, 1979). (We will discuss these experiments in greater detail in Chapter 9.) Studies of the importance of CS-US similarity for conditioning have uncovered additional stimulus-relevance relations, discussed below.

Importance of CS-US similarity. Although there is no doubt that CS-US relevance is a major factor in classical conditioning, at present it is not known what makes a CS relevant to a US. One promising answer is that similarity in the time course of conditioned and unconditioned stimuli is important (Testa, 1974). This idea explains the results of the Garcia/Koelling experiment because the combinations of CS and US that were easily associated involved stimuli that have similar time courses. Tastes are generally considered long-duration stimuli because even if presented briefly, they often leave a slow-fading aftertaste or trace. This is particularly true with certain tastes, such as garlic and onion. One often continues to feel the taste of fresh onions long after the onions have been eaten. Malaise induced by radiation or drug treatment is also lengthy. The similarity in the length of taste and sickness experiences may be critical to their rapid association. The relevance between audiovisual cues and shock may be explained in comparable terms. Audiovisual cues are typically short-lasting and do not have long traces. The foot shock used in these experiments was also brief, and that is perhaps why audiovisual cues became rapidly associated with shock.

The CS-US-similarity hypothesis is not an entirely convincing explanation of the taste/illness and audiovisual/shock relevance effect because we do not have precise information about the time course of the stimuli involved. Although we are probably correct in saying, for example, that tastes and sickness are both long-lasting stimuli, we do not know exactly how long they are in any particular case or which is longer. However, good evidence for the CS-US-similarity hypothesis is provided by experiments on higher-order conditioning performed by Robert Rescorla and his associates (for example, Rescorla & Cunningham, 1979; Rescorla & Furrow, 1977; Rescorla & Gillan, 1980). One set of experiments showed that associations develop more rapidly between stimuli of the same modality (both auditory or both visual, for example) than between stimuli of different modalities (auditory and visual or visual and auditory). Another experiment involved all visual stimuli. Two of the stimuli were colors (blue and green), whereas the other two were orientation cues (horizontal and vertical lines). Pigeons learned associations more rapidly if both stimuli in the association were of the same type (color or orientation) than if one stimulus was color and the other was orientation. In a final set of experiments, it was shown that animals learn associations between stimuli much more readily if the stimuli are presented in the same location. All these experiments manipulated the similarity between two CSs in higher-order conditioning rather than in first-order conditioning. Nevertheless, they provide clear evidence that stimulus similarity is an important determinant of associations.

Although there is good evidence for the CS-US-similarity hypothesis, the hypothesis may not be able to explain all instances of CS-US relevance. One difficulty for the hypothesis may be that different types of CS-US-relevance relations may occur in different species. Not much research has been performed on this problem so far. However, one suggestive experiment compared the relative effectiveness of taste and visual cues in ingestional aversion learning in rats and quail (Wilcoxon, Dragoin, & Kral, 1971). The results with the rats were as expected on the basis of Garcia's research: rats learned stronger aversions to the taste than to the visual CS. However, the opposite outcome was observed with the quail. The birds learned stronger aversions to the visual than to the taste aspect of the substance that had been paired with illness. Wilcoxon and his associates did not compare the effectiveness of taste and visual cues in association with different unconditioned stimuli in the quail. Therefore, their experiment did not demonstrate a CS-US-relevance relation in the birds. However, their results strongly suggest that visual cues are more relevant to illness in birds than they are in rats. The CS-US-similarity hypothesis may not be able to explain such species differences in CS-US relevance. (For additional information on the mechanisms of visual aversion learning in birds, see Lett, 1980.)

How conditioned and unconditioned stimuli become associated

In the previous section we described what makes certain events particularly effective as conditioned stimuli and other events effective as unconditioned stimuli. Once the CS and US have been identified, how do they become associated, and what factors facilitate or hinder their association? In Chapter 4 we described certain procedures that are particularly effective in producing conditioning. In the present section we will describe the mechanisms of the formation of associations in greater detail.

Two views of the acquisition process

One of the fundamental facts about classical conditioning is that not every pairing of the CS with the US produces the same increase in the performance of the conditioned response. Figure 5.5 shows a hypothetical learning curve in classical conditioning. The first few pairings of the CS and US produce large increases in performance of the conditioned response. Thus, initially each point on the learning curve is much higher than the previous point. These changes in the conditioned response are represented by ΔCR in Figure 5.5. (The symbol Δ, delta, is used to represent change.) As conditioning proceeds, the increases in the performance of the conditioned response become much smaller after each CS-US pairing. The value of ΔCR becomes less and less. With sufficient training, a stable level of responding is reached, and ΔCR is close to zero. This part of the learning curve is called the **asymptote.**

Why do early conditioning trials produce much larger increases in the performance of the conditioned response than later trials? One cannot attribute this effect to fatigue or decreases in motivation, because similar results are obtained even if subjects receive only one trial per day. There are two plausible explanations. One of these analyzes the learning curve in terms of changes in the ability of the conditioned stimulus to become associated with the US or gain associative strength. According to this view, there is a limit to how strongly a CS can become associated with the US. With repeated conditioning trials, the CS comes increasingly closer to this limit, and therefore further increments in the associative strength of the CS become progressively smaller. This idea

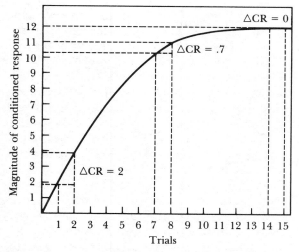

Figure 5.5. Idealized learning curve. The magnitude of the conditioned response increased 2 units ($\Delta CR = 2$) between the first and second conditioning trials, .7 unit ($\Delta CR = .7$) between the seventh and eighth trials, and 0 unit ($\Delta CR = 0$) between the fourteenth and fifteenth trials.

may be called the **CS-saturation hypothesis.** Once the CS becomes "saturated" with association to the US, additional increases in associative strength become impossible, and ΔCR becomes zero.

A second approach to the analysis of acquisition assumes that there are changes in the ability of the unconditioned stimulus to produce learning. According to this idea, the unconditioned stimulus is fully effective during the first few conditioning trials and therefore produces large increments in the conditioned response. However, as training progresses, the US gradually loses this ability to produce conditioning in the situation, and increases in the conditioned response become smaller and smaller. At asymptote, the US is assumed to be entirely incapable of producing further conditioning, and CR is zero. This view may be called the **US-reduction hypothesis.** As conditioning proceeds, the effectiveness of the US gradually becomes reduced, and progressively less conditioning occurs.

Traditionally the acquisition of classically

conditioned responses has been viewed in terms of the CS-saturation hypothesis. However, contemporary investigators, starting with Kamin, Wagner, and Rescorla, have advocated the US-reduction hypothesis, and this is the dominant view of conditioning today. The hypothesis, though, is certainly not self-evident. What direct evidence is there that the US loses its effectiveness through conditioning? What is responsible for this loss in US effectiveness? Are the mechanisms of the loss of US effectiveness relevant to a variety of learning phenomena, or are they applicable only to the initial learning of a conditioned response? We will address questions such as these in the discussion to follow.

The blocking effect

Animals conditioned outside the laboratory typically encounter numerous stimuli. Events that signal danger, for example, may involve multiple visual, auditory, and olfactory stimuli. It is advantageous for the organism to use only those cues that signal danger most effectively. Other cues that either do not signal danger consistently or are redundant are best ignored. Otherwise, the organism might be in a constant state of alertness or tension, ready to flee or fight unnecessarily. The US-reduction hypothesis suggests how uninformative and redundant stimuli may be prevented from becoming conditioned. Conditioning one CS with a particular US to asymptote reduces the ability of the US to produce further conditioning in that situation. Therefore, if a new CS is added to the situation, little, if any, conditioning of the new stimulus should occur. This implication has been borne out in a series of experiments on what has come to be called the **blocking effect.** These experiments, initiated by Leon Kamin, delineate specific instances in which conditioning procedures fail to produce conditioning.

The blocking effect has been most extensively investigated using the conditioned-suppression procedure with rats (Kamin, 1968, 1969). The basic procedure involved three phases (see Figure 5.6). In Phase I, the experimental group received repeated pairings of conditioned stimulus A with the unconditioned stimulus. This phase of training was continued until stimulus A was conditioned to asymptote, when animals completely suppressed their lever-press responses as stimulus A was presented. This conditioning of stimulus A presumably reduced the effectiveness of the unconditioned stimulus. To evaluate the loss in US effectiveness, an attempt was made to condition a new stimulus, B, with the same US. In Phase II of the procedure, stimuli A and B were presented simultaneously and paired with the US. After several such conditioning trials, stimulus B was presented alone in a test trial to see to what degree the animals learned to suppress their behavior in the presence of stimulus B. The control group was given the same Phase II training with stimulus B as the experimental subjects, but for them stimulus A was not conditioned in Phase I. Therefore, the US presumably was not reduced in effectiveness in Phase II. The US-reduction hypothesis predicts less conditioning of stimulus B in the experimental group than in the control group. Tests with stimulus B presented alone at the end of the experiment confirmed this result. In many replications of the experiment, stimulus B invariably produced less conditioned suppression of behavior in the experimental group than in the control group.

Group	Phase I	Phase II	Test
Experimental	A → US	[A + B] → US	B
Control		[A + B] → US	B

Figure 5.6. Diagram of the blocking procedure. During Phase I, stimulus A is conditioned with the US in the experimental group, while the control group does not receive conditioning trials. During Phase II, both the experimental and control groups receive conditioning trials in which stimulus A is presented simultaneously with stimulus B and paired with the US. A later test of response to stimulus B alone shows that less conditioning occurs to stimulus B in the experimental than in the control group.

In addition to demonstrating the blocking effect, Kamin (1968, 1969) performed many experiments to find out what aspects of his procedure were responsible for interference with the conditioning of stimulus B in the experimental group. These and other experiments have shown that the conditioning of stimulus B will be blocked if stimulus B is redundant—that is, if B adds no new information about the US. Two aspects of the blocking procedure are critical in meeting this requirement. First, stimulus A must be present together with stimulus B. Second, stimulus A has to be an adequate predictor of the US during the conditioning trials for stimulus B. These features ensure that stimulus A alone is sufficient to signal the US, and B is redundant (unnecessary). If the conditions that make stimulus B redundant are not met, blocking will not occur. For example, stimulus A does not block the conditioning of stimulus B if stimulus A is not present during Phase II (see Figure 5.6). Blocking also does not occur if stimulus A is not conditioned with the US during Phase I or if the conditioned properties of stimulus A are extinguished between Phases I and II. In both these cases, the result is that stimulus A does not signal occurrences of the US during Phase II, and therefore stimulus B is not redundant. These findings indicate that the conditioning of stimulus A to asymptote does not reduce the effectiveness of the unconditioned stimulus in all circumstances. Rather, US effectiveness is reduced only in those situations in which the unconditioned stimulus is signaled by stimulus A. When stimulus A is absent or after extinction of stimulus A, when it no longer signals the US, the effectiveness of the unconditioned stimulus remains in full force.

Why is it that a redundant stimulus does not become conditioned by the US? The presence of stimulus A during the conditioning trials for stimulus B in Phase II of the blocking procedure makes the US entirely expected. Thus, the US is not surprising in Phase II. These considerations suggested to Kamin that the unconditioned stimulus has to be *surprising* to produce conditioning. If the unconditioned stimulus is not surprising, it does not startle the animal and stimulate the "mental effort" that is required for the formation of an association. Expected events do not require new adjustments by the organism and therefore do not stimulate new learning. By definition, unexpected events are stimuli to which the organism has not yet adjusted. Therefore, unexpected events are much more likely to create new learning.

The idea that the unconditioned stimulus has to be surprising to produce new learning is consistent with the blocking effect. It is also consistent with the US-reduction explanation of the shape of typical learning curves. Presumably, learning occurs rapidly during the first few pairings of the CS and US because during these initial conditioning trials the US is not yet predicted by the CS and is therefore surprising. As conditioning proceeds, the CS becomes an increasingly better predictor of the US, and occurrences of the US during later conditioning trials therefore become less and less surprising.

Hence, less conditioning is produced by the later conditioning trials. Eventually, the CS fully predicts the US on each conditioning trial, and no further increments in the conditioned response are observed.

The Rescorla/Wagner model of conditioning

The idea that the unconditioned stimulus has to be surprising to promote classical conditioning is a central concept in contemporary theories of conditioning. One of the first and most systematic developments of this idea into a theory of conditioning was provided by Robert Rescorla and Allan Wagner (Rescorla & Wagner, 1972; Wagner & Rescorla, 1972). These investigators formulated a mathematical model of the concept of US surprisingness. The mathematical model provides two important advantages over earlier verbal descriptions of the idea. First, it is a highly precise treatment of the concept of US surprisingness. Second, with the use of mathematical derivations and com-

---

Box 5.3. Selective Attention in Autistic Children

The blocking effect illustrates one way in which organisms respond selectively to stimuli in their environment. It suggests that individuals do not respond to or pay attention to redundant or uninformative stimuli in a situation. Such selective attention no doubt has adaptive significance. Organisms are constantly exposed to a large array of stimulation. If one were to respond to all the available stimuli indiscriminately, behavior would be inefficient and disorganized. It is far more effective to respond only to those cues that are good predictors of significant events.

Research has shown that psychotic and autistic children often select uninformative stimuli. Schreibman and Lovaas (1973), for example, compared how normal and autistic children distinguish between two lifelike human figures. Normal children made the distinction on the basis of various enduring characteristics of the figures, especially features of the head. In contrast, autistic children focused on characteristics

that are not constant features of an individual and therefore cannot be used effectively to identify someone. One child, for example, used the shoes as the distinguishing feature between the two figures. When the shoes were removed, the child could no longer tell the figures apart. The autistic children failed to respond to relevant and effective identifying traits.

Lovaas and his colleagues suggest that failure to attend to relevant stimuli may be one cause of the severe behavior problems that autistic children have (see Lovaas & Newsom, 1976). Autistic children, for example, do not make social attachments to individuals who should be highly familiar to them, such as their parents and caretakers. It may be that from the autistic child's point of view even a frequently encountered person is a stranger because the child fails to attend to enduring identifying features of the person. Failure to recognize a parent, for example, as the same person on each encounter may prevent the child from developing a social bond with the parent.

puter simulations, the implications of the concept of US surprisingness can be extended to a wide variety of conditioning phenomena.

What might constitute a mathematical expression of the concept of surprise? By definition, an event is surprising if what is expected differs from what actually occurs. When the difference between the expected and actual events is small, the surprisingness of the event is small. If you expect a small gift for your birthday and that is what you get, you will not be very surprised. In contrast, if you expect a small gift and you receive a car for your birthday, you will be much more surprised. Accordingly, if we have a measure of the strength of the expectation and a measure of what actually occurs, we can calculate the surprisingness of the event by noting the difference between the two measures.

How do we know what degree of expectation an animal has for the unconditioned stimulus? One possible index of expectation is the strength of the conditioned response elicited by the CSs in the situation. If a very strong conditioned response is elicited, presumably the subject has a strong expectation of the US. If a CR is not elicited, presumably the subject does not expect the US. Therefore, we can represent the strength of expectation by the strength of the conditioned response. This solves one of our problems in calculating the surprisingness of the US. The other problem is to measure the strength of the actual event. Rescorla and Wagner suggested that the asymptote of conditioning supported by a particular US is a good measure of the strength of that US. According to this suggestion, to measure the strength of a US, we can simply conduct conditioning with that US until the asymptote is reached and no further increments in the conditioned response occur. This is a reasonable proposition because stronger unconditioned stimuli will condition responses to higher asymptotes. With this measure, we can calculate the surprisingness of the US by calculating the difference between the asymptote of the conditioning

possible with the US (the actual event) and the magnitude of the conditioned response elicited by the CSs that signal the US (the degree of expectation). This is stated in the following mathematical expression:

$$\lambda - CR \qquad (1)$$

where λ (lambda) is a measure of the asymptote of conditioning possible and CR is a measure of the conditioned response to all the CSs that signal the US.

Given our measure of US surprisingness, how do we predict how much learning will take place on a given conditioning trial? The basic idea is that conditioning will be proportional to the extent of US surprisingness. If the US is highly surprising on a given trial, a great deal of conditioning will take place, and hence there will be a large increase in the conditioned response. If the US is not surprising, not much conditioning will take place, and little change in the conditioned response will result. These ideas are summarized in the equation

$$\Delta CR = k(\lambda - CR) \qquad (2)$$

where ΔCR is the change in the conditioned response that occurs as a result of the conditioning trial, λ is the asymptote of conditioning possible, CR is the strength of the conditioned response that was elicited on that trial, and k is a constant. On the first conditioning trial, the animal does not make the conditioned response. Therefore, CR is equal to zero, and nothing is subtracted from λ in Equation 2. Thus, as a result of the first conditioning trial, the increment in the conditioned response will be $k\lambda$. As conditioning proceeds, CR will become larger, and therefore the value of the difference between λ and CR will become smaller. This will make for smaller increments in the conditioned response. Finally, when the subject is responding at the asymptotic level, no further increments in the conditioned response will occur, because CR will be equal to the asymptotic value, λ. Substituting λ for CR in Equation 2 yields

$$\Delta CR = k(\lambda - CR) = k(\lambda - \lambda) = k(0) = 0 \quad (3)$$

In our development of the ideas that led to the Rescorla/Wagner model, we strayed a bit from the equation Rescorla and Wagner proposed. We used the strength of the conditioned response on a particular trial to indicate the degree of expectancy of the US. However, the conditioned responses subjects perform do not always perfectly reflect the strength of the association between CS and US. Therefore, instead of stating their equation in terms of the strength of conditioned responses, Rescorla and Wagner used the more abstract concept of associative strength, or value. Associative strength is reflected in the magnitude of conditioned responses in that a CS more strongly associated with a US will elicit larger conditioned responses. By using the concept of associative strength, Rescorla and Wagner avoided having to worry about other variables that sometimes also influence performance of the CR. Another difference between our treatment and Rescorla and Wagner's model is the constant k in Equation 2. Rescorla and Wagner broke down the constant k into two components, α (alpha) and β (beta). α represents the salience or novelty of the CS, and β represents the salience or novelty of the US. (We will not say anything further about these terms because they remain constant in most experiments.) Thus, the Rescorla/Wagner equation is as follows:

$$\Delta V = \alpha\beta(\lambda - V_T) \quad (4)$$

where ΔV represents the change in the associative strength, or value, of a particular CS, α and β are constants, λ is the asymptote of conditioning possible with the US, and V_T is the total associative strength, or value, of all the stimuli that precede the US during the conditioning trial. As you can see, Equation 4 is very similar to Equation 2. In both equations conditioning is driven by the discrepancy between the asymptote of conditioning and the amount of conditioning that has already taken place with the stimuli present on the conditioning trial.

Application of the Rescorla/Wagner model to the blocking effect.   One of the important phenomena that stimulated the development of the Rescorla/Wagner model was the blocking effect. Therefore, Equation 4 should predict blocking of the conditioning of a new stimulus, B, by the presence of a previously conditioned stimulus, A (as in the experimental group in Figure 5.6). To apply Equation 4 to the conditioning of stimulus B, one first has to calculate the total associative strength (V_T) of all the CSs present during conditioning trials in Phase II of the blocking procedure. There are two CSs in Phase II, stimulus A and stimulus B. The associative strength of stimulus B (V_B) on the first Phase II conditioning trial is zero because stimulus B has not been paired with the US so far ($V_B = 0$). The associative strength of stimulus A (V_A) on the first Phase II conditioning trial is determined by its conditioning in Phase I. Recall that stimulus A was paired with the US a sufficient number of times in Phase I so that it became conditioned to the asymptotic value, λ. Therefore, $V_A = \lambda$. The associative strength of all the CSs in the situation (V_T) can be calculated by adding up the associative strength of the individual stimuli A and B. Thus,

$$V_T = V_A + V_B \quad (5)$$

We have calculated V_A to be λ and V_B to be 0. Substituting these values into Equation 5, we have

$$V_T = V_A + V_B = \lambda + 0 = \lambda \quad (6)$$

Substituting λ for V_T (as calculated in Equation 6) into Equation 4, we have the following:

$$\Delta V_B = \alpha\beta(\lambda - V_T) = \alpha\beta(\lambda - \lambda) \quad (7)$$
$$= \alpha\beta(0) = 0$$

Equation 7 indicates that stimulus B will not change in associative strength as a result of the first conditioning trial of Phase II in the blocking procedure. Since the associative strength of stimulus B is zero at the beginning of Phase II, stimulus B will not gain (or lose) associative strength in Phase II. In other words, stimulus B will not become conditioned in the experimental group.

In contrast to the lack of conditioning predicted in the experimental group, the Rescorla/Wagner model predicts that conditioning will occur in the control group. At the beginning of Phase II, the associative strengths of stimuli A and B in the control group are both zero because neither stimulus was conditioned previously (see Figure 5.6). The total associative strength, V_T, of the two stimuli is $V_A + V_{B'}$ or $0 + 0 = 0$. To calculate the increase in the associative strength of stimulus B in Phase II for the control group, we apply Equation 4 to stimulus B as follows:

$$\Delta V_B = \alpha\beta(\lambda - V_T) = \alpha\beta(\lambda - 0) = \alpha\beta\lambda \quad (8)$$

This calculation indicates that stimulus B will gain associative strength (by the amount of $\alpha\beta\lambda$) on the first conditioning trial of Phase II. Thus, the Rescorla/Wagner model predicts conditioning of stimulus B in the control group but not in the experimental group in the blocking experiment. This prediction is consistent with the observed results.

Unusual predictions: Loss of associative strength despite continued reinforcement. In addition to predicting the blocking effect, the Rescorla/Wagner model makes numerous very unusual predictions about conditioning. We will describe one of these as an example (see Figure 5.7). It involves two conditioned stimuli, A and B. The animal first receives conditioning trials in which stimulus A is presented by itself and paired with the unconditioned stimulus. These trials are conducted until stimulus A is conditioned to asymptote. Stimulus B is then

presented without stimulus A and paired with the US a sufficient number of times so that it also reaches asymptotic associative strength. It is important to keep in mind that in Phase I of the experiment, stimuli A and B never appear at the same time. In the next phase of the experiment, stimuli A and B are presented simultaneously for the first time and paired with the unconditioned stimulus. What will happen to the associative strengths of stimuli A and B as a result of the procedure in Phase II? Because the US continues to be presented in Phase II, the Phase II conditioning trials of the experiment are not extinction trials in the ordinary sense. Therefore, most people would not expect that stimuli A and B would lose some of their conditioned properties as a result of the Phase II conditioning trials. However, this is precisely what the Rescorla/Wagner model predicts and what occurs (see Kremer, 1978).

Why does the Rescorla/Wagner model predict loss of associative strength in stimuli A and B? Before using equations to show how the model treats this example, let us consider the problem conceptually. As a result of the Phase I conditioning trials, stimuli A and B each independently fully predict the unconditioned stimulus. Therefore, when the two stimuli are presented simultaneously for the first time in Phase II, the unconditioned stimulus is overpredicted. Stated another way, simultaneous exposure to stimuli A and B in Phase II makes the subjects expect a much larger unconditioned stimulus than what actually occurs. The unconditioned stimulus is surprisingly small. Under these circumstances, the model predicts, expectations will be brought in line with what actually occurs by reductions in the associative strengths of stimuli A and B. These downward adjustments will continue until the simultaneous presence of stimuli A and B in Phase II no longer causes an overprediction of the US.

To see how the equations of the model can be applied to this case, let us first consider what the model predicts about stimulus A in Phase II. The change in the associative strength of stimulus A as a result of the first Phase II conditioning trial can be predicted by applying Equation 4 to stimulus A:

$$\Delta V_A = \alpha\beta(\lambda - V_T) \tag{9}$$

The terms α and β are constants in the experiment. Therefore, we do not have to worry about their value. λ is the asymptote of conditioning that the US employed can support, and V_T is the sum of the associative strengths of all the cues presented during the Phase II trials. There are two such stimuli, A and B. Each stimulus was conditioned to the asymptotic level, λ, in Phase I. Therefore, the associative strength of each stimulus at the start of Phase II is λ. The sum of the associative strengths of stimuli A and

B is $\lambda + \lambda$, or 2λ. Substituting this value for V_T in Equation 9, we have the following:

$$\Delta V_A = \alpha\beta(\lambda - V_T) = \alpha\beta(\lambda - 2\lambda) = \alpha\beta(-\lambda)$$
$$= -\alpha\beta\lambda \tag{10}$$

This calculation indicates that the *change* in the associative strength of stimulus A as a result of the first Phase II conditioning trial is negative. In other words, stimulus A will lose associative strength. Predictions about what will happen to stimulus B in Phase II are made in a similar fashion. These calculations predict that stimuli A and B will lose associative strength in Phase II despite the fact that they continue to be paired with the US. The losses in associative strength will end when the sum of the associative

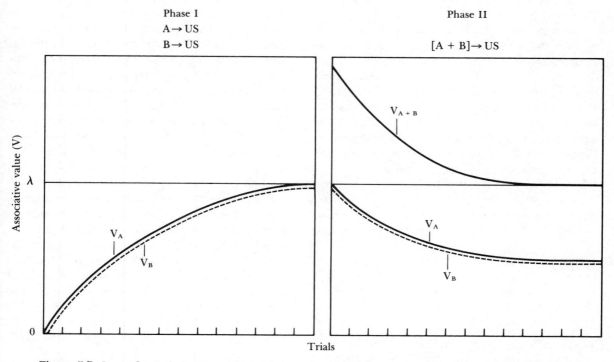

Figure 5.7. Loss of associative strength despite continued reinforcement. Stimuli A and B are conditioned separately to asymptote in Phase I, so that $V_A = \lambda$ and $V_B = \lambda$ at the end of Phase I. In Phase II stimuli A and B are presented simultaneously and paired with the US. This produces a loss in the associative strengths of both stimulus A and stimulus B until the sum of the associative strengths of the two stimuli is equal to λ.

strengths of A and B no longer exceeds λ, so that simultaneous exposure to stimuli A and B does not cause an overprediction of the US.

The Rescorla/Wagner model and conditioned inhibition. The treatment of conditioned inhibition in the Rescorla/Wagner model is very similar to its treatment of conditioned excitation. In both cases, conditioning is assumed to result from a discrepancy between what is expected and what actually occurs. Subjects may be surprised either by unexpectedly receiving the unconditioned stimulus or by unexpectedly *not* receiving the US. According to the Rescorla/Wagner model, the unexpected absence of the unconditioned stimulus produces conditioned inhibition (Wagner & Rescorla, 1972). This state of affairs is satisfied by all the conditioned-inhibition procedures we discussed in Chapter 4.

Negative changes in associative strength are the key to understanding how the Rescorla/Wagner model treats the phenomenon of conditioned inhibition. If a stimulus starts out with no associative strength, so that V = 0, negative changes in associative strength will make the net associative strength of the stimulus less than zero. According to the Rescorla/Wagner model, negative values of associative strength indicate that the stimulus is inhibitory. All conditioned-inhibition procedures produce negative associative strength. Consider, for example, the standard procedure for conditioned inhibition, reviewed in Figure 5.8. This procedure involves

$$A \rightarrow US \qquad\qquad [A + B] \rightarrow \text{no US}$$

Result: $\qquad V_A > 0 \qquad\qquad V_B < 0$

$$V_A + V_B = 0$$

Figure 5.8. Procedure for and results of inhibitory conditioning of stimulus B. On some trials CS_A is paired with the US, and on other trials CS_A is presented together with CS_B but without the US. CS_A acquires excitatory conditioned properties ($V_A > 0$) and CS_B acquires inhibitory conditioned properties ($V_B < 0$), such that $V_A + V_B = 0$.

two types of trials. On some trials stimulus A is presented alone and paired with the US. On other trials, stimulus A is presented together with stimulus B and the unconditioned stimulus is omitted. Through this training, stimulus B acquires conditioned inhibitory properties. How does the Rescorla/Wagner model predict this outcome?

The change in associative strength of stimulus B is calculated by applying Equation 4 to stimulus B as follows:

$$\Delta V_B = \alpha\beta(\lambda - V_T) \qquad (11)$$

Recall that in excitatory conditioning λ reflects the maximum amount of responding a US will support. What will the value of λ be for inhibitory conditioning? On inhibitory conditioning trials, the unconditioned stimulus is not presented. Repeated trials without an unconditioned stimulus ordinarily result in complete loss of the conditioned response. Therefore, the asymptote supported by the outcome of inhibitory conditioning trials is zero. This makes the value of λ in Equation 11 equal to zero. The value of V_T in Equation 11 is computed by adding together the associative strengths of stimuli A and B ($V_A + V_B$). The associative strength of stimulus A is some positive value because stimulus A is periodically paired with the US. For purposes of illustration, let us say the associative strength of stimulus A is $+.5$. The associative strength of stimulus B cannot be greater than zero because stimulus B is never paired with the US. Initially, the associative value of stimulus B is zero. Therefore, the sum of the associative strengths of stimuli A and B is $.5 + 0$, or $.5$. Substituting in Equation 11 the values of λ and V_T we arrived at, we have

$$\Delta V_B = \alpha\beta(\lambda - V_T) = \alpha\beta(0 - .5) = -.5\alpha\beta \quad (12)$$

This equation indicates that stimulus B will lose associative strength on inhibitory conditioning trials. Because stimulus B starts out with no associative strength, this decline will give stimulus

B a net negative associative strength, which is interpreted as reflecting conditioned inhibition.

Conditioned inhibition results from the unexpected absence of the US. On inhibitory conditioning trials of the procedure summarized in Figure 5.8, the subjects expect the unconditioned stimulus because of the presence of stimulus A (which is paired with the US on other occasions). However, the US does not occur on inhibitory conditioning trials. The absence of the US is a surprising event and stimulates a downward readjustment of expectancies. Eventually, the inhibitory strength of stimulus B becomes great enough to cancel the excitatory strength of stimulus A. At this point, simultaneous presentation of stimuli A and B on inhibitory conditioning trials leads to a net zero expectancy that the US will occur, and the animal is not surprised by the outcome of the trial. This outcome represents the asymptote of inhibitory conditioning.

Importance of situational cues in conditioning. As we have seen in the preceding examples, according to the Rescorla/Wagner model, the amount and type of conditioning that occurs to a CS depend critically on the conditioned properties of other stimuli that are also present during the conditioning trial. A particular CS may not become conditioned if other stimuli are present that already predict the US (the blocking effect). A particular stimulus may lose associative strength as a result of pairings with the US if all the stimuli in the situation together "overpredict" the US. Finally, a particular stimulus will acquire inhibitory properties if it is not followed by the US but other stimuli in the situation predict the US. Thus, classical conditioning depends not only on the nature of the particular CS and US that are used and their temporal relations but also on the stimulus context in which the CS and US are presented.

Another way to view the above examples is that the effectiveness of an unconditioned stimulus does not depend solely on its physical properties and its relevance to the CS. Rather, the effects of an unconditioned stimulus depend a great deal on the situation in which the US is presented (or not presented). The critical thing for producing learning is that the US (or its absence) be surprising. The type of learning that results depends on what makes the US (or its absence) surprising. If the US is surprising because it is underpredicted, positive changes in the associative strength of the CSs will result. If the US is surprising because it is overpredicted, negative changes in the associative strength of the CSs will result. Through these adjustments, conditioned stimuli gain and lose associative strength until the subject comes to predict accurately what unconditioned stimuli actually occur. Thus, classical-conditioning mechanisms serve to protect subjects from being surprised by regularly occurring unconditioned stimuli in their environment.

What is learned in classical conditioning?

Our discussions of classical conditioning so far have told us a great deal about factors that govern the development of an association between the CS and US. In Chapter 4 we described various conditioning procedures and noted that some of these are much more effective in producing learning than others. In Chapter 5 we have described so far how the progress of conditioning depends on the events that are used as the conditioned and unconditioned stimuli and on other stimuli present during the conditioning trials. In all of this discussion, conditioning was identified by the development of new responses to the conditioned stimulus. We noted that a large variety of responses can become conditioned, including salivation, eye blinking, fear, locomotor approach and withdrawal, and aversion responses. However, we did not explain why one set of responses becomes conditioned in one situation and other responses become conditioned in other situations. Several models have been offered to predict what responses will become conditioned in various circumstances. We will describe some of the important models and discuss what evidence supports or contradicts each idea.

The stimulus-substitution model

The oldest idea about what animals learn in classical conditioning is based on a model of conditioning proposed by Pavlov. As noted in Chapter 4, Pavlov was primarily a physiologist. Not unexpectedly, therefore, his model of conditioning has a greater physiological orientation than other models. For purposes of theorizing, Pavlov viewed the brain as consisting of discrete neural centers (see Figure 5.9). He suggested that one brain center was primarily responsible for processing the unconditioned stimulus, and a different center was primarily responsible for processing the conditioned stimulus. A third brain center was assumed to be responsible for generating the unconditioned response. Because the unconditioned response occurred whenever the unconditioned stimulus was presented, Pavlov assumed that there was a neural connection between the neural center for the US and the neural center for the UR (see Figure 5.9). Furthermore, because the reaction to the US was not learned, the functional path-

way between the US and UR centers was assumed to be innate (see Figure 5.9).

According to Pavlov's model, the learning of conditioned responses takes place through the establishment of new functional neural pathways. During the course of repeated pairings of the conditioned and unconditioned stimuli, a connection develops between the brain center for the CS and the brain center for the US. Presentation of the conditioned stimulus then results in excitation of the US neural center by way of this new neural pathway. Excitation of the US center in turn generates the unconditioned response because of the inborn connection between the US and UR centers. Therefore, conditioning enables the conditioned stimulus to elicit the unconditioned response. The response to the conditioned stimulus may not always be identical to the response to the unconditioned stimulus. Differences between the two may occur if, for example, the conditioned stimulus is not as intense as the unconditioned stimulus and therefore produces less excitation of the UR center. However, the Pavlovian model predicts that the general nature and form of the conditioned response will be similar to those of the unconditioned response. Because of the new functional pathway established between the CS center and the US center, the conditioned stimulus comes to have similar effects on the nervous system to the effects of the unconditioned stimulus. In a sense the CS becomes a surrogate US or substitute for the US. That is why the model is called **stimulus substitution.**

The US as a determining factor for the CR. According to the stimulus-substitution model, each unconditioned stimulus is assumed to have its own unique brain center, which is connected to a unique unconditioned-response center. If conditioning turns a CS into a surrogate US, the model predicts that CSs conditioned with different USs will come to elicit different types of conditioned responses. This is

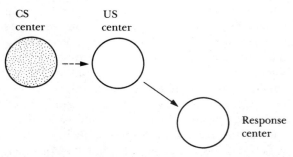

Figure 5.9. Diagram of Pavlov's stimulus-substitution model. The solid arrow indicates an innate neural connection. The dashed arrow indicates a learned neural connection. The CS comes to elicit a response by activating the US center, which innately elicits the response.

obviously true. Animals learn to salivate when conditioned with food and to blink when conditioned with a puff of air to the eye. Salivation is not conditioned in eyeblink conditioning experiments, and eyeblink responses are not conditioned in salivary conditioning experiments.

The above comparison of salivary and eyeblink conditioning provides evidence that different unconditioned stimuli lead to different conditioned responses. The stimulus-substitution model also predicts that the form of the conditioned response will be similar to the form of the unconditioned response. In some situations this prediction is also confirmed. Consider, for example, conditioning with food and water in pigeons. Food and water are both ingestible, rewarding stimuli. However, the unconditioned response in pigeons (and many other animals) is very different for these two stimuli. A pigeon eating grain makes rapid, hard pecking movements directed at the grain with its beak slightly open at the moment of contact. In contrast, it drinks by lowering the beak into the water, sucking up some water, and then raising the head gradually to allow the water to flow down the throat. Thus, the unconditioned responses of eating and drinking differ in both speed and form.

Jenkins and Moore (1973) compared sign tracking in pigeons with food and with water as the unconditioned stimulus. In both experimental situations, the conditioned stimulus was illumination of a small disk or response key for 8 sec before delivery of the unconditioned stimulus. With repeated pairings of the key light with presentation of grain, the pigeons gradually started pecking the illuminated key. Pecking also developed with repeated pairings of the key light with presentation of water. However, the form of the conditioned response was very different in the two situations. In the food experiment, the pigeons pecked the response key as if eating: the pecks were rapid with the beak slightly open at the moment of contact. In the water experiment, the pecking movement was slower, made with the beak closed, and was often accompanied by swallowing. Thus, the form of the conditioned response was determined by and resembled the form of the unconditioned response. Eatinglike pecks occurred in conditioning with food, and drinkinglike pecks occurred in conditioning with water. These findings provide strong support for the stimulus-substitution model (see also Peterson, Ackil, Frommer, & Hearst, 1972).

Difficulties with the stimulus-substitution model. Doubts arose about the stimulus-substitution model very early in American investigations of classical conditioning. The problem was that in certain situations the forms of the conditioned and unconditioned responses are significantly different. Hilgard reviewed several examples many years ago (Hilgard, 1936). He noted, for example, that whereas the unconditioned response to shock is an increase in respiration rate, the conditioned response to a CS paired with shock is a decrease in the rate. Detailed study of the form of conditioned eyeblink responses also showed that humans blink differently in response to conditioned and unconditioned stimuli. In other research of this type, Zener (1937) carefully observed both salivation and motor responses to a bell that had been paired with food in dogs. The unconditioned response to food always involved lowering the head to the food tray and chewing one or more pieces of food. After conditioning, the bell rarely elicited chewing movements, and if chewing occurred, it was not sustained. The conditioned response to the bell only sometimes included orientation to the food tray. On some trials the dog looked toward the bell instead. On other trials the dog's orientation vacillated between the food tray and the bell, and on still other occasions the dog held its head between the food tray and the bell when the bell sounded. Thus, the conditioned responses elicited by the bell were often different from the unconditioned responses elicited by the food.

Modern approaches to stimulus substitution. Because the form of the conditioned response is not invariably similar to the form of the unconditioned response, some researchers have become skeptical about the stimulus-substitution model. In addition, modern theorists believe that neural mechanisms of learning are much more complex than the stimulus-substitution model implies. Nevertheless, the unconditioned stimulus appears to be very important in determining characteristics of the conditioned response other than its form. Manipulations that directly influence the unconditioned response have an impact on the conditioned response as well. Therefore, some modern theorists have proposed a variant of the stimulus-substitution model. This model retains the idea that the conditioned response is elicited by way of a US "center" of some sort. However, in an effort to avoid misleading implications about neural mechanisms, the contemporary view does not make reference to the nervous system. Rather, it is stated in more abstract language. The new model states that animals learn two things from repeated pairings of a CS with a US. First, they learn an association between the CS and the US. Second, they form an image or representation of the unconditioned stimulus. According to the model, the conditioned response depends on both these factors. The CS elicits the CR because of its association with the US representation. If either the CS-US association or the US representation is weak, the conditioned response will not occur.

Strong evidence for the importance of the US representation in classical conditioning is provided by experiments in which the US representation is manipulated without changing the CS-US association. One set of these studies involved reducing the value of the US representation after conditioning. The basic strategy and rationale involved in one experiment (Rescorla, 1973) are illustrated in Figure 5.10. During Phase I of the experiment, both the experimental and the control groups received conventional conditioned-suppression training with a loud noise as the unconditioned stimulus. This phase of the procedure was assumed to

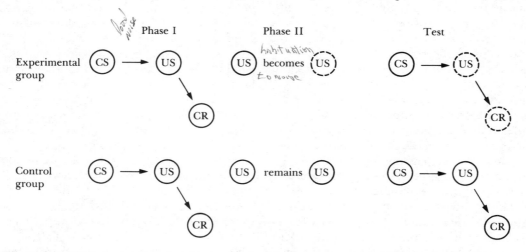

Figure 5.10. Basic strategy and rationale involved in US-devaluation experiments. In Phase I, the experimental and control groups receive conventional conditioning to establish an association between the CS and the US and to lead subjects to form a representation of the US. In Phase II the US representation is devalued for subjects in the experimental group. The US representation remains unchanged for subjects in the control group. If the conditioned response (CR) is elicited by way of the US representation, devaluation of the US representation in the experimental group is expected to reduce responding to the CS.

establish an association between the CS and the US for both groups as well as to lead the subjects to form a representation of the loud-noise US. In the next phase of the experiment, the experimental group received a treatment designed to devalue the US representation. The loud noise was repeatedly presented to reduce (habituate) subjects' response to the US. The control group was not exposed to the noise during this phase. Thus, the US representation was assumed to remain intact for the control group (see Figure 5.10). The effects of the devaluation of the US representation were then measured by testing subjects with the conditioned stimulus. The experimental group suppressed its responding during the CS significantly less than the control group. Thus, the US-devaluation treatment reduced the power of the CS to elicit the conditioned-suppression response. This experiment shows in an ingenious way that the conditioned response is elicited by way of a US representation.

The effects of US devaluation on elicitation of the conditioned response have also been investigated in classical conditioning with food. However, because animals do not become habituated to food in the same way that they become habituated to loud noises, other techniques had to be used to devalue the US representation. Two such procedures have been tested. One was to satiate the animals with food. The other was to condition an aversion to the food by pairing the food with sickness induced either by rapid rotation of the animals on a platform or by injection of a drug. Both the satiation and food-aversion procedures reduced the extent to which a food-conditioned stimulus elicited the conditioned response (Holland & Rescorla, 1975a; Holland & Straub, 1979).

The experiments described above, together with other research (Rescorla, 1974; Rescorla & Cunningham, 1977; Rescorla & Heth, 1975; but see Bouton & Bolles, 1979), show that the status of the US representation is very important for certain types of classical conditioning. In the situations described above, the conditioned response appears to have been elicited by way of the representation of the unconditioned stimulus. This mediation of the CR by the US representation is similar to Pavlov's suggestion that the CR is elicited by stimulation of the US center by the CS. However, in contrast to the stimulus-substitution model, the US-representation approach does not assume that the form of the conditioned response will always be similar to that of the unconditioned response.

Second-order conditioning and the stimulus-representation model. Although there is good evidence for the US-representation model in first-order conditioning, the model is not applicable to all instances of second-order conditioning. Recall that in second-order conditioning, learning occurs because of the pairings of a novel second-order stimulus (CS_2) with a previously conditioned stimulus (CS_1). The relation of CS_2 and CS_1 in second-order conditioning is procedurally comparable to the relation of CS_1 to the US in first-order conditioning. Therefore, extension of the stimulus-representation model to second-order conditioning implies that the second-order CS (CS_2) elicits the conditioned response by way of the representation of the first-order stimulus (CS_1). This possibility is illustrated by Model A in Figure 5.11. In tests of the importance of the first-order-CS representation for responding to the second-order stimulus, investigators extinguished the conditioned response to the first-order CS. (This manipulation is analogous to devaluation of the US for first-order conditioning). Extinction of the first-order CS did not influence the conditioned response to the second-order CS in fear conditioning (Rizley & Rescorla, 1972). This manipulation also did not influence second-order conditioning with a food reward in rats when the conditioned response was an increase in activity (Holland & Rescorla, 1975a, 1975b). These results show that the second-order conditioned stimulus did not elicit the conditioned response because of

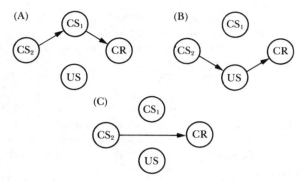

Figure 5.11. Three models of second-order conditioning. In Model A, the second-order stimulus, CS_2, elicits the conditioned response by way of an association of CS_2 with the representation of the first-order stimulus, CS_1. In Model B, CS_2 elicits the conditioned response by way of an association with the representation of the US. In Model C, CS_2 comes to elicit the CR directly. Model A best describes the results of sign-tracking experiments with pigeons. Model C best describes activity- and fear-conditioning experiments with rats.

its association with the representation of the first-order CS.

According to another model of second-order conditioning, the second-order stimulus, CS_2, comes to elicit the conditioned response by way of an association with the representation of the US. This possibility is illustrated by Model B in Figure 5.11. Model B predicts that devaluation of the US should reduce the strength of the conditioned response elicited by CS_2. However, several studies have shown that US devaluation does not reduce the second-order conditioned response in fear- or activity-conditioning situations (Holland & Rescorla, 1975a; Rescorla, 1973). Thus, both Models A and B are inapplicable to second-order fear conditioning or the appetitive conditioning of increased activity. These findings suggest that second-order conditioning in these situations involves the learning of a direct association between CS_2 and the neural mechanisms involved in producing the conditioned response. This possibility is illustrated by Model C in Figure 5.11.

The evidence described above in fear condi-

tioning and appetitive conditioning of activity does not support the stimulus-representation model of second-order conditioning. However, second-order conditioning of sign tracking with food as the US in pigeons appears to involve the representation of the first-order CS. In this situation, extinction of the first-order stimulus reduces the response to the second-order conditioned stimulus (Rashotte, Griffin, & Sisk, 1977; Rescorla, 1979). Further research is needed to determine why second-order conditioning of sign tracking is governed by stimulus-representation processes whereas such mechanisms are not involved in second-order conditioning of fear or increased activity.

The preparatory-response model

Several ideas have been proposed to explain why the conditioned response is sometimes different from the unconditioned response. One of the more interesting is based on a functional and adaptive view of classical conditioning. It is elegantly described in the following passage concerning signals for shock (and other aversive events):

> [Without a signal] the animal would still be forced to wait in every case for the [shock] stimulus to arrive before beginning to meet it. The veil of the future would hang just before his eyes. Nature began long ago to push back the veil. Foresight proved to possess high survival-value, and conditioning is the means by which foresight is achieved. Indeed, this provision gave the distance-receptors most of their value. Neither sight nor sound of an approaching enemy is intrinsically hurtful; without conditioning, these exteroceptors would have lost their phylogenetic significance [Culler, 1938, p. 136].

According to this interpretation, animals have evolved to make conditioned responses because these reponses allow them to become prepared for the unconditioned stimulus. Conditioning allows animals to "make preparatory adjustments for an oncoming stimulus" (Culler, 1938, p. 136).

The preparatory-response model is not committed to the idea that the form of the conditioned response will be similar to the form of the unconditioned response. It also does not claim that the conditioned and unconditioned responses will always be different. It simply states that in classical-conditioning situations animals learn to make responses that best prepare them for the forthcoming presentation of the unconditioned stimulus. Sometimes these responses are similar to the unconditioned response; in other situations they are different from the unconditioned response. If food is the unconditioned stimulus, anticipatory salivation effectively prepares the oral cavity for the arrival of food. Therefore, salivation develops as the conditioned response. If shock (which results in increased breathing) is the unconditioned stimulus, decreased breathing in anticipation of shock protects the subject from hyperventilation. Therefore, decreased breathing develops as the conditioned response.

There are two difficulties with the preparatory-response model. First, it is difficult to predict the form of the conditioned response on the basis of this model. Not all responses that can prepare animals for the unconditioned stimulus become learned as the conditioned response. In addition, it is not always clear ahead of time what responses will effectively prepare subjects for the US. (For example, what would best prepare a rat in a small enclosure for a loud-noise US?) Because of these problems, in many cases explanations of the preparatory function of the conditioned response are developed after the form of the response has been discovered. Such explanations are thus post hoc.

The second difficulty with the preparatory-response idea is that, at least in some artificial experimental situations, the conditioned response is obviously maladaptive. Consider, for example, the "long box" sign-tracking experiment described in Chapter 4. As you may recall, pigeons were placed in a long alley (Figure 4.5), and food was periodically presented in the middle of the alley. Each presentation of food was preceded by the brief illumination of a key light at one end of the alley. As the key light became associated with the food presentations, the pigeons would run to the end of the alley, peck the key light, and then run back to the middle to get the food. Thus, the sign-tracking response to the light CS took the animals away from the food source. It is difficult to see how this prepared them for the food. Some conditioning experiments using a drug as the US also involve the learning of poor preparatory responses. For example, rats suppress their drinking of water in the presence of stimuli that have been paired with the injection of lithium chloride. However, increased drinking in response to lithium-conditioned stimuli would better prepare them for the drug because the increased fluid intake would promote excretion of lithium.

The compensatory-response model

In many classical-conditioning situations involving drugs as unconditioned stimuli, the form of the conditioned response is opposite the form of the unconditioned response. For example, epinephrine causes a decrease in gastric secretion as an unconditioned response. In contrast, the response to a CS for epinephrine is increased gastric secretion (Guha, Dutta & Pradhan, 1974). Dinitrophenol causes increased oxygen consumption and increased temperature. The response to a CS for dinitrophenol involves decreased oxygen consumption and decreased temperature (Obál, 1966). These and many similar examples (see Siegel, 1977b) have provided the impetus for the compensatory-response model. The model has been most often discussed in reference to drug conditioning situations. According to the model, responses conditioned by drug unconditioned stimuli are expected to be compensatory for the unconditioned responses elicited by the drug. Thus, if the drug causes a change in behavior in one direction, the model predicts that CSs for the drug will result in changes in behavior in the opposite direction.

The compensatory-response model is more precise than the preparatory-response model in that the conditioned response is always predicted to be opposite in form to the unconditioned response. However, this precision also makes the model inapplicable to many situations. In some cases the response conditioned by a drug is similar to the unconditioned response to the drug. For example, amphetamine causes increased activity as an unconditioned response, and this behavior can be conditioned to stimuli that reliably precede the presence of amphetamine (Pickens & Dougherty, 1971). Insulin causes decreased activity, convulsions, and unresponsiveness to applied stimulation; this pattern of behavior also occurs in response to a CS for insulin (Siegel, 1975a). In yet other cases, measurement of several response systems indicates that some conditioned responses are similar to the unconditioned response and others are opposite to it. For example, after conditioning with anticholinergic drugs, the conditioned stimulus elicits pupillary dilation and increased salivation (Korol, Sletten, & Brown, 1966; Lang, Brown, Gershon, & Korol, 1966). The pupillary-dilation CR is similar to the unconditioned response to the drugs, whereas the increased salivation is opposite the direct effects of the anticholinergic agents. These diverse findings are embarrassing to the compensatory-response model. However, future research will, one hopes, lead to a specification of the boundary conditions for the model. We will then know when to predict compensatory conditioned responses and when not to.

Although the compensatory-response model is inadequate as a comprehensive account of the nature of conditioned responses, it has provided an interesting analysis of drug tolerance. Tolerance is said to develop when repeated administrations of a drug have progressively less effect on the subject. The development of drug tolerance is sometimes a serious problem in the use of drugs because progressively higher doses

are required to produce the same effect. Shepard Siegel recently proposed a model of drug tolerance based on conditioned compensatory responses. The model assumes that with repeated presentations of a drug, the stimuli that always accompany drug administrations will become conditioned by the drug. These stimuli might be the time of day, the sensations involved in preparing a syringe, or the stimuli involved in getting out a pill to swallow. The conditioned drug-administration cues are assumed to elicit conditioned responses that are opposite to the unconditioned reactions to the drug. These conditioned compensatory responses subtract from the reaction otherwise elicited by the drug. Therefore, the response to the drug is attenuated when the drug is taken in the presence of these conditioned stimuli (see Figure 5.12).

The conditioning model of drug tolerance attributes tolerance to compensatory responses conditioned to environmental stimuli paired with drug administration. If the model is correct, then manipulations of the external envi-

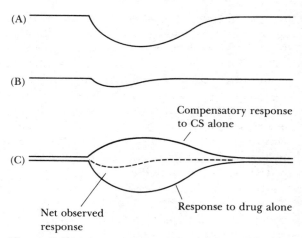

Figure 5.12. Diagram of the Pavlovian-conditioning model of drug tolerance. The strength of the reaction is indicated by deviations from the horizontal line. (A) Reaction to the CS plus the drug before conditioning. (B) Reaction to the CS plus the drug after extensive experience with the drug. (C) Components of the reaction after conditioning, showing that drug tolerance is due to a compensatory response conditioned to the CS.

ronment should influence the effectiveness of drugs. Various aspects of this prediction have been confirmed by Siegel and his colleagues in experiments with opiates, such as morphine and heroin (Siegel, 1975b, 1976, 1977a, 1978; Siegel, Hinson, & Krank, 1978). Morphine has a long history of medical use as a painkiller. However, patients quickly develop tolerance to it, so that a given amount of the drug becomes progressively less effective in reducing pain. However, the analgesic effects of the drug may be restored, if the usual drug-administration cues are removed, as by administering the drug with a novel procedure or in a new room. Drug tolerance is also less likely if subjects are made highly familiar with the drug-administration stimuli before being treated with the drug, because such CS familiarity interferes with condi-

tioning. Finally, drug tolerance can be reversed by extinguishing the drug-administration cues by repeatedly presenting the cues without the drug.

The conditioned stimulus and the form of the conditioned response

According to the models of conditioning described above, the form of the conditioned response is determined by the unconditioned stimulus used. The exact nature of this relation is different in each model. In one model the CR is expected to be similar to the UR, in another the CR "prepares" subjects for the US, and in the third the CS "compensates" for the US. These interpretations of conditioning, and the evidence that supports them, emphasize the im-

Box 5.4. Heroin Overdose from the Absence of Drug-Conditioned Stimuli

Heroin overdose is a leading cause of death among heroin users. It is also one of the most perplexing causes of death. Victims rarely take more heroin before they die than they usually use. On occasion, death occurs while the syringe is still in the victim's arm—before he or she has finished injecting the intended amount. Therefore, heroin-related deaths are rarely caused by excessive amounts of the drug. Why do the addicts die, then? One answer is suggested by the conditioning model of drug tolerance. Long-term users of heroin have a set ritual they go through when taking the drug. They may use the drug only at certain times, when they are in the company of certain people, or in special locations. These drug-related stimuli are expected to become conditioned by the heroin use. The conditioning model predicts that heroin-compensatory physiological reactions will come to be elicited by the usual drug-administration ritual. If experienced users take heroin at an unusual time, with a new group of people, or in a new place, the conditioned compensatory responses will not occur. Hence, the usual amount of heroin will have a much larger physiological

effect than it has ordinarily. This unexpectedly large drug effect may be sufficient to cause physical complications and death.

Not all people who experience heroin overdose die. Prompt medical attention can be a lifesaver. Interviews with survivors of heroin overdose indicate that the adverse reaction to the drug often occurs when the heroin is taken in unusual circumstances. Animal research also indicates that the absence of drug-conditioned stimuli places subjects at increased risk of heroin-induced death (Siegel, Hinson, & Krank, 1979). Rats in this research first received several heroin injections in connection with a distinctive set of environmental stimuli. The animals were then given a higher test dose of the drug. For some subjects the test dose was administered in the presence of the usual drug-administration stimuli. For another group, the drug was given in an environment where the subjects had never received heroin before. The test dose of heroin resulted in a greater proportion of deaths among animals that received the drug in the absence of the drug-conditioned environmental cues. These findings support an explanation of the heroin-overdose phenomenon in terms of the conditioning model of drug tolerance.

portance of the unconditioned stimulus in establishing the form of the conditioned response. However, the nature of the US is not the only important factor. The form of the conditioned response also depends on the conditioned stimulus used.

Earlier in this chapter we discussed how the speed of learning of the conditioned response is influenced by various aspects of the conditioned stimulus. The *rate* of learning depends on the intensity and novelty of the CS and the relevance of the CS to the US. Aspects of the conditioned stimulus also influence the *form* of the conditioned response. In an unusual experiment, for example, Timberlake and Grant (1975) investigated classical conditioning in rats with food as the unconditioned stimulus. One side of the experimental chamber was equipped with a sliding platform that could be moved in and out of the chamber through a flap door (see Figure 5.13). Instead of using the conventional

light or tone as the conditioned stimulus, the experimenters restrained a live rat on the stimulus platform. Ten seconds before each delivery of food, the platform was moved into the experimental chamber, thereby transporting the stimulus rat through the flap door. The stimulus rat was withdrawn from the chamber at the end of the trial. Thus, presentation of the stimulus rat served as the conditioned stimulus for food.

The stimulus-substitution model predicts that the experimental subjects will come to respond to the CS for food as they respond to food. Therefore, they are expected to gnaw or bite the stimulus rat that serves as the CS. It is unclear what the preparatory- and compensatory-response models predict in this situation. In fact, as the CS rat was repeatedly paired with food, the CS came to elicit orientation, approach, and sniffing movements, as well as social contacts. Such responses did not develop if

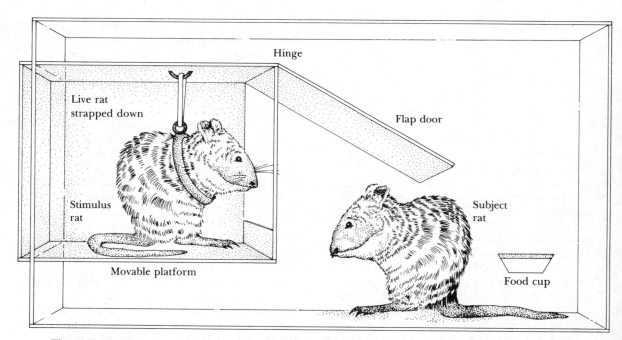

Figure 5.13. Diagram of experiment by Timberlake and Grant (1975). The conditioned stimulus for food is presentation of a stimulus rat on a movable platform through a flap door on one side of the experimental chamber. *(Based on Timberlake, 1980b.)*

the CS rat was not paired with food or was presented at random times with respect to food. This outcome does not support any model that explains the form of the conditioned response solely in terms of the unconditioned stimulus used. The pattern of conditioned responses, particularly the social behavior elicited by the CS rat, was no doubt determined by the unusual conditioned stimulus used in this experiment (see also Timberlake, 1980a). Other kinds of food-conditioned CSs elicit different conditioned responses. For example, Peterson et al. (1972) inserted an illuminated response lever into the experimental chamber immediately before presenting food to rats. With the protruding metal lever as the conditioned stimulus, the conditioned responses were "almost exclusively oral and consisted mainly of licking responses and gnawing behavior" (Peterson et al., 1972, p. 1010).

One of the most careful and systematic investigations of the role of the conditioned stimulus in determining the nature of the conditioned response was performed by Holland (1977). He compared visual and auditory stimuli in experiments involving a food US in rats. Conditioned auditory cues of various types invariably resulted in head-jerk and startle movements and standing by the food dish. The conditioned head-jerk and startle reactions were not evident with visual conditioned stimuli. When diffuse light was paired with food, the predominant conditioned response was standing by the food dish. When the conditioned visual stimulus was localized at the top of the experimental chamber, conditioned rearing on the hind legs was also often observed (see also Holland, 1980).

The conditioned response as an indicator of learned associations

We have reviewed a diversity of ideas and findings concerning the form of the conditioned response. Our discussion has also revealed that the form of the conditioned re-

sponse depends on a variety of factors, some relevant to the unconditioned stimulus and others relevant to the conditioned stimulus. Can all this information be integrated into a single, comprehensive view of classical conditioning? What that view might be is as yet unclear. However, it is quite likely that any integration of the findings of classical-conditioning experiments will have to involve a strong distinction between the *learning* of an association of the CS with the US and the *performance* of the conditioned response. According to this distinction, issues in classical conditioning can be separated into two categories. One category of issues is concerned with how the CS and US become associated— how the learning takes place. Another category of issues concerns what animals do about what they have learned—the performance of the conditioned response.

A strong learning/performance distinction assumes that animals do not learn particular responses in classical-conditioning experiments. Rather, they learn associations between the CS and the US, or expectancies of the unconditioned stimulus. The conditioned response that develops during the CS is assumed to be simply a reflection or indication of the association formed between the CS and US. With this approach, a variety of responses to the conditioned stimulus that develop during the course of conditioning may be used as indicators of the association being established.

Traditionally, Western psychologists have been concerned mainly with the mechanisms of learning and have not addressed in great detail issues concerned with the performance of conditioned responses. The Rescorla/Wagner model, for example, describes the conditions that produce changes in "associative strength." The assumption is that these changes will be reflected in conditioned responses. However, the correspondence of associative strength and conditioned responses may not be perfect. Given the emphasis on learning mechanisms, we have obtained much more information about learning processes than about processes relevant to the performance of responses. At present there is no entirely satisfactory explanation for the diversity of responses observed in classical-conditioning experiments. Furthermore, it seems unlikely that a single model will be able to predict the nature of the conditioned response in every example of classical conditioning. It may be that one set of mechanisms will be needed to explain the form of physiological conditioned responses, and a different set of processes will have to be postulated to explain conditioned responses that involve overt skeletal movements, such as approach toward or withdrawal from a conditioned stimulus.

The conditioned response as an interaction between conditioned and innate behavioral processes

Although a comprehensive performance model does not exist for all classically conditioned responses, a model of conditioned overt skeletal movements is beginning to take shape in contemporary thinking. The basic idea is that the effects of a conditioned stimulus on behavior result from an interaction between the conditioned properties of the stimulus and the innate behavior repertoire or tendencies of the organism. Such stimuli as lights, tones, and tastes all elicit innate responses in the absence of conditioning. Animals also have innate reactions to the expectation of significant biological events, such as food, water, or cutaneous pain. When such stimuli as lights, tones, and tastes become conditioned, the responses they come to elicit represent the integration of the original innate responses to these stimuli and the innate responses to the *expectancy* of the unconditioned stimulus. This view of the conditioned response emphasizes that the form of the CR is determined both by the nature of the conditioned stimulus and by the nature of the unconditioned stimulus. The nature of the CS is important because animals have different innate reactions to various stimuli before conditioning. The nature of the unconditioned stimulus is

important because it in part determines what animals learn to expect on the basis of the CS, and different expectancies are assumed to elicit different innate responses or response tendencies.

The interaction between conditioned and innate behavioral processes in determining the form of the conditioned response is nicely illustrated by an experiment on the conditioning of baby chicks with heat as the unconditioned stimulus. When baby chicks are cold and seek warmth in their natural environment, they approach the mother hen, peck at the feathers on the underpart of her body, and snuggle up to her (rub and push their heads up into her feathers). In contrast, the presence of heat elicits reduced locomotion, extension of the wings, twittering, and eye closure in the chicks. Wasserman (1973) used a small lighted disk as the conditioned stimulus and paired it with brief exposure to heat in young chicks. As the lighted disk became conditioned, the chicks started to approach and peck it. Later the pecking responses became less forceful as the chicks pushed the disk and shook their heads in a snuggling type of movement. These conditioned responses were very different from the reactions to the heat unconditioned stimulus itself. However, they are nicely predicted from what the chicks do naturally when they expect to receive heat from the mother hen. Because of the conditioning procedure, the naturally occuring heat-seeking response came to be directed toward the conditioned stimulus (see also Hogan, 1974; Wasserman, 1974).

The idea that conditioned responses represent an interaction between conditioned and innate behavioral processes is a promising development in behavior theory. However, much still remains to make the hypothesis useful in predicting the form of conditioned responses. In many cases we do not know exactly what the animal's innate responses to the expectancy of a particular unconditioned stimulus are. The hypothesis also does not specify how innate reactions to the expectancy of a significant biological event become "integrated" with the innate reactions to the stimulus that is to serve as the CS. Further research is required on the relation between instinctive behavior and conditioning processes for these details to be worked out.

Concluding comments

Traditionally, classical conditioning has been regarded as a relatively simple and primitive type of learning that is involved only in the regulation of glandular and visceral responses, such as salivation. The establishment of CS-US associations was assumed to occur fairly automatically with the pairing of a CS and a US. Given the simple and automatic nature of the conditioning and its limitation to glandular and visceral responses, it was not viewed as very important in explaining the complexity and richness of human experience. This view of classical conditioning is no longer tenable. The research reviewed in Chapters 4 and 5 has shown that classical conditioning is a rather complex process and is involved in the conditioning of a wide variety of responses, including not only glandular secretory responses but also emotional behavior and locomotor movements. The learning does not occur automatically with the pairing of a CS with a US. Rather, it depends on the subject's prior experience with each of these stimuli, the presence of other stimuli during the conditioning trial, and the extent to which the CS and US are relevant to each other. Furthermore, the processes of classical conditioning are not limited to CS-US pairings. Learned associations can occur between two biologically weak stimuli (sensory preconditioning), in the absence of an unconditioned stimulus (higher-order conditioning), or in the absence of conventional conditioned stimuli (counterconditioning). Given these and other complexities of classical-conditioning processes, it is a mistake to disregard classical conditioning in attempts to explain complex forms of behavior. The richness of classical-conditioning mechanisms make them potentially quite relevant to the richness and complexity of human experience. Tremendous advances have occurred in the understanding of classical-conditioning processes during the last 15 years. It will be interesting to see how this new knowledge comes to be used in the analysis of complex forms of human and animal behavior.

CHAPTER SIX

Instrumental Behavior: Foundations

The goal of Chapter 6 is to describe the theoretical and empirical foundations of the study of instrumental behavior. We will begin with a discussion of various types of contingencies that can exist between instrumental behavior and its consequences. We will then present a historical overview of the ways instrumental behavior has been studied. Finally, we will examine certain features that are inherent in every instrumental-conditioning situation and must be considered in any experimental analysis of instrumental behavior.

In the preceding chapters we discussed various aspects of how responses are elicited by discrete stimuli. Studies of habituation, sensitization, and classical conditioning are all concerned mainly with an analysis of the mechanisms whereby stimuli trigger responses. Because of this emphasis, experiments on habituation, sensitization, and classical conditioning use procedures in which animals have no control over the stimuli to which they are exposed. Certain events, such as CSs and USs, are periodically introduced into the situation according to a schedule determined by the experimenter. The procedures for studying and modifying elicited behavior mimic many situations in the lives of both animals and people. There are many occasions when the organism has no control over the events or stimuli that it encounters. However, there are also many circumstances in which events are a direct result of the individual's be-

havior. By studying hard, a student can learn the material in a course and get a good grade; by turning the car key in the ignition, a driver can start the engine; by putting a coin in a vending machine, a child can obtain a piece of candy. In all these instances, some aspect of the subject's behavior is instrumental in producing a consequent stimulus. Furthermore, the behavior occurs because of the consequences it produces. Students would not study if studying did not result in the learning of interesting information or in good grades; drivers would not turn the ignition key if this did not start engine; and children would not put coins in a candy machine if they did not get something in return. Responses that occur mainly because they are instrumental in producing certain consequences are called **instrumental behavior.**

Because instrumental behavior is governed primarily by the events that it produces, such behavior may be characterized as goal-directed. Instrumental responses occur because the goal would not be reached without them. Goal-directed behavior represents a large proportion of all animal and human behavior. Consider a morning routine. One gets out of bed in order to go to the bathroom and get cleaned up. One gets cleaned up to be ready to get dressed. One gets dressed to keep warm and avoid social embarrassment. The next step may involve making breakfast to reduce hunger. Then the person may drive a car to get to work. On the job, one performs various tasks to receive praise and a salary. One's daily life is filled with actions, large and small, that are performed in order to produce certain consequences.

The fact that response consequences influence the future occurrence of the behavior is clear to everyone. How such consequences affect behavior is not as readily apparent. Much of the remainder of this book will be devoted to a discussion of how or by what mechanisms the environmental consequences of responses alter behavior. In this chapter we will first clarify what is meant by *instrumental behavior* and describe the various types of contingencies that can exist between instrumental behavior and its consequences. We will then explore some of the ways instrumental behavior has been studied. Different researchers have approached instrumental behavior from different points of view, and their theoretical perspectives have greatly influenced the course of their investigations. Finally, we will present some basic preliminary considerations in the experimental analysis of instrumental behavior.

Definition and types of instrumental contingencies

The instrumental contingency

As we have already stated, there are many instances of instrumental behavior in everyday life. In the laboratory, psychologists have stud-

ied many kinds of instrumental behavior: rats running in mazes to obtain food; pigeons pecking keys to obtain grain; dogs jumping hurdles to avoid electrical shock; and monkeys pulling chains to watch electric trains. All these responses are instrumental because they produce some stimulus or change in the environment. In more technical terms we define *instrumental behavior* as behavior that is influenced by an **instrumental contingency.** We have used the word *contingency* before in connection with classical conditioning. In classical conditioning the contingency is between the CS and US. Whether the CS is a good signal for the US depends on the contingent relation between the two stimuli. The US is predictable from the occurrence of the CS, for example, if there is a positive contingency between the CS and US. In instrumental conditioning the critical contingency is between the instrumental response and its consequence. If the response always produces the consequence, then we say the consequence is contingent on the response. As in classical conditioning, the degree of **contingency between the instrumental response and the reinforcer** may vary. The consequence may follow the response with varying degrees of predictability. The consequence may also depend on the absence of a response. In many cases "doing nothing" produces certain effects.

Types of instrumental contingencies

We classify instrumental contingencies by whether the consequence of behavior is contingent on a response or on the absence of a response. We also classify instrumental contingencies by the nature of the consequence itself. If the consequence is something desired, such as food, it is called a reward or a **positive reinforcer.** If the consequence is unpleasant, such as shock, it is called an **aversive stimulus** or a **negative reinforcer.** Figure 6.1 shows four possible instrumental contingencies. The response consequences on the left involve a reward, or positive reinforcer; the response con-

Positive S^R		
	Response	No response
Positive reinforcement	S^R presented or continued	S^R not presented or terminated
Negative punishment	S^R not presented or terminated	S^R presented or continued

Negative S^R		
	Response	No response
Positive punishment	S^R presented or continued	S^R not presented or terminated
Negative reinforcement	S^R not presented or terminated	S^R presented or continued

Figure 6.1. Consequences of responding and not responding in two types of instrumental contingencies involving a reward, or positive reinforcer, and two types of instrumental contingencies involving an aversive, or negative, reinforcer. S^R is the reinforcing stimulus.

sequences on the right involve an aversive, or negative, reinforcer. For each contingency the figure shows how the occurrence or non-occurrence of the instrumental response is related to the consequence. Let us examine each case in more detail.

Positive reinforcement.   The term **positive reinforcement** refers to a class of situations in which there is a positive contingency between the instrumental response and a reinforcing stimulus. In other words, if the subject performs the instrumental response, it receives the reinforcing stimulus; if the subject does not perform the response, the reinforcing stimulus is not presented. Giving a hungry rat a food pellet whenever it presses a response lever, but not when it does not press the lever, is a laboratory example of positive reinforcement. There are many examples of positive reinforcement outside the laboratory. A mother may give her child a cookie only when he puts away his toys; a teacher may praise a student only when the student hands in a good report; or an employee may receive a bonus check only when he or she performs well on the job. The intention of the mother, the teacher, and the employer is to make sure that the instrumental response con-

tinues to occur and maybe even increases in frequency.

Sometimes continuous rewarding events are used in positive-reinforcement procedures. In these cases, the rewarding event continues (or may even increase) as long as the instrumental response is being performed. If the instrumental response stops, the rewarding stimulus also stops or is decreased. In an interesting application of this type of positive reinforcement, infants were conditioned to kick in order to operate a mobile suspended over the crib (Rovee & Rovee, 1969). The harder they kicked, the more movement they could produce in the mobile. The infants showed a rapid and sustained increase in kicking under these circumstances.

Laboratory procedures in which a continuous reinforcing stimulus is used resemble situations outside the laboratory in which there is a direct mechanical connection between behavior and the environment. For example, as long as your foot is on the accelerator, the car continues to move; as long as you eat your dessert, you continue to have the pleasure of tasting the food in your mouth; as long as you sit in the Jacuzzi, you continue to enjoy the water surrounding your body. Although these examples involve continuous reinforcers, they nevertheless represent positive reinforcement because there is a positive contingency in each case between the instrumental response and the reinforcer. As soon as the instrumental responses are terminated, the reinforcing stimuli are also terminated.

Positive punishment. The term **positive punishment** refers to a class of situations in which there is a positive contingency between the instrumental response and an unpleasant, or aversive, stimulus. If the subject performs the instrumental response, it receives the aversive stimulus; if it does not perform the instrumental response, the aversive stimulus is not presented. A mother may reprimand her child for running into the street but not for playing quietly in the yard; your boss may criticize you for being late to a meeting; your teacher may give you a failing grade for answering too many test questions incorrectly. Such procedures decrease the future likelihood of the instrumental response. Procedures that actively discourage instrumental behavior are called **punishment** procedures. The cases that we have described involve positive punishment because the decrease in the instrumental behavior is produced by a positive contingency between the response and the aversive reinforcer.

Laboratory experiments on punishment usually also involve some type of positive reinforcement to get the instrumental behavior to occur occasionally. The subject may be initially trained to make some response for positive reinforcement, such as pressing a lever or running down a runway for food. Once the lever response is established, an aversive stimulus, such as shock, may be presented after each lever press. In the runway, the subject may receive a brief shock in the goal box. The result is a decrease in lever pressing or running.

What we have called "positive punishment" is often simply referred to as "punishment" in other writings. We have used the term *positive punishment* here to emphasize that this type of procedure involves a positive response/reinforcer contingency. Later in the text we will follow the more conventional usage of referring to a positive contingency between a response and an aversive stimulus simply as "punishment."

Negative reinforcement. The first two situations we described involved a positive contingency between the instrumental response and the reinforcer. If the response occurred, the reinforcer was delivered; if the response did not occur, the reinforcer was not delivered. In positive reinforcement, the reinforcer was a rewarding, or pleasant, stimulus; in positive punishment, the reinforcer was an unpleasant, or aversive, stimulus. We now turn to procedures that involve a **negative contingency** between the instrumental response and reinforcer. In a negative contingency the response turns off or prevents the presentation of the reinforcer. If the response occurs, the reinforcer is withheld; if the response does not occur, the reinforcer is delivered. Such a procedure increases the likelihood of behavior if the reinforcer is an aversive stimulus. Situations in which the occurrence of an instrumental response terminates or prevents the delivery of an aversive stimulus are called **negative reinforcement** procedures.

There are two types of negative reinforcement procedures. In one case the aversive stimulus is continuously present but can be terminated by the instrumental response. This type of procedure is called **escape.** Prisoners may escape the unpleasantness of a jail by breaking out. You may escape the unpleasant sounds of a radio that is receiving only static by turning it off. People may leave a movie theater to escape the experience of a bad movie. In the laboratory, a rat may be exposed to a continuous shock at the beginning of a trial. By jumping over a barrier or pressing a lever, the rat can escape the shock. In all these cases, the presence of the aversive stimulus sets the occasion for the instrumental response. The instrumental response is reinforced by termination of the aversive stimulus only if the response occurs during the aversive stimulus. If the rat presses the lever when the shock is not activated, the lever-press response is not reinforced by shock termination.

The second type of negative reinforcement procedure involves an aversive stimulus that is scheduled to be presented sometime in the future. In this case the instrumental response prevents delivery of the aversive stimulus. This type of procedure is called **avoidance.** There are many things we do to prevent the occurrence of something bad. Students often study before an examination only to avoid receiving a bad grade; fire alarms are installed to avoid damage to health and property that can be caused by accidental fires; people get their cars tuned up regularly to avoid unexpected breakdowns. In the laboratory, a rat may be scheduled to receive shock at the end of a warning stimulus. However, if it makes the instrumental response during the warning stimulus, the shock is not delivered. We will have much more to say about avoidance behavior in Chapter 10.

Negative punishment. Another type of situation that involves a negative contingency between the instrumental response and the reinforcer is called **negative punishment.** Negative punishment differs from negative reinforcement in that a pleasant, or rewarding, stimulus serves as the reinforcer. In a negative punishment procedure, the instrumental response prevents the delivery of the positive reinforcer. If the subject makes the instrumental response, the positive reinforcer is not delivered; if the subject does not respond, the positive reinforcer is presented. Thus, the reinforcer is delivered only if the subject withholds the instrumental response. As you might suspect, this type of procedure leads to a decrease in the likelihood of the instrumental behavior. That is why it is considered a punishment procedure.

Negative punishment is often preferable to positive punishment in human applications be-cause it reduces the likelihood of the instrumental response without introducing an aversive stimulus. Negative punishment is being used when a child is told to go to her room after doing something bad. The parents are not introducing an aversive stimulus when they tell the child to go to her room. There is nothing aversive about the child's room. Rather, by sending the child to the room, the parents are withdrawing sources of positive reinforcement, such as playing with friends or watching television. Suspending someone's driver's license for drunken driving also constitutes negative punishment (withdrawal of the reinforcement or privilege of driving). In contrast, locking someone in jail for drunken driving is an example of positive punishment. In this case an aversive stimulus (being in jail) is instituted following the instrumental response (drunken driving).

Negative punishment is also called **omission training** or **differential reinforcement of other behavior** (DRO). Omission training and differential reinforcement of other behavior are merely two alternative ways to institute negative punishment. Both involve a negative contingency between the instrumental response and delivery of a positive reinforcer. In the omission-training procedure, the positive reinforcer is terminated or not presented (omitted) when the instrumental response occurs. In the DRO procedure, the subject periodically receives the positive reinforcer provided that it performs responses other than the target instrumental response. Thus, the procedure involves reinforcement of "other" behavior. Whether negative punishment is put into practice by way of an omission-training procedure or by differential reinforcement of other behavior, it reduces the likelihood of the instrumental response specified in the procedure.

Final note on terminology. Often there is considerable confusion about the terms used to describe instrumental behavior. For example, many people confuse negative reinforcement and punishment because both procedures involve aversive stimuli, such as shock. However, the response/reinforcer contingency is different in the two cases. In what is commonly called punishment, there is a positive contingency between the instrumental response and the aversive stimulus. (The response results in delivery of the aversive stimulus.) In contrast, in negative reinforcement, there is a negative response/reinforcer contingency. (The response either terminates or prevents the delivery of the aversive stimulus.) This difference in the contingencies produces very different outcomes. The instrumental response is decreased by the punishment procedure and increased by negative reinforcement.

The terms *positive reinforcer* and *positive reinforcement* are often used interchangeably, as are *negative reinforcer* and *negative reinforcement* or *punisher* and *punishment*. To avoid confusion, we we will limit use of words with the suffix *-er* to refer to the stimulus or event that is the consequence of the response. Thus, the term *positive reinforcer* will be used only to refer to rewarding stimuli, such as food. The terms *negative reinforcer* and *punisher* will be used only in reference to aversive stimuli, such as shock. We will use terms ending in *-ment* (*positive reinforcement, negative reinforcement, punishment*) to refer to the procedures defined above or their effects. Thus, we will speak of experiments using positive reinforcement and punishment procedures. The resulting increases and decreases in responding will be referred to as positive reinforcement and punishment effects.

Instrumental behavior in the laboratory: Problems and approaches

Preliminary problems

It is obvious that much of animal and human behavior can be called instrumental. How, though, should we investigate instrumental behavior? We could go to the natural environment and look for examples of positively reinforced behavior, avoidance behavior, and the like. However, this approach is often very cumbersome because it is difficult to isolate and control variables we might want to study. The type of research we will discuss brings instrumental behavior into the laboratory. The idea, as with elicited behaviors, is to study representative responses in the hope of discovering general principles. However, as we shall see, the task is complicated by a number of factors.

In elicited behavior it is relatively simple to produce a response to study. One has only to select a stimulus that elicits a particular response. As our study of elicited behavior reveals, there is a regularity between what the experimenter does and what the organism does. The situation for instrumental behavior is less reliable because the factors that control the behavior come *after* a response has been made. The experimenter has to induce the organism to make the response so that the consequences of the behavior can occur and influence the future likelihood of the behavior. In this sense instrumental behavior is voluntary, or, as Skinner (1953) suggests, it is *emitted* rather than elicited. We may do many things to increase or decrease the likelihood that the response will or will not occur. However, the ultimate initiation of a response belongs with the organism.

Because instrumental behavior is emitted, laboratory analyses of it require providing the organism with a situation in which the instrumental behavior is likely to occur. For purposes of analysis, laboratory procedures usually allow for a response to be made repeatedly. Animals have been repeatedly placed in confinement so that their escape response can be studied. In other experiments subjects have been deprived of food in order to induce them to make many responses that produce small units of food. Each situation that has been used has its own unique properties. Selection of the experimental situation depends on the intent of the investigator. Which experimental situation is used also determines in part the types of conclusions that may be reached.

The fact that instrumental behavior is determined by its consequences poses a special problem for theorists. How can an event that comes after the response influence the response? Several answers to this question have been proposed. The solutions represent different ways of looking at the instrumental-conditioning situation as a whole. General theories of behavior based on the analysis of instrumental behavior were developed during the first half of this century. We will not discuss in detail their development or the research they generated. The reader is referred to other sources for such information (for example, Hilgard & Bower, 1975). Rather, we will focus on a few central ideas. Our purpose is to present those ideas that have played a particularly dominant role in the development of research to the present day. We will meet these ideas again in later chapters.

Thorndike and the law of effect

The first laboratory and theoretical analyses of instrumental behavior were performed by E. L. Thorndike. Thorndike's original intent was to study animal intelligence (Thorndike, 1898). The appearance of Darwin's theory of evolution led people to speculate about the extent to which human intellectual capacities, such as reasoning, are present in animals. Figure 6.2 shows a puzzle box that Thorndike designed to study intelligent behavior in cats. In a typical experiment, a cat was placed in the puzzle box. The box could be opened by loosening a latch. Random movements by the cat sometimes resulted in release of the latch, thus allowing escape. The cat eventually developed a set of responses that resulted in quick release of the latch. Figure 6.2 shows the progress of one cat over several trials. As trials progressed, the cat required less and less time to escape from the box.

Thorndike interpreted the results of his studies as reflecting the learning of an association. When the cat was initially placed in the box, it displayed a variety of responses that are typical of a confined animal. Eventually one of these responses, such as clawing, resulted in opening the box. Thorndike believed that such successful escapes led to the learning of an association between the stimuli inside the puzzle box and the escape response. As the connection, or

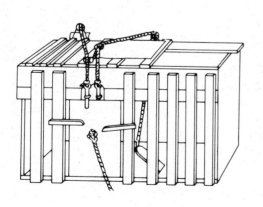

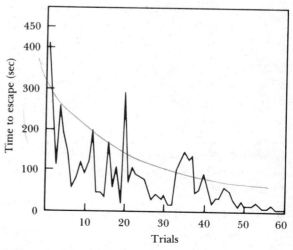

Figure 6.2. Thorndike's puzzle box and data obtained from one cat. The time it took the cat to escape from the box gradually decreased over trials of training. *(After Thorndike, 1898.)*

association, between the box and the successful response became stronger, the cat came to make that particular response whenever it was confined in the puzzle box. The consequence of the successful response—escaping the box—strengthened the association between the box stimuli and the response.

Box 6.1. Edward Lee Thorndike

Thorndike was born in 1874. As an undergraduate at Wesleyan University, he became interested in the work of William James, then at Harvard. Thorndike himself entered Harvard as a graduate student in 1895. During his stay he began his research on instrumental behavior. He started out using chicks as subjects. Since there was no laboratory space at Harvard at that time, he set up his project in William James' cellar. After a short time, he was offered a fellowship at Columbia University. This time his laboratory was located in the attic of psychologist James Cattell. Thorndike received his Ph.D. from Columbia in 1898 for his work entitled "Animal Intelligence: An Experimental Analysis of Associative Processes in Animals." This included the famous puzzle-box experiments. Thorndike stayed on in New York at Columbia University Teachers College, where for many years he served as professor of educational psychology. Among other things, he attempted to apply to children the principles of trial-and-error learning he found with animals. He also became interested in psychological testing and became a leader in this newly formed field. Several years before his death, Thorndike returned to Harvard as the William James Lecturer, a fitting honor for this great psychologist.

Thorndike observed animals in a variety of puzzle boxes that arranged different environmental consequences for the behavior. From these observations he formulated the **law of effect.** The law of effect states that *if a response in the presence of a stimulus is followed by a satisfying event, the association between the stimulus and the response is strengthened. If the response is followed by an annoying event, the association is weakened.* It is important to stress here that according to the law of effect, animals learn an association between the response and the stimuli present at the time of the response. The consequence of the response is not involved in the association. The satisfying or annoying consequence simply serves to strengthen or weaken the bond, or association, between the response and the stimulus situation.

Instrumental behavior and the study of learning

Thorndike's approach to instrumental behavior focused on the acquisition (learning) of a response. Learning was also the primary consideration for Edwin Guthrie (1886–1959), Clark Hull (1884–1952), and Edward Tolman (1886–1959), who followed. These men are often called learning theorists. All of them were in fact interested in behavior as a whole. However, the acquisition of new responses was central to their analyses.

Traditional experimental situations for the study of instrumental learning. Figure 6.3 shows two pieces of apparatus used extensively to study instrumental learning. The **runway** contains a start box at one end and a goal box at the other end. The rat is placed in the start box at the beginning of each trial. The movable barrier separating the start box from the main section of the runway is then lifted. The rat is allowed to make its way down the runway until it reaches the goal box, which usually contains a reward, such as food or water.

The behavior of animals in the runway can be measured in several ways. We can measure how long the animal takes to traverse the alley and reach the goal box. This is called the **running time.** With repeated trials, animals typically require progressively less time to get to the goal box. Some experimenters prefer measuring the *speed* at which the animals run down the alley. Running time can be easily converted to running speed by dividing the length of the

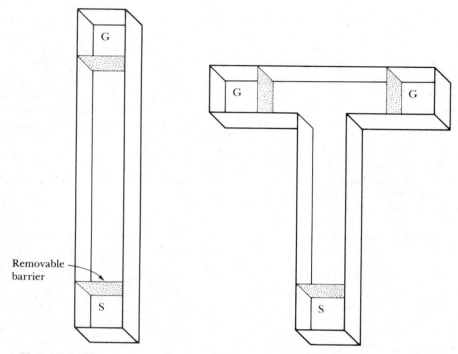

Figure 6.3. Top view of a runway and a T maze. S is the start box; G, the goal box.

runway by the running-time measure. The running-time and speed measures are both reflections of the vigor of the running response. Another aspect of what animals do in this situation is how long they take to leave the start box and begin moving down the alley. How long the animal waits to leave the start box after the start-box door is lifted is called the **latency of the running response.**

A variant of the runway is the **T maze** (see Figure 6.3). Mazes of all sorts have been used to study animal learning. We present the T maze in particular because many theoretically important experiments were performed using this type of maze. The T maze consists of a start box and a T-shaped runway with goal boxes at both ends. Because it has two goal boxes, the T maze is well suited to studying instrumental *choice* behavior. The experimenter may bait one goal box with food, leaving the other empty. The experimenter tests to see how often the subject makes the correct turn at the choice point. Ini-

tially, the rat may choose the baited side with a probability of .50. With repeated trials, the subject will choose the baited side more and more often.

Learning is studied in the runway and T maze by placing a naive rat repeatedly in the situation. With repeated experience the rat's behavior improves. In the runway, the running time and latency of the response decrease over trials. In the T maze, the frequency of correct choices increases with reinforcement. Further analyses attempt to isolate and examine the factors that influence acquisition of the response. The most important of these is, of course, the consequence, or reinforcer. How reinforcement influences behavior is a critical theoretical issue.

S-R theories of learning. Thorndike proposed that reinforcement brings about an association between the instrumental response and the stimuli present when the response is made. This stimulus-response association increases the likelihood that the subject will repeat the response whenever it again experiences the stimulus. Thorndike also speculated about the neural basis of stimulus-response associations (Thorndike, 1931). He assumed that because of the experience with reinforcement, a connection became established between certain sensory neurons and response neurons. Thus, reinforcement was assumed to stamp in a stimulus-response association in a mechanistic fashion. Once the association is established, the stimulus is assumed to produce the instrumental response in much the same way that a classically conditioned stimulus elicits a conditioned response.

Edwin Guthrie proposed an equally mechanistic idea of learning, but one that gave less importance to the law of effect (see Guthrie, 1952). Guthrie thought simply that whatever response is performed in the presence of a particular stimulus gets associated with that stimulus irrespective of the consequences. In short, "we learn what we do." The only necessary condition for learning, according to Guthrie, is stimulus-response **contiguity**—that is, the response must occur at the same time as the stimulus. Other theorists stressed the importance of stimulus-response contiguity as well. Guthrie's work is noteworthy because he attempted to apply the concept to account for a great variety of behavioral phenomena both in and out of the laboratory. Reinforcement, in Guthrie's scheme, helps learning because it produces a dramatic change in the stimulus environment, as when a cat escapes from a puzzle box. This

---

Box 6.2. Applications of Guthrie's Theory

Guthrie's works include one of the earliest attempts to apply a principle of learning from the laboratory to understanding and altering human fears, neuroses, and psychoses. He reasoned that the mechanisms responsible for behavior disorders are the same as those responsible for normal behavior. For example, he suggested that a phobia is the result of an association with the phobic stimulus, which was accidentally present in a fear-eliciting situation. Because the phobic tends to avoid situations that elicit fear, he or she does not get the opportunity to unlearn, or break, this stimulus-response bond. According to Guthrie, to overcome a fear, the phobic must reexperience the fear-provoking situation so that new responses other than fear become associated with the situation. This idea was carried out in the treatment of an elevator phobia by a somewhat unscrupulous therapist:

In order to get rid of a fear of elevators the first essential is an experience with elevators. But the elevator-phobe will not ride elevators. His one terrifying experience has led him to the habitual avoidance of them. One hasty cure of such an elevator fear which had per-

sisted for many years and became a serious handicap to the businessman who suffered it was achieved by enticing the possessor into a tall office building on the excuse that he must at least look at an elevator. He was assured he need not ride in it. When he and his impatient counselor had arrived before the elevator the phobic was seized by the arm and literally pushed into the car. He was frightened but made no scene, perhaps because of the presence of the elevator girl. He was told that the ride was to continue and that an attempt to get out would lead to his being taken for an insane man in custody.

The terror whose effects had operated for over ten years did not fully materialize. The man was annoyed and somewhat frightened, but such a state is usually not maintained for long, and after a number of rides up and down he was willing to go to other office buildings and try elevators [Guthrie, 1938, pp. 278–279.]*

---

*From *Pschology of Human Conflict*, by E. R. Guthrie. Copyright © 1938 by Harper & Row. Reprinted by permission.

change keeps the stimulus-response association for the escape response relatively uncontaminated by irrelevant stimuli.

Another approach to stimulus-response learning was incorporated into the general behavior theory of Clark Hull (see Hull, 1952). Hull, like Thorndike, held that the consequences of behavior are critical for learning. Hull referred to the connections between stimuli and responses as *habits*. His main variable, habit strength, is a measure of how reliably a response occurs in the presence of a given stimulus. The strength of a habit, according to Hull, depends on the number of times the stimulus-response connection is reinforced. The mechanism responsible for this effect is *drive reduction*. That is, before making the response, the organism is in a state of drive because of food deprivation or the like. Running in a runway or making the correct turn in a T maze is strengthened because the food in the goal box reduces the hunger. This account of reinforcement dominated psychology for many years. We will return to it, along with modern developments, in Chapter 8.

Hull's theory of behavior is one of the most ambitious undertakings in the study of conditioning and learning. Hull tried to develop a total behavior theory based on a few axioms. It was both mathematical and deductive. The aim was to identify certain fundamental relations from which various aspects of behavior could be derived and predicted. Hull's theory is no longer the focus of much research. Certain aspects of the theory became too cumbersome to permit experimental proof or disproof. In addition, some aspects of the theory failed to be confirmed by experimental evidence. However, the impact of Hull and his work are still immense. Some of his ideas were later developed by Kenneth Spence and remain important and useful today.

S-R versus sign learning. All the work discussed so far considers stimulus-response bonds to be the basis of learning. However, this posi-

tion was not held universally. Another leading theorist of the time, Edward Tolman, took a more cognitive approach (see Tolman, 1932). He proposed that animals do not learn to make particular responses but rather learn various sign relations in their environment. In running a maze, for example, a rat is assumed to follow signs to the desired goal rather than repeating stamped-in responses. It learns a behavior route rather than a fixed pattern of responses. The learning itself involves the formation of expectancies. With repeated trials, the rat comes to expect that the goal will be reached via the behavior route.

Much research has been devoted to testing predictions of the S-R and sign-learning approaches. We can exemplify the controversy with the following experiment. The research question is whether rats in a maze learn to make a certain response, as the S-R theorists would say, or whether they learn where food is located in their environment, as sign-learning theorists would say. Figure 6.4 shows a maze that was used to investigate this question. The maze has

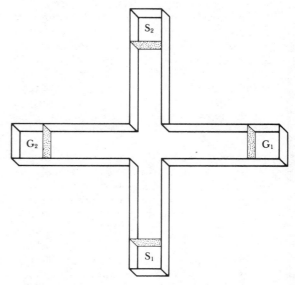

Figure 6.4. Design of maze used in the experiment by Tolman, Ritchie, and Kalish (1946). S_1 and S_2 are the start boxes; G_1 and G_2, the goal boxes.

two start boxes and two goal boxes. Two groups of rats were used. For one group, food was always located in the same goal box, but at the beginning of successive trials, the subjects were randomly placed in one or the other start box. If the food was always located in G_1, for example, the animals had to make a right turn if they were started from S_1 and a left turn if they were started from S_2. Therefore, these animals could not learn the maze on the basis of a fixed response but had to learn on the basis of the location of the food. In contrast, for the second group food was available in the goal box only if they made a specified turn. For some animals the correct turn was always going right, for others it was always going left, regardless of which start box they were placed in. If a subject for which going right was the correct response was placed in S_1, it had to go to G_1 for the reward; if it was placed in S_2, it had to go to G_2. Therefore, these animals had to learn on the basis of the response required, not the location of the food reward. Tolman and his colleagues found that the group that had to learn on the basis of the location of the food learned the task more rapidly (Tolman, Ritchie, & Kalish, 1946).

This study was criticized by proponents of stimulus-response learning theories. The ensuing controversy led to repetition of the basic experiment with more and more refinements. Many groups of rats were tested without providing a definitive answer to the question. It seems that animals are more likely to learn a maze on the basis of the location of the food in situations where there are many distinctive cues to indicate where the food is located. In situations where location cues are not prominent (where there are no distinctive visual, olfactory, or auditory stimuli), animals are more likely to learn the maze in terms of a sequence of motor movements.

Psychologists are no longer concerned with the construction and testing of comprehensive theories like those of Hull and Tolman. This type of work appears to have run its course. The theories are no longer considered accurate

or useful representations of all learning. New ideas have been proposed in the continuing effort to develop a comprehensive account of the effects of reinforcement. Many of these new issues have come into the forefront of our thinking as a reaction to the failure of the older theories.

Operant behavior

In many instances we are interested not so much in the learning of an instrumental response as in the performance of a response already in the subject's repertoire. For example, a mother may want to get her son to clean his room more often. The mother does not doubt that the son knows how to do the job; the problem is to get the learned behavior to occur. Performance of learned behavior can be and has been studied using runways and T mazes. However, methods developed by B. F. Skinner have become far more popular in such investigations. Skinner's methods are based on a different perspective from the learning theorists'. Because of the impact of his methods on modern research, we will examine his perspective and rationale in some detail.

The Skinner box. T mazes and the like measure behavior as discrete events. After one trial in the apparatus, the subject is removed and returned to the start box for another trial. Skinner devised a way to study behavior in a more continuous manner. Figure 6.5 shows a typical **Skinner box** used for this purpose. It is a small experimental chamber that contains something, such as a lever, that the animal can manipulate. The chamber also has a mechanism that can deliver a reward, such as food or water. In the simplest experiment, a hungry rat is placed in the box. The lever is electronically connected to the food-delivery system. If the rat should hit the lever, a food pellet falls into the food tray.

Most rats, when placed in a Skinner box, do not press the lever frequently. There are two

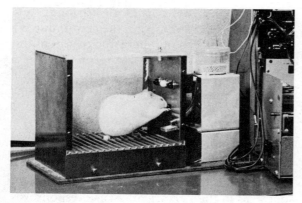

Figure 6.5. A Skinner box equipped with a response lever and an automatic food-delivery device. Electrical equipment is used to program procedures and record responses automatically.

preliminary steps for establishing the lever press as a frequent response. First the animals are taught when food is available in the food cup. This is done by repeatedly pairing the sound of the food-delivery device with the delivery of a food pellet into the cup. After enough such pairings, the sound of the delivery of food comes to serve as a conditioned stimulus for the presence of food in the cup. This preliminary phase of conditioning is called **magazine training.**

After magazine training, the subject is ready to learn the required instrumental response. Most instrumental responses can be analyzed in terms of components. For example, lever pressing requires that the subject approach the response lever, raise its front paws above the lever, and then push down. To facilitate lever pressing, the experimenter may begin by giving the subject food for performing preliminary components of the lever-press response. Initially, the subject may be rewarded for just approaching the vicinity of the lever. Then, reward may be delivered only if the subject sniffs or touches the lever. Finally, reward may be delivered only if the animal actually presses down on the lever. Such a sequence of training

steps is called **shaping by successive approximations.** The experimenter requires increasingly closer and closer approximations to the desired behavior before delivering the reward.

The cumulative recorder. The repetitive occurrences of a response such as lever pressing in a Skinner box are usually recorded with a special kind of automatic event recorder known as the **cumulative recorder** (see Figure 6.6). A rotating drum pulls paper out of the recorder at a constant speed, and a pen rests on the paper. If no responses occur, the pen remains stationary and makes a horizontal line as the paper comes out of the machine. If the animal performs a lever-press response, the pen moves one step vertically on the paper. Since each lever-press response causes the pen to move one step up the paper, the total vertical distance traveled by the pen represents the cumulative (total) number of responses the subject has made. Because the paper comes out of the recorder at a constant speed, the horizontal distance on the cumulative record is a measure of how much time has elapsed in the session. The slope of the line made by the cumulative recorder represents the rate of responding.

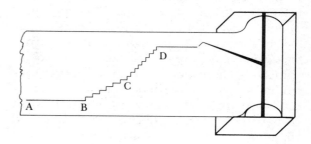

Figure 6.6. Cumulative recorder used for the continuous recording of behavior. The paper moves out of the machine toward the left at a fixed rate. Each response causes the pen to move up the paper one step. No responses occurred between points A and B. A moderate rate of responding occurred between points B and C, and a rapid rate occurred between points C and D.

The **cumulative record** provides a complete visual representation of when and how frequently the animal responds during a session. In the cumulative record shown in Figure 6.6, for example, the animal did not perform the response between points A and B. A slow rate of responding occurred between points B and C. Responses occurred more frequently between points C and D, and the animal quit responding after point D.

The concept of the operant.   Skinner was interested in the laboratory analysis of a form of behavior that is representative of all naturally occurring ongoing activity. However, before behavior can be experimentally analyzed, a measurable unit of behavior has to be defined. Casual observations of ongoing behavior indicate that behavior is continuous. One activity leads to another. Behavior does not fall neatly into units like molecules of a chemical solution. Skinner proposed the concept of the **operant** as a way of dividing behavior into meaningful and measurable units.

Operant responses such as the lever press are defined in terms of the effect that they have on the environment. Activities that have the same effect on the environment are considered to be instances of the same operant. The critical thing is not the muscles that are involved in the behavior but how the behavior "operates" on the environment. For example, the lever-press operant response in rats is typically defined as a depression of the lever sufficient to cause the closure of a microswitch. The subject may press the lever with its right paw, its left paw, or its tail. All these different muscle responses constitute the same operant if they all depress the lever the required amount. Various ways of pressing the lever are assumed to be functionally equivalent because they all have the same effect on the environment—namely, closing the microswitch.

The terms *operant* and *instrumental* are frequently used interchangeably. However, there

---

Box 6.3.   Defining Responses in Behavior Therapy

The concept of the operant is useful in defining behaviors in the clinic as well as the laboratory. A mother brings her child to the clinic complaining that the child is hyperactive or undisciplined. She describes her child with comments like "He wreaks havoc whenever he enters the room" or "He drives me crazy" or "He is completely uncontrollable." Similarly, a distraught husband and wife may seek help because they feel the love has disappeared from their marriage. Both the mother and the married couple describe their problem in general terms even though the difficulty comes from a series of specific responses. Treatment in many cases must start with a more precise definition of the activities that are problematic. What does the child actually do when he enters a room? What specific responses lead the husband and wife to conclude that love is lost? Sometimes defining the specific problem responses is enough to alleviate the difficulty. At other times the clinician has to help the clients find out what kinds of events or situations promote the problem responses. It may then be possible to change the environment in a way that encourages more desirable responses to replace the problematic activities.

---

is a subtle distinction. Instrumental behavior as conceptualized by the learning theorists (with the exception of Tolman) referred to particular muscle movements and responses. Fixed sequences of muscle movements were assumed to become attached to various stimuli. In contrast, an operant may consist of any of a variety of muscle movements, provided that each movement has the same effect on the environment.

It should be noted that because of the way operant responses are defined, they do not represent "natural" units of behavior or inherent properties of ongoing activity. Rather, operant behavior units are determined by what the experimenter is interested in investigating and measuring. For example, the experimenter may define the operant in such a way that it involves a highly discrete response, such as pressing a lever with a force between 4.5 and 5.5 grams. Alternatively, the experimenter may define the operant in such a way that it involves a long chain of complex responses, such as walking down a tunnel, making a left turn, and turning a dial to open a door. Depending on how the operant is being measured, the changes in the environment produced by an operant may allow for only a small number of effective responses or may permit a large variety of activities. Skinner assumed that reinforcement strengthens all operant behavior in the same way. The same mechanisms are assumed to be involved in the operant conditioning of complex response chains and of small, discrete muscle movements. Given this belief in the generality of operant-conditioning processes, Skinner proposed that the principles of all operant behavior could be discovered by studying only one or two *arbitrary operants*. He selected lever pressing in rats and pecking a small disk or key in pigeons as arbitrary operants for this purpose. These particular operants were assumed to be special only in that they are easy to measure. Lever-pressing and key-peck responses can be easily detected by the closure of switches attached to the response lever or key. These switch closures can then be automatically recorded, enabling precise monitoring of the behavior for long periods. Recent investigators have begun to question whether lever pressing and key pecking are truly representative of all operant behavior, as Skinner assumed. We will discuss some of this controversy later.

Response rate as a measure of operant behavior. Skinner, like Thorndike and Hull, emphasized the importance of reinforcement. Reinforcement changes the subject's tendency to respond. According to Skinner, saying that the tendency to respond has increased is equivalent to saying that the probability that the response will occur has increased. If we say, for example, that Joe Smith has an increased tendency to study, we really mean that we are more likely to find Joe studying now than before. In actuality, however, we do not evaluate response probabilities. Instead, we measure the frequency with which a response occurs. We say events are highly probable when they occur frequently or at high rates. Skinner therefore proposed that response rate, or frequency, be used to measure the strength of operant behavior.

The behavioral-baseline technique. When a subject is first put in a Skinner box, it engages in a wide variety of activities. Each activity has a particular rate of occurrence before conditioning. A naive rat, for example, has a high rate of sniffing and a low rate of lever pressing. This initial rate of responding before the introduction of experimental manipulations is called the **free-operant baseline** or the **operant level.** The free-operant baseline can be used to assess the change in behavior that occurs when a conditioning procedure is introduced. Reinforcement of lever pressing, for example, will increase the rate of this response from its low operant level to a much higher rate.

The free-operant baseline, or operant level, is useful in revealing the effects of procedures such as reinforcement that *increase* the rate of responding. However, if the operant level of a response is low to begin with, it cannot be used to detect the effects of experimental manipulations that might further *decrease* the rate of the the behavior. In such cases, it is desirable to regularly reinforce the operant response so that it will occur at a stable rate higher than the operant level. This level of responding maintained by reinforcement is also called a baseline. The baseline rate of a reinforced operant response can be used to evaluate the effects of procedures, stimuli, or other manipulations that may either increase or decrease the rate of operant behavior. The effects of the experimental manipulations are revealed by changes in the baseline rate of the operant response.

In Chapter 4 we described the use of a **behavioral baseline** to evaluate the effects of aversive classical-conditioning procedures. The technique, known as conditioned suppression or the conditioned-emotional-response procedure, first involves getting rats to lever-press for food reinforcement at a steady rate. A light or tone CS is then paired with shock. The effects of this classical conditioning are then evaluated by presenting the conditioned stimulus while the subject is pressing the response lever. As can be seen in Figure 6.7, the animal stops lever-pressing when the CS is presented. The cumulative record is flat during the CS. Before and after presentation of the CS, the animal presses the lever at a steady rate. Thus, the effects of the classical-conditioning procedure are clearly evident in a change in the baseline rate of the operant behavior.

The behavioral-baseline technique is a novel methodological approach to the analysis of behavior. Most of the research of Hull, Tolman, and their associates, for example, was conducted with various types of runways and mazes, and large groups of subjects were exposed to each experimental condition. The effects of these conditions were then evaluated by comparing the performance of subjects across groups. The results were based on the average performance of groups of subjects. Skinner ob-

jected to this group-statistical approach and advocated exposing individual subjects to the same reinforcement procedure until the behavior was stable and predictable. He then observed how a manipulation influenced this stable baseline. As long as the baseline was indeed stable, the results of the experimental manipulation could be easily observed. Given that stable baselines can be produced, Skinner argued that large groups of subjects are unnecessary in behavioral research. The effects of experimental manipulations should be evident with individual subjects. As it turned out, both the group-statistical and individual-subject approaches have their place in the experimental analysis of behavior. Some questions are more easily answered using a single-subject baseline technique. Other types of questions necessitate the use of groups of subjects. Throughout the remainder of the book we will discuss both types of research.

Experimental analysis of instrumental behavior: Preliminary considerations

The basic problem in the analysis of instrumental behavior is understanding how the consequences of behavior influence the future occurrence of the behavior. Basically, this is a study of relations. The focus is on relations between environmental events and behavior. We will deal with various aspects of this problem in the next five chapters. Before we begin, however, certain other important aspects of instrumental-conditioning situations also have to be considered. The generality of every instance of instrumental conditioning, whether it occurs in a runway, a maze, or a Skinner box, is limited by certain variables. For example, the response required for reinforcement may vary in how easy it is or how "natural" it is for the subject to perform. The consequences selected may be mild or strong, and they may be more or less appropriate for the subject. In addition, there is

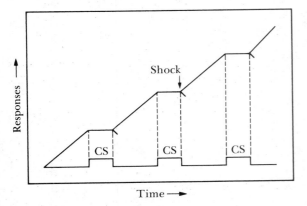

Figure 6.7. Cumulative record showing effects of conditioned-emotional-response training. Subjects are given a brief shock at the end of each CS presentation and consequently suppress their lever-press responding during the CS. (Hypothetical data.)

the subject itself. The subject may be hungry or thirsty, intelligent or dull, highly experienced in the situation or experimentally naive. Consideration of such variables is preliminary to an analysis of relations between environmental events and instrumental behavior.

Subject variables

The learning and performance of instrumental responses can be greatly influenced by various characteristics of the subject. Some of these characteristics may be relatively long-lasting features of the organism, such as its intellectual capacity, neurophysiology, and skeletal-muscular structure. Other characteristics are more transient, such as its motivational state, health, or alertness. Limitations of space prevent us from describing the effects of all possible subject variables on instrumental behavior. We will focus on only two important types of factors, motivation and the subject's previous experience.

Motivation. One of the most important characteristics of the subject that determine the learning and performance of instrumental behavior is the subject's motivation. Motivational state in part determines the effectiveness of reinforcers. If an animal is not hungry, it will not press a lever for a food reward. If it is not sexually aroused, it will not work to gain access to a sexual partner. In lay language, the term *motivation* usually refers to some kind of force or impetus that drives the behavior, and motivational states are used to explain why the behavior occurs. We may say, for example, that Mary is eating because she is motivated by hunger. However, for such an explanation to be informative, we have to have reason to believe that Mary is hungry independent of the fact that she is eating. If we do not have such independent evidence for hunger, our explanation of Mary's eating behavior may be incorrect. Mary may be eating because she likes the taste

of the food or is trying to please the person who gave her the food.

Independent evidence for a motivational state is often provided by the procedures that are used to create the motivation. Perhaps the most common procedure for producing a motivational state is **deprivation.** Food, for example, is made an effective reinforcer for rats by first depriving them of it. Generally, animals perform an instrumental response for food more often after longer periods of food deprivation. This direct relation between rate of responding and food deprivation is illustrated in Figure 6.8. Eating can also be influenced by brain lesions or the injection of hormones or drugs. Each of these types of manipulations can be used to provide independent evidence of the motivational basis for eating.

Another important manipulation that changes the animal's motivational state is to provide unlimited access to the reinforcer. This procedure, called **satiation,** reduces the animal's motivation to obtain that reinforcer. Therefore, satiation usually reduces the rate of instrumental behavior. The effects of satiation for food, for example, can be easily observed by

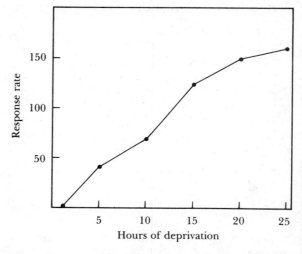

Figure 6.8. Rate of response as a function of number of hours of food deprivation. (Hypothetical data.)

giving the animals unlimited access to food before testing them in a food-reinforcement procedure. The effects of satiation can also be observed during the course of long instrumental-conditioning sessions. If a rat is allowed to press a lever for a food reward until it has completely satisfied its hunger, its rate of lever pressing will decline.

Motivational states can influence behavior in several ways in addition to determining the effectiveness of reinforcers. For example, sometimes food deprivation raises or lowers the level of general activity. Experimenters often take advantage of this effect of food deprivation in shaping new responses. By food-depriving the animal, the experimenter can sometimes increase the subject's activity and thereby make it more likely that the animal will perform the desired responses during the shaping process. Motivational variables can be used to set the occasion for learning in other ways as well. In an interesting procedure for toilet-training young children, Azrin and Foxx (1974) suggest that parents set aside a day for training the child. Preceding and during the training period, the child is to be given as much fluid to drink as possible, to increase the probability that the child will urinate. The more the child urinates, the more opportunity the parent has to shape appropriate toileting responses in the child.

Learning to learn. Another important characteristic of subjects that determines how they learn and perform instrumental responses is their previous experience. Certain types of previous experience can facilitate the learning of instrumental responses. Other types of experiences may hinder instrumental performance. One of the earliest rigorous demonstrations of the influence of previous experience on the learning of instrumental behavior was performed by Harry Harlow with monkeys (Harlow, 1949). The subject was seated in an apparatus similar to the one shown in Figure 6.9. A tray containing two visually distinctive objects was placed in front of the animal at the start of each trial. One of the objects, designated as correct, always had a piece of food hidden under it, and the monkey was allowed to find the food. The positions of the two objects—left or right—were randomly varied from one trial to the next. The subject received six successive training trials with a given pair of objects. The animal was then given a new problem with a new pair of objects. Again, one of the objects was designated as correct and had a piece of food hidden under it at the start of each trial. Nothing was hidden under the other object. After six trials with the second problem, the monkey was tested with a third set of objects for six trials, and so on. The procedure was continued until each animal had received training with about 300 pairs of objects.

The interesting outcome of the learning-to-learn experiment was that the animals' rates of learning improved with successive pairs of objects. With the first pair of objects, the monkeys did not learn perfectly to pick the correct object in the six trials that were administered. As the animals received more practice with the problems, they learned the problems faster and faster. In fact, after a couple of hundred problems, they learned each problem in one presentation of a pair of objects. On the first trial with a new pair of objects, their choice was random because they had not yet received reinforcement for the correct response. However, on the second trial with a new pair of objects, nearly all the animals always chose the object with the food under it. Thus, they achieved near-perfect performance after experiencing the outcome of only one choice, whether or not this response uncovered the food.

The learning-to-learn findings raise an interesting issue concerning what is learned in instrumental conditioning. The fact that the monkeys' rate of learning increased with successive problems indicates that the animals were learning more than specific stimulus-response associ-

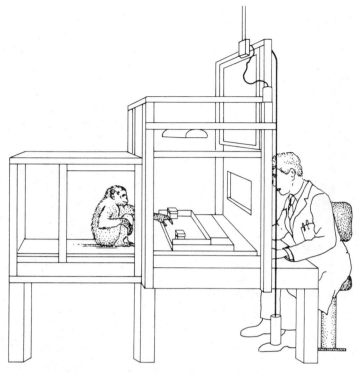

Figure 6.9. Wisconsin General Test Apparatus used by Harlow in experiments on learning sets. The monkey sits in a cage with access to a stimulus tray. The tray holds two objects that cover wells. A raisin or peanut is under one of the objects. *(After Harlow, 1949.)*

ations. Indeed, an S-R association could not have been the learning mechanism, because the problem was changed every six trials. Harlow suggested that the monkeys learned not only what was the correct response for each problem but also how to learn the problems. They learned a strategy, or **learning set.** The strategy might have been as follows: if food is found under object A, then object A is correct; if food is not found under object A, then object B is correct. This type of solution is called the **win-stay, lose-shift strategy.**

Learning sets describe many instances of human learning. We do not approach each new learning situation naively. Rather, our accumulation of experience helps us quickly learn what is the correct response when we encounter new situations. In calculus, for example, learning

how to solve one problem helps us solve others. Tactics found to be successful in one situation are carried over and facilitate the learning of solutions to new problems.

Learned helplessness. In the learning-to-learn experiments, animals are given experience with problems that they can learn to solve to obtain reinforcement, and this facilitates their learning in subsequent situations. The opposite result occurs if animals are first exposed to an insoluble problem. Such prior experience interferes with learning in subsequent situations. One example, the **learned-helplessness effect,** was originally investigated by Seligman, Overmier, and Maier (for example, Overmier & Seligman, 1967; Seligman & Maier, 1967) and has since attracted the attention of many other investigators as well (see reviews by Alloy & Seligman, 1979; Maier & Jackson, 1979; Maier & Seligman, 1976; Seligman, 1975).

Most of the learned-helplessness experiments on animals have used aversive stimulation. For example, in many of the original experiments dogs were first placed in a restraining apparatus and given a series of shocks that they could neither escape nor avoid. (The "problem" was insoluble.) The next day, the animals were placed in a shuttle box for instrumental-escape training. The shuttle box contained two compartments separated by a barrier. The animal was put in one of the compartments, and shock was administered through a grid floor. The dog could escape the shock by jumping across the barrier into the other compartment, which was not electrified. Naive dogs ordinarily learn this barrier-jump escape response very quickly. However, the dogs that had received exposure to uncontrollable shocks the day before behaved in a most peculiar fashion. Seligman (1975) described the behavior of one of these dogs as follows:

> The dog's first reactions to shock in the shuttle box were much the same as those of a naive dog; it ran around frantically for about thirty seconds. But, then it stopped moving; to our surprise, it lay down and quietly whined. After one minute of this we turned the shock off; the dog had failed to cross the barrier and had not escaped from shock. On the next trial, the dog did it again; at first it struggled a bit, and then, after a few seconds, it seemed to give up and to accept shock passively. On all succeeding trials, the dog failed to escape [p. 22].

Seligman and his associates proposed the **learned-helplessness hypothesis** to explain why exposure to uncontrollable shocks results in a deficit in subsequent instrumental learning. According to this explanation, during exposure to inescapable shocks, animals learn that the shocks are independent of their behavior—that there is nothing they can do to control the shocks. Having learned that shocks occur re-

gardless of what they do, the animals make little effort to control the shocks when the shocks are later made escapable. This explanation assumes that animals have to learn two things when they are exposed to escapable shocks after learned-helplessness training. First, they have to learn that their behavior can now control the shock. They then have to learn what the required instrumental response is that allows them to escape from the shock. In contrast, normal animals have only to learn to make the correct instrumental response. Since they have not had learned-helplessness training, they already know that their behavior is likely to be effective in controlling the environment.

Many carefully controlled experiments have been performed to substantiate the learned-helplessness hypothesis (for example, Maier, 1970; Maier, Albin, & Testa, 1973; Seligman & Beagley, 1975). The goal of these studies was to isolate the uncontrollability of shock as the critical manipulation for learned-helplessness training. Three groups of animals have typically been used in these investigations. During the initial phase of the experiment, one control group is given escapable-shock training. The animals in this group are periodically exposed to shock but can escape from it by making an instrumental response, such as pressing on a panel. The experimental group receives the same shocks for the same duration as the escape control group. However, for these subjects the shocks are inescapable. A third group of animals is not exposed to shocks during the first phase. All subjects are then given escape or avoidance training, usually in a shuttle box. The significant finding is that animals exposed to inescapable shocks are slower to learn the shuttle response later than animals in either control group. It is important to realize that this learned-helplessness group was not the only one exposed to shocks during the first phase of the experiment. The escape control group was also exposed to shocks initially. However, the escape control subjects could turn off the shocks. The results of these experiments show that it is the uncontrollability of shocks that produces the learned-helplessness effect, not merely exposure to shock per se.

There has been considerable controversy about the learned-helplessness interpretation of the learning deficit that occurs in animals exposed to inescapable shock (for example, Black, 1977; Levis, 1976). In some situations inescapable shock produces a decrease in motor movement, and this is what is responsible for the deficit in later learning (for example, Anisman, de Catanzaro, & Remington, 1978; see also Anderson, Crowell, Cunningham, & Lupo, 1979). However, there are also situations in which the deficit in learning cannot be attribut-

ed to the suppression of movement caused by inescapable shock (for example, Jackson, Alexander, & Maier, 1980). Thus, it appears that inescapable shock can have several effects in animals, only one of which is learned helplessness (Maier & Jackson, 1979).

The learned-helplessness phenomenon has been observed in several species, including college sophomores. Hiroto (1974), for example, performed an experiment in which human subjects could turn off a loud noise by moving a finger across a barrier in a finger apparatus modeled after animal shuttle boxes. Subjects given pretraining with uncontrollable loud noise failed to learn the shuttle response. They

---

Box 6.4.   Helplessness and Depression

In a provocative book, *Helplessness: On Depression, Development, and Death,* Seligman (1975) suggests that learned helplessness may be an appropriate model for understanding human depression. Many similarities exist between helpless laboratory animals and depressed human patients. In both cases there is a reduction in overall activity. Depressed persons typically do not do much. They may, for example, remain in bed all day. Laboratory subjects show a similar lethargy, which extends to activities that could result in reinforcement. Depressed persons do poorly on instrumental-learning tasks. Both helpless animals and depressed persons show reductions in aggressive tendencies, sexual activity, and appetite. Research also indicates that an imbalance of neuroactive hormones may occur in both cases.

Seligman suggests that depression may result from the same kind of process that produces helplessness in animals—namely, experiences in which the subject learns that responding is futile. A wife may become depressed if nothing she does seems to please her husband. A student may become depressed if he or she continues to get bad grades after trying various study techniques. Cancer patients may become depressed when they come to realize that a variety of attempted

treatments are all unsuccessful.

The learned-helplessness model suggests not only causes of depression but also treatments and prevention procedures. It suggests that we can prevent depression by providing experiences in which the person's actions are effective in controlling the environment. People should be careful to avoid situations in which everything is determined by others and in which the necessary coping responses far exceed their ability. The suggested treatment of depression involves providing experiences that serve to demonstrate to the patient that his or her responses can in fact control the environment. If the depression is very severe, the therapist may begin by showing the patient that he or she can in fact get out of bed, prepare breakfast, go shopping, and so on. As progress permits, increasingly complex tasks are presented, and the subject is guided to perform the responses necessary to produce the relevant outcome. Of course, treatment procedures have to be combined with an analysis of what caused the depression for the particular person, to reduce the risk of relapse. Eliminating the cause of the depression may be a very difficult task, depending on the life circumstances of the patient. (For a further discussion of learned helplessness as a model of depression, see Huesmann, 1978.)

merely sat out the duration of the loud noise. In contrast, control subjects, who had either previous noise-escape training with a pushbutton or no previous training, readily learned the finger shuttle response.

Although the majority of learned-helplessness experiments have involved aversive stimuli, Seligman (1975) proposes that results of the same type may also occur in positive-reinforcement situations. Helplessness should result if the subject learns that reinforcers occur irrespective of behavior. Can we turn a subject into a "spoiled brat" by giving it everything it needs without responding? Preliminary studies (see Engberg, Hansen, Welker, & Thomas, 1972) suggest that this can happen. Further research is needed, however, to establish the mechanisms involved.

Seligman has also suggested that learning about the controllability of events may be an important aspect of human development. Even in infancy, children learn that their responses have certain consequences. A baby may coo at his father, who may coo back in return. Infants are able to elicit smiles, hugs, and vocalizations from their caretakers depending on what the infants do. Seligman points out that children who do not have these basic experiences show severe behavioral and even physiological disturbances. Children raised in orphanages with only routine physical care may have severe problems as a result. Learning early in life that the environment can be controlled by one's behavior may be important to "inoculate" the person against the effects of the many instances in life when events occur outside one's control.

Response variables

One of the key assumptions in Skinner's approach to the study of instrumental behavior is that pressing a lever in rats and pecking a key in pigeons are representative of all other operant responses. Analysis of lever-press and key-peck conditioning was therefore expected to yield universally applicable principles of behavior.

However, research suggests that these as well as some other commonly used instrumental responses may not be as representative as was originally hoped. Certain responses seem to be far easier to condition with reinforcement than others. In addition, innate response patterns like those discussed in Chapter 2 may play a more important role in instrumental conditioning than some investigators originally believed.

Belongingness in instrumental conditioning. We saw in Chapter 5 that classical conditioning occurs at different rates depending on the combination of CS and US that is used. Rats readily learn to associate tastes with sickness, for example, whereas associations between tastes and shock are not as easily learned. We suggested that a CS has to "belong" to a US, or be "relevant" to the US, for conditioning to occur rapidly. Analogous belongingness, or relevance, relations are found in instrumental conditioning.

Thorndike was the first to observe differences in the conditionability of various responses with reinforcement. In many of the puzzle-box experiments, the cat had to manipulate a latch or string to escape from the box. However, Thorndike also tried to condition such responses as yawning and scratching. The cats could learn to make these responses. Interestingly, however, the form of the responses changed as training proceeded. At first, the cat would scratch itself vigorously to be let out of the box. On later trials, it would only make "aborted" scratching movements. It might put its leg to its body but would not make a true scratch response. Similar results were obtained in attempts to condition yawning. As training progressed, the animal might open its mouth to be let out of the box, but it would not give a *bona fide* yawn.

Thorndike proposed the concept of **belongingness** to explain the failures to train such responses as scratching and yawning. According to this concept, certain responses naturally belong with certain reinforcers because of the subject's evolutionary history. Operating a latch or pulling a string are manipulatory responses that naturally belong with release from confinement. In contrast, scratching and yawning have not evolved to help animals escape from confinement and therefore do not belong with release from the puzzle box. Presumably this is why scratching and yawning do not persist as vigorous *bona fide* responses when reinforced by release from the box.

Thorndike's observations are supported by the more recent work of Breland and Breland (1961). They encountered interesting difficulties in attempts to condition instrumental responses with food reinforcement in several species. Their goal was to train amusing response chains in animals with operant-conditioning procedures for displays to be used in amusement parks and zoos. During the course of this work they observed dramatic behavior changes that were not consistent with the reinforcement procedures they were using. For example, they describe a raccoon that was reinforced for picking up a coin and depositing it in a coin bank:

> We started out by reinforcing him for picking up a single coin. Then the metal container was introduced, with the requirement that he drop the coin into the container. Here we ran into the first bit of difficulty: he seemed to have a great deal of trouble letting go of the coin. He would rub it up against the inside of the container, pull it back out, and clutch it firmly for several seconds. However, he would finally turn it loose and receive his food reinforcement. Then the final contingency: we [required] that he pick up [two] coins and put them in the container.
>
>   Now the raccoon really had problems (and so did we). Not only could he not let go of the coins, but he spent seconds, even minutes, rubbing them together (in a most miserly fashion), and dipping them into the container. He carried on this behavior to such an extent that the practical application we had in mind—a display featuring a raccoon putting money in a piggy bank—simply was not feasible. The rubbing behavior became worse and

worse as time went on, in spite of non-reinforcement [p. 682].*

The Brelands had similar difficulties with other species. Pigs, for example, also could not learn to put coins in a piggy bank. After initial training, they began rooting the coins along the ground. The Brelands called the development of such responses as rooting in the pigs and rubbing coins together in the raccoons **instinctive drift.** As the term implies, the extra responses that developed in these food-reinforcement situations were activities the animals instinctively perform when obtaining food. Pigs root along the ground in connection with feeding, and raccoons rub and dunk food-related objects. These innate food-related responses are apparently very strong and can take over to the extent that they compete with the responses required by the experimenter. The Brelands emphasized that such instinctive response tendencies have to be taken into account in the analysis of behavior. (For other investigations of such limitations on instrumental conditioning, see Annable & Wearden, 1979; Boakes, Poli, Lockwood, & Goodall, 1978; Pearce, Colwill, & Hall, 1978; Shettleworth, 1975.)

The concept of preparedness. A popular approach to thinking about differences in the rate of learning in various situations involves the concept of **preparedness,** introduced by Seligman (1970). According to this idea, differences in the ease of learning reflect differences in the extent to which animals' evolutionary history has prepared them to learn the required responses and associations. If the animal is well adapted to learn a particular task—if performance of the task "comes naturally"—the subject is said to be highly **prepared** for it. Responses and associations for which the animal is evolutionarily prepared are readily learned

---

*From "The Misbehavior of Organisms," by K. Breland and M. Breland. In *American Psychologist*, 1961, *16*, 682. Copyright 1961 by the American Psychological Association.

Box 6.5. Teaching Violin Playing

The research on response limitations in instrumental conditioning indicates that it is important to consider the subject's naturally occurring response tendencies in designing training procedures. This principle serves as the basis for a novel and highly successful method for teaching violin playing developed by the Japanese violinist Shinicki Suzuki. Traditional approaches to violin playing typically begin with teaching students to associate printed notes on a page with the position of their fingers on the violin. In addition, the students are required to draw the bow slowly across the strings to produce a smooth sound. Suzuki observed that neither of these tasks is close to naturally occurring response tendencies in young children. Instead, very young children find it much easier to associate the *sound* of a note with the position of their fingers on the violin. Suzuki likened this feature of learning to the way children naturally learn language. They initially learn meanings of words through listening, not through reading. Suzuki also observed that young children find it much easier to move the bow with quick, short movements over the strings than to draw the bow slowly. He successfully capitalized on these observations in his teaching method. With his method, which has been adopted in many parts of the world, children do not begin by learning to read music. Rather, they listen to recordings of their pieces and place their fingers on the violin so as to imitate these sounds. In addition, the beginning pieces use short, quick bowing movements exclusively. Long, smooth motions are not attempted until the child has considerable skill. The result is that many children have been taught highly complex violin-playing skills that teachers in the past thought were impossible at very young ages. Furthermore, because the technique makes use of responses that occur more naturally for the children, they can begin to play tunes early in their training and hence derive more enjoyment from their playing.

with very little training. In contrast, if the task requires responses and associations that are opposite to what the animal has evolved to be able to learn, the animal is said to be **contraprepared** for the task. Because such tasks are contrary to the animal's natural behavioral tendencies, learning the tasks is very difficult and perhaps impossible. Finally, if the responses and associations involved in the task are neither consistent with nor opposite to the animal's natural behavior tendencies, the animal is said to be **unprepared** for the task. Animals can learn responses and associations for which they are unprepared. However, the rate of learning is intermediate between the rapid learning observed in situations for which the animal is prepared and the laborious learning observed in situations for which the animal is contraprepared. Thus, according to the concept of preparedness, various learning tasks can be arranged along a continuum according to the relation between the required responses and associations and the animal's evolutionary history.

The concept of preparedness has done a great deal to increase our awareness of the importance of evolutionary factors in learning situations. However, it has not been useful in stimulating research or in furthering our understanding of the mechanisms of learning. The concept has two important weaknesses as a tool in the analysis of behavior. First, it is very difficult, if not impossible, to find the relative positions of various learning tasks on the continuum of preparedness. Seligman has suggested, for example, that we should use the rate of learning as one yardstick with which to measure preparedness. But how can we compare the rate of learning across different learning tasks? Consider, for example, the suggestion that taste-aversion learning in rats and language acquisition in children are both highly prepared types of learning. Because these two tasks are extremely different, involving very dissimilar responses, stimuli, and organisms, it is unlikely that one could find a common measure of behavior that could be applied equally to measure the rate of learning in both situations.

The other analytic weakness of the concept of preparedness is its implication that there is a continuous process that systematically varies as a function of preparedness. According to this idea, all prepared or all contraprepared tasks should have something in common that determines their degree of preparedness. However, this is highly unlikely. Consider, for example, tasks that are very difficult to learn and therefore can be considered contraprepared. Difficulty in learning tasks could be due to a myriad of factors. Perhaps the subject's musculature precludes performing the required response. Perhaps the subject is unable to sense the relevant stimuli. The subject's nervous system may not be sufficiently developed to permit the association, or it may have developed in ways that make formation of the required association impossible. Prepared associations, similarly, may be determined by a multiplicity of factors. Therefore, to say that the subject is prepared, unprepared, or contraprepared for a learning task does not give us much insight into why the learning occurs rapidly, slowly, or not at all.

Reinforcer variables

Another important factor that determines the learning and performance of instrumental behavior concerns characteristics of the stimulus that is delivered as a consequence of the instrumental response—the reinforcer. Two aspects of the reinforcer that have been extensively analyzed are its magnitude, or quantity, and its quality. Many experiments have evaluated the influence of the quantity and quality of the reinforcer in both reinforcement and punishment situations. The basic finding in these experiments has been that the behavioral effect of the instrumental-conditioning procedure increases as the quantity and quality of the reinforcer or punisher increases. For example, food-reinforced responding increases with increases in the amount or quality of food presented consequent to the response, and shock-punished responding is suppressed more as the intensity of the shock is increased.

Although the quantity and quality of the reinforcer are logically different characteristics, often it is difficult to separate them experimentally. A change in the quantity of the reinforcer may also make the reinforcer qualitatively different. An increase in shock intensity, for example, may result in a qualitatively different type of discomfort. In an interesting experiment involving positive reinforcement, Hutt (1954) tried to isolate the effects of quantity and quality on instrumental behavior. Nine groups of rats were trained to press a bar for a liquid reinforcer. The reinforcer was varied in both quantity and quality for the various groups. Three of the groups received a small amount of fluid, three a medium amount, and three a large amount. The fluid was a mixture of water, milk, and flour. One of the three groups given a particular amount of fluid received this basic mixture. For another group, the quality of the mixture was

improved by adding saccharin to the basic mixture. For the third group, the quality of the fluid was reduced by adding a small amount of citric acid. Figure 6.10 shows the average rates of bar pressing for each group. Increases in either the quality or the quantity of the reinforcer produced higher rates of responding.

An even more important variable than amount or quality of a reinforcer is the way the reinforcer is delivered. The reinforcer may be delivered immediately after every instance of the behavior or in one of many other patterns involving various relations between the response and the reinforcer. We will describe the effects of such variations in the response/reinforcer relation starting in Chapter 7.

Concluding comments

The goal of this chapter has been to introduce the basic issues related to the investigation of instrumental behavior. We have seen that a wide variety of behavioral situations can be

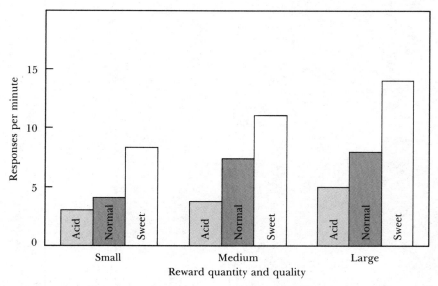

Figure 6.10. Average rates of responding in independent groups of subjects for which responding was reinforced with reinforcers varying in quantity and quality. *(After Hutt, 1954.)*

called instrumental. After all, there are many ways in which behavior influences the course of events. The study of instrumental behavior centers on one question: how does a consequence of behavior influence the occurrence of that behavior? Experimental investigations of this question have been closely connected to behavior theory from the beginning. The next chapters on instrumental behavior will continue to reflect the close association between theory and experiment.

Experimental investigation of instrumental behavior necessitates creating a situation in which an instrumental response can be made and measured. This involves selecting a subject, a response, a reinforcer, and a motivating procedure. We have seen that these selections can greatly influence what happens. Important though they may be, however, subject, response, and reinforcer variables are only preliminary to the study of the central issue of how a consequence influences behavior. The experimental analysis of this central issue involves varying the way the response produces the consequence. Must the consequence always follow the response immediately? Must there be a causal connection? How do the frequency and probability of response-produced consequences influence behavior? These are questions we will consider in the next two chapters.

CHAPTER SEVEN

Instrumental Behavior: Experimental Analysis

The performance of an instrumental response is highly dependent on the schedule of reinforcement used to reward or punish the behavior. A schedule of reinforcement is a program, or rule, that determines the conditions under which the occurrence of a response is followed by presentation of the reinforcer. A great many schedules of reinforcement are possible and have been investigated. We will describe some of the most important of these and the patterns of responding produced by each.

One of the most important factors that govern instrumental behavior is the relation between occurrences of the response and delivery of the reinforcer. The way we have discussed instrumental conditioning up to this point might imply that instrumental responses are always followed by the reinforcer. However, even casual reflection shows that in the natural environment rarely does every occurrence of an instrumental response produce the reinforcer. You do not get a high grade on a test every time you spend many hours studying. You cannot get on a bus every time you go to the bus stop, and inviting someone over for dinner does not always result in a pleasant evening. In fact, in most cases the relation between instrumental responses and consequent reinforcement is rather complex. Attempts to study how these complex relations control the occurrence of in-

strumental responses has led to laboratory investigations of schedules of reinforcement.

A **schedule of reinforcement** is a program, or rule, that determines how and when the occurrence of a response will be followed by a reinforcer. There are an infinite number of ways that such a program could be set up. The delivery of a reinforcer may depend on the occurrence of a certain number of responses, the passage of time, the presence of certain stimuli, the occurrence of other responses of the animal, or any number of things. One might expect that cataloging the behavioral effects produced by the various possible schedules of reinforcement would be a very difficult task. However, research so far has shown that the job is quite manageable. Reinforcement schedules that involve similar relations among stimuli, responses, and reinforcers usually produce similar patterns of behavior. The exact rate of responding may differ from one situation to another. However, the *pattern* of response rates is usually amazingly predictable. This regularity has made the study of the effects of reinforcement schedules both interesting and fruitful.

Schedules of reinforcement influence both how an instrumental response is learned and how it is then maintained by reinforcement. Traditionally, however, investigators of schedule effects have been most concerned with maintenance of behavior. Reinforcement schedules have been most extensively investigated in Skinner boxes that permit continuous observation of behavior so that fluctuations in the rate of responding can be readily observed and analyzed (for example, Ferster & Skinner, 1957). How the operant response is initially shaped and conditioned is rarely of interest. Often a given schedule of reinforcement will produce its characteristic pattern of instrumental behavior irrespective of how the operant response was originally learned. Thus, investigations of reinforcement schedules have provided a great deal of information about the factors that control the maintenance and performance, rather than the learning, of instrumental behavior.

Investigation of the mechanisms of reinforcement that maintain instrumental responding is just as important for the understanding of behavior as investigation of the mechanisms that promote the learning of new responses. More of an animal's behavior is devoted to repeating responses that were previously learned than to acquiring new responses. Humans also spend much of their day doing highly familiar tasks. Conditions of reinforcement that maintain behavior are of great concern to managers, who have to make sure their employees continue to perform the jobs that they learned earlier. Even teachers are more often concerned with encouraging the occurrence of already learned responses than with teaching new responses. Many students who do poorly in school know how to do their homework and how to study but simply choose not to. Teachers can use information about the effects of reinforcement schedules to motivate more frequent studying.

Delay of reinforcement

One of the first parameters of the response/reinforcer relation to be studied was the time between the response and the reinforcer. Early investigations of this variable were performed with mazes, such as the T maze, in which the instrumental response consists in making the correct turn. Groups of rats were used, each group receiving a different delay of reinforcement. Reinforcement was delayed by confining the rat to a compartment after it made its choice but before it was allowed to enter the goal box with the reinforcer. Results

---

Box 7.1. Praise: Bridging the Delay-of-Reinforcement Interval

Perhaps the greatest hindrance to the application of instrumental-conditioning principles in various training situations is that it is often inconvenient to deliver reinforcers immediately after occurrences of the desired response. Trainers of animal circus acts often carry pieces of food with them during the performance to reinforce correct responses. However, they cannot always deliver the treats, because the animal may be too far away, or eating the treat may distract the animal from making the next response. Therefore, it is not uncommon for the trainers to use verbal praise. Words such as *good* and *nice* can be conditioned to serve as conditioned reinforcers for a variety of animals by saying the words whenever the animals are given pieces of food. The praise can then be used to provide immediate reinforcement and bridge the interval between performance of the desired response and the actual delivery of the primary reward. This is one reason trainers frequently talk to their animals during a performance.

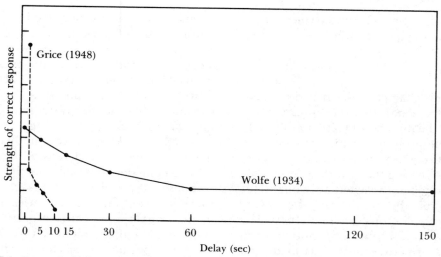

Figure 7.1. Strength of the correct response as a function of delay of reinforcement in two experiments (Wolfe, 1934; Grice, 1948).

from two such studies are shown in Figure 7.1. In both experiments, learning was best with no delay of reinforcement, and it gradually decreased with longer delays. The data from Wolfe (1934) show a much flatter gradient than the data from Grice (1948). Learning occurred with extensive delays in Wolfe's experiment, although quite slowly. What accounts for this difference between the two studies?

Grice's experiment was specifically designed to eliminate cues other than the reinforcer that might signal that food would be forthcoming after a correct response. Such cues are called **secondary** or **conditioned reinforcers.** These may be such things as the position of the food cup in the maze (right or left), differential lighting over the arm of the maze that contains the food, or even the proprioceptive cues from making a right or left turn. In Grice's experiment, the correct choice was to go to the white arm of the maze. However, the white arm was sometimes on the right and sometimes on the left, so that the secondary cues from going right or left could not be used to find food. Under these conditions, learning was severely retarded with delays of reinforcement greater

than .5 sec. From results such as these, investigators have concluded that the emergence of an instrumental response requires the immediate delivery of the reinforcer in the absence of secondary cues. (For a further discussion of secondary reinforcement, see Chapter 9.)

Simple schedules of intermittent reinforcement

Another important factor that determines the learning and performance of instrumental responses is the frequency of reinforcement. If the subject is reinforced after each occurrence of the instrumental response, a **continuous reinforcement schedule** is said to be in effect. Continuous reinforcement is rarely found in nature. It is much more common for occurrences of instrumental responses to result in reinforcement only some of the time. Situations in which responding is reinforced only some of the time are said to involve a **partial** or **intermittent reinforcement schedule.** There are many ways to arrange for responding to be reinforced intermittently. We begin with a discussion of schedules that use relatively simple rules for determining which responses will be reinforced.

Ratio schedules

The defining characteristic of **ratio schedules** of reinforcement is that reinforcement depends only on the number of responses the subject makes. The program relating responses to reinforcement requires merely counting the responses and delivering the reinforcer each time the required number is reached. One might, for example, deliver the reinforcer after every tenth lever-press response in rats. In such a schedule, there would be a fixed ratio between the number of responses the subject made and the number of reinforcers it got. (There would always be ten responses per reinforcer.) This makes such a procedure a **fixed-ratio schedule.** More specifically, the procedure would be called a fixed-ratio 10 schedule (abbreviated FR 10). Fixed-ratio schedules may be found in daily life wherever a fixed number of responses are always required for reinforcement. The delivery person who always has to visit the same number of houses to complete his or her route is working on a fixed-ratio schedule. Piecework in factories is usually set up on a fixed-ratio schedule: workers get paid for every so many "widgets" they put together. Flights of stairs provide another example. In a given staircase, you always have to go up the same number of steps to reach the next landing.

Strictly speaking, a continuous reinforcement schedule is also a fixed-ratio schedule. Reinforcement depends only on the number of responses the subject makes. Furthermore, there is a fixed ratio of responses to reinforcements: one response per reinforcer. Therefore, continuous reinforcement is a fixed ratio of 1.

On a continuous reinforcement schedule, subjects typically respond at a steady and moderate rate. Pauses in responding are not predictable, if they occur at all. A rat, for example, will press a lever steadily at first and then slow down as it becomes satiated. A very different pattern of responding occurs when an intermittent fixed-ratio schedule of reinforcement is in effect. Figure 7.2 provides a sample cumulative record. The delivery of reward is indicated on

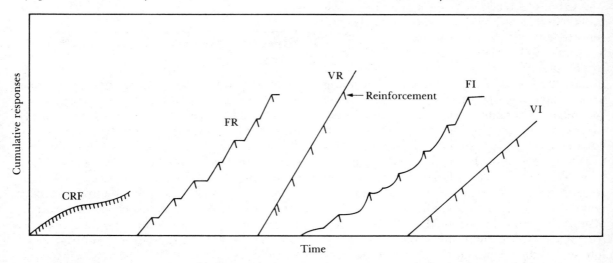

Figure 7.2. Sample cumulative records of lever pressing on various simple reinforcement schedules. Horizontal displacements in the records indicate passage of time. Vertical displacements indicate cumulative responses. Hatch marks indicate times when the reinforcer is delivered. CRF is the continuous reinforcement; FR, the fixed ratio; VR, the variable ratio; FI, the fixed interval; and VI, the variable interval. (Hypothetical data.)

the record by the small downward deflections of the pen, or hatch marks. As you can see, the animal stops responding after each reinforcement. However, when the subject resumes responding, it responds at a high and steady rate. Thus, responding on a fixed-ratio schedule has two characteristics. The zero rate of responding that occurs just after reinforcement is called the **postreinforcement pause.** The high and steady rate of responding that completes each ratio requirement is called the **ratio run.** If the ratio requirement is increased a little (from FR 15 to FR 30, for example), the rate of responding during the ratio run usually does not change. However, with higher ratio requirements the postreinforcement pause is longer. If the ratio requirement is suddenly increased a great deal (from FR 15 to FR 100, for example), the animal is likely to pause periodically before the completion of the ratio requirement. This effect is called *ratio strain.* In extreme cases ratio strain may be so great that the animal stops responding altogether.

The postreinforcement pause in fixed-ratio schedules is a result of the predictably large number of responses required for the next delivery of the reinforcer. Given enough experience with a fixed-ratio procedure, the subject learns that after reinforcement, it always has to make a certain number of responses to receive the next reinforcer. This predictability can be disrupted by varying the number of responses required for reinforcement from one occasion to the next. Such a procedure is still a ratio schedule because reinforcement still depends on how many responses the subject makes. However, a different number of responses is counted for the delivery of each reward. Such a procedure is called a **variable-ratio schedule.** We may, for example, require the subject to make 10 responses to earn the first reward, 13 to earn the second reward, 7 for the next one, and so on. The numerical value of a variable-ratio schedule indicates the average number of responses required per reinforcement. Thus, our procedure would be a variable-ratio 10

schedule (abbreviated VR 10). Because the number of responses required for reinforcement is no longer predictable, there are no predictable pauses in the rate of response on a variable-ratio schedule. Rather, the subject responds at a fairly steady rate until it becomes satiated (see Figure 7.2).

Variable-ratio schedules are found in daily life wherever an unpredictable amount of effort is required to obtain a reinforcer. Each time a custodian goes into a room on his rounds, he knows that some amount of cleaning will be necessary, but he does not know exactly how dirty the room will be. Gamblers playing a slot machine are also responding on a variable-ratio schedule. They always have to play the machine a certain number of times to win. However, they never know how many plays will produce the winning combination. Variable-ratio schedules are also common in sports. A certain number of strokes are always required to finish a hole in golf, for example. However, players can never be sure how many strokes they will need to use when they start.

Interval schedules

Reinforcement does not always depend solely on the amount of effort or the number of responses the subject makes. Sometimes responses are reinforced only if they occur at certain times. **Interval schedules** of reinforcement illustrate this type of situation. In a simple interval schedule, a response is reinforced only if it occurs more than a set amount of time after the last reinforcer delivery. In a **fixed-interval schedule,** the set time is constant from one occasion to the next. Consider, for example, a fixed-interval 2-min schedule (FI 2 min) for lever pressing in rats. Animals exposed to this schedule always get reinforced for the first response they make after 2 min has passed since the last reward. Because responses that occur shortly after a reward are never reinforced, animals on a fixed-interval schedule learn to wait to make the instrumental response until the end of the fixed 2-min interval. The resulting pattern of responding is somewhat complicated (see Figure 7.2). Very few responses occur at the beginning of the interval after a reward. As the time for the availability of the next reinforcer draws closer, the response rate rapidly increases. The animal responds at a high rate at the end of the 2-min interval and therefore usually receives the reinforcer as soon as the 2 min is finished. There is a curve in the cumulative record as the animal speeds up responding toward the end of the interval. The pattern of response that develops with fixed-interval reinforcement schedules is accordingly called the **fixed-interval scallop.**

It is important to realize that a fixed-interval schedule of reinforcement does not ensure that the animal will be reinforced at fixed intervals of time. Thus, rats on an FI 2-min schedule do not automatically receive the reinforcer every 2 min. Instrumental responses are required for the reinforcer in interval schedules, just as in ratio schedules. The interval only determines when the reinforcer becomes available. In order to receive the reinforcer when it becomes available, the subject still has to make the instrumental response.

Fixed-interval schedules are found in situations in which a fixed amount of time is required to prepare or set up the reinforcer. Consider, for example, washing clothes in an automatic washer. A certain amount of time is required to complete the wash cycle. No matter how many times you open the washing machine before the required amount of time has passed, you will not be reinforced with clean clothes. Once the cycle is finished, the reinforcer becomes available, and you can pick up your clean clothes any time after that. Making Jell-O provides another example. After the gelatin is mixed in hot water, it has to chill for a certain amount of time to gel. To be able to eat the Jell-O, you have to wait until it is ready. No matter how many times you check the refrigerator before the required amount of time has

elapsed, the Jell-O will not have the proper consistency. If you are particularly eager to eat the Jell-O, the rate of your opening the refrigerator door will be similar to an FI scallop.

Like ratio schedules, interval schedules can be unpredictable. In a **variable-interval schedule,** the reinforcer is provided for the first response that occurs after a variable amount of time has elapsed since the previous reward. We may set up a schedule, for example, in which one reward is delivered when the animal makes a response more than 4 min after the last reward, the next reinforcer is given for the first response that occurs more than 5 min after that, and the next one is given for the first response that occurs at least 3 min later. In this procedure, the average interval that has to pass before successive rewards become available is 4 min. Therefore, the procedure is a variable-interval 4-min schedule, abbreviated VI 4 min. Like variable-ratio schedules, variable-interval schedules maintain steady and stable rates of responding without pauses (see Figure 7.2).

Variable-interval schedules are found in situations in which an unpredictable amount of time is required to prepare or set up the reinforcer. If your mechanic cannot tell you when your car will be fixed, he has imposed a variable-interval schedule on you. You have to wait a certain amount of time before attempts to get your car will be reinforced. However, the amount of time involved is unpredictable. A taxi dispatcher is also controlled by variable-interval schedules. After a cab has completed a trip, it is available for another assignment, and the dispatcher will be reinforced for sending the cab on another errand. However, once an assignment is made, the cab is unavailable for an unpredictable period, during which time the dispatcher cannot use the same cab for other trips.

In simple interval schedules, once the reward becomes available, the subject can receive the reward any time thereafter, provided it makes the required response. On a fixed-interval

2-min schedule, for example, reward becomes available 2 min after the previous reinforcement. If the animal responds at exactly this time, it will be reinforced. If it waits to respond for 90 min after the previous reinforcement, it will still get the reward. Outside the laboratory, it is more common for reinforcers to become available for only limited periods in interval schedules. Consider, for example, a dormitory cafeteria. Meals are served only at certain times. Therefore, going to the cafeteria is reinforced only if you wait long enough after the last meal. However, once the next meal becomes available, you have a limited amount of time in which to get it. This kind of restriction on how long reward remains available is called a **limited**

Box 7.2. The Postreinforcement Pause, Procrastination, and Cramming for Exams

The postreinforcement pause that occurs in fixed-ratio and fixed-interval schedules is a very common human experience. In fixed-ratio schedules, the pause occurs because a predictably large number of responses are always required to produce the next reward. In a sense, the animal is "procrastinating" before embarking on the large effort necessary for reinforcement. Similar procrastination is legendary in human behavior. Consider, for example, a term in which you have several papers to write. You are likely to work on one term paper at a time. However, when you have completed one paper, you probably will not start working on the next one right away. Rather, there will be a postreinforcement pause. After completing a large project, people tend to take some time off before starting the next task. In fact, procrastination between tasks or before the start of a new job is the rule rather than the exception. Laboratory results provide a suggestion for overcoming such procrastination. Fixed-ratio-schedule performance in the laboratory indicates that once animals begin to respond on a ratio run, they respond at a high and steady rate until they complete the ratio requirement. This suggests that if somehow you got yourself to start on a job, chances are you would not find it difficult to keep working to finish it. Only the beginning is hard. One technique that works pretty well in getting started is to tell yourself that you will begin with only a small part of the new job. If you are trying to write a paper, tell yourself that you will write only one paragraph to start with. You may very well find that once you have completed the first paragraph, it will be easier to write the second one, then the one after that, and so on. If you are procrastinating about spring cleaning, do not think about doing the entire job. Instead, start with a small part of it, like washing the kitchen floor. The rest will then come more easily.

On a fixed-interval schedule, postreinforcement pauses may occur because once a reward has been delivered, there is no chance that another will be available for some time. Scheduling of tests in college courses has important similarities to the basic fixed-interval schedule. In many courses there are few tests, and the tests are evenly distributed during the term. There may be a midterm and a final exam. The pattern of studying that such a schedule maintains is very similar to what is observed in the laboratory. There is no studying at all at the beginning of the semester or just after the midterm exam. Many students begin to study only a week or so before each test, and the rate of studying rapidly increases as the day of the test approaches. Studying at the beginning of the term or after the midterm exam is not reinforced by the receipt of good grades on tests at that time. Therefore, students do not study at these points in the term. More frequent studying can be motivated by giving more frequent tests. The highest rate of responding would occur if unannounced tests were given at unpredictable times, in a manner analogous to a variable-interval schedule. This is the well-known "pop quiz" technique.

hold. Limited-hold restrictions can be added to both fixed-interval and variable-interval schedules.

Comparison of ratio and interval schedules

There are striking similarities between the patterns of responding maintained by simple ratio and interval schedules. As we have seen, both fixed-ratio and fixed-interval schedules produce a predictable pause in responding after each reinforcement. In contrast, variable-ratio and variable-interval schedules both maintain steady rates of responding, without predictable pauses. Despite these similarities, there is a very important difference betwen ratio and interval schedules. This involves the extent to which the occurrence of responding determines how often the subjects are reinforced. A very strong and direct relation exists between the rate of response and the frequency of reinforcement in ratio schedules. Because the only thing that determines whether the subject will be reinforced is the number of responses it makes, the rate of responding totally determines the frequency of reinforcement. By responding more often, the subject can always earn the reinforcer more often. This relation makes ratio schedules extremely motivating. The subject is driven by the schedule to respond at high rates because each response gets it closer to the payoff.

In interval schedules the rate of response does not determine the frequency of reinforcement in the same manner as in ratio schedules. Consider, for example, a fixed-interval 2-min schedule. Each reward becomes available 2 min after the last reward. If the subject responds right away when the reward is set up, the reward is delivered and the next cycle begins. However, no matter how frequently the subject responds, it will never be reinforced any more often than once every 2 min. Therefore, the interval schedule sets a maximum limit on the frequency of reinforcers the subject can earn. In the FI 2-min example, the limit is 30 reinforcers per hour. If the subject does not re-

spond as soon as each reward becomes available, it will not earn reinforcers as often as possible. Therefore, the rate of responding determines the frequency of reinforcement to some extent. However, the delivery of reward depends more on exactly *when* the subject responds than on how often it responds.

Because the rate of responding does not entirely determine the frequency of reinforcement in interval schedules, such schedules typically do not motivate as high response rates as ratio schedules, even if subjects receive the same number of reinforcements in the two types of schedules. In an important experiment on this topic, Reynolds (1968) compared the rate of key pecking in pigeons reinforced on variable-ratio and variable-interval schedules. Two pigeons were trained to peck the response key for food reinforcement. One of the birds was reinforced on a variable-ratio schedule. Therefore, for this animal the frequency of reinforcement was entirely determined by its rate of response. The other animal was reinforced on a variable-interval schedule. However, the availability of the reinforcer for this animal was controlled by the behavior of the other pigeon. Each time the variable-ratio pigeon was just one response short of the required number, the experimenter reinforced the next response that each subject made. Thus, the variable-ratio bird controlled the variable-interval schedule for its partner. This yoking procedure ensured that the frequency of reinforcement was virtually identical for the two subjects.

Figure 7.3 shows the pattern of responding exhibited by each subject. Even though the two subjects received the same frequency of reinforcers, they behaved very differently. The pigeon reinforced on the variable-ratio schedule responded at a much higher rate than the pigeon reinforced on the variable-interval schedule. The variable-ratio schedule motivated much more vigorous instrumental behavior.

Ratio schedules motivate higher rates of responding than interval schedules outside the laboratory as well. Doctors, for example, usually work on a schedule that has very strong ratio characteristics. The more patients they see, the more money they make. Every patient whom they refuse to see represents the loss of a certain amount of income. This direct relation between rate of response and rate of reinforcement may contribute to their diligence. Because ratio characteristics in a schedule of reinforcement provide a strong impetus for responding, such schedules are usually strongly resisted by employees. In a labor/management negotiation, management is likely to want to build ratio characteristics into the contract, whereas represen-

tatives of labor will insist that interval-schedule characteristics be instituted.

Response-rate schedules of reinforcement

As we have seen, ratio schedules of reinforcement encourage subjects to respond at higher rates than interval schedules. However, neither schedule requires that subjects perform at a specified rate in order to get reinforced. Therefore, differences in the rate of response ob-

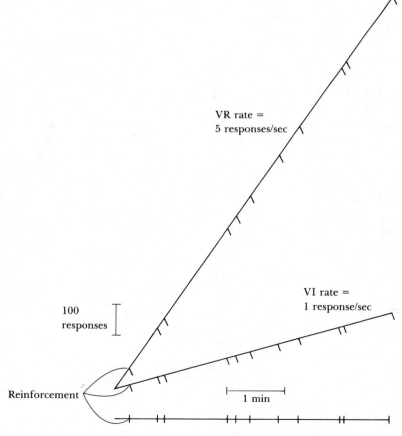

Figure 7.3. Cumulative records for two pigeons, one reinforced on a variable-ratio (VR) schedule and the other yoked to it on a variable-interval (VI) schedule. Although subjects received the same reinforcements at about the same time, the VR bird responded five times as fast as the VI bird. *(From Reynolds, 1968.)*

served are indirect effects of the schedules. In contrast, other types of procedures specifically require that subjects respond at a particular rate to get reinforced. Such procedures are called **response-rate schedules** of reinforcement.

In response-rate schedules, whether a response is reinforced depends on how soon it occurs after the preceding response. The interval between successive responses is called the **interresponse time,** abbreviated **IRT.** A reinforcement schedule could be set up, for example, in which a response is reinforced only if it occurs sooner than 5 sec after the preceding response. If the subject makes a response every 5 sec, its rate of response will be 12 per min. Thus, the schedule provides reinforcement if the rate of response is 12/min or greater. The subject will not be reinforced if its rate of response is less than 12/min. As you might suspect, this procedure encourages responding at high rates. Therefore, it is called **differential reinforcement of high rates,** or **DRH.**

In DRH schedules, a response is reinforced only if it occurs *less than* a certain amount of time after the preceding response. The opposite result is achieved if a response is reinforced only if it occurs *more than* a certain amount of time after the previous response. This type of procedure is called **differential reinforcement of low rates,** abbreviated **DRL.** As you might suspect, DRL schedules encourage subjects to respond slowly.

Response-rate schedules are found outside the laboratory in situations that require particular rates of responding. An assembly line provides a good example. The speed of movement of the line dictates the rate of response for the workers. If an employee responds more slowly than the specified rate, he or she will not be reinforced and may, in fact, get fired. However, workers have to be careful not to work too rapidly, because of social pressure imposed by fellow workers. Those who respond at very high rates are likely to earn the enmity of their peers. Social pressure in some work situations differentially reinforces low rates of responding.

Box 7.3. DRL and the Cure of Hysterical Blindness

In an interesting clinical case study, Brady and Lind (1961) used a DRL schedule to initiate the treatment of hysterical blindness. Hysterical symptoms are physical disabilities that occur in the absence of physical pathology. Although no physical cause can be found, the symptoms can be as real to the patient as those arising from physical disease. In this case a 40-year-old man became blind. No physical cause could be found. However, from the case history, it appeared that the blindness enabled him to escape from a difficult life situation involving, among other things, a demanding wife and difficulties at work. Traditional forms of therapy had been unsuccessful.

Brady and Lind instituted treatment sessions in which the patient was reinforced for pushing a button on a DRL schedule. If he pushed the button every 18 to 23 sec, he received praise and tangible rewards. After several sessions, a light was introduced that signaled the end of the 18-sec wait period. If the patient made use of the visual cue, he could greatly improve his performance and his reinforcement rate. At first the patient became agitated and tried to ignore the light. However, as the differential-reinforcement schedule was maintained, he gradually started to use the visual cue. After several sessions, he was able to say that he could see the light. This acknowledgment appears to have been a breakthrough in the case. Once the patient's functional sight returned, he was able to benefit from more traditional types of therapy to alleviate the problems that had made him hysterically blind.

Concurrent schedules: The study of response choice

The reinforcement schedules we have discussed thus far have involved an analysis of the relation between occurrences of a particular response and reinforcement of that response. However, the study of situations in which only one response is being measured is not likely to provide us with a complete understanding of behavior. Animal and human behavior involves a great deal more than just the repetition of individual responses. Even in a simple situation such as a Skinner box, organisms engage in a wide variety of activities and are continually making choices among the various responses that they are able to perform. Furthermore, the occurrence of a particular response very much depends on the availability of other response alternatives. A teenager may trim the neighbor's grass for $15 if the sky is overcast and his friends are out of town. However, if the weather is good and his friends are home, he is more likely to spend the afternoon at the beach with them. We are constantly having to make choices about what to do. Should we go to the movies or stay at home and study? Should we go shopping tonight or watch television tonight and go shopping tomorrow? Understanding the mechanisms of response choice is fundamental to the understanding of behavior because the choices organisms make determine the occurrence of individual responses.

The choices available to animals and people can be very complex. For example, a person may have a choice of 12 different responses (reading the newspaper, watching television, going for a walk, playing with the dog, and the like), each of which produces a different type of reinforcer according to a different reinforcement schedule. Analyzing all the factors that may control the individual's behavior in such a situation would be formidable, if not impossible. Therefore, psychologists have begun experimental investigations of the mechanisms of choice by studying simpler situations. The simplest choice situation is one in which the subject has two response alternatives and each response is followed by a reinforcer according to some schedule of reinforcement.

Historically, much of the research on choice behavior has been conducted using mazes, particularly the T maze. As noted in Chapter 6, choice can be measured by the frequency with which the subjects turn to the left or the right. In a classic paper entitled "The Determiners of Behavior at a Choice Point," Tolman (1938) advanced the argument that all behavior is essentially choice behavior. The choice may be one response or another or, more simply, responding or not responding. Tolman argued that the determinants of behavior (such as magnitude of reward available on each side) advanced by his theory likewise apply to choice (see Woodworth & Schlosberg, 1954, for a good review of the choice experiments using T mazes).

More recent approaches to the study of choice use Skinner boxes equipped with two manipulanda, such as two response levers. In the typical experiment, responding on each manipulandum is reinforced on some schedule of reinforcement. The two schedules are in effect at the same time, and the subject is free to switch from one manipulandum to the other. This type of procedure is called a **concurrent schedule of reinforcement.** Concurrent schedules of reinforcement allow for continuous measures of choice because the subject is free to change back and forth between the response alternatives. Preference (choice) is measured by the rates of response on each manipulandum or the time spent responding on each.

Figure 7.4 shows an example of a concurrent schedule for pigeons. The experimental chamber has two response keys. If the pigeon pecks the key on the left, it receives food reinforcers according to a variable-interval 60-sec schedule. Pecks on the right key produce food reinforcers according to a fixed-ratio 10 schedule. The animal is free to peck either response key at any time. The point of the experiment is to see how the animal distributes its pecks on the two keys and how the schedule of reinforcement on each key influences its choices.

On some concurrent schedules, particularly those involving interval-schedule components, the pigeon may be reinforced for the very first peck it makes after switching from one key to the other. This "accidental" reinforcement may

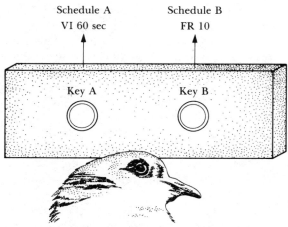

Schedule A
VI 60 sec

Schedule B
FR 10

Key A

Key B

Figure 7.4. Diagram of a concurrent schedule. Pecks on key A are reinforced according to a VI 60-sec schedule of reinforcement. Pecks on key B are reinforced according to an FR 10 schedule of reinforcement.

encourage the subject to change frequently from one key to the other. To assess the effects of concurrent schedules without this reinforcement of switching, experimenters often add the constraint that the first one or two pecks after a switch will not be reinforced. This feature is called a **change-over delay (COD)** because it delays reinforcement after a change from one response key to the other.

Measures of response choice

The animal's choice in a concurrent schedule is reflected in the distribution of its behavior between two response alternatives. This can be measured in several ways. One common technique is to calculate the **relative rate of response** on each alternative. The relative rate of response on key A, for example, is calculated by dividing the response rate on key A by the total rate of response (rate on key A plus rate on key B): $R_A/(R_A + R_B)$, where R_A is the rate of response on key A and R_B is the rate of response on key B. If the subject pecks equally often on the two response keys, this ratio will be .5. If the rate of response on key A is greater than the

rate of response on key B, the ratio will be greater than .5. If the rate of response on key A is less than the rate of response on key B, the ratio will be less than .5. The relative rate of response on key B can be calculated in a comparable manner.

The matching law

As you might suspect, the distribution of the subject's behavior between the two response alternatives is greatly influenced by the reinforcement schedule for each alternative. If the same reinforcement schedule is available for each response alternative, as in a concurrent VI 60-sec VI 60-sec procedure, the pigeon will peck the two keys equally often. The relative rate of response for pecks on each side will be .5. This result is intuitively reasonable. If the pigeon spent all its time pecking on one side, it would receive only the reinforcers programmed for that side. The subject can get more reinforcers by pecking on both sides. Since the reinforcement schedule available on each side is the same, there is no advantage in spending more time on one side than on the other.

By responding equally often on each side of a concurrent VI 60-sec VI 60-sec schedule, the subject will also earn reinforcers equally often on each side. The **relative rate of reinforcement** earned for each response alternative can be calculated in a manner comparable to the relative rate of response. For example, the relative rate of reinforcement for alternative A is the rate of reinforcement of response A divided by the total rate of reinforcement (the sum of the rate of reward earned on side A plus the rate of reward earned on side B). This is expressed in the formula $r_A/(r_A + r_B)$, where r_A and r_B represent the rates of reinforcement earned on each response alternative. On a concurrent VI 60-sec VI 60-sec schedule, the relative rate of reinforcement for each response alternative will be .5 because the subject earns rewards equally often on each side.

Effects of variations in the concurrent schedule. As we have seen, in the concurrent VI 60-sec VI 60-sec schedule, both the relative rate of response and the relative rate of reinforcement for each response alternative are .5. Thus, the relative rate of response is equal to the relative rate of reinforcement. Will this equality also occur if the two response alternatives are not reinforced according to the same schedule in the concurrent procedure? This important question was asked by Herrnstein (1961). Herrnstein studied the distribution of responses on various concurrent VI VI schedules in which the maximum total rate of reinforcement the subject could earn was 40 per hour. However, depending on the exact value of each VI schedule, different proportions of the total 40 rewards/hour could be obtained by

each response alternative. For example, with a concurrent VI 6-min VI 2-min schedule, a VI 6-min schedule is in effect on the right key and a VI 2-min schedule on the left key. A maximum of 10 reinforcers per hour could be obtained by responding on the right, and a maximum of 30 reinforcers per hour could be obtained by responding on the left.

Herrnstein studied the effects of a wide variety of concurrent VI VI schedules. There was no constraint on which side the pigeons could peck. They could respond exclusively on one side if they chose, or they could distribute their pecks between the two sides in any proportion they chose. In fact, however, the pigeons distributed their responding in a uniform and predictable fashion. The results, summarized in Figure 7.5, indicate that the relative rate of re-

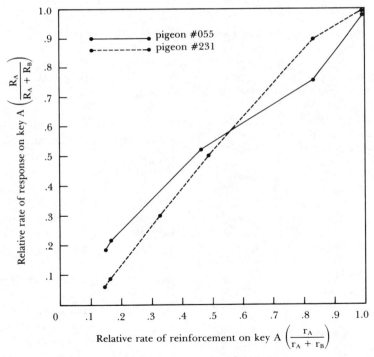

Figure 7.5. Results of two pigeons pecking on concurrent VI VI schedules. Each data point represents one combination of VI schedules whose combined reinforcement rate is 40 reinforcements per hour. Note that at each point the relative rate of response nearly equals (matches) the relative rate of reinforcement. *(From Herrnstein, 1961.)*

sponse on a given alternative was always very nearly equal to the relative rate of reinforcement earned on that alternative. If the pigeons earned a greater proportion of their reinforcers on alternative A, they made a greater proportion of their responses on alternative A. According to these results, *the relative rate of response on an alternative matches the relative rate of reinforcement for that alternative.* This relation has been found in many situations and has been considered a law of behavior. It is called the **matching law** and is expressed symbolically as follows:

$$\frac{R_A}{R_A + R_B} = \frac{r_A}{r_A + r_B}$$

where R_A and R_B are the rates of response on side A and side B, and r_A and r_B are the rates of reinforcement earned on each side. The matching law represents a fundamental fact about choice behavior and indicates that choices are not made capriciously but show a particular relation to rates of reinforcement.

Much of current research on operant conditioning is devoted to issues concerning the matching law. One reason for this interest is that the matching relation is found in a wide variety of situations and with every species that has been tested. Baum (1975), for example, investigated matching in human subjects responding in a signal-detection game. Each subject was seated in front of two screens. Target missiles were projected on each screen according to a variable-interval schedule. The subject could watch one screen or the other. If the subject was watching the screen when a missile appeared, he or she could score a " hit" by pressing a lever. Subjects were paid for the number of hits they made. Baum varied the values of the variable-interval schedules. He found that the time the subjects spent watching each screen matched the rate of hits (rewards) they received on that screen.

Box 7.4.   Matching in Social Interactions

Many social situations can be regarded as a concurrent schedule. Consider a party at which you are talking with several persons. Some things you say will be of interest to some of these persons, and they will respond with smiles, attention, and comments. Other persons may be less attentive to your conversation. The relative amounts of time you spend talking to various persons may very well depend on the relative levels of enthusiasm (reinforcement for conversation) they show. Two psychologists, Conger and Killeen (1974), tested this hypothesis in a social-psychology experiment. They told the subject of the experiment that he or she would be participating in a discussion with three other persons. The three others were in fact "confederates" of the experimenters. Two of the confederates were instructed to reinforce the subject's comments according to a certain schedule. Reinforcement consisted of positive comments and the like. The third confederate was present to keep the discussion moving. The researchers found that the behavior of the subject was consistent with the matching law. That is, the relative time spent talking to each confederate discussant matched the relative rate of reinforcement.

Extension of the matching law to simple reinforcement schedules.   If the matching law represents a fundamental fact about behavior, then it should also characterize responding on simple schedules of reinforcement. In a simple reinforcement schedule, only one response manipulandum is provided (such as a lever or a key), and the subject is reinforced for responses on this manipulandum according to some program. The matching law describes the distribution of responses among several alternatives. How can it be applied to single-response situations? As Herrnstein (1970) pointed out, even single-response situations can be considered to involve a choice. The choice is between making the specified response (bar pressing or pecking a key, for example) and engaging in other possible activities (grooming, walking around, pecking the floor, sniffing holes in the experimental chamber). Subjects receive explicit reinforcers programmed for occurrences of the specified operant response. In addition, they no doubt receive intrinsic rewards for the other activities in which they engage. Hence, the total reinforcement in the situation has to be considered to include the programmed rewards and the intrinsic rewards. This type of analysis permits application of the matching law to single-response reinforcement schedules. Consider R_A to represent the rate of the specified operant response in the schedule, R_O the rate of the animal's other activities, r_A the rate of the explicit programmed reinforcement, and r_O the rate of the intrinsic reinforcement for the other activities. The matching law for single-response situations may be stated as follows:

$$\frac{R_A}{R_A + R_O} = \frac{r_A}{r_A + r_O}$$

By mathematically fitting a variation of this equation to single-response data, Herrnstein provides evidence that the matching law holds in such situations.

Matching and the concept of reinforcement value. The distribution of responses organisms make matches not only the relative rates of reinforcement they earn for the response alternatives but also other features of reinforcement. Catania (1963), for example, varied the *amount* of reinforcement available for responding on each of two alternatives in a concurrent schedule. He found that the relative rates of response the subjects made on each alternative matched the relative magnitude of reinforcement they could earn on the alternatives. This relation may be expressed as

$$\frac{R_A}{R_A + R_B} = \frac{A_A}{A_A + A_B}$$

where R_A and R_B are the response rates on alternatives A and B, and A_A and A_B are the amounts of reward provided for responding on A and B, respectively. Matching has also been found with delays of reinforcement (Chung, 1965; Chung & Herrnstein, 1967). The relative rate of response for one of two alternatives matches the relative delay of reinforcement for responding on that alternative. The shorter the relative delay, the higher the relative response rate.

Such features of reinforcers as amount and delay can be considered aspects of the quality, or value, of the reinforcer. We can assume that subjects prefer reinforcers that occur frequently, are of a large amount, and are delivered with short delays. Accordingly, we may think of the matching law more generally as the matching of relative rates of response to the relative values of the alternative reinforcers. Furthermore, we could use relative rates of response to measure the relative values of reinforcers. Let us suppose that we want to find out whether two reinforcers are equal in value to the subject. Does John like chocolate ice cream as much as he likes vanilla? To answer this question, we have to look at how frequently John eats each flavor when given a choice. If 50% of the time he eats the chocolate and 50% of the time he eats the vanilla, we may conclude that the two flavors are of equal value for John. Similarly, two reinforcement schedules are said to be of equal value if the subject chooses to respond 50% of the time on each alternative when the two schedules are simultaneously available in a concurrent procedure. Because the relative values of reinforcers are determined by relative response rates, the relative values of reinforcers cannot be used to *explain* why subjects distribute their responses between alternative reinforcers in particular ways. Relative rates of response and relative values of reinforcers are just two sides of the same coin. They are reflections of the same basic behavior process involved in making choices (see Rachlin, 1971).

Matching and maximizing rates of reinforcement

If the relative values of reinforcers and the relative rates of response in a choice situation are reflections of the same behavioral process, is there some other factor that controls this basic choice process? This is the most important question in contemporary investigations of behavioral choice. The answer is not yet clear. However, many investigators have considered what can be called the **maximizing hypothesis.** According to this hypothesis, subjects in a choice situation distribute their responses so as to receive the maximum possible frequency of reinforcement for the number of responses they perform. That is, they switch back and forth between the response alternatives so as to get as many reinforcers as possible.

An early explanation of matching as maximizing was proposed by Shimp (1966, 1969). Shimp suggested that the subject switches from one schedule to another so as to maximize the immediate rates of reinforcement. He proposed, and found some experimental support for, the idea that the subject switches from one schedule to the other as the probability of reinforcement for the alternate schedule increases. Consider a pigeon on a concurrent VI VI schedule. As the pigeon pecks key A, the timer controlling the schedule for key B is still operating. The longer the pigeon stays on key A, the greater the probability is that the interval for key B has elapsed and the time for reinforcement is at hand. By switching, the pigeon picks up the reinforcer on key B. Now the longer it remains on key B, the more likely key A will be set for reinforcement. Shimp proposed that the matching relation is a by-product of the pigeon's prudent switching when the probability of reinforcement on the alternate schedule is high.

Attempts to substantiate matching as the result of such a molecular maximizing process have not as yet worked. Another approach is to look at maximizing over the entire session rather than from moment to moment. This approach appears to be more fruitful at present. The maximizing hypothesis applied to entire sessions was developed to explain observations of choice behavior in concurrent schedules involving ratio components. In concurrent ratio schedules, subjects rarely switch back and forth between the alternatives. Rather, they choose the ratio component that requires the fewest responses for reinforcement and respond only on this alternative. On a concurrent FR 20 FR 10 schedule, for example, the subject is likely to respond only on the FR 10 alternative. In this way it maximizes the rate of reinforcement it receives. This choice is intuitively reasonable. Why should anyone work on the leaner FR 20 schedule? If a concurrent FR VI schedule is used, the subject's behavior will be similarly biased. If the ratio is sufficiently small, the subject will spend more time responding on the ratio schedule than on the VI schedule. Some time, however, will be spent on the VI schedule. The longer the subject works on the FR schedule, the greater is the probability that sufficient time has elapsed to make reward available on the VI schedule. Therefore, to maximize the number of reinforcers it gets, the subject should respond on the VI schedule once in a while. In contrast, if the ratio schedule requires a great many responses per reinforcer, the subject will bias its responding toward the VI schedule to maximize the number of reinforcers it gets.

Feedback functions.   To empirically evaluate the maximizing hypothesis, one has to determine whether subjects in choice situations in fact receive the maximum rate of reinforcement. This requires first finding out the maximum rate of reinforcement possible for various response rates. Obviously, this will depend on the schedule of reinforcement. The relation between rate of response and the rate of reinforcement for a given schedule is called a **feedback function.** For a ratio schedule it is very easy to determine the rate of reinforcement for a given rate of response. Consider, for example, a fixed-ratio 10 reinforcement schedule. The subject gets reinforced for every tenth response. Therefore, the rate of reinforcement will always be 1/10 of the rate of response. This is true for all possible response rates. Therefore, the feedback function for an FR 10 schedule is given by the equation r = .10R, where r is the rate of reinforcement and R is the rate of response.

Specifying the feedback function for interval schedules is much more difficult. Consider, for example, a variable-interval schedule. Subjects typically respond much more often than what is actually necessary in such a procedure. If the pigeon had extrasensory perception (ESP) and knew when the reinforcer became available each time, it would need to make only one response to earn each reinforcer. The rate of reinforcement would equal the response rate. Evidently, from the behavior of pigeons, we can conclude that if they have ESP, they do not use it. The rate of reinforcement on variable-interval schedules is much less than the rate of responding. Although we know that much, it is impossible to specify the relation between response rate and reinforcement rate as precisely for interval schedules as for ratio schedules. The problem is that the delivery of reward depends a great deal on exactly when the responses occur, not just on the overall response rate. If the subject makes a lot of responses just after each reward, it will receive few rewards for a high response rate. In contrast, if it waits after each reward and then spaces out its responding more evenly, it will earn many more rewards for the same overall high response rate. These characteristics make it impossible to specify the maximum rate of reinforcement possible for a given response rate. The rate of reinforcement may be very high, very low, or anywhere in between, depending on exactly how the responses are distributed.

The relation between responding and reinforcement is even more complicated in concurrent schedules. Here we have to consider the distribution of responses between the two alternatives and also the rates of reinforcement that this distribution produces. Since we cannot specify the feedback function, it is difficult to say whether maximizing is achieved. Various researchers have tried different approaches to this problem. For example, Rachlin, Green, Kagel, and Battalio (1976) used a computer to simulate responses on many concurrent VI VI schedules. The computer was programmed to distribute responses between two alternatives in various ways. The number of reinforcers that resulted from each distribution of responses was measured. Interestingly, response distributions that produced the greatest number of reinforcers also satisfied the matching law. This outcome suggests that maximizing may indeed underlie the matching phenomenon.

Matching and the law of effect. Thus far, research has not yet resolved whether matching is a product of maximizing or is a fundamental behavior process that does not result from more elementary principles. Nevertheless, matching experiments clearly indicate that organisms are highly sensitive to the relation between the responses they make and the reinforcers they receive in return. Research on matching has provided us with a modern revision of the law of effect: organisms adjust their behavior according to the consequences of behavior so that the relative rates of responding equal the relative rates of reinforcement. Exactly how this adjustment takes place is as yet unclear. One cannot help being amazed that organisms are sensitive to the relation between their behavior and its consequences in ways that still confound scientists after the decades of research Thorndike started.

Concurrent chained schedules: The study of complex choice

In the choice situations described above, animals had two response alternatives and could switch from one to the other at any time. Many choice situations outside the laboratory are of this type. If you are eating a dinner of roast beef, vegetables, and mashed potatoes with gravy, you can switch from one food to another at any time during the meal. You can similarly switch back and forth between radio stations you listen to or parts of the newspaper you read. However, other situations involve much more complex choices. Choosing one alternative may make other alternatives unavailable, and the choice may involve assessing complex, long-range goals. Should you go to college and get a degree in engineering or start in a full-time job without a college degree? One cannot switch back and forth between these two alternatives frequently. Furthermore, to make the decision, you need to consider more than merely whether you enjoy taking engineering courses more or less than you enjoy holding a job. This choice also involves long-range goals. A degree in engineering may enable you to get eventually a higher-paying job, but it may require significant economic sacrifices initially. Getting a job would enable you to make money sooner, but in the long run you might not be able to earn as much money.

Obviously, we cannot conduct experiments that directly involve complex choices such as choosing between college and employment. However, simplified analogous questions may be posed to laboratory animals. For example, does a pigeon prefer to work on an FR 10 schedule of reinforcement for 15 min, or does it prefer to work on a VI 60-sec schedule for the same amount of time? Answers to such questions can be obtained with the use of **concurrent chained schedules of reinforcement.** A concurrent chained schedule involves at least two components (see Figure 7.6). In the first component, the subject is allowed to choose between two alternatives by making one of two responses. In the example diagramed in Figure 7.6, the pigeon makes its choice by pecking either response key A or response key B. Pecking key A produces alternative A, the opportunity to peck key A for 15 min on an FR 10 schedule of reinforcement. If the pigeon pecks key B at the beginning of the cycle, it thereby produces alternative B, which is the opportunity to peck key B for 15 min on a VI 60-sec schedule. Re-

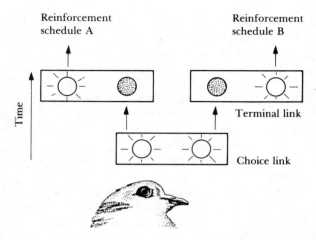

Figure 7.6. Diagram of a concurrent chained schedule. Pecking key A in the choice link puts into effect reinforcement schedule A in the terminal link. Pecking key B in the choice link puts into effect reinforcement schedule B in the terminal link.

sponding on either key A or key B during the initial component of the schedule does not produce reinforcement. The opportunity for reinforcement occurs only after the initial choice has been made and the pigeon has produced one or the other terminal components.

The pattern of responding that occurs in the terminal component of a concurrent chained schedule is characteristic of whatever schedule of reinforcement is in effect during that component. In our example, if the pigeon has produced alternative A, its pattern of pecking during the terminal component will be similar to the usual response pattern in FR 10 schedules. If the pigeon has produced alternative B, its pattern of pecking during the terminal component will be characteristic of a VI 60-sec schedule.

The animal's choice between the schedules of reinforcement in effect in the terminal components of a concurrent chained schedule is measured by the proportions in which it chooses key A and key B during the initial choice component. Research has shown that the choice behavior is largely determined by the overall reinforcement characteristics of each of the terminal components. The pigeon will show a preference for the terminal schedule that results in more frequent or greater reinforcement. In concurrent chained schedules of punishment, the pigeon will prefer the terminal component that has the least frequent punishment. The concurrent-chained-schedule method can be used to determine how various aspects of reinforcement combine to influence choice behavior.

An interesting application of a concurrent chained schedule is the experimental investigation of self-control. As every dieter knows, self-control is often a matter of choosing the greater delayed reward (being thin) over the immediate smaller reward (eating the piece of cake). When the piece of cake is there in front of you, it is very difficult to choose the delayed reward. Rachlin and Green (1972) set up a laboratory analogue of self-control with pigeons. When given a direct choice between an immediate, small reward or a delayed, large reward, pigeons often chose the small, immediate reward. However, under certain circumstances they could be trained to exhibit self-control. The basic concurrent chained schedule used in this research is shown in Figure 7.7. In the terminal components of the schedule, responding was rewarded by either immediate access to a small amount of grain (alternative A) or access

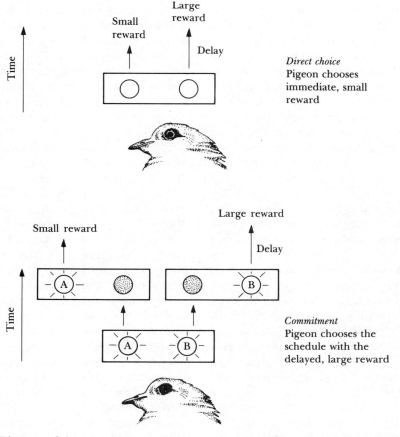

Figure 7.7. Diagram of the experiment by Rachlin and Green (1972) on self-control. Top panel shows the direct-choice procedure. Bottom panel shows the concurrent chained procedure.

to a large amount of grain that was delayed by 4 sec (alternative B). The pigeons could choose between these two alternatives by pecking either key A or key B during the initial component of the schedule.

Under what circumstances did the pigeons show self-control? Everyone who diets knows that it is easier to refuse a piece of cake that is to be eaten at tomorrow's luncheon than to refuse one that is to be eaten in the next few minutes. A similar effect occurred in the pigeons. The subjects were more likely to choose the delayed large reward over the immediate small reward if the terminal components of the concurrent chained schedule were delayed after the pigeons made their initial choice. The terminal components were delayed by requiring the subjects to respond ten times on the choice keys (FR 10) during the initial component of the schedule instead of only once. Behavior in the concurrent schedule appeared to be controlled by the proportion between the delays of reinforcement associated with the two alternatives. Increasing the response requirement during the initial component of the concurrent chained schedule made the difference between immediate and delayed reward in the terminal components, expressed as a ratio, much smaller.

The ratio between the delays of reinforcement can be calculated as follows. Let us say that it takes the animal 10 sec to complete the FR 10 response requirement in the choice component of the schedule and 1 sec to make the required response in each of the terminal components. If the animal chooses terminal component A (immediate small reward), the total delay between its initial choice and the reward will be 10 sec (for all the choice responses) plus 1 sec (for the terminal-component response), or 11 sec. If it chooses terminal component B (large reward delayed 4 sec), the total delay between its initial choice and the reward will be 10 + 1 + 4 sec (choice responses, terminal response, and reward delay in the terminal component), or 15 sec. Thus, the ratio of the delays of reinforce-

ment for the two components in this case is 11/15.

A much larger proportional difference results if the terminal components are presented immediately after the first choice response. In this case, we do not have to include 10 sec for the time from the first to the tenth response in the choice component, because only one response occurs. Let us still assume that it takes the pigeon 1 sec to make the required response in each of the terminal components. If it chooses terminal component A (immediate small reward), the total delay between its initial choice and reinforcement will be 1 sec (for the terminal component response). If the pigeon chooses component B (large reward delayed 4 sec), the total delay between its initial choice and reinforcement will be 5 sec (1 sec for the terminal response and 4 sec for reward delay in the terminal component). Thus, the ratio of the delays of reinforcement for the two choices is 1/5. This is a much larger disproportion than 11/15, and pigeons do not show self-control under these circumstances. Such calculations indicate that the *comparative* delay of reinforcement is the critical variable in self-control. Self-control occurs only if the additional delay required for the large reward is small compared with the delay for the lesser reward.

The laboratory analogue research suggests that dieting will be more successful if the dieter avoids confrontations with immediate small rewards. One must keep the ratio between the delays of reinforcement from eating and from being thin as close to 1 as possible. This is particularly true for dieting because being thin is a reward that is usually very delayed. One can add delay to the small immediate rewards of eating fattening foods by increasing the response requirement for obtaining food. If you do not have ready-to-eat foods in the house, the time and energy required to purchase and prepare the food may make it easier to forgo the small immediate reward of eating in favor of the delayed reward of being thin. (Interestingly, other lines of research also make this recommendation; see Schachter, 1971b.)

Extinction

So far we have discussed how organisms behave when their responses are reinforced according to various schedules of reinforcement. A related and very important issue concerns what responses occur when reinforcement is no longer available. Not many reinforcement schedules in nature remain in effect throughout the organism's lifetime. Responses that are successful in producing reinforcement at one time may cease to be effective as circumstances change. Children, for example, are praised for drawing crude representations of people and objects, but the same type of drawing is not considered good if made later in life. Dating someone may be extremely pleasant and rewarding until the person finds another special friend and no longer encourages your approaches. The nonreinforcement of a response that was previously rewarded is called **extinction.** We encountered extinction earlier in the book in connection with classical conditioning. There, *extinction* referred to the reduction in a response when the conditioned stimulus was no longer followed by the unconditioned stimulus. In instrumental conditioning, extinction is the reduction in an instrumental response when it is no longer followed by the reinforcer.

Effects of extinction procedures

Instrumental extinction procedures—withdrawal of reinforcement—have two important types of effects on the organism. First, of course, the procedure results in a gradual decrease in the rate of the instrumental response. During the first extinction session, the subject may respond rapidly at first and then gradually slow down until it stops making the instrumen-

tal response. If the subject is placed back in the experimental situation the next day, there may be a slight and temporary recovery in rate of responding. This is called **spontaneous recovery.** However, the amount of spontaneous recovery decreases with repeated extinction sessions, until the subject ceases to make the instrumental response altogether. Figure 7.8 shows the course of a response during the first two extinction sessions.

In addition to the expected decline in the instrumental response, extinction procedures also produce strong emotional effects and behavioral arousal. If the subject has become accustomed to receiving reinforcement for a particular response, it may become extremely upset and aggressive when rewards are no longer delivered. This emotional reaction induced by withdrawal of rewards is called **frustration.** Frustrative aggression induced by extinction procedures is dramatically demonstrated by experiments in which two animals (pigeons, for example) are placed in the same Skinner box (Azrin, Hutchinson, & Hake, 1966). One of them is initially rewarded for pecking a response key, while the other animal is restrained in a corner of the experimental chamber. The key-pecking bird largely ignores the other one as long as reinforcement is provided. However,

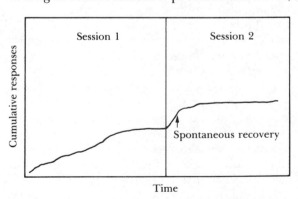

Figure 7.8. Cumulative record of responding during the first and second sessions of extinction. The burst of responding at the beginning of the second session is spontaneous recovery. (Hypothetical data.)

when reinforcement ceases, the previously rewarded animal is likely to attack its innocent partner. Similar aggression occurs if a stuffed model instead of a real animal is placed in the Skinner box.

Frustrative reactions to withdrawal of rewards are also common outside the laboratory. When a vending machine breaks down and no longer delivers a soft drink or candy for the coins that are put into it, people often become abusive and pound and kick the machine. Vending machines have to be built very sturdily to withstand this frustrative aggression. Frustration is also common in interpersonal interactions when extinction is introduced by one of the parties. If a husband is accustomed to having his clothes always laundered, the first time his wife fails to do the laundry, he may become very angry. If a child is accustomed to being driven to school every day by her parents, she is likely to become upset if one day she has to walk or take the bus. If you and your special friend usually go on a date every Saturday evening, you will surely be very disturbed if unexpectedly your friend calls off the date.

Determinants of extinction effects

The most important variable that determines the magnitude of both the behavioral and emotional effects of an extinction procedure is the schedule of reinforcement in effect for the instrumental response before the extinction procedure is introduced. Various subtle features of reinforcement schedules can influence the subsequent extinction of instrumental responses. However, the dominant schedule characteristic that determines extinction effects is whether the instrumental response was reinforced every time it occurred (continuous reinforcement) or only some of the times it occurred (intermittent, or partial, reinforcement). Most of the schedules of reinforcement described earlier in the chapter involve partial reinforcement. We discussed these schedules in great detail because the pattern of responding that occurs when re-

inforcement is available closely depends on the special features of each schedule. However, the difference between continuous and partial reinforcement is much more important in the study of extinction effects than differences among the various possible partial reinforcement schedules. The general finding is that extinction is much slower and involves fewer frustration reactions if the subjects previously experienced a partial reinforcement schedule than if they previously experienced continuous reinforcement (see Figure 7.9). This phenomenon is called the **partial-reinforcement extinction effect,** or PRE.

The persistence in responding that is created by intermittent reinforcement can be remarkable. Aspiring actors and actresses study hard and persist in their eagerness to pursue an acting career even though they may get very few important roles. Habitual gamblers are similarly at the mercy of intermittent reinforce-

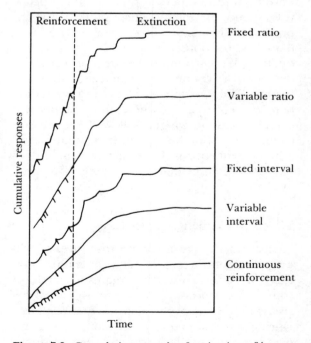

Figure 7.9. Cumulative records of extinction of instrumental behavior following various simple schedules of reinforcement. (Hypothetical data.)

ment. The few times they win big strongly encourage them to continue gambling during long strings of losses. Partial reinforcement also occurs often in interpersonal situations. If you are not really interested in dating someone who finds you extremely attractive, you may accept only a small proportion of his or her invitations. By doing this, you will be reinforcing the person intermittently and thus may make the person much more persistent in trying to win your favor. Intermittent reinforcement can also have undesirable consequences if parents give in to various demands from a child only after the child has made the request repeatedly. Consider, for example, a child riding in a grocery cart while the parent is shopping. The child asks the parent to buy a piece of candy. The parent says no. The child asks again and again and then begins to throw a temper tantrum because the parent continues to say no. At this point, the parent is likely to give in to avoid public embarrassment. By buying the candy, the parent will have reinforced the temper tantrum and also provided intermittent reinforcement for the repeated demands for candy. The schedule of reinforcement the parent used will make the child very persistent in making requests in the future and will also encourage tantrums. If such interactions between parent and child occur frequently, the child is likely to become someone who is casually referred to as a "brat."

Mechanisms of the partial-reinforcement extinction effect

Perhaps the most obvious explanation of the PRE is that animals continue responding more when reward is withdrawn after intermittent reinforcement than after continuous reinforcement because the withdrawal of reward is more difficult to detect in this case. If the subject does not receive reward after each response during training, it may not notice right away when reward ceases. The change in reinforcement conditions is presumably much more dramatic if reward ceases after continuous reinforcement.

This explanation of the partial-reinforcement extinction effect is called the **discrimination hypothesis.**

Although the discrimination hypothesis provides an intuitively satisfactory explanation of the PRE, the phenomenon is not so straightforward. In an ingenious test of the discrimination hypothesis, Jenkins (1962) and Theios (1962) first trained one group of animals with partial reinforcement and another group with continuous reinforcement. Both groups then received a period of continuous reinforcement before reinforcement for each group was withdrawn. Because the extinction procedure was introduced immediately after continuous reinforcement training for both groups, it was presumably equally noticeable or discriminable. Nevertheless, the subjects that initially received partial reinforcement training responded more during the extinction period. These experiments show that the advantage of partial reinforcement does not come from making the start of the extinction procedure more difficult to detect. Rather, it seems that subjects learn something important during partial reinforcement training that is not lost if they also receive continuous reinforcement before the extinction procedure.

What do organisms learn during partial reinforcement training that makes them respond more often when rewards are no longer available? Numerous complicated experiments have been performed in attempts to answer this question. These studies indicate that partial reinforcement training promotes persistence during extinction in two ways. One of the mechanisms of the partial-reinforcement extinction effect was proposed by Amsel (for example, 1958, 1967, 1979) and has come to be known as *frustration theory.* Frustration theory assumes that animals reinforced on an intermittent schedule go through several stages in their training. During the course of partial reinforcement, subjects receive some rewarded and some nonrewarded trials. Consequently, they develop conflicting expectations. Rewarded trials lead them to expect reinforcement, and non-rewarded trials lead them to expect non-reinforcement. Initially, the anticipation of reward encourages the subjects to go ahead and make the instrumental response, whereas the anticipation of nonreinforcement discourages them from making the instrumental response. Thus, early in training the subjects are in a conflict about what to do. However, on some occasions when the subjects expect nonreward, performance of the instrumental response may in fact be followed by the reinforcer. Because of such experiences, performance of the instrumental response becomes conditioned to the expectation of nonreward. According to frustration theory, this is the key to persistent responding in extinction. Because animals learn to make the instrumental response in expectation of nonreward, subjects trained with intermittent reinforcement continue to make the instrumental response when extinction procedures are introduced. In contrast, there is nothing about the experience of continuous reinforcement that teaches animals to respond when they expect not getting rewarded. Therefore, these subjects stop responding much sooner in extinction. (For a further discussion of frustration theory, see Chapter 11.)

The second prominent mechanism that promotes responding in extinction after intermittent reinforcement was proposed by Capaldi (for example, 1967, 1971) and is known as *sequential theory*. Sequential theory relies heavily on memory mechanisms. It assumes that animals can remember very well whether or not they were reinforced for performing the instrumental response in the recent past. The theory assumes, further, that animals on a partial reinforcement schedule learn to make the instrumental response when they remember not having been rewarded on the preceding trials. Thus, the memory of not having been rewarded recently comes to motivate the subjects to perform the instrumental behavior. Precisely how this happens depends a great deal on the sequence of rewarded (R) and nonrewarded (N) trials that are administered in the intermittent reinforcement schedule.

Consider the following sequence of trials: RNNRRNR. In this sequence the subject is rewarded the first time it makes the instrumental response, not rewarded on the next two occasions, then rewarded twice, then not rewarded, and then rewarded again. The fourth and last trials are critical in this schedule. The subject is reinforced for responding on the fourth trial. It is assumed that on this trial the subject remembers not having been rewarded on the preceding two trials. Because of the reinforcement on the fourth trial, it is assumed, the subject learns that it will be reinforced for responding when its memory indicates that it was not rewarded on the preceding two trials. A similar mechanism is activated by the reinforcement on the last trial of the above sequence. Here the subject is rewarded for responding when its memory indicates that it was not reinforced on the single immediately preceding trial. With enough experiences of this type, subjects learn to respond whenever they remember not having been reinforced on the preceding trials. This learning, in turn, creates persistent responding in extinction after intermittent reinforcement. A continuous reinforcement schedule does not permit animals to learn such persistence. On a continuous reinforcement schedule, subjects are rewarded for every occurrence of the instrumental response. Therefore, they cannot learn that they will be rewarded for responding on occasions when they remember not having been reinforced on preceding trials. Nonreinforced trials during extinction therefore do not motivate them to continue responding.

Some have regarded frustration theory and sequential theory as competing explanations of the partial-reinforcement extinction effect. However, since the two mechanisms were originally proposed, a very large and impressive body of evidence has been obtained in support of each theory. Therefore, we cannot regard one of the theories as correct and the other as incorrect. Rather, the two theories point out two different ways in which partial reinforcement can promote responding during extinction. In some situations one or the other mechanism may be operative, and in other cases both processes could contribute to persistent responding in extinction.

Concluding comments

The basic principle of instrumental conditioning is very simple: reinforcement increases (and punishment decreases) the future probability of an instrumental response. However, as we have seen, the experimental analysis of instrumental behavior can be rather intricate.

Many important aspects of instrumental behavior are determined by the schedule of reinforcement. There are numerous schedules by which responses can be reinforced. Reinforcement can depend on how many responses have occurred, the passage of time, or the rate of responding, and more than one reinforcement schedule may be available to the subject at the same time. The pattern of instrumental behavior, as well as choices among various response alternatives, is strongly determined by the schedule of reinforcement that is in effect. Reinforcement schedules also determine the extent to which subjects persist in responding when rewards become no longer available. These various findings have told us a great deal about how reinforcement controls behavior in a wide variety of circumstances.

CHAPTER EIGHT

Reinforcement: Theories and Experimental Analysis

Chapter 8 is devoted to a detailed discussion of the mechanisms whereby reinforcement increases the future probability of certain responses. We begin with a discussion of what aspects of instrumental-conditioning procedures are critical for producing reinforcement effects. This is followed by a discussion of exactly what it is about reinforcers that makes them effective in strengthening behavior. The chapter ends with a discussion of a theory that views reinforcement as involved in the selection of responses rather than the strengthening of behavior.

Chapters 6 and 7 described how instrumental behavior is influenced by various kinds of experimental manipulations. This research has provided us with a great deal of information about the characteristics of instrumental behavior in many circumstances. The present chapter will analyze in greater detail precisely how it is that reinforcement changes the future probability of behavior. A complete account of the mechanisms of reinforcement has to provide answers to three key questions: what is the effective feature of instrumental-conditioning procedures, what makes reinforcers reinforce, and what do organisms learn during the course of instrumental conditioning? The answers to these questions involve some of the most exciting and important aspects of behavior theory

today. We are witnessing a major reorientation in how theoreticians conceptualize the mechanisms of reinforcement. Early investigators followed Thorndike in assuming that reinforcement involved the strengthening of a specific response by the presentation of a specific kind of stimulus (a reinforcer) after occurrences of the response. Thus, the emphasis was on changes in a single response brought about by delivery of a particular type of stimulus. More recent conceptualizations of the reinforcement process take a broader view of the animal's behavior. They recognize that reinforcement involves much more than the presentation of a stimulus. Reinforcing stimuli must be consumed or used in some way. Consummatory responses (approach, chewing, and swallowing, for example, in the case of food) now play a broader role in our understanding of the reinforcement process. We are now concerned with how all the responses in the animal's repertoire are changed during reinforcement. This chapter will first discuss traditional theories of reinforcement and will then describe the theoretical developments and insights into behavior that have been provided by the broader contemporary conceptualizations of the reinforcement process.

What is the effective feature of instrumental-conditioning procedures?

Correlation and contiguity

It is a common observation that presenting grain to a hungry pigeon whenever it pecks a key is sufficient to increase its key pecking above the operant level. As we well know by now, setting up such an operant-conditioning procedure involves several steps: specifying the response and the reinforcer, motivating the subject (deprivation), and specifying the relation between the response and the reinforcer. We usually think of the relation between response and reinforcer as a simple cause-and-effect relation. In fact, however, the typical operant procedure involves at least two relations. First, there is the **correlation between the instrumental response and the reinforcer.** This is determined by the schedule of reinforcement. As we noted in Chapter 7, the correlation between response and reinforcer can be described in various ways. One can describe it in terms of the feedback function—the amount of reinforcer received as a function of the number of responses performed. Alternatively, one can specify the conditional probabilities between the reinforcer and the response. In a continuous reinforcement schedule, for example, the conditional probability of the reinforcer given a response is 1.0. The probability of a reinforcer

given no response is 0.0. Another important aspect of operant-conditioning procedures is the **temporal relation between the response and the reinforcer.** In most operant procedures, the reinforcer immediately follows the response. This relation is called **temporal contiguity.**

Are both response/reinforcer correlation and temporal contiguity necessary for reinforcement to increase the probability of the response? What aspects of behavior does each of these relations govern? In Chapter 7 we discussed some experiments related to these questions. Experiments on delay of reinforcement show that little if any conditioning occurs if there is a long delay between the response and the reinforcer without secondary reinforcers to bridge the delay. In these experiments, the temporal contiguity was disrupted while the correlation between response and reinforcer remained unchanged. The resulting failure in conditioning reflects the necessity of temporal contiguity.

What would happen if we removed the correlation but retained the contiguous relation between response and reinforcer? Such an experiment was first performed by Skinner in 1948. It is one of the most widely cited and analyzed experiments in conditioning and learning. As we shall see, fundamental arguments concerning reinforcement have been based on this simple experiment. All major reinforcement theorists deal with the results in one way or another.

The superstition experiment. Skinner placed several naive pigeons in separate experimental chambers and programmed the food hoppers to deliver a bit of grain periodically. The food was presented every 15 sec irrespective of what the pigeons were doing. They were not required to peck a key or perform any other response to get the food. This kind of response-independent schedule is called a fixed-time (FT) schedule of reinforcement. After a while, Skinner returned to see what the pigeons were doing. He described some of what he saw as follows:

> In six out of eight cases the resulting responses were so clearly defined that two observers could agree perfectly in counting instances. One bird was conditioned to turn counter-clockwise about the cage, making two or three turns between reinforcements. Another repeatedly thrust its head into one of the upper corners of the cage. A third developed a "tossing" response, as if placing its head beneath an invisible bar and lifting it repeatedly. Two birds developed a pendulum motion of the head and body. . . . Another bird was conditioned to make incomplete pecking or brushing movements directed toward but not touching the floor [Skinner, 1948, p. 168].

The pigeons appeared to be responding as if their behavior controlled the delivery of the reinforcer when in fact the rewards were delivered independent of behavior. Accordingly, Skinner called the behavior **superstitious behavior,** and his study is the **superstition experiment.**

Skinner's explanation of superstitious behavior rests on the notion of **accidental,** or **adventitious, reinforcement.** Animals are always doing something even if no particular responses are required to obtain reinforcers. Skinner suggested that whatever response the pigeon happens to make just before a reinforcer is delivered becomes strengthened and subsequently increases in frequency because of the reward. The accidental pairing of a response with delivery of the reinforcer is called "adventitious reinforcement." One accidental pairing with a reinforcer increases the chance that the same response will occur just before the next delivery of reward. This second fortuitous response/reinforcer contiguity further strengthens the probability of the response. In this way, each accidental pairing helps to "stamp in" a particular response. After a while, the response will occur frequently enough to be identified as superstitious behavior.

Herrnstein and Morse (reported in Herrn-

stein, 1966) replicated Skinner's superstition experiment. However, instead of using naive pigeons, they initially trained an animal to peck a response key for a food reward on a fixed-interval 11-sec schedule. After the key-pecking response was well established, a response-independent schedule of food delivery was instituted. The animal was no longer required to peck the response key. Rather, the food was delivered automatically every 11 sec regardless of the pigeon's behavior. The rate of pecking throughout the experiment is summarized in Figure 8.1. We see that pecking decreased somewhat when responding was no longer required for reinforcement. However, the pigeon still continued to peck at a steady rate.

After the superstition phase of the experiment, the fixed-interval reinforcement schedule was reinstituted for the next 18 sessions to reestablish high rates of pecking. Reinforcement was then entirely withheld during the last phase of the experiment (extinction). In such an extinction procedure the response/reinforcer correlation is eliminated, as it is in a fixed-time (superstitious) schedule. However, there is also no chance for temporal contiguity between responses and reinforcement, because no food at all is presented. Figure 8.1 shows that extinction resulted in a much lower rate of pecking than the fixed-time schedule.

Implications of the superstition experiment. On the basis of these results, Herrnstein elaborated on Skinner's interpretation of the superstition experiment. He suggested that the experiment illustrates three fundamental aspects of the reinforcement process. First, and most important, the superstition experiment illustrates that temporal contiguity between a response and a reinforcer is both a necessary and a sufficient condition for the strengthening of the response. The response does not have to physically cause reward delivery, and there does not have to be a correlation between the

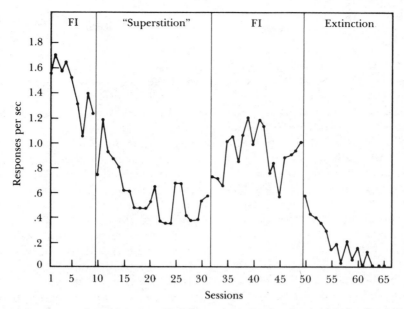

Figure 8.1. A pigeon's rate of pecking over 65 daily sessions. During Sessions 1–9 a fixed-interval 11-sec schedule of reinforcement was in effect for the pecking behavior. During Session 10–31 food was delivered every 11 sec regardless of what the pigeon did. The fixed-interval schedule was reinstituted during Sessions 32–49. Extinction was in effect during Sessions 50–65. *(After Herrnstein, 1966.)*

response and the reinforcer. Second, the superstition results imply that once a response has been conditioned, the reinforcer does not have to occur perfectly contiguously with the response in order to maintain frequent occurrences of the behavior. If perfect contiguity were required, the rate of response should have decreased more sharply in Herrnstein and Morse's experiment when the fixed-time schedule was introduced. It seems that once a response is learned, longer delays between response and reinforcement can occur without jeopardizing the reinforcement effect. Third, Herrnstein suggested that acquisition is a faster process than extinction. That is, one accidental pairing of a response and a reinforcer does more to promote the response than one accidental nonpairing does to extinguish it. In the initial phases of acquisition of a superstitious response, one would expect many nonpairings. If these extinction trials had as strong an effect

as the accidental response/reinforcer pairings, it would be very difficult for a particular response to become established as superstitious behavior. Extinction processes can be minimized in fixed-time superstitious schedules by keeping the interval between successive food deliveries very short. In Skinner's (1948) experiment this interval was 15 sec, and in Herrnstein and Morse's study it was 11 sec. Had the interval been much longer, there would have been more opportunity for extinction, and probably less superstitious behavior would have been evident.

The correlation effect. The superstition experiment suggests that the correlation between response and reinforcer is not necessary to produce a reinforcement effect. This is not to say that the correlation has no effect at all on behavior. In light of the data shown in Figure 8.1, Herrnstein suggested that operant procedures that involve both response/reinforcer contiguity and correlation are maximally effective in strengthening behavior because they ensure that the reinforcer is always contiguous with a *particular form* of the operant response. This explanation is based on the assumption that there is natural variation or drift in behavior. On a fixed-time (superstitious) schedule, the pecking response may be initially directed at the response key but then might drift away from the key or change in some other way. For example, the pigeon may start pecking spots on the wall near the response key. Pecking may be occurring at the same rate as before, but only some of the pecks will be recorded on the response key. A schedule that retains the correlation between the response and the reinforcer limits this behavioral drift. If the pigeon starts pecking somewhere other than at the key, it will not be reinforced as often, and this will discourage the response drift. Such a decrease in reinforcement does not happen on a fixed-time schedule. Hence, the rate of recorded key pecking is lower on a fixed-time (superstition) schedule than on a response-contingent schedule (see Figure 8.1).

The differential effects of a correlation between response and reinforcement are also illustrated by the experiment by Reynolds (1968) discussed in Chapter 7. You may recall that the performance of pairs of pigeons was compared. For one animal in a pair, pecking a key was reinforced on a variable-ratio schedule. For the other pigeon, a variable-interval schedule was in effect. However, the availability of reinforcement on the variable-interval schedule was determined by the delivery of reward for the variable-ratio subject. This yoking procedure ensured that the two pigeons received the reinforcer at approximately the same times. The reinforcer was also delivered immediately after a pecking response for both pigeons. However, the correlation between response and reinforcement was not the same for the two birds in each pair. For the pigeon reinforced on the variable-ratio schedule, the rate of reinforce-

ment was directly correlated with the rate of response. The faster the pigeon pecked, the faster it completed the ratio requirement and received food. Such a correlation did not exist for the pigeon reinforced on the variable-interval schedule. The VI bird had only minimal control over reinforcement. The only response that "counts" on a variable-interval schedule is the one that occurs when the reinforcer is available. As long as this response is properly timed, no other responses are necessary. Increases in response rate do not effectively increase the rate of reinforcement. The results of the experiment bear out this difference in the response/reinforcer correlation between the two schedules of reinforcement. The variable-ratio schedule yielded much higher rates of responding than the variable-interval schedule. Thus, the pigeons' behavior was consistent with the correlation between responses and reinforcement.

Cause and effect as an epistemological problem

The superstition experiment implies that temporal contiguity between response and reinforcer alone is necessary and sufficient to strengthen and maintain behavior. Pigeons in superstition experiments appear to be locked into a needless expenditure of responses because of the stamping-in force of reinforcement. In essence, the pigeon fails to recognize that there is no causal relation between its behavior and the food. Is this an accurate picture of reinforcement? In Chapter 6 we described experiments on learned helplessness in which subjects learned that they had no control over environmental events. This learning impeded the later learning of an instrumental response when the subjects were subsequently allowed to control the presence and absence of the reinforcer. Why does the pigeon behave as if it did not perceive the absence of a correlation between responses and reinforcers in the superstition experiment, when learned-helplessness effects occur in other situations? One might suggest that the pigeon is simply too "stupid" to realize that it has no control. Perhaps a more reflecting organism, such as a human, would do better. Although there may be organismic differences in this area, it is also true that even humans fail to perceive cause and effect accurately in many instances. The old joke about the man who paints his lawn blue to keep elephants away is a case in point. His neighbor comments "There is no need to paint your lawn blue, because there are no elephants for thousands of miles around." The painter merely replies "You see how effective it is!"

Another approach is to ask what differences exist in various situations that might be re-sponsible for different perceptions of cause/ effect relations. There are many differences between superstition and learned-helplessness experiments that may lead to differences in perceptions of causality. The superstition experiment, for example, involves shorter inter-reinforcement intervals than most learned-helplessness experiments. To what extent such features influence perceptions of control must await further experimental study.

Historical considerations of the perception of causality. The analysis of the conditions giving rise to the perception of causality is a very old area of study. According to Hume, our understanding that two events are causally re-

---

Box 8.1. Thoughts on the Perception of Causality and Control

The superstition experiment raises some thought-provoking questions about perceptions of control in our daily lives. The pigeon behaves as if its responses controlled the delivery of food when in fact the food is delivered independent of behavior. Perhaps the true controlling variables in our lives are as obscure to us as the schedule of response-independent reinforcement is to the pigeon. Might our behavior be controlled by forces we are not aware of? Writers throughout literature have proposed that at times this is a reasonable hypothesis. The consequences of human behavior have been attributed not to the desires, will, or control of the individual but to a higher authority or order. On a very pessimistic note, Shakespeare wrote,

As flies to wanton boys are we to th' gods.
They kill us for their sport.
King Lear, IV, 1

Tolstoy discussed the perception of control at length from a historical perspective in *War and Peace*. He argued that human behavior does not exert as much control over the course of events as we think. The forces that shape history are external to the individual. Our mistaken impressions about our own control are as ridiculous as the impression that the earth stands still while the universe revolves. He writes:

As with astronomy the difficulty in the way of recognizing that the earth moves consisted in having to rid oneself of the immediate sensation that the earth was stationary accompanied by a similar sense of the planets' motion, so in history the obstacle in the way of recognizing the subjection of the individual to the laws of space and time and causality lies in the difficulty of renouncing one's personal impression of being independent of those laws. But as in astronomy the new view said: 'True, we are not conscious of the movement of the earth but if we were to allow that it is stationary we should arrive at an absurdity, whereas if we admit the motion (which we do not feel) we arrive at laws,' likewise in history the new theory says: 'True, we are not conscious of our dependence but if we were to allow that we are free we arrive at an absurdity, whereas by admitting our dependence on the external world, on time and on causality we arrive at laws' [1957, pp. 1443–1444].*

*From *War and Peace*, Vol. 2, by L. N. Tolstoy. Translated by R. R. Edmonds Harmondsworth. Copyright © by Rosemary Edmonds, 1957. Reprinted by permission of Penguin Books Ltd.

lated is based on repeated experiences in which these two events occur together. We never perceive directly any energy or force that we would call "cause." We only perceive two events happening together. Thus, Hume writes:

> In all single instances of the operation of bodies or minds, there is nothing that produces any impression, nor consequently can suggest any idea of power or necessary connexion. But when many uniform instances appear, and the same object is always followed by the same event; we then begin to entertain the notion of cause and connexion [1777/1902, p. 78].

Michotte, a French psychologist, performed the first experimental work on the perception of causality (see Michotte, 1963). Like Hume, he assumed that causality is a structure that we impose on our sensations. Michotte tried to determine what experiences lead to causal inferences. Subjects in his experiments were asked to describe the motion of two moving figures. Michotte varied the way in which the figures moved and analyzed his subjects' statements for inferences of causality. He found temporal contiguity to be very important. Other research following the work of Michotte (see Duncker, 1945) showed that spatial contiguity also plays a role in some instances. This should not be surprising, as temporally contiguous events tend to occur in the same place as well as at the same time. In addition, pairs of events that are perceived as causally related often share physical properties. For example, water, which we perceive as making objects wet, feels wet and makes other things feel wet as well.

Contiguity, necessity, and sufficiency. Temporal contiguity is only one of three possible characteristics of the relation between two events that sometimes occur together. Necessity and sufficiency are other such characteristics. One of the events may be necessary for occurrence of the other, and/or the second event may be sufficient for assuming that the first event

has occurred. The properties of necessity and sufficiency may or may not accompany temporal contiguity. Consider the superstition experiment again. From the pigeon's point of view, food occurs contiguously with a response. However, the response is not *necessary* for the food delivery. In addition, food delivery is not *sufficient* information to know whether the response was made. This absence of necessity and sufficiency is the logical essence of response-independent schedules.

Modern research is just beginning to elucidate the role of contiguity, necessity, and sufficiency in human perception of causation. For example, Siegler and Liebert (1974) and Dammond (1978) asked children to decide when or whether a little computer was causing a light to become illuminated. The relation of the computer's behavior to the light bulb was manipulated so that sometimes there was temporal contiguity, sometimes the computer's activity was necessary for operation of the light bulb, and sometimes the light bulb was sufficient to tell that the computer was active. The results, though still sketchy, indicate that children, by and large, use temporal contiguity to infer causality. However, as they get older, they tend to make use of the sufficiency property as well.

Causality without contiguity. Causality is sometimes inferred even when there is no temporal contiguity between the events. For example, cause and effect is understood to exist between sexual behavior and pregnancy. However, this inference of causality is usually not arrived at on the basis of individual experience. Even in our culture there are some women who conceive but do not know how conception comes about. The long delay between sexual activity and visible signs of pregnancy no doubt makes it difficult to infer a causal relation between the two. Complex causal inferences of this sort are, by and large, learned from other people rather than through individual effort.

What makes reinforcers reinforce?

If we were to name all the stimuli that have been used as reinforcers, we would have a very long list. Included would be the more popular stimuli, such as food, water, and sexual partners, and other diverse stimuli, such as oxygen, increases in atmospheric temperature, saccharin solution, and even electrical shock. The list would also include such activities as watching a moving electric train, playing pinball, and running in a running wheel. Finally, we might include reinforcers that are not always easily defined, such as the approval of others, self-satisfaction, and the like. What do all these stimuli have in common that makes them effective reinforcers? We might presume that where there is reinforcement, there is pleasure. Thorndike used a slightly different wording. In the law of effect he described what we now call reinforcing stimuli as events that produce "satisfying states of affairs." What, though, is a satisfying state of affairs? Or what is pleasurable? It is tempting to define *pleasure* or *satisfying state of affairs* as any event or stimulus that the subject will work for—in other words, whatever will reinforce behavior. However, such a definition provides a circular answer to our original question of what makes reinforcers reinforce. What is needed is a definition of *pleasure* or *satisfying state of affairs* that is not stated in terms of a reinforcement effect.

One way out of the circularity in the answer to "What makes reinforcers reinforce?" is to restrict the scope of the question. Instead of trying to answer the question for all circumstances, we can try to provide an answer for only a particular reinforcing stimulus that is used to strengthen a particular response in a unique situation. For example, what makes food an effective reinforcer for lever pressing in rats placed in a Skinner box? A circular answer to this question would be that food reinforces lever pressing because it is a reinforcer in this situation. This is not an informative statement. Meehl (1950) suggested that the **principle of transsituationality** can be of help in cases like this. The principle of transsituationality assumes that reinforcers are effective in strengthening behavior in a variety of situations. Food, for example, is expected to reinforce not only lever pressing in a Skinner box but also running in a runway and swimming in a tank of water. Given this transsituationality, one can use the outcome of the effects of reinforcement in one situation to explain the effects in another. Thus, we can say that food strengthens behavior in a lever-press experiment because food has been identified as a reinforcer in a runway experiment. This explanation is not circular. The reinforcing properties of food are identified in a situation (the runway experiment) that is different from the situation in which we are trying to explain the reinforcement effect (the lever-press experiment).

Although the principle of transsituationality helps to avoid circularity, it is not entirely satisfactory. Assume that we use the fact that food is an effective reinforcer in a runway experiment to explain why food strengthens behavior in a lever-press experiment. Such an explanation would not provide much insight into behavior. The fundamental question of why reinforcers reinforce would remain unanswered until we knew why food is an effective reinforcer in a runway experiment. Another weakness of this approach is that reinforcers are not always effective across a broad range of situations. As we discussed in Chapter 6, there are serious constraints on operant conditioning. A reinforcer that is effective in strengthening one response may not be useful in reinforcing other types of behavior.

The theories of reinforcement that we will examine in the coming pages represent a more analytical approach to the question of what makes a reinforcer reinforce. Basically, there are two central problems in the analysis. One problem is to determine the essential characteristics of reinforcers. If these were known, one could identify reinforcers readily by the presence or absence of the critical characteristics. The second problem is describing the mechanism involved. That is, what does the reinforcer do, and how does it do it? We have already discussed some ideas on this issue in Chapter 6. The earliest ideas concerning this problem were based on the assumption of an associative bond between stimulus and response. Thorndike, for example, suggested that reinforcement brings about the association between a response and the stimuli present when the response is made. The view suggested by Skinner and elaborated by Herrnstein with respect to the superstition experiment is that reinforcement "stamps in" whatever response happens to be occurring at the time. Whereas Thorndike stressed the association between stimuli and responses, Skinner's view stresses the relation between the response and the reinforcer.

The theories of reinforcement that we will discuss analyze the characteristics of reinforcers and the mechanisms involved in reinforcement in greater detail. Like Skinner's approach, they by and large focus on the relation between the reinforcer and the response. The first group of theories describe the mechanisms thought to be responsible for the stamping-in effect. These theories take what we will call the biological approach: they characterize reinforcers and reinforcement mechanisms in terms of their biological significance. A second set of theories have a more behavioral emphasis. Although not denying the importance of biological considerations, they analyze reinforcement in terms of a reorganization of behavior. The third approach represents a combination of the biological and behavioral theories.

THEORIES INVOLVING BIOLOGICAL MOTIVATING FORCES

Much of the research on instrumental learning uses biologically relevant stimuli, such as food and water, as reinforcers. Subjects are deprived of a substance such as food, and the return of this substance is the reinforcer. Because these stimuli are necessary to the organism's survival, it is not surprising that much of the work on reinforcement proposes biological mechanisms for the reinforcement effect.

Biological homeostasis and drive reduction

Some reinforcement theorists have described the procedures of deprivation and reinforcement as two opposing processes that alter the organism's physiological state. The concept of **biological homeostasis** is useful here to describe the results of these two processes. By "biological homeostasis" we mean that state of the organism in which all physiological systems are in proper balance. Deprivation procedures typically used upset this balance. In contrast, reinforcement returns the organism to homeostasis, the balanced state. The motivation to perform the instrumental response is seen as the result of the loss of homeostasis. According to this view, reinforcement works because organisms always seek to return to homeostasis.

One of the first theorists to make extensive use of a biological homeostatic mechanism was Hull. As we discussed in Chapter 6, Hull believed that the deprivation procedures used in experiments that employ food and water as reinforcers create a biological drive state. Reinforcers were assumed to have the common characteristic of reducing this drive state. According to this hypothesis, the mechanism of reinforcement involves a homeostatic process. Each time the subject obtains the reinforcer, it moves a step closer to homeostasis. The inborn tendency of the organism to return to homeostasis is the motivation for the response. Therefore, according to Hull, the degree of drive determines (in part) the degree of responding.

Biological needs or drives are assumed to be related to elements of the environment that are necessary for survival of the individual or the species. Therefore, need or drive states presumably can be identified with physiology experiments. Consistent with this view, food, water, oxygen, and temperature changes have all been successfully used as reinforcers. However, a serious weakness of a strict drive-reduction model is that there are reinforcers that do not have a corresponding biological need or drive. Activities such as watching an electric train can be used to reinforce the behavior of monkeys. To explain such reinforcers, one might hypothesize the existence of a curiosity drive. However, this approach is not very productive. The only evidence for the existence of a curiosity drive is that moving trains and the like are effective reinforcers. This reintroduces the same type of circularity problem we discussed earlier. We would be saying that a moving train reinforces behavior because it reduces the curiosity drive and that we know that there is a curiosity drive because the sight of a moving train reinforces behavior. The need- and drive-reduction theory compels us to add an item to our list of drives each time we find a reinforcer that does not satisfy a biological drive that has been identified by other means. However, if we do this, we will not have a way to identify reinforcers independently. Therefore, the drive-reduction hypothesis has not been entirely successful in specifying a common feature of reinforcers independent of their reinforcement effects.

Reinforcement and the sources of motivation

The drive-reduction hypothesis exemplifies the fact that the analysis of reinforcement is often cast as part of the broader field of motivation. Reinforcement is one way of forcing behavior to change. Where, though, does the force lie? Sometimes the force seems to lie within the organism as a drive state. Motivation induced by a drive state is called **primary motivation.** Motivation for behavior may also come from the reinforcer itself. Sometimes just the presence of food, water, or a sexual partner can trigger behavior. Such motivation created by the sensory properties of a reinforcer is called **incentive motivation.** Sheffield, Wulff, and Backer (1951) demonstrated, for example, that a male rat will run down a runway in order to gain access to a female. The male will persist in the instrumental response even though it is not allowed to complete the sexual response. The behavior thus continues in order to obtain the stimulus without drive reduction. Motivating behavior by a stimulus alone is a common everyday phenomenon. You may, for example, be enticed into eating a piece of cake just by the sight of the cake even though you are not hungry. Motivating behavior in this manner by the mere presence of a stimulus constitutes a large part of commercial advertising. At times it appears that a drive state can be induced when there may be no physiological basis for it.

One way of characterizing an incentive stimulus such as food is by the behavior involved in consuming it. Most reinforcers must be "taken in" or experienced in some way in order to be effective. There are many sensations involved in this process that may be important. We describe eating after a fast as intensely satisfying or pleasurable. Hedonists through the centuries have told us that the force behind our actions is that we seek pleasure and avoid pain. This philosophy suggests that we should look to the sensations produced by consuming, utilizing, or experiencing reinforcers as the source of motivation for instrumental behavior. Sheffield and his colleagues proposed a theory of reinforcement along these lines. The so-called **consummatory-response theory** asserts that it is the behavior of eating, drinking, and the like that gives rise to the reinforcement effect. A key experiment here involved the use of saccharin as a reinforcer. Saccharin cannot reduce any physiological drive state, because it has no nutritive value. However, it gives what we usually call pleasurable taste sensations. Furthermore, it is effective in reinforcing instrumental behavior (Sheffield, Roby, & Campbell, 1954). (For a further discussion of incentive motivation, see Black, 1969.)

We thus have two possible sources of mo-

Box 8.2.   Drive-Stimulus Control of Eating in Obese Persons

It is a common experience that certain stimuli will induce a behavior typical of a drive state even if the drive state is absent. Even though you are not hungry, you may eat a peanut because it is there. Once you eat one peanut, the taste stimuli may induce you to eat another. Thus, we have the adage that it is impossible to eat just one peanut. Research by Schachter and his colleagues (Schachter, 1971b) suggests that the eating behavior of obese persons is especially under the influence of food stimuli. A series of experiments has shown that obese persons differ from normal-weight persons in the extent to which food stimuli, as opposed to physiological hunger, control their eating. For instance, one study compared the effects of physiological hunger on the eating behavior of normal and obese subjects. Hungry normal persons ate more crackers than normal subjects who were less hungry because they had recently eaten a roast-beef sandwich. In contrast, the same manipulation of hunger had no effect on the intake of obese persons. The obese subjects ate the same number of crackers irrespective of whether they had recently eaten a roast-beef sandwich. In another study, Nisbett (1968) found that hungry obese subjects ate less than hungry normal subjects when the food was not visible, but they ate more when the food was readily available. The hungry normal subject is more likely to seek out food that is hidden from view. Decke (cited in Schachter, 1971a) found that the taste of food is also an important determinant of intake. Obese subjects will drink more of a standard milkshake than normal-weight people. However, if the milkshake is laced with quinine so that it tastes bad, the obese person drinks far less than the normal control subject. Such findings suggest that obese persons may eat less if they are exposed to fewer positive food stimuli. To reduce ingestion, food may be hidden from view and made less accessible and less appetizing.

ogy literature at length. At present it appears that reinforcement is neither solely drive reduction nor solely incentive motivation. Both aspects play a role. Miller and Kessen (1952), for example, compared the reinforcement effects of food delivered directly into the stomach through a fistula and food consumed in the normal fashion. They found that fistula feeding could serve effectively as a reinforcer. Drive reduction from fistula feeding appears to be sufficient. However, the effect was not as powerful as that produced by normal eating.

At present, it is convenient to think of all sources of motivation as contributing to reinforcement effects. Modern research on brain stimulation, physiology, and biochemistry has made important contributions to our understanding of the motivational processes involved in reinforcement.

Brain stimulation: Reinforcement and motivation

Two physiological psychologists, James Olds and Peter Milner, implanted electrodes in the septal area of the brain of rats. The rats were then observed in a large compartment where they were given brief, mild electrical pulses to the brain through the electrodes. The rats tended to move toward the area of the chamber where they had last received the brain stimulation. Olds and Milner then connected a response lever to the electrical stimulator and discovered that the rats would press the lever at extremely high rates for many hours to receive the brain stimulation. The phenomenon was called **intracranial self-stimulation** (Olds & Milner, 1954). Olds and Milner's study sparked interest in several areas. The implications of the research were tremendous. The prospects of having such a powerful reinforcer available raises moral as well as practical issues in the control of behavior (see Box 8.3). Reinforcement theorists, however, were interested in the less glamorous aspects of the phenomenon. The self-stimulation research raised hope that a

tivation: (1) the drive state and (2) the incentive properties of the reinforcer. The role of each of these sources has been discussed in the psychol-

mechanism common to all reinforcers could be analyzed on a physiological level.

The findings of Olds and Milner stimulated several lines of investigation. Many experiments were performed to map out the various areas of the brain that, when stimulated, yield a reinforcement effect. In addition, there have been neurochemical analyses of the various neural pathways involved. Another set of experiments has explored the similarity of self-stimulation to other types of reinforcers. One outstanding feature of self-stimulation is that it is persistent and the response rates are high compared with other types of instrumental responding. In other respects self-stimulation appears to be similar to the traditional reinforcers when the two are compared under carefully controlled situations (see Mogenson & Cioe, 1977, for a review). Thus, the explanations for the effects of self-stimulation have followed the explanations for the traditional reinforcers. In general, it is assumed that one physiologically based explanation can serve for both.

One early explanation of brain-stimulation reinforcement involved drive reduction. It was hypothesized that brain stimulation activated the neural circuits that are involved when drives are reduced by consummatory behavior. However, this explanation turned out to be too simplistic. It was discovered that the same electrical stimulation of the brain that reinforces lever pressing can also elicit responses such as eating, drinking, and sexual behavior when the appropriate stimulus (food, water, or a sexual partner) is available (for example, Caggiula & Hoebel, 1966; Herberg, 1963; Hoebel & Teit-

---

Box 8.3. "Pleasure-Seeking Brains: Artificial Tickles, Natural Joys of Thought"

In an article with the above title, the physiologist H. J. Campbell (1971) has discussed the significance of self-stimulation research in light of evolutionary theory and what it means to be "human." Campbell's own research involves the natural stimulation of the limbic system of the brain. He proposes that for lower animals sensory stimulation leads to limbic-system stimulation. When animals are given the opportunity merely to stimulate themselves sensorily with an electric "tickler," they will do so in much the same way as they will self-stimulate more-central brain structures. The major difference is that sensory stimulation satiates or habituates whereas limbic-system stimulation does not. However, as Campbell notes, when one sensory system is satiated, the animal switches to another. It does not simply sit back and do nothing.

Campbell therefore suggests that the underlying principle of behavior is keeping the limbic system stimulated. Phylogeny determines the ways this can be done. We may assume that plants, unlike animals, do not have central pleasure centers. As we move along the phylogenetic scale, the interconnections between the limbic system and other neural systems become increasingly complicated. In lower animals the limbic system receives input primarily from sense organs. In people, however, neural connections involving the limbic system are more extensive and include the cortex of the brain. For this reason, complex cortical activities, such as thinking or problem solving, may stimulate the limbic structures. Thus, these activities help to keep our limbic system activated. Of course, the limbic system is also linked to sense organs in higher organisms as well. Behavior that we sometimes label subhuman or animalistic—vandalism for sheer pleasure, excessive eating, and the like—also is known to occur in humans. Campbell proposes that our social institutions exist to keep these forms of pleasure seeking under control and to promote higher intellectual forms of limbic stimulation. If the electrical circuitry that allows us to seek pleasure by intellectual pursuits is the result of evolution, in a flight of fantasy we can imagine that evolution may yet produce another creature capable of intellectual pleasures. Campbell's proposal gives us the possibility that in a million years the octopus may prove mathematical theorems!

elbaum, 1962; Margules & Olds, 1962; Mogenson & Stevenson, 1966). Thus, brain stimulation appears in part to *in*duce rather than *re*duce drives. Deutsch (1960) concluded that reinforcement in general requires both drive induction and subsequent drive reduction. Glickman and Schiff (1967) offered a slightly different interpretation of the experiments that is similar to Sheffield's consummatory-response theory. They suggested that the source of the reinforcement effect is the species-specific responses such as eating and drinking that help the organism adapt to its environment. Brain stimulation and instrumental deprivation/reinforcement procedures have the same effects on behavior because they are simply two ways of eliciting these adaptive responses.

Other research suggests that self-stimulation involves incentive motivation. Pfaffman (1960) proposed that self-stimulation is the result of activating the pathways that generally transmit such sensations as the taste of food. According to this view, brain stimulation reinforces behavior for the same reason that saccharin is an effective reinforcer—not by drive reduction but through the sensations involved in the consummatory responses. Campbell (1971) found evidence in support of this hypothesis. He showed that brain-stimulation reinforcement can be produced by electrical stimulation of the peripheral neural pathways that are generally known to transmit sensations from natural reinforcers. Campbell proposed that the physiological basis for reward lies in the activation of the central reward pathways by means of any one of several inputs. Generally we think of the inputs as triggered by exteroceptive stimuli, such as taste and smell. However, other types of inputs are possible. In the human brain, the pathways could presumably be activated by cognitive processes. This would explain why some people get pleasure from doing puzzles, studying mathematics, and the like and why those activities can sometimes serve as reinforcers.

As with traditional reinforcers, research on brain stimulation supports the idea that reinforcement is the result of both drive state and incentive motivation. Evidence for this point of view arises from the fact that the rate of self-stimulation can be enhanced or reduced by altering either the drive state or incentive stimuli. For example, a rat will self-stimulate faster if it is also food-deprived (Olds, 1958). If the site of stimulation also induces drinking, self-stimulation is enhanced if water is available (Mendelson, 1967; Mogenson & Kaplinsky, 1970; Mogenson & Morgan, 1967). If the water is made tastier by adding saccharin, the response rate is enhanced even more (Phillips & Mogenson, 1968). Results such as these have led theorists to conclude that reinforcement occurs when an external stimulus (such as water) is present in conjunction with an overall drive state (such as thirst). This is, of course, what happens in the typical instrumental situation. Both elements also appear to be present with brain stimulation, albeit artificially induced or mimicked. Several theorists have suggested mechanisms to describe these dual effects more precisely (for example, Bindra, 1969; Mogenson & Huang, 1973). We will briefly describe the model by Milner because it draws directly on both brain stimulation and conventional reinforcers.

Milner (1970) suggested that when an organism is deprived, general behavioral arousal ensues. Behavioral arousal is characterized by exploratory behavior and other increased motor responses. The organism's behavior involves switching from one response to another. If the organism finds an appropriate stimulus by making a particular response, a response-hold mechanism is activated. The animal no longer switches from one behavior to another. Rather, it remains locked into the response that keeps it in contact with the stimulus until the drive state is reduced. In the case of brain stimulation, Milner has proposed that some of the neural pathways are short-circuited. The response-switch mechanism may be inhibited for a long time, giving rise to the persistent self-stimulating behavior. Milner's model is bolstered by concurrent work on the catecholamine pathways in the brain. These pathways appear to be involved in brain stimulation and may exert the response-inhibiting processes Milner's model requires (Milner, 1976). A complete understanding of the workings of the neural mechanisms of reinforcement awaits further research.

THEORIES INVOLVING BEHAVIORAL HOMEOSTASIS

The general aim of the preceding theories is to describe the biological mechanisms for reinforcement. Underlying the biological approaches is the common assumption that reinforced behavior is trained or stamped into the organism's behavioral repertoire. The underlying assumption of the next set of theories is much different. For one, these models do not look for underlying biological processes. Reinforcement is described in terms of how the organism must adjust its behavior to meet the demands of a particular situation. Behavior is not necessarily stamped in, but rather reorganized. The theories of reinforcement describe how this reorganization takes place.

Homeostasis, as we have said, is a balanced physiological state of the organism. Homeostasis becomes relevant to reinforcement when deviations from the stable state occur and the organism attempts to rectify the situation. The second group of theories assume that a similar homeostatic mechanism exists with respect to behavior. That is, we may consider the behaving organism as having a particular balance of responses to maintain. The organism has particular things to do: it must eat, breathe, drink, keep warm, exercise, entertain itself, and so on. All these activities have to occur in particular proportions. If the normal balance of activities is upset, behavior is assumed to change so as to correct the deviation from behavioral homeostasis. The actual behavioral balance may in fact be dictated by physiological homeostasis. Eating, drinking, and exercise are all part of maintaining physiological homeostasis. However, behavioral theories of reinforcement are stated in

terms of behavioral rather than physiological processes. As in the consummatory-response theory, reinforcers are defined in terms of responses rather than in terms of stimuli. The focus is on the relation between the reinforcing responses and the antecedent instrumental responses they alter.

Premack's theory of reinforcement

Drive-reduction and incentive-motivation theories of reinforcement share an implicit assumption that reinforcers constitute a particular class of stimuli. Together with the consummatory-response theory, these theories also assume that the responses that accompany reinforcing stimuli are fundamentally different in some way from responses that can serve as instrumental behavior. Premack took issue with this distinction and suggested that instrumental responses and responses accompanying reinforcing stimuli differ only in their likelihood of occurrence. He pointed out that responses involved with commonly used reinforcers are activities that the subject is highly likely to pursue. For example, animals in a food-reinforcement experiment are highly likely to engage in eating responses. Deprivation procedures serve to ensure that eating will be the most likely behavior in the situation. In contrast, instrumental responses are typically low-probability activities. An experimentally naive rat, for example, is quite unlikely to press a response lever. Premack (1965) proposed that this difference in response probabilities is critical for reinforcement. Formally, his reinforcement principle may be stated as follows: *Given two responses arranged in an operant-conditioning procedure, the more probable response will reinforce the less likely behavior; the less probable response will not reinforce the more likely behavior.*

Eating will reinforce bar pressing because eating is typically more probable than bar pressing. Under ordinary circumstances, bar pressing cannot reinforce eating. However, Premack's theory suggests that if for some reason bar pressing became more probable than eating, it would reinforce eating. Thus, Premack's theory denies that there is a fundamental distinction between reinforcers and instrumental responses. The particular characteristic that makes a reinforcer reinforce is not something intrinsic to the reinforcing response. Rather, the reinforcing response is simply more likely to occur than the instrumental response. Consequently, it is possible to use a wide variety of responses as reinforcers.

Experimental evidence. Premack and his colleagues conducted many experiments to test his theory (see Premack, 1965, 1971a). One of the early studies was a very simple test using young children. Premack first gave the children two response alternatives (eating candy and playing a pinball machine) and measured which response was more probable for each child. Some of the children preferred eating candy over playing pinball; others preferred pinball. In a second phase of the experiment (see Figure 8.2), the children were tested with one of two procedures. In one procedure, eating was specified as the reinforcing response and play-

ing pinball was the instrumental response. That is, the children had to play the pinball machine in order to get the opportunity to eat the candy. The question was whether all the children would increase their pinball playing. Consistent with Premack's theory, only those children who preferred eating to playing pinball showed a reinforcement effect under these circumstances. In the second procedure, the roles of the two responses were reversed. Eating was the instrumental response, and playing pinball was the reinforcing response. The children had to eat candy to get the opportunity to play pinball. In this situation only those children who preferred playing pinball to eating showed a reinforcement effect.

In another experiment, Premack (1962) altered the probabilities of the responses by changing deprivation conditions. Rats were tested using the responses of drinking and running in a rotating wheel. The experiment is diagramed in Figure 8.3. In one study the rats were water-deprived but not deprived of the opportunity to run in the wheel. Under these circumstances drinking was more probable than running, and the opportunity to drink could be effectively used to reinforce running. In the second study, the rats were not deprived of water. Under these circumstances, they were more likely to run in the wheel than to drink. Now, the opportunity to run in the wheel could be effectively used to reinforce drinking. However, drinking could no longer be used to reinforce running. Thus, running and drinking could be interchangeably used as instrumental and reinforcing responses, depending on the animal's state of water deprivation.

Measuring response probability. Both the experiments described above had two parts. In the first part, behavior was measured in a situation in which the subject had unlimited opportunity to engage in either of the responses to be used later as the instrumental and the reinforcing responses. This situation is assumed to reflect the behavioral homeostatic balance of

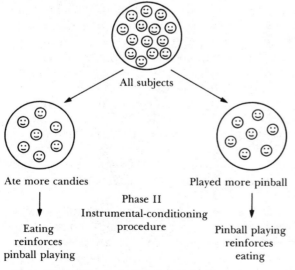

Phase I Free eating and pinball playing

All subjects

Ate more candies

Played more pinball

Phase II
Instrumental-conditioning
procedure

Eating
reinforces
pinball playing

Pinball playing
reinforces
eating

Figure 8.2. Diagram of Premack's (1965) study.

Experiment 1

1. Rat is water deprived

2. Rat drinks more than it runs

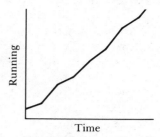

3. Drinking reinforces running

Experiment 2

1. Rat is not water deprived

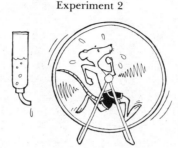

2. Rat runs more than it drinks

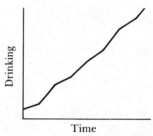

3. Running reinforces drinking

Figure 8.3. When a rat is water-deprived (Experiment 1), it drinks more than it runs. Therefore, drinking reinforces running. When a rat is not water-deprived (Experiment 2), it runs more than it drinks. This time running reinforces drinking. *(Based on Premack, 1962.)*

the organism in the absence of any constraints on responding. We call this the *baseline phase.* In the second part of the experiments, the *instrumental-conditioning phase,* the opportunity to engage in the high-probability reinforcer response was provided only when the subject made the lower-probability instrumental response. As we saw, what happened in the second phase depended on the relative probabilities of the two responses during the baseline phase. Therefore, before we can make precise predictions about how one response will (or will not) reinforce another, we must have some way to measure and compare the baseline probabilities of the two responses.

One possible measure of response probability is the frequency with which each response occurs in a set amount of time. This measure is fine as long as we are comparing responses that require similar amounts of time, such as pressing two alternative but otherwise identical response levers. What would we do, however, if we wanted to compare the probability of two very different responses, such as doing a crossword puzzle and eating? Comparing frequencies of response here would be very cumbersome and difficult. One would have to define what is an instance or unit of puzzle-solving behavior and what is an instance or unit of eating. Is completing one word in a crossword puzzle a unit of puzzle-solving behavior, or is completing all the items in a certain direction (horizontal or vertical) one unit of this behavior? Does a unit of eating mean taking one bite, completing one course, or eating an entire meal? We then have to decide which possible unit of puzzle solving should be considered equivalent to which unit of eating. Is each answer in a puzzle comparable to each bite of eating?

As the above discussion suggests, it is difficult to formulate comparable units of behavior for diverse activities. However, a common dimension to all responses is *time*. Premack suggested that response probability may be measured in terms of the amount of time the subject spends engaged in the response in a specified period. We can express this idea in the following equation:

$$\text{probability of response} = \frac{\text{time spent on response}}{\text{total time}}$$

By this definition, responses taking up a greater proportion of the available time are considered more probable than responses on which the subject spends less time. If in an hour you spend 45 minutes eating and 15 minutes working on a puzzle, we would say that eating was more probable than working on the puzzle during this hour. Therefore, eating should reinforce working on the puzzle.

Although Premack's measure of response probability provides a means of comparing diverse responses, it is counterintuitive in some instances. Consider, for example, a comparison between sexual behavior and studying. A student may spend a good deal more time studying than engaging in sexual behavior. Nevertheless, most students would rate sexual behavior as more pleasant and reinforcing. This paradox may be resolved if we take into account the duration of the baseline observations. Given an unlimited choice between sex and studying in a two-hour period, sex will most likely predominate. However, over a two-year period, studying may be the more probable response. The baseline observation period is also critical for assessing the probability of responses that occur only periodically. For example, although you spend a good deal of time eating in a 24-hour period, eating is not uniformly distributed during the course of a day. Rather, it is highly likely only at certain times. In addition, the more time

you devote to an activity such as eating, the less likely the response becomes for a while. After an hour has been spent in gastronomic pursuits, eating can become very *un*likely.

Because response probabilities vary with time itself, Premack further suggests that the more appropriate response measure is momentary probability. The use of this measure is illustrated in a hypothetical experiment using two responses whose frequencies change in different ways during a session. The experiment is summarized in Figure 8.4. Response A decreases in probability as the session progresses. In contrast, the probability of response B increases. Over the entire session, the subject spends more time engaged in response A than in response B. However, response A can reinforce response B only during the first part of the session, because the momentary probability of response A is higher only during this time. During the second part of the session, response B has a greater momentary probability and therefore will effectively reinforce response A.

Response probability as a measure of response value.   Implicit in our discussion is the notion that more probable responses are more preferred or more valuable. Indeed, Premack suggests that value underlies all behavior. Organisms scale all response alternatives in terms of their value. At any given moment, the more valuable responses have more time allotted to them. If this is true, response probability should fit with other measures of value. In Chapter 7 we discussed concurrent schedules as a way of measuring reinforcement value. The matching law states that the relative rate of response equals the relative value of reinforcement. If we measure the time spent responding on an alternative rather than the response rate, we have

$$\frac{T_1}{\text{total time}} = \frac{V_1}{\text{total value}}$$

and

$$\frac{T_2}{\text{total time}} = \frac{V_2}{\text{total value}}$$

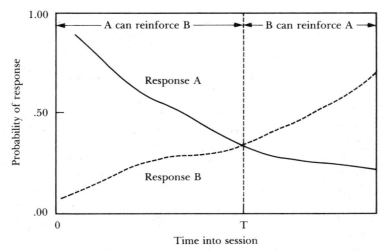

Figure 8.4. Diagram of hypothetical response probabilities for two responses with different probabilities over time. At the beginning of the session (time = 0), response A has a greater momentary probability than response B. Hence response A can reinforce response B. At time T, response B becomes more probable than response A. From this point on, response B can reinforce response A.

for each of two alternatives. Thus, Premack's measure of response probability can be used as a measure of value if we consider responding on schedule 1 as one behavior and responding on schedule 2 as a second behavior.

The idea that value underlies the time allocated to various responses is central to a homeostatic theory of reinforcement. The changes in behavior that we ordinarily attribute to motivational procedures can be considered to result from changes in response value (Premack, 1971a). Hunger, thirst, and increased sexual arousal reflect increased values of eating, drinking, and sexual behavior. Any procedure (such as deprivation) that increases the value of a response relative to the instrumental behavior will enable this response to serve as a reinforcer. The actual reasons that the value has changed are not necessarily important for predicting reinforcement effects.

Momentary probability and restrictions on the reinforcing response. In most instrumental-conditioning procedures, the momentary probability of the reinforcing response is kept at

a high level through two procedures. One, already discussed, is deprivation. Deprivation can effectively increase the probability of certain responses and is often a necessary precondition for reinforcement. However, deprivation procedures are not directly a part of the basic instrumental-conditioning paradigm. In contrast, the second method of increasing momentary probabilities is a component of the instrumental-conditioning procedure itself. It involves restricting the opportunity to engage in the reinforcing response. A rat lever-pressing for food typically does not receive a whole meal for each lever-press response. The importance of this limitation on the reinforcing response should not be underestimated. If we were to give the rat a full meal for making one lever-press response, chances are we would not increase its rate of lever pressing very much. Restrictions on the opportunity to engage in the reinforcing response complement deprivation procedures to increase momentary response probability. In general, we can characterize instrumental-conditioning procedures as requiring the subject to do *more* of the instrumental response for *less* of the reinforcing response than it would do in an unrestricted situation.

Restrictions on the reinforcing response, as we have said, make sure that the momentary probability of the response remains high. In fact, these restrictions should be taken into account in measuring baseline response probabilities. That is, during the baseline session, the amounts of time spent engaged in various responses should be measured under the same constrained circumstances that will occur during the instrumental-conditioning session. For example, the probability of eating should be measured in terms of the amount of time spent eating when food is periodically doled out in small pellets, as during instrumental conditioning.

The fact that the reinforcing response is restricted is a very important aspect of the instrumental-learning situation. According to Premack (1965), it is one of the necessary conditions for reinforcement. Restriction of the reinforcer results in loss of behavioral homeostasis. That is, providing the reinforcer only when the instrumental response has occurred inflicts an imbalance on the natural flow of behavior. The subject cannot allocate time to the various responses in the way it would ordinarily. We may think, then, of the response restriction imposed by the instrumental procedure as giving rise to a kind of behavioral tension. Scholars and artists for centuries have suggested that something akin to this tension is necessary to produce great creative works. Although there are many examples to the contrary, it is often thought that a certain amount of suffering is necessary to produce great works. Premack's theory of reinforcement suggests that some degree of "suffering" or behavioral tension generated by behavioral deprivation may be necessary for even the smallest reinforcement effect.

The deprivation hypothesis

As we have seen, measuring response proba-

bility is not always a simple matter. A complete analysis of response probabilities requires extensive information about the time course and interdependence of the various responses the subject is apt to perform in a particular situation. Timberlake and Allison (1974) have suggested a simpler approach. They note, as discussed above, that restricting the opportunity to make a response increases the value of that response. If we know how much time the organism tends to spend on a particular activity in the absence of restrictions, we can increase the momentary probability of the activity by limiting access to the response. Any response can serve as a reinforcer if the subject is restricted from performing the response as often as it would if given unlimited opportunity. Timberlake and Allison called this the **deprivation hypothesis.**

Experimental application of the deprivation hypothesis requires two phases, just as tests of Premack's theory do. In the first phase, the baseline levels of the various responses are measured. This step provides information about how the subject allocates its time to the various response alternatives when there are no artificial restrictions on any behavior. In the second phase, the subject is deprived of the opportunity to perform the reinforcing response. In response-independent schedules such as the superstition experiment, the reinforcing response is simply made available periodically for a limited time. In response-dependent schedules, a relation between the instrumental response and the reinforcing response is specified. So much reinforcing response is available for so much instrumental response. On a fixed-ratio 10 schedule, for example, 3 sec of eating could be available for the number of seconds required to peck 10 times (FR 10). In both the response-independent and response-dependent reinforcement situations, the way the subject distributes its behavior among response alternatives is partly determined by these experimentally imposed restrictions.

Parameters of time allocation

The schedule of response-dependent reinforcement specifies the feedback function. That is, it specifies the amount of the reinforcing response the subject obtains for its instrumental responses. The actual time devoted to these responses, however, may vary. The subject may spend very little time on the instrumental response and obtain relatively little of the reinforcing response, or it may devote nearly all the available time to the instrumental behavior. We thus see the subject as reallocating time within the limits imposed by the instrumental procedure. What factors determine the actual allocation of time?

One important factor in the reallocation of time in instrumental-conditioning procedures is related to the reinforcing response. We know that such features as the quantity and quality of the reinforcer influence the instrumental-response rate. In behavioral-homeostasis models, these reinforcer characteristics are assumed to alter the value of the reinforcing response. Indeed, research has shown that the baseline level of the reinforcing response strongly influences the reallocation of time among responses in instrumental-conditioning procedures (Brownstein, 1962; Landford, Benson, & Weisman, 1969; Premack, 1961, 1963). A second important factor is the baseline level of the instrumental response. An instrumental procedure in which you were reinforced for watching television would most likely yield very different results than one that used dishwashing as the instrumental response. A third important factor in time reallocation is the time the subject is required to spend on the instrumental response compared with the time available for the reinforcing response. We discussed the role of this variable in the previous sections. Each of the three factors determining time allocation has been extensively investigated (see Burkhard, 1981; Timberlake & Allison, 1974, for reviews). More important, however, is the combination of these factors. You may be willing to wash dishes for an hour in order to watch television for an hour. You are not likely to wash dishes for five weeks for the same reinforcer. However, if the opportunity to spend $3 million were added to the reinforcer, washing dishes for five weeks would no doubt become much more attractive. It is the combination of what you want and what you have to do to get it that determines how you allocate your time among response alternatives.

Various theorists have combined the individual factors that determine time allocation into a kind of rule to describe the redistribution of behavior. For example, Timberlake and Allison's deprivation hypothesis emphasizes the deprivation of the reinforcing response. The reallocation of time to the response alternatives depends on the degree of deprivation of the reinforcing response (D_R). This deprivation, D_R, is in turn assumed to be a function of a particular combination of other factors, according to the formula

$$D_R = B_R - \frac{B_I R}{I}$$

where B_R and B_I are the baseline levels of the reinforcing and instrumental responses respectively, R is the amount of the reinforcing response that is available at each presentation of the reinforcer, and I is the instrumental-conditioning requirement. Allison (1976) has proposed yet another arrangement of these same variables. This proposal, called the "conservation hypothesis," is based on the idea that the instrumental and the reinforcer responses involved always retain a particular relation to each other from one session to another. The combined time on the two responses in the instrumental-conditioning phase is assumed to be some constant function of the combined times for these responses in the baseline phase. The subject thus conserves something akin to energy expended on the two activities between the baseline and the reinforcement phases.

Multiple-response approaches

Both the deprivation and conservation hypotheses provide rules for how the time devoted to the instrumental and the reinforcing responses is reallocated from baseline to instrumental-conditioning sessions. Recent research indicates, however, that the scope of these rules is severely limited (see Rachlin & Burkhard, 1978). Quantitative predictions using these rules work only over a limited range of schedules. Furthermore, the rules are confined to situations in which only the instrumental and reinforcer responses are affected by the conditioning procedure. There is much evidence now that in many cases other responses may be altered as well. The introduction of an instrumental-conditioning procedure often causes a total reshuffle of many activities of the organism, not just the two responses that are directly involved in the instrumental procedure. In some cases ordinarily low-valued activities emerge and compete with the instrumental response when the response requirement is imposed as a condition for access to the reinforcer. You know, for example, that if you study hard or work diligently on a term paper, you will do better in your course of study. However, it is when you settle down to study that you may have a sudden desire to do your laundry, catch up on writing long-overdue letters, or run some errands. The necessity of analyzing multiple responses in studies of instrumental conditioning is exemplified by studies of schedule-induced behavior.

Schedule-induced adjunctive behavior.
Most research on instrumental behavior is performed in laboratory situations devoid of many response options. This is, of course, done to minimize variability in the data. When the environment is made just a little more complicated, dramatic effects are sometimes observed. For example, Falk (1961) added a water bottle to Skinner boxes in which rats were reinforced with food for pressing a response lever on a variable-interval schedule. Although the animals were not water-deprived, they consumed huge quantities of water. In some instances, the fluid intake during a 3-hour session was nearly half the body weight of the rat! This excessive drinking is called **schedule-induced polydipsia.** Schedule-induced polydipsia is particularly curious because it has defied various traditional physiological and behavioral explanations. It does not involve known physiological mechanisms of thirst. Nor does it seem to be the result of accidental reinforcement, classical conditioning, or mediating responses for the instrumental response (see Falk, 1972, for a review). The excessiveness of the behavior suggests that it is part of an emotional reaction of some kind. However, attempts to elucidate this idea have not gone very far.

Drinking is not the only kind of "extra" behavior that develops in reinforcement situations. Schedule-induced aggression has been observed in a number of animals. Monkeys will bite a rubber hose after reinforcement (Hutchinson, Azrin, & Hunt, 1968). Pigeons will attack another pigeon or a stuffed model of a pigeon (for example, Gentry, 1968). Monkeys will eat wood shavings (Villareal, 1967), and rats will run in a running wheel (Levitsky & Collier, 1968) or lick a stream of air (Mendelson & Chillag, 1970) when these response alternatives are available in the experimental situation.

Falk (1972) has suggested that the above responses be classified together as **adjunctive behavior** because they have certain similar characteristics. First, they all develop during exposure to schedules of intermittent reinforcement even though these responses are not involved in obtaining or consuming the reinforcer. They all tend to be excessive and to occur shortly after reinforcement. In addition, although adjunctive behavior is observed with response-

Box 8.4. Schedule-Induced Behavior in Humans

Schedule-induced behavior such as polydipsia has often been observed in animals. Recent research suggests that schedule-induced behaviors are also readily apparent in human subjects. In one experiment by Wallace, Singer, Wayner, and Cook (1975), adult humans were observed as they operated a slot machine. The subjects were initially told that the study concerned the effects of gambling on blood pressure. In fact, the gambling was the operant response that was reinforced on an FI 15-sec or FI 60-sec schedule of reinforcement. That is, the payoff was scheduled by the experimenters. While the subjects "gambled," the experimenters recorded other behaviors, including various motor activities and eating and drinking of snacks that had been provided. The results showed clear increases in adjunctive activity produced by the schedules of reinforcement; the FI 60-sec schedule induced more activity than the FI 15-sec schedule. The particulars of the behavior are described as follows:

> Although no consistent polydipsia or hyperphagia [was] induced. . . , occasionally copious drinking occurred and large amounts of food were consumed. Several instances of other bizarre behaviors were observed such as blending cheezels and Coca-Cola and drinking the mixture, tearing scrap paper into hundreds of pieces and arranging them in symmetrical patterns, pressing the space bar with a bare foot, tossing cheezels into a paper cup, vocalizations, and play eating [p. 653].

Skinner and Morse (1957) and later Kachanoff, Leveille, McClelland, and Wayner (1973) have entertained the hypothesis that bizarre psychotic behavior may be schedule-induced by the natural schedules affecting the person. The descriptions of schedule-induced behavior by Wallace et al. are relevant in this connection. However, far more research is required to substantiate this interesting idea.

dependent instrumental-conditioning procedures, the response requirement does not seem to be necessary. Intermittent food delivery is sufficient to produce adjunctive behavior without any response requirement for obtaining the reinforcers. Finally, the magnitude of adjunctive behavior is related to the interval between successive food presentations. Figure 8.5 shows the level of adjunctive drinking and aggression as a function of time between reinforcers. Adjunctive behavior first increases and then decreases as a function of the interreinforcement interval.

Models for reallocation of time with multiple responses. Elucidating the effects of reinforcement on the total behavior of an organism is a complicated task. Just defining and measuring all or most of an organism's activities is very difficult. Anyone who doubts this need only try to describe completely everything a 4-year-old child does in an hour! Understanding how and why reinforcement procedures change this response profile is even more problematic. However, several models are currently being developed. The goal is to describe the relation between behavior in an unconstrained situation and behavior in the presence of instrumental-conditioning limitations. How and why does the time allocated to various responses change from one situation to the other?

One approach to the redistribution of behavior is modeled after economic theory (Rachlin & Burkhard, 1978; see also Staddon, 1976). Economists try to explain how money is allocated to various commodities under circumstances involving different incomes and prices. They assume that individuals allocate money so as to maximize the value, or utility, of their purchases. The amount of each commodity purchased therefore depends on individual preferences (values) for the commodities, together with income and price restrictions. If you go to the store to buy apples. bananas, and oranges,

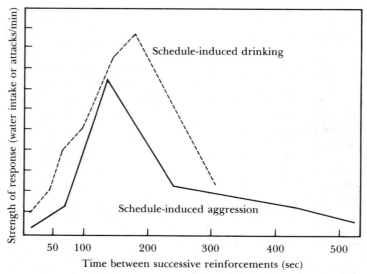

Figure 8.5. Amount of adjunctive behavior as a function of the interreinforcement interval. [Schedule-induced-drinking data are adapted from Falk (1972). Schedule-induced-aggression data are adapted from Flory (1969).]

your actual purchases will depend on the price of each fruit, how much money you have, and how you value the three fruits.

The multiple-response model also assumes that subjects maximize value—the value of their total behavioral output. There are restrictions on behavior, just as there are restrictions on purchases in the marketplace. Behavior is restricted by the total time available (time income) and how long it takes to complete each response (behavioral price). Let us assume that in an evening you may watch television, study, eat a good meal, and sleep. How much time you actually spend on each of these activities depends on how much time you have, how much time each response requires, and the structure of your preferences for the activities. Response/ reinforcer contingencies and the like can add further restrictions. Nevertheless, the time spent on each response presumably results from obtaining the highest possible value under the restrictions. The actual time expended in each activity is determined jointly by the temporal restrictions and the preferences, or values, placed on the responses.

We will not describe the details of the economic model of response reallocation (see Burkhard, 1981; Rachlin & Burkhard, 1978). However, several important aspects of the model should be mentioned. The multiple-response approach represents a far more complicated analysis of behavior than that provided by the earlier learning theorists. Instead of focusing merely on changes in the instrumental response, the model considers all of the animal's activities. Thus, the view of behavior is broader and more closely related to the natural behavioral repertoire of the organism. In contrast, the associationist approaches typical of earlier learning theorists are rather mechanistic (reinforcement simply "stamps in" instrumental responses). Furthermore, earlier learning theorists viewed individual responses as being far more plastic, or malleable, to reinforcement procedures than the contemporary multiple-response approaches do. Reinforcement procedures are viewed as reorganizing the organism's entire behavioral repertoire rather than just changing the likelihood of an individual response. Therefore, the effects of reinforcement on the instrumental response depend on the organism's full range of activities and the values of these activities.

REINFORCEMENT AS RESPONSE SELECTION

The last approach to the study of reinforcement is based largely on the work of Staddon and Simmelhag (1971). This model, like the multiple-response approach, ·takes an all-encompassing view of the animal's behavior. Reinforcement is viewed as one way in which particular responses are selected out of the animal's repertoire to predominate at certain times and in certain places. To understand this treatment of reinforcement, it is necessary first to understand the view of behavior that underlies it.

The model of behavior proposed by Staddon and Simmelhag incorporates observations about behavior that have been problematic to more traditional approaches. The first of these includes data on belongingness, preparedness, and instinctive drift, described in Chapter 6. You will recall that these observations indicate that some responses are amenable to reinforcement whereas others defy or compete with reinforcement effects. A second set of observations incorporated into the Staddon/Simmelhag model concerns the adjunctive-behavior phenomena described earlier in this chapter. Traditional accounts of behavior have not been successful in explaining these "extraneous" schedule effects. A third area of research incorporated into the model involves the phenomenon of sign tracking, described in Chapter 4. You may recall that pigeons will come to peck a key that is illuminated just before each periodic delivery of food. This phenomenon was problematic for theories of operant conditioning when it was discovered, because up to that time it was believed that pecking could be strengthened only with operant-conditioning procedures. Finally, the Staddon/Simmelhag model is concerned with the superstition experiment.

What do all these areas of research—superstition, adjunctive behavior, sign tracking, and belongingness—have in common? They all involve responses to periodic delivery of reinforcement, and many of them appear to be biologically determined. The Staddon/Simmelhag model describes how intermittent reinforcement reorganizes behavior.

Staddon and Simmelhag's superstition experiment

The approach to behavior advocated by Staddon and Simmelhag is illustrated by their analysis of the superstition experiment. In their replication of the study, they compared the behavior of pigeons on three schedules of reinforcement. In two of the schedules, reinforcers were periodically delivered irrespective of the pigeons' behavior (superstition schedules). One of these schedules involved a fixed amount of time between successive reinforcers, as in Skinner's original superstition experiment. The other was a response-independent variable-time schedule. The third schedule was a standard fixed-interval schedule in which pigeons were required to peck a response key for reinforcement.

Unlike other researchers, Staddon and Simmelhag carefully observed the total behavior of the pigeons throughout the experiment. They defined and measured the occurrence of many responses, such as orienting responses to the food hopper, pecking the response key, wing flapping, turning in quarter circles, and preening. The frequency of each response was recorded according to when it occurred during the interval between successive deliveries of the reinforcer. Data for several responses for one pigeon are shown in Figure 8.6. The figure shows that some of the responses occurred predominantly toward the end of the interval between successive reinforcers. For example, R_1 and R_7 (orienting to the food magazine and pecking at something on the magazine wall) were much more likely to occur at the end of the

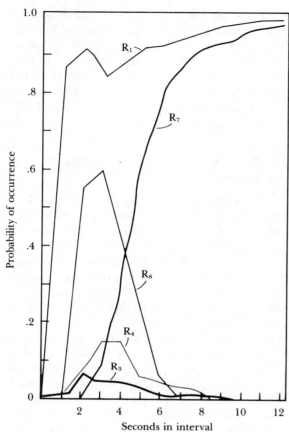

Figure 8.6. Probability of several responses as a function of time between successive deliveries of a food reinforcer. R_1 (orienting toward the food magazine wall) and R_7 (pecking at something on the magazine wall) are terminal responses, having their highest probabilities at the end of the interreinforcement interval. R_3 (pecking at something on the floor), R_4 (a quarter turn), and R_8 (moving along the magazine wall) are interim responses, having their highest probabilities somewhere near the middle of the interreinforcement interval. *(From Staddon & Simmelhag, 1971.)*

and making a quarter turn) somewhere near the middle of the interreinforcement interval. These activities were called **interim responses.** Which actions were terminal responses and which were interim responses did not vary very much from one pigeon to another. The terminal responses by and large appeared to include activities that are a part of the pigeon's natural eating pattern—pecking, putting head in food hopper, and so on. In contrast, activities not related to eating, such as preening and turning, tended to make up the interim-response category.

Distinctive interim and terminal responses developed with all three reinforcement schedules tested. The results of the response-dependent schedule differed from the results of the response-independent schedules (fixed time and variable time) only in that key pecking was always a strong terminal response on the response-dependent schedule. This outcome suggests that a response/reinforcer contingency facilitates the selection of one particular terminal behavior from the set of all possible terminal responses. Furthermore, Staddon and Simmelhag failed to find evidence of accidental-reinforcement effects. Responses did not always increase in frequency merely because they occurred coincidentally with food delivery. Food delivery appeared to influence only the strength of terminal responses, even in the initial phases of training. (For other experiments of this type, see Reberg, Innis, Mann, & Eizenga, 1978; Reberg, Mann, & Innis, 1977.)

The evolutionary model of behavior

Staddon and Simmelhag's superstition experiment, together with the research on sign tracking, belongingness, and adjunctive behavior, suggests that there is a biological basis for all the effects of periodic food delivery on behavior, including the increase in the probability of the response required for reinforcement. The model of behavior Staddon and Simmelhag

interreinforcement interval than at other times. Staddon and Simmelhag called these **terminal responses.** Other activities increased in frequency after the delivery of a reward and then decreased as the time for the next reward drew closer. The pigeons were most likely to engage in R_8 and R_4 (moving along the magazine wall

propose is fashioned after Darwin's theory of evolution. Darwin saw the emergence of particular physical characteristics in a species as the result of an interplay between two processes, variation and selection. Individuals of a species vary naturally in many of their characteristics (for example, height, hair color, and agility). Those characteristics that facilitate the transmission of genes from one generation to the next are selected out as individuals bearing maladaptive characteristics fail to reproduce or have unhealthy offspring.

Staddon and Simmelhag proposed that processes of variation and selection analogous to those entertained by Darwin are at work with behavior. There are always variations in behavior. Organisms in nature do not persist in doing the same thing for very long. Behavior is forever changing because of experience and learning, transitory changes in physiological state, variations in the stimulus environment, and the like. Certain events or characteristics of the environment are assumed to select from the variability in behavior certain responses that come to predominate at particular times and in particular situations. One of these selection mechanisms is provided by the delivery of a reinforcer, whether the reinforcer is response-contingent or response-independent. According to this point of view, reinforcement does not "stamp in" particular responses. Rather, it limits behavioral variability at particular times. The subject is not victimized by accidental response/reinforcer pairings. Rather, the subject does what it usually does with the particular reinforcer; if the reinforcer is grain, we expect responses such as pecking to emerge in pigeons. If the reinforcer comes on a periodic or intermittent schedule, the subject simply shifts its pattern of behavior to accommodate this schedule. When a particular reinforcer is not likely to be delivered, there is more variability in behavior, or responses are selected out by other reinforcers.

According to the Staddon/Simmelhag model, superstitious behavior and sign tracking are products of the same process. Both are considered to emerge as terminal responses. In sign tracking, the behavior is directed to the lighted key. The selective feature of reinforcement is also consistent with the belongingness and instinctive-drift phenomena. Each reinforcer is assumed to give rise to its own set of terminal responses. Hence, responses and reinforcers have a special relation to each other. Instinctive drift is apt to occur when the response required for reinforcement is not one of the terminal responses for that reinforcer.

Reinforcement as response selection explains the operation of reinforcement outside the laboratory as well. Consider, for example, starting an old car on a cold morning. Each time you turn the key in the ignition, you will undoubtedly go through a number of responses, such as pulling out the choke, pressing the accelerator down, and turning the ignition key for sometimes long and sometimes short periods. You may also engage in such responses as sneezing, wrapping your scarf more tightly around your neck, or making a rash of verbal reprimands at the jalopy. Let us assume the car finally starts. The start of the engine is far more likely to reinforce activities related to the ignition than the other responses you performed just before the car started. We might think of the ignition-related responses as terminal responses for getting the car started. All the things you do related to the ignition may not in fact be necessary for getting the engine started. Jiggling the key in the ignition, for example, may not actually help. However, it is unlikely that you will ever limit your responses to only those actions that are absolutely necessary to get the car started. Rather, you will probably repeat the entire pattern with superfluous responses. In contrast, nonterminal responses, such as fixing the scarf, sneezing, or making verbal reprimands, will not be reinforced by the start of the engine and will not necessarily occur the next time you try to start the car.

Concluding comments

We have presented research and theories about reinforcement representing several points of view. No one approach is comprehensive. Each approach starts from a particular set of ideas about what a reinforcer is. Whether one regards a reinforcer as a stimulus or as a response leads one, as we have seen, in different directions. In fact, a reinforcer in most cases involves both stimuli and responses. Determining a common feature for all reinforcers is therefore an extremely complex task.

Explaining the mechanism of reinforcement likewise rests on a set of starting assumptions about instrumental behavior. We began our discussion with the simple notion that instrumental behavior is "stamped in" by reinforcement. The instrumental response was originally viewed as a single behavior that increases in frequency with reinforcement. The drive-reduction theorists suggested a biologically based mechanism to account for the "stamping in" ef-

fect. However, with more research it became clear that the motivating circumstances are not so simple. Drive states and incentive stimuli interact in complex and not completely understood ways. The behavioral theories tend to view instrumental behavior as a by-product of a total reorganization of behavior under less than optimal conditions. The idea of maximizing behavioral value plays a central role in these models. Subjects reallocate their time to various responses so as to maximize behavioral value. Most comprehensive approaches in the future may well follow in the direction proposed by Staddon and Simmelhag. This type of model may bring together the biological approaches with the behavioral. Terminal behaviors do seem to have a "stamped in" quality that may be better called "selected." This selection, however, is going on within the framework of a reallocation of time to various responses within the constraints of an instrumental-conditioning procedure.

CHAPTER NINE

Signal Value in Instrumental Conditioning: Stimulus Control and Secondary Reinforcement

In Chapter 9 we begin our discussion of the role of stimulus/reinforcer relations in instrumental conditioning. We will first describe how instrumental behavior can come to be controlled by stimuli that precede and accompany the performance of reinforced responses. We will then describe the ways secondary, or conditioned, reinforcers (stimuli that accompany the delivery of the primary reinforcer) can influence instrumental behavior.

In our discussion of instrumental behavior so far, we have emphasized the relation between the instrumental response and the reinforcer. As we have seen in Chapters 7 and 8, the response/reinforcer relation is a very important aspect of instrumental conditioning. However, responses and reinforcers do not occur in a vacuum. Animals typically experience particular stimuli when they perform the instrumental response, and the response is often followed not only by the reinforcer but also by other cues that reliably accompany the delivery of the reward. This sequence of events is diagramed in Figure 9.1. Consider, for example, the reinforcement of lever pressing in rats with pellets of food. The lever-press response (R) is made in the presence of many ambient stimuli (S_A), such as the sight, smell, and sounds of the experi-

mental chamber. The lever-press response itself is accompanied by other stimuli (S_B). For example, the depression of the lever may produce an audible click. It may also activate the food-delivery device, which makes certain noises in the process of delivering the food reinforcer (S^{R+}). The stimuli S_A and S_B that precede and follow the response can have very important

Figure 9.1. Stimulus relations in instrumental-conditioning procedures. The instrumental response (R) is performed in the presence of certain stimuli (S_A) and produces other cues (S_B) that are paired with the reinforcer (S^{R+}).

roles in the control of instrumental behavior.

The sight, smell, and sounds of the experimental chamber (stimuli S_A) provide the stimulus context for the instrumental behavior. Because the instrumental response is rewarded in the presence of these cues, these stimuli can come to control occurrences of the response. Stimulus control of instrumental behavior is evident in many spheres of life outside the laboratory. For most students, for example, studying is under the strong control of school-related stimuli. College students who have fallen behind in their course work often make determined resolutions to do a lot of studying when they return home during the Thanksgiving, Christmas, or spring vacation. However, not much work ever gets accomplished during these holidays. The stimulus context of the holidays is usually very different from the stimuli experienced when classes are in session. Therefore, the holiday stimuli do not evoke effective studying behavior. Traveling businesspeople often have a similar problem. They may find it difficult to get much work done on airplanes because the stimulus context of an airplane is too different from the stimuli of their offices.

Stimulus control of behavior is an important aspect of behavioral adjustments to the environment. The survival of animals in the wild frequently depends on their ability to perform responses that are appropriate to the stimulus circumstances. With seasonal changes in their food supply, for example, animals may have to adopt different foraging responses to obtain food. Within the same season, one type of behavior is required in the presence of predators or intruders, and other types of responses are reinforced in the absence of nearby danger. In cold weather, animals may seek comfort by going to areas warmed by the sun; on rainy days they may seek comfort by going to shaded areas. To be effective in obtaining comfort and avoiding pain, animals always have to behave in ways that are appropriate to their changing circumstances.

Performance of instrumental responses appropriate to the stimulus situation is so important that failure to do this is often considered abnormal. Many instrumental acts that are evident in psychologically disturbed persons are pathological only in that they occur in situations where they should not. Getting undressed, for example, is acceptable instrumental behavior in the privacy of your bedroom. The same behavior on a public street is considered highly abnormal. Staring at a television set is considered appropriate if the set is turned on. Staring at a blank television screen may be a symptom of behavior pathology. If you respond in a loving way in the presence of your spouse or other family members, your behavior generally has positive consequences. The same behavior directed toward strangers on the street can have quite different effects. Yelling and screaming is reinforced by social approval at football games. The same responses are frowned on if they occur in a church, a classroom, or a supermarket.

The stimuli that follow an instrumental response and signal the delivery of the reinforcer (S_B in Figure 9.1) are also important in the control of behavior. Such stimuli initially may have no particular effect on the organism. However, because these cues accompany the delivery of the reinforcer, they become conditioned by the reinforcer. Therefore, they are called **secondary** or **conditioned reinforcers.** Secondary, or conditioned, reinforcers can be identified in many aspects of life. Words of praise are conditioned reinforcers because they often accompany other reinforcers, such as a financial bonus, a hug, or a special present. The sight and smell of good food are conditioned reinforcers because they accompany a satisfying meal. Money is a conditioned reinforcer because it is accompanied by all sorts of other rewarding stimuli, such as food, clothes, entertainment, or whatever else money can buy. The fact that conditioning is required for money to have reinforcing properties is clearly evident when you consider how children react to money. Young children do not understand the relation between value and size. They may prefer a nickel to a dime because the nickel is bigger. They will use money as toys rather than as a way of obtaining other desired items.

In the present chapter we will consider in some detail how instrumental behavior is related to the stimuli that are present when the response is made and to conditioned reinforcers that are delivered following the response. Much of the research we will describe borrows from the study of classical conditioning. Some of the terms and concepts that we will use are similar to what we previously discussed in our treatment of classical conditioning. The present chapter illustrates some of the ways classical-conditioning processes are involved in the control of positively reinforced instrumental behavior. We will consider the role of classical conditioning in aversive instrumental-conditioning situations in Chapter 10, followed by a more general treatment of the interaction of the two types of conditioning in Chapter 11.

Stimulus control of instrumental behavior

As noted above, reinforcement of an instrumental response typically occurs in the presence of particular stimuli, and these stimuli may come to control the performance of the instrumental behavior. How can we tell that instrumental behavior has come under the control of such stimuli? How do stimuli gain control over instrumental behavior? In what sense do these stimuli control behavior, and what do subjects learn about the stimuli? Questions such as these have been extensively discussed and investigated. We will review some of the highlights of this research.

Differential responding and stimulus discrimination

The first problem that has to be solved in an investigation of stimulus control is how to identify and measure instances of it. How can we tell

that an instrumental response has come under the control of certain cues? Consider, for example, a pigeon pecking for food on a variable-interval reinforcement schedule in a Skinner box. While in the Skinner box, the pigeon is exposed to a wide variety of stimuli, including the color and texture of the walls of the chamber, the sight of the nuts and bolts holding the chamber together, the odor of the chamber, and the noises of the ventilating fan. In addition, let us assume that the circular response key in the box is illuminated by a pattern consisting of a white triangle on a red background. The pigeon in this situation is probably also stimulated by internal sensations provided by its degree of food deprivation and its general physical well-being. How can we determine whether these external and internal stimuli control the pigeon's key-pecking behavior?

Reynolds (1961a) conducted an experiment using stimuli similar to those described above. Two pigeons were reinforced on a variable-interval schedule for pecking a circular response key. Reinforcement for pecking was available whenever the response key was illuminated by a visual pattern consisting of a white triangle on a red background (see Figure 9.2). The stimulus on the key, thus, had two components, the white triangle and the red color of the background. Reynolds was interested in finding out which of these stimulus components gained control over the pecking behavior. Therefore, after the pigeons learned to peck steadily at the triangle on the red background, Reynolds measured the amount of pecking that occurred when only one of the component stimuli was presented. On some of the test trials, the white triangle was projected on the response key without the red color. On other test trials, the red background color was projected on the response key without the white triangle.

The results are summarized in Figure 9.2. One of the pigeons pecked a great deal more when the response key was illuminated with the red light than when it was illuminated with the white triangle. This outcome shows that its

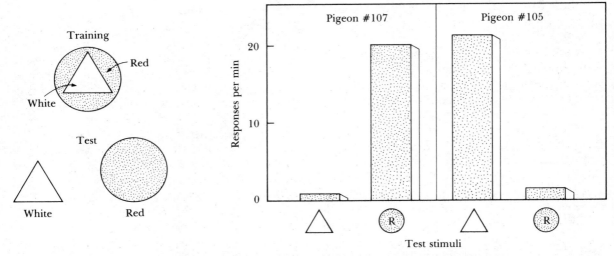

Figure 9.2. Summary of procedure and results of experiment by Reynolds (1961a). Two pigeons were first reinforced for pecking whenever a compound stimulus consisting of a white triangle on a red background was projected on the response key. The rate of pecking was then observed in each subject when the white triangle and the red background stimuli were presented separately.

pecking behavior was much more strongly controlled by the red color than by the white triangle. In contrast, the other pigeon pecked a great deal more when the white triangle was projected on the response key than when the key was illuminated by the red light. Thus, for this subject, the pecking behavior was more strongly controlled by the triangle than by the color stimulus.

Reynolds' experiment illustrates several important ideas. First, it shows how we can experimentally determine whether instrumental behavior has come under the control of a particular stimulus. *Stimulus control of instrumental behavior is demonstrated by differential responding in the presence of different stimuli.* If a subject responds in one way in the presence of one stimulus and in a different way in the presence of another stimulus, we may conclude that its behavior has come under the control of the stimuli involved. Such differential responding was evident in the behavior of both the pigeons Reynolds tested. Both animals responded more frequently in the presence of one of the stimuli

(red color or triangle) than in the presence of the other.

Differential responding to two or more stimuli also indicates that the subjects are discriminating among the stimuli—that they are treating each stimulus as being different from the other cues. Such stimulus discrimination does not always occur. If the pigeons had ignored the visual cues that were projected on the response key or if the pigeons had been blind, they would have responded the same way to the white triangle and the red background. The fact that they responded differently to the two stimuli shows that they discriminated between the two cues. Thus, *stimulus discrimination exists whenever subjects respond differently to different stimuli.* Stimulus discrimination and stimulus control are two ways of considering the same phenomenon. One cannot have either one without the other. If a subject does not discriminate between two stimuli, its behavior is not under the control of those cues.

Another interesting aspect of the results was that the pecking behavior of each animal came under the control of a different stimulus component. The behavior of one bird came under the control of the red color, and the behavior of the other came under the control of the triangle. The procedures used in the experiment did not direct the animals to attend especially to either the red light or the triangle. Therefore, it is not surprising that different stimuli came to control pecking behavior in the two subjects. The experiment was comparable to showing a group of schoolchildren a famous picture in a beautiful gold frame without telling them what to look at. Some of the children may become captivated by the beauty of the frame, others by the beauty of the picture. In the absence of special procedures of the sort we will discuss below, one cannot always predict which of the various stimuli that an organism experiences will gain control over its instrumental behavior.

Although only one of the stimulus components evoked much pecking in each of the pigeons, one cannot conclude from this information that the other stimulus had no effect whatever. Perhaps measurement of some other response to the stimuli or some other aspect of key pecking, such as its duration, would have provided evidence of control by both stimulus components. As the experiment was conducted, it yielded information only about the stimulus control of the rate of key pecking. The conclusions that can be reached from the study are also limited to the stimulus features that were varied in the tests. The fact that one pigeon responded more frequently to the white triangle than the red background allows us to conclude only that some property or properties of the triangle were important. It does not tell us that the shape of the triangle was the critical feature of the stimulus. The pecking behavior may have been controlled instead by the color or brightness of the triangle. Further tests are required to identify exactly which of these stimulus characteristics controlled the pecking behavior. These considerations indicate that *the conclusions that can be reached about stimulus control are limited to the particular responses and stimuli used in a particular test procedure.*

Stimulus generalization

In our discussion so far, we have treated stimuli as if they were clearly identifiable and distinguishable entities in the world. However, identifying and differentiating various stimuli is not a simple matter. Stimuli may be defined in all kinds of ways. Sometimes widely different objects or events are considered instances of the same stimulus because they all share the same function. Whether an object can be used as a stimulus in a toy-playing experiment, for example, depends on whether it can function as a toy; the exact physical characteristics of the object are not important. In contrast, in other studies stimuli are identified and distinguished in terms of precise physical features such as the frequency of sound waves or the wavelength of light. How stimuli are defined in a particular experiment largely depends on the purposes of the investigation.

Psychologists and physiologists have been concerned for a long time with how organisms identify and distinguish different stimuli. This area of research is a part of the study of psychophysics, but it is also related to the problems of stimulus control. One of the main phenomena of interest here is **stimulus generalization.** In a sense, stimulus generalization is the opposite of differential responding or stimulus discrimination. Stimulus generalization is said to exist *whenever the subject fails to respond differentially to various stimuli*—whenever the same level of behavior is observed in the presence of different stimuli.

The phenomenon of stimulus generalization was first observed by Pavlov. He found that after a particular stimulus was conditioned, subjects would also make the conditioned response to other, similar stimuli. That is, they failed to respond differentially to stimuli that were similar to the original conditioned stimulus. Stimulus generalization has also been investigated in instrumental conditioning. In a landmark experiment, Guttman and Kalish (1956) first reinforced pigeons on a variable-interval schedule for pecking a response key illuminated by a light whose wavelength was 580 nanometers (this has a yellowish-orange color). After training, the animals were tested with a variety of other colors projected on the response key, and the rate of responding in the presence of each color was recorded. The results of the experiment are summarized in Figure 9.3. The highest rate of pecking occurred in response to the original 580-nm light. The subjects also made substantial numbers of pecks when lights of 570 and 590 nm wavelength were tested: the responding generalized to the 570-nm and 590-nm stimuli. However, as the color of the test stimuli became increasingly different from the color of the original training stimulus, progressively fewer responses occurred. The results show a gradient of responding as a function of how similar each test stimulus was to the original training stimulus. This type of outcome is called a **stimulus-generalization gradient.**

Stimulus-generalization gradients as a measure of stimulus control. Stimulus-generalization gradients are often used to evaluate stimulus control because they provide information about how sensitive the subject's behavior is to variations in environmental stimulation. With the use of stimulus-generalization gradients, we can determine exactly how much a stimulus has to be changed in order for behavior to change. Consider, for example, the gradient in Figure 9.3. Subjects responded much more when the original 580-nm training stimulus was presented than when the response key was illuminated by lights whose wavelengths were 520, 540, 620, and 640 nm. Thus, differences in color controlled different levels of responding. However, this control was not very precise. Responding to the 580-nm color generalized to the 570- and 590-nm stimuli. The wavelength of the 580-nm training stimulus

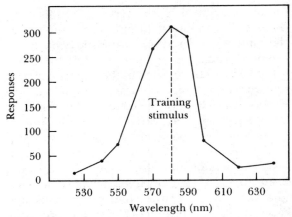

Figure 9.3. Stimulus-generalization gradient for pigeons that were trained to peck in the presence of a colored light of 580 nm wavelength and then tested in the presence of other colors. (*After Guttman & Kalish, 1956.*)

had to be changed by more than 10 nm before a decrement in performance was observed.

The fact that substantial rates of responding occurred in the presence of stimuli between 570 and 590 nm indicates that the color of the response key did not have to have a wavelength of exactly 580 nm to evoke the pecking response. How do you suppose pigeons would have responded in this experiment if they had been color-blind? If the subjects had been color-blind, they could not have distinguished lights of different wavelengths. Therefore, they would have responded in much the same way regardless of what color was projected on the response key. Hypothetical results of an experiment of this sort are presented in Figure 9.4. If the pigeons did not respond on the basis of the color of the key light, similar high rates of responding would have occurred as different colors were projected on the key. Thus, the stimulus-generalization gradient would have been flat.

A comparison of the results obtained by Guttman and Kalish and our hypothetical experiment with color-blind pigeons indicates that *the steepness of a stimulus-generalization gradient can be used as a measure of the extent to which the*

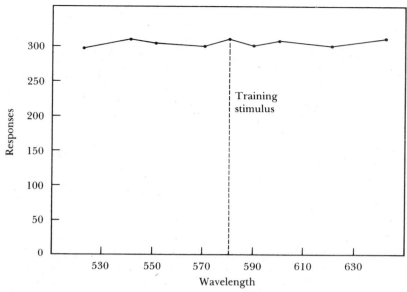

Figure 9.4. Hypothetical stimulus-generalization gradient for color-blind pigeons trained to peck in the presence of a colored light of 580 nm wavelength and then tested in the presence of other colors.

stimulus feature being varied controls the behavior of the subjects. A flat generalization gradient (Figure 9.4) is obtained if subjects respond the same way to a variety of stimuli. This lack of differential responding shows that the stimulus feature that is varied in the generalization test does not control the instrumental behavior. In contrast, a steep generalization gradient (Figure 9.3) is obtained if subjects respond more to some of the test stimuli than to others. This differential responding is evidence that the instrumental behavior is under the control of the stimulus feature that is varied among the test stimuli. We may think of generalization and differential responding as opposites. If a great deal of generalization occurs, there is little differential responding. If responding is highly differential to stimuli, little generalization is obtained.

Mechanisms of stimulus generalization.
The phenomenon of stimulus generalization is remarkable because it shows that responding can occur with stimuli that have never been

presented or paired with reinforcement during training. Why should new stimuli that have not occurred in training evoke the conditioned behavior? The first person to suggest an answer to this question was Pavlov. Pavlov observed stimulus-generalization effects in his classical-conditioning experiments. He noted, for example, that if a tactile stimulus applied to one part of the skin was conditioned with a US, tactile stimuli applied to nearby areas of the skin would also elicit the conditioned response. However, the strength of the conditioned response was less as the test stimuli were applied to areas farther and farther from the location of the original CS. From such observations, Pavlov formulated a model of stimulus generalization based on the **irradiation of excitation.**

Pavlov assumed that every stimulus produces excitation in a particular area of the cortex, and similar stimuli activate physically adjacent areas. He proposed that when a CS is presented and paired with reinforcement, excitation occurs in the brain locus corresponding to the CS, and this excitation irradiates to adjacent brain locations, much as circular waves irradiate from the point of contact when a pebble is tossed into a calm lake. The irradiation of excitation was assumed to be progressively weaker with increasing distance from the center of excitation. You may recall from Chapter 5 that simultaneous excitation of the CS and US centers was assumed to result in an association between the two stimuli. Because of the irradiation of excitation, whenever the CS was presented, nearby areas also became activated, and Pavlov assumed that these nearby areas of the brain also became associated with the US center. Thus, during the course of conditioning, the US was assumed to become associated with not only the CS but also stimuli that were similar to the CS.

The neural mechanism Pavlov proposed to explain stimulus generalization was greeted with skepticism, but the basic idea that effects of training spread to stimuli similar in some way to the training cues was adopted by major behavior theorists, such as Hull and Spence. However, some psychologists argued that even this formulation was unacceptable. Consider, for example, our hypothetical experiment on stimulus generalization in color-blind pigeons. We suggested that such animals would respond equally to stimuli of various colors. They would show perfect stimulus generalization. Such a result could not be explained in terms of the spread of effect of excitation, because in color-blind animals the presentation of a particular color during training presumably does not produce excitation of a brain area corresponding to that particular color. A much more reasonable explanation of our results with color-blind subjects is that they responded similarly to all the colors because they could not distinguish differences among them. This type of alternative account of stimulus generalization was proposed by Lashley and Wade (1946) in a spirited attack on the irradiation-of-excitation hypothesis. Lashley and Wade suggested that the generalization of a conditioned response from one stimulus to another reflects a failure of subjects to discriminate differences between the stimuli. They suggested that animals have to learn to treat stimuli as similar to or different from one another. Thus, in contrast to Pavlov, they considered the shape of a stimulus-generalization gradient to be determined entirely by the subject's previous sensory experiences rather than by the physical properties of the stimuli tested. Experimental investigations have not confirmed all of Lashley and Wade's ideas. However, as we shall see, there is ample evidence that the shape of stimulus-generalization gradients is a function of the subjects' previous experience with the stimuli involved.

Classical conditioning and instrumental behavior: The pairing hypothesis

Having defined what constitutes stimulus control and how it can be measured, we can begin to discuss how stimuli come to control behavior. The first analyses of stimulus control were based on what may be called the **pairing hypothesis.** According to this idea, the mere presence of a stimulus when a response is reinforced is sufficient for that stimulus to gain control over the behavior. Because this hypothesis is the basis for much subsequent research, we will examine it in some detail.

We have noted that the instrumental-conditioning situation is made up of several elements, including the ambient stimuli (S_A), the response (R), and the response consequence, or reinforcer (S^{R+}). Various relations exist between these elements (see Figure 9.5). We discussed the instrumental contingency in great detail in Chapters 7 and 8. The analysis of stimulus control involves the relations of the ambient stimuli (S_A) to the response and to the reinforcer. These relations have the components of a classical-conditioning procedure. Figure 9.5 illustrates that whenever the response is reinforced, stimuli S_A are paired with the reinforcer. In this sense, *every instrumental-conditioning procedure has a classical-conditioning procedure embedded in it.*

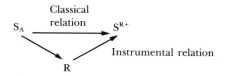

Figure 9.5. Relations between the instrumental response (R), the stimuli experienced when the response is performed (S_A), and the reinforcer in instrumental conditioning.

In early analyses of instrumental behavior, such as those of Thorndike and Guthrie, the ambient stimuli that are present when the response is reinforced were thought to have a very important role in the control of the behavior. The ambient stimuli were assumed to become conditioned to elicit the instrumental response in much the same way that a classically conditioned stimulus elicits a conditioned response. For example, in his law of effect, Thorndike stated that if a response in the presence of a stimulus is followed by a satisfying event, the association between the stimulus and the response is strengthened (see Chapter 6). Because of this association, the instrumental response comes to be controlled by the stimulus. The only requirement for the formation of such a stimulus-response association was considered to be contiguity of the stimulus with the reinforced response. Thus, stimuli were thought to gain control over behavior simply by being present when the behavior was reinforced.

The pairing hypothesis has turned out to be a much too simplistic view of how stimuli gain control over behavior. Casual observation, as well as laboratory studies, shows that not all stimuli coincident with a reinforced response come to control the behavior. If all such stimuli gained control, organisms would end up responding to all kinds of minute and irrelevant events in their environment. Such an expenditure of effort would be wasteful and maladaptive. In fact, only a few of the many stimuli that are contiguous with a reinforced response

actually gain control over the behavior. Staying within the framework of the pairing hypothesis, Hull (1952) suggested that stimuli gain control according to their salience. More intense stimuli, for example, are expected to gain control over behavior more readily than weak stimuli. As we shall see, amending the pairing hypothesis with the concept of stimulus salience is not enough to provide a complete account of stimulus control. We will review some of the extensive investigations that have been conducted to determine the principles by which some stimuli are more likely to gain control of behavior than others.

The environment as viewed from the subject's perspective

The presentation of an environmental event with certain stimulus features of interest to us does not guarantee that the subject will respond to these same stimulus characteristics. One must always consider the subject's perspective in an analysis of stimulus control. We cannot simply note certain features of the events we present to an organism and assume that the subject will perceive the cues as we do. Rather, we have to let the subject tell us by its behavior what it perceives of the stimuli we present.

What does the world look like from the subject's perspective? One of the most obvious determinants of what the subject perceives of its environment is the organism's sensory capacities. A subject's behavior can come under the control of a particular stimulus only if the organism is sensitive to that stimulus. Events outside the range of what the subject can detect with its sense organs simply do not exist for that individual unless the stimuli are amplified or transduced into something the organism can detect. People, for example, cannot detect sounds whose pitch is above about 20,000 cycles per second. Such stimuli are called "ultrasounds" because they are outside the range of human hearing. Because ultrasounds are inaudible to people, such sounds cannot come to control human behavior. Other species, however, are able to hear ultrasounds. Dogs, for example, can hear whistles outside the range of human hearing and therefore can be trained to respond to such sounds.

Limitations on what stimuli can come to control behavior are also set by whether the subject comes in contact with the stimulus. Consider, for example, a child's crib. Parents often place mobiles and other decorations on and around the crib to provide interesting stimuli for the child to look at. The crib shown in Figure 9.6 is decorated with such a mobile. The mobile consists of several thin, knitted animal figures mounted on cardboard (a giraffe, a seal, and a lion). Which aspects of this stimulus complex can potentially control the child's behavior? To answer this question, one has to consider what the child sees about the mobile rather than what the mobile looks like to adults. From the child's vantage point under the mobile, only the bottom edges of the animal figures are visible. The shapes of the animals and surface decorations cannot be seen very well from below. Therefore, these other features are not likely to gain control of the child's looking behavior. These considerations illustrate that the subject's orientation with respect to the various features of its environment greatly influences what stimuli can gain control over its behavior.

Another important determinant of stimulus control is the subject's previous experience. The crib shown in Figure 9.6 is decorated with a picture of a smiling elephant behind it. The parents picked this picture because they thought it was particularly cute and entertaining. However, the child is not likely to be entertained by the same aspects of the picture as the parents. For the child, the picture is merely an abstract collection of dark connected lines with spots of color. The child cannot react to the fact that the picture portrays an animal or that the animal is looking up. Special kinds of experience are required before these aspects of the picture can gain control over behavior.

The above examples illustrate that stimulus control is determined by a number of factors, including the sensory capabilities of the organism, orientations to various aspects of the environment, and experience. Laboratory experiments have shown that stimulus control is also a function of the type of reinforcement provided, the response subjects have to perform to obtain reinforcement, the relative ease of conditioning the various stimuli in the situation, and the relative effectiveness of the stimuli in predicting the availability of reinforcement. The sections to follow will discuss in greater detail how these factors determine control. The experimental analysis of stimulus control is a very difficult undertaking because we know very little about how organisms order, organize, and use the various sensory experiences to which they are constantly exposed. The research we will present constitutes beginning attempts to understand how stimuli influence behavior.

Figure 9.6. An infant looking up at a mobile.

Effects of past experience on stimulus control

One of the most important determinants of stimulus control is the subject's past experience. Encouraged in part by Lashley and Wade's proposals, investigators have been very much interested in this variable. Lashley and Wade assumed that animals learn to distinguish similarities and differences among stimuli by experiencing natural variations of the stimuli. Exposure to various colors during one's normal course of activities, for example, was assumed to produce discriminations among colors. If this is true, then animals exposed to very few colors from birth should not respond differentially when tested with various colors later in life. Several experimental tests of this prediction have been conducted. Peterson (1962), for example, raised ducks in cages illuminated by a sodium light that provided little if any variation in color. The ducks were then conditioned to peck a response key of a particular color. A control group of animals that had been raised in normal light and exposed to various colors in the usual manner received the same kind of key-peck training. Both groups were then tested in the presence of various colors for stimulus generalization. Consistent with Lashley and Wade's prediction, the ducks reared in the monochromatic sodium light showed a flat generalization gradient. They responded approximately equally to all the colors presented during the generalization test. In contrast, the normally reared ducks showed the more familiar bell-shaped gradient, indicating differential responding to the various colors. From the difference in these generalization gradients, one can conclude that color controlled the pecking behavior of only the normally reared ducks.

Peterson's findings clearly indicate that previous experience is important for stimulus control. However, the results have not been widely replicated. In addition, it is not clear what aspect of the experimental group's abnormal experience was responsible for the results. Raising ducks without exposure to various colors may alter the development of their visual system. Proper development of various parts of the eye and brain involved in color vision may require exposure to different colors early in life.

Stimulus-discrimination training. A possible reason why ducks raised without normal exposure to various colors do not respond differentially to colors is that they have not had different types of experiences with color stimuli. Color cues have not distinguished various objects in the environment for them. To examine this possibility, we have to give subjects experiences with color stimuli. This can be done in laboratory experiments using **stimulus-discrimination procedures**. In a stimulus-discrimination procedure, the subject is exposed to at least two different stimuli—let us say a red and a green light. However, reinforcement for performing the instrumental response is available only in the presence of one of the colors. Thus, the subject will be reinforced for responding on trials when the red light is on but not when the green light is on. This type of procedure is diagramed in Figure 9.7. In this procedure the red light signals the availability of reinforcement for responding. The green light signals that responding will not be reinforced. The stimulus that signals the availability of reinforcement is often called the **S+** or **S^D** (pronounced "ess dee"). In contrast, the stimulus that signals the lack of reinforcement is often called the **S−** or **S$^\Delta$** (pronounced "ess delta").

With sufficient exposure to a discrimination procedure, subjects will come to respond whenever the S+ is presented and withhold responding whenever the S− is presented. The acquisition of this pattern of responding is illustrated in the graph in Figure 9.7. Initially subjects respond similarly in the presence of the S+ and the S−. However, as training progresses, responding in the presence of the S+ persists and responding in the presence of the S− declines. The fact that the subjects respond much

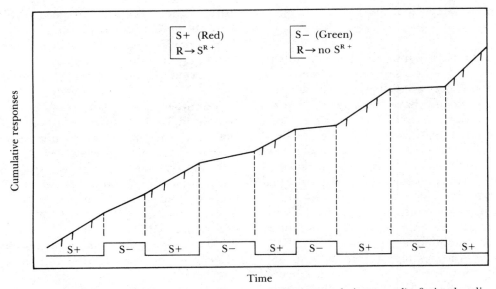

Figure 9.7. Procedure and hypothetical results (presented as a cumulative record) of stimulus-discrimination training. Responding is reinforced in the presence of the S+ (a red light) and is not reinforced in the presence of the S− (a green light). Differential responding gradually develops to the two stimuli. (Hatch marks on the cumulative record indicate reinforcements.)

more to the S+ than to the S− indicates differential responding to the S+ and S− stimuli. Thus, stimulus-discrimination procedures establish control by the stimuli that signal when reinforcement is and is not available. Once S+ and S− have gained control over the subject's behavior, they are called **discriminative stimuli.** S+ is a discriminative stimulus for performing the instrumental response, and S− is a discriminative stimulus for not performing the response.

The procedure diagramed in Figure 9.7 is the standard procedure for stimulus-discrimination training in instrumental conditioning. Stimulus discriminations can be also established with the use of classical-conditioning procedures. In this case one CS (the CS+) is paired with the unconditioned stimulus and another CS (the CS−) is presented in the absence of the US. With repeated pairings of the CS+ with the US and presentations of the CS− by itself, subjects will gradually learn to make the conditioned response to the CS+ and inhibit the conditioned response when the CS− is presented. (We discussed this procedure in Chapter 4; see Figure 4.9.) Instrumental stimulus-discrimination procedures are different from classical-conditioning procedures only in that the subject has to perform the instrumental response in the presence of the S+ in order to receive reinforcement. Thus, the S+ does not signal that reinforcement will be automatically provided. Rather, the S+ indicates that performance of the instrumental response will be reinforced.

Multiple schedules of reinforcement. The stimulus-discrimination procedure shown in Figure 9.7 is just one way that differential responding can be established. Differential responding to two (or more) stimuli can develop whenever each stimulus signals a different schedule of reinforcement for the instrumental response. Thus, for example, we could reinforce responding in the presence of a red light

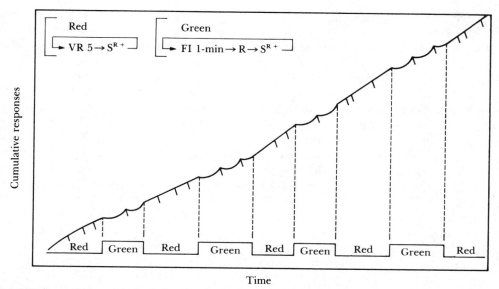

Figure 9.8. Procedure and hypothetical results (presented as a cumulative record) of a multiple schedule of reinforcement. Responding is reinforced on a variable-ratio 5 schedule in the presence of a red light and is reinforced on a fixed-interval 1-min schedule in the presence of a green light. A steady rate of responding characteristic of a VR 5 schedule occurs during the red light, and a scalloped pattern of responding characteristic of an FI 1-min schedule occurs during the green light. (Hatch marks on the cumulative record indicate reinforcements.)

on a variable-ratio 5 schedule of reinforcement (VR 5) and reinforce responding in the presence of a green light on a fixed-interval 1-min schedule (FI 1 min). Such a procedure is diagramed in Figure 9.8. You may recall from Chapter 7 that a variable-ratio schedule maintains a stable rate of responding. In contrast, on a fixed-interval schedule subjects pause just after each reinforcement and gradually increase their rate of responding after that until the next reinforcement (producing the scalloped pattern). In a multiple schedule, subjects will gradually come to perform the appropriate pattern of instrumental behavior in the presence of each stimulus. Whenever the red light is on, a steady rate of responding will occur, corresponding to the variable-ratio schedule; whenever the green light is on, a scalloped pattern will be evident, corresponding to the fixed-interval schedule. This outcome is illus-

trated in the graph in Figure 9.8. The different patterns of responding that occur in the presence of the red and green lights indicate that these stimuli control differential responding. To conclude that there is differential responding to stimuli, one does not necessarily have to see responding to one stimulus and no responding to a different stimulus.

A procedure of the sort shown in Figure 9.8 is called a **multiple schedule of reinforcement.** In a multiple schedule, different schedules of reinforcement are in effect consecutively in the presence of different stimuli. Stimulus-discrimination procedures are a special type of multiple schedule in which the reinforcement schedule provided in the presence of one of the stimuli is extinction. The general result with multiple schedules is that the pattern of responding that occurs in the presence of a particular stimulus corresponds to whatever reinforcement schedule is in effect with that stimulus. Multiple schedules illustrate that the patterns of responding produced by various schedules of reinforcement can come under the control of stimuli present when each schedule is in effect.

Stimulus discrimination and multiple schedules outside the laboratory.   Nearly all reinforcement schedules that exist outside the laboratory are in effect only in the presence of particular stimuli. Playing a game yields reinforcement only in the presence of enjoyable or challenging partners. Hurrying is reinforced in the presence of stimuli that indicate that you will be late and is not reinforced in the presence of stimuli that indicate that you will not be late. Driving rapidly is reinforced when you are on the highway but not when you are on a city street. Loud and boisterous discussions with your friends are reinforced at a party Saturday night. The same type of behavior is not reinforced during a sermon in church. Eating with your fingers is reinforced when you are on a picnic but not when you are in a fine restaurant. Getting dressed in your best clothes is reinforced when you are going to the senior prom but not when you are preparing to paint the garage. One's daily activities typically consist in going from one situation to another (to the kitchen to get breakfast, to the bus stop, to your office, to someone else's office, to the grocery store, and so on), and in each situation reinforcement is provided on different schedules for different people.

Effects of discrimination training on stimulus control.   We have noted that discrimination training brings the instrumental response under the control of the stimuli used. We reached this conclusion because discrimination training produces differential responding to the S+ and S− stimuli. How precise is the control that S+ acquires over the instrumental behavior, and what factors determine the precision of the stimulus control that is achieved? To answer such questions, it is not enough to note differential responding to S+ versus S−. One must also find out how steep the generalization gradient is when subjects are tested with stimuli that systematically vary from the S+ along some stimulus dimension. Furthermore, one must find out what aspect of the discrimination-training procedure is responsible for the type of stimulus-generalization gradient obtained. These issues were first addressed in classic experiments by Jenkins and Harrison (1960, 1962).

Jenkins and Harrison investigated how auditory stimuli of different frequencies (pitches) come to control the pecking behavior of pigeons reinforced with food. They measured how pigeons responded to tones of various frequencies after three types of training procedures. One group of subjects was reinforced during training for pecking in the presence of a 1000-cycle-per-second tone and received no reinforcement when the tone was off. Therefore, for these subjects the 1000-cps tone served as the S+ and the absence of tones served as the S−. A second group of pigeons also received discrimination training. The 1000-cps tone again served as the S+. However, for the second group the S− was a 950-cps tone. Thus, these pigeons were reinforced for pecking whenever the 1000-cps tone was presented and were not reinforced whenever the 950-cps tone was presented. The third group of pigeons served as a control group and did not receive discrimination training. The 1000-cps tone was continuously activated for these animals, and they could always receive reinforcement for pecking in the experimental chamber.

After the training procedures described above, each pigeon was tested for pecking in the presence of tones of various frequencies to see how precisely pecking was controlled by the pitch of the tones in each group. The generalization gradients obtained in the experiment are shown in Figure 9.9. The control group, which had not received discrimination training, responded nearly equally in the presence of all the test stimuli: the pitch of the tones did not

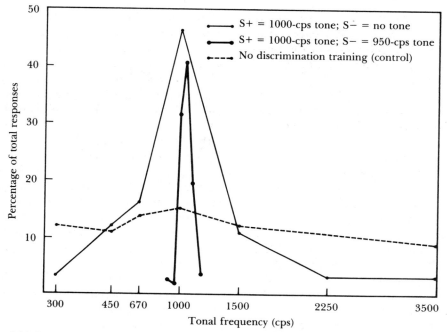

Figure 9.9. Generalization gradients of response to tones of different frequencies after various types of training. One group received discrimination training in which a 1000-cps tone served as the S+ and the absence of tones served as the S−. Another group received training in which a 1000-cps tone served as the S+ and a 950-cps tone served as the S−. The control group did not receive discrimination training before the generalization test. *(After Jenkins & Harrison, 1960, 1962.)*

control behavior. Each of the other two training procedures produced control over the pecking behavior by the frequency of the tones. The strongest stimulus control (steepest generalization gradient) was observed in animals that had been reinforced for responding in the presence of the 1000-cps tone (S+) and not for responding to the 950-cps tone (S−). Subjects that received discrimination training between the 1000-cps tone (S+) and the absence of tones (S−) showed an intermediate degree of stimulus control by tonal frequency.

Jenkins and Harrison's experiment shows that *discrimination training increases the stimulus control of instrumental behavior.* Furthermore, a particular stimulus dimension, such as tonal frequency, is most likely to gain control over responding if the S+ and S− stimuli used in the discrimination procedure differ along precisely

that stimulus dimension. The most precise control by tonal frequency was observed in subjects that had received discrimination training in which the S+ was a tone of one frequency (1000 cps) and the S− was a tone of another frequency (950 cps). Discrimination training did not produce as strong control by pitch if the S+ was a 1000-cps tone and the S− was the absence of tones. In this case subjects learned a discrimination between the presence and absence of the 1000-cps tone and could have been responding in part on the basis of the loudness or timbre of the tone in addition to its frequency.

Some investigators have used results of the sort obtained by Jenkins and Harrison to argue that stimuli come to control instrumental behavior only if subjects experience differential reinforcement in connection with the stimuli (for example, Terrace, 1966b). According to this suggestion, if subjects are not exposed to different reinforcement schedules in the presence of different stimuli, these stimuli will not gain control over their behavior. In analyzing why a particular type of stimulus has gained control over instrumental behavior, it is important to consider not only what differential reinforcement is provided during an experiment but also what differential reinforcement may occur outside the experimental context. Thomas, Mariner, and Sherry (1969), for example, replicated the control group tested by Jenkins and Harrison and confirmed that the generalization gradient for tonal frequencies is flat when subjects do not receive discrimination training. They also tested a second group of pigeons that had received experience with a 1000-cps tone in the home cage. For these subjects the 1000-cps tone was sounded every time food was delivered in the home cage. Key-peck training in the experimental chamber was conducted in the same way for these animals as for the control group. Tests of stimulus generalization using tones of various frequencies resulted in a steep generalization gradient for the group that had experienced the tone paired with food delivery. Thus, the effects of differential training conducted in the home cage with the 1000-cps tone transferred to the experimental chamber and resulted in greater stimulus control of pecking by the frequency of the tones.

The idea that differential reinforcement is necessary for the development of stimulus control is intuitively attractive. However, the hypothesis is also nearly impossible to refute with experimentation. Any time we find a case in which stimulus control occurs in the absence of explicit differential training, one can always postulate a possible source of inadvertent differential training that might have occurred outside the experimental situation. The mere fact, for example, that different responses are required to obtain food in a Skinner box than in the home cage may be sufficient to produce control by the stimuli in the Skinner box.

Discrimination training and the predictive value of stimuli. Although the *necessity* of discrimination training for stimulus control is debatable, such training clearly has a profound effect. Why should this be so? One possibility is that discrimination training ensures an adequate pairing of the S+ stimulus with the reinforcer. In addition, the S+ is the best predictor of the availability of reinforcement in a discrimination procedure. Other stimuli, such as various sights and sounds of the experimental chamber, are also paired with the reinforcer each time the reward is presented. However, these ambient stimuli are experienced when reinforcement is not available as well. Therefore, cues other than the S+ are not as good predictors of reinforcement.

We noted in the study of classical conditioning that the signal value of the CS is an important factor for conditioning. Simply pairing the CS with the US does not necessarily result in conditioning. If the US occurs both in the presence and in the absence of the CS, the CS may not become conditioned even though it is periodically paired with the US. Similar findings have been observed with discriminative stimuli. The procedures used in one such investigation (Wagner, Logan, Haberlandt, & Price, 1968) are summarized in Figure 9.10. Two groups of rats were conditioned with a discrete-trial procedure in which the subjects were reinforced on 50% of the trials for pressing a lever in the presence of a compound stimulus consisting of a light and one of two tones. For both groups, one of the tones (tone 1) was presented simultaneously with the light on half of the trials, and the other (tone 2) was presented simultaneously with the light on the remaining trials. For group 1, responding was reinforced on 50% of the trials on which the light/tone-1 compound stimulus was presented and on 50% of the trials on which the light/tone-2 compound stimulus was presented. Before describing the procedure for group 2, let us consider the relative predictive value of the two tones and the light stimulus in the pro-

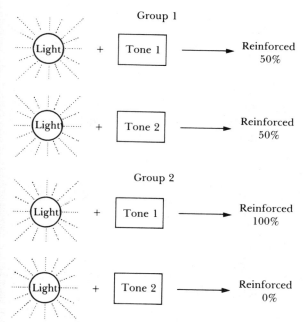

Figure 9.10. Diagram of experiment by Wagner, Logan, Haberlandt, and Price (1968). Relative to the two tones, the light was a better predictor of reinforcement for group 1 than for group 2. Consequently, subjects responded to the light more in group 1 than in group 2.

cedure for group 1. Note that the subjects received reinforcement for responding 50% of the time that tone 1 was presented. The procedure also provided reinforcement 50% of the time that tone 2 was presented. Finally, the subjects were also reinforced 50% of the time that the light appeared, even though the light was presented on a greater total number of trials than the tones. Because reinforcement was delivered on 50% of the times that tone 1, tone 2, and the light were each presented, the three stimuli were equally good predictors of reinforcement in the situation.

The procedure for group 2 was similar to that for group 1 in many respects. Again tone 1 was presented with the light on half the trials, and tone 2 was presented with the light on the remaining trials. However, this time reinforcement was always available on trials with the light/tone-1 compound stimulus. In contrast,

responses were never reinforced on trials with the light/tone-2 stimulus. This procedure ensured that, as in group 1, reinforcement was available 50% of the time that the light stimulus was presented. However, this time the light was not as good a predictor of the availability of reinforcement as tone 1. Of the three stimuli, tone 1 was the best predictor of reinforcement because subjects could obtain reinforcement on 100% of the trials on which tone 1 was presented. Tone 2 was the least valid predictor of reinforcement because subjects were never reinforced on tone-2 trials. The value of the light as a signal for reinforcement was intermediate between the two tones.

Relative to the tones in the experiment, the light stimulus was a better predictor of the availability of reinforcement for group 1 than for group 2. Therefore, if the relative predictive value of the cues is important in determining stimulus control, we would expect the light to have greater control over the behavior of the animals in group 1 than in group 2. This is precisely what Wagner and his associates observed. In tests with the light stimulus presented alone at the end of the experiment, subjects in group 1 responded much more than subjects in group 2. It is important to realize that this outcome cannot be explained in terms of the percentage of time that reinforcement was available when the light stimulus was presented. In both groups 1 and 2, subjects could obtain reinforcement on 50% of the trials on which the light was presented. The critical difference between groups 1 and 2 was that relative to the other stimuli in the situation (tones 1 and 2), the light was a better predictor of reinforcement for group 1 than for group 2.

Results of the sort obtained by Wagner et al. (1968) clearly indicate that the pairing hypothesis is inadequate to account for stimulus control. The two groups in the experiment received the same number of pairings of the light stimulus with reinforcement. The results suggest that discriminative stimuli have a powerful effect on behavior not because they are paired with the reinforcement but because they signal how or when a reinforcer is to be obtained. Other things being equal, if a stimulus is a better predictor of the availability of reinforcement than another cue, it is more likely to gain control of instrumental behavior.

What is learned in discrimination training?

As we have seen, if the instrumental response is reinforced in the presence of one stimulus (S+) and not reinforced in the presence of another stimulus (S−), these stimuli will come to control occurrences of the instrumental behavior. Because of the profound effect that discrimination training has on stimulus control, investigators have been interested in what subjects learn during discrimination training. Consider the following relatively simple situation: responses are reinforced whenever a red light is turned on (S+) and not reinforced whenever a loud tone is presented (S−). What strategies could the subject use to make sure that most of its responses were reinforced in this situation? One possibility is that the subject will learn simply to respond whenever the S+ is present and will not learn anything about the S−. If it followed the rule "Respond only when S+ is present," the subject would end up responding much more to S+ than to S− and would obtain the available reinforcers. Another possibility is that the subject will learn to not respond during S− but will not learn anything about what to do during S+. This would constitute following the rule "Suppress responding only when S− is present." If the subject followed this rule, it would also end up responding much more to S+ than to S−. A third possibility is that the subject will learn both to respond to S+ and to not respond to S−. Thus, it may learn something about the significance of both the stimuli in the discrimination procedure.

Spence's theory of discrimination learning.
One of the first and most influential theories of discrimination learning was proposed by Ken-

neth Spence in 1936. Spence advocated the third of the possibilities described above. According to his theory, reinforcement of a response in the presence of the S+ conditions excitatory properties to the S+ that come to evoke the instrumental behavior on future presentations of this stimulus. In contrast, nonreinforcement of responding during presentations of S− is assumed to condition inhibitory properties to S− that serve to inhibit or to suppress the instrumental behavior on future presentations of S−. Differential responding to S+ and S− is assumed to reflect the excitation and inhibition that become conditioned to S+ and S−, respectively.

How can we experimentally evaluate the excitation/inhibition theory of discrimination learning? As noted above, mere observation that subjects respond more to S+ than to S− is not sufficient to argue that they have learned something about both these stimuli. More sophisticated experimental tests are required. One possibility is to use stimulus-generalization gradients. If an excitatory tendency has become conditioned to S+, then stimuli that increasingly differ from S+ should be progressively less effective in evoking the instrumental response. In other words, we should observe a steep generalization gradient, with the greatest amount of responding occurring to S+. Such an outcome is called an **excitatory stimulus-generalization gradient.** If an inhibitory tendency has become conditioned to S−, then stimuli that increasingly differ from S− should be progressively less effective in inhibiting the instrumental response. Such an outcome is called an **inhibitory stimulus-generalization gradient.**

Behavioral techniques were not sufficiently sophisticated when Spence proposed his theory to allow direct observation of the kind of excitatory and inhibitory stimulus-generalization gradients his theory assumed. However, experimental tests conducted decades later proved that his ideas were correct. In one important experiment, two groups of pigeons received discrimination training with visual stimuli before tests of stimulus generalization (Honig, Boneau, Burstein, & Pennypacker, 1963). One group of subjects was reinforced for pecking when the response key was illuminated by a white light that had a black vertical bar superimposed on it (S+) and was not reinforced when the white light was presented without the vertical bar (S−). The second group of animals received the same type of discrimination training. However, for them the S+ and S− stimuli were reversed. This time the black vertical bar

served as the S−, and the white key without the bar served as the S+. After both groups learned to respond much more to S+ than to S−, Honig et al. conducted tests of stimulus generalization to see how much control the vertical bar had gained over the instrumental behavior in the two groups. The test stimuli consisted of the black bar on a white background, with the bar tilted at various angles away from the vertical position.

The results of the experiment are summarized in Figure 9.11. Let us first consider the

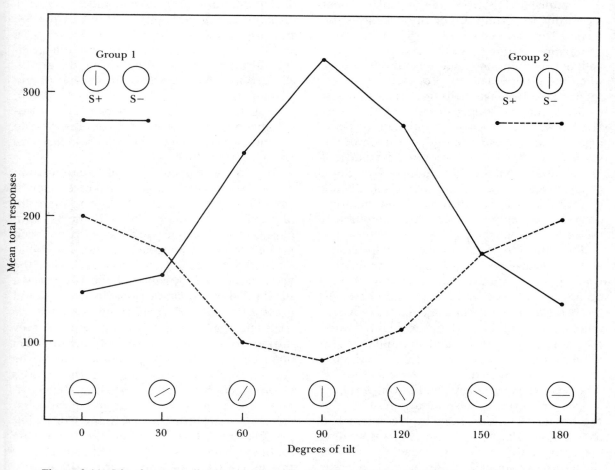

Figure 9.11. Stimulus-generalization gradients for line-tilt stimuli in two groups of subjects after discrimination training. For group 1 a vertical black bar on a white background served as the S+ and the white light without the bar served as the S−. For group 2 the functions of the stimuli were reversed. *(After Honig, Boneau, Burstein, & Pennypacker, 1963.)*

outcome for group 1. Recall that for this group the vertical bar had served as the S+ during discrimination training. Therefore, these subjects came to respond in the presence of the vertical bar. During the generalization test, the highest rate of responding occurred when the bar was presented in the original vertical position, and progressively less responding was observed when the bar was tilted farther and farther away from the vertical. These results indicate that the position of the vertical bar gained control over the pecking behavior when the stimulus served as S+. Let us consider next the results for group 2. For these subjects the vertical bar had served as the S− during discrimination training. At the end of discrimination training, these subjects did not peck when the vertical bar was projected on the response key. Results of the generalization test indicated that this failure to respond to the vertical bar was due to active inhibition of the pecking behavior in response to the position of the vertical bar. As the bar was tilted farther and farther away from the original vertical position, progressively more pecking occurred. Stimuli that were increasingly different from the original S− produced progressively less inhibition of the pecking behavior.

The outcome of the experiment by Honig and his colleagues shows that discrimination training can produce both excitatory conditioning to S+ and inhibitory conditioning to S−. An excitatory stimulus-generalization gradient around the vertical bar was obtained when the bar served as the S+, and an inhibitory gradient of generalization around the vertical bar was obtained when the bar served as the S−. The excitatory gradient had an inverted-U shape, with greatest responding occurring to the original S+. The inhibitory gradient had the opposite shape, with the least responding occurring to the original S−. The fact that gradients of excitation and inhibition can occur around S+ and S− provides strong support for Spence's theory of discrimination learning.

Errorless discrimination training.   The results reviewed above show that discrimination training can result in excitatory tendencies conditioned to the S+ and inhibitory tendencies conditioned to the S−. However, this experiment does not tell us whether all discrimination-training procedures produce both kinds of learning. In fact, subsequent research has shown that discrimination training does not always result in inhibitory tendencies conditioned to the S−. In the typical discrimination procedure, the S+ and S− stimuli are not altered during the course of training. Initially, subjects respond during both presentations of the S+ and presentations of the S− (see Figure 9.7). However, because reinforcement is not available during S−, responding during S− gradually becomes extinguished. In a series of important experiments, Terrace (1964, 1966b) investigated whether subjects can learn a discrimination without ever making a response to S− and experiencing the fact that responses are not reinforced during S−.

Terrace developed a novel discrimination procedure in which subjects make very few if any responses during S− ("errors"). The technique involves gradually fading in the S− stimulus. Let us assume that we wish to train pigeons to peck when the response key is illuminated by a red light and to not peck when the key is illuminated by a green light. If we used a standard discrimination procedure, we would present the red and green stimuli on alternate trials and reinforce the pecking response only during the red light. The intensity and duration of the S+ and S− stimuli would remain the same during the course of training. In Terrace's errorless discrimination procedure the S+ is presented at the same intensity and duration on every S+ trial throughout training (for example, Terrace, 1972). However, this is not true for the S−; the S− is gradually faded in. During the initial trials of the discrimination procedure, the S− is presented so briefly and at such a low intensity that the subject does not respond to it. The duration and intensity of the S− are gradually increased in small steps on successive S− trials as discrimination training progresses. If these fading steps are small enough, subjects may never respond to the S−.

To condition a discrimination in pigeons between red (S+) and green (S−) lights using an errorless procedure, we may begin by just turning the key light off briefly during S− trials. (Pigeons rarely if ever peck a dark response key.) We might then gradually increase how long the key light is off on successive S− trials until the animal is exposed to the full duration of the S− without responding. With this procedure we have faded in the duration of the S−. Now we may begin to fade in the color of the S−. We could begin by shining only an extremely faint and brief green light on the response key on S− trials. We may then gradually increase the intensity of the brief green light on successive presentations of it. When the green light is at its full intensity, we may gradually increase its duration. With the proper fading steps, the S− can be gradually introduced without the subjects' ever making a response to it. Thus, the fading procedure enables the discrimination to be learned without errors.

Early results suggested that errorless discrimination training leads to fundamentally different types of reactions to S− than more standard discrimination techniques. As we have seen, during the course of conventional discrimination training, the S− comes to actively inhibit the instrumental response (see Figure 9.11). The S− also becomes aversive to the subject and may elicit aggressive responses and attempts to escape and avoid the S−. Another possible result of conventional discrimination training is the peak-shift effect, described in the following section. Terrace found that after errorless discrimination training, the S− does not produce any of these effects. During errorless discrimination training, the S− does not come to actively inhibit responding or produce aggression or escape and avoidance attempts, and

the peak-shift effect does not occur. He therefore proposed that the performance of nonreinforced responses to S− ("errors") during the course of discrimination training is neces-

---

Box 9.1. Programmed Instruction

Errorless learning may also occur outside the laboratory with special training procedures. Learning with a minimum of errors is one of the goals of programmed instruction. Many students are familiar with programmed instruction textbooks, which present information in small steps analogous to the fading steps Terrace used in his pigeon experiments. The student is asked a question to which he or she readily knows the answer. New material is incorporated into the succeeding questions. Learning occurs as succeeding questions or problems are solved. If the program is well designed, the student can progress through the series of problems or questions and answer each without ever giving an incorrect response. The student is given immediate confirmation (reinforcement) for the answer before proceeding to the next question. The process is illustrated by the following sample questions taken from *The Analysis of Behavior* by James Holland and B. F. Skinner (1961). In this program the student fills in the blank in each statement on the right. The correct answer appears in the small box on the left before the next item in the program is presented.

	A doctor taps your knee (patellar tendon) with a rubber hammer to test your _____ .
reflexes (reflex)	If your reflexes are normal, your leg _____ to the tap on the knee with a slight kick (the so-called knee jerk).
responds (reacts)	In the knee jerk or patellar-tendon reflex, the kick of the leg is the _____ to the tap on the knee.
response (reaction)	The stimulation *object* used by the doctor to elicit a knee jerk is a(n) _____ .

sary for the S− to actively inhibit responding and produce the various other side effects of conventional discrimination training (for example, Terrace, 1972). However, subsequent research has shown that the absence of errors is probably not the critical factor. Rather, the fading technique used to introduce the S− in the errorless procedure may be what prevents the S− from becoming conditioned to actively inhibit responding and produce the other emotional effects of more conventionally trained S− stimuli (Rilling, 1977).

Effects of intradimensional discrimination training

So far we have discussed general characteristics of stimulus-discrimination training that can be found with any combination of stimuli serving as the S+ and the S− in a discrimination procedure. In addition to the effects already described, certain special problems and phenomena arise if the S+ and S− in a discrimination procedure differ from each other in only one stimulus characteristic, such as color, brightness, or pitch. Instances in which the S+ and S− are identical except in one stimulus characteristic are called **intradimensional discrimination** procedures. Consider, for example, discrimination training in which the S+ and S− are identical in every respect except color. What effect will the similarity in the colors of S+ and S− have on the control of S+ over the instrumental behavior? Will the rate of response to S+ be determined mainly by the availability of reinforcement in the presence of S+, or will the rate of response to S+ also be influenced by how similar the color of S+ is to the color of S−?

The peak-shift phenomenon.   In an important experiment, Hanson (1959) investigated the effects of intradimensional discrimination training on the extent to which various colors controlled the pecking behavior of pigeons. All the subjects in the experiment were reinforced

for pecking in the presence of a light whose wavelength was 550 nanometers. Thus, the S+ was the same for all animals. The groups differed in how similar the S− was to the S+. One group, for example, received discrimination training in which the S− was a color of 590 nm wavelength. For another group the S− was much more similar to the S+; the wavelength of the S− was 555 nm, only 5 nm away from the S+. The performance of these subjects was compared with the behavior of a control group that did not receive discrimination training but was also reinforced for pecking in the presence of the 550-nm S+ stimulus. After these different types of training, all subjects were tested for their rate of pecking in the presence of stimuli of various wavelengths.

The results are shown in Figure 9.12. Let us consider first the performance of the control group. These animals showed the highest rates of response to the S+ stimulus, and progressively lower rates of responding occurred as the subjects were tested with stimuli increasingly different from the S+. Thus, the control group showed the usual excitatory stimulus-generalization gradient around the S+. Animals that had received discrimination training with the 590-nm color as S− yielded slightly different results. They also responded at high rates to the 550-nm color that had served as the S+. However, these subjects showed much more generalization of the pecking response to the 540-nm color. In fact, their rate of response was slightly higher to the 540-nm color than to the original 550-nm S+. This shift of the peak responding away from the original S+ was even more dramatic in subjects that had received discrimination training with the 555-nm color as S−. These subjects showed much lower rates of responding to the original S+ (550 nm) than either of the other two groups. Furthermore, their highest response rates occurred to colors of 540 and 530 nm wavelength. This shift of the peak of the generalization gradient away from the original S+ is remarkable because in the earlier phase of

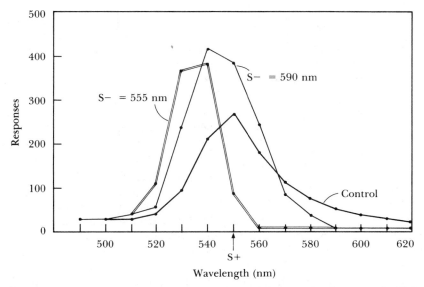

Figure 9.12. Effects of intradimensional discrimination training on stimulus control. All three groups of pigeons were reinforced for pecking in the presence of a 550-nm light (S+). One group received discrimination training in which the S− was a 590-nm light. Another group received discrimination training in which the S− was a 555-nm light. The third group served as a control and did not receive discrimination training before the test for stimulus generalization. *(After Hanson, 1959.)*

discrimination training, responding was never reinforced in the presence of the 540-nm or 530-nm stimuli. The highest rates of pecking occurred to stimuli that had never even been presented during the original training.

The shift of the peak of the generalization gradient away from the original S+ is called the **peak shift** phenomenon. The results of Hanson's experiment indicate that the peak-shift effect occurs following intradimensional discrimination training. A shift in the peak of the generalization gradient did not occur in the control group, which had not received discrimination training. The peak of the generalization gradient is shifted away from S+ in a direction opposite the stimulus that was used as the S− in the discrimination procedure. In addition, the peak-shift effect was a function of the similarity of the S− to the S+ used in discrimination training. The greatest shift in peak responding occurred in subjects for which the S− had been very similar to the S+ (555 nm, compared with

550 nm). The peak-shift effect was much less for subjects that had received discrimination training with more widely different colors (590 nm, compared with 550 nm).

Transposition and relational learning. The peak-shift effect is remarkable because it shows that the only stimulus in whose presence responding is reinforced (the S+) is not necessarily the stimulus that evokes the highest rate of responding after intradimensional discrimination training. This kind of outcome can also be observed in choice situations. Köhler (1939), for example, exposed chickens to a choice between two stimuli differing in brightness. Both stimuli were gray, but one was a slightly lighter gray than the other. The subjects were reinforced for choosing the lighter of the two stimuli (see Figure 9.13); the lighter stimulus was the S+. After the subjects learned to select the lighter stimulus, Köhler introduced an interesting test. He presented the original S+, but

Transposition

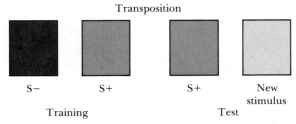

S−	S+	S+	New stimulus
Training		Test	

Figure 9.13. The phenomenon of transposition. During training the subject is reinforced for choosing the lighter of two shades of gray. During the test session, the subject is given a choice between the original S+ and a new stimulus that is a lighter shade of gray than the S+. The new stimulus is chosen during the test session.

this time the alternative was a stimulus that was even lighter than the old S+. Thus, the relation between the stimulus alternatives was the same during the test as it had been during original training—that is, one was lighter than the other. The test stimuli involved a transposition of the "lighter-than" relation between the original S+ and S−. Would the chickens pick the S+ that they had been reinforced for picking during training, or would they pick the new, lighter alternative stimulus? Remarkably, the chickens picked the lighter alternative: they responded more to the new stimulus, the lighter gray, than to the medium shade of gray that they had learned to pick during the initial phase of the discrimination training. This phenomenon is called **transposition.**

Köhler explained his findings in terms of the concept of **relational learning.** He proposed that during training with stimuli that differ on a particular stimulus dimension, subjects learn to respond on the basis of the relation between the stimuli rather than on the basis of their absolute stimulus characteristics. Thus, in his experiment the chickens presumably learned to respond on the basis of the relation between the brightness of the two stimuli present on a given trial: they learned to pick the lighter of the two cues available. During the test session, the lighter of the two stimuli was one they had never encountered before. However, because

the subjects were responding on the basis of the relative brightness of the stimuli, they again chose the lighter stimulus, even though this meant rejecting the original S+. The test stimuli consisted of a transposition of the original stimuli in such a way that the relation that existed between the two cues during training (one being lighter than the other) was maintained during the test session. The presence of the original relation in the test stimuli presumably controlled the choice behavior.

Relational versus stimulus learning in intradimensional discrimination. The phenomena of peak shift and transpositional choice seem to challenge the idea that the absolute stimulus features of events that signal the availability of reinforcement acquire control over the instrumental response. These phenomena also appear to be inconsistent with the notion that discrimination learning involves the learning of excitatory tendencies surrounding S+ and inhibitory tendencies surrounding S−. Can the phenomena of peak shift and transposition be explained in terms of the excitatory and inhibitory gradients that we have assumed develop as a result of discrimination training, or do we have to accept different mechanisms, such as relational learning? In an ingenious analysis, Spence (1937) suggested that excitatory and inhibitory gradients may in fact produce the peak-shift and transposition phenomena. This analysis is particularly remarkable because it was proposed more than 20 years before the peak-shift effect was experimentally demonstrated.

Spence's explanation of peak shift and transposition is based on two assumptions. First, Spence assumed that intradimensional discrimination training produces excitatory and inhibitory stimulus generalization gradients centered at S+ and S−, respectively, in much the same way as other types of discrimination training. Second, he assumed that the tendency to respond to a particular stimulus is determined by the generalized excitation to that stimulus *minus* the generalized inhibition to that stimulus. By subtracting the assumed gradient of inhibition centered at S− from the assumed gradient of excitation centered at S+, Spence was able to predict the phenomena of both peak shift and transposition.

Consider, for example, two gray stimuli that are very similar except that one is somewhat lighter. Let us assume that the lighter stimulus serves as S+ in a discrimination procedure and the darker gray shade serves as S−. What is learned about the S+ and S− stimuli will presumably generalize along the dimension of shades of gray. Figure 9.14 shows the excitatory and inhibitory generalization gradients that will presumably develop around the S+ and S− stimuli. Notice that because S+ and S− are close together on the stimulus dimension, the excitatory and inhibitory gradients overlap to some extent. To predict the level of response that will occur to various shades of gray, one has simply to subtract the level of inhibition that is assumed to be generalized to a particular stimulus from the level of excitation generalized to that stimulus. The inhibitory gradient in Figure

9.14 does not extend to stimuli S₃ and S₄. Therefore, no generalized inhibition is subtracted from the generalized excitation for these test stimuli. The greatest amount of inhibition is subtracted from the generalized excitatory strength of stimulus S−, with lesser amounts subtracted from the S+ and test stimuli S₁ and S₂. The dots connected with a solid line in Figure 9.14 represent the net excitatory strength of S−, S+, and test stimuli S₁ through S₄.

The net excitatory gradient in Figure 9.14 is a prediction of the subject's behavior. This prediction is consistent with the phenomena of both peak shift and transposition. Note that the peak of the net generalization gradient calculated in Figure 9.14 is not at the S+ but is displaced away from S+ in a direction opposite S−. This is precisely what is observed in peak-shift experiments (see Figure 9.12). The net generalization gradient also predicts transposition if subjects are given a choice between two stimuli within a certain range of shades of gray. If subjects are given a choice between the original S+ and the S−, they will choose S+ (the lighter of the two stimuli) because there is a

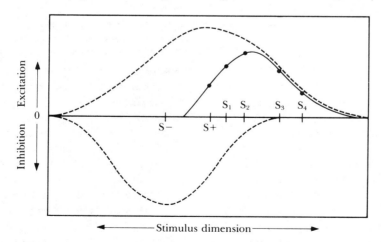

Figure 9.14. Spence's model of intradimensional discrimination learning. Excitatory and inhibitory stimulus-generalization gradients (dashed curves) are assumed to become established around S+ and S−, respectively. The subject's behavior is predicted from the net generalization gradient (solid curve), which is calculated by subtracting the inhibitory gradient from the excitatory gradient.

greater net excitatory strength associated with S+. If the subjects are given a transpositional choice between S+ and a new stimulus S_1 that is a lighter shade of gray than S+, they will choose the new stimulus because S_1 has a greater net excitatory strength than S+. According to the data in Figure 9.14, the lighter of the two stimuli will also be selected if subjects are given a choice between S_1 and S_2. Thus, the transposition phenomenon is predicted between stimuli S− and S_2 along the dimension of shades of gray. However, if the subjects are tested with stimuli S_2 and S_3, they will no longer choose the lighter cue. Instead, in this choice test, Spence's model predicts that they will select the darker of the two stimuli (S_2) because S_2 has a greater net excitatory strength than S_3. Thus, Spence's model of intradimensional discrimination learning not only predicts that transposition will take place but also indicates that the phenomenon is limited to stimuli that are close to S+ and S− on the stimulus dimension. Subsequent experimental work has confirmed that the phenomenon of transposition breaks down when subjects are tested with stimuli that are too far from the original training stimuli (for example, Kendler, 1950; Spence, 1937).

Precise predictions from Spence's model depend on the exact shape of the excitatory and inhibitory gradients that are assumed to exist around S+ and S−, respectively. At the time that Spence proposed his model, experimental techniques were unavailable to obtain direct evidence of excitatory and inhibitory gradients and their net effects. However, more recent research conducted with modern operant-conditioning techniques has provided impressive evidence for the types of generalization gradients Spence assumed served as the basis for peak shift and transposition (see Hearst, 1968, 1969; Klein & Rilling, 1974; Marsh, 1972). Thus, tests of stimulus generalization have typically provided supportive evidence for Spence's model. However, the model has been less successful with data on how subjects choose among stimuli. The model has particular difficulty in explaining results with the intermediate-choice problem.

In the intermediate-choice problem, subjects are reinforced for selecting the intermediate stimulus in a group of three. During initial training, subjects may be exposed to three squares of different sizes, for example, and reinforced for selecting the mid-size square (see Figure 9.15). Subjects can learn a discrimination like this without too much difficulty. Notice that in this case there are two incorrect (S−) stimuli, one on each side of the correct stimulus (S+), along the dimension of size. Spence would predict that inhibitory generalization gradients will develop around each S− stimulus and an excitatory gradient will develop around S+ (see Figure 9.15). If the inhibitory gradients are subtracted from the excitatory gradient, the net result is an excitatory gradient that remains centered at the original S+ (see Figure 9.15). The original S+ has the greatest net excitation associated with it. Therefore, Spence's model predicts that if the subjects are tested with a new group of three stimuli, they will always choose whichever stimulus is most similar to the original S+, whether or not this is the intermediate-size stimulus. Contrary to this prediction, however, research has shown that subjects sometimes will continue to pick the intermediate-size stimulus when tested with new sets of three stimuli (for example, Gonzalez, Gentry, & Bitterman, 1954). Thus, in the intermediate-choice problem, subjects can respond on the basis of the relation among the stimuli rather than the absolute feature of the S+.

Where does all this evidence leave interpretations of the effects of intradimensional discrimination training? Clearly, the relational-learning account is not entirely correct or entirely incorrect. Similarly, an analysis in terms of learning about specific stimulus features is also not entirely correct or entirely incorrect. The evidence indicates that animals can learn to respond on the basis of the relation between rein-

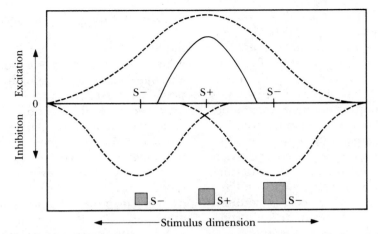

Figure 9.15. Analysis of the intermediate-choice problem in terms of Spence's theory of discrimination learning. Subjects are presented with three stimuli and are reinforced for choosing the intermediate one (for example, intermediate in size). An excitatory gradient is assumed to become established around the intermediate-size stimulus (S+), and inhibitory gradients are assumed to develop around the non-reinforced (S−) stimuli. (Dashed lines represent these gradients.) The net excitatory gradient (solid line) is centered at the original S+.

forced and nonreinforced stimuli. They can also learn to respond on the basis of the absolute features of the S+ and S− stimuli. It may be that different aspects of their learning are measured by stimulus-generalization and transpositional-choice tests. In stimulus-generalization tests, the results no doubt reflect what animals have learned about specific stimulus features. Subjects cannot respond on the basis of a relation between stimuli in a generalization test because they are exposed to only one stimulus at a time. In contrast, choice tests are likely to reflect both stimulus learning and relational learning. The results indicate that both types of learning can occur.

Control by elements of a compound stimulus

We have already noted that not all the stimuli in a situation gain control over behavior. The control exerted by a particular stimulus can be greatly enhanced by making the cue a discriminative stimulus for the response—by making it a good predictor of when the response will be reinforced. In most instances of differential reinforcement outside the laboratory, the events that signal the availability of reinforcement are not unitary stimuli. Rather, they consist of a complex of cues. During a football game, for example, cheering and jumping up and down are reinforced by social approval if the people near you are all rooting for the same team as you are. If you cheer and shout your approval when the opposition scores, you are likely to be booed and heckled. Here the discriminative stimulus for cheering consists of all the visual stimuli that indicate that the appropriate team has scored, the sound of the announcer stating the score, and the complex visual and auditory cues provided by everyone else cheering around you. Most other discriminative stimuli are equally complex. Consider, for example, the discriminative stimulus that tells you that pushing your grocery cart up to the checkout counter after waiting in line will be reinforced. The customer before you has to have finished checking out, the checkout counter has to be free of other carts, the checkout person is likely to say something like "Next," and if you hesitate in making the response, the people behind you are likely to encourage you to move along.

When the discriminative stimulus for reinforcement consists of a rich array of stimulation, which components of the entire stimulus complex gain control over the instrumental behavior, and what factors determine whether one stimulus component rather than another will gain the greatest degree of control? It is difficult to experimentally analyze discriminative stimuli as complex as the ones found at a football game or a grocery checkout counter. Laboratory analyses of how elements of a compound stimulus come to control instrumental behavior are most often conducted with discriminative stimuli that consist of only two simple elements, such as a light and a tone. Research has shown that which of the component stimuli gains control over behavior depends in part on the type of reinforcement used, what responses subjects are required to perform for reinforcement, and the relative ease of conditioning the stimuli.

Effects of type of reinforcement on stimulus control.   Stimulus control depends not only on differential reinforcement but also on the type of reinforcement used. Different categories of stimuli are more likely to gain predominant control over the instrumental response with positive than with negative reinforcement. This relation has been most clearly demonstrated in experiments with pigeons (see LoLordo, 1979, for a review). In one study, for example, two groups of pigeons were given discrimination training to press a foot treadle in the presence of a compound stimulus consisting of a red light and a 440-cps tone (Foree & LoLordo, 1973). Responses in the absence of the light/tone compound were not reinforced. For one group of animals, reinforcement for treadle pressing in the presence of the light/tone S+ stimulus consisted of food. For the other group, treadle pressing was reinforced by the avoidance of shock. If these subjects pressed the treadle in

the presence of the S+, no shock was delivered on that trial; if they failed to respond during the S+, a brief shock was periodically applied until a response occurred. Both groups of pigeons learned the discrimination. The animals pressed the treadle much more frequently in the presence of the light/tone stimulus than in its absence. Once this occurred, Foree and LoLordo sought to determine which of the two components of the complex S+, the light or the tone, was primarily responsible for the responses during the S+. Subjects received test trials in which the light or the tone stimulus was presented alone. Responding during these tests with the stimulus elements was then compared with the behavior of the subjects when the light and the tone were presented simultaneously, as during the initial discrimination training.

The results are summarized in Figure 9.16. Pigeons that received discrimination training with food reinforcement responded much more when tested with the light stimulus alone than when tested with the tone alone. In fact, their rate of treadle pressing in response to the isolated presentation of the red light was nearly as high as when the light was presented simultaneously with the tone. We can conclude that the behavior of these subjects was nearly exclusively controlled by the red-light stimulus. A very different pattern of results occurred with the animals that had received discrimination training with shock-avoidance reinforcement. These animals responded much more when tested with the tone alone than when tested with the light alone. Thus, with shock avoidance reinforcement the tone acquired more control over the treadle response than the red light.

Similar results have been obtained in several experiments by LoLordo and his associates (for example, Foree & LoLordo, 1975; LoLordo, 1979; LoLordo & Furrow, 1976). These findings indicate that the stimulus control of instrumental behavior is determined in part by the type of reinforcement used. Visual stimuli appear to be more likely to gain control over positively reinforced behavior than auditory

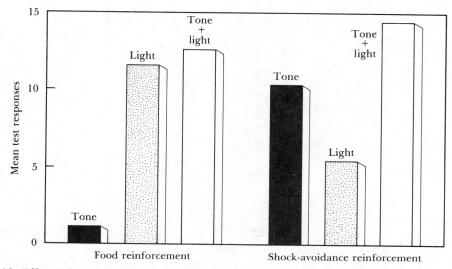

Figure 9.16. Effects of type of reinforcement on stimulus control. A treadle-press response in pigeons was reinforced in the presence of a compound stimulus consisting of a tone and a red light. With food reinforcement, the light gained much more control over the behavior than the tone. With shock-avoidance reinforcement, the tone gained more control over behavior than the light. *(After Foree & LoLordo, 1973.)*

cues, and auditory cues are more likely to gain control of negatively reinforced behavior than visual cues. This dependence of stimulus control on type of reinforcement is probably the result of the evolutionary history of pigeons. Responding to visual cues may be particularly useful for pigeons in seeking food, whereas responding to auditory cues may be particularly adaptive in avoiding danger. Unfourtunately, we do not know enough about the evolutionary history of pigeons to be able to identify the evolutionary advantages of different types of stimulus control in different situations. We also do not know how stimulus control varies as a function of type of reinforcement in other species. This question is a fertile area for future research.

Effects of type of instrumental response on stimulus control.   Another factor that can determine which of several components of a discriminative stimulus gains control over behavior is the nature of the response required for reinforcement. The importance of the in-

strumental response for stimulus control is illustrated by an experiment by Dobrzecka, Szwejkowska, and Konorski (1966). These investigators studied discrimination learning in dogs with auditory stimuli. The dogs were gently restrained in a harness, with a metronome placed in front of them and a buzzer placed behind them. The metronome and buzzer provided qualitatively different types of sounds: the metronome produced a periodic beat and the buzzer produced a continuous rattle. The two stimulus sources also differed in location, one in front of and the other behind the animal. Dobrzecka et al. were interested in which of these two stimulus characteristics (quality of the sound or its location) would come to control behavior.

Two groups of dogs served in the experiment (see Figure 9.17). The two groups differed in what responses were required for reinforcement in the presence of the buzzer and the metronome stimuli. Group 1 received training on what can be called a right/left discrimination. When the metronome was sounded, subjects in

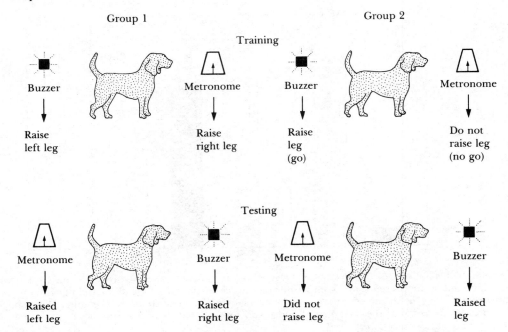

Figure 9.17. Diagram of experiment by Dobrzecka, Szwejkowska, and Konorski (1966). Dogs were conditioned in a left/right or go/no-go discrimination (groups 1 and 2, respectively) with auditory stimuli that differed both in location (in front or in back of the subjects) and in quality (the sound of a buzzer or a metronome). During testing the location of the two sounds was reversed. The results showed that the left/right differential response was controlled mainly by the location of the sounds, whereas the go/no-go differential response was controlled mainly by the quality of the sounds.

this group were reinforced for raising the right leg; when the buzzer was sounded, they were reinforced for raising the left leg. Thus, the location of the response (right/left) was important for reinforcement in this group. Group 2 received training on what may be called a go/no-go discrimination. In this case the subjects learned to raise the right leg to the buzzer (S+) but to leave it down when the metronome (S−) was on. Thus, the quality of the response (go/no-go) was important for reinforcement for this group rather than its location.

What aspect of the sounds of the metronome and buzzer—quality or location—gained control over the instrumental behavior in the two groups of subjects? To answer this question, Dobrzecka et al. tested the animals with the positions of the metronome and buzzer reversed. During these tests, the buzzer was placed in

front of the animals and the metronome behind them (see Figure 9.17). This manipulation produced very different results in the two groups. Subjects trained on the right/left discrimination (in which the location of the response was critical for reinforcment) had learned to respond mainly on the basis of the location of the auditory cues rather than their quality. Subjects in group 1 raised their right leg in response to sound from the front, regardless of whether the sound was made by the metronome or the buzzer. When the sound came from the back, they raised the left leg, again regardless of whether the sound was made by the metronome or the buzzer. Thus, the location of the sounds controlled their behavior much more than sound quality. The opposite outcome was observed in subjects trained on the go/no-go discrimination. These dogs responded mainly on the basis of the quality of the sound rather than its location. They raised a leg in response to the buzzer regardless of whether the sound came from the front or the back, and they did not raise a leg when the metronome was sounded, again irrespective of the location of the metronome.

These results indicate that responses that are differentiated by location (right/left) are more likely to come under the control of the location of discriminative stimuli. In contrast, responses that are differentiated by quality (go/no-go) are more likely to come under the control of the quality of discriminative stimuli. It is not known at present why such relations exist. However, the results clearly indicate that the activities required for reinforcement can determine which aspects of discriminative stimuli come to control the instrumental behavior.

Effects of the relative ease of conditioning various stimuli. Research on the effects of the type of reinforcement and the type of instrumental response on stimulus control has not been very extensive. Therefore, the range of discrimination situations in which these variables are important is not yet known. Another determinant of stimulus control, the relative ease of conditioning the various stimuli in the situation, has been known for a long time and is likely to be important in most instances of stimulus-discrimination learning. Pavlov (1927) observed a long time ago that if two stimuli are presented simultaneously, the presence of the stimulus that is easier to condition may hinder the conditioning of the other stimulus. This phenomenon is called **overshadowing.** The presence of the stimulus that becomes conditioned rapidly overshadows the conditioning of the other stimulus. In many of Pavlov's experiments the two stimuli were of the same modality (two tones, for example) but differed in intensity. As we noted in Chapter 5, more intense stimuli become conditioned more rapidly. Pavlov found that a low-intensity stimulus could become conditioned (somewhat slowly) if it was

presented by itself and repeatedly paired with the US. However, much less conditioning occurred if the weak stimulus was presented simultaneously with a more intense stimulus. Later research has shown that overshadowing can occur between stimuli of different modalities as well, provided that one stimulus is more easily conditioned than the other (for example, Kamin, 1969).

Although the phenomenon of overshadowing was first discovered in classical conditioning, it also occurs in instrumental discrimination procedures (see Sutherland & Mackintosh, 1971, for a review). If a stimulus is composed of two components, acquisition of control by the weaker component may be disrupted by the presence of the more effective component. From the research of LoLordo and his associates, for example, we would expect that in food-reinforcement situations the acquisition of control by an auditory stimulus would be overshadowed by the presence of a visual stimulus. We previously discussed studies of auditory-stimulus control of food-reinforced pecking in pigeons performed by Jenkins and Harrison (1960, 1962). The response key in these experiments was always illuminated with a white light, and unless one of the auditory cues was used as a discriminative stimulus, the pecking behavior did not come to be controlled by the auditory cues. This result was interpreted as showing that a stimulus must be an S+ in order to acquire control over behavior. However, a later experiment by Rudolph and van Houten (reported in Mackintosh, 1977) challenges this conclusion. They found steep auditory generalization gradients, indicating strong control by the auditory cues, provided that the pigeons pecked a dark key. This finding suggests that Jenkins and Harrison (1960, 1962) may not have found stimulus control of pecking by auditory cues in the absence of discrimination training (see Figure 9.9) because the response key they used was illuminated with a light. Perhaps the light overshadowed the auditory stimulus during training.

The phenomenon of overshadowing indicates that stimuli may, in a sense, compete for control over behavior. Two or more stimuli, each of which can gain control over behavior when presented alone, may not all come to control the instrumental response when they are presented simultaneously. Acquisition of control by less effective stimuli can be hindered by the presence of more easily conditioned stimuli. Some investigators believe that competition among stimuli is a major factor determining stimulus control (see Mackintosh, 1977). Organisms may have limits on their capacity to process various stimuli, or reinforcers may be effective in conditioning only a limited set of stimuli at the same time. In either case, only the "best" stimuli in a situation may acquire control over behavior. The problem is to determine what the "best" stimuli are for any given circumstance.

Applications of stimulus control: Self-control

Most people at some time in their lives experience problems with self-control. Students who wish to improve their grades have trouble improving their study habits; smokers who want to quit cannot resist a cigarette; people who want to lose weight have trouble controlling their food intake. Problems with self-control often involve behaviors occurring at inappropriate times and places that interfere with long-range goals. Behavior therapists, in helping people improve their self-control, have suggested techniques that limit the control various stimuli have over certain behaviors. For example, principles of stimulus control have been applied to study behaviors (see Fox, 1966, for an examination of the problems). Some suggestions for improving study habits are as follows:

1. Select a suitable place for study, with adequate lighting and free from distractions.

2. Study at this place and only at this place. (Do not study on your bed, as this will probably lead to sleeping rather than studying.) Do not use the study area for other tasks, such as letter writing or drawing.

3. Remain at the study area only as long as you are studying. If you begin to daydream, prepare to leave the area.

4. Before actually leaving the area, complete one small unit of work. Finish reading the page or complete one problem.

The goal of these suggestions is to establish the study area as a discriminative stimulus for concentrated study as opposed to other behaviors, such as letter writing, sleeping, or socializing. As in many cases of application, the laboratory principles are only loosely applied here. You may have noted that no true differential contingency is in effect here—the student is not actually constrained. The hope is, nevertheless, that by limiting the behavior that occurs in the presence of the study space, this stimulus situation will come to control the study behavior. In fact, many students find these suggestions quite helpful.

A similar approach has been taken in weight-reduction programs. Weight-reduction programs strive to reduce caloric intake through diet and increase caloric output through exercise. Many weight-reduction programs now include a behavioral component as well. Research has shown that altering the conditions under which people eat helps to alter the amount eaten (see Stunkard & Mahoney, 1976). This occurs because eating is frequently triggered by stimuli when there is no real need for food. Eating may be triggered by such things as time of day, the presence of ready-made snacks, turning on the television, or sitting down to talk with a friend. Weight-reduction programs try to counteract the effects of such stimuli by requiring participants to eat only in a limited setting. The dieter is instructed, for example, to eat only at a particular table with a proper table setting. The stimulus conditions can be made highly specific by using only a particular table-cloth and china. In addition, only food that is properly prepared and served is to be eaten. We must repeat here that these suggestions are only part of a total program for weight reduction. They are not sufficient in and of themselves. They are very useful in many cases because it is often easier to limit where one eats than how much one eats. Moreover, in restricting where one eats, one often reduces the amount eaten as well. For more details the interested reader may want to consult a highly successful diet plan proposed by Stuart and Davis (1972) in a book entitled *Slim Chance in a Fat World.*

Secondary reinforcement

Instrumental behavior always occurs in the presence of particular stimuli. In the preceding section we described how discriminative stimuli that signal what schedule of reinforcement is in effect at a particular time come to control instrumental behavior. Another category of stimuli that can also be important in the control of behavior consists of the events that occur just before each delivery of the reinforcer. Cues that signal delivery of the reinforcer are called **secondary reinforcers.** Both discriminative stimuli and secondary reinforcers are paired with reinforcement. However, there is an important difference between the two types of events concerning when they occur in relation to the instrumental behavior. Discriminative stimuli are experienced before the occurrence of the instrumental response. In contrast, secondary reinforcers are presented after the instrumental behavior. In a Skinner box, for example, pressing a lever may be reinforced with food only when a red light is on, and the food presentation may be accompanied by noises of the food-delivery device. In this example, the red light serves as the discriminative stimulus

(S+) and is present before the reinforced response occurs. The noise of the food-delivery device serves as the secondary reinforcer and is present only after the reinforced response has occurred. The food is the primary reinforcer in this situation. Because secondary reinforcers are repeatedly paired with delivery of the primary reinforcer, they become conditioned by the primary reinforcer through the mechanisms of classical conditioning. Therefore, secondary reinforcers are also called **conditioned reinforcers.**

Secondary, or conditioned, reinforcers play a major role in the control of behavior outside the laboratory. Our work is rarely compensated directly by need-fulfilling items such as food, clothing, or shelter. Rather, we receive tokens, such as money, which can later be exchanged for primary reinforcers. Studying in school is not directly rewarded by a good job and success in life. Rather, studying is rewarded by good grades, which may play a role in obtaining a good job. Certain comments, gestures, and facial expressions are also secondary reinforcers because they gain control over behavior only through conditioning with primary reinforcers. A parent taking care of an infant is constantly pairing verbal stimuli with primary positive and negative reinforcers. Comments such as "Good boy" and "Good girl" are paired with hugs, smiles, and the like. "No!" is paired with tones of anger or sometimes a physical slap or restraint. We may consider these words secondary reinforcers because initially the verbal stimuli have no effect on the child. The first time a child hears a stern "No!," he is likely to turn around, smile sweetly, and continue in the forbidden behavior. With sufficient experience, the same "No!" will come to elicit cries or, ideally, a change in his actions.

Three functions of secondary reinforcers

The above examples illustrate various roles that stimuli associated with primary reinforcement can have. Some secondary reinforcers, such as money, may substitute for a primary reinforcer. In substituting for a primary reinforcer, the stimulus helps to bridge the delay between the performance of a response and delivery of primary reinforcement. As noted in Chapter 7, very little learning occurs if there is a substantial delay between a response and its consequences. However, primary reinforcers in the real world rarely follow immediately the responses that produce them. Rather, responses result in certain stimuli, which in turn signal the later delivery of the primary reinforcer. These stimuli stand in the place of the primary reinforcer in maintaining behavior. Thus, one function of secondary reinforcers is to *substitute for immediate primary reinforcement.* You may feel jubilant, for example, after buying a ticket to go on an exciting cruise even though the cruise is not to take place for several months. The ticket substitutes for the cruise and helps to bridge the interval between buying the ticket and enjoying the trip.

Another important function of secondary reinforcers is to *provide feedback* for the desired instrumental response. A grade of A on a test tells you that you studied in an effective fashion for the test. This information can help you decide how to study for the next test. By saying "Good boy" or "Good girl" during the course of teaching a child to read, the parent can inform the child which words are being read correctly. The response-feedback function of secondary reinforcers is particularly important when the correct response is difficult for the subject to discern. The feedback serves to identify clearly the response to be reinforced.

Secondary reinforcers often also serve as *discriminative stimuli* for responses involved in obtaining the primary reinforcer. The smell of cooking at dinnertime is a secondary reinforcer because it signals that a good meal is about to be served. However, it is also a discriminative stimulus that indicates that certain responses, such as setting the table and sitting down to eat, will be reinforced. In the laboratory, the sound of

the food-delivery device that follows the occurrence of a lever-press response indicates that approaching the food cup will be reinforced. Thus, the sound of the food-delivery device is a discriminative stimulus for approaching the food cup.

Any conditioned reinforcer may have any one or all three of the functions we have described. Which function of a secondary reinforcer is most prominent depends in part on what we look at. The phrase "Good boy" or "Good girl," for example, may appear to substitute for a primary reinforcer if we consider what changes occur in the responses that precede this stimulus. If the responses that precede the phrase are increased in likelihood, we may conclude that the phrase substitutes for a reinforcer. If we look only at the immediate effects of the stimulus and see that it elicits a self-satisfied grin, we may think of the phrase more as a feedback stimulus. In contrast, if we consider what actions follow the phrase and find that the child approaches the parent and seeks to be hugged, we may think of the phrase as a discriminative stimulus for approach and affection responses. The role of secondary reinforcers in laboratory situations can be similarly analyzed from different points of view. Which function of secondary reinforcers is emphasized depends in part on the procedures used to measure their effects. In some cases, secondary reinforcers can function in all three ways.

Laboratory analyses of secondary reinforcement

Extinction tests. Early conceptualizations of secondary reinforcement emphasized the view that secondary reinforcers are substitutes for primary reinforcement because they are conditioned by primary reinforcers. This view developed readily from the stimulus-substitution model of conditioning that was widely accepted during the first few decades after Pavlov's work became well known in the United States. As we noted in Chapter 5, Pavlov believed that during the course of conditioning, the CS acquires many of the same properties as the US. Applying this idea to secondary reinforcement suggests that secondary reinforcers acquire many of the properties of primary reinforcers and can therefore come to serve in the same capacity.

In an effort to evaluate the substitution function of secondary reinforcers, early investigators used extinction procedures to test for the effects of secondary reinforcement. If secondary reinforcers substitute for primary reinforcement, then instrumental responding should continue to occur if it is reinforced by nothing more than secondary reinforcement. Experimental evaluations of this prediction involved a two-stage procedure and two groups of subjects. During Phase 1, both groups of subjects were reinforced for performing an instrumental response, and each instance of reinforcement was accompanied by a stimulus, such as a brief noise. In Phase II, the primary reinforcer was no longer delivered after responding in either group. For one of the groups, performance of the instrumental response during this phase was not followed by any stimuli arranged by the experimenter. For the second group, performance of the response was followed only by the brief noise that had previously been paired with the primary reinforcer. Responding during the extinction phase was expected to continue longer for the second group than for the first. The results of such experiments indicated that extinction indeed occurs more slowly when secondary reinforcement is provided. However, the effect was usually rather small. One reason for its smallness may have been that the extinction procedure actually involved two types of extinction simultaneously. During the extinction phase, both the instrumental response and the secondary reinforcer occurred in the absence of primary reinforcement. The relatively small secondary-reinforcement effects that were observed may reflect the fact that the secondary reinforcer was also being extinguished during the ex-

tinction phase of the experiment. Overlooking this possibility may have led to an underestimation of the power of secondary reinforcement.

Second-order schedules of reinforcement. Because extinction tests may underestimate the strength of secondary-reinforcement effects, other strategies have been devised to study secondary reinforcement. One method, developed by Fred Kelleher, involves a **second-order schedule of reinforcement.** A second-order schedule consists of a subordinate schedule embedded in a master schedule. Each completion of the subordinate schedule is counted as a "response" in determining whether the master schedule has been satisfied. Meeting the requirements of the master schedule results in delivery of the primary reinforcer (food, for example). In contrast, each completion of the subordinate schedule only results in the delivery of a secondary reinforcer. The master schedule determines when satisfaction of the subordinate schedule results in primary reinforcement. These interrelations between the subordinate and master schedules may be illustrated by an example.

In one of Kelleher's experiments pigeons were reinforced for pecking on a second-order schedule in which the master schedule was fixed-ratio 15 and the subordinate schedule was fixed-interval 4 min (Kelleher, 1966). The primary reinforcer was food. To obtain the food, the pigeons had to complete the requirements of the subordinate FI 4-min schedule 15 times in a row to satisfy the FR-15 master schedule. Upon each completion of the FI 4-min subordinate schedule, the response key was briefly illuminated by a white light. The 15th time the FI 4-min component was satisfied, the key was again briefly lit, and the subjects received access to food. Thus, the white light was paired with food and presumably became a conditioned reinforcer.

Panel A of Figure 9.18 shows a sample cumulative record of responding that occurred on

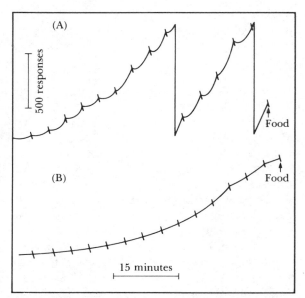

Figure 9.18. Cumulative records of key pecking for a pigeon reinforced on an FR 15 (FI 4 min) second-order schedule. In panel A, the key light was briefly illuminated by a white light each time the FI 4-min requirement was completed. In panel B, the brief white light was always omitted. Hatch marks indicate completions of the FI 4-min requirement. Food was presented only upon the 15th completion of the FI 4-min requirement. *(After Kelleher, 1966.)*

the second-order schedule of reinforcement. Presentations of the secondary reinforcer are indicated by hatch marks on the cumulative record. The most remarkable aspect of these results is that the subject responded for the secondary reinforcer in much the same way that organisms ordinarily respond for primary reinforcement. The subordinate FI 4-min schedule maintained a scalloped pattern of responding very similar to what is observed with an FI 4-min schedule of primary reinforcement. The rate of response was near zero just after the delivery of the secondary reinforcer and gradually accelerated after that until the next delivery of the brief light.

Kelleher was interested in determining to what extent the presentation of the brief white light was responsible for the scalloped pattern that occurred on the subordinate FI 4-min

schedule. Therefore, in another phase of the experiment he omitted the brief light at each completion of the subordinate schedule. The response requirements of the second-order schedule were not changed in any way except that completions of the subordinate schedule were no longer marked by the light. A sample cumulative record of pecking under these circumstances is shown in panel B of Figure 9.18. The hatch marks on the cumulative record indicate each time that the subordinate FI 4-min schedule was satisfied and the secondary reinforcer would have been presented. Omitting the secondary reinforcer produced two dramatic changes in the behavior of the pigeons. First, their overall rate of responding was much less than when secondary reinforcers were provided. Second, responding on the subordinate FI 4-min schedule was no longer characterized by the scalloped pattern. The pigeons did not respond at a low rate at the start of each FI 4-min component and accelerate their rate of responding toward the end of the 4-min interval. These findings show that marking each completion of the subordinate schedule with a brief stimulus change was responsible for the high rates of responding and the scalloped pattern observed in panel A of Figure 9.18.

The results shown in Figure 9.18 indicate that a brief stimulus can lead to increased response rates and can also influence the pattern of responding that occurs. However, the results do not prove that the brief light that was delivered at the end of each FI 4-min component had to be a conditioned reinforcer to produce these effects. Perhaps presenting a stimulus at each completion of the FI 4-min requirement would lead to high response rates and a scalloped pattern even if the stimulus were never paired with primary reinforcement. To evaluate this possibility, investigators have studied procedures in which a brief stimulus is presented at the end of each subordinate-schedule component except the last one, which results in the presentation of food. Because the stimulus is omitted when food is presented, the stimulus cannot become conditioned by the food. Such experiments have yielded conflicting results (see Gollub, 1977). If the stimulus that marks the end of each subordinate-schedule component is also presented when food is delivered, results of the sort shown in panel A of Figure 9.18 are always obtained. If the end of each subordinate-schedule component is marked by a stimulus that is not present when food is delivered, increased response rates and patterns of responding appropriate to the subordinate schedule occur only in some situations. Gollub (1977) has concluded that whether these effects are observed depends on the type and salience of the stimulus that marks the end of each subordinate-schedule component and on the nature of the reinforcement schedules used.

Why should a stimulus that is never paired with primary reinforcement ever produce reinforcementlike effects in second-order schedules? No definite answer to this question is available. One possibility is that such stimuli are effective because they provide feedback for each completion of the subordinate schedule. The pigeon may use the stimulus to mark its position with respect to the master schedule. Such stimulus feedback provides information that one subordinate component of the master schedule has been completed and that at least one additional component must be completed for food to be presented. Thus, second-order schedules of reinforcement are particularly useful in studying the response-feedback function of secondary reinforcers.

Choice and stimulus validity. The research on second-order schedules shows that secondary reinforcers are like primary reinforcers in their capacity to enhance behavior and to produce patterns of responding appropriate to the schedule of reinforcement. Do secondary reinforcers also acquire reinforcement value in the sense that they are sought out like primary reinforcers? If secondary reinforcers share the properties of primary rein-

forcers in this respect, then subjects should prefer situations rich in secondary reinforcement to situations where secondary reinforcement is infrequent. Schuster (1969) conducted an experiment to test this idea with pigeons. The subjects could peck either one of two response keys. The schedule of primary reinforcement was the same for responding on both keys—a variable-interval schedule. The two response keys differed in the availability of secondary reinforcement. For one key, the secondary reinforcer, a light and buzzer, occurred only with primary reinforcement. For the other key, the secondary reinforcer occurred after responses at other times as well. Therefore, this key was richer in the absolute number of secondary reinforcers delivered. The first key, however, maintained a more valid predictive relation between the light/buzzer stimulus and food. Every instance of the light/buzzer ended with food on the first key. On the second key, the secondary reinforcer was presented more often but was only occasionally paired with food.

The results of the experiment were very interesting. When the pigeons pecked the key rich in secondary reinforcement, their response rate was higher than when they pecked the other key. The extra secondary reinforcers had an enhancing effect on the rate of responding. However, the pigeons *preferred* to peck the key with the fewer but more valid secondary reinforcers. They spent more time pecking this key. Thus, the secondary reinforcer did not function as a primary reinforcer in the sense of having a positive value for choice behavior, even though it could enhance the rate of responding once a choice had been made. The predictive relation between the light/buzzer and food seemed to be critical in controlling choice behavior.

Chained schedules of reinforcement. The techniques for studying the effects of secondary reinforcers we have discussed so far have stressed the reinforcement and response-feedback functions of secondary reinforcement. Secondary reinforcers can also act as discriminative stimuli for certain responses. In some of the examples that we have described, the secondary reinforcers served as discriminative stimuli indicating that going to the food cup would be reinforced. The discriminative-stimulus functions of secondary reinforcers have been most extensively investigated with the use of **chained schedules of reinforcement.** In a chained schedule, the subject has to make a series, or chain, of responses to obtain primary reinforcement. Each response in the chain occurs in the presence of a particular stimulus, and performance of each response produces the stimulus for the next response in the chain.

Many examples of chains of responses may be found outside the laboratory. Consider, for example, making a peanut-butter-and-jelly sandwich. The finished product may be considered to be the primary reinforcer. However, before the sandwich is ready to be eaten, many responses have to be performed. First you have to get out the ingredients—bread, peanut butter, and jelly. These responses occur in the presence of the cabinet that houses the ingredients. In the presence of the jars of peanut butter and jelly, the appropriate response is opening the jars. In the presence of the bag of bread, the appropriate response is taking out two slices. These responses create new stimuli: open jars and two free slices of bread. In the presence of these cues, the appropriate response is spreading the peanut butter and jelly on the slices of bread. This in turn results in new stimuli (pieces of bread with peanut butter and jelly spread on them), in the presence of which the proper response is putting the slices together to make the sandwich. Once the stimulus of the sandwich is produced, the sandwich may be eaten, completing the response chain. In this and all other examples of chained schedules, each response produces certain stimuli, in the presence of which the next response in the chain has to be performed. Therefore, *each stimulus serves both as a reinforcer for the response that produced it and as*

a discriminative stimulus for the next response in the chain.

Laboratory studies of chained schedules usually do not involve as many components as are required to prepare a peanut-butter-and-jelly sandwich. An example of a much simpler chained schedule is presented in Figure 9.19. In this case, a rat is required to pull a cord when a tone is sounded. The first pull response that occurs after a variable interval averaging 1 min produces a light stimulus. In the presence of the light, the rat has to complete a fixed ratio of 10 lever-press responses to obtain food. The delivery of food completes the chain. At this point the investigator can turn the tone on again and start another trial of the chained schedule. The light stimulus in this procedure has two functions. It serves as a discriminative stimulus for lever pressing because lever pressing is reinforced (with food) only during the light. The light also becomes a conditioned reinforcer because it is present only during the food-reinforcement component of the chained schedule. Because the light becomes a secondary reinforcer, its presentation serves to reinforce the cord-pull responses that are required to produce the light. In contrast to the two functions of the light stimulus, the tone in the present procedure serves only as a discriminative stimulus for pulling the cord.

With sufficient training on a chained schedule of the sort diagramed in Figure 9.19, subjects learn to perform the appropriate response during the light and tone stimuli. That is, they will pull the cord only during the tone and press the response lever only during the light. In addition, a pattern of responding will develop in the presence of each stimulus that corresponds to the schedule of reinforcement in effect during that stimulus. In our example, pulling the cord during the tone was reinforced by the onset of the light according to a variable-interval schedule. We would expect cord pulling during the tone to be characterized by the same steady rate of response that occurs with primary reinforcement delivered on a variable-interval

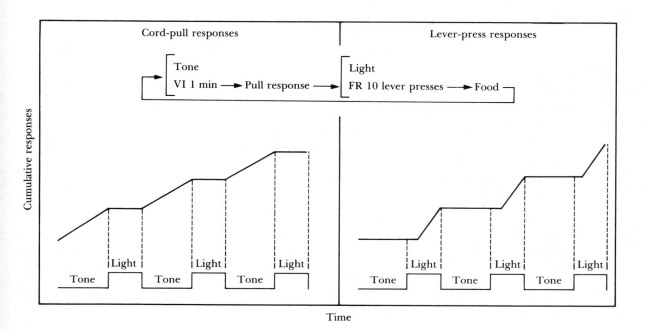

Figure 9.19. Illustration of a chained schedule of reinforcement. The first cord-pull response that occurs more than a variable interval averaging 1 min after the tone is presented results in presentation of the light. In the presence of the light a fixed ratio of 10 lever-press responses results in delivery of food. The tone is then presented again, and the chain is repeated. The hypothetical cumulative records show that subjects learn to pull the cord only during the tone and to press the lever only during the light. In addition, the pattern of responding that occurs on each manipulandum is appropriate to the reinforcement schedule for that response.

schedule. During the light, responding was reinforced according to a fixed-ratio schedule. Therefore, we would expect the rat to pause for a while when the light was turned on and then produce a high and steady rate of lever pressing to complete the ratio requirement, as is characteristic of performance reinforced on a fixed-ratio schedule. These hypothetical results are illustrated in the bottom panel of Figure 9.19.

As we have noted, the pattern of responding that occurs in each component of a chained schedule corresponds to the schedule of secondary or primary reinforcement available in that component. However, the absolute rate of responding is determined only by the primary reinforcement. The closer a particular component of the chained schedule is to the primary reinforcement, the higher will be the rate of responding in that component. This relation was discovered in an important experiment by Gollub (1958). He used chain schedules with equal schedules of secondary reinforcement in each component. Responding in each component was reinforced by the presentation of the stimulus for the next component according to the same fixed-interval schedule. The chained schedule had four stimulus components before the final component, and subjects could obtain food only in the final component.

Box 9.2.   Teaching Children How to Tie Shoelaces

Learning to tie shoes is a complex problem for a four-year-old. Shoe-tying lessons usually begin with the first step, the half-hitch, and proceed to the end. Since the task involves fine motor responses that are difficult for the child, the desired result may not be attained until after many slow and unsuccessful attempts. The whole affair can be quite frustrating for student and teacher alike.

An alternative approach makes use of the methods used in the laboratory to shape chained-schedule responding. Training a rat to perform a chained sequence begins with the last response in the chain—the response that is most immediately reinforced with food. Once this response is established, the next-to-last response is shaped. The reinforcer for the next-to-last response is not the food but the discriminative stimulus for the last response. The subject makes the next-to-last response, receives the discriminative stimulus, and then makes the last response in the chain for the food reinforcer. By working backward from the food-reinforced response, a chain with several components can be readily shaped. In tying a shoe, the recommended procedure is to begin not with the half-hitch but with the last response in the chain. The teacher ties the laces all the way except for pulling the "rabbit ears" to produce the bow. This the child does, and *voilà*, the shoe is tied! The child will probably be pleased with this initial success (reinforced) and ready to try again. This time the teacher leaves a little more for the child to do. By working backward, the teacher ensures that the child's efforts are almost always successful and hence reinforced. Children taught by this method learn to tie shoelaces quite readily.

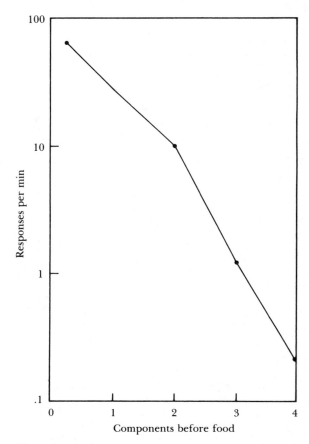

Figure 9.20. Rate of responding in various components of a chained schedule before the presentation of food. Each component of the chained schedule provided secondary reinforcement on an FI 30-sec schedule. Note that, the further a component is from primary reinforcement, the lower the response rate is in that component. *(After Gollub, 1958.)*

Figure 9.20 shows the rate of responding that occurred in each component. Higher response rates occurred in stimulus components closer to the delivery of food.

Chained schedules illustrate the discriminative properties of secondary reinforcers because each stimulus in the chain serves as a dis-criminative stimulus for the response required in that component. A strong test of the discriminative properties of the stimuli involves modifying the order of the components in the chained schedule. What would happen if, in our example (see Figure 9.19), we presented the light stimulus before the tone once the subjects had received extensive training with the components presented in the opposite order? Generally, the discriminative control of behavior will not be disrupted by such a manipulation. The subjects will continue to press the bar when the light is on and to pull the cord during the tone. However, if food is now delivered in the tone component, the absolute rate of responding will gradually come to be greater during the tone than during the light (see Gollub, 1977).

Applications of secondary reinforcement: Token economies

One of the more controversial applications of learning principles is the token economy. A token economy is a system in which subjects can earn tokens by performing specified desirable behaviors. The tokens can be exchanged for various goods and services the subject chooses, such as candy, cigarettes, magazines, a pass to see a movie, or the opportunity to engage in certain games or watch television. The tokens thus function as secondary reinforcers. Token economies have been widely used and studied in institutional settings, such as hospitals for the chronic mentally ill or schools for the mentally retarded (see Kazdin & Bootzin, 1972, for a detailed review). Such institutions invariably have patients who are very apathetic, listless, and dependent on the staff for their basic needs. They may not groom, dress, or feed themselves, make their beds, and keep their belongings tidy, and they may rarely engage in any activities such as talking to others, drawing or doing craft work, or exercising. They may not perform such activities because these responses do not provide intrinsic rewards (pleasures) for them. By setting up a token economy with chronic mentally ill patients, the therapist hopes to reinstate common coping behaviors by applying reinforcers that have extrinisic value. The therapist hopes that once productive behaviors are reinstated, the intrinsic value of the self-care and other responses will again come to control the activities. With mentally retarded persons, a token economy provides extra motivation to learn and use new skills. If someone's level of functioning is particularly low, the tokens can be used to reinforce components of

or successive approximations to the desired behaviors.

In many token economies tremendous improvements in performance have been reported. In one dramatic example (McReynolds & Coleman, 1972), 48 patients from a "back" ward were studied. These patients were nearly without self-care and social behaviors. For instance, only 10% of them could dress themselves and only 40% could feed themselves. The average time of hospitalization was 13 years. No one had been discharged from this ward in two years. After one year with the token economy, 30 patients could dress themselves and all of them could eat properly. Thirteen patients had been transferred to more open wards in the institution, five had been home on visits, and seven had been discharged to the community.

Despite successes such as those reported by McReynolds and Coleman, token economies are not without problems. Implementation of a token economy is often difficult and raises ethical problems. The most effective primary reinforcers in many cases are food and accommodations. Should a patient be denied these things if he or she has not earned the required tokens? In most token economies the problem is solved by providing adequate food and accommodations free and allowing patients to "buy" better accommodations in exchange for tokens. Another problem is that although the reinforcement contingencies are effective in strengthening self-care, social, and work skills, the patient may continue to have problems with delusions and the like. The token economy does not provide the basic cure. Like other procedures, it must be used judiciously as a part of a total treatment program.

Concluding comments

In this chapter we have begun our analysis of how organisms make use of signals in their environment in making instrumental responses. We have discussed stimuli of two types that signal different aspects of the instrumental situation. The first signals the response/reinforcer contingency. The second signals when the reinforcer is available. In both cases we have seen that organisms make use of signals in a variety of ways. It is not a simple matter for the psychologist to discern how signals are being used. The problems of determining what the subject is "doing" with a particular stimulus in a particular situation make this area of research quite challenging. The problems are far from solved.

The ideas presented in this chapter form a basis for the research presented in the next two chapters. Chapter 10 will deal with issues related to aversive stimulation. Issues related to stimulus control have been of great theoretical importance in the analysis of avoidance and punished behavior. In Chapter 11 we will deal further with theoretical ideas that relate classical and instrumental behavior.

CHAPTER TEN

Aversive Control: Avoidance and Punishment

In the present chapter we will discuss how behavior can be controlled by aversive stimulation. We will limit the presentation to two types of instrumental-conditioning procedures involving aversive stimuli—avoidance and punishment. We will describe both the major experimental findings on avoidance and punishment and the major theoretical concepts that have been proposed to explain these findings.

Our discussion of instrumental behavior so far has involved positively reinforced behavior. We now turn to behavior controlled by events that are regarded as noxious, or aversive. In the laboratory, the most commonly studied aversive stimulus is electrical shock. However, such stimuli as loud noise and intense heat have also been used. In addition, the absence of an expected positive reinforcer can have effects similar to those of common noxious stimuli. Our discussion will focus on two types of procedures involving aversive stimuli—avoidance and punishment. In both these procedures animals learn to minimize their exposure to aversive events. Precisely how this takes place has been the subject of a great deal of research and considerable debate. We will describe the highlights of these areas of investigation.

Avoidance behavior

Avoidance is a type of instrumental behavior in which the organism's responses prevent the occurrence of an aversive stimulus. Effective avoidance behavior is critical for survival. Animals have to avoid predators and exposure to extreme climatic conditions, as well as more mundane things, such as slipping and falling or running into objects. Avoidance also constitutes much of human behavior. Grabbing a handrail while walking on an uneven surface helps you avoid falling, holding your hands in front of you as you walk in a dark room helps you avoid bumping into things, and making adjustments in the position of the steering wheel as you drive helps you avoid driving off the road. These and numerous other activities constitute avoidance behavior because in each case the instrumental response is responsible for preventing an aversive situation that would otherwise occur.

In most cases the avoidance response is followed by nothing more than the absence of the aversive situation. Given the proper avoidance responses, you will not fall, bump into things, or drive off the road. No particular pleasure is derived from these avoidance responses. You simply fail to experience pain. The absence of an aversive situation is presumably the reason that avoidance responses are made. However, how can the absence of something provide reinforcement for instrumental behavior? This is the fundamental question in the study of avoidance. Mowrer and Lamoreaux (1942, p. 6) pointed out some years ago that "not getting something can hardly, in and of itself, qualify as rewarding." Since then much intellectual effort has been devoted to figuring out what else is involved in avoidance-conditioning procedures that might provide reinforcement for the behavior. In fact, the investigation of avoidance behavior has been dominated by this theoretical problem.

Origins of the study of avoidance behavior

The study of avoidance behavior was initially closely allied to investigations of classical conditioning. The first avoidance-conditioning experiments were conducted by the Russian psychologist Bechterev (1913) as an extension of Pavlov's research. Unlike Pavlov, however, Bechterev investigated conditioning mechanisms in human subjects. In one situation, participants were asked to place a finger on a metal plate. A warning stimulus (the CS) was periodically presented, followed by a brief shock (the US) through the plate. As you might suspect, the subjects quickly lifted the finger off the plate upon being shocked. With repeated conditioning trials, they also learned to make this response to the warning stimulus. The experiment was viewed as a standard example of clas-

sical conditioning. However, in contrast to the standard classical-conditioning procedure, in Bechterev's method the subjects determined whether they were exposed to the US. If they lifted their finger off the plate in response to the CS, they did not experience the shock scheduled on that trial. Thus, they could avoid the shock by making the finger-withdrawal response. This aspect of the procedure constitutes a significant departure from Pavlov's methods because in standard classical conditioning the delivery of the US does not depend on the subject's behavior.

The fact that Bechterev and others who followed his example did not use a standard classical-conditioning procedure went unnoticed for many years. Starting in the 1930s, several investigators attempted to compare directly the effects of a standard classical-conditioning procedure with a procedure that had the added instrumental avoidance component (for example, Schlosberg, 1934, 1936). One of the most influential of these comparisons was performed by Brogden, Lipman, and Culler (1938). They tested two groups of guinea pigs in a rotating wheel apparatus (see Figure 10.1). A tone served as the CS, and shock again served as the US. The shock stimulated

Figure 10.1. Modern running wheel for rodents.

the guinea pigs to run and thereby rotate the wheel. For one group of subjects, the shock was always presented 2 sec after the beginning of the tone (classical group). The second group (avoidance group) received the same type of CS-US pairings when they did not make the conditioned response (a small movement of the wheel). However, if these subjects moved the wheel during the tone CS before the shock occurred, the scheduled shock was omitted. The percentage of trials on which each group made the conditioned response is shown in Figure 10.2. It is evident from the results that the avoidance group quickly learned to make the conditioned response and was responding on 100% of the trials within eight days of training. In contrast, the classical group never achieved this high level of performance, even though training was continued much longer for them.

These results clearly show that there is a critical difference between standard classical conditioning and procedures that include an instrumental avoidance component. The avoidance procedure produces a much higher level

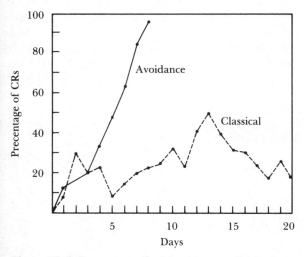

Figure 10.2. Percentage of trials with a conditioned response on successive days of training. The conditioned response prevented shock delivery for the avoidance group but not for the classical group. *(After Brogden, Lipman, & Culler, 1938.)*

of responding than what is observed with mere pairings of the CS with shock. Furthermore, this facilitation of behavior cannot be explained solely by what is known about classical conditioning. In fact, the results obtained by Brogden et al. are paradoxical when viewed just in terms of classical conditioning. For the avoidance group, the CS is often presented without the US because the subjects often prevent the occurrence of shock. These CS-alone trials constitute extinction trials and hence should attenuate the development of the conditioned response. In contrast, the classical group never receives CS-alone trials because it can never avoid shock. Therefore, if CS-US pairings were the only important factor in this situation, the classical group should have performed better than the avoidance group. The fact that the opposite result occurred indicates that analysis of avoidance behavior requires more than classical-conditioning principles.

Although avoidance behavior is not just another case of classical conditioning, the classical-conditioning heritage of the study of avoidance behavior has greatly influenced its subsequent experimental and theoretical analysis. Investigators have been greatly concerned with the importance of signals for the aversive event in avoidance conditioning and with the relation of the warning signal to the instrumental response and the aversive US. Experimental questions of this type have been extensively investigated with procedures similar to that used by Brogden and his colleagues. This method is called **discriminated** or **signaled avoidance**, and its standard features are diagrammed in Figure 10.3.

The first thing to note about the signaled avoidance technique is that it involves discrete trials. Each trial is initiated by the CS. The events that occur after that depend on what the subject does. There are two possibilities. If the subject makes the response required for avoidance during the CS but before the shock is scheduled, the CS is turned off, and the US is

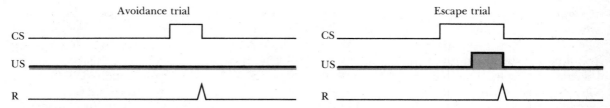

Figure 10.3. Diagram of the discriminated, or signaled, avoidance procedure. *Avoidance trial:* If the subject makes the response required for avoidance during the CS (the signal) but before the US (for example, shock) is scheduled, the CS is turned off, and the US is omitted on that trial. *Escape trial:* If the subjects fails to make the required response during the CS-US interval, the scheduled shock is presented and remains on until the response occurs, whereupon both the CS *and* the US are terminated.

omitted on that trial. This is a successful **avoidance trial**. If the subject fails to make the required response during the CS-US interval, the scheduled shock is presented and remains on until the response occurs, whereupon both the CS and the US are terminated. In this case, the instrumental response results in escape from the shock. Hence this type of trial is called an **escape trial**. During early stages of training, most of the trials are escape trials, whereas avoidance trials predominate once the avoidance response is well established.

Discriminated avoidance procedures can be conducted using a variety of experimental situations. One may, for example, use a Skinner box in which a rat has to press a response lever during a tone to avoid shock (Hoffman, 1966). Another experimental situation that has been extensively used in studies of discriminated avoidance is the shuttle box, an example of which is shown in Figure 10.4. The shuttle box consists of two compartments separated by a low barrier and a guillotine door. The animal is placed in one side. At the start of the trial, the CS is presented (a light or a tone, for example), and the door between the two compartments is opened. If the animal crosses over to the other side before the shock is scheduled, no shock is delivered, and the door is closed until the next trial. The next trial can be administered starting with the animal in the second compartment. With this procedure, the animal shuttles back and forth between the two sides on successive

trials. The response is therefore called **shuttle avoidance**.

In the shuttle avoidance procedure, the animal can be shocked on either side of the apparatus. For example, if the subject is on the left side when a trial starts and it fails to make the shuttle response, it will receive shock on the left side. If it is on the right side when a trial begins and it again fails to cross, it will receive shock on the right side. A variation of the shuttle avoidance procedure has also been extensively investigated in which the subject is always placed on the same side of the shuttle box at the start of each trial. For example, it may always be placed in the left compartment. In this case, the animal would have to run to the right compartment on each trial to avoid (or escape) shock. At the end

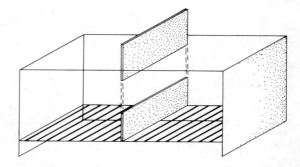

Figure 10.4. Shuttle box. The box has a metal grid floor and is separated into two compartments by a low barrier and a guillotine door. The door is raised at the start of each trial. The instrumental response consists in crossing from one side of the box to the other.

of the trial it would be removed from the right compartment and replaced in the left compartment to start the next trial. Such a procedure is called a **one-way avoidance** procedure because the animal always has to cross in the same direction. An important aspect of the one-way procedure is that the animal can be shocked in only one of the two compartments (the one it is placed in at the start of each trial). This part of the apparatus is called the **shock compartment**, and the other side is called the **safe compartment**.

Two-process theory of avoidance

It is clear from the results of experiments such as that by Brogden et al. (1938) that procedures in which a warning signal is repeatedly paired with shock do not produce as much responding as procedures that also allow for the instrumental response to prevent the delivery of the aversive stimulus. The addition of the avoidance contingency provides some kind of instrumental reinforcement for the avoidance response. Exactly what this source of reinforcement is has been the central question in investigations of avoidance learning. The first and most influential answer to the puzzle of avoidance behavior was proposed by Mowrer (1947) and elaborated by Miller (for example, 1951) and others, and it is known as the two-process theory of avoidance. The two-process theory in one form or another has been the dominant theoretical viewpoint on avoidance learning for many years. As we shall see, the theory has some serious shortcomings, and it is no longer viewed as a complete explanation of avoidance learning. Nevertheless, it continues to be important, at least to the extent that it is the standard against which other explanations of avoidance behavior are always measured.

As its name implies, two-process theory assumes that two mechanisms are involved in avoidance learning. The first is a classical-conditioning process activated by pairings of the warning stimulus (CS) with the aversive event (US) on trials when the subject fails to make the avoidance response. As was common at the time, Mowrer assumed that classical conditioning occurs by stimulus substitution. Because the US was an aversive event, Mowrer assumed that it elicited fear. Through classical conditioning with the US, the CS presumably also comes to elicit fear. Thus, the first component of two-process theory is the *classical conditioning of fear to the CS*. Fear is an emotionally arousing state that motivates the organism. It is also aversive, so that a reduction in fear can provide negative reinforcement. Since fear is elicited by the CS, termination of the CS presumably results in a reduction in the level of fear. The second process in two-process theory is based on these considerations. Mowrer assumed that the instrumental avoidance response became learned because it terminated the CS and thereby reduced the conditioned fear elicited by the CS. Thus, the second component is *instrumental reinforcement of the avoidance response through fear reduction*.

There are several noteworthy aspects of two-process theory. First, and perhaps most important, is that the classical and instrumental processes are not assumed to provide independent sources of support for the avoidance behavior. Rather, the two processes very much depend on each other. Instrumental reinforcement through fear reduction is not possible until fear has been conditioned to the CS. Therefore, the classical-conditioning process has to occur first. After that, the instrumental-conditioning process may create extinction trials for the classical-conditioning process. This occurs because each successful avoidance response prevents the occurrence of the US. Thus, two-process theory predicts a constant interplay between classical and instrumental processes. Another important aspect of two-process theory is that it explains avoidance behavior in terms of escape from conditioned fear rather than in terms of the prevention of shock. The fact that the avoidance response prevents shock is seen as a by-product in two-process theory, not as the critical event that motivates avoidance behavior. Escape from conditioned fear provides the critical reinforcement for avoidance behavior. Thus, according to two-process theory, the instrumental response is reinforced by a tangible event (fear reduction) rather than merely the absence of something (aversive stimulation).

Experimental analysis of avoidance behavior

A great deal of research has been conducted concerning avoidance behavior, much of it stimulated in one way or another by two-process theory. We cannot review all the evidence. However, we will consider several important types of results that have to be considered in any effort to fully understand the mechanisms of avoidance behavior.

Acquired-drive experiments. In the typical avoidance procedure, the classical conditioning of fear and instrumental reinforcement through fear reduction occur intermixed in a series of trials. However, if these two processes in fact exist, it should be possible to demonstrate their operation in situations in which the two types of conditioning are not intermixed. This is the goal of acquired-drive experiments. The basic strategy is to first condition fear to a CS with a "pure" classical-conditioning procedure in which the organism's responses do not influence whether the US is presented. In the next phase of the experiment, the animals are periodically exposed to the fear-eliciting CS and allowed to perform an instrumental response that is effective in terminating the CS (and thereby reducing fear). No shocks are scheduled in this phase. Therefore, the instrumental response is not required to avoid shock presentations. If two-process theory is correct and escape from the fear-eliciting CS can reinforce instrumental behavior, then subjects should be able to learn the instrumental response in the second phase of the experiment.

This type of experiment is called an **acquired drive** study because the drive to perform the instrumental response (fear) is learned through classical conditioning. (It is not an innate drive, such as hunger or thirst.)

One of the first and most famous acquired-drive experiments was performed by Miller (1948). However, because of certain problems with that study, we will describe a follow-up experiment by Brown and Jacobs (1949). Rats were tested in a shuttle box. During the first phase of the procedure, the door between the two shuttle compartments was closed. The rats were individually placed on one side of the apparatus and a pulsating-light/tone CS was presented, ending in shock through the grid floor. Twenty-two such Pavlovian conditioning trials were conducted, with the rats confined on the right and left sides of the apparatus on alternate trials. The control group received the same training except that no shocks were delivered. During the next phase of the experiment,

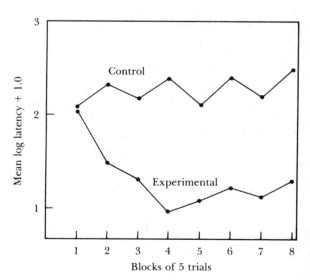

Figure 10.5. Mean latencies to cross from one side to the other in the shuttle box for control and experimental groups. The shuttle crossing resulted in termination of the CS on that trial. For the experimental group, the CS was previously conditioned with shock. Such conditioning was not conducted with the control group. *(After Brown & Jacobs, 1949.)*

Box 10.1. Phobic and Obsessive-Compulsive Behavior as Avoidance

In Chapter 4 we noted that clinical psychologists sometimes consider phobias to be fear responses that have been conditioned to particular stimuli. Frequently, however, the problem involves more than the fear itself. People who complain of phobias do not merely suffer from an irrational fear but more often than not also exhibit problematic behaviors that are instrumental in avoiding the fear. Agoraphobics, for example, experience anxiety or fear reactions when they are in crowded areas. To avoid such situations, some persons remain shut in their homes all the time. The fear of crowded situations may have been established through classical conditioning. Returning home or staying home reduces the anxiety elicited outside the home.

The problem of obsessive-compulsive persons can also be described within the context of avoidance. Obsessive-compulsive behavior is ritualistic behavior, such as handwashing, that occurs in the absence of a reasonable cause. One woman reported by Leon (1974) washed repeatedly and excessively (sometimes showering) after urinating, out of fear of contamination. For this woman the ritualistic behavior became so severe, taking up the better part of her day, that she was unable to pursue other projects effectively. Obsessive-compulsive persons report that they experience overwhelming anxiety if they cannot perform the ritualistic behavior. These reports suggest that the ritual reduces some classically conditioned anxiety response.

In actual clinical practice there is no way to know whether avoidance behavior and two-factor theory are actually at work. There are no experimental controls to rule out other interpretations, and frequently not all the relevant information to warrant the avoidance hypothesis is known. The basic research, however, provides a model for understanding certain aspects of the behavior. (For a further discussion of compulsive ritualistic behavior, see Rachman and Hodgson, 1980.)

each subject was placed on one side of the shuttle box, the center barrier was removed, and the CS was presented. The CS remained on until the subject crossed over to the other side, when the CS was turned off. The animal was then removed until it received its next trial. A one-way procedure was used, with the animals placed on the same side at the start of each trial. No shocks were delivered during this second phase of the experiment. The investigators were interested to see whether the rats would learn to cross rapidly from one side to the other when the only reinforcement for crossing was termination of the previously conditioned light/tone CS.

The amount of time each subject took to cross the shuttle box and turn off the CS was measured for each trial. These response latencies are summarized in Figure 10.5 for both the shock-conditioned and the control group. The two groups of subjects had similar response latencies at the beginning of instrumental training. However, as training progressed, the shock-conditioned animals learned to cross the shuttle box faster (and thus turn off the CS sooner) than the control group. This outcome shows that termination of a fear-conditioned stimulus is sufficient to provide reinforcement for an instrumental response. Such findings have been obtained in a variety of experimental situations (for example, Dinsmoor, 1962; McAllister & McAllister, 1971). In addition, other experiments have shown that delaying the termination of the CS after the instrumental behavior reduces the reinforcement effect, just as it does with instrumental responses maintained by positive reinforcement (for example, Delprato, 1969; Israel, Devine, O'Dea, & Hamdi, 1974; Katzev, 1967, 1972). These results provide strong support for two-process theory.

Concurrent measurement of fear and avoidance behavior. Another important strategy that has been used in investigations of avoidance behavior has involved concurrently measuring fear and instrumental avoidance responding. If two-process theory is correct in assuming that fear provides the motivation for avoidance behavior, then animals should appear fearful in avoidance situations. However, conditioned fear and avoidance responding are not always highly correlated (see review by Mineka, 1979). Fairly early in the investigation of avoidance learning, it was noted that animals become less fearful as they learn the avoidance response (Solomon, Kamin, & Wynne, 1953; Solomon & Wynne, 1953). Since then, more systematic measurements of fear have been used. One popular behavioral technique for measuring fear involves the conditioned-suppression procedure described in Chapters 4 and 6. In this technique, animals are first conditioned to make an instrumental response (such as lever pressing) for a food reward. A shock-conditioned CS is then presented while the subjects are responding to obtain food. Generally, the CS produces a suppression in the lever-press behavior, and the extent of this response suppression is assumed to reflect the amount of fear elicited by the CS. If the warning signal in an avoidance procedure comes to elicit fear, then presentation of the warning stimulus in a conditioned-suppression experiment should result in suppression of food-reinforced behavior. This possibility was first investigated in a famous experiment by Kamin, Brimer, and Black (1963).

Kamin et al. initially trained their rats to press a response lever for food reinforcement on a variable-interval schedule. The animals were then trained to avoid shock in response to an auditory CS in a shuttle box. Training was continued for independent groups of subjects until they successfully avoided shock on 1, 3, 9, or 27 consecutive trials. The animals were then returned to the lever-press situation. After their rate of responding had stabilized, the auditory CS that had been used in the shuttle box was periodically presented to see how much sup-

pression in responding it would produce. The results are summarized in Figure 10.6. Lower values of the suppression index indicate greater disruptions of the lever-press behavior by the shock-avoidance CS. Increasing degrees of response suppression were observed among groups of subjects that had received avoidance training until they successfully avoided shock on 1 to 9 successive trials. This outcome is consistent with two-process theory. Contrary to the theory, however, less response suppression occurred among subjects that had avoided shock on 27 consecutive trials. These subjects showed less suppression to the CS than subjects that had not received as extensive avoidance training. This outcome indicates that fear as measured by conditioned suppression decreases during ex-

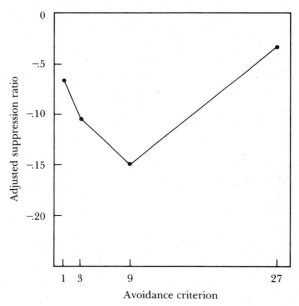

Figure 10.6. Suppression of lever pressing for food during a CS that was previously conditioned in a shock-avoidance procedure. Independent groups received avoidance training until they met a criterion of 1, 3, 9, or 27 consecutive avoidance responses. The suppression scores were adjusted for the degree of suppression produced by the CS before avoidance conditioning. Lower values of the adjusted ratio indicate greater suppression of lever pressing. *(After Kamin, Brimer, & Black, 1963.)*

tended avoidance training and is at a minimal level after extensive training (see also Linden, 1969; Starr & Mineka, 1977). However, the decrease in fear is not accompanied by a decrease in the strength of the avoidance response (Mineka & Gino, 1980).

Asymptotic avoidance performance. Two-process theory of avoidance not only specifies the mechanisms of the acquisition process for avoidance behavior but also makes predictions concerning the nature of performance once the response has been well learned. More specifically, it predicts that the strength of the avoidance response will fluctuate in cycles. Whenever a successful avoidance response occurs, the shock is omitted on that trial. This is assumed to be an extinction trial for the conditioned fear response. Repetition of the avoidance response (and thus the CS-alone extinction trials) should lead to extinction of fear. As the CS becomes extinguished, there will be less reinforcement resulting from the reduction of fear, and the avoidance response will also become extinguished. As this happens, the avoidance response will cease to occur in time to prevent the US. However, when shock is not avoided, the CS is paired with the US. This pairing should reinstitute fear to the CS and reestablish the potential for reinforcement through fear reduction. Hence, the avoidance response should become reconditioned. Thus, the theory predicts that after initial acquisition, the avoidance response will go through cycles of extinction and reacquisition. Although evidence of this sort has been observed on occasion (for example, Sheffield, 1948), avoidance behavior usually does not fluctuate in cycles. Rather, one of the most noteworthy aspects of avoidance behavior is that it is highly resistant to extinction when shocks no longer occur, as long as the response continues to be effective in terminating the CS. After shuttle avoidance conditioning with an intense shock in dogs, for example, the animals continue to make the avoidance

response for hundreds of trials without receiving shock. One dog was observed to make the avoidance response on 650 successive trials after only a few shocks (Solomon et al., 1953).

The extreme resistance to extinction of avoidance behavior is difficult to explain in terms of two-process theory. To accommodate such results, Solomon and Wynne (1954) proposed two modifications of the theory. First, they suggested that with extensive training, the latency of the avoidance response to the CS becomes shorter than the latency of the conditioned fear response. Therefore, the animal terminates the CS before the fear response has a chance to occur, and fear is not actually elicited on most trials after extensive training. Solomon and Wynne called this mechanism **anxiety conservation**. Anxiety conservation is not enough for a complete explanation of the resistance to extinction of avoidance behavior. If fear is not elicited, there is also no reinforcement through fear reduction, and the avoidance response should extinguish. Therefore, Solomon and Wynne also proposed that after conditioning with intense shocks, conditioned fear is *partly irreversible*. That is, no matter how many CS-alone exposures the subject receives, it will always have some residual fear of the CS. Subsequent research has not found this second assumption to be very useful (see Mineka, 1979).

Extinction of avoidance behavior through response blocking and CS-alone exposure. As we noted above, if the avoidance response is effective in terminating the CS and no shocks are presented, avoidance responding persists for a long time. Is avoidance behavior always highly resistant to extinction, or are there procedures that result in fairly rapid extinction? The answer is very important not only for a theoretical analysis of avoidance behavior but also for extinguishing maladaptive or pathological avoidance responses in human patients (see Box 10.2). One of the most effective and extensively investigated extinction procedures for avoidance behavior is called **flooding** or **response prevention** (Baum, 1970). It involves presenting the CS in the avoidance situation but with the apparatus altered in such a way that the subject is prevented from making the avoidance response. Thus, the subject is exposed to the CS without being permitted to terminate it. In a sense, it is "flooded" with exposure to the CS.

One of the most important variables determining the effects of a flooding procedure is the duration of the forced exposure to the CS. This is nicely illustrated in an experiment by Schiff, Smith, and Prochaska (1972). Rats were trained to avoid shock in response to an auditory CS warning stimulus in a one-way avoidance situation. After all the animals avoided shock on ten consecutive trials, the safe compartment was blocked off by a barrier, and subjects received various amounts of exposure to the CS without shock. Independent groups of subjects received 1, 5, or 12 blocked trials, and on each of these trials, the CS was presented for 1, 5, 10, 50, or 120 sec. The barrier blocking the avoidance re-

sponse was then removed, and all subjects were tested for extinction. At the start of each extinction trial, the subject was placed in the apparatus, and the CS was presented until the animal crossed into the safe compartment. Shock never occurred during the extinction trials, and subjects were tested until they took 120 sec or longer to cross into the safe compartment on three consecutive trials. The strength of the avoidance response was measured in terms of the number of trials subjects took to reach this extinction criterion.

As expected, blocked exposure to the CS facilitated extinction of the avoidance response. Furthermore, this effect was determined mainly by the total duration of exposure to the CS. The number of flooding trials administered (1, 5, or 12) facilitated extinction only because each trial added to the total amount of time the subjects were exposed to the CS without being allowed to escape from it. The results of the experiment are summarized in Figure 10.7. Increases in the total duration of blocked exposure to the CS resulted in more rapid ex-

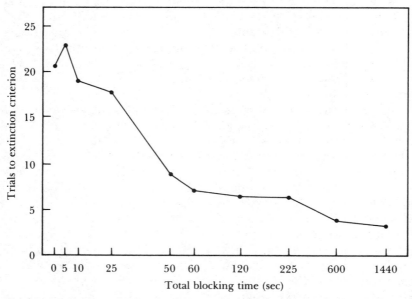

Figure 10.7. Trials to extinction criterion for independent groups of animals that previously received various durations of blocked exposure to the CS. *(From Schiff, Smith, & Prochaska, 1972.)*

tinction of the avoidance response (see also Baum, 1969; Weinberger, 1965).

Two-process theory predicts that flooding will extinguish avoidance behavior because forced exposure to the CS is expected to produce extinction of fear. The fact that more extensive exposure to the CS results in more rapid extinction of the avoidance response (for example, Schiff et al., 1972) is consistent with this view. However, detailed investigations of the role of fear in flooding procedures have also provided evidence contrary to two-process theory. Independent measurements of fear (with the conditioned-suppression technique, for example) have shown that fear does not extinguish as rapidly as does the avoidance behavior in flooding experiments (for example, Coulter, Riccio, & Page, 1969; Mineka & Gino, 1979; Page, 1955). This outcome suggests that extinction of fear is only one factor responsible for the effects of flooding procedures. Other variables may be related to the fact that during flooding, subjects not only receive forced exposure to the CS but are prevented from making the avoidance response. In certain situations, blocking of the avoidance response can contribute to extinction of the avoidance behavior independent of CS exposure. One demonstration of this fact was performed by Katzev and Berman (1974).

Katzev and Berman first conditioned rats to avoid shock in a shuttle box. Fifty extinction trials were then conducted. Pairs of subjects were set up for this phase of the experiment. For one subject of each pair, the shuttle response was not blocked during the extinction trials, so that the rat could turn off the CS by crossing to the other side. The other subject of each pair received the identical CS exposures that the first rat received, except that the shuttle response was blocked by a barrier. Thus, CS exposure was equal for the two types of subjects, but only one of the subjects in each pair could terminate the CS by making the shuttle response. A third group of rats served as a control group and was not exposed to the CS (or

the shuttle box) during this phase. All the subjects were then given a series of standard extinction trials. The barrier was removed altogether, and the CS was periodically presented until the subjects crossed to the other side of the apparatus. The results are summarized in Figure 10.8. The control group made the greatest number of shuttle crossings. The least number of responses occurred in subjects that had received blocked exposure to the CS. In fact, these animals were much less likely to respond than animals that had received the identical exposure to the CS but could always terminate the CS presentations by making the shuttle response. These results show that response blocking can facilitate extinction of avoidance behavior independent of variations in CS exposure. Thus, evidently the flooding procedure involves more than just Pavlovian extinction of the CS (see Baum, 1970; Mineka, 1979, for a more detailed discussion). Perhaps subjects learn a response that is incompatible with the

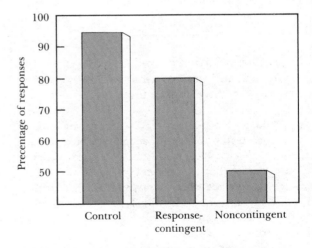

Figure 10.8. Percentage of shuttle responses that occurred during the first ten test trials. In the previous phase of the experiment, the control group was not exposed to the CS, the response-contingent group received CS exposures that could be terminated by a shuttle response, and the noncontingent group received yoked CS exposures independent of behavior. Initially all subjects received discriminated avoidance training. (*After Katzev & Berman, 1974.*)

Box 10.2. Extinction of Phobic and Obsessive-Compulsive Behavior

The research we have reviewed on extinction of avoidance shows that avoidance behavior will persist if the response is effective in terminating the CS even if the aversive stimulus is no longer presented. Similarly, phobic and obsessive-compulsive behavior often persists in the absence of truly traumatic events. The ritualistic hand-washing of some compulsive people persists even though there is no real contamination. Someone with a snake phobia may continue to avoid outdoor areas even though the chances of seeing a snake, let alone being harmed by one, are remote. The avoidance behavior in these situations prevents the person from testing the reality of the basis for fear.

Procedures that enhance extinction in the laboratory, such as flooding and response prevention, have been tried in the clinic as treatment techniques. Although there is not much in the way of well-controlled clinical research, individual case studies provide some evidence for the efficacy of these procedures. Meyer (1966) studied two women who engaged in persistent obsessive-compulsive rituals. These women were requested to perform threatening activities, such as touching dirty objects. They were then prevented by the nursing staff from engaging in their usual rituals. This procedure initially caused a great deal of distress. However, gradually the distress and the ritual behaviors subsided (see also Rachman & Hodgson, 1980).

Because response prevention and flooding can cause severe distress, some clinicians have done the flooding in graduated steps to keep the distress at tolerable levels. Grossberg (1965), for example, used a graduated procedure to cure a student of a public-speaking phobia. This phobia was preventing the student from completing a 1-min speech in front of a class in public speaking. The student was initially asked to read a familiar passage from a book to the therapist. Gradually, the speaking situation was made increasingly similar to the normal speech-class conditions: the size of the audience was increased, and the nature of the speech was changed in graduated steps. After 17 sessions the student was able to give the required speech for class and received a B in the course.

avoidance behavior during blocked exposures to the CS, and this contributes to the observed loss of avoidance responding.

Relative importance of various effects of the instrumental response in signaled avoidance. As we have stated, two-process theory emphasizes that the critical effect of the avoidance response is that it terminates the CS. The resulting reduction of the fear conditioned to the CS is assumed to reinforce the avoidance response. However, as we have seen, some aspects of avoidance behavior cannot be explained in terms of this fear-reduction mechanism. In actuality the avoidance situation is more complicated. There are other potential sources of reinforcement for the avoidance response in addition to fear reduction. If the response occurs during the CS-US interval, the response prevents delivery of the US. In contrast, if it occurs after the US has been presented, the response can terminate the US. Thus, the instrumental response actually has three possible effects in a standard avoidance procedure: CS termination (T), US avoidance (A), and US escape (E). Two-process theory assumes that the avoidance and US-escape components are not critical. This proposition can be investigated by comparing the standard avoidance-conditioning procedure with various modifications of the standard method that allow for only one or two of the three customary effects of the instrumental response.

Several studies have made such comparisons (for example, Kamin, 1956). One of the most extensive was conducted by Bolles, Stokes, and Younger (1966). Bolles et al. compared the performance of eight groups of animals during the course of 100 training trials. The procedures and results are summarized in Table 10.1. Four

TABLE 10.1. *Percentage of trials on which an instrumental response occurred as a function of whether the CS could be terminated (T), shock could be avoided (A), or shock could be escaped (E) in the shuttle box and the running wheel*

Possible effects of the instrumental response	Shuttle box	Running wheel
TAE	70	85
TA-	37	79
T-E	31	38
T--	10	48
-AE	40	75
-A-	15	62
--E	9	26
---	14	28

Based on Bolles, Stokes, and Younger (1966) and Bolles (1972).

of the groups could immediately terminate the conditioned stimulus (a 10-sec burst of loud noise) by making the instrumental response. For the first of these groups (group TAE), the instrumental response was also effective in both avoiding the US and escaping from it if the shock was not prevented. The second group (group TA-) could terminate the CS and avoid the US but could not escape the shock once the shock occurred. The shock lasted .3 sec regardless of what these animals did. The third group (group T-E) was allowed to terminate the CS and escape from the US but could not avoid the shock by responding during the CS-US interval. For them, the shock was presented on every trial. The fourth group (group T--) could only terminate the CS; they could neither avoid nor escape from the US. For the remaining animals, the CS was always presented for 10 sec and could not be terminated early by the instrumental response. For one of these groups (group -AE), a response during the CS-US interval was effective in avoiding shock on that trial, and a response during shock terminated the US. Another group (group -A-) was allowed to avoid the shock but could not escape from it once the shock occurred. The next group (group --E) could never avoid the shock but was allowed to escape from it, and the last group (group ---) could neither avoid nor escape the shock. This last group just received the CS followed by shock on every trial regardless of what they did.

The eight procedures described above were tested in two experiments. In one experiment, a shuttle box was used, and the rats had to cross from one side to the other to make the specified instrumental response. In the second experiment, the rats had to run enough to rotate a running wheel through one-fourth of a revolution from a stationary position to make the instrumental response. The results of both experiments are summarized in Table 10.1. Let us first consider the outcome of the shuttle-box experiment. The first thing that is obvious from these results is that none of the three possible effects of the instrumental response was sufficient by itself to produce any learning. Animals that could only terminate the CS (group T--), only avoid the shock (group -A-), or only escape the shock (group --E) all performed the instrumental response as infrequently as the control group (group ---), whose behavior had none of these effects. Thus, contrary to the prediction of two-process theory, termination of the CS was not enough to condition the instrumental behavior. However, if the animals were also allowed to either avoid or escape shock, the CS-termination component of the procedure greatly facilitated performance. You can see this by comparing pairs of groups that received identical treatment except that one could terminate the CS whereas the other could not: group TAE performed much better (70%) than group -AE (40%), group TA- performed better (37%) than group -A- (15%), and group T-E performed better (31%) than group --E (9%). This outcome supports two-process theory.

Although the shuttle-box results indicate that CS termination is important, contrary to two-process theory, CS termination was not the only significant factor. In combination with CS termination and/or US escape, avoidance of shock also facilitated performance. Groups that were allowed to avoid the shock performed better than comparable groups that did not have this opportunity: group TAE performed better

(70%) than group T-E (31%), group TA- performed better (37%) than group T-- (10%), and group -AE performed better (40%) than group --E (9%). The experiment provides a similar conclusion concerning the shock-escape component. Groups that were allowed to escape shock performed better than comparable groups that always received shock for a fixed duration (compare groups TAE and TA-, groups T-E and T--, and groups -AE and -A-). Thus, the presence of the avoidance and the escape components of the standard avoidance procedure significantly facilitated learning. As we will discuss later (see p. 256), these results might have been due to the fact that when avoidance or escape was not possible, occurrences of the instrumental response were followed by the shock. This constituted punishment of the instrumental response and might have been responsible for the lower levels of performance observed when the avoidance and escape components were absent from the procedure.

The pattern of results observed in the running-wheel apparatus was very different from the outcome of the shuttle-box experiment. For example, the shock-avoidance component alone was sufficient to produce learning in the running wheel. Group -A- responded on 62% of the trials, whereas the control group, ---, responded only 28% of the time. The CS-termination procedure in isolation also produced substantial levels of responding (group T--, 48%). However, when added to the avoidance and/or escape components, the CS-termination procedure did not increase the behavior very much (compare groups -AE and TAE, groups -A- and TA-, and groups --E and T-E). The escape component also did not add much to the learning. In fact, in one pair of groups, the addition of the escape component detracted slightly from performance (compare groups T-- and T-E). In contrast to these small effects produced by adding the CS-termination or US-escape components, adding the avoidance component always substantially increased

learning. Group TAE performed much better (85%) than group T-E (38%), group TA- performed much better (79%) than group T-- (48%), and group -AE performed much better (75%) than group --E (26%). Therefore, the major finding in the running-wheel experiment was that the avoidance component is the most important aspect of the avoidance procedure. This outcome, together with the fact that the patterns of results were very different in the shuttle-box and running-wheel experiments, presents a strong challenge to two-process theory.

Nondiscriminated (free-operant) avoidance. The Bolles, Stokes, and Younger study illustrates that prevention of the US may play a greater role in avoidance conditioning than previously considered by two-factor theory. However, in all the procedures tested in this study, the shock was always preceded by a warning stimulus (the CS). (In some cases the subjects could terminate the CS; in other cases it remained on for a fixed duration even if the avoidance response occurred.) Could animals also learn to avoid shock even if there were no external warning stimulus in the situation? Within the context of two-factor theory, this would seem to be almost a heretical question. However, science often progresses when investigators ask bold questions, and Sidman (1953a, 1953b) did just that. He devised what has come to be known as the **nondiscriminated** or **free-operant avoidance** procedure. (It is also sometimes called **Sidman avoidance**.) In this procedure shock is scheduled to occur periodically without warning, let us say every 10 sec. Some behavior is specified as the avoidance response, and each occurrence of this response prevents the delivery of the scheduled shocks for a fixed period—say, 30 sec. Animals will learn to avoid shocks under these conditions even though there is no warning stimulus. The procedure is constructed from only two time intervals (see Figure 10.9). One of these is the interval between shocks in the absence of a re-

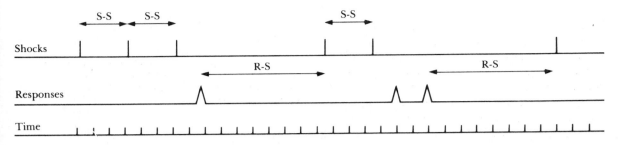

Figure 10.9. Diagram of the nondiscriminated, or free-operant, avoidance procedure. Each occurrence of the response initiates a period without shock, as set by the R-S interval. In the absence of a response, the next shock occurs a fixed period after the last shock, as set by the S-S interval. Shocks are not signaled by an exteroceptive stimulus and are usually brief and inescapable.

sponse. This is called the **S-S** (shock-shock) **interval.** The other critical time period is the interval between the response and the next scheduled shock. This is called the **R-S** (response-shock) **interval.** The R-S interval is the period of safety created by the response. In our example, the S-S interval is 10 sec and the R-S interval is 30 sec.

In addition to lacking a warning stimulus, the free-operant avoidance procedure differs from discriminated avoidance in allowing for avoidance responses to occur at any time. In discriminated avoidance procedures, the avoidance response is effective in preventing the delivery of shock only if it is made during the CS. Responses in the absence of the CS (the intertrial interval) have no effect. In fact, in some experiments (particularly those involving one-way avoidance), the animals are removed from the apparatus between trials. In contrast, in the free-operant procedure, an avoidance response occurring at any time will reset the R-S interval. If the R-S interval is 30 sec, shock is scheduled 30 sec after each response. However, by always responding just before this R-S interval is over, the subject can always reset the R-S interval and thereby prolong its period of safety indefinitely.

There are several striking characteristics of free-operant avoidance experiments. First, these studies generally involve much longer periods of training than discriminated avoidance experiments. It is rare, for example, for a dis-

criminated avoidance experiment to be conducted long enough so that the animals receive 100 shocks. However, 100 shocks is not excessive in free-operant avoidance studies, in part because sometimes it takes a lot of experience with shock before subjects learn to make the avoidance response regularly. Extensive training is also often used because the investigators are specifically interested in what steady-state adjustment the animals will make to such schedules of aversive stimulation. Thus, in many cases the initial learning of the avoidance behavior is not the primary focus of the experiment. Another general characteristic of these experiments is that even after extensive training, animals often never get good enough to avoid all shocks. Finally, there are often large differences between subjects in how they respond to the identical free-operant avoidance procedure.

Figures 10.10 and 10.11 illustrate the kinds of results that can be obtained with free-operant avoidance training. Each figure shows cumulative records of lever pressing during successive 1-hour periods of the first time that two rats were exposed to the avoidance procedure. In the absence of lever presses, the subjects received shock every 5 sec (the S-S interval). Each lever-press response initiated a 20-sec period without shocks (the R-S interval). Shocks are indicated by downward deflections of the cumulative-recorder pen. Rat H-28 (Figure

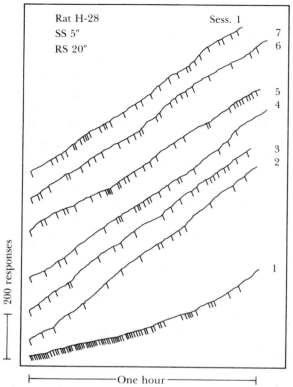

Figure 10.10. Cumulative record of lever pressing for a rat the first time it was exposed to a nondiscriminated avoidance procedure. Numerals at the right label successive hours of exposure to the procedure. Oblique slashes indicate delivery of shock. *(From Sidman, 1966.)*

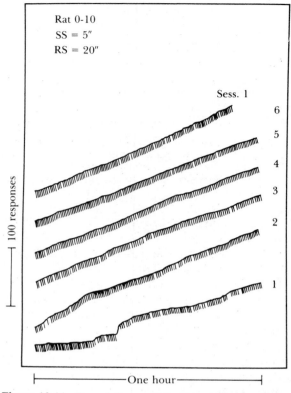

Figure 10.11. Cumulative record of lever pressing for a rat the first time it was exposed to a nondiscriminated avoidance procedure. Numerals at the right label successive hours of exposure to the procedure. Oblique slashes indicate delivery of shock. *(From Sidman, 1966.)*

10.10) received a lot of shocks at first but started to press the lever even during the first hour of training. It responded a great deal during the second hour of the session and then settled down to a steady rate of lever pressing for the next 5 hours that the procedure was in effect. This was its stable response pattern under these conditions. Rat H-28 was a particularly fast learner. However, even at the end of the 7 hours of training it received more than 30 shocks/hour.

Rat O-10 (Figure 10.11) did not perform as well as rat H-28. It received a great many more shocks and never achieved a high rate of responding. Its stable pattern of behavior after several hours of training was always to wait for the shock to occur at the end of an R-S interval before responding again. It usually did not respond to reinstitute the R-S interval and did not obtain prolonged periods free from shock. Therefore, it received a shock about every 20 sec, as set by the R-S interval.

Numerous experiments have been conducted on free-operant avoidance behavior (see Hineline, 1977; Sidman, 1966). The rate of responding is controlled by the values of the S-S and R-S intervals. The more frequently shocks are scheduled in the absence of responding (the S-S interval), the more likely the animal is to learn the avoidance response. Increasing the periods of safety produced by the response (the R-S interval) also promotes the avoidance behavior. In addition, the relative values of the S-S and R-S intervals are also important. For example, the animal is not likely to make the instrumental response if the R-S interval is shorter than the S-S interval because responding could increase the number of shocks it received.

Nondiscriminated avoidance behavior presents a challenge for two-process theory because there is no explicit CS to elicit conditioned fear and it is not clear how the avoidance response reduces fear. However, two-process theory has not been entirely abandoned in attempts to explain free-operant avoidance (see Anger, 1963). The S-S and R-S intervals used in effective procedures are usually rather short (less than 1 min). Furthermore, they remain fixed during an experiment, so that the intervals are highly predictable. Therefore, it is not unreasonable to suggest that the animals might learn to respond to the passage of time as a signal for shock. The assumption of temporal conditioning allows for application of the mechanisms of two-process theory to free-operant avoidance procedures. The basic strategy is to assume that the passage of time after the last shock (in the case of the S-S interval) or after the last response (in the case of the R-S interval) becomes conditioned to elicit fear. Since the timing starts anew with each occurrence of the avoidance response, the response effectively removes the fear-eliciting temporal cues. Termination of these time signals can then reinforce the avoidance response through fear reduction. Thus, the temporal cues involved in getting near the end of the S-S or R-S interval are assumed to have the same role that the explicit CS has in discriminative avoidance procedures.

The above analysis of free-operant avoidance in terms of two-process theory predicts that subjects will not distribute their responses randomly in time. Rather, they will be more likely to respond as the end of the R-S interval gets closer, because it is here that the temporal cues presumably elicit fear. Results consistent with this prediction have been obtained. However, many animals successfully avoid a great many shocks without distributing their responses in the manner predicted by two-process theory. Furthermore, the predicted distribution of responses often develops only after extensive training, after the subject is avoiding a great many of the scheduled shocks (see Sidman, 1966). In addition, avoidance behavior has been successfully conditioned with the use of free-operant procedures in which the S-S and R-S intervals are varied throughout the experiment (for example, Herrnstein & Hineline, 1966). When the S-S and R-S intervals are of unpredictable duration, subjects are much less likely to be able to learn to use the passage of time as a signal for shock. It is therefore difficult to adapt two-process theory to explain their avoidance learning. These types of results have discouraged some investigators from accepting two-process theory as an explanation of free-operant avoidance learning (see Herrnstein, 1969; Hineline, 1977, for further details).

Alternative theoretical accounts of avoidance behavior

In the preceding review of experimental investigations of avoidance behavior, we used two-process theory to provide the conceptual framework for the discussion. This was reasonable because many of the research questions were stimulated in one way or another by two-process theory. However, as we saw, the theory is not fully supported by the experimental evidence in every case. Accordingly, various modifications and alternatives to two-process theory have been proposed. We will discuss some of the more important of these. In two-process theory, reinforcement for the avoidance response is assumed to be provided by the reduction of fear. This is a case of negative reinforcement—reinforcement due to removal of an aversive state. Several recent theoretical treatments have proposed that avoidance procedures also provide for positive reinforcement

of the avoidance response. The first three theories we will discuss are of this type. In contrast,
the last theory emphasizes the role of punishment and innate response mechanisms in
avoidance behavior.

Relaxation theory.   Relaxation theory, proposed by Denny (for example, 1971), accepts
the idea that a stimulus that signals shock comes
to elicit fear. However, it assumes that termination of a fear CS not only removes an aversive
state of affairs but also has positive consequences. More specifically, Denny proposed
that termination of a fear CS is followed by relaxation. Relaxation is assumed to be a desirable
state that can reinforce the instrumental avoidance response through conventional mechanisms of positive reinforcement. In discriminated avoidance procedures, this source of
reinforcement is available only if the animal
performs the instrumental response during the
fear CS, because it is only at this time that the
response can terminate the CS and lead to relaxation. Therefore, the fear CS comes to serve
as a discriminative stimulus for the avoidance
behavior. According to this account, then, the
avoidance response occurs not because the organism is escaping from the CS but because it is
seeking relaxation.

Many aspects of avoidance behavior are consistent with relaxation theory (see review by
Denny, 1971). However, one weakness of the
theory is that there are few experimental
findings that cannot also be explained in other
ways. You may recognize, for example, that the
basic assumption that a state of relaxation follows fear is similar to the ideas of the opponent-
process theory, discussed in Chapter 3. Relaxation theory also has difficulty explaining why
flooding procedures facilitate the extinction of
avoidance behavior. Denny (1971) suggested
that flooding works because the subject begins
to relax while it receives prolonged exposure to
the CS. However, it is not clear why relaxation
should begin before the CS has been terminated. Application of the theory to free-operant
avoidance behavior is also rather cumbersome.

**Positive reinforcement through condi-
tioned inhibition of fear.**   In all avoidance-
conditioning procedures, the avoidance response is followed by a period free from shock.
There are also always distinctive feedback stimuli that accompany the instrumental response.
These may be provided by a change in location,
as when a rat moves from one side to the other
in a shuttle box; they may be tactile or other
external stimuli involved in making the response, such as those provided by touching and
manipulating a response lever. The response-
feedback stimuli may also be proprioceptive (internal) cues provided by the muscle movements
involved in making the response. Regardless of
what they are, because the instrumental response produces a period without shock, the
stimuli accompanying the response are negatively correlated with shock. As we discussed in
Chapter 4, this is one of the circumstances that
lead to the development of conditioned inhibition. Therefore, response-feedback cues
may become conditioned to signal the absence
of shock. Since a shock-free period is desirable,
a conditioned inhibitory stimulus may serve as a
positive reinforcer. In this way, the stimuli that
accompany avoidance responses may provide
positive reinforcement for the instrumental behavior. (This hypothesis is sometimes also called
the safety-signal theory of avoidance.)

In most avoidance experiments, no special
steps are taken to ensure that the avoidance
response is accompanied by vivid feedback
stimuli that could become conditioned inhibitors. Spatial, tactile, and proprioceptive
stimuli that are not specifically programmed
but inevitably accompany the avoidance response serve this function. However, one can
easily modify any avoidance procedure to provide a distinctive stimulus, such as a brief light
or tone, after each occurrence of the avoidance
response. The conditioned-inhibition rein-

forcement model predicts that introducing an explicit feedback stimulus will facilitate the learning of an avoidance response. Numerous experiments have found this to be true (for example, Bolles & Grossen, 1969; D'Amato, Fazzaro, & Etkin, 1968; Keehn & Nakkash, 1959). Other studies have shown that during the course of avoidance training, a response-feedback stimulus becomes a conditioned inhibitor of fear (for example, Morris, 1974; Rescorla, 1968). Furthermore, there is also direct evidence that a feedback stimulus that has been conditioned to inhibit fear during the course of avoidance training thereby becomes an effective positive reinforcer for new responses (Morris, 1975; Weisman & Litner, 1972; see also Dinsmoor & Sears, 1973). Thus, there is considerable evidence for the conditioned-inhibition reinforcement factor in avoidance learning.

The conditioned-inhibition reinforcement mechanism is not necessarily a substitute for the negative reinforcement process assumed by two-process theory. That is, CS-termination reinforcement and conditioned inhibition could well coexist and both contribute to the strength of the avoidance behavior (see Cicala & Owen, 1976; Owen, Cicala, & Herdegen, 1978). It is also important to realize that the reinforcement provided by a conditioned inhibitor is similar to that provided by CS termination in that both involve the reduction of fear. (A conditioned inhibitor actively inhibits fear, whereas CS termination leads to the dissipation of fear.) Therefore, the subject has to be fearful for a conditioned inhibitor to act as a reinforcer. However, in contrast to two-process theory, the state of fear does not necessarily have to be elicited by a fear CS. The fear could be elicited by the entire situation in which the experiment is conducted. This makes the conditioned-inhibition model well suited to explain free-operant avoidance behavior. Shocks occur frequently in a free-operant avoidance procedure if the subject fails to make the avoidance re-

sponse. Therefore, it is quite likely that the entire experimental situation will come to elicit fear. Because shocks never occur for the duration of the R-S interval after a response is made, the proprioceptive and tactile stimuli that accompany the response can become conditioned inhibitors of fear. Thus, the response-associated feedback cues can come to provide positive reinforcement for the free-operant avoidance response (Dinsmoor, 1977; Rescorla, 1968). Conditioned inhibition of fear by feedback stimuli also helps explain instances in which discriminated avoidance behavior persists during extensive training despite a reduction of the level of fear elicited by the CS (for example, Kamin et al., 1963; Mineka & Gino, 1980).

Reinforcement of avoidance through reduction of shock frequency. The conditioned-inhibition reinforcement mechanism does not present a radical alternative to the two-process theory of avoidance. In contrast, another reinforcement mechanism, shock-frequency reduction, has been proposed as an alternative to two-process theory (deVilliers, 1974; Herrnstein, 1969; Herrnstein & Hineline, 1966; Sidman, 1962). By definition, avoidance responses prevent the delivery of shock and thereby reduce the frequency of shocks the subject receives. The theories of avoidance we have discussed so far have viewed the reduction of shocks as a by-product of avoidance responses rather than as something that is involved in causing the behavior. In contrast, the shock-frequency-reduction position views the avoidance of shock as critical to the motivation of avoidance behavior.

Shock-frequency reduction as the cause of avoidance behavior was first entertained by Sidman (1962) as a way of explaining results he obtained in a concurrent free-operant avoidance experiment. Rats were exposed to two free-operant avoidance schedules at the same time. Responses on one response lever prevented shocks on one of the schedules, and responses on the other lever prevented shocks on the second schedule. Sidman concluded that the subjects distributed their responses between the two response levers so as to reduce the overall frequency of shocks they received. The idea that shock-frequency reduction can serve to reinforce avoidance behavior was later encouraged by evidence of learning in a free-operant avoidance procedure specifically designed to minimize the role of fear-conditioned temporal cues (Herrnstein & Hineline, 1966). In addition, as we noted earlier, studies of the relative importance of various components of the discriminated avoidance procedure have also shown that the avoidance component significantly contributes to the learning (for example, Bolles et al., 1966; Kamin, 1956). In fact, prevention of shock was the critical feature when wheel turning served as the avoidance response in the experiment by Bolles et al. (see Table 10.1).

Despite the types of evidence cited above, the shock-frequency-reduction hypothesis has not been widely accepted. Several experiments have shown that animals can learn to make an avoidance response even if the response does not reduce the frequency of shocks delivered (for example, Gardner & Lewis, 1976; Hineline, 1970). Responding in these studies delayed the onset of the next scheduled shock but did not prevent its delivery. Thus, overall shock frequency was unchanged by the instrumental response. Such evidence shows that shock-frequency reduction is not necessary for avoidance. Nevertheless, one might argue that it can facilitate learning in situations in which the avoidance response is allowed to reduce shock frequency. However, the experimental results that have shown this to be true can also be explained in other ways.

Much of the evidence that supports the shock-frequency-reduction hypothesis may be explained either as conditioned-inhibition reinforcement or as the punishing effects of shocks in the absence of the avoidance component. If a

response reduces the frequency of shocks, external and proprioceptive stimuli involved in making the response will come to signal the absence of shock and become a conditioned inhibitor. The conditioned inhibitory properties of these stimuli can then reinforce the behavior. This conditioned-inhibition mechanism is a plausible alternative to the shock-frequency-reduction interpretation, particularly for free-operant avoidance experiments (for example, Herrnstein & Hineline, 1966). In fact, it is a more broadly applicable explanation. Unlike the shock-frequency hypothesis, the conditioned-inhibition account can also explain the results reviewed in the preceding section concerning the properties of response-feedback cues in avoidance experiments.

The possible role of punishment is another important factor to consider in experiments that emphasize the role of shock-frequency reduction. Consider, for example, the discriminated wheel-turn avoidance experiment by Bolles et al. (1966), discussed earlier. In the standard procedure, turning the running wheel during the CS prevented the delivery of shock on that trial. When this shock-avoidance component of the procedure was unavailable, the animals' performance was substantially impaired (see Table 10.1). However, in the absence of the avoidance component, responses that occurred during the CS were followed by shock at the end of the CS-US interval. This contingency may have led to suppression of the instrumental response through punishment. Thus, higher rates of responding may have been observed when responses prevented shock because the instrumental behavior was not punished under these circumstances. An appeal to shock-frequency reduction (or shock avoidance) as reinforcement is not required to explain the results.

Avoidance behavior and species-specific defense reactions.   The theories discussed so far have been concerned mainly with how the events that precede and follow the avoidance response control avoidance behavior. The specific nature of the instrumental response required to prevent scheduled shocks was not a primary concern of these theories. In addition, the reinforcement mechanisms assumed by the theories all required some time to develop. Before fear reduction could be an effective reinforcer, fear first had to be conditioned to the CS; before feedback cues could come to serve as reinforcers, they had to become signals for the absence of shock; and before shock-frequency reduction could work, subjects had to experience enough shocks to be able to assess shock frequencies. Therefore, these theories tell us very little about what determines the organism's behavior during the first few trials of avoidance training. The lack of concern with what the subject does during the first few trials is a serious weakness. For an avoidance mechanism to be very useful to the subject in its natural habitat, the process has to generate successful avoidance responses very quickly. If an animal is trying to avoid being eaten by a predator, for example, it may not be alive to experience repeated training trials.

In contrast to the theories we considered earlier, the account of avoidance behavior we will discuss in the present section focuses on the specific nature of the instrumental response required to prevent shock and addresses what controls the subject's behavior during the early stages of avoidance training (Bolles, 1970, 1971). The theory starts by recognizing that aversive stimuli and situations elicit strong unconditioned, or innate, responses in animals. It is assumed that many of these innate responses have evolved because they enable the organism to cope with or obtain protection from the aversive event. Therefore, Bolles has called these innate responses **species-specific defense reactions** (SSDRs). We have already seen some examples of SSDRs. The mobbing behavior of birds directed toward a potential predator (Chapter 3) is a particularly complicated social SSDR. Another example is the tendency of the young of mouthbreeding cichlids to swim toward dark areas when the water is disturbed (Chapter 2). In rats and many other animals, species-specific defense reactions include flight (running), freezing (immobility), and fighting. Which of these responses is observed depends on the circumstance. If there is an obvious way out of the situation, running may be the predominant response. When running is not possible, freezing may occur. If there is another animal in the situation, fighting may be the most likely behavior.

The SSDR account of behavior in avoidance situations states that species-specific defense reactions predominate during the initial stages of avoidance training. If the most likely SSDR is successful in preventing shocks, this behavior will persist as long as the avoidance procedure is in effect. If the first SSDR is not effective, it will be followed by shock, which will suppress the behavior through punishment. The animal will then make the next-most-likely SSDR. If shocks persist, this second SSDR will also become suppressed by punishment, and the organism will make the third-most-likely SSDR. The process will end when a response is found that is effective in avoiding shocks, so that the behavior is not suppressed by punishment. Thus, according to the SSDR account, mechanisms of punishment are responsible for the selection of the instrumental avoidance response from the organism's range of activities. Furthermore, the range of responses available to the subject in an aversive situation is assumed to be restricted to its species-specific defense reactions. Reinforcement, be it positive or negative, is assumed to have a minor role, if any, in avoidance learning. The correct avoidance response is not strengthened by reinforcement. Rather, it occurs because other SSDRs are suppressed by punishment.

One obvious prediction of the SSDR theory is that some types of responses will be more easily learned in avoidance experiments than other types. Consistent with this prediction, Bolles (1969) found that rats can rapidly learn to run in a running wheel to avoid shock. In contrast, their performance of a rearing response (standing on the hind legs) did not improve much during the course of avoidance training. Presumably, running was learned faster because it was closer to the rat's species-specific defense reactions in the running wheel. In another study (Brener & Goesling, 1970), rats were placed on a platform. One group was required to remain still to avoid shock, whereas another group was required to engage in some type of movement (exactly what the movement was did not matter). The rats required to remain still were more successful in avoiding shocks. This can also be interpreted in terms of the SSDR theory because remaining still is presumably very close to the innate response of freezing that is common in such situations. Unlike these first two experiments, a third study (Grossen & Kelley, 1972) initially documented the subjects' responses to shock before selecting the avoidance response. The rats were placed on a large, flat grid surface. When shocked, the animals were highly likely to freeze near the side walls of the apparatus (thigmotaxis). A platform was then placed on the grid floor either in the center or near the side walls, and the animals were required to jump onto the platform to avoid shock. Faster learning occurred when the platform was near the sides of the apparatus than when it was in the center of the grid surface. Thus, the avoidance performance was accurately predicted from the subjects' innate reactions to shock. In an important follow-up experiment, Grossen and Kelley also showed that the position of the platform did not make any difference if the subjects were reinforced with food for making the jump response rather than shock avoidance.

The avoidance puzzle: Concluding comments

We have learned a great deal about avoidance behavior in the 40 years since Mowrer and Lamoreaux puzzled about how "not getting something" can motivate avoidance responses (Mowrer & Lamoreaux, 1942). As we saw, numerous ingenious answers to this puzzle have been provided. Two-process theory, relaxation theory, conditioned inhibition, and shock-frequency reduction all provide different views of what happens after an avoidance response to reinforce it, whereas the SSDR account suggests a punishment alternative to reinforcement theories. None of these theories can explain all the data. However, each provides useful ideas in understanding various aspects of avoidance behavior. For example, none of the more recent formulations is as useful in explaining the acquired-drive experiments as two-process theory. The conditioned-inhibition theory is particularly useful in explaining free-operant avoidance behavior, the results of studies of the role of response-feedback stimuli in avoidance conditioning, and the maintenance of avoidance behavior in the absence of much fear elicited by a warning stimulus. In contrast, the SSDR theory is very useful in considering what happens during the early stages of avoidance training. It is also important in considering why certain responses are much more easily learned than others. Given the complexities of avoidance learning, the use of several conceptual frameworks to explain all the data may be inevitable.

Punishment

Although most of us engage in avoidance behavior of one sort or another every day, there is little public awareness of or concern about what is involved in making avoidance responses. The reason may be that avoidance conditioning is rarely used in efforts to control the behavior of others. In contrast, the other aversive conditioning process we will discuss, punishment, has always been of great concern to people. In some situations punishment is used as a form of retribution or as a price for undesirable behavior. The threat of punishment is also frequently used to encourage adherence to religious and civil codes of conduct. Many institutions and rules have evolved to ensure that punishment will be administered in ways that are deemed ethical and acceptable to society. Furthermore, what constitutes justified punishment in the criminal justice system, in child rearing, in schools, and elsewhere is a matter of continual debate.

In contrast to societal concerns about punishment, for many years experimental psychologists did not devote much attention to the topic. On the basis of a few experiments, Thorndike (1932) and Skinner (1938, 1953) concluded that punishment is not a very effective method for controlling behavior and has only temporary effects at best (see also Estes, 1944). This claim was not seriously challenged until the 1960s, when punishment processes began to be much more extensively investigated (Azrin & Holz, 1966; Campbell & Church, 1969; Church, 1963; Solomon, 1964). We will describe the effects of punishment on positively reinforced instrumental behavior. In such situations punishment can be a very successful means of changing behavior. In fact, punishment often suppresses responding in just one or two trials. Thus, punishment typically produces a change in behavior much more rapidly than other forms of instrumental conditioning, such as positive reinforcement or avoidance.

Experimental analysis of punishment

The basic punishment procedure involves presenting an aversive stimulus after a specified response. The usual outcome of the procedure is that the specified response becomes suppressed. By suppressing the punished response, the subject avoids the aversive stimulation. Because punishment involves the suppression of behavior, it can be observed only if the response is likely to occur in the absence of aversive stimulation. Therefore, in experimental investigations, the punished response is usually also reinforced with a positive reinforcer, such as food or water. This procedure provides a conflict between responding to obtain positive reinforcement and not responding to avoid punishment. The degree of response suppression that occurs is determined both by variables related to presentation of the aversive stimulus and by variables related to the availability of positive reinforcement.

Characteristics of the aversive stimulus and its method of introduction.   A great variety of aversive stimuli have been used in punishment experiments. The most extensively studied stimulus has been electrical shock. Other primary (unconditioned) aversive stimuli that have been used include a blast of air (Masserman, 1946), loud noise (for example, Azrin, 1958), and a physical slap (Skinner, 1938). Punishment can also be produced by exposure to a cue that has been conditioned with shock rather than by direct exposure to shock itself (for example, Hake & Azrin, 1965). An even more complicated procedure involves using time out from positive reinforcement as the aversive event (for example, Thomas, 1968). *Time out* refers to removal of the opportunity to obtain positive reinforcement. Time out is often used to punish children for engaging in undesirable behavior, as when a child is told "Go to your room" for doing something bad. Another effective punishment procedure with human beings is overcorrection (Foxx & Azrin, 1973). In this case, the person is made not only to rectify what was done badly but to overcorrect for the mistake. For example, a child who has placed an object in his or her mouth may be asked to remove the object and also wash out the mouth with an antiseptic solution.

The response suppression produced by punishment depends on certain features of the aversive stimulus. The effects of various characteristics of the aversive event have been most extensively investigated with shock. The general finding is that more response suppression results from the use of more intense or longer shocks in a punishment procedure (see reviews by Azrin & Holz, 1966; Church, 1969; Walters

& Grusec, 1977). Low-intensity aversive stimulation produces only moderate suppression of responding, and the disruption of behavior may recover with continued exposure to the punishment procedure (for example, Azrin, 1960). In contrast, if the aversive stimulus is sufficiently intense, responding may be completely suppressed for a long time. In one experiment, for example, high-intensity punishment completely suppressed the instrumental response for 6 days (Azrin, 1960).

Another very important factor in punishment is how the aversive stimulus is introduced. If a high intensity of shock is used when the punishment procedure is first introduced, the instrumental response will be severely suppressed. Much less suppression of behavior will occur if initially a mild punishment is used, with the shock intensity gradually increased during the course of continued punishment training (Azrin, Holz, & Hake, 1963; Miller, 1960). Thus, subjects can be protected from the effects of intense punishment by first being exposed to lower levels of shock that do not produce much response suppression. It appears that because a low intensity of punishment does not disrupt responding very much, subjects learn to persist in making the instrumental response in the presence of the aversive stimulation. This learning then generalizes to higher intensities of shock, with the result that the instrumental response continues to be made when the more aversive punishment is used.

According to the above explanation, subjects adopt a particular mode of responding during their initial exposure to punishment, and this type of behavior generalizes to new punishment situations (Church, 1969). This idea has an interesting implication. Suppose that subjects are first exposed to intense shock that results in a very low level of responding. The mode of behavior adopted during initial exposure to punishment is severe suppression of responding. If the shock intensity is subsequently reduced, the severe suppression of behavior should persist, resulting in less responding than if the mild

shock had been used throughout the procedure. Results consistent with this prediction have been obtained by Raymond (reported in Church, 1969). Thus, initial exposure to mild aversive stimulation that does not disrupt behavior very much *reduces* the effects of later intense punishment. In contrast, initial exposure to intense aversive stimulation *increases* the suppressive effects of later mild punishment.

Response-contingent versus response-independent aversive stimulation. Another important variable that determines the extent to which aversive stimulation suppresses behavior is whether the aversive stimulus is presented whenever the specified response occurs or is presented periodically independent of behavior. Response-independent aversive stimulation can result in the suppression of instrumental behavior. However, the general finding is that significantly more suppression of behavior occurs if the aversive stimulus is produced by the instrumental response (for example, Azrin, 1956; Camp, Raymond, & Church, 1967; Frankel, 1975). In one experiment (Church, 1969), three groups of rats were reinforced for pressing a response lever on a variable-interval 1-min schedule of food reinforcement. Then punishment was introduced while the food reinforcement was continued. One group was never shocked. The second group received response-independent aversive stimulation. A brief shock was presented every 2 min, on the average, irrespective of the rats' lever pressing. The third group received response-contingent aversive stimulation. The brief shock became available on the average of every 2 min but was delivered to the subjects only if they made a lever-press response, at which time it was delivered immediately after the response. The results are summarized in Figure 10.12. The data are presented in terms of suppression ratios that compare the rate of responding during the punishment phase of the experiment to the rate of responding observed before punishment was introduced. A score of .5 indicates no sup-

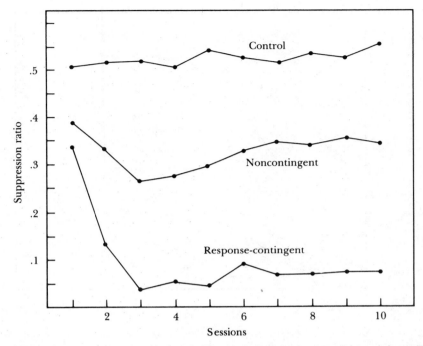

Figure 10.12. Degree of response suppression observed during ten successive sessions. The control group did not receive shock. The noncontingent group received shocks independent of behavior, and the response-contingent group was shocked when it responded. *(From Church, 1969.)*

pression of responding, and a score of 0 indicates complete suppression of the lever-press behavior. As you can see, the response-independent shocks produced a small suppression of responding that started to dissipate after the third session. In contrast, response-contingent shocks produced a severe and lasting suppression of lever pressing. Thus, response-produced aversive stimulation was much more effective in suppressing behavior than response-independent aversive stimulation.

Effects of delay of punishment. In response-independent procedures, the aversive stimulus may occur immediately after the instrumental response on some occasions and a long time after the response on other occasions. Explicit investigation of the interval between instrumental behavior and aversive stimulation

has shown that this variable greatly influences the degree of response suppression. The general finding is that increasing the interval between the instrumental response and delivery of punishment results in less suppression of behavior (for example, Baron, 1965; Camp et al., 1967). This relation is particularly important in attempts to use punishment to modify behavior outside the laboratory. Inadvertent delays may occur if the undesired response is not detected right away, if it takes time to investigate who is actually at fault for an error, or if preparing the aversive stimulus requires time. Such delays may preclude the effective use of punishment procedures.

Effects of schedules of punishment. Just as positive reinforcement does not have to be provided for each occurrence of the instrumental response, punishment may also be delivered

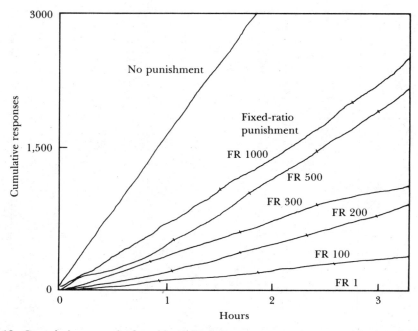

Figure 10.13. Cumulative record of pecking when the response was not punished and when the response was punished according to various fixed-ratio schedules of punishment. The oblique slashes indicate the delivery of punishment. Responding was reinforced on a variable-interval 3-min schedule. *(From Azrin, Holz, & Hake, 1963.)*

only intermittently. For example, instead of punishing every occurrence of the instrumental response, punishment may be provided after a fixed number of responses. Such a procedure is called a "fixed-ratio punishment schedule." In one study of fixed-ratio punishment, pigeons were first reinforced with food on a variable-interval schedule for pecking a response key (Azrin, Holz, & Hake, 1963). When the key-pecking behavior was occurring at a stable and high rate, punishment was introduced. Various fixed-ratio punishment procedures were tested while food reinforcement continued to be provided for the pecking behavior. The results are summarized in Figure 10.13. When every response was shocked (FR 1 punishment), key pecking ceased entirely. With the other punishment schedules, the rate of responding depended on the frequency of punishment. Higher fixed-ratio schedules allow more re-

sponses to go unpunished. Not surprisingly, therefore, higher rates of responding occurred when higher fixed-ratio punishment schedules were used. However, some suppression of behavior was observed even when only every 1000th response was followed by shock.

Fixed- and variable-interval punishment schedules have also been investigated. These schedules are arranged in a manner similar to fixed- and variable-interval schedules of positive reinforcement. As we noted in Chapter 7, a fixed-interval schedule of positive reinforcement provides reinforcement for the first response that occurs more than a fixed amount of time after the last reward, and animals increase their rate of responding as they get closer to the end of the fixed interval. In a fixed-interval schedule of punishment, the first response is punished that occurs more than a fixed amount of time after the last delivery of the aversive stimulus. As subjects get closer to the end of the fixed interval (and thus closer to the possibility of punishment), their rate of responding decreases (Azrin, 1956). This makes the pattern of behavior produced by a fixed-interval punishment schedule in some ways the opposite of the pattern produced by fixed-interval positive reinforcement. In variable-interval punishment schedules, the delivery of the aversive stimulus is triggered by the first response that occurs more than a variable amount of time after the last punished response. The occurrence of punishment is therefore less predictable than in fixed-interval schedules. The result is a steady but low rate of responding that lacks the predictable pauses observed with fixed-interval schedules (Azrin, 1956).

Effects of the schedule of positive reinforcement.   As we noted earlier, in most studies of punishment the instrumental response is simultaneously maintained by a positive reinforcement procedure so that there is some level of responding available to be punished. As it turns out, the effects of a punishment procedure are in part determined by this positive reinforcement. When behavior is maintained by either a fixed- or a variable-interval schedule of positive reinforcement, punishment produces a decrease in the overall rate of responding. However, the temporal distribution of the behavior is not disturbed. That is, during the punishment procedure, variable-interval positive reinforcement produces a suppressed but stable rate of responding (see Figure 10.13), whereas fixed-interval positive reinforcement produces the typical scalloped pattern of responding (for example, Azrin & Holz, 1961). The outcome is considerably different if the behavior is maintained by a fixed-ratio positive reinforcement schedule. As we noted in Chapter 7, fixed-ratio schedules produce a pause in responding just after reinforcement (the postreinforcement pause), followed by a high and steady rate of responding to complete the number of responses necessary for the next reinforcement

(the ratio run). Punishment usually increases the length of the postreinforcement pause but has little effect on the ratio run (Azrin, 1959). The initial responses of a fixed-ratio run are much more susceptible to punishment than later responses. Thus, shock delivered early in a ratio run increases the postreinforcement pause more than shock delivered later in the completion of the ratio (Dardano & Sauerbrunn, 1964; see also Church, 1969). Another important aspect of positive reinforcement schedules is the frequency of reinforcement provided. Generally, punishment has less effect on instrumental responses that produce more frequent positive reinforcement (for example, Church & Raymond, 1967).

Availability of alternative responses for obtaining positive reinforcement.   In many experiments, the punished response is also the only response the subject can perform to obtain positive reinforcement, such as food. By decreasing its rate of responding, the subject may decrease the number of food pellets it receives. Therefore, the subject is in a conflict between suppressing its behavior to avoid punishment and responding to obtain positive reinforcement. This predicament does not exist if alternative responses for obtaining positive reinforcement are available. In this case, the subject can entirely cease making the punished response without having to forgo positive reinforcement. As one might expect, the availability of an alternative source of reinforcement greatly increases the suppression of responding produced by punishment. In one study, for example, adult males were seated in front of two response levers, and pressing either response lever was reinforced with a cigarette on a variable-interval schedule (Herman & Azrin, 1964). After the behavior was occurring at a stable rate, responses on one of the levers resulted in a brief obnoxious noise. In one experimental condition, only one response lever was available during the punishment phase. In another condition, both response levers were accessible, and responding on one of them was punished with the loud noise. The results are summarized in Figure 10.14. When the punished response was the only way to obtain cigarettes, punishment produced a moderate suppression of behavior. In contrast, when the alternative response lever was available, responding on the punished lever ceased altogether. Thus, the availability of an alternative response for obtaining positive reinforcement greatly increased the suppressive effects of punishment. Similar results have been obtained in other situations. For example, children punished for playing with certain toys are much less likely to play with these if they are allowed to play with other toys instead (Perry & Parke, 1975).

Effects of a discriminative stimulus for punishment.   As we saw in Chapter 9, if positive reinforcement is available for responding in the presence of a distinctive stimulus but is not available in its absence, the subject will learn

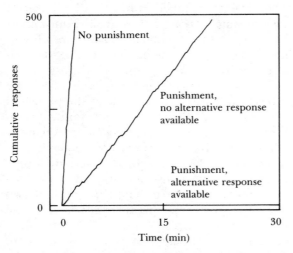

Figure 10.14. Cumulative record of responding when responses are not punished, when responses are punished and there is no alternative source of reinforcement, and when responses are punished but an alternative reinforced response is available. *(From Azrin & Holz, 1966; after Herman & Azrin, 1964.)*

to respond only when the stimulus is present. The suppressive effects of punishment can also be brought under stimulus control. This occurs if responding is punished in the presence of a discriminative stimulus but is not punished when the stimulus is absent. Such a procedure is called **discriminative punishment**. With continued exposure to discriminative punishment, the suppressive effects of punishment will come to be limited to the presence of the discriminative stimulus. In one of the first experiments of this type, Dinsmoor (1952) reinforced rats with food on a variable-interval 2-min schedule for pressing a response lever. After responding had stabilized, successive 5-min periods of punishment were alternated with 5-min periods of no punishment. During the punishment periods, the lights in the experimental chamber were turned off, and each lever-press response resulted in a brief shock. During the safe periods, the lights were turned on and no shocks were delivered. The rats quickly learned to restrict their lever-press responses to the safe periods. When the lights were turned off, signaling that the punishment procedure was in effect, responding was suppressed. However, responding resumed whenever the lights were turned back on, signaling that responses would not be punished.

The fact that the suppressive effects of punishment can be limited to the presence of discriminative stimuli is often problematic in applications of punishment. In many situations, the person who administers the punishment also serves as a discriminative stimulus for punishment, with the result that the undesired behavior is suppressed only as long as he or she is present. If one teacher is more strict about discipline than another, children will learn to suppress their rambunctious behavior in that class more than in other classes. If one parent is stricter than another, children will be better behaved in the presence of the stricter parent. A Highway Patrol car is a discriminative stimulus for punishment for speeding. Drivers are more likely to obey speed laws in areas where they see many patrol cars than in unpatrolled stretches of highway.

Punishment as a signal for the availability of positive reinforcement. Punishment does not always suppress behavior. In fact, in certain situations people seem to seek out punishment. Does this represent a breakdown of the normal mechanisms of behavior, or can such behavior be explained by the principles we have discussed so far? Experimental evidence suggests that conventional behavioral mechanisms may lead to such seemingly abnormal behavior. Punishment seeking can result from a situation in which positive reinforcement is available only when the instrumental response is also punished. Punishment comes to serve as a signal for the availability of positive reinforcement, and subjects may therefore respond at a higher rate in the presence of punishment than in its absence.

In one experiment on this phenomenon, pigeons were first trained to peck a response key for food reinforcement on a variable-interval schedule (Holz & Azrin, 1961). Each response was then punished by a mild shock sufficient to reduce the response rate by about 50%. In the

---

Box 10.3.   When Punishment Doesn't Work

Sometimes children are brought to a therapist because their behavior is out of control. In a typical example the child is unruly and does not respond to the disciplinary practices of parents or teachers. Even punishment, used as a last resort, does not work. The parents or teachers complain that punishing the child only makes the behavior worse. It is not uncommon for children with a severe problem of this type to be diagnosed as hyperactive or emotionally disturbed. These labels suggest there is something fundamentally wrong with the child. Behavior therapists, however, have found that in some cases the problem may be nothing more than the result of mismanaged discipline. The parents or teachers may have inadvertently established punishment as a discriminative stimulus for positive reinforcement. Instead of decreasing some undesirable behavior, punishment increases it. How can this happen?

Let us take the hypothetical situation of Johnny, who lives in a home with two busy parents. Johnny, like most children, is rather active. If he is quietly playing in his room, the parents are likely to ignore him and engage in activities of their own. In contrast, if Johnny behaves badly or makes demands, the parents are forced to attend to him. The parents may be giving Johnny attention only when he is misbehaving or making demands. Any time he is not being a problem, the parents may be thankfully relieved to have a moment's peace. Thus, rather than reinforcing cooperative or peaceful behavior, the parents can come to ignore Johnny at these times. What we have then is a vicious cycle. The more Johnny misbehaves, the less attention he is given for nondisruptive behavior, because the parents come to cherish quiet moments as a chance to do something on their own. Misbehavior becomes his main means of obtaining attention. The punishments and reprimands that go with the behavior signal to the child that the parents are caring and attending.

In actuality the therapist does not have the opportunity to observe how behavior problems of this type originate. The "discriminative value of punishment" explanation is supported by the outcome of attempts to change the situation. The hypothesis suggests that if one changes the attention patterns, Johnny's behavior problem can be alleviated. Indeed, clinical psychologists often show parents how to attend to appropriate and constructive activities and to use punishment with as little attention as possible. In many cases dramatic improvement ensues when parents are able to positively reinforce cooperative behavior with their attentions and ignore disruptive activities as much as possible.

next phase of the experiment, periods in which the punishment procedure was in effect were alternated with periods in which punishment was not scheduled. In addition, the pecking response was reinforced with food only during the punishment periods. The punishment and safe periods were not signaled by an exteroceptive stimulus, such as a light or a tone. Therefore, the only way for subjects to tell whether reinforcement was available was to see whether they were punished for pecking. Under these circumstances higher rates of pecking occurred during punishment periods than during safe periods. Punishment became a discriminative stimulus for food reinforcement.

Punishment and response reallocation. In Chapter 8 we discussed how reinforcement of a particular response may cause a reorganization or reallocation of the organism's entire behavioral repertoire. Reinforcement often increases the future likelihood of the reinforced response and decreases some other activities the subject might perform. Punishment likewise produces a reallocation of the subject's behavior. Suppression of the punished response may be accompanied by increases in some other activities as well as, possibly, decreases in certain nonpunished responses. In one experiment, for example, thirsty rats were given access to a running wheel and a drinking tube at the same time (Dunham, 1972). The rats were then punished for drinking. As expected, punishment suppressed the drinking response. However, punishment also increased the amount of time the rats spent running in the wheel. Such compensatory increases in nonpunished responses have been observed in a variety of situations. Typically not all the animal's nonpunished responses increase when one response is selected out for punishment. Rather, it is often the most likely of the nonpunished responses that becomes increased (Dunham, 1971, 1978). Reorganization of the subject's response profile can also involve decreases in the rate of nonpunished responses. For example, in guinea pigs the punishment of

certain responses (open-rearing, scrabbling, or face washing) results in an increase in freezing and a walk/sniff behavior as well as a decrease in unpunished wall-rearing and gnawing (Shettleworth, 1978). Research on such reorganizations of behavior is still in its infancy, and it is not entirely clear precisely what mechanisms determine the outcome in punishment situations (see Dunham, 1978; Shettleworth, 1978).

Theories of punishment

In contrast to the study of avoidance behavior, investigations of punishment, by and large, have not been motivated by theoretical considerations. Most of the evidence available about the effects of punishment has been the product of empirical curiosity. The investigators were interested in finding out how punishment is influenced by various manipulations rather than in testing certain theoretical formulations. In fact, there are few systematic theories of punishment, and most of these were formulated in some form more than 30 years ago. We will describe three of the most prominent theories.

Conditioned-emotional-response theory of punishment. One of the first systematic theoretical treatments of punishment was provided by Estes (1944). The theory is based on the discovery by Estes and Skinner (1941) that a conditioned stimulus that has been paired with shock will suppress the performance of food-reinforced instrumental behavior. We discussed this conditioned-suppression, or conditioned-emotional-response, procedure earlier in this chapter as well as in Chapters 4 and 6. The standard conditioned-suppression experiment involves first conditioning animals to make an instrumental response, such as a lever press, for food reinforcement. Classical conditioning is then conducted in which a CS (a tone or light, for example) is paired with a brief shock. The conditioned aversive stimulus is then presented while the animal is allowed to lever-press for the food reinforcement. The usual result is that responding is disrupted during presentations of the CS. This response suppression was originally interpreted as resulting from competing responses elicited by the CS. The basic idea was that the conditioned stimulus came to elicit certain emotional responses (such as freezing) by virtue of being paired with shock. These conditioned emotional responses were presumably incompatible with making the lever-press response (the rat could not freeze and press the lever at the same time). Therefore, the rate of lever pressing was suppressed during presentations of the CS.

Estes (1944) proposed that punishment suppresses behavior through the same mechanism that produces conditioned suppression to a shock-paired CS. In contrast to the conditioned-suppression experiment, however, punishment procedures usually do not involve an explicit CS that signals the impending delivery of shock. Estes suggested that the various stimuli the subject experiences just before making the punished response serve this function. For example, just before the rat presses a response lever, it experiences the visual and other spatial cues that exist near the lever, the tactile cues of the lever, and perhaps proprioceptive stimuli that result from its posture just as it is about to make the lever press. When the response is punished, all these stimuli become paired with shock. With repetition of the punishment episode, the various preresponse stimuli become strongly conditioned by the shock. As these cues acquire conditioned aversive properties, they will come to elicit conditioned emotional responses that are incompatible with the punished behavior. Thus, the punished response will become suppressed.

The conditioned-emotional-response theory can explain a great many facts about punishment. For example, the fact that more intense and longer-duration shocks produce more response suppression can be explained by assuming that the stimuli conditioned by these aversive events elicit more vigorous conditioned emotional responses. The theory can also explain why response-contingent aversive stimulation produces more response suppression than response-independent delivery of shock. If shock is produced by the instrumental response, the stimuli that become conditioned by the shock are more likely to be closely related to performance of this behavior. Therefore, the conditioned emotional responses are more likely to interfere with the punished response.

In a recent reformulation of the conditioned-emotional-response theory, Estes (1969) has proposed an alternative account of the mechanisms of conditioned suppression. The new formulation may be paraphrased in motivational terms. The basic idea is that a shock-conditioned stimulus disrupts food-reinforced responding because it evokes an emotional or motivational state (let us say fear) that is incompatible with the motivation maintaining the food-reinforced behavior. The shock-conditioned stimulus is assumed to inhibit the motivation to respond based on positive reinforcement. This revision is compatible with modern two-process theory, which we will discuss in Chapter 11. Both theories assume that motivational states elicited by a classically conditioned stimulus can interact with or influence the motivational state inherent in an instrumental-conditioning procedure.

Avoidance theory of punishment. An ingenious alternative to the conditioned-emotional-response theory regards punishment as a form of avoidance behavior. This theory is most closely associated with Dinsmoor (1954, 1977) and follows the tradition of the two-process theory of avoidance behavior. Dinsmoor accepted the notion that the stimuli that set the occasion for the instrumental response become conditioned by the aversive stimulus when the response is punished. Thus, these stimuli were assumed to acquire conditioned aversive properties in much the same manner as stated in the conditioned-emotional-response theory. However, Dinsmoor added a second process to the mechanism of punishment. He proposed that subjects learn to escape from the conditioned aversive stimuli related to the punished response by engaging in some other behavior that is incompatible with the punished activity. Since this behavior is incompatible with the punished response, by engaging in this behavior the subject can effectively avoid getting shocked. Thus, the basic idea of the avoidance theory is that during the course of punishment, responses incompatible with the punished response become learned as avoidance responses, and performance of these responses results in suppression of the punished behavior.

The avoidance theory of punishment is an intellectually ingenious effort. It suggests that all changes in behavior, be they increases or decreases in the likelihood of a response, can be explained by the same response-strengthening mechanisms. Suppression of behavior is not viewed as reflecting the weakening of the punished response. Rather, it is explained in terms of the strengthening of competing responses that effectively avoid the aversive stimulation. Thus, a single theoretical framework is used to explain two different types of experimental outcomes. Such an economy of theoretical concepts has always been considered one of the criteria of desirable scientific explanations.

Despite its cleverness and parsimony, the avoidance theory of punishment is not uniformly applauded. First, because it explains punishment in terms of avoidance mechanisms, all the theoretical problems that have been troublesome in the analysis of avoidance behavior become problems that have to be solved in the analysis of punishment as well. Another challenge for the theory is that its critical elements are not stated in a way that makes them easily accessible to experimental verification (Rachlin & Herrnstein, 1969; Schuster & Rachlin, 1968). The stimuli that are assumed to acquire conditioned aversive properties are not under the direct control of the experimenter. Rather, they are events that one assumes the subject experiences when it is about to make the punished

response. Similarly, the activities the subject learns to perform to avoid making the punished response are ill specified. The theory does not tell us what these responses will be in a given situation or how one might look for them. The theory also provides a rather cumbersome explanation of the outcome of experiments on concurrent chained schedules of punishment (for example, Schuster & Rachlin, 1968). However, the theory has remained compatible with most of the facts about punishment, perhaps because it is stated in a way that makes experimental tests of it difficult.

Punishment and the negative law of effect. The third and last concept about punishment that we shall consider is also the oldest. Thorndike (1911) originally proposed that positive reinforcement and punishment involve symmetrically opposite processes. Just as positive reinforcement strengthens behavior, so punishment weakens it. In later years Thorndike abandoned the idea that punishment weakens behavior because he failed to find supporting evidence in some of his experiments (Thorndike, 1932). However, the belief that there is a negative law of effect that is comparable but opposite to the familiar positive law of effect has retained favor with some investigators (for example, Azrin & Holz, 1966; Rachlin & Herrnstein, 1969). One approach to the analysis of the negative law of effect has been initiated by Premack and his colleagues. As we discussed in Chapter 8, Premack proposed that positive reinforcement occurs when the opportunity to engage in a highly valued activity is made dependent on the prior performance of an activity of lower value. The subject allocates time according to this restriction. The instrumental response is increased and the reinforcing behavior is decreased by the contingency. According to Premack, the punishment contingency reverses this relation. Here, a low-valued activity is made to occur contingent on the performance of a higher-valued behavior. Undergoing shock, for example, has a much lower probability than pressing a lever for food. Hence, shock can punish lever pressing.

Premack and his colleagues tested this idea about punishment using a motor-driven running wheel equipped with a drinking tube. In one experiment (Weisman & Premack, 1966), rats were deprived of water, so that drinking was more probable than running. Then a punishment procedure was introduced in which a bout of drinking was followed by a period of running. (The motor driving the running wheel was turned on to force the rats to run.) Under these conditions, drinking was suppressed by running. Thus, a punishment effect was obtained. This and other experiments (see Premack, 1971a) illustrate that the punishing effects of forced running are similar to those of shock. The studies by Premack and his colleagues also illustrate the comparability of reinforcement and punishment. In the Weisman/Premack experiment, the same contingency (running after drinking) produced the opposite effects if the relative values of the behaviors involved were reversed. To reverse the values of the activities, the rats were no longer water-deprived. Running was then more probable than drinking. In this case drinking increased if the rats performed the running response after a drinking episode—a reinforcement effect. Thus, running after drinking punished or reinforced drinking, depending on the relative values of the two activities.

With a reinforcement procedure the instrumental response is increased and the reinforcing response is decreased relative to a baseline free-responding situation. With a punishment procedure the instrumental response is decreased and the reinforcing or punishing response is increased relative to a baseline condition. Moreover, in both cases the response that increases is the low-valued behavior and the one that decreases is the higher-valued behavior. Viewed in this way, the procedures of reinforcement and punishment produce the same effects. Operationally, there is only one signifi-

cant difference. In punishment the subject has to be forced to engage in the lower-valued activity. Rats do not ordinarily apply electrical shocks to themselves or run more than they want. In reinforcement the subject is "induced" to engage in the lower-valued activity by the contingency itself.

Premack's analysis, as we have said, suggests that reinforcement and punishment are essentially the same when the total range of the organism's activities is considered rather than just the instrumental response alone. This proposition was investigated in a toy-playing experiment with children (Burkhard, Rachlin, & Schrader, 1978). In a baseline phase, children were observed playing with three toys. The toys were ranked high, medium, and low on the basis of how much time the children spent with each one. The children were assigned to reinforcement and punishment groups. For the reinforcement group 1 min of playing with the high-ranked toy was allowed after 1 min of play with the low-ranked toy. For the punishment group, 1 min of play with the low-ranked toy was required after 1 min of play with the high-ranked toy. In both cases the medium toy provided background activity and could be used freely. If Premack's punishment hypothesis is correct, the two procedures should result in the same overall allocation of time to the three toys. This in fact was the result. The reinforcement and punishment groups were indistinguishable in how much time they ended up playing with each toy. Playing with the low-ranked toy increased and playing with the high-ranked toy decreased to comparable levels for the two groups.

Research along the lines Premack has proposed is continuing. As in the case of positive reinforcement, the work suggests that punishment imposes a restriction against which behavior has to be adjusted. The negative law of effect, in light of this approach, is a statement of the way behavior changes under these restrictions: a low-valued activity produces a decrease in a higher-valued activity. Economically minded theorists propose, as in the case of positive reinforcement (see Chapter 8), that the subject responds so as to maximize overall value. The maximization process, with both reinforcement and punishment procedures, involves an increase in a low-valued activity balanced against a decrease in a high-valued activity and may include effects on other behaviors as well.

Use of punishment outside the laboratory

Nowhere in the application of the principles of learning and conditioning is there more controversy than in the application of aversive control procedures. Books to guide parents in the use of discipline disagree on whether punishment is useful or should be used at all; controversy rages in the courts and on school boards over whether punishment may be used by teachers in the classroom and by therapists in hospitals; much debate has occurred over the centuries on the proper use of aversive control in the criminal justice system. What is the basis for all this debate? On closer inspection we see that the issues concern both the practical problems involved in the application of aversive control procedures and moral questions that arise when one person does harm to another.

Practical problems in the use of punishment. One argument that has been used against the application of punishment is that it does not work. However, this is likely to be true only if punishment is used inappropriately. The laboratory research we discussed earlier has numerous implications for the effective use of punishment. For best results, punishment has to be delivered immediately after the undesired behavior. If punishment cannot be applied immediately, it is less likely to be effective and perhaps should be omitted altogether. Another important consideration is the intensity of the punishment. If punishment is to be used at all, it is best to use a high-intensity aversive stimulus

from the beginning. To use mild punishment for initial transgressions only leads to adaptation, or habituation, to the punishment procedure. Once punishment is used, it must be applied to every occurrence of the undesired behavior for best results. One must also be sure to minimize the amount of positive reinforcement available for the punished response as well as provide alternative means whereby the individual can obtain positive reinforcement. Finally, one must be careful not to have the punishment signaled by some stimulus or have the punishment serve as a cue for the availability of positive reinforcement. Often applications of punishment outside the laboratory violate these prescriptions for the effective use of punishment.

Punishment has also been criticized on the grounds that it produces an overall suppression in the individual's behavior rather than just a suppression of the punished response. This idea, originally entertained by theoreticians, has been extended to situations outside the laboratory. Some people claim that using punishment as a means of disciplining a child merely stifles the child's normal overall activity. More recent research, however, does not support this claim. Earlier in the chapter we reviewed evidence that punishment indeed suppresses particular responses. In addition, we know that punishment leads to a reallocation of behavior that often includes an increase in certain nonpunished responses (for example, Dunham, 1978). Some suppression of other nonpunished responses may also occur. However, this decrease is rarely as great as the suppression of the punished response (for example, Church, Wooten, & Matthews, 1970).

Another reservation about the use of punishment is that it has undesirable side effects, such as aggression, escape, and hostility. Some parents and teachers do not like to use punishment because the child may become hostile, throw tantrums, try to run away, or come to hate the parents, teachers, or school. The adult may find these side effects far more difficult to deal with than the original undesired responses. Advocates of criminal justice reform often cite the fact that a prison sentence frequently does not produce the hoped-for reform in the criminal. Rather, the convict may return to society with more hostility than before. This hostility, together with newly acquired antisocial skills learned from other prisoners, may be more detrimental to society in the long run than the original transgression.

Laboratory investigations have documented the undesirable side effects of punishment. Several investigators have studied behaviors elicited by aversive events used in punishment procedures. Shock, for example, can elicit aggression. If two animals are placed in an experimental chamber together and shocked, they will assume an attack posture and fight for the duration of the shock (for example, Ulrich, Hutchinson, & Azrin, 1965). Similarly, monkeys will bite a rubber hose (Hutchinson, Azrin, & Hake, 1966), and humans will show jaw-clenching movements when aversively stimulated. These elicited responses occur when aversive stimuli are presented contingent on an instrumental response, as in punishment (see Hutchinson, 1977). Hence, it is not surprising that children may turn and hit the parent after punishment or that a prisoner may strike out at available objects of aggression on being sentenced or incarcerated.

Punishment can also motivate escape from the punishment situation. Laboratory experiments have shown that rats and pigeons will learn an instrumental response whose only consequence is escape from a punishment situation (for example, Azrin, Hake, Holz, & Hutchinson, 1965; Hearst & Sidman, 1961). Outside the laboratory such escape may present a serious problem because the goal of the application of punishment is rarely to drive the individual out of the situation. When we punish a child for not doing house chores or not doing homework, we do not want him or her to run away from home. When we punish a teenager for smoking in school, we do not want the student to drop out of school or escape the situation by taking psychoactive drugs.

Another undesirable side effect of punishment is that the motivating and eliciting properties of the aversive stimulus may become conditioned to other stimuli present in the situation by way of classical conditioning. Thus, a person administering punishment may become associated with the aversive stimulation. We know that stimuli conditioned by shock and other aversive USs themselves acquire aversive properties. Through this mechanism, the punished subject may come to dislike the teacher, playmate, or parent who delivered the punishment.

A final difficulty concerns the effects on the person who is delivering the aversive stimulus. Delivering punishment is often accompanied by certain reactions in the person who does the punishing. Parents become upset or angry with the undesired activities of their children. It is a rare parent or teacher who can deliver punishment in a purely detached manner. Delivery of punishment can be seen in many cases as an aggressive act elicited by the child's unruly behavior. As such, it may go out of control. Child abuse, battered adults, brutality by prison guards and prisoners are all examples in which punishment has gone out of control. Unfortunately, these are serious problems in our society that we do not understand very well or know how to solve as yet.

Moral considerations. It is a safe generalization that most people do not like to be punished. In addition, at least in our more relaxed moments we do not like to inflict punishment on others. Parents do not like to see their children unhappy, teachers do not want to be disliked or perceived as "executioners" by inevitably errant children, and judges do not want to see human life spent unproductively in jail. When we use punishment, we may be reminded of the baser side of human nature, revealed in torture, concentration camps, and the like. However, there are cases in which we purposefully inflict pain in order to prevent a greater pain. We do not think we are executioners if we recommend a trip to the dentist, a vaccination, or a spoon of codliver oil. We do not regard these practices as immoral, because even though they inflict discomfort, they are performed in pursuit of a greater good.

The same rationale is often used in advocating the use of punishment. We punish inappropriate behaviors in order to allow the emergence of a better person. Hence, we have the expression "Spare the rod and spoil the child." Most parents do not feel that slapping a toddler for approaching a hot stove or touching an electrical wire is wrong. The overall safety of the child is at stake, and the pain of a slap is insignificant by comparison. Punishment has the tremendous advantage over other behavioral procedures that the suppression of behavior is sometimes immediate when the procedure is applied properly. With alternative methods, such as extinction, the response suppression usually takes longer. To ensure that a toddler will not get burned by a stove, for example, immediate suppression of the behavior is of paramount importance.

The moral dilemma of punishment can be illustrated by the controversy surrounding the use of punishment with autistic children. Autistic children frequently engage in self-injurious behavior, such as banging their heads against a wall, pulling out their hair, or biting themselves. Sometimes the self-injurious behavior is so severe that the child's hands must be bound together to prevent injury. In extreme cases, the child's hands and feet have to be tied to the corners of his or her bed. Lovaas and his colleagues studied self-injurious behavior in many children (see Lovaas & Newsom, 1976, for a review). They concluded that in the cases they observed, the behavior was maintained largely by attention given to the children whenever they mutilated themselves. In attempting to soothe the children, caretakers appeared to be inadvertently reinforcing the self-injurious responses. When the caretakers ignored the behavior, the responses eventually extinguished. However, the extinction period could be long and sometimes began with an initial increase in self-inflicted injury. In some cases to allow the child to go through extinction would have been very dangerous; the child could have severely injured himself or herself during the extinction process. Lovaas and his colleagues turned to punishment to treat the severe cases. Each instance of self-mutilation was followed by a slap or a brief electrical shock. The result was a quick suppression of the self-injurious behavior.

Naturally, the punishment procedures that were used met with objections. It is our common belief that hitting or shocking children whom we regard as severely ill is fundamentally wrong. However, the research seems to show that our love and attention only serve to promote the self-injurious behavior. Lovaas and Newsom suggest that the use of punishment with autistic children is a case of small pain inflicted for the greater good of the child. Suppressing the self-mutilating behavior is only one step in the treatment procedure. The fact that the child is no longer engaging in this self-destructive compulsive behavior enables the therapist to go on and establish more socially appropriate behaviors through love and affection. However, the research has not yet elucidated all aspects of the punishment procedures. There are many unanswered questions about the long-range effects of punishing self-mutilation and the effects of this punishment on other behaviors. Such questions have to be answered before a fully informed decision on the therapy of choice can be made.

Although punishment can be effective in certain situations, it must be used with great care. The problems that go along with the use of punishment are very real. Punishment should never be used indiscriminately. However, when used properly in a morally justified situation, punishment can be a useful technique for the suppression of undesired activities.

CHAPTER ELEVEN

Interactions of Classical and Instrumental Conditioning

Chapter 11 is devoted to a general discussion of how classical and instrumental conditioning processes may interact. We begin with a description of experiments that have evaluated the possible role of instrumental reinforcement in classical-conditioning procedures. We will then describe some of the extensive theoretical and experimental work that has been done to assess the role of classical conditioning in instrumental-conditioning situations.

Classical and instrumental conditioning are clearly distinguishable conceptually and according to the standard procedures used to investigate them. As we saw in Chapters 4 and 5, classical conditioning is assumed to involve the learning of relations, or associations, between stimuli (usually the CS and the US), and classical-conditioning procedures focus on when the stimuli occur in relation to each other independent of what the animal does. In contrast, as we noted in Chapters 6–8, instrumental conditioning is assumed to involve the learning or redistribution of the animal's responses, and instrumental-conditioning procedures focus on the relation between occurrences of a specified (instrumental) response and delivery of the reinforcer. Despite these conceptual and procedural distinctions between classical and instrumental conditioning, in practice most conditioning procedures involve both instrumental and classical components, and it is often difficult, sometimes impossible, to isolate them.

We already saw examples of the interaction of classical and instrumental conditioning processes in analyses of discrimination learning (Chapter 9) and avoidance behavior and punishment (Chapter 10). In the present chapter we will consider the interaction of classical and instrumental conditioning more generally. We will first describe the potential role of instrumental-conditioning processes in classical-conditioning experiments and ways instrumental conditioning can be ruled out as a factor in classical-conditioning procedures. We will then describe the potential role of classical-conditioning processes in instrumental learning. With the use of special procedures, experiments have shown that classical conditioning can occur without the opportunity for instrumental reinforcement. However, procedures do not exist that permit the occurrence of instrumental conditioning in the absence of the opportunity for classical conditioning. Therefore, a great deal of theoretical and experimental effort has been devoted to elucidating the role of classical conditioning in instrumental learning situations.

Role of instrumental reinforcement in classical-conditioning procedures

In a typical classical-conditioning procedure, the conditioned stimulus is periodically presented, followed by the unconditioned stimulus. As such CS-US trials are repeatedly conducted, the subject comes to make a conditioned response during the CS-US interval. However, the occurrence of the conditioned response does not determine whether the US is presented. The US is presented irrespective of the conditioned response. In fact, this aspect of classical-conditioning procedures is the primary basis used to distinguish classical from instrumental training procedures. Nevertheless, for a long time investigators of conditioning mechanisms have been concerned with the fact that there is an opportunity for instrumental reinforcement in many classical-conditioning procedures, and this reinforcement may be in part responsible for the learning that occurs (Coleman & Gormezano, 1979; Gormezano & Coleman, 1973).

The potential for instrumental reinforcement in classical conditioning is most obvious in situations in which the subject makes anticipatory conditioned responses. Anticipatory conditioned responses occur before presentation of the unconditioned stimulus on a given trial. This pairing of the CR with the US provides at least two possible opportunities for instrumental reinforcement. First, if the US is a positive reinforcer, such as food, its presentation shortly after the CR may result in adventitious (accidental) reinforcement of the CR. Second, the occurrence of the CR may somehow alter the unconditioned stimulus so as to make the US either more rewarding or more effective in conditioning (for example, Hebb,

1956; Perkins, 1955, 1968). The possibility that conditioned responses may make the US more effective or rewarding was first recognized by Schlosberg (1937). He proposed, for example, that dogs may learn to salivate in a conditioning experiment using food as the US because anticipatory salivation makes it easier to dissolve and swallow dry food. Correspondingly, salivation may be learned in a classical-conditioning situation with a drop of acid as the US because anticipatory salivation helps to dilute the aversive taste of the acid. Such instrumental modifications of the US can be postulated to occur in all classical-conditioning experiments.

Two experimental strategies have been devised to evaluate the role of instrumental reinforcement in classical-conditioning situations. One of these effectively eliminates the possibility of adventitious reinforcement of the conditioned response. The other technique is designed to assess the role of modifications in the unconditioned stimulus caused by the occurrence of the CR, by specifically arranging for such changes in the US. Experiments using both strategies have indicated that instrumental reinforcement is not necessary for the learning that takes place in classical-conditioning procedures. Consequently, classical conditioning can be observed even if the situation does not permit the occurrence of instrumental reinforcement.

The omission control procedure

As we noted above, if the US is a positive reinforcer, such as food, presentation of the US following the CR may result in adventitious reinforcement of the CR. The opportunity for this kind of instrumental reinforcement is very easy to eliminate with a simple modification of the standard classical-conditioning procedure. The modified technique, called the **omission control procedure**, is diagrammed in Figure 11.1. Whether the US is presented on a given trial depends on whether the conditioned response occurs. On trials without a CR, the CS is fol-

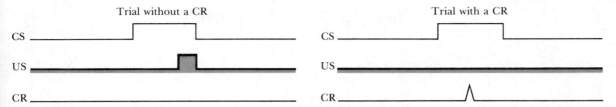

Figure 11.1. Diagram of the omission control procedure. On trials without a conditioned response, the CS is followed by the US in the usual manner (left panel). On trials with a conditioned response, the US is omitted (right panel).

lowed by the US in the usual manner. However, on trials with a CR, the US is omitted. Thus, the CR is never followed by the US. Therefore, there is no opportunity for the US to accidentally reinforce the conditioned response.

The omission control procedure was introduced by Sheffield (1965) in the study of salivary conditioning in dogs. He tested dogs in conditioning with food and acid in the mouth as unconditioned stimuli. In both types of conditioning, omitting the US when a CR occurred did not prevent development of conditioned salivation. Acquisition of conditioned salivation was generally slower with the omission control procedure than with presentations of the US on all trials. Nevertheless, the omission procedure was remarkably effective. One dog, for example, continued to salivate on about 50% of trials after 800 trials on the omission control procedure.

Since its introduction by Sheffield, the omission control procedure has been tested in a variety of classical-conditioning situations (for example, Gormezano & Hiller, 1972; Patten & Rudy, 1967). It has been perhaps most frequently used in studies of sign tracking. As we have noted, in sign tracking, animals come to approach and touch (sometimes manipulate) stimuli that signal the delivery of a positive reinforcer, such as food. Investigators originally questioned whether sign tracking is actually learned through classical conditioning. Some suggested that accidental reinforcement of responding by the food presentation that follows each CS is necessary for the acquisition of sign

tracking. The omission control procedure can be used to evaluate this possibility. Although the experiments are not uniform in their conclusions (for example, Hursh, Navarick, & Fantino, 1974; Wessells, 1974), the preponderance of the evidence is that sign tracking can occur in the absence of the opportunity for accidental reinforcement (for example, Stiers & Silberberg, 1974; Williams & Williams, 1969).

One particularly noteworthy demonstration of sign tracking in the absence of the opportunity for adventitious reinforcement by the food US is provided by Peden, Browne, and Hearst (1977). Pigeons were tested in an experimental chamber that had a food hopper built into one wall and a response key built into an adjacent wall 35 cm away. The key light was periodically illuminated for 8 sec, followed by access to grain for 5 sec. Approaching the key light was considered to be the conditioned response. In the first phase of the experiment (omission control), food delivery at the end of a trial was canceled if the pigeon approached within 20–25 cm of the key-light CS. In phase II, food always followed illumination of the key light regardless of what the pigeons were doing. The investigators measured the percentage of trials on which the animals approached the light CS during each phase of the experiment.

The results are shown in Figure 11.2. The remarkable finding was that pigeons persisted in approaching the key light CS during the first phase of the experiment even though such approach responses canceled the delivery of food. Fifty trials were conducted each day, and even

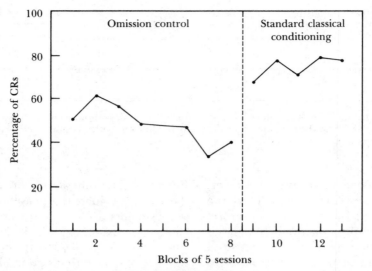

Figure 11.2. Percentage of trials on which a conditioned response (approach to the CS) was observed during blocks of five sessions. Each session consisted of 50 trials. During the first eight blocks of sessions (2000 trials) an omission control procedure was in effect. During the remainder of the experiment a standard classical-conditioning procedure was in effect. *(After Peden, Browne, & Hearst, 1977.)*

after about 2000 trials, the pigeons were observed to approach the CS approximately 40% of the time. Other research demonstrated that many fewer CS-approach responses occur if the CS and food presentations occur randomly so that the CS does not signal the delivery of food (Peden et al., 1977, Experiment 2). In addition, on only about 2% of the trials were the subjects near the response key at the start of the trial. Therefore, the high level of CS-approach behavior observed during the omission control phase was due to the association of the CS with food. Approach responses increased during the next phase of the experiment, when every trial ended in food delivery. The higher level of performance in the standard classical-conditioning procedure (phase II) than in the omission control procedure (phase I) is commonly observed in studies of this kind (for example, Schwartz & Williams, 1972). What is responsible for this outcome is open to debate (Jenkins, 1977). In the present study it may be that the pigeons made more approach responses in phase II because here all trials ended in food. Classical con-

ditioning generally leads to higher levels of performance if each occurrence of the CS ends in presentation of the US. Another possibility is that the omission control procedure slightly discouraged approach behavior in phase I because the subjects received food only when they failed to approach the key light. Thus, avoiding the key light may have been strengthened to some extent as an instrumental response. Finally, it may be that adventitious reinforcement was responsible for some of the approach responses in phase II, and this is why more approach responses occurred in phase II than in phase I. Nevertheless, results of the type shown in Figure 11.2 clearly demonstrate that highly persistent sign tracking can occur with omission control procedures, which preclude having the CR shortly followed by the US.

Conditioned-response modifications of the US

Studies with the omission control procedure provide strong evidence that accidental reinforcement is not necessary for the learning that occurs in classical-conditioning experiments. Omission control experiments also provide evidence against the importance of modifications in the unconditioned stimulus caused by the CR. Because the US is omitted on trials in which a CR occurs, subjects cannot alter the US by making the conditioned response. (They can only prevent the US from being presented.) Another experimental technique that has been used to evaluate the importance of modifications in the US caused by the CR involves explicitly arranging changes in the US whenever the CR occurs. Consider, for example, a classical-conditioning situation in which the US is an aversive stimulus. It may be suggested that in such cases the subject learns to make the CR because the CR somehow reduces the aversiveness of the US. (Perhaps by making the CR, the subject "braces" itself against the US.) If this is true, then explicitly arranging for the intensity of the US to be reduced when the CR occurs should facilitate acquisition of the conditioned response.

The importance of modifications of the US caused by the CR was investigated in an experiment on the conditioning of the nictitating-membrane response in rabbits (Coleman, 1975). The CS was a tone, and the US was a brief shock to the skin near one of the eyes. Retraction of the nictitating membrane over the eyes was measured as the conditioned (and unconditioned) response. Four groups of rabbits were tested. All groups received a 5.0-milliampere shock after the CS on trials in which a conditioned response did not occur. For group 5-5, the shock was also 5.0 ma when the rabbits made a conditioned response. For the other groups, the shock intensity was decreased when a conditioned response occurred. For group 5-3, the shock was decreased to 3.3 ma on trials when the CR occurred. For group 5-1, the CR decreased the shock intensity to 1.7 ma, and for group 5-0, the CR prevented delivery of the shock altogether (essentially, group 5-0 received an omission control procedure). If

shock reduction provides important instrumental reinforcement for the conditioned response in this type of classical conditioning, better learning should occur in groups 5-3, 5-1, and 5-0 than in group 5-5.

The results are shown in Figure 11.3. Contrary to the instrumental-reinforcement prediction, the speed and level of conditioning were not increased by explicitly reducing the shock intensity whenever the conditioned response occurred. Groups 5-3, 5-1, and 5-0 did not learn the nictitating-membrane response faster than group 5-5. In fact, the only difference evident

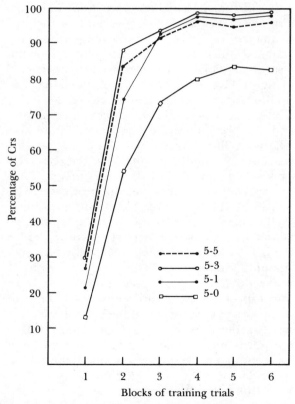

Figure 11.3. Percentage of conditioned responses in an experiment on nictitating-membrane conditioning with rabbits. The conditioned response resulted in reduction of the intensity of the shock US for groups 5-3 and 5-1 and omission of the US for group 5-0. In contrast, the conditioned response had no effect on the delivery of the US in group 5-5. *(From Coleman, 1975.)*

among the groups was that completely reducing the shock intensity to 0 ma whenever the conditioned response occurred (group 5-0) resulted in a lower level of conditioning than observed in all other groups. These results indicate that modifications in the US caused by the CR are not necessary for classical conditioning and may not even facilitate learning in this situation.

Role of classical conditioning in instrumental-conditioning procedures

As we noted in Chapters 6 and 9, in an instrumental-conditioning procedure, the instrumental response occurs in the presence of certain distinctive stimuli and is followed by the reinforcer. This sequence of events is reviewed in Figure 11.4. S_A represents the stimuli that are present when the instrumental response is made, R represents the instrumental response, and S^{R+} represents the reinforcing stimulus. The wavy line between the response and the reinforcing stimulus signifies that the response causes the delivery of the reinforcer. This causal relation ensures that the reinforcer will be paired with the subject's exposure to stimuli S_A. The pairing of stimuli S_A with the reinforcer allows for the occurrence of classical conditioning, and an association can develop between stimuli S_A and the reinforcer.

We discussed in the preceding section how classical-conditioning processes may be investigated in the absence of the opportunity for instrumental conditioning. To accomplish this, one needs only to make sure that occurrences of the conditioned response are not followed by presentation of the unconditioned stimulus. Unfortunately, an analogous strategy cannot be used to eliminate the occurrence of classical conditioning in instrumental procedures. To prevent classical conditioning, one cannot omit presenting the reinforcer after the animal's exposure to stimuli S_A, because this will also result

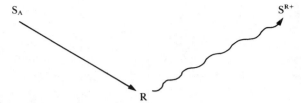

Figure 11.4. Relations that exist in instrumental conditioning. The instrumental response (R) occurs in the presence of distinctive stimuli (S_A) and results in delivery of the reinforcer (S^{R+}). The reinforcement of response R in the presence of stimuli S_A allows for the classical conditioning of S_A by the reinforcer.

in nonreinforcement of the instrumental response.

Specification of an instrumental response ensures that the animal will always experience certain distinctive stimuli (S_A) in connection with making the response. These stimuli may involve the place where the response is to be made, the texture of the object the subject is to manipulate, or distinctive odor or visual cues. Whatever they may be, reinforcement of the instrumental response will inevitably result in a pairing between stimuli S_A and the reinforcer. The only way to prevent this pairing is not to present the reinforcer after the instrumental response. However, this will also prevent instrumental conditioning. One cannot assume that pairings of stimuli S_A with the reinforcer will inevitably produce classical conditioning. As we noted in Chapters 4 and 5, the occurrence of classical conditioning depends on much more than just stimulus pairings. Nevertheless, pairings of stimuli S_A with the reinforcer provide the potential for the occurrence of classical conditioning. Consequently, many important theories have been concerned with the role of classical conditioning in the control of instrumental behavior.

The r_g-s_g mechanism

One of the earliest and most influential accounts of the role of classical conditioning in instrumental behavior was originally proposed by Clark Hull (1930, 1931) and was later elaborated by Kenneth Spence (1956). Essentially, Hull and Spence added a classical-conditioning component to the mechanism of instrumental behavior proposed by Thorndike. You may recall from Chapter 6 that according to Thorndike, reinforcement of an instrumental response increases the future likelihood of the behavior by establishing an association between the response and the stimuli present at the time the response is made. Using the symbols in Figure 11.4, Thorndike's view assumes that reinforcement establishes an association between S_A and R. Therefore, the presence of the stimuli S_A in the future directly triggers the occurrence of the instrumental response. This direct stimulation of the instrumental response is the instrumental-conditioning process. Hull and Spence suggested that there is also a classical-conditioning process that encourages or motivates the instrumental behavior. More specifically, they assumed that during the course of instrumental conditioning, animals not only learn to make response R in the presence of stimuli S_A but also acquire an expectation that they will be rewarded. This reward expectancy is learned through classical conditioning and also motivates the instrumental response.

It seems intuitively reasonable that instrumental behavior occurs in part because organisms learn to expect reward. If you were to introspect about why you perform certain instrumental responses, the answer would probably be that you expect to be rewarded. You go to work because you expect to get paid; you study for a test because you expect that doing so will help you get a higher grade. To incorporate these ideas into a systematic account of instrumental behavior, one has to specify in greater detail what expectations are, how they are learned, when they occur in relation to the instrumental response, and how they motivate the instrumental behavior. The r_g-s_g mechanism provides answers to all these questions.

Hull and Spence recognized that whenever the instrumental response R is followed by the reinforcer S^{R+}, the stimuli S_A present at the time of the response will become paired with the reinforcer. This pairing is assumed to result in the classical conditioning of stimuli S_A by the reinforcer S^{R+}. Hull and Spence believed that classical conditioning occurs by stimulus substitution. As we noted in Chapter 5, according to the stimulus-substitution hypothesis, the conditioned stimulus is assumed to acquire the properties of the unconditioned stimulus to some extent. In the instrumental-conditioning paradigm, S_A acts in the role of the CS, and the reinforcer acts in the role of the US. Therefore, Hull and Spence assumed, S_A will come to elicit some of the same responses that are elicited by the reinforcer. If the reinforcer is food, during the course of instrumental training, the animal will presumably come to salivate and perhaps make chewing movements when it experiences stimuli S_A. These classically conditioned responses are rarely as vigorous as the salivation and chewing elicited by the food itself, and they occur in anticipation of the food delivery. Therefore, they are called **fractional anticipatory goal responses**. The conventional symbol for such a response is r_g.

The fractional anticipatory goal response is assumed to be similar to other types of responses. As noted in Chapter 2, responses typically produce some type of sensory feedback. That is, the act of making a response usually creates distinctive bodily sensations. The sensory feedback produced by the fractional anticipatory goal response is represented by the symbol s_g.

The fractional anticipatory goal response, with its feedback stimulus s_g, is assumed to constitute the expectancy of reward. The full sequence of events in the r_g-s_g mechanism is illustrated in Figure 11.5. The fractional anticipatory goal response r_g is elicited by S_A before the instrumental response occurs. Thus, the instrumental response is made in the presence of

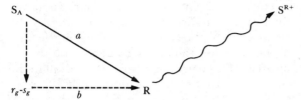

Figure 11.5. The r_g-s_g mechanism. During instrumental conditioning, the instrumental response R is followed by the reinforcer S^{R+}. Because this happens in the presence of distinctive situational cues S_A, an association is formed between S_A and R (arrow *a*). Delivery of the reinforcer following exposure to S_A results in the classical conditioning of S_A by the reinforcer. Therefore, S_A comes to elicit a classically conditioned fractional anticipatory goal response r_g with its feedback cues s_g. Because the instrumental response R is reinforced in the presence of s_g, an association also becomes established between s_g and R (arrow *b*).

the sensory feedback s_g from r_g. Because the instrumental response is reinforced when it is made after experience with s_g, a connection becomes established between s_g and the response R. The outcome of these events is that as instrumental conditioning proceeds, the instrumental response comes to be stimulated by two factors. First, the presence of S_A comes to evoke the instrumental response directly by association with R. Second, the instrumental activity also comes to be made in response to the expectancy of reward (r_g-s_g) because of an association between s_g and R (see Figure 11.5).

The fractional anticipatory goal response mechanism (r_g-s_g) is assumed to have two important functions. First, it is assumed to contribute to the general level of motivation of the animal and thereby enhance instrumental behavior. The subject's general level of motivation, or arousal, is increased in situations that elicit stronger fractional anticipatory goal responses, and this higher level of motivation presumably produces more vigorous activity. The second important function of the r_g-s_g mechanism is that it directs behavior. Because of the association of the instrumental response (R) with the stimulus feedback (s_g) from fractional anticipatory goal response (see arrow

b in Figure 11.5), the instrumental response is predicted to occur whenever the fractional anticipatory goal response is elicited. Once the instrumental response has been conditioned to s_g, it will occur in the presence of any stimulus that elicits the fractional anticipatory goal response. As we will see, the general motivational properties of r_g-s_g have been abandoned in contemporary theorizing. However, the second function of r_g-s_g—directing behavior—continues to be recognized.

The r_g-s_g mechanism and positive instrumental reinforcement. The r_g-s_g mechanism is consistent with numerous aspects of positively reinforced instrumental behavior. It predicts, for example, that classical-conditioning procedures will influence the performance of positively reinforced instrumental behavior in certain ways. Consider, for example, a discrimination procedure in which rats are reinforced for pressing a response lever in the presence of a tone (S+) and not reinforced in the absence of the tone. How might this discriminated lever pressing be influenced by classical-conditioning procedures involving the tone? The r_g-s_g mechanism predicts that performance of the lever-press response in the presence of the tone will be facilitated by initially conducting classical conditioning in which the tone is repeatedly paired with food. The response lever can be removed from the experimental chamber during this phase to avoid accidentally reinforcing lever presses. Classical conditioning of the S+ with food should condition the fractional anticipatory goal response to the tone S+. Elicitation of r_g by the tone should increase motivation for the instrumental behavior and thereby increase lever pressing during the tone. In contrast, once the discriminated lever-press response has been established, extinguishing the fractional anticipatory goal response should produce a decrement in the instrumental behavior. Such extinction can be accomplished by removing the response lever from the experimental chamber and repeatedly presenting the S+ without food. Extinguishing the fractional anticipatory goal response is expected to reduce both its motivational and response-directing functions. Evidence consistent with these and similar predictions of the r_g-s_g mechanism has been obtained (for example, Trapold & Winokur, 1967).

Frustration theory.   The basic ideas of the fractional anticipatory goal response mechanism have been used extensively in the analysis of the frustrative effects of nonreinforcement (see Amsel, 1958, 1967, 1979). We described frustration theory in general terms in Chapter 7 in our discussion of the partial-reinforcement

extinction effect. The details of the theory provide a good illustration of fractional anticipatory goal response mechanisms. Frustration theory was developed to characterize what subjects learn during intermittent reinforcement of an instrumental locomotor response in a runway. Figure 11.6 shows what happens, according to the theory, on rewarded and nonrewarded trials. On rewarded trials, locomotion in the runway (R_{Loc}) is reinforced by food (S^{R+}). On nonrewarded trials the reinforcer is not presented. As training progresses, the fractional anticipatory goal response r_g becomes classically conditioned to the cues of the runway (S_A). Because the subject can never tell ahead of

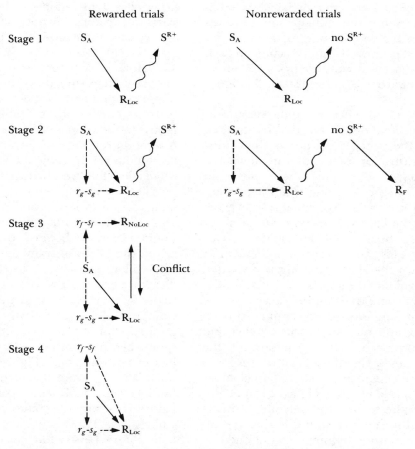

Figure 11.6. Outline of frustration theory. *(After Amsel, 1958. See text for explanation.)*

time what the outcome of a trial will be, r_g is elicited by S_A on both rewarded and non-rewarded trials. Rewarded trials simply serve to strengthen r_g. In contrast, drastically different things happen on nonrewarded trials (see Stage 2, Figure 11.6). The fact that S_A elicits r_g may be interpreted to mean that the subject expects to be rewarded. Nonreward in the face of the expectation of reinforcement is assumed to elicit a primary (unconditioned) frustration response (R_F). The primary frustration response is assumed to be subject to classical conditioning just like unconditioned responses to food. Therefore, repeated experiences of frustration are assumed to lead to the classical conditioning of a fractional anticipatory frustration response r_f, which has feedback cues that are symbolized as s_f. r_f-s_f represents the anticipation of frustration. With the conditioning of anticipatory frustration, the runway stimuli S_A come to elicit both anticipation of frustration (r_f-s_f) and anticipation of reward (r_g-s_g) (see Stage 3, Figure 11.6).

In the absence of special training, organisms tend to avoid situations that lead to frustration. Therefore, the initial reaction to the anticipation of frustration is to not run down the runway (R_{NoLoc}). This puts the subjects in conflict in Stage 3 of training. They are stimulated to perform the instrumental response because of r_g-s_g and are stimulated *not* to perform the response because of anticipatory frustration, r_f-s_f. This conflict is resolved in favor of running down the alley. Running is rewarded more than avoiding the goal box because food is presented on some trials and because even on trials without food the animal is removed from the goal box and thereby has its conflict and frustration reduced. The resolution of the conflict involves having the locomotor response (R_{Loc}) conditioned to the cues of anticipatory frustration, s_f (see Stage 4, Figure 11.6). Thus, according to the theory, the outcome of intermittent reinforcement training is that the instrumental response becomes conditioned to

the cues of anticipatory frustration (s_f) as well as to the cues of anticipatory reward (s_g).

Frustration theory has been very successful in explaining various aspects of instrumental conditioning and extinction. One important implication of the theory is that after an instrumental response has become conditioned to the cues of anticipatory frustration, that response will occur whenever the subject anticipates being frustrated. This prediction has been confirmed in several ways. Consider the following experiment, diagrammed in Figure 11.7. One group of rats (group A) is given runway training in two runways, one white and the other black. The subjects are reinforced every time they run in the white alley (CRF) and thus never experience frustration in the white alley or learn anticipatory frustration there. In contrast, they receive intermittent, or partial, reinforcement (PRF) for running in the black alley. Therefore, anticipatory frustration is learned in the black alley, and the running response becomes conditioned to the cues of anticipatory frustration. After this training, the running response in the white (CRF) alley is extinguished. A second group of rats (group B) receives only continuous reinforcement training (CRF) in the white alley, followed by extinction in this alley.

Will the running response extinguish at the same rate for groups A and B? If external stimulus control were the only relevant factor, one would expect so because the two groups received the identical training experience in the white alley. However, frustration theory predicts that group A, which also received partial reinforcement training in the black alley, will extinguish slower in the white (CRF) alley. For group A, but not for group B, the running response became conditioned to the cues of anticipatory frustration (see Figure 11.7). During extinction in the white alley, frustration is elicited by the absence of reinforcement, and anticipatory frustration becomes conditioned to the white alley. The feedback cues (s_f) from this anticipatory frustration elicit the running re-

Group A

	White alley	Black alley
Training	Continuous reinforcement (CRF)	Partial reinforcement (PRF)
	r_g-s_g ----→ running	r_g-s_g ----→ running
	no r_f-s_f	r_f-s_f ----→ running
Extinction	r_f-s_f ----→ running	

Group B

	White alley
Training	Continuous reinforcement (CRF)
Extinction	r_f-s_f ----→ no running

Figure 11.7. Experiment illustrating that responses conditioned to the cues of anticipatory frustration occur whenever anticipatory frustration is elicited. In group A, the running response becomes conditioned to the cues of anticipatory frustration (s_f) because of partial reinforcement for running in the black alley. Therefore, the running response occurs when anticipatory frustration is elicited during extinction in the white alley. Group B never receives partial reinforcement training for running. Therefore, avoidance of the goal area (not running) occurs as an innate reaction to the anticipation of frustration during extinction in the white alley for group B.

sponse in group A but not in group B. Therefore, frustration theory predicts slower extinction of the running response in group A than in group B. Results such as these have been repeatedly obtained (for example, Amsel, Rashotte, & MacKinnon, 1966).

In the above experiment, PRF training in one situation (the black alley) produced persistent responding during extinction in a different apparatus (a white alley). Does partial reinforcement training always increase persistence in extinction, or does the result depend on what response becomes conditioned to the cues of anticipatory frustration during PRF training? The response that is learned to cues of anticipatory frustration appears to be critical. In a very interesting experiment, Ross (1964) first conditioned two groups of animals to perform a climbing response in a short, wide, black box for food reinforcement. Group A was given partial reinforcement training during this phase. Therefore, for these subjects the climbing response became conditioned to the cues of anticipatory frustration. In contrast, group B was

given continuous reinforcement for climbing and therefore never experienced frustration in the climbing situation. Both groups were then given continuous reinforcement training with a water reward for running in an alley that was very different from the climbing box. (The alley was long, narrow, and white.) After the continuous reinforcement training, the running response was extinguished in the second apparatus for both groups. During extinction of the running response, 14 of 16 subjects in group A were observed to perform the climbing response in the alley apparatus. Such extensive climbing did not occur in group B. The climbing behavior in group A led to more rapid loss of the running response in group A than in group B. Apparently, in group A the cues of anticipatory frustration experienced during extinction in the alley elicited the climbing response that had been reinforced on an intermittent schedule in a different apparatus. Such findings provide good evidence for the response-directing functions of the fractional anticipatory goal response mechanism. We will return to this type of results at the end of the chapter.

Concurrent measurement of instrumental behavior and classically conditioned responses

The experiments described above involved somewhat indirect predictions from r_g-s_g mechanisms. One direct implication of the r_g-s_g mechanism is that classically conditioned responses develop during instrumental conditioning. In addition to this general prediction, the r_g-s_g mechanism also specifies how these classically conditioned responses should be related to the occurrence of the instrumental response. The r_g-s_g mechanism treats classically conditioned responses as reflections of a reward expectancy that motivates the instrumental response. Therefore, the classically conditioned responses are predicted to begin before the instrumental behavior on any trial (see Figure 11.5).

Perhaps the simplest and most direct approach to investigating the role of classical conditioning in instrumental learning is to measure classically and instrumentally conditioned responses at the same time. This is the approach taken by **concurrent-measurement experiments**. Numerous investigations of this type have been carried out in positive and negative reinforcement situations (see Black, 1971; Rescorla & Solomon, 1967, for reviews). All these experiments provide evidence that classically conditioned responses are learned during instrumental conditioning. However, the relation between the two types of conditioned responses varies from one situation to another. Rather than summarize all the evidence, we will describe the results of a few important experiments with positive reinforcement to illustrate the kinds of outcomes that can be obtained.

In some experimental situations the relation between classically and instrumentally conditioned responses is as predicted by the r_g-s_g mechanism. That is, the classically conditioned responses begin before the instrumental activity. In one such demonstration, Miller and De-Bold (1965) conditioned rats to press a response lever for water reinforcement. The water was squirted into each rat's mouth through a small metal tube permanently attached to the animal's head. In addition to recording occurrences of the lever-press response, Miller and DeBold measured how often the rats licked at the water delivery tube. It was assumed that licking was classically conditioned by the water reinforcement. Lever-press responses were almost always accompanied by licking behavior. The rats were also observed to lick the tube at other times. However, licking was much less vigorous when it occurred without lever pressing. The relation between licking and lever pressing is illustrated in Figure 11.8, which shows the rate of licking for 1/2-sec periods before and after lever-press responses. As you can see, the rate of licking gradually increased just before the lever-press response. The highest rate of licking occurred just after the response, when the reinforcer was ordinarily delivered, and licking subsided after that. Similar results have been observed by Shapiro (1962), using dogs reinforced for pressing a lever on a differential reinforcement of low rates (DRL) schedule. Salivation usually began just before the dogs pressed the response lever and continued for a little while after the response.

Contrary to the findings of Miller and De-Bold (1965) and Shapiro (1962), in some cases classically conditioned responses coincide with occurrences of the instrumental behavior during instrumental conditioning. A good example is provided by the behavior of two dogs tested by Williams (1965). The animals were required to press a response lever on a fixed-interval 16-sec schedule for food reinforcement. The first response that occurred 16 sec or more after the last reinforcement was rewarded. As we noted in Chapter 7, a fixed-interval schedule typically produces a "scalloped" pattern of responding. The instrumental response occurs at a very low rate, if at all, at the beginning of the

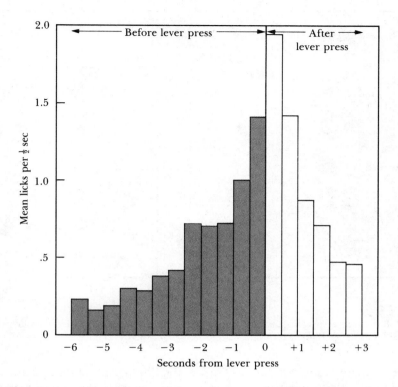

Figure 11.8. Rate of licking a water tube for 1/2-sec periods before and after a lever-press re-sponse. *(From Miller & DeBold, 1965.)*

fixed interval. As the end of the interval (and the availability of the reinforcer) gets closer, the rate of the instrumental response gradually increases. In addition to recording the lever-press responses of the dogs, Williams measured their rate of salivation during the fixed interval. He was interested in whether the pattern of salivation during each trial would match the pattern of lever pressing.

The results are shown in Figure 11.9 for each dog. The data represent the animals' performance after extensive training. Each graph shows the average number of lever-press responses and drops of saliva each dog produced during successive 1-sec periods of the 16-sec fixed-interval cycle. As you can see, at the beginning of the fixed-interval cycles, the dogs hardly ever pressed the response lever and salivated

very little. However, as the end of the FI period approached, both lever pressing and salivation gradually increased. Furthermore, the general pattern of this increased responding toward the end of the interval was nearly indistinguishable for the instrumental (lever pressing) and classically conditioned (salivation) responses. This coincidence of salivation and instrumental responding on a fixed-interval schedule has also been observed by other investigators (Shapiro, 1960, 1961). In addition, Kintsch and Witte (1962) noted that the scalloplike temporal pattern of lever pressing is learned faster than the scalloplike pattern of salivation.

So far we have seen instances in which classically conditioned responses precede and/or coincide with instrumental behavior. In other situations, the classically conditioned responses

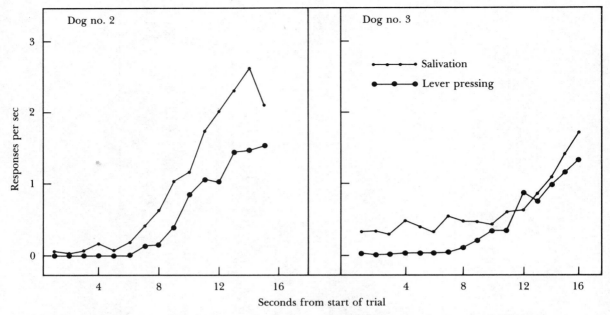

Figure 11.9. Rate of lever pressing and salivation by two dogs during successive 1-sec periods of a 16-sec fixed-interval trial. *(After Williams, 1965.)*

occur after the instrumental response. This happens, for example, if the instrumental behavior is reinforced on a fixed-ratio schedule. You may recall from Chapter 7 that on a fixed-ratio schedule the only factor that determines the delivery of reward is how many responses the subject has made. When these responses occur does not matter. Williams (1965) reinforced dogs with food for pressing a lever on a fixed-ratio 33 schedule and also measured salivation during this instrumental conditioning. What he found with two of his subjects is shown in Figure 11.10. Each graph presents the rates of lever pressing and salivation that occurred during successive seconds from the previous reward. For dog 4, data are shown for the first 13 sec after reinforcement; for dog 7, the first 24 sec. Each dog started lever-pressing within several seconds and achieved a stable rate of responding (between 1.5 and 2 responses per sec) by the fourth second. However, salivation did not appear until much later, when

the animal was close to completing its ratio requirement. Dog 4 did not show substantial salivation until the 10th second after the previous reward, and dog 7 did not consistently increase its salivation until more than 18 sec had elapsed. A similar dissociation between instrumental behavior and conditioned salivation has been observed by Ellison and Konorski (1964).

Implications of the concurrent-measurement experiments for the r_g-s_g mechanism. As we have seen, concurrent measurement of instrumental behavior and classically conditioned responses has failed to reveal a consistent pattern of results. In different situations classically conditioned responses may precede, coincide with, or follow the instrumental behavior. This varied pattern of results is not limited to classically conditioned salivation or positive reinforcement procedures (see Black, 1971; Rescorla & Solomon, 1967). Where does this leave the r_g-s_g mechanism? As we noted earlier, the

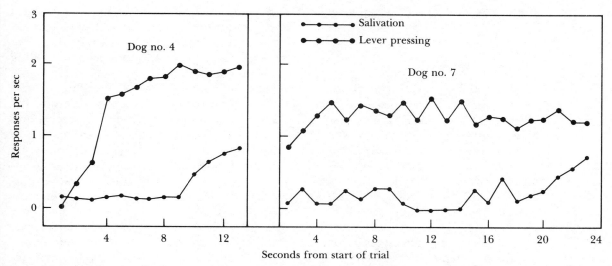

Figure 11.10. Rate of lever pressing and salivation by two dogs during successive 1-min periods in a fixed-ratio trial. Lever pressing was reinforced on a fixed-ratio 33 schedule. *(After Williams, 1965.)*

r_g-s_g mechanism predicts that classically conditioned responses will precede the instrumental response. However, sometimes the opposite is observed.

There are several possible reactions to this type of evidence. One is to maintain that the r_g-s_g mechanism provides a useful account of the relation between classical and instrumental conditioning but to claim that r_g does not represent a measurable classically conditioned response (Logan, 1959; MacCorquodale & Meehl, 1948). According to this approach, r_g is considered to represent a hypothetical construct, a theoretical entity, whose characteristics are governed by the rules of classical conditioning. It is assumed that r_g cannot be observed directly but may be inferred from certain aspects of instrumental behavior. If this approach is adopted, evidence from concurrent-measurement experiments cannot be used to disprove the r_g-s_g mechanism.

A second possible approach is to maintain that r_g is a measurable response but to suggest that it is only one of several classically conditioned responses that may occur during instrumental training. Perhaps the experiments we cited did not measure the appropriate response as an index of r_g. However, if this alternative is accepted, it has to be accompanied by independent criteria for deciding in advance what response will be a good measure of r_g in a particular situation.

A third possible approach to the inconsistent relations observed between classically conditioned responses and instrumental behavior is to abandon the r_g-s_g mechanism and consider alternative ways to conceptualize the relation between classical and instrumental conditioning. This is the approach adopted by modern two-process theory, to which we turn next. Modern two-process theory has been very influential in stimulating a great deal of research on the interaction of classical and instrumental conditioning. However, as we shall see, this theory has not been entirely successful, and it has turned out to be necessary to retain the response-directing functions of the r_g-s_g mechanism to fully account for the available evidence.

Modern two-process theory

The model of the interrelation of classical and operant conditioning we will discuss in this section was brought into focus in 1967 by Rescorla and Solomon. However, it was developed from ideas entertained as early as the 1940s, especially in connection with theorizing about the mechanisms of avoidance learning (see Mowrer, 1960; Rescorla & Solomon, 1967, for a more detailed discussion). We term the model "modern two-process theory" to distinguish it from the two-process theory of avoidance learning we discussed in Chapter 10. Modern two-process theory is similar to the r_g-s_g mechanism in that it assumes that classical conditioning is important in motivating instrumental behavior. However, it adopts a different view of classical conditioning and a different view of the role of classical conditioning in motivation.

Rather than regarding classical conditioning as involving the learning of particular responses (such as r_g), modern two-process theory assumes that the primary outcome of classical conditioning is that previously "neutral" stimuli come to elicit a particular type of motivation, or **central emotional state,** that corresponds to the unconditioned stimulus used. Classical conditioning is viewed as changing the emotional properties of stimuli for the animal. Unlike the r_g-s_g mechanism, modern two-process theory does not view classical conditioning as contributing to the *general* motivation, or arousal, of the subject. Rather, classical conditioning is assumed to enable stimuli to elicit *particular* emotions, or types of motivation. The emotional state that comes to be elicited by a conditioned stimulus is specific to the type of unconditioned stimulus used and is considered to be a characteristic of the central nervous system—a mood, if you will. Emotional states do not invariably lead to particular responses. On the contrary, they may be manifest in any one of a variety of actions. Anger, for example, may result in fighting, shouting, a frown, or refusal to acknowledge someone's presence, depending on the circumstances.

Because instrumental-conditioning procedures contain the circumstances necessary for classical conditioning, modern two-process theory assumes that central emotional states are conditioned during ordinary instrumental training. These states become conditioned either to situational cues or to discriminative stimuli that accompany the reinforcement procedure. Furthermore, the emotional states are assumed to motivate the instrumental behavior. The fact that classically conditioned emotional states are not always manifest in the same responses makes modern two-process theory much less precise than the r_g-s_g mechanism. It also makes the concurrent measurement of instrumental behavior and classically conditioned responses irrelevant to evaluation of the theory. Because modern two-process theory does not specify what responses a conditioned emotional state will lead to, it cannot be disproved by the type of evidence concurrent-measurement experiments provide.

If modern two-process theory cannot be disproved by concurrent-measurement experiments, how can it be empirically tested? As it turns out, the theory makes one very important and unambiguous prediction about behavior—namely, that *the rate of an instrumental response will be modified by the presentation of a classically conditioned stimulus*. This prediction is based on the following considerations. During instrumental conditioning, a conditioned central emotional state is assumed to develop to motivate the instrumental response. Classically conditioned stimuli are also assumed to elicit central emotional states. Therefore, presentation of a classically conditioned stimulus to a subject while it is performing on an instrumental reinforcement schedule will alter the emotional state that was maintaining the instrumental response. This will be evident in a change in the rate of the instrumental behavior. We have already seen an example in the conditioned-emotional-response (CER) procedure, described in earlier chapters. You may recall that in the CER procedure, animals are first trained to press a response lever for food reinforcement. A discrete stimulus, such as a light or a tone, is then repeatedly paired with shock. This classically conditioned fear stimulus is then presented to the animals while they are lever-pressing for food. Consistent with the prediction of modern two-process theory, presentation of the shock-conditioned CS produces a change in the rate of the lever-press response. The rate of lever pressing for food decreases when the shock-conditioned CS is presented.

Classically conditioned stimuli do not always suppress instrumental behavior, as in the CER procedure. According to two-process theory, exactly what kinds of changes will be produced by various kinds of classically conditioned stimuli will depend on the emotional state created by these CSs and the emotional state created by the instrumental reinforcement schedule. If the classically conditioned stimulus produces emotions that are opposite to those that motivate the instrumental behavior, the rate of the instrumental response will decrease. This is presumably what happens in the CER procedure. The food-reinforcement schedule motivates lever pressing by way of a positive emotional state conditioned by food. This emotion is disrupted when the shock-conditioned CS is presented because the CS elicits an aversive emotional state. In other situations the classically conditioned stimulus may evoke an emotion that is similar to the emotional state created by the instrumental reinforcement schedule. When this occurs, the two emotions will summate, and the rate of the instrumental behavior will increase.

Specific predictions of modern two-process theory. Specific predictions about how classically conditioned stimuli will influence instrumental behavior can be made by considering the types of emotions that are elicited by various types of CSs and by instrumental reinforcement schedules. Borrowing language introduced by Mowrer (1960), Table 11.1 provides metaphorical labels for the emotional states that are presumably elicited by some common types of classically conditioned stimuli. Let us first consider classical conditioning with a positive (appetitive) unconditioned stimulus, such as food or water. If the stimulus is a CS+—that is, if it becomes associated with the impending presentation of the US—we may refer to the emotional state created by the CS as **hope**. In contrast, if the stimulus is a CS−, meaning that it has become associated with the removal or the absence of the appetitive US, we may refer to the emotional state created as **disappointment**. In the case of a CS+ for the impending presentation of an aversive US, such as shock, the conditioned emotional state is called **fear**. Finally, if the conditioned stimulus is a CS− associated with the removal or absence of an aversive US, we may presume that **relief** is elicited by presentations of the CS. Using this same terminology, we may assume that instrumental behavior reinforced by the presentation of food (or other appetitive reinforcers) is motivated by "hope" and that instrumental behavior reinforced by the avoidance or removal of shock (or other aversive events) is motivated by "fear." It is important to note that these labels are used for convenience only and do not imply that the

TABLE 11.1. *Emotional states elicited by the CS after various types of classical conditioning*

Conditioned stimulus	Unconditioned stimulus	
	Appetitive (such as food)	Aversive (such as shock)
CS+	hope	fear
CS−	disappointment	relief

Pavlovian CSs involved necessarily elicit the same emotions that people experience when they describe their feelings using the terms *hope, disappointment, fear,* and *relief*.

If presentation of a classically conditioned stimulus alters instrumental behavior solely by changing the emotions that motivate the instrumental response, what should we expect in various situations? Table 11.2 lists the predicted outcomes when classically conditioned stimuli eliciting hope, disappointment, fear, and relief are presented to animals responding either to obtain food (positive reinforcement) or to avoid shock (negative reinforcement). Let us first consider the predictions in the case of positive reinforcement (cells 1–4). The underlying emotional state created by positive reinforcement is hope. Hope is incompatible with fear, and hence the rate of the instrumental response is expected to decline when a CS+ for an aversive US is presented (cell 1). Hope and relief may be considered compatible emotional states because both are positive (desirable) emotions. Therefore, we predict that when a CS− for an aversive US is presented (creating relief), it will increase the rate of positively reinforced instrumental behavior (cell 2). In cell 3, the classically conditioned stimulus facilitates the instrumental response because it elicits hope, which is the same type of emotion as the motivational state conditioned by the positive reinforcement schedule. A decrease in responding is predicted in cell 4 because the disappointment created by the classically conditioned stimulus presumably subtracts from the hope that motivates the instrumental behavior.

Cells 5–8 state the predictions when the instrumental procedure involves negative reinforcement, such as shock avoidance. The underlying emotion that motivates the instrumental behavior in this case is fear. This fear is enhanced when a CS is presented that also elicits fear (cell 5). Hence, an increase in the rate of the instrumental response is predicted. The fear is reduced by presentation of a CS that has been associated with the removal or absence of an aversive US (cell 6). Instrumental responding therefore declines. Fear is presumably also reduced when the classically conditioned stimulus elicits hope (cell 7) because fear and hope are incompatible emotions. However, the motivation for the instrumental response is expected to increase when a CS− for an appetitive US is presented (cell 8) because disappointment and fear are both aversive emotional states. Therefore, an increase in responding is expected in this case.

Results consistent with modern two-process theory. We have already noted that the concurrent measurement of instrumental behavior and classically conditioned responses cannot be used to evaluate modern two-process theory. How, then, can the predictions in Table 11.2 be experimentally tested? The experiments that have been performed to evaluate modern two-process theory were modeled after the CER procedure and are called **transfer-of-control**

TABLE 11.2. *Effects of classically conditioned stimuli on the rate of instrumental behavior*

Instrumental schedule	Aversive US		Appetitive US	
	CS + (fear)	CS − (relief)	CS + (hope)	CS − (disappointment)
Positive reinforcement (procurement of food) (hope)	1 decrease	2 increase	3 increase	4 decrease
Negative reinforcement (avoidance of shock) (fear)	5 increase	6 decrease	7 decrease	8 increase

experiments. Such experiments basically consist of three phases. Phase I involves instrumental conditioning of an operant response using some schedule of positive or negative reinforcement. In phase II, the subjects are given classical conditioning in which an explicit CS is associated with either the presence or absence of an unconditioned stimulus. Phase III is the critical transfer phase. Here the animal is allowed to engage in the instrumental response, and the explicit CS from phase II is periodically presented to see what effect it has on the rate of the instrumental behavior. In some applications of the transfer-of-control design, the classical-conditioning phase is conducted before instrumental conditioning. In some other experiments, phases I and II are conducted concurrently. That is, classical-conditioning trials with the CS and US are periodically presented while the subject is being trained on the instrumental reinforcement schedule. These variations in the basic design are often unimportant to the results observed in phase III, the critical transfer phase.

Modern two-process theory has stimulated a great deal of research testing predictions of the type in Table 11.2 using the transfer-of-control design. Many of the results of these experiments have been consistent with the predictions. We will not review all the evidence here but will cite some illustrative examples. Let us first consider the effects of classically conditioned stimuli on the performance of instrumental behavior maintained by positive reinforcement (cells 1–4 in Table 11.2). As we have already noted, cell 1 represents the conditioned-emotional-response procedure. The common finding is that a CS+ conditioned with an aversive US suppresses the rate of positively reinforced instrumental behavior (see reviews by Blackman, 1977; Davis, 1968; Lyon, 1968). The effects of a signal for the absence of an aversive US (a CS−) on positively reinforced responding (cell 2) have not been as extensively investigated. However, the available data are again consistent with the prediction. Hammond

(1966), for example, found that lever pressing in rats reinforced by food increased when a CS− for shock was presented. In certain situations, food-reinforced instrumental behavior is also increased by presentation of a CS+ for food, consistent with the prediction in cell 3 (for example, Estes, 1943, 1948; LoLordo, 1971). Research on the effects of a signal for the absence of an appetitive reinforcer (CS−) on positively reinforced responding (cell 4) has not been very extensively pursued. However, evidence consistent with two-process theory (a suppression of the instrumental response) has been observed in what studies there are (for example, Gutman & Maier, 1978; Hearst & Peterson, 1973).

Many experiments have been performed to determine how stimuli that signal an aversive US (CS+) or its absence (CS−) influence the rate of negatively reinforced instrumental behavior (cells 5 and 6). These studies generally support predictions of modern two-process theory. Numerous studies have shown that the rate of avoidance behavior is increased by the presentation of a CS+ for shock and decreased by the presentation of a CS− for shock (for example, Bull & Overmier, 1968; Desiderato, 1969; Rescorla & LoLordo, 1965; Weisman & Litner, 1969). Presentation of a signal for the presence of food (CS+) has also been noted to decrease the rate of instrumental avoidance behavior, as cell 7 predicts. Several investigators have noted this effect (for example, Bull, 1970; Davis & Kreuter, 1972; Grossen, Kostansek, & Bolles, 1969). The effects of a signal for the absence of food (CS−) on avoidance behavior (cell 8) have not been extensively investigated. One experiment that included a test of the prediction in cell 8 failed to find any effect on avoidance responding (Bull, 1970). However, in another study (Grossen et al., 1969), a classically conditioned CS− for food facilitated instrumental avoidance behavior, as predicted in cell 8. Taken together, these studies offer considerable empirical support for the predictions of modern two-process theory listed in Table 11.2.

Role of response interactions in the effects of classically conditioned stimuli on instrumental behavior

In our discussions of the results of the transfer-of-control experiments so far, we have emphasized the interaction between the emotional state elicited by the classically conditioned stimulus and the emotional state established by the instrumental reinforcement procedure. However, a classically conditioned stimulus may also influence instrumental behavior through the overt responses it elicits. Consider, for example, a hypothetical situation in which the classically conditioned stimulus makes the animal remain still, and the instrumental response is shuttling back and forth in a shuttle box. In this case, presentation of the CS will decrease the instrumental response simply because the tendency to stop moving elicited by the CS will interfere with the shuttle behavior. An appeal to the interaction between emotional states elicited by the CS and the instrumental reinforcement schedule is not necessary to understand such an outcome. Facilitation of responding would occur if the classically conditioned stimulus elicited overt responses that were similar to the instrumental behavior. In this case, presentation of the CS would increase the observed rate of the instrumental behavior because the responses elicited by the CS would be added to the responses the animal was performing to receive instrumental reinforcement. Assumptions about central emotional states would again be unnecessary in explaining the results.

Investigators have been very much concerned with the possibility that the results of transfer-of-control experiments are due to the fact that Pavlovian CSs elicit overt responses that either interfere with or facilitate the behavior required for instrumental reinforcement. Various strategies have been used to rule out this possibility (see Overmier & Lawry, 1979, for a recent review). These efforts have been generally successful in showing that many transfer-of-control effects are not produced by interactions between overt responses (see, for example, Grossen et al., 1969; Overmier, Bull, & Pack, 1971; Scobie, 1972). However, overt classically conditioned responses can have an important role in some transfer-of-control experiments. This is particularly true when the classically conditioned CS is a discrete localized stimulus, such as a spot of light, because such CSs elicit sign tracking. As we noted earlier, when a localized stimulus becomes a conditioned CS+ for food, animals tend to approach it. In contrast, if the localized stimulus becomes a CS+ for shock, it will elicit **negative sign tracking.** That is, the subject will tend to move away from the CS (for example, Leclerc & Reberg, 1980). Positive and negative sign tracking elicited by classically conditioned CSs may increase or decrease the performance of an instrumentally reinforced response, depending on whether the sign-tracking responses are compatible or incompatible with the instrumental response (for example, LoLordo, McMillan, & Riley, 1974).

Response interactions involving sign tracking in pigeons. If a spot of light is used as the CS and is repeatedly paired with food, pigeons will not only learn to move toward the CS but will also learn to peck it. Thus, the CS comes to determine where the pigeon moves and where it pecks. If such sign tracking is important in transfer-of-control experiments, we would expect that CSs located in different places would have different effects on performance of instrumental behavior. In one experiment designed to evaluate this prediction (Schwartz, 1976), pigeons were tested in a chamber provided with two circular keys that could be illuminated (see Figure 11.11). One of the keys was designated as the instrumental response key, and pecks here provided food reinforcement according to a variable-interval schedule. When the key-pecking response was occurring at a stable rate, classical-conditioning trials were periodically introduced. The CS was a red light turned on for 12 sec preceding the automatic

Instrumental response key   Side key

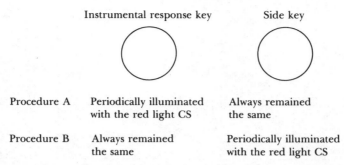

Procedure A	Periodically illuminated with the red light CS	Always remained the same
Procedure B	Always remained the same	Periodically illuminated with the red light CS

Figure 11.11. Diagram of procedures used by Schwartz (1976). In procedure A, the red light CS was periodically presented on the instrumental response key and ended with the automatic delivery of grain. In procedure B, the red light CS (followed by food) was periodically presented on the side key.

presentation of 4 sec access to grain. (The pigeons did not have to peck anywhere to obtain grain at the end of each presentation of the red light.) In one experimental procedure (procedure A in Figure 11.11), the red light CS appeared on the response key the pigeons had to peck for instrumental reinforcement. In a second procedure (procedure B in Figure 11.11), the red light CS appeared on the side key in the experimental chamber. The red light CS was conditioned with food in both cases.

If the emotional effect of the CS+ for food is the only factor determining its effects on instrumental behavior, it should not matter whether the CS appears on the instrumental key or on the side key. However, if sign tracking is also involved, the location of the CS should make a big difference. More specifically, when the CS+ for food appears on the instrumental response key (procedure A), the CS is expected to elicit approach and pecking (sign tracking), and this pecking should add to the instrumentally reinforced pecks the animal ordinarily makes on this key. Thus, pecking at the instrumental response key should increase when the CS is presented. In contrast, when the CS+ for food is presented on the side key (procedure B), the sign-tracking approach and pecks are expected to be directed to this second key and away from the instrumental response key. Hence, presentation of the CS should decrease pecking at the instrumental response key.

The results of the experiment are summarized in Figure 11.12. First, let us consider what happened when the CS was presented on the same response key the subjects had to peck for instrumental reinforcement (procedure A). As predicted by the sign-tracking hypothesis, the rate of pecking on this key was much higher when the red light CS was present than when it was absent. Thus, the CS+ for food increased the rate of pecking measured on the instrumental key. This result is consistent with modern two-process theory (see cell 3 in Table 11.2) because the CS+ for food is assumed to elicit the same type of emotional state (hope) that is created by the positive instrumental reinforcement procedure. However, response facilitation was not observed when the CS was presented on the side key (procedure B); in fact, pecks on the instrumental key decreased. Such suppression in the rate of positively reinforced instrumental behavior has been observed in many experiments when an appetitive CS+ is presented (for example, Azrin & Hake, 1969; Konorski & Miller, 1930; Meltzer & Brahlek, 1970; Miczek & Grossman, 1971). This response suppression is contrary to the predictions of modern two-process theory. Although it is not known in every case why such suppression occurs, in the present study the reason was that the pigeon moved to the side key with the CS and pecked it instead of pecking the instrumental key. The rate of pecking on both keys combined during

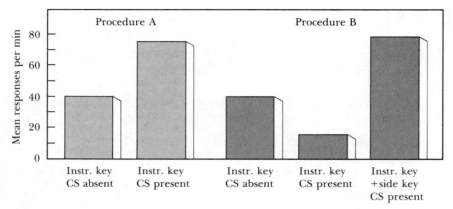

Figure 11.12. Rates of pecking in procedure A and procedure B of the experiment by Schwartz (1976). In procedure A the CS was presented on the instrumental response key; in procedure B the CS was presented on the side key (see Figure 11.11). *(After Schwartz, 1976.)*

the CS periods was higher than the rate of pecking on the instrumental key in the absence of the CS. Thus, in procedure B response facilitation by the CS was observed only if all the pecks made by the pigeons were taken into account.

Behavioral contrast and the interaction of classical and instrumental conditioning. The experiment by Schwartz (1976) shows that sign-tracking key pecks can summate with instrumentally reinforced pecking if a classically conditioned visual stimulus for food is projected on the response key. This type of result has profound implications for a phenomenon known as **positive behavioral contrast.** Positive contrast effects were documented in a classic experiment by Reynolds (1961b). Pigeons were first reinforced on a VI 3-min schedule for pecking whenever either of two colors was projected on the response key (red or green, for example). Thus, a multiple VI VI schedule of reinforcement was in effect. The pigeons learned to respond steadily in both components of the multiple schedule because reinforcement was available in each component. Once responding stabilized on the multiple VI VI schedule, the procedure was changed. Pecking

during the first component (with the red light) continued to be reinforced on the VI 3-min schedule. However, responding during the second component (with the green light) was now on extinction. Thus, the procedure was changed to a multiple VI Ext schedule. As expected, the pigeons decreased their pecking during the green-light extinction component. Reynolds was particularly interested in how the introduction of extinction during the green light influenced pecking during the red light, which continued to be reinforced on the VI 3-min schedule. Interestingly, responding increased during the red light. This type of outcome, illustrated in Figure 11.13, is called "positive behavioral contrast." Positive behavioral contrast is a remarkable phenomenon because it involves an increase in the rate of behavior during a stimulus even though the reinforcement schedule remains unchanged during that stimulus.

Why does responding increase in the presence of a stimulus when extinction is introduced in the presence of another stimulus? Many explanations of positive behavioral contrast have been offered, and the phenomenon has stimulated extensive investigations. Schwartz and Gamzu (1977) have proposed that positive be-

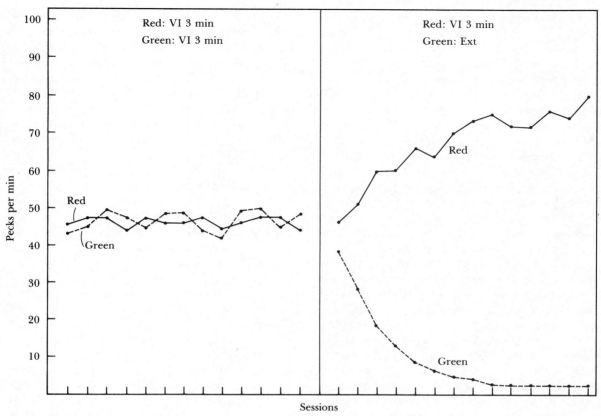

Figure 11.13. Hypothetical results demonstrating the phenomenon of positive behavioral contrast. In the left panel, pigeons are reinforced for pecking a response key on a multiple VI 3-min VI 3-min schedule. The procedure is then changed to a multiple VI 3-min Ext schedule (left panel). The rate of responding during the unchanged component (with the red light) increases when extinction is introduced in the other component (with the green light).

havioral contrast represents the summation of classically conditioned sign-tracking pecks and instrumentally conditioned pecks. They argue that the added responses that occur in the first (unchanged) component of the multiple VI Ext schedule are sign-tracking responses. These responses emerge when the multiple VI VI procedure is changed to multiple VI Ext because the key colors in the multiple VI Ext schedule come to signal differential reinforcement. The red light comes to signal the presence of the VI reinforcement schedule, and the green light comes to signal extinction. Such conditioning of

the key colors does not occur during the earlier multiple VI VI procedure because there the two colors accompany the same VI schedule of reinforcement.

Schwartz and Gamzu's analysis of positive behavioral contrast is supported by several lines of evidence. If sign tracking is the basis for behavioral contrast, then the location of the stimuli for the multiple schedule should make a big difference in the results. Keller (1974) tested this prediction with the same type of approach that Schwartz (1976) used in the experiment described in the preceding section (see Figure

11.11). Red and green lights were used to signal the different components of a multiple schedule. In one procedure, the lights were projected on the same key that the pigeons were required to peck for instrumental reinforcement. (This is comparable to procedure A in Figure 11.11 and the procedure originally used by Reynolds.) In this situation, positive behavioral contrast was obtained. In a second condition, the red and green lights associated with the components of the multiple schedule were projected on a side key different from the instrumental response key. (This is comparable to procedure B in Figure 11.11.) In this situation positive behavioral contrast was not obtained if only the pecks directed at the instrumental response key were counted. However, the pigeons also pecked the side key whenever the color there signaled the availability of reinforcement in the multiple VI Ext procedure. Evidence of positive behavioral contrast was obtained in the second procedure only if the sign-tracking pecks at the side key were added to the pecks directed at the instrumental key. These findings are comparable to the results obtained by Schwartz (1976) in procedure B (see Figure 11.12) and provide strong support for the sign-tracking analysis of behavioral contrast.

Another source of support for the sign-tracking analysis is provided by research with other species and other responses. According to the hypothesis, contrast is in a sense an artifact of the similarity of the responses conditioned by the classical and instrumental aspects of a multiple schedule. If these responses are different, they will not be added together in the same response measure, and behavioral contrast should not occur. Consistent with this prediction, contrast is usually not found when pigeons are required to perform such responses for instrumental reinforcement as hopping on a treadle or pressing a bar, which are not similar to sign-tracking responses. Similarly, experiments with rats typically do not result in behavioral contrast. In fact, responding sometimes decreases in the unchanged VI component of the

multiple schedule when extinction is introduced in the other component. In rat experiments, the signal for food is usually a tone or a light above the response lever. Sign-tracking responses in this situation would most likely be directed toward the tone or light. Therefore, they do not summate with the instrumental lever-press response. In fact, they may compete with lever pressing. Hence, positive behavioral contrast is not obtained.

Response interactions involving sign tracking in rats. The experiments by Schwartz (1976) and Keller (1974) have shown that whether instrumentally reinforced pecking is increased by a CS for food depends on the location of the CS. Stimulus location can also determine the effect of an appetitive CS+ on positively reinforced instrumental responding in rats. In one experiment (Karpicke, Christoph, Peterson, & Hearst, 1977), rats were trained to pull a chain suspended from the top of the experimental chamber for milk reinforcement. When the chain-pulling operant was occurring at a stable rate, classical-conditioning trials were superimposed on the instrumental reinforcement schedule. These trials consisted in turning on a localized light CS shortly before the delivery of several drops of free milk. For one group of rats the light CS was close to the chain manipulandum; for another group it was located in another part of the experimental chamber. After conditioning, the light CS disrupted instrumental chain pulling in both groups. Therefore, the experimenters reported their results in terms of suppression ratios (see Chapter 4). The lower the value of this ratio, the more suppression in the instrumental response was produced by the CS. A score of .5 was achieved if presentation of the CS had no discernible effect on instrumental responding.

The results are summarized in the left portion of Figure 11.14. When the CS was located near the chain manipulandum, presentation of the CS had only a minor disruptive effect on instrumental chain pulling. In contrast, when the CS was located in another part of the experimental chamber, chain pulling was much more severely disrupted during the CS presentations. More-detailed observations of the animals indicated that the response suppression occurred because the animals tended to approach the CS. When the CS was located far from the chain manipulandum, approaching the CS took the rats away from the chain and thereby reduced their chain-pulling behavior.

Sign tracking elicited by the classically conditioned CS can also determine transfer-of-control effects when the CS is conditioned with an aversive rather than an appetitive US. As we noted earlier, if a localized CS+ is conditioned with an aversive stimulus, such as shock, animals will tend to move away from it (negative sign tracking). Karpicke et al. (1977) repeated the experiment described above, with a shock-conditioned CS+ that was either close to or far from the location where the instrumental response was performed. Rats again served as subjects and were first trained to pull a chain to obtain milk. When the chain-pulling operant was well established, classical-conditioning trials were conducted in which presentation of a localized light ended in shock. For one group the light was near the chain manipulandum, whereas for a second group it was in another part of the experimental chamber. If animals tend to move away from a CS+ for shock, this should disrupt chain pulling more when the CS is near the chain manipulandum than when it is far away.

The results are summarized in the right panel of Figure 11.14. As predicted by the response-interaction hypothesis, the CS+ disrupted the instrumental chain-pulling response much more when it was close to the chain than when it was farther away. It is interesting to note that this effect is opposite to what occurred when the CS was conditioned with milk (left panel of Figure 11.14). In that case, the far CS disrupted chain pulling more than the near CS. Thus, the location of the CS is not the sole determinant of what effect the CS has on chain

pulling. Rather, the transfer-of-control results depend on whether the CS is conditioned with a positive or negative reinforcer (milk or shock) and whether the sign tracking elicited by the CS makes the animal move away from the location where the instrumental response has to be performed.

Experiments on the role of sign tracking in transfer-of-control studies are significant because they show that the emotional interactions emphasized by modern two-process theory cannot explain all transfer-of-control results. However, it is important to keep in mind that transfer-of-control experiments do not invariably involve sign tracking. Sign tracking is most likely to develop in situations where localized CSs are used that elicit approach or withdrawal. Experiments in which the CS is a diffuse stimulus (flooding the experimental chamber with a tone, for example) are not likely to be complicated by sign-tracking effects.

Discriminative-stimulus properties of classically conditioned states

We have described the results of many experiments showing that classically conditioned

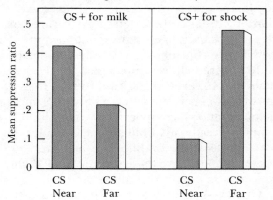

Figure 11.14. Suppression of chain pulling reinforced by milk in rats when a CS+ for milk or shock is presented. The CS was located either near or far from the chain manipulandum. (Lower values of the suppression ratio indicate greater disruptions of instrumental behavior.) *(After Karpicke, Christoph, Peterson, & Hearst, 1977.)*

stimuli can influence the performance of instrumental behavior. In analyzing these effects we have emphasized two aspects of classically conditioned stimuli: the emotional state or particular type of motivation evoked by the stimuli and the overt responses these stimuli elicit. However, explanation of all the ways that classically conditioned stimuli can influence instrumental behavior requires postulating a third variable as well. We must assume that classically conditioned stimuli evoke a theoretical state that has not only particular motivational and response-eliciting properties but also stimulus characteristics. The idea is that the state of neural excitation in the brain created by classically conditioned stimuli leads to particular sensations in addition to eliciting particular types of motivation (emotions) and overt responses. These sensations can come to serve as discriminative stimuli for the instrumental behavior and thereby influence instrumental performance.

How might classically conditioned states acquire discriminative-stimulus properties? Theoretically the answer is rather straightforward. We know from Chapter 9 that a stimulus acquires discriminative control of behavior if responses in the presence of the stimulus are reinforced and responses in its absence are not reinforced. Therefore, stimulus features of a classically conditioned state should acquire discriminative control over instrumental behavior with differential reinforcement in the usual manner. However, this is easier to say than it is to prove experimentally. The experimental demonstration is complicated by the fact that we cannot directly manipulate the stimulus features of classically conditioned states; we cannot present and remove these stimuli at will the way we can turn a light or tone on and off.

One experimental approach to the study of discriminative-stimulus properties of classically conditioned states involves an instrumental discrimination procedure. Consider, for example, the procedure diagramed in Figure 11.15. Subjects are placed in a two-way shuttle box and are reinforced with food for crossing from one side to the other when a clicker is sounded but are not reinforced in the absence of the clicker. Thus, the clicker becomes an appetitive S+. Because subjects receive food during the S+ (and not during its absence), the S+ also becomes classically conditioned by the food and presumably comes to elicit a classically conditioned state, denoted by the symbol T in the lower part of Figure 11.15. The classically conditioned state T presumably has stimulus features, denoted by s_T in Figure 11.15. These sensations (s_T) are present when the instrumental response is reinforced because the classically conditioned state (T) is elicited by the S+. However, the s_T sensations are not present on nonreinforced trials because the S− is not conditioned to elicit the classically conditioned state T. The presence of s_T on reinforced but not on nonreinforced trials may enable these stimuli to

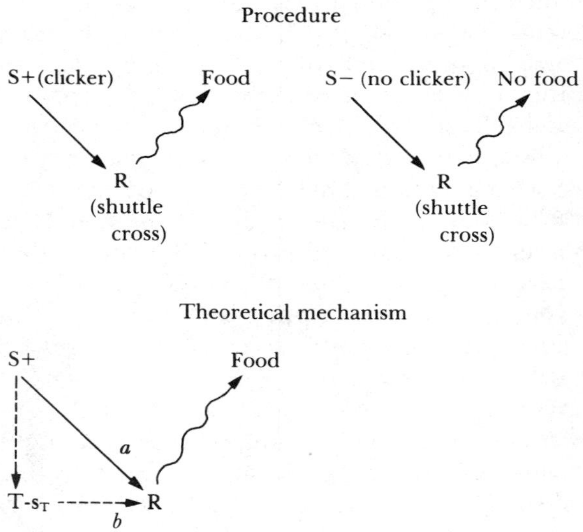

Figure 11.15. Procedure and theoretical mechanism for discrimination training of an instrumental shuttle response (R). Shuttle crossings are reinforced with food during a clicker (S+) and not reinforced in the absence of the clicker (S−). The S+ comes to elicit a classically conditioned state T with its stimulus properties s_T. The instrumental response can be evoked by the S+ either directly (arrow *a*) or by way of the discriminative-stimulus properties of the classically conditioned state (arrow *b*).

serve as discriminative cues for the instrumental response, as denoted by arrow *b* in the lower part of Figure 11.15.

The schema presented in Figure 11.15 makes it plausible that during discrimination training the stimulus properties (s_T) of a classically conditioned state may acquire discriminative control over the instrumental behavior. However, according to the theoretical model outlined in Figure 11.15, there are two means whereby the S+ can come to evoke the instrumental response. The S+ may evoke the instrumental response directly, as denoted by arrow *a* in the lower part of the figure, or may evoke the response indirectly by way of the stimulus properties of the classically conditioned state (arrow *b*). Therefore, if we find that subjects make the shuttle response during the S+ and not during the S−, this does not tell us specifically that the stimulus properties s_T of the classically conditioned state have gained discriminative control over the behavior. Behavior elicited by the S+ could just as well have occurred because of a direct connection between the S+ and the response.

To prove that s_T can evoke the instrumental response by itself, we have to present s_T without the S+. In this case any shuttling that is observed can only be attributed to s_T. But how can this be done, since we do not have direct control over s_T? One possibility is to condition some stimulus other than the S+ to also elicit the classically conditioned state T. Let us add a second phase to the experiment we have been considering. After the discriminative shuttle-response training that we have conducted with the clicker as the S+, let us put the subjects in a distinctively different apparatus and conduct simple classical conditioning in which a pure tone (CS+) is paired with the presentation of food and a different pure tone (CS−) is given without food. This procedure, together with the first phase of the experiment we have been considering, is summarized in Figure 11.16. Keep in mind that the second phase of the experiment involves only classical conditioning. The

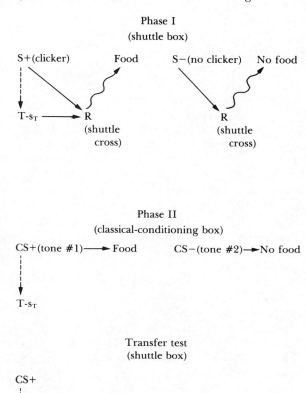

Figure 11.16. Outline of the experiment by Overmier and Lawry (1979). Instrumental discrimination training is conducted in a shuttle box in phase I. Classical conditioning is then conducted in a separate apparatus that does not permit subjects to make the shuttle response. The CS+ is then tested in the shuttle box to see whether it increases shuttle responding.

subject is not required to perform any particular instrumental response for the food to be delivered. Shuttle responses are not reinforced in this phase of the experiment. In fact, the conditioning is carried out in an apparatus where the subject cannot make shuttle crossings. Thus, in the second phase, the only thing that happens is that one tone becomes a CS+

for food and another tone becomes a CS− for food.

Both phase I and phase II of the experiment depicted in Figure 11.16 involve conditioning with food. Therefore, the pure tone CS+ presumably comes to elicit the same classically conditioned state T in phase II that was conditioned to the S+ in phase I. We can assume that after conditioning of the CS+, the CS+ will elicit the classically conditioned state T, with its accompanying stimulus properties s_T. This brings us to the most important aspect of this complicated experiment. Recall that we are trying to prove that the stimulus properties s_T of the classically conditioned state came to serve as discriminative stimuli for the shuttle response in phase I of the experiment. If this is true, then any time the subjects experience s_T in the shuttle box, shuttle crossings should increase. Therefore, presentation of the food-conditioned CS+ should evoke increased shuttle responding. Such a result would provide conclusive proof that the stimulus properties of the food-conditioned state acquired discriminative control over the shuttle behavior. The shuttle response was never reinforced in the presence of the CS+ in phase II. Therefore, the CS+ could not have become conditioned to elicit the shuttle response directly. Rather, the CS+ can only evoke shuttling indirectly by eliciting the food-conditioned state T, with its stimulus properties s_T.

The experiment that we have been describing was carried out by Overmier and his associates (see Overmier & Lawry, 1979). Dogs served as subjects. In describing the study, we omitted several aspects to simplify the presentation. Between phases I and II of the experiment, subjects received free-operant avoidance training in the shuttle box in the presence of a bright light. (Each shuttle crossing here postponed the next scheduled shock by 30 sec.) This free-operant avoidance schedule was in effect during the final phase of the experiment when the food-conditioned CS+ was presented in the shuttle box. The point of interest was

whether shuttle crossings would be increased by presentation of the CS+. The final transfer test also involved presentations of the food-conditioned S+ (from phase I) and the food-conditioned CS− (from phase II).

The results of the experiment are summarized in Figure 11.17. The data are presented in terms of the percent change (increase or decrease) in shuttle responding caused by presentation of the food-conditioned S+ and the food-conditioned CS+ and CS− stimuli. The free-operant avoidance schedule remained in effect for the shuttle behavior during these stimulus presentations. Let us first consider the effects of the food-conditioned S+. The rate of shuttle crossings increased during this stimulus. This outcome cannot be explained as due to the emotional effects of the S+. Since the S+ was conditioned with food, it presumably elicited the emotion of hope, which should have subtracted from the emotion of fear that was maintaining the baseline shuttling behavior. However, the increased responding elicited by the S+ can be accounted for in terms of the responses that had been conditioned to

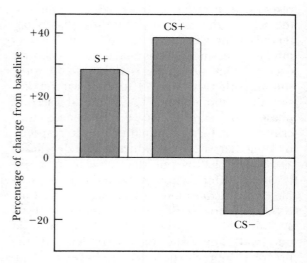

Figure 11.17. Percent change in shuttle shock-avoidance responding when a food-conditioned S+ for shuttling is presented or a food-conditioned CS+ or CS− is presented. *(From Overmier & Lawry, 1979.)*

the S+. Recall that in phase I of the experiment the subjects were reinforced (with food) for shuttle crossings during the S+. Thus, the S+ was conditioned to evoke shuttle responses, and perhaps this is why shuttling increased during the transfer test when the S+ was presented.

Let us consider next what happened when the food-conditioned CS+ was presented while the subjects were responding in the shuttle box on the free-operant avoidance schedule. The CS+ also increased shuttling. This is a very significant finding because it cannot be explained by either the emotional properties of the state elicited by the CS+ or the responses elicited by the CS+. Since the CS+ was conditioned with food, the emotional state it evoked (hope) should have subtracted from the emotion (fear) maintaining the baseline avoidance behavior, and there should have been a decrease in shuttle responding. The responses conditioned to the CS+ cannot explain the increased shuttle behavior, because the CS+ was conditioned in a classical-conditioning procedure and special precautions were taken to make sure that the shuttle response would not become conditioned to the CS+ in the second phase of the experiment. The increased responding evoked by the CS+ is best explained by the discriminative-stimulus properties (s_T) of the classically conditioned state (T) elicited by the CS+. These cues (s_T) presumably gained control over the shuttle response because of the training subjects received in phase I of the experiment.

Let us next consider what happened when the food-conditioned CS− was presented in the transfer test. This time a small decrease in shuttle crossings occurred. This is an important control observation because it shows that not all stimuli will produce increases in shuttling in this situation. Therefore, we can be sure that the effects observed with the S+ and the CS+ were due to the specific conditioning history of these stimuli.

Finally, one other aspect of the results of this experiment is particularly interesting—namely, that the food-conditioned CS+ did not produce a smaller increase in shuttle crossings than the S+. Theoretically, it is possible for the S+ to evoke the shuttle response in two ways (see lower portion of Figure 11.15). The S+ may evoke the response directly, as depicted by arrow *a* in Figure 11.15. Alternatively, the S+ may evoke the response by way of the discriminative-stimulus properties of the classically conditioned state T, as depicted by arrow *b*. In contrast, the CS+ can evoke the shuttle behavior only by way of the discriminative properties of the conditioned state T. Because of the way that the CS+ was conditioned in phase II, there was no opportunity for the shuttle response to become directly associated with the CS+. If the S+ in fact activated the shuttle response both directly and indirectly (by way of the classically conditioned state), the S+ should have produced a larger increase in shuttle crossings than the CS+. The fact that this did not occur suggests that all the effectiveness of the S+ was mediated by the classically conditioned state that it elicited. Thus, the present findings suggest that only the connection depicted by arrow *b* in Figure 11.15 became established during the initial discrimination training.

Overmier and his colleagues have conducted several experiments of the sort that we have described (see Overmier & Lawry, 1979). These studies provide strong support for the idea that classically conditioned states have stimulus properties that can acquire discriminative control over instrumental behavior. Furthermore, the discriminative properties of classically conditioned states can override the emotional properties of the states, as in the experiment just described. This set of experiments also provides strong evidence that classical conditioning plays a crucial role in discrimination training. That is, as a result of discrimination training, the instrumental response becomes associated with the stimulus properties of the classically conditioned state elicited by the S+, and this is in large measure why the S+ comes to evoke the instrumental response. Thus, the S+ is conditioned to evoke the instrumental response indirectly, by way of the stimulus properties of classically conditioned states.

It is interesting to note that the present theoretical analysis in terms of discriminative-stimulus properties of classically conditioned states (see Figure 11.15) is very similar to the r_g-s_g mechanism discussed earlier (see Figure 11.5). As in the r_g-s_g mechanism, the stimuli present during instrumental conditioning (S+) are assumed to become classically conditioned, and the classically conditioned entity is assumed to have stimulus characteristics that come to serve as discriminative cues for the instrumental response. Thus, the present model has the same type of response-directing function that we previously discussed in connection with the fractional anticipatory goal response mechanism (see especially our earlier discussion of frustration theory). However, the present account differs from the r_g-s_g mechanism in that a classically conditioned intervening state (T) is assumed to be acquired rather than a fractional anticipatory goal response (r_g). In addition, in the contemporary theoretical model, the classically conditioned entity elicited by the S+ is also assumed to have emotional properties that can add to or subtract from other elicited emotions, in accordance with the predictions of modern two-process theory.

Concluding comments

Classical and instrumental conditioning procedures are clearly different from each other. However, instrumental reinforcement can be involved in classical-conditioning procedures, and classical-conditioning processes can be involved in instrumental-conditioning procedures. Experimental investigations have shown that classical conditioning can take place in the absence of the opportunity for instrumental reinforcement. However, comparable investigations cannot be conducted to show that instrumental conditioning is possible without the occurrence of classical conditioning.

All instrumental-conditioning procedures allow for the occurrence of classical conditioning. Concurrent-measurement experiments confirmed that classically conditioned responses in fact develop during instrumental-conditioning procedures. However, the concurrent measurement of classically and instrumentally conditioned responses has not proved very helpful in elucidating the interrelation of these two processes. Another experimental technique, the transfer-of-control design, has provided much more enlightening information. This type of experiment has confirmed in numerous instances the basic tenet of two-process theory—that classically conditioned stimuli can influence the performance of an independently established instrumental response. The transfer of control from Pavlovian conditioned stimuli to instrumental behavior appears to be governed by three factors. One important factor is the nature of the central emotional state elicited by the Pavlovian CS in comparison with the central emotional state that is established by the baseline instrumental reinforcement schedule. (This factor has been emphasized by modern two-process theory.) A second important variable concerns the overt responses elicited by the Pavlovian CS and how these interfere with or facilitate the instrumental behavior. (Of course, this factor is important only when the Pavlovian CS elicits marked overt responses.) The third important variable in transfer-of-control experiments concerns the discriminative-stimulus properties of the classically conditioned states. (This factor has been emphasized by theories similar to the r_g-s_g mechanism.) One or another of these three factors may predominate in various transfer-of-control situations, allowing for a variety of experimental outcomes.

CHAPTER TWELVE

Cognitive Aspects of Animal Behavior

In Chapter 12 we will consider one of the most recently developed areas of research relevant to the study of conditioning and learning, cognitive aspects of animal behavior. We begin with a discussion of cognitive aspects of classical conditioning. We will then discuss research on memory mechanisms in animals and the relation of memory to conditioning and learning. In the last part of the chapter we will introduce some of the most recent and controversial aspects of the study of animal cognition: serial-pattern learning, concept formation, and the learning of language.

One of the most prominent contemporary developments in the study of conditioning and learning is a renewed interest in cognitive processes in animal behavior (for example, Griffin, 1976; Hulse, Fowler, & Honig, 1978). Although cognitive issues were entertained in considerations of animal behavior decades ago (for example, Tolman, 1932), such concepts have not been extensively used in scientific analyses of animal behavior until recently. This resurgence of interest in cognitive concepts can be traced to two coincidental developments. First, research in animal behavior has shown that the strict S-R behaviorist approach does not provide an entirely adequate conceptual framework for certain aspects of animal behavior. Second, great advances have been made in the last 20 years in the development of a scientific approach to the study of human cognitive functions. The significant success that has been

achieved in the experimental investigation of human cognitive behavior has encouraged similar investigations in animal behavior.

The word *cognition* comes from the Latin meaning "knowledge or thinking" and is used in common parlance to refer to thought processes. To most people, thought processes have two prominent characteristics. First, we tend to regard thinking as involving the voluntary, deliberate, and conscious consideration of some topic, usually with the use of language. Thus, thinking is informally considered to be a kind of "talking to oneself." The second prominent characteristic of thinking is that it can lead to actions that cannot be explained on the basis of the external stimuli the person happens to experience at the time. For example, on your way to work, you may remember that you did not lock up when you left home. This thought may make you return home and lock the door. Your returning cannot be explained by the external stimuli to which you are exposed as you go to work. You encounter these same stimuli every day, but they usually do not make you return home. Rather, your behavior is attributed to the thought of the unlocked door.

In the scientific study of animal behavior, the term *cognition* is used in a more restricted sense than in common language. A clear consensus has not yet emerged concerning the definition of **animal cognition.** However, animal cognition is not defined as voluntary or conscious reflection about a topic. It does not refer to thinking in the ordinary sense. Rather, *animal cognition refers to the use of an internal representation, or code, as a basis for action.* An internal representation is the form in which information is held in memory. Internal representations ("mental" codes, if you will) may consist of various types of information. They may involve, for example, information about particular features of stimuli or information about relations among previously experienced events. We know very little about how animals form representations of stimuli in their environment, what determines which aspects of experience become incorporated into an internal representation, or where and how representations are stored in the nervous system. However, the concept of an internal representation is useful because it allows us to explain the occurrence of responses that are not entirely governed by external stimuli. Behavior can be guided by internal representations of events and relations rather than by concrete external stimuli. Consequently, cognitive mechanisms are often invoked when an animal's actions cannot be entirely explained in terms of the external stimuli the animal is exposed to at the time.

The assumption that animals have cognitive mechanisms should not be taken to mean that their behavior is voluntary and involves conscious free will. Animal cognition probably has little in common with ordinary thinking and is assumed to be fully determined by strict laws of nature. It is presumably just as automatic and

subject to experimental control as any other aspect of behavior. The only difference is that cognitive aspects of behavior are only indirectly controlled by the stimuli the subject experiences. External stimuli are assumed to trigger an image or representation, which in turn guides the behavior that actually occurs. This can take place in various ways, as we will see in the ensuing discussion.

As we noted earlier, the serious study of cognitive mechanisms in animal behavior follows great advances in the understanding of human cognitive functions. The investigation of animal cognitive behavior will no doubt further the understanding of animal behavior. Can this investigation also be useful for the understanding of human cognitive functions? It remains to be seen. Investigators of human cognition have had little interest in the animal research so far. However, this disinterest may be due to the fact that studies of animal cognition are still in their infancy. The results of the research may become more useful for human applications as more complex techniques are devised that will allow investigation of more complex experimental questions. With these developments, research on animal cognition may become very useful in the understanding of certain aspects of human cognitive functions. One particularly fertile area in this regard is the study of cognitive processes in prelinguistic human infants. Very young human infants cannot be tested with most of the procedures used in the study of adult human cognition. However, procedures developed in animal research can be adapted for this purpose, since animal research techniques typically do not depend on linguistic abilities (for example, Cohen, 1976).

We will begin our discussion of animal cognition by describing aspects of classical conditioning that involve cognitive mechanisms. We will then describe some of the extensive research on the mechanisms of animal memory. (Memory is one of the most important topics in the study of both human and animal cognition.) Finally, we will discuss some recent research on complex cognitive processes in animals. Throughout our treatment, we will be concerned with aspects of behavior that are not caused directly by external stimuli but are guided by internal representations of certain aspects of the environment.

Cognitive aspects of classical conditioning

Cognitive mechanisms are clearly involved in some aspects of behavior, such as memory and language, that we have not described in earlier chapters. However, cognitive mechanisms are also important in conditioning. Much of our discussion of classical conditioning in Chapters 4 and 5 followed the strong cognitive orientation of contemporary research in this area. We have also mentioned some cognitive mechanisms in instrumental conditioning. The learned-helplessness hypothesis, for example, is a cognitive formulation. As we noted in Chapter 6, according to the learned-helplessness hypothesis, subjects exposed to inescapable and unavoidable aversive stimulation learn that the aversive event is independent of their behavior. They acquire a representation or view of the environment according to which their behavior cannot have control over the aversive stimulation. The relational-learning hypothesis, discussed in Chapter 9, is also a cognitive mechanism. A particular relation between two stimuli (one being bigger than the other, for example) is not a physical attribute of either stimulus. To respond on the basis of a relation between two stimuli, subjects have first to abstract certain features of each stimulus (size, for example) and then to compare these features. Thus, relational learning requires the formation of representations of the stimuli in the situation. In the present section we will describe in greater detail the kind of evidence that has encouraged a cognitive approach to the study of classical conditioning. Cognitive formulations have been much more important in the study of classical

conditioning than in the study of instrumental behavior.

S-R versus S-S learning

Originally, classical conditioning was viewed as a mechanism whereby organisms learned to make something like the unconditioned response to a new stimulus, the CS. This approach to classical conditioning focuses on the formation of new stimulus-response connections (connections between the CS and the UR) and therefore is called the **S-R learning** approach. The S-R learning approach states that the most important aspect of classical conditioning is the attachment of a new response to the CS, and *the effects that the CS has on the organism can be entirely explained by the responses that have been conditioned to it.* We did not emphasize the S-R approach in our discussion of classical conditioning in Chapters 4 and 5 because it is no longer the dominant view of classical conditioning. The S-R approach is based on the assumption that the unconditioned response (or some component of it) becomes conditioned to the CS during classical conditioning. As we noted in Chapter 5, such stimulus substitution does not occur in many classical-conditioning situations. The shift away from the S-R approach has also been encouraged by studies showing that classical conditioning is strongly influenced by the extent to which the CS is a good predictor of the forthcoming presentation of the US or its absence (see Chapters 4 and 5). These results, together with the type of evidence we will describe below, have encouraged viewing classical conditioning as a form of **S-S learning.**

The S-S learning approach assumes that during classical conditioning organisms do not learn to make a particular response to the CS. Rather, they learn *an association between two stimuli,* the CS and the US. In many cases this S-S association involves learning that the CS is a good signal for the forthcoming presentation of the US. However, S-S associations may be based on other types of relations between the CS and

US, such as their similarity (see Chapter 5). Nevertheless, according to this view, classical conditioning involves the learning of a relation between stimuli (S-S), not the learning of particular responses to stimuli (S-R). If subjects do not learn to make the conditioned response to the CS, how does the conditioned stimulus come to control their behavior? The S-S approach assumes that the conditioned response is not elicited directly by the CS. Instead, the CS is assumed to elicit or activate a representation ("mental image") of the US because of the S-S association, and the conditioned response occurs because of this representation of the US.

Simple demonstrations of classical conditioning do not help us decide between the S-R and S-S interpretations. Consider, for example, the simple acquisition of conditioned salivation. The sound of a bell is repeatedly paired with food, and the animal comes to salivate in response to the bell. This could occur either because a connection has been established between the bell and salivation (the S-R view) or because the bell has become associated with the food (the S-S view). To distinguish between S-S and S-R learning, more sophisticated approaches are required.

Evidence for S-S learning from conditioning with lights and tones

One strategy for obtaining evidence of S-S as opposed to S-R learning in classical conditioning has involved taking advantage of the fact that in rats visual and auditory conditioned stimuli come to elicit different types of responses after pairings with food. As we noted in Chapter 5, the predominant response to an auditory stimulus conditioned with food is a startlelike head-jerk movement. In contrast, the predominant response to a visual stimulus conditioned with food is standing by the food dish and sometimes rearing up on the hind legs during the CS. The S-R approach would interpret these results as showing that animals learn different things when a light is conditioned with

food and when a tone is. Different S-R connections are presumably established, resulting in the different types of responses to the conditioned stimuli. In contrast, the S-S approach assumes that the same CS-food association is learned when different types of stimuli are conditioned with food. However, it is acknowledged that this CS-food association may lead to different types of responses because of differences in the nature of the CSs (for example, Bindra, 1974). How might the S-S and S-R interpretations be experimentally distinguished in this case? One possibility is to look for evidence that the same kind of thing is learned regardless of whether a light or a tone is conditioned with food. Holland (1977) obtained evidence relevant to this issue using tone and light stimuli in blocking and second-order conditioning experiments.

In one experiment Holland (1977) evaluated whether a light-conditioned stimulus could block the conditioning of a tone and vice versa. You may recall that demonstration of the blocking of CS by a previously conditioned stimulus involves a three-stage experiment (see "The Blocking Effect," Chapter 5). In the first phase of blocking experiments, one CS (let us say stimulus X) is strongly conditioned by having it repeatedly paired with the US. During the second phase of the experiment, a novel stimulus (let us say A) is presented together with stimulus X during each conditioning trial. The subjects are then tested to see to what extent stimulus A became conditioned during its pairings with the US. The typical outcome is that the presence of stimulus X during phase II interferes with, or blocks, the conditioning of stimulus A.

The blocking effect may be explained by assuming that learning to stimulus A does not take place if what is to be learned is already elicited by some other stimulus in the situation (such as stimulus X). Holland (1977) tested whether animals learn the same thing when a light or a tone CS is paired with food by determining whether a tone CS would block the conditioning of a light CS and vice versa. Since a tone and a light CS elicit different responses when conditioned with food, the S-R approach predicts that neither of these CSs will block conditioning of the other. In contrast, blocking is predicted by the S-S approach because the same type of CS-food association is assumed to be established during pairings of a light and of a tone with food. The results were in line with the S-S approach. Stimulus X did not have to elicit the same response that was to be conditioned to the novel stimulus A for blocking to occur. A tone CS that was first conditioned with food to elicit a head-jerk movement successfully blocked the conditioning of standing by the food dish in response to a light CS. Similarly, a light CS that was first conditioned to elicit standing by the food dish blocked the conditioning of head-jerk movements to the tone CS.

The blocking procedure is one way to determine whether the same kind of thing is learned when a light or a tone is conditioned with food. Another strategy is to see whether food-conditioned light and tone CSs lead to similar or different outcomes when they are used in a second-order conditioning experiment. You may recall from Chapter 5 that in the second-order conditioning procedure, one stimulus, CS_1, is first conditioned with a US in the usual manner. CS_1 is then used to condition a new stimulus, CS_2. According to the S-R approach, the responses initially conditioned to CS_1 critically determine what is learned when CS_1 is used in second-order conditioning of the new stimulus, CS_2. CS_2 presumably becomes conditioned to elicit the same types of responses that are elicited by CS_1. In contrast, the S-S approach emphasizes the importance of the association formed between CS_1 and the US. Similar CS_1-US associations are expected to lead to similar results in second-order conditioning, regardless of the particular responses conditioned to CS_1.

Holland (1977) tested the above predictions by first conditioning either a light or a high-pitched tone with food as the unconditioned stimulus. As expected, different responses be-

came conditioned to the light and tone CS_1 stimuli. These primary conditioned stimuli were then used in second-order conditioning of a low-pitched tone (CS_2). The S-R approach predicts that different responses would be conditioned to the low-pitched tone (CS_2) because different responses were elicited by the light and high-pitched primary CSs. In contrast, the S-S approach predicts that the two CS_1 stimuli would condition the same type of response to CS_2 because the two CS_1 stimuli were associated with the same US (food). The results supported the S-S approach. Similar conditioned responses developed to the low-pitched tone regardless of whether the light or high-pitched tone was used as the CS_1 during second-order conditioning.

The US representation as a determinant of the conditioned response

Another experimental method for distinguishing S-S and S-R learning involves manipulating the subject's representation of the unconditioned stimulus. If the conditioned response occurs because the CS activates a representation of the US, then changes in the US representation should be accompanied by changes in the conditioned response. A great deal of evidence of this sort has been obtained. We will only touch on the highlights of these results here because we have already reviewed many of the important experiments in Chapter 5 (see "Modern Approaches to Stimulus Substitution"). The basic approach in these studies involves first conducting classical conditioning in the standard manner by pairing a CS with a US. The subject's reactions to the US are then altered in various ways. For example, if the US is a burst of loud noise, reactions to it may be reduced by habituating the subject to the loud noise. If the US is food, reactions to it can be reduced by diminishing the subject's level of hunger or by conditioning an aversion to the food with poisoning (for example, Holland & Rescorla, 1975a; Rescorla, 1973). These manipulations are designed to devalue or weaken the representation of the unconditioned stimulus. After this US devaluation, the animals are tested for their reaction to the CS that was conditioned in the first phase of the study. The typical finding is that a devaluation of the US representation diminishes the conditioned responses elicited by the CS.

Experiments in which the US representation is altered after the establishment of a conditioned stimulus provide strong evidence in favor of the S-S learning interpretation of classical conditioning. If classical conditioning involved learning to make a particular response to the CS (the S-R view), then manipulations of the unconditioned stimulus after the CS has been conditioned should not alter the extent to which the CS elicits the CR. That such manipulations in fact change responding to the CS indicates that the conditioned response is not elicited directly by the CS but occurs because of the US representation evoked by the CS.

We stated earlier that cognitive mechanisms are often invoked to explain behavior that cannot be explained entirely by the external stimuli present in the situation. This was the case for all the experiments described above. Let us first consider the blocking and second-order conditioning experiments with light and tone CSs. The results could not be predicted on the basis of the responses that were elicited by the light and tone conditioned stimuli. After pairings with food, a light CS blocked the conditioning of a tone (and vice versa), even though the two types of stimuli elicited very different types of responses. Furthermore, light and tone CSs produced the same kind of second-order conditioning even though each elicited a different pattern of conditioned responses. The results of experiments involving changes in the subject's representation of the unconditioned stimulus also cannot be explained by the external stimuli present in the situation. As we noted, devaluation of the unconditioned stimulus reduced the extent to which the CS elicited conditioned responses. This result was produced by

various manipulations of the subjects' reaction to the US. A food US, for instance, was devalued by satiating the subjects with food or pairing the food with poison. These manipulations never involved the conditioned stimulus. Furthermore, the devalued US was not actually present when the animal was tested for its response to the CS. Nothing about the CS was changed and no new stimuli were introduced during the test session. Therefore, the reduction in responding to the conditioned stimulus that was observed after US devaluation cannot be explained in terms of the stimuli present at the time the responses were measured. However, the results are consistent with the idea that animals form a representation of the US. The CS presumably activates this US representation, which is in turn responsible for the responses that occur.

Memory mechanisms in animal behavior

Memory is one of the most extensively investigated cognitive processes. Much of the research and theorizing dealing with memory has been concerned with the performance of human subjects. However, investigators of animal behavior have also become very much interested in the study of memory mechanisms during the past decade or so (for example, Honig & James, 1971; McGaugh & Herz, 1972; Medin, Roberts, & Davis, 1976; Spear, 1978; Spear & Miller, 1981). In the present section we will describe some of the prominent techniques used in the study of animal memory and also discuss a few of the major theoretical issues in the field.

The term **memory** is commonly used to refer to the ability to reproduce or recount information that was experienced at an earlier time. Thus, we are said to remember what happened in our childhood if we can tell stories of childhood experiences. We are said to remember a phone number if we can state it accurately, and we are said to remember someone's name if we call him or her by the correct name. Unfortunately, similar tests of memory with animals are usually impractical. We cannot ask an animal to tell us what it did last week. Instead, we have to use the animal's overt responses as a clue to its memory. If your cat wanders far from the house and finds its way back home, you might conclude that it remembered where you live. If your dog has grown fond of a particular person and eagerly greets him after a long separation, you might conclude that it remembered that person. These and similar cases illustrate that *the existence of memory in animals is identified by the fact that their current behavior can be predicted on the basis of some aspect of their earlier experiences.* Any time the animal's behavior is determined by past events, we can conclude that some type of memory mechanism is involved in the control of that behavior.

You may notice that our definition of *memory* is very similar to how we defined *learning.* In Chapter 1 we characterized learning as an enduring change in the mechanisms of behavior that results from prior exposure to environmental events. The major difference between the definitions of *memory* and *learning* is that *learning* refers to "enduring" effects of prior experience. In contrast, memory mechanisms do not preclude instances in which the control of behavior by past experiences is short-lasting. Things can be remembered for either short or long periods. We can say that something is remembered even if the memory lasts only briefly. All instances of learning involve memory. If the subject is incapable of remembering past events, past experiences cannot produce an enduring change in its behavior. However, not all instances of memory involve learning. Temporarily remembered experiences that influence an animal's actions involve memory but not learning.

Because the concepts of learning and memory are so similar, the concept of memory is superfluous in the interpretation of many learning experiments. Consider, for example, salivary conditioning to a tone. With repeated pairings of a tone with food, the dog comes to salivate in response to the tone. After the conditioned response has been well established, we may wait for a month before testing the animal again. When the subject is returned to the experimental situation, chances are that it will again salivate in response to the tone. We do not need the concept of memory to explain this outcome. It would be sufficient to conclude that the subject's performance of the conditioned response after a month's rest simply indicated that it had learned the response to the tone. However, one cannot do without the concept of memory in explaining the control of behavior by past experiences in situations in which learning is not involved. The concept of memory is indispensable in at least two types of situations. One involves instances in which past events have only a short-lasting effect on the organism's actions, thus precluding a learning interpretation. Memory mechanisms are also required to explain cases in which responses to past events are changed by procedures that do not produce learning in and of themselves. We will describe examples of both temporary memory effects and modifications of memory by procedures that do not involve learning. Finally, we will discuss some theoretical issues concerning the interrelation of learning and memory.

Short-term, or working, memory

As noted above, one aspect of behavior that involves memory and can be clearly distinguished from learning concerns short-lasting effects of past events. One of the earliest investigations of this phenomenon was carried out by Hunter (1913). He was interested in the ability of animals to retain a "mental" representation of a stimulus and tested rats, dogs, and raccoons in a simple memory task. The apparatus consisted of a start area from which the animals could enter any one of three compartments. One of the three compartments was illuminated by a light bulb and had a piece of food in it. The other two compartments were not illuminated or baited with food. After the subjects had learned to choose the illuminated compartment on each trial, Hunter made the task a bit more difficult. Now the light signaling food remained on for only a short time, and after the signal was turned off, the subject was detained in the start area before being allowed to choose among the three compartments. Therefore, the animal had to remember somehow which compartment had been illuminated in order to find the food. The longer subjects were delayed before being allowed to make a choice, the less likely they were to go to the correct compartment. The maximum delay rats could withstand was about 10 sec. The performance of dogs did not deteriorate until the delay interval was extended to more than 5 min, and raccoons performed well as long as the delay was no more than 25 sec. The species also differed in terms of what they did during the delay interval. Rats and dogs were observed to maintain a postural orientation toward the correct compartment during the delay interval. No such postural orientations were observed in the raccoons.

Since the raccoons did not maintain a postural orientation during the delay interval, explanation of their behavior requires the concept of some kind of memory mechanism. In order to respond accurately in the delay procedure, the animals could not use any stimuli present when they were allowed to choose among the three compartments. Rather, they had to remember which compartment had been illuminated at the start of the trial. The fact that performance quickly deteriorated as the delay interval was increased indicates that the animals could not remember the correct compartment very long. This experiment illustrates what is commonly called **short-term** or **working memory.** Short-term, or working, memory is a theoretical entity inferred from the behavior of the animals. We do not observe short-term memory directly. Rather, it is assumed to be involved in situations in which past experiences exert only a short-lasting influence over behavior. Short-

term memory is usually contrasted with **long-term memory.** Long-term memory is assumed to be involved when past experiences have an enduring effect on behavior. Because of its persistence, long-term memory invariably involves learning. Short-term memory does not. There are no set rules about how quickly a memory has to decay to be considered an example of short-term memory or how persistent it can be before it becomes an example of long-term memory. However, long-term memory is assumed to last at least several days. In contrast, short-term memory is usually lost within a few minutes, although, as we will see, there are examples of short-term memory that persist for several hours.

Since Hunter's research, increasingly sophisticated techniques have been developed for the study of short-term memory. We will describe two prominent contemporary procedures. One of these, the delayed-matching-to-sample procedure, can be adapted to the study of how animals remember any one of a variety of stimuli. The other technique has much more restricted applicability and is used primarily in the investigation of memory for spatial stimuli. However, it has also yielded some very interesting and significant results.

Delayed matching to sample.   The delayed-matching-to-sample procedure, one of the most versatile techniques for the study of short-term memory, represents a substantial refinement of the technique that Hunter originally used. As in Hunter's procedure, the subject is exposed to a cue indicating which is the correct response on that particular trial, and this stimulus is removed before the animal is permitted to perform the designated behavior. In the typical experiment with pigeons, for example, the experimental chamber contains three response keys arranged in a row, as in Figure 12.1. The point of the study is to see whether the pigeons can remember a sample stimulus long enough to pick it out when they are given a choice between the sample and some other stimulus. The center

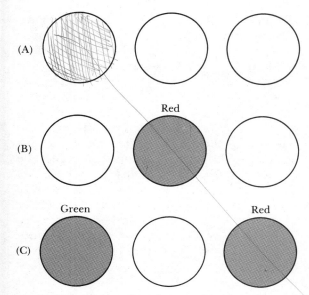

(A)

Red

(B)

Green   Red

(C)

Figure 12.1. Diagram of the delayed-matching-to-sample procedure for pigeons. The experimental chamber has three response keys arranged in a row (A). At the start of a trial, the sample stimulus (red) is presented on the center key (B). This stimulus is then removed, and after a delay two choice stimuli (red and green) are presented on the side keys (C). Pecks at the choice stimulus that matches the sample are reinforced.

key is used to present the sample stimulus, and the two side keys are later used to present the choice cues. The test stimuli might be illumination of the response keys from the rear with either a red or a green light. At the start of a trial, the center key is illuminated with a white light. After the pigeon pecks the white center key, the color of that key changes to one of the test stimuli—let us say, red. This is the sample for that trial. Usually several pecks to the sample stimulus are required, after which the sample is turned off and the two side keys are lit up. One of the side keys is illuminated with the sample for that trial (red), and the other key is illuminated with the alternate color (green). If the pigeon pecks at the side key that matches the sample (in this case the red key), the pigeon is reinforced. If it pecks the alternate color, no reward is provided. Thus, the reinforced re-

sponse is to "match" the sample. Which of the test stimuli serves as the sample is randomly varied from one trial to the next, and the matching stimulus is equally likely to be presented on the right or left key during the choice. Therefore, the pigeon can never predict which stimulus will be the sample on a given trial or where the matching stimulus will appear during the choice.

During the initial stages of matching-to-sample training, the sample stimulus is allowed to remain visible until the subject has made the correct choice. Thus, in our example, the red light on the center key would remain illuminated until the subject correctly pecked the red side key. Such a procedure is called **simultaneous matching to sample** and does not require memory processes because the cue for the correct response is visible when the response is made. Once subjects have mastered the simultaneous-matching procedure, the sample stimulus can be presented only briefly and removed before the choice stimuli are provided. Introduction of a delay between exposure to the sample stimulus and the availability of the choice cues changes the procedure to **delayed matching to sample.**

In most applications, as we mentioned, the matching stimulus is equally likely to appear on the left or the right choice key. Hence, subjects cannot make the correct choice by orienting to the right or left when the sample appears on the center key and holding this body posture until the choice stimuli are presented. Thus, in contrast to Hunter's procedure, simple postural orientations cannot be used to increase the likelihood of making the correct choice. Subjects are forced to use more complicated memory processes to obtain reinforcement in the delayed-matching procedure.

The delayed-matching-to-sample procedure has been extensively used in research with monkeys (D'Amato, 1973; Jarrard & Moise, 1971) and pigeons (Blough, 1959; Roberts & Grant, 1976). It has also been used with dolphins (Herman & Gordon, 1974), goldfish (Steinert, Fallon, & Wallace, 1976), and rats (Wallace, Stein- ert, Scobie, & Spear, 1980). Two aspects of the procedure appear to be critical in determining the accuracy of performance: the delay interval and the duration of exposure to the sample stimulus at the start of the trial. In one experiment, for example, Grant (1976) tested pigeons in the standard three-key apparatus after they had received extensive training on delayed matching to sample with visual stimuli. At the start of each trial, the center key was illuminated with a white light. When the subject pecked the center key, the sample color for that trial appeared briefly on the center key. The side keys were then illuminated, one with the matching color and the other with a different color. Two pairs of colors were used on alternate trials—red/green and blue/yellow. Before the side keys were illuminated, the sample stimulus remained on the center key for 1, 4, 8, or 14 sec. The choice keys were illuminated 0, 20, 40, or 60 sec after the sample stimulus was turned off on the center key. After the subject made its choice, all the keys were turned off for a 2-min intertrial interval.

The results of the experiment are summarized in Figure 12.2. If subjects pecked the choice keys randomly, they would be correct 50% of the time. Higher scores indicate that subjects responded on the basis of their memory for the sample stimulus. For all the sample durations evaluated, the accuracy of matching decreased as longer delays were introduced between exposure to the sample and opportunity to make the choice response. In fact, if the sample was presented for only 1 sec and the opportunity to make a choice was delayed 40 sec or more, the pigeons responded at a chance level. Performance improved if they were exposed to the sample for longer periods. When the sample was presented for 4, 8, or 14 sec, the subjects performed above chance levels even when the delay interval was as long as 60 sec. These results show that memory for the sample colors decreased as a function of the delay interval and

increased as a function of the duration of exposure to the sample.

Results like those shown in Figure 12.2 have encouraged a **trace decay** interpretation of short-term memory (Roberts & Grant, 1976). This hypothesis assumes that presentation of a stimulus produces changes in the nervous system that gradually decrease, or decay, after the stimulus has been removed. The initial strength of the stimulus trace is assumed to reflect the physical energy of the stimulus. Thus, longer or more intense stimuli are presumed to result in stronger stimulus traces. However, no matter what is the initial strength of the trace, it is assumed to decay at the same rate after the stimulus ends. The extent to which the memory of an event exerts control over the organism's actions depends on the strength of the stimulus trace at that moment. The stronger the trace, the stronger is the effect of the past stimulus on the subject's behavior. The trace-decay model predicts results of exactly the sort summarized in Figure 12.2. Increasing the delay interval in the matching-to-sample procedure reduces the accuracy of performance presumably because the trace of the sample stimulus is weaker after longer intervals. In contrast, increasing the duration of exposure to the sample improves performance presumably because longer exposures to the sample establish stronger stimulus traces.

The trace-decay hypothesis emphasizes the physical characteristics of the sample stimulus as the critical factor in short-term, or working, memory. The initial strength and decay characteristics of the stimulus trace are presumed to be directly related to the physical nature of the sample stimulus and the sensory neural processing that the stimulus activates. However, other types of research have shown that short-term memory does not depend entirely on the physical features of the event to be remembered. First, delayed-matching-to-sample performance improves with practice with the same types of sample stimuli. A dramatic example is

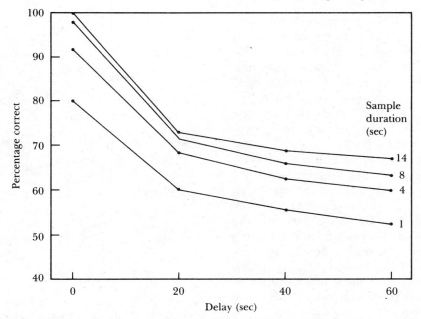

Figure 12.2. Percentage of correct responses in a delayed-matching-to-sample task as a function of duration of presentation of the sample stimulus (1–14 sec) and delay between the sample and the choice stimuli (0–60 sec). *(From Grant, 1976.)*

provided by the learning history of a monkey named Roscoe. After 4500 training trials, Roscoe could not perform above chance level if a 20-sec interval was introduced between the sample and choice stimuli. However, after 17,500 trials he correctly matched the sample stimulus nearly 80% of the time with a 2-min sample-to-choice delay interval, and after approximately 30,000 trials his performance was better than chance with a 9-min delay interval (D'Amato, 1973). Another important determinant of short-term memory is the extent to which the stimulus is surprising. Several lines of investigation have shown that surprising events are remembered better than expected events (Maki, 1979; Terry & Wagner, 1975). Finally, recent research suggests that memory processes can be brought under stimulus control. It appears possible to facilitate forgetting in a short-term memory task by presenting a forgetting cue that indicates subjects will not be tested for

their memory of the sample stimulus (Grant, 1981b; Maki & Hegvik, 1980; Rilling, Kendrick, & Stonebraker, 1981). These types of findings indicate that the control of behavior by short-term memory processes can be more complicated than the trace-decay hypothesis implies (see Grant, 1981a, for a detailed discussion).

Spatial memory in a radial maze. The delayed-matching-to-sample procedure has been adapted to investigate how animals remember a variety of stimuli, including visual shapes, numbers of responses performed, and the presence or absence of reward (for example, D'Amato, 1973; Maki, Moe, & Bierley, 1977). Another type of information that is important for animals to remember concerns the spatial configuration of their habitat. To be able to move about efficiently, animals have to remember how their environment is laid out—where open spaces, sheltered areas, or potential food sources are located. In many environments, once food has been eaten at one location, it is not available there again for some time until it is replenished. Therefore, in foraging, animals have to remember where they last found food and avoid that location for a while. Such foraging behavior has been nicely documented (Kamil, 1978) in a species of Hawaiian honeycreeper, the amakihi *(Loxops virens).* These birds feed on the nectar of mamane flowers. After feeding on a cluster of flowers, they avoid returning to the same flowers for about an hour. By delaying their return to clusters they have recently visited, the birds increase the chance that they will find nectar in the flowers they search. They appear to remember the spatial location of recently visited flower clusters.

Spatial memory—memory for locations in space—has been studied in the laboratory with the use of complex mazes (for example, Olton, 1979). In one investigation, for example, rats were tested in a maze similar to that shown in Figure 12.3 (Olton & Samuelson, 1976). The maze had eight arms radiating from a central choice area. A pellet of food was placed at the end of each arm. In each test, the rat was placed in the center of the maze and was free to enter each arm to obtain the food there. Once a food pellet had been consumed, that arm of the maze remained without food for the rest of the trial. How should the rat go about finding food in this situation? One possibility is to select randomly which alley to enter each time. Thus, the rat might enter an alley, eat the food there, return to the center area and then randomly select another arm of the maze to enter next, and so on. However, this would involve going down alleys from which the rat had already taken the food. A more efficient strategy would be to enter only those arms of the maze that the animal had not visited yet on that trial. This is in fact what most of the animals learned to do. Entering an arm that had not been visited previously (and therefore contained food) was considered to be a correct choice. The number of correct choices subjects made during the first

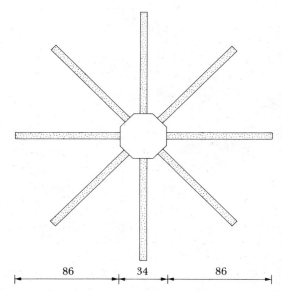

Figure 12.3. Top view of an eight-arm radial maze used in the study of spatial memory. Numbers indicate dimensions in centimeters. *(From Olton & Samuelson, 1976.)*

eight choices of successive tests is summarized in Figure 12.4. During the first five test runs after familiarization with the maze, the rats made a mean of nearly seven correct choices during each test. With continued practice, the mean number of correct choices was consistently above seven, indicating that the subjects rarely entered an arm they had previously chosen in that trial.

The fact that animals nearly always chose an arm from which they had not yet removed the food makes for efficient food gathering. However, this information is not enough to show that the animals were using some kind of spatial-memory mechanism. There are several ways in which they could have entered only previously unchosen arms without necessarily remembering the locations of all the arms they had already visited. For example, the rats might have been able to smell the food at the entrance to unvisited alleys. Another possibility is that the rats marked each arm they visited with something like a drop of urine and then just avoided

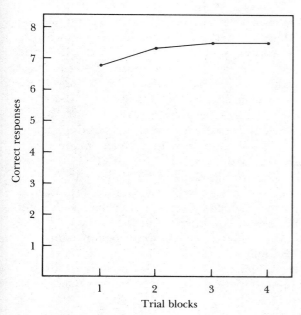

Figure 12.4. Mean number of correct responses rats made in their first eight choices during blocks of five test trials in the eight-arm radial maze. *(After Olton, 1978.)*

arms of the maze that had this odor marker. Alternatively, the animals might have learned a response chain of some sort, always selecting arms in a fixed sequence. For example, they might have learned to enter successive arms in a clockwise direction.

Numerous experiments have been performed to determine whether the performance of rats in a radial maze is in fact governed by spatial memory, and these studies have generally upheld the memory interpretation. One of these experiments was conducted to determine whether the rats were using the odor of food as a cue for entering an alley. The rats were allowed to remove food from six of the eight arms of the maze as usual. Before the subjects were permitted to make their remaining choices, those six arms were rebaited with food. If the rats were using the odor of food as a cue for entering an alley, replacing the food was expected to get them to reenter previously chosen alleys. However, this did not happen. Subjects did not return to previously chosen arms on

their next two choices even if the arms were rebaited, and after that they were no more likely to enter rebaited arms than arms that did not have food (Olton & Samuelson, 1976).

In another study the maze was doused with aftershave lotion to mask any odor trails the rats might have made as they walked through the maze (Olton & Samuelson, 1976). In a related study, the animals' sense of smell was surgically disrupted (Zoladek & Roberts, 1978). Neither of these manipulations decreased the animals' performance. In another type of procedure, animals were allowed to enter several alleys during a test session. They were then confined to the center of the maze before being allowed to enter the remaining arms. During the confinement period, some of the arms of the maze were interchanged, or the entire maze was rotated 45°. The partitions blocking the entrances to the alleys were then removed, and the animals were free to make additional choices. The point of interest was whether the rats would reenter previously chosen arms if these were now in new locations or whether they would avoid the previously chosen arms regardless of where these arms were. The results indicated that the rats responded on the basis of spatial location rather than on the basis of the odor or other characteristics of the maze arms (Olton, Collison, & Werz, 1977; Olton & Samuelson, 1976; see also Suzuki, Augerinos, & Black, 1980). Once subjects had removed food from an alley in a particular location, they avoided reentering that location even if a new maze arm was placed there. However, they did not avoid visiting old maze arms that were now in new locations.

The available evidence also suggests that rats in a radial-maze experiment do not learn specific response chains or sequences of maze arms to enter. For example, rats do not always make their selections in the same order. For purposes of illustration, the order of choices made by four rats during ten daily sessions of testing is shown in Table 12.1. Each arm of the maze was assigned a number (from 1 to 8), and each sequence of numbers in the "Order" columns indicates the sequence of alleys a subject entered. Each day the subjects were placed in the center of the maze and were left in the maze until they had obtained all eight food pellets or until 10 min elapsed, whichever occurred first. A careful study of Table 12.1 and similar data indicates that although there are some regularities in the choices, the subjects rarely chose alleys in a given sequence more than once or twice. Consider rat number 1. On the first day it started with alley 7, followed by alleys 6 and 5. This sequence (7-6-5) was repeated only once during the ten days of testing, on day 7. Further, on day 7 the sequence 7-6-5 was followed by alley 4, whereas on day 1, the sequence 7-6-5 was followed by alley 1. (For a further study of the role of response sequences, see Olton et al., 1977.)

The radial-maze performance of rats is rather remarkable. In an important test of the limits of spatial memory, Beatty and Shavalia (1980b) allowed rats to make four choices in the eight-arm radial maze in the usual manner. The subjects were then detained in their home cages for various periods up to 24 hours. After the delay interval, they were returned to the maze and allowed to make choices 5–8. An entry into an alley they had not previously chosen was considered a correct choice, and an entry into a previously used alley was considered an error. The percentage of correct choices made by the animals as a function of the delay interval is summarized in Figure 12.5. A delay interval of up to 4 hours imposed after the first four choices did not disrupt performance. Longer periods of confinement in the home cage produced progressively poorer performance. In fact, only one rat out of five showed significant retention of the first four choices after a 24-hour period. These data show that spatial

TABLE 12.1. *Order in which rats entered successive arms of an eight-arm maze*

Rat	Day	Order	Rat	Day	Order
1	1	76512678365824	3	1	7878351246
	2	71237463845		2	418514687356142
	3	75567823451		3	712856134
	4	67543218		4	14536827
	5	37812456		5	42537146217348
	6	5678134562		6	12437518425417836
	7	32187654		7	24682467351
	8	35781246		8	24782513476
	9	16373135675428		9	634671378245
	10	2187573456		10	31753885264
2	1	671348625	4	1	18431748751826
	2	783624715		2	32164871864325
	3	8573246851		3	45231786
	4	74568123		4	86431752
	5	687413245		5	48632175
	6	4632571478		6	32876541
	7	67824513		7	16572843
	8	68345712		8	53286417
	9	67814523		9	48762513
	10	72345186		10	65482173

Note. The numbers in the "Order" columns refer to arms 1–8 of the maze.

After Olton & Samuelson (1976).

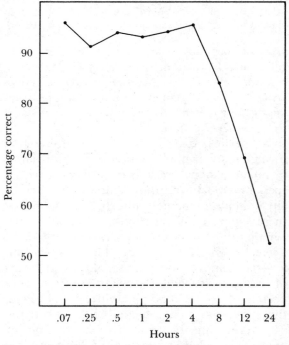

Figure 12.5. Percentage correct responses on choices 5–8 in an eight-arm radial maze. Between choices 4 and 5 the animals were returned to their home cages for varying intervals ranging from .07 to 24 hours. The dashed line indicates chance performance (41%). *(After Beatty & Shavalia, 1980b.)*

memory is not permanent. However, it lasts at least several hours. Other research has shown that spatial memory is also remarkably immune to disruption by other experiences during this period (Beatty & Shavalia, 1980a; Maki, Brokofsky, & Berg, 1979).

Disruption and facilitation of memory

Short-term memory is one way in which past events can control behavior in the absence of learning. The concept of memory is also necessary to explain instances in which the control of behavior by past experiences is either disrupted or facilitated by procedures that do not produce new learning in and of themselves. To explain such results, we assume that the subject's memory for the past experiences has been altered somehow. There are many ways that memories can be either disrupted or facilitated without producing new learning. You may, for example, tie a string around your finger to remind yourself to call someone. The string by itself does not tell you whom to call or what the person's phone number is. Rather, it facilitates your memory of a name and a phone number that you previously learned. In an analogous fashion, exposure to various experiences can either disrupt or facilitate the memory of animals without producing new learning. For example, certain stimuli experienced before or after a to-be-remembered event can disrupt memory for that event. Memory can also be disrupted by various neurophysiological treatments. Exposure to other types of stimuli can facilitate memory of past events without producing new learning. We will describe each of these types of modifications of memory.

Proactive and retroactive interference.
Perhaps the most common source of memory disruption is exposure to prominent stimuli either before or after the to-be-remembered event. Consider, for example, a cocktail party. If the only person there you do not know is your neighbor's brother, chances are you will not have much trouble remembering his name.

However, if you are introduced to a number of new people before and/or after you meet your neighbor's brother, you may find it much more difficult to remember his name. There are numerous well-documented and analyzed situations in which memory is disrupted by exposure to a prominent stimulus prior to the event to be remembered. Because in these cases the interfering stimulus occurs *before* the target event, the disruption of memory is called **proactive interference.** In other instances memory is disrupted by exposure to a prominent stimulus after the to-be-remembered event. Because in these situations the interfering stimulus occurs *after* the target event, the disruption of memory is called **retroactive interference.** The mechanisms of proactive and retroactive interference have been extensively investigated in human memory (Postman, 1971; Slamecka & Ceraso, 1960; Underwood, 1957). Proactive and retroactive interference have also been investigated in animals with tasks involving delayed matching to sample (for example, Grant, 1975; Grant & Roberts, 1973, 1976) and spatial memory (for example, Gordon, Brennan, & Schlesinger, 1976; Gordon & Feldman, 1978; Maki et al., 1979).

Proactive interference can be investigated in the delayed-matching-to-sample procedure by exposing subjects to an interfering stimulus just before presentation of the sample stimulus on each trial. In the standard matching-to-sample procedure, animals are given a sample (let us say S_1), followed by two choice stimuli (let us say S_1 and S_2), one of which (S_1) matches the sample. The subjects are reinforced only for responding to the matching stimulus. In one study of proactive interference with monkeys, illumination of stimulus panels with a red or a green light served as the S_1 and S_2 stimuli (Jarvik, Goldfarb, & Carley, 1969). The experimental chamber had three stimulus panels arranged in a row. The sample was always presented on the center panel. One second after presentation of the sample stimulus, the two side panels were illuminated with the choice stimuli. To investigate the effects of proactive interference, subjects were exposed to an interfering stimulus for 3 sec at various intervals ranging from 1 to 18 sec before presentation of the sample. The interfering cue was always the incorrect choice for that trial. If the sample on a given trial was the green color, the preceding interfering stimulus was exposure to the red color on the center key, and vice versa. Subjects also received control trials not preceded by exposure to an interfering stimulus.

The results are summarized in Figure 12.6. On control trials—that is, when no interfering cues were presented before exposure to the sample—the monkeys made the correct choice nearly 100% of the time. They responded less accurately when the sample stimulus was preceded by an interfering cue. Furthermore, greater disruptions of performance occurred when the interfering stimulus more closely preceded the sample stimulus. No proactive interference occurred if the interfering stimulus was presented more than 8 sec before the sample.

Retroactive interference can be investigated in the delayed-matching-to-sample procedure by introducing an interfering stimulus between exposure to the sample and presentation of the choice stimuli. If the delayed-matching-to-

sample task involves visual cues, memory for the sample is more likely to be disrupted by visual than by auditory cues presented during the delay interval (for example, Worsham & D'Amato, 1973). Perhaps the simplest way to present interfering visual stimuli is to turn on a light so that the animals can see various features of the experimental chamber. Several experiments have shown that illumination of the experimental chamber during the delay interval impairs memory for visual stimuli in a matching-to-sample task (for example, Grant & Roberts, 1976; Worsham & D'Amato, 1973). In one experiment, pigeons highly experienced in delayed matching to sample were tested with two visual cues as sample and choice stimuli (Roberts & Grant, 1978). The test cues, three vertical or horizontal white stripes on a black background, were projected on circular response keys in the usual 3-key experimental chamber. The choice stimuli were presented 0–12 sec after exposure to the sample, and the experimental chamber was either illuminated or dark during the delay period. The results are shown in Figure 12.7. Subjects correctly chose

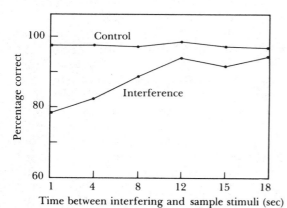

Figure 12.6. Percentage correct responses in a delayed-matching-to-sample task. On some trials an interfering stimulus was presented for 3 sec 1–18 sec before the sample stimulus. On control trials no interfering stimulus was presented. *(After Jarvik, Goldfarb, & Carley, 1969.)*

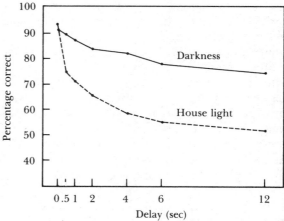

Figure 12.7. Percentage of correct responses in a delayed-matching-to-sample task as a function of increasing delays (0–12 sec) between the sample and the choice stimuli. On some trials the delay interval was spent in darkness. On other trials the house lights were on during the delay interval. *(From Roberts & Grant, 1978.)*

the matching stimulus more than 90% of the time when there was no delay after the sample stimulus. Accuracy decreased as the interval between the sample and choice cues was increased. However, this decrement in performance was much greater when the house lights were on during the delay interval. Thus, if subjects could see various features of the experimental chamber during the delay interval after exposure to the sample stimulus, their memory for the sample was impaired.

Two kinds of mechanisms may lead to proactive and retroactive interference in short-term memory tasks of the sort that we have described. One possibility is that the interfering stimulus elicits responses that compete with the correct choice response in the matching-to-sample task. Competing responses are especially likely to occur when the interfering stimulus is the incorrect choice on a particular matching trial, as in the proactive-interference experiment we described. Here the animals were first exposed to the incorrect stimulus on a particular trial; they were then presented with the sample stimulus, followed by a choice between the sample and the incorrect stimulus. It is quite possible that the subjects often made the incorrect choice because they remembered both the incorrect and the sample stimuli when they were required to choose between them.

Another possible source of interference effects is that the interfering stimulus disrupts memory for the sample on a given trial. In a matching task, the information about the sample stimulus on a given trial is presumably held in some type of short-term memory structure. We may assume that the short-term memory structure has a limited capacity. If the short-term memory structure becomes overloaded, some information will be lost. Interfering stimuli may disrupt performance by overloading the capacity of short-term memory and thereby leading to the loss of information about the sample stimulus. The example of retroactive interference we described was probably produced by this type of mechanism. The interfering

stimulus here was illumination of the experimental chamber rather than exposure to the incorrect choice. Illumination of the experimental chamber provides the subject with a large array of visual stimuli (all the colors, shades, and contours of various features of the environment). This richness of visual stimulation may exceed the capacity of short-term memory for visual cues and thereby lead to forgetting about the sample stimulus on that trial. Thus, two different mechanisms may be invoked to account for interference effects in animal short-term memory: response competition at testing and disruption of memory storage.

Neurophysiological sources of disruption of memory. People who suffer brain damage because of accident or disease may experience **amnesia** (loss of memory) as a result. For example, someone who receives a strong blow to the head may forget some things. However, information is not forgotten randomly. Rather, the person is most likely to forget events that took place just before the injury and remember earlier experiences. Thus, the person may forget how the injury occurred, where the accident took place, or who else was there. However, the person will still remember more long-term information, such as his or her name and address and the names and ages of brothers and sisters. The first extensive study of memory loss following brain injury in humans was conducted by Russell and Nathan (1946). In general, they found that there is a temporal gradient of memory loss going back in time from the point of injury. The closer an episode is to the time of injury, the more likely the person is to forget that information. This phenomenon is called **retrograde amnesia.**

Retrograde amnesia has been extensively investigated in animal laboratory experiments. The first studies of this sort used electroconvulsive shock (ECS) to induce amnesia. Electroconvulsive shock, introduced as a treatment for mental illness many years ago (Cerletti & Bini, 1938), is a brief electrical current passed through the brain between electrodes placed on each side of the head. It is not known exactly how ECS produces changes in disturbed patients. Investigators interested in memory started to study the effects of ECS because patients often report retrograde amnesia after ECS treatment (for example, Mayer-Gross, 1943).

In the first laboratory investigation of the amnesic effects of ECS, Duncan (1949) trained rats to perform an instrumental response to avoid aversive stimulation. One conditioning trial was conducted on each of 18 days of training. All subjects except those in the control group received an electroconvulsive shock after each training trial. For independent groups of animals, the ECS was delivered at various times ranging from 20 sec to 4 hours after the training trials. The question of interest was whether and to what extent ECS would disrupt learning of the task. The results are summarized in Figure 12.8. Subjects treated with electroconvulsive shock 1 hour or more after each training

trial performed as well on the avoidance task as the control group, which did not receive ECS. In contrast, the performance of the animals given ECS within 15 min of the training trials was disrupted. In fact, there was a gradient of interference: administration of ECS closer to the training trials resulted in poorer avoidance performance.

The pattern of results Duncan obtained is consistent with a retrograde-amnesia interpretation. Electroconvulsive shock is assumed to produce a gradient of amnesia such that events close to the ECS are not remembered as well as earlier events. Therefore, delivery of ECS shortly after a conditioning trial disrupts retention of that conditioning experience more than delivery of ECS at a longer period after the conditioning trial. It is possible to explain Duncan's results without the concept of amnesia (for example, Coons & Miller, 1960). However, numerous subsequent experiments have provided convincing evidence of experimentally induced retrograde amnesia in a wide variety of learning tasks (see McGaugh & Herz, 1972; Spear, 1978, for reviews). In addition, experiments have shown that retrograde amnesia can be produced by many treatments that affect the nervous system, including anesthesia (McGaugh & Petrinovich, 1965), temporary cooling of the body, or hypothermia (Riccio, Hodges, & Randall, 1968), and injection of drugs that inhibit protein synthesis (for example, Flexner, Flexner, & Stellar, 1963).

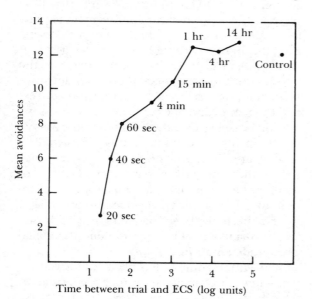

Figure 12.8. Mean number of avoidance responses for independent groups of rats given electroconvulsive shock (ECS) at various intervals after each avoidance trial. The control group was not given ECS. *(From Duncan, 1949.)*

Failure of consolidation versus failure of retrieval. Why do treatments such as ECS produce a graded loss of memory? One explanation of retrograde amnesia is the *memory-consolidation hypothesis* (see McGaugh & Herz, 1972). This hypothesis assumes that when an event is first experienced, it is in a short-term, or temporary, state. While in short-term memory, the information is vulnerable and can be lost because of presentation of interfering stimuli or other disruptive manipulations. However, if the proper conditions are met, the information gradually becomes consolidated into a relatively permanent form. **Memory consolidation** is assumed to be some kind of physiological process that gradually puts information into a long-term or permanent state. Neurophysiological disturbances such as electroconvulsive shock, anesthesia, body cooling, or inhibition of protein synthesis are assumed to interfere with the consolidation process and thereby disrupt the transfer of information to long-term memory. Because the memory is not consolidated, it is assumed to be lost to the subject forever. Disruption of consolidation produces amnesia only for information stored in short-term memory. Once information has been consolidated and transferred to long-term memory, it cannot be lost because of disruptions of consolidation. Amnesic agents presumably lead to loss of memory for recently experienced events but not earlier experiences because only the recent events are in short-term memory and thus are susceptible to disruptions of consolidation.

Disruptions of performance caused by amnesic agents can also be explained in a very different way. According to this alternative account, amnesia results not from loss of the memory but from inability to retrieve it from the long-term storage system (Lewis, 1979; Miller & Springer, 1973; Spear, 1973). This explanation is called the *retrieval-failure hypothesis*. **Retrieval** refers to the recovery of information from long-term memory. The consolidation and retrieval-failure hypotheses can be highlighted by an analogy. To make sure that you do not lose the information in your grandfather's will, you may decide to put the will into a safety-deposit box. Your grandfather dies some time later, and you find that you are unable to produce the will to see what is in it. Why might you be unable to gain access to the information in the will? One possibility is that the will never got put into the safety-deposit box. Perhaps you lost it on the way to the bank. This type of loss is analogous to a failure of consolidation. The alternative is that the will is in fact in the safety-deposit box but you lost the key to the box or do not remember where the box is located. This type of loss is analogous to a failure of retrieval.

A distinction between alternative theoretical explanations such as consolidation failure and retrieval failure is unimportant if we cannot find evidence to decide between the two. What kinds of experimental results would favor one explanation over the other? The consolidation-failure hypothesis states that once a memory is lost, it cannot be recovered. In contrast, the retrieval-failure view holds that amnesia can be reversed if the proper procedure is found to "remind" subjects of the memory. Thus, to decide between the alternatives, we have to find techniques that can reverse the effects of amnesic agents. Several such procedures have been developed, some of which are described in the next section. The fact that amnesia can be reversed makes it very difficult, if not impossible, to prove the memory-consolidation hypothesis. Given that many presumably "lost" memories have been reactivated by various reminder treatments, it is possible to argue that every loss of memory represents a failure of retrieval rather than a failure of consolidation (Miller & Springer, 1973). Even if one reminder treatment is found ineffective in reversing a case of amnesia, one can never be sure that some other reactivation treatment will not be discovered that will be successful. Thus, one can never be sure that a memory is irretrievable, as is required by the consolidation-failure position.

Facilitation of memory retrieval by "reminder" treatments. Numerous experiments have shown that memory for earlier conditioning trials can be reinstated by exposing subjects to some aspects of the stimuli that were present during the training trials (see reviews by Gordon, 1981; Spear, 1976, 1978). In early investigations of this phenomenon, exposure to the reinforcer independent of behavior was often used as the "reminder" treatment. In one experiment, for example, memory loss produced by electroconvulsive shock was counteracted by reexposing subjects to the aversive unconditioned stimulus before the retention test (Quartermain, McEwen, & Azmitia, 1970). However, experiments in which the "reminder" episode involves the unconditioned stimulus have been criticized on the grounds that such procedures permit new learning to occur (for example, Gold, Haycock, Macri, & McGaugh, 1973; Schneider, Tyler, & Jinich, 1974). If the "reminder" treatment produces new learning, the improved performance of subjects given this treatment may be due to the new learning rather than the reinstatement or retrieval of an old memory.

It is always important to consider the possibility of new learning when evaluating the effects of "reminder" treatments. However, many aspects of recent research on the facilitation of memory retrieval are difficult to explain using the new-learning hypothesis. Perhaps the most convincing way to make sure that a reminder treatment does not produce new learning is to use an extinction trial to reinstate the old memory. Improved performance after an extinction trial clearly cannot be attributed to new learning that is compatible with the old memory. Several experiments have demonstrated the facilitation of memory retrieval by an extinction trial. In one such study (Gordon & Mowrer, 1980), four groups of rats were conditioned to make a one-way avoidance response. The apparatus consisted of two compartments, one white and the other black. At the beginning of each trial, the subject was placed in the white compartment. Several seconds later the door to the black compartment was opened, simultaneously with the onset of a flashing light. If the subject crossed over to the black side within 5 sec, it avoided shock. If it did not cross in time, the shock was presented until the rat entered the black compartment. Subjects received repeated conditioning trials until they successfully avoided shock on three consecutive trials. Immediately after this training, two groups of rats were given electroconvulsive shock to induce amnesia.

Memory for the avoidance response was tested 72 hours after the end of training. During the retention test, subjects received five trials conducted the same way as during conditioning, except now the shock was never turned on no matter how long the rats took to cross to the black side. The most important aspect of the experiment involved giving an extinction ("reminder") trial to some of the subjects 15 min before the beginning of the retention test. This reminder treatment consisted in placing the rats in the white compartment of the apparatus for 60 sec with the flashing light turned on. No shock was delivered at the end of this stimulus exposure. Ordinarily we would expect such an extinction trial to decrease avoidance performance. The critical question was whether the extinction trial would also decrease the performance of rats made amnesic by electroconvulsive shock. If the extinction trial serves as a reminder treatment and facilitates retrieval of the memory of avoidance conditioning after ECS, it should facilitate avoidance behavior.

The results of the study are summarized in Figure 12.9. The data are presented in terms of the latency of avoidance responses during the retention test. Lower scores indicate that subjects performed the avoidance response faster. Higher scores indicate poorer performance. Let us first consider the two groups of rats that had not been given electroconvulsive shock. For these subjects, administration of the reminder extinction trial 15 min before the retention test resulted in slower avoidance behavior. This is the usual outcome of extinction. Let us next consider the results for subjects that had received ECS. Electroconvulsive shock in the absence of a reminder treatment (ECS, no reminder) resulted in the slowest avoidance responses. This outcome indicates that ECS produced amnesia for the prior avoidance training. However, if ECS-treated subjects were also given the extinction reminder trial before the retention test, their performance was much improved. In fact, the ECS rats given the re-

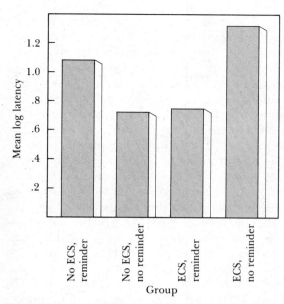

Figure 12.9. Latency of the avoidance response during a retention test for four groups of rats. Two of the groups were not given electroconvulsive shock (ECS) after training and were tested either after a reminder extinction trial or without the reminder trial. The other two groups were treated with ECS after training and were also tested either after a reminder extinction trial or without the reminder trial. *(After Gordon & Mowrer, 1980.)*

minder treatment responded as fast as subjects that had not received either ECS or the extinction trial. These results suggest that the reminder treatment fully restored the memory of the prior avoidance training. Thus, the amnesic effects of ECS were eliminated by exposing the subjects to the extinction trial. Since the extinction trial produced a decrement in performance in the absence of ECS, these results cannot be explained in terms of any new learning produced by the reminder treatment.

Much has been learned about the processes involved in facilitation of memory retrieval by reminder treatments (see Gordon, 1981; Spear, 1976, 1978). In addition to exposure to the reinforcer alone or the conditioned stimuli alone (an extinction trial), various reminder procedures have been found to facilitate memory

retrieval. Other effective reminder treatments have included, for example, exposure to the background stimuli of the experimental room (for example, Deweer, Sara, & Hars, 1980) and exposure to the nonreinforced stimulus in a discrimination procedure (for example, Campbell & Randall, 1976). Another very important aspect of the facilitation of memory retrieval is that memories retrieved because of a reminder treatment are also susceptible to disruption by amnesia-producing agents such as electroconvulsive shock or body cooling. Thus, if a reminder of a conditioning trial is followed by ECS or hypothermia, subjects will forget the original conditioning trial (Mactutus, Riccio, & Ferek, 1979; Misanin, Miller, & Lewis, 1968). Finally, reminder treatments can be used to reverse various types of memory loss in addition to memory loss due to administration of amnesia-producing agents like ECS. Reminder treatments, for example, can facilitate memory retrieval from short-term memory (Feldman & Gordon, 1979). They can also be used to remind older animals of early-life experiences that are often rapidly forgotten (for example, Campbell & Randall, 1976; Haroutunian & Riccio, 1979; Rovee-Collier, Sullivan, Enright, Lucas, & Fagen, 1980).

Interrelations of learning and memory

So far we have focused on various behavioral phenomena that involve manipulations of memory rather than learning. However, as we noted earlier, memory is obviously involved in learning. If organisms were incapable of remembering past events, learning could not take place. Acknowledging that memory and learning are interrelated, however, is not enough to tell us precisely what their relations are. Advances in our knowledge of memory mechanisms in animals have been accompanied by increased interest in integrating this information with what we know about conditioning and habituation. One of the most systematic efforts of this type has been pursued by Allan Wagner and his associates and has resulted in a theoretical model of memory, conditioning, and habituation known as *rehearsal theory* (Wagner, 1976, 1978, 1979; see also Wagner, 1981, for an elaboration and greater specification of the concepts in the form of a detailed mathematical model).

Rehearsal theory accepts the common assumption that there are two types of memory, long-term and short-term. Short-term memory (abbreviated STM) is assumed to have a limited capacity, so that presentation of a new stimulus may interfere with the processing of other events in STM. In contrast, the capacity of long-term memory is assumed to be much larger and is never exceeded in the usual experiment. All stimuli the subject is exposed to are first assumed to enter short-term memory. From here the information may simply be lost with the passage of time, or if a stimulus becomes associated with another stimulus, the information learned will be stored in long-term memory. The extent to which information in short-term memory influences the subject's behavior or leads to learning is assumed to depend on the extent to which the information is "rehearsed." **Rehearsal** may be thought of as a means of maintaining the memory in an active state. The more vigorously a stimulus is rehearsed, the more likely it is to influence the subject's immediate behavior (elicit some response). Rehearsal is also important in conditioning and the transfer of information to long-term memory. It is assumed that two stimuli (a CS and a US, for example) will become associated with each other to the extent that they are simultaneously rehearsed in short-term memory. Once the association between the CS and the US has been established, presentation of the CS will result in retrieval of the memory of the US from long-term to short-term memory. Thus, the subject becomes "reminded" of the US when it experiences the CS after conditioning has taken place.

The concept of rehearsal has a critical role in the theory. Another important concept is **priming.** A stimulus is said to be primed in short-term memory if it is already being rehearsed. There are two ways a stimulus can come to be rehearsed in STM. First, it may be rehearsed because it was recently presented. This type of priming is called **self-generated priming:** the stimulus is primed by a prior presentation of itself. The second way a stimulus can come to be primed in STM is for the stimulus to be retrieved from long-term memory by an associated stimulus (such as a CS). For example, a US can become primed in STM by the prior presentation of a CS that was associated with the US. This type of priming is called **retrieval-generated priming.** This technical language may seem a bit burdensome. However, the ideas involved are not very obscure. If you are actively thinking of a stimulus, it is said to be primed. You can be thinking of a stimulus because it was recently presented (self-generated priming) or because you were exposed to another event that reminded you of the stimulus (retrieval-generated priming).

At this point we are ready to consider the most important aspect of rehearsal theory—the relation between priming and rehearsal. The critical assumption of the theory (the feature that leads to most of its interesting predictions) is that *priming of a stimulus in STM interferes with rehearsal of another presentation of the same stimulus.* Thus, an event will not receive much rehearsal if the same stimulus was presented in the recent past (self-generated priming) or if an associated stimulus was presented in the recent past (retrieval-generated priming). The assumption that priming blocks rehearsal has important implications for both the responses elicited by a stimulus and the new learning in which a stimulus may participate. Recall that the extent to which a stimulus influences the subject's behavior or leads to new learning depends on the extent to which the stimulus is rehearsed. Because priming disrupts rehearsal, the priming of a stimulus in STM reduces the extent to which that stimulus will elicit responses or will be involved in new learning. These implications of rehearsal theory are compatible with many findings in habituation and conditioning. We will describe some of the more important results below.

Priming and habituation phenomena. As we noted in Chapter 3, repeated presentations of a stimulus often result in a reduction of the subject's response to the stimulus. There are two types of habituation effects. One is a short-term decrement in reactivity to a stimulus from which the subject recovers spontaneously if it is not exposed to the stimulus for some time. The second type of habituation is much more long-lasting and does not dissipate with a period of rest. Both these phenomena are consistent with rehearsal theory. The temporary loss of responsiveness to a stimulus may be explained in terms of self-generated priming (for example, Whitlow, 1975). Each presentation of a stimulus primes that stimulus in STM for a limited period. If the event is repeated while the subject is still rehearsing the previous stimulus presentation, the subject will not rehearse the new occurrence of the stimulus and therefore will not react to it. This decrement in reactivity will dissipate with time as the subject finishes rehearsing earlier stimulus presentations. Thus, response decrements due to self-generated priming will show spontaneous recovery.

Long-lasting habituation effects are explained in terms of retrieval-generated priming. The idea is that during repeated presentations of a test stimulus in a particular situation, an association is established between background cues of the situation and the test stimulus. Because of this association, the subject is "reminded" of the test stimulus whenever it is in the experimental situation. Thus, the test stimulus is primed by way of a retrieval-generated priming process. This retrieval-generated priming reduces the extent to which the subject will rehearse presentations of the test stimulus and therefore reduces the extent to which the subject will react to them. An interesting implication of this interpretation is that the decrement in responsiveness should be reversed by extinguishing the association between the background cues of the experimental situation and the test stimulus. This can be done by simply leaving the subject in the experimental situation for a long time without presentations of the test stimulus. After such an extinction experience, the background cues of the situation should no longer "remind" the subject of the test stimulus and therefore should no longer produce retrieval-generated priming. In confirmation of this predicted outcome, Whitlow and Pfautz (reported in Wagner, 1976) found that a rest period spent in the experimental chamber without stimulus presentations resulted in recovery from long-term habituation.

Priming and classical conditioning. The assumption that priming interferes with the degree of rehearsal a stimulus ordinarily elicits also has interesting implications for classical conditioning. Rehearsal theory assumes that an association will be established between the CS and the US to the extent that the two stimuli are simultaneously rehearsed in STM. This simultaneous rehearsal can be disrupted by the priming of either the CS or the US in STM before the conditioning trial. One way to accomplish this is to present either the CS or the US by itself shortly before the conditioning trial. Such a CS or US preexposure episode would produce self-generated priming of the CS or US, respectively, and should interfere with establishment of the CS-US association. Consistent with this prediction, several investigations have shown that presentation of the CS or the US by itself shortly before a conditioning trial interferes with conditioning (for example, Best & Gemberling, 1977; Domjan & Best, 1977; Terry, 1976).

Another way to disrupt conditioning by priming of either the CS or the US before the conditioning trial involves retrieval-generated priming. Retrieval-generated priming of the US can be accomplished by presenting a stimulus that was previously associated with the US. Thus, exposure to a previously conditioned stimulus should block the formation of an association between a new CS and the US. As we discussed in Chapter 5, this outcome, known as the blocking effect, has been demonstrated in many conditioning experiments. Retrieval-generated priming of the CS can be accomplished through the mechanisms we discussed above in connection with long-term habituation effects. Repeated presentations of the CS (without the US) in an experimental situation should establish an association between the CS and the background stimuli of the situation. These background cues will then prime the memory of the CS in STM, and this will interfere with establishment of a new association between the CS and a US. Evidence in support of this prediction has been obtained by Wagner, Pfautz, and Donegan (reported in Wagner, 1979) in both rabbit eyelid conditioning and fear conditioning in rats.

Final note. We have presented rehearsal theory as an example of the kind of integration that should be possible between the mechanisms of learning and the mechanisms of memory. Rehearsal theory is not the final word on how this integration will take place. The theory is deficient in that it fails to make quantitative predictions and fails to address certain important phenomena of conditioning, such as conditioned inhibition. Some of these shortcomings have been remedied in a new theory of memory and learning proposed by Wagner (1981), called the SOP model (for Standard Operating Procedures of memory). The model has stimulated some important new research (for example, Donegan & Wagner, 1981) and is applicable to a much broader range of conditioning phenomena than rehearsal theory (Mazur & Wagner, 1981). It will be exciting to see how future research will shape our understanding of the interrelations of learning and memory mechanisms.

Complex cognitive processes in animals

In the present section we will consider three important complex cognitive skills that are clearly present in human beings—serial-pattern learning, concept formation, and language use. Animal research on these topics is in its formative stages. Some provocative results have been obtained in each area. However, in some cases the interpretation of the results is in serious dispute, and in all three cases we are very far from a complete understanding of the mechanisms responsible for the results. Nevertheless, these areas of research are significant because they present new challenges for the experimental analysis of animal learning and behavior.

Serial-pattern learning

Stimuli in the environment rarely occur randomly and independently of other events. Rather, many aspects of the environment involve orderly patterns of stimulation. Behavior in response to serial patterns of stimuli has been extensively investigated in humans (for example, Jones, 1974; Restle & Brown, 1970; Simon & Kotovksy, 1963). Consider, for example, what you would do if you were asked to memorize the following list of numbers: 1234234534564567. You could learn the numbers by memorizing which number was in each of the 16 positions of the list. If you knew that 1 was in the first position, 2 in the second and fifth positions, 3 in the third, sixth, and ninth positions, and so on, you could recall the numbers in the correct order. However, this would be the hard way. A much simpler strategy would be to look for a pattern to the numbers. If you could figure out the pattern, you would have a rule that you could use to generate the sequence of numbers. The numbers listed above were generated by a relatively simple rule, which might be stated as follows: start counting with the number 1, but every four numbers subtract 2. Memorizing this rule is much easier than learning what number is located in each of the 16 positions of the list.

Experiments on serial-pattern learning in rats.

Abstracting a rule from a sequence of stimuli involves responding to the pattern of the stimuli. It is clear that people respond on the basis of the patterns inherent in the stimuli they experience. Do animals also learn about the serial patterns of stimuli? This question was put to laboratory rats by Stewart Hulse and his colleagues (Hulse, 1978; Hulse & Campbell, 1975; Hulse & Dorsky, 1977, 1979).

An experimental analysis of how animals respond to serial patterns of stimuli first requires selecting effective stimuli. To start such a research project, one would want to use stimuli of some biological significance to the subjects. Hulse and his students chose to use different numbers of food pellets as the stimuli. Food-deprived subjects were tested in a runway and received different numbers of food pellets in the goal box at the end of each run. In one experiment, the goal box contained either 14, 7, 3, 1, or 0 food pellets. Subjects were given sets of five runs in the runway. In each series of five runs, one group of subjects received 14 food pellets on the first run, 7 pellets on the second, then 3, then 1, and finally 0. Thus, these subjects received less food on a given run than they got on the preceding run. This sequence of stimuli (14-7-3-1-0) is called a **monotonic sequence**. A simple rule ("less than the preceding") can be used to generate the list. The second group of rats were exposed to the same stimuli. However, for them the sequence of stimuli could not be generated by a simple rule. In this case 14 pellets were given on the first run, 1 pellet on the second, 3 on the next, 7 on the next, and 0 on the fifth run. Thus, the sequence was 14-1-3-7-0. This is a **non-monotonic sequence** because a simple rule ("less than the preceding" or "more than the preceding") cannot be used to generate the entire list of stimuli.

The experiments measured how fast the rats ran down the alley on the five runs of a series. In both the monotonic (14-7-3-1-0) and the nonmonotonic (14-1-3-7-0) sequences, the first run was rewarded with 14 pellets. Therefore, we would expect both groups to run rapidly on the first run. Both sequences also involved 0 pellets on the fifth run. Therefore, as the subjects learned what the reward sequence was, we would expect that they would slow down as they traversed the alley on the fifth run. The critical prediction in the experiment concerned which group would run slower on the fifth run. The monotonic sequence (14-7-3-1-0) has a much simpler pattern than the nonmonotonic sequence (14-1-3-7-0). Therefore, if subjects were responding on the basis of the pattern of food-pellet quantities, we would expect that the rats given the monotonic sequence would learn to slow down on the fifth run after fewer repetitions of the series of five than the rats given the nonmonotonic sequence. We might also expect that subjects given the monotonic sequence would run slower on the fifth run than those given the nonmonotonic sequence.

The outcome of the experiment was as predicted by the serial-learning hypothesis. Figure 12.10 shows how long the subjects took to go down the alley on each of the five runs of a sequence at the end of the experiment. Both groups took much longer to run down the alley on the nonreinforced (fifth) run of a sequence than on the earlier runs. Other aspects of the results indicate that subjects exposed to the monotonic sequence (14-7-3-1-0) learned to take longer on the fifth run after less training than subjects exposed to the nonmonotonic sequence (14-1-3-7-0). In addition, as Figure 12.10 shows, subjects in the monotonic group took longer to go down the alley on the fifth run than subjects in the nonmonotonic group.

The two sequences used in the preceding experiment (14-7-3-1-0 and 14-1-3-7-0) are very

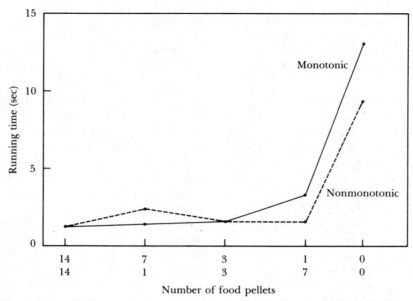

Figure 12.10. Asymptotic running times on five successive runs reinforced by different numbers of food pellets. One group of rats received a monotonic, decreasing series of food quantities (14-7-3-1-0 pellets). The other group received a nonmonotonic series of food quantities (14-1-3-7-0 pellets). *(From Hulse, 1978.)*

different. One is strongly monotonic, and the other has a much more complicated pattern. What would happen if animals were tested with two reward sequences that were much more similar? Consider, for example, the sequences 14-7-3-1-0 and 14-5-5-1-0. Both involve decreasing numbers of food pellets for successive runs in a series of five runs. Thus, both may be considered monotonic. However, in the second sequence (14-5-5-1-0) there is a temporary interruption of the decreasing pattern: both the second and third runs are reinforced with 5 pellets. Therefore, the second sequence may be described as weakly monotonic. The first sequence (14-7-3-1-0) is strongly monotonic because there is no interruption of the rule "less than the preceding." One may assume that a strong monotonic pattern is easier to learn than a weak monotonic pattern. Therefore, if rats respond on the basis of the pattern of reinforcement, we may expect appropriate performance in subjects exposed to the strong

monotonic pattern than in subjects exposed to the weak monotonic pattern.

Figure 12.11 summarizes the results of an experiment that compared running times in the runway for animals reinforced with the strong and weak monotonic patterns described above. As in the preceding experiment, subjects took very little time to go through the alley on reinforced runs. Both groups took significantly longer to get to the end of the alley on the fifth (nonreinforced) run of each series. However, the animals exposed to the strong monotonic sequence (14-7-3-1-0) ran much slower on the nonreinforced run than the animals exposed to the weak monotonic sequence (14-5-5-1-0). Thus, this experiment provides further evidence consistent with the idea that animals respond on the basis of the pattern that exists in a series of pellet-quantity stimuli.

Alternatives to serial-pattern learning. The types of experiments we have described

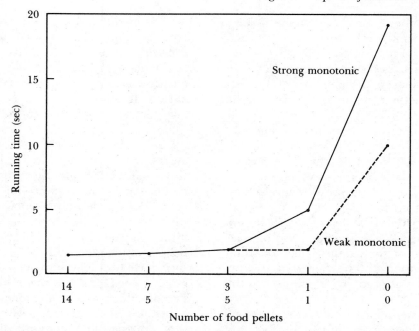

Figure 12.11. Asymptotic running times on five successive runs reinforced by different numbers of food pellets. One group of rats received a strong monotonic series of food quantities (14-7-3-1-0 pellets). The other group received a weak monotonic series (14-5-5-1-0 pellets). *(From Hulse, 1978.)*

can also be analyzed using theoretical concepts that do not assume pattern learning (see Hulse & Dorsky, 1977, 1979, for detailed discussions of this issue). The most prominent alternative view is the sequential theory proposed by Capaldi (for example, 1967, 1971). We discussed this theory in Chapter 7 as it applies to instrumental behavior during extinction. The theory assumes that on any given run, subjects can remember the reward outcome of the preceding run. Whether this memory stimulates (or inhibits) the instrumental response depends on whether the response is reinforced (or not reinforced) in the presence of the memory. Consider the sequence 14-7-3-1-0. In this sequence the subjects are reinforced for responding (on the second run) when they remember receiving 14 pellets on the preceding run (S^{14}). They are also reinforced for responding (on the third and fourth runs) when they remember receiving 7 and 3 pellets on the preceding runs (S^7 and S^3),

respectively. Thus, the memories S^{14}, S^7, and S^3 become positive discriminative stimuli (S+s) for the instrumental response. In contrast to the first four runs, when subjects are reinforced, they are not reinforced on the fifth run, after receiving a 1-pellet reward on the fourth run. Therefore, the memory of receiving 1 pellet on the preceding trial (S^1) becomes a negative discriminative stimulus (S−) for the instrumental response. According to this analysis, animals are slow to respond on the fifth run because the memory of 1 pellet on the preceding trial acts as an S−. This general line of reasoning predicts that the more distinctive the S+ memory is from the S− memories, the faster the animals will learn to slow down on nonreinforced trials, and the slower they will run on such trials.

As Capaldi and his associates have noted (see Capaldi & Molina, 1979), an analysis in terms of the discriminative-stimulus properties of the memory for prior reinforcements does not readily predict the results summarized above. Consider, for example, the difference between the strong (14-7-5-3-1-0) and weak (14-5-5-1-0) monotonic sequences shown in Figure 12.11. In both these sequences, the memory of 1 pellet (S^1) is a negative discriminative stimulus. In the strong sequence (14-7-5-3-1-0), the most similar positive discriminative stimulus is the memory of 3 pellets (S^3). In contrast, in the weak monotonic sequence (14-5-5-1-0), the most similar positive discriminative stimulus is the memory of 5 pellets (S^5). More stimulus generalization should occur from S^3 to S^1 than from S^5 to S^1. Therefore, S^1 should be less effective in inhibiting running in the strong monotonic sequence (14-7-3-1-0) than in the weak monotonic (14-5-5-1-0) sequence. The fact that the opposite outcome was observed is contrary to this prediction.

The sequential-memory analysis does not provide a satisfactory account of the types of results presented in Figure 12.11. However, this does not mean that the discriminability of memories on reinforced and nonreinforced trials does not control behavior when a sequential pattern of reinforcements is used. Capaldi and Molina (1979) have shown that with certain reward sequences the discriminability of the memories is more important in predicting behavior than the structural pattern of the sequence (whether it is monotonic or nonmonotonic, for example). Thus, behavior appears to be governed by both the structural pattern of the sequence of rewards and the discriminability of memories on reinforced and nonreinforced trials. Future research will, we hope, specify the circumstances in which each of these mechanisms is activated. (For a further discussion of these issues, see Capaldi, Verry, & Davidson, 1980; Hulse, 1980.)

Concept formation in animals

Organisms experience a great variety of stimuli during their lifetime. However, as we have seen, they often do not respond to these stimuli as independent and isolated events. We discussed one type of perceptual organization in the preceding section. Animals may (and humans in fact do) respond to a series of stimuli on the basis of the structural pattern of the series. Reactions to stimuli can also be organized by classes, or categories, that an individual stimulus may represent. Consider, for example, seeing a chair. You may note some of its specific features, such as its color, shape, height, firmness, and materials. However, you will also note that it is an instance of the category "chair." We can all agree on what things are chairs and what things are not. Specifying the critical features that constitute the concept "chair" is much more difficult. Many chairs are brown, have four legs, have a seat at about knee level, are hard, and are made of wood. However, something can be a chair without having any of these characteristics. Although it is not well understood how human beings form concepts, there is no doubt that concepts are very important in human behavior. We have concepts of physical entities, such as chairs, houses, trees, water, cats, and dogs. We also have concepts of events, such as a thunderstorm or a fight, and abstract concepts, such as loyalty, fairness, and intelligence. One reason concepts are very important in human behavior is that they form the building blocks of language. Words, in large measure, are labels for concepts.

Because complex concepts are critical to language, the investigation of concept formation in animals has been an integral part of efforts to teach linguistic skills to animals (for example, D. Premack, 1976). Much of this research has been conducted with chimpanzees. There is no doubt that chimpanzees are capable of learning complex concepts. However, chimpanzees have a much more developed nervous system than most animals. Therefore, one may well wonder whether a lower organism such as the pigeon is also capable of responding on the basis of a concept. There have been numerous investigations of this possibility (for example, Herrnstein & Loveland, 1964; Lubow, 1974;

Malott & Siddall, 1972; Siegel & Honig, 1970; Zentall & Hogan, 1974).

One of the most thorough analyses of concept formation in the pigeon was carried out by Herrnstein, Loveland, and Cable (1976). They investigated pigeons' ability to respond to instances of three concepts—tree, water, and a particular person—on the basis of two-dimensional pictures illustrating these concepts. Their method basically involved discrimination training. In the "tree" experiment, for example, color slides of various scenes were projected on the wall of the experimental chamber near a response key. If the scene contained a tree or some part of a tree, the pigeons were reinforced with food for pecking the response key. If the picture did not contain a tree or any part of one, pecking was not reinforced. Each experimental session consisted of 80 slide presentations, about 40 of which included a tree. During training the stimuli for any given day were randomly selected from 500–700 pictures depicting various scenes from all four seasons of the year in New England. The reinforced stimuli included trees (or parts of trees) of all descriptions. However, the trees were not necessarily the main point of interest in the pictures. Some slides showed a tree far away, others had trees in the foreground, and still others showed trees that were partly obstructed so that only some of the branches were visible, for example.

During training the same photographs were occasionally used more than once. Subjects soon learned the requirements of the task and pecked the response key at a much higher rate in the presence of pictures containing a tree. However, this discrimination could have been specific to the training stimuli. That is, the pigeons may have learned to peck in the presence of certain pictures and not peck when other scenes appeared. To evaluate this possibility, the animals were tested at the end of the experiment with pictures they had never seen before. The pigeons performed nearly as accurately on the new pictures as on the pictures used during the initial training. Much higher rates of pecking occurred in the presence of new slides that contained a tree (or a part of one) than in the presence of new slides that did not contain trees. Similar results were obtained in experiments involving the presence or absence of water (lakes, ocean, puddles, and so on) or the presence or absence of a particular person (in various types of clothing, in various situations, doing various things).

Although the pigeons clearly learned the relevant discrimination in each experiment, precisely what was responsible for their correct behavior is not easy to specify. There are two possible approaches to this issue. A noncognitive analysis would assume that all the reinforced stimuli had certain stimulus characteristics in common and that the instrumental response became conditioned to these common features. Presumably, the subjects responded appropriately to new pictures because the correct new pictures also contained the relevant stimulus features. Herrnstein et al. (1976) reject this analysis on the grounds that it is difficult to see what the common features of the correct stimuli might have been. Many of the trees, for example, had green coloration and were leafy, vertical, woody, and branching. However, the pigeons also responded to pictures of trees that did not have these characteristics. In addition, they failed to respond to pictures that did not have a tree but had some green, leafy, vertical, woody, and branching components. The problem of identifying a tree in terms of critical stimulus features is similar to the problem of specifying the concept "chair" in this way. It is difficult to pinpoint or abstract the critical stimulus features or combinations of features.

Assuming that the pigeons did not respond on the basis of some common stimulus features of trees, how did they correctly identify trees in pictures they had never seen before? Herrnstein et al. (1976) suggest that animals have an innate predisposition to form concepts of certain things. However, the precise form of the concept is shaped by the stimuli to which the subjects are exposed. According to this view, "Pigeons tend innately to infer a tree category from instances of trees, a familiar-person category from varying instances, and so on, more or less as we do ourselves. The properties of the inferred class arise from the joint constraints imposed by the stimuli and by innate factors" (Herrnstein et al., 1976, p. 301). This is a provocative proposal for how animals acquire concepts. However, assuming that the concept of a tree, for example, is not derived entirely from the presented pictures but is in part innate does not account for how the pigeons identified a given picture as an instance of the concept. Since only visual cues were available to them, one must assume that they used some aspects of the visual stimuli to make the decision. Thus, it seems that a complete analysis of this type of behavior still has to come to grips with the problem of specifying what stimulus features allow pigeons (and people) to identify a particular tree as illustrative of the concept of a tree. It will be interesting to see how this theoretical problem is resolved.

Teaching language to chimpanzees

Perhaps the most complex cognitive skill is the use of language. In fact, many have assumed that langauge use is so complex and specialized that it exists only in human beings. According to this view, the ability to engage in language depends on certain innate processes that have evolved only in our own species (for example, Chomsky, 1972; Lennenberg, 1967). In contrast, others have proposed that human beings engage in language because they are especially intelligent and because they have had the necessary training—not because they are the only organisms with the required genetic background. This second view suggests that nonhuman animals may also acquire language, provided that they are sufficiently intelligent and receive the proper training. Encouraged by this possibility, a number of people have tried to

teach language skills to animals. If this effort were successful, it would end, once and for all, debates about the uniqueness of human beings in the acquisition of language. If we could teach language to animals, we would also be able to communicate with them and thereby gain unique insights into their lives. Talking to an animal would be something like talking to someone from outer space. We might see for the first time how the world looks through the experiences of nonhuman individuals. We might also gain unique insights into ourselves. We would see for the first time how our own actions are viewed by an organism not biased by human experiences and ethnocentricity.

Most efforts to teach animals language have involved the chimpanzee because of all the primates, the chimpanzee is the most similar to human beings. Despite many similarities, however, chimpanzees do not learn to speak when they are given the same types of experiences that children have as they learn to speak. This became clear through observations of chimpanzees reared as children in the homes of people. Nadezhda Kohts, of the Darwinian museum in Moscow, raised a chimpanzee in her home from 1913 to 1916 without once having it imitate the human voice or utter a word of Russian (see A. J. Premack, 1976). More detailed accounts of life with a chimpanzee are available from the experiences of Winthrop and Louise Kellogg, who raised a baby chimpanzee along with their baby boy in the 1930s (Kellogg, 1933). Their adopted charge also did not learn to speak in the normal manner. Undaunted by this evidence, Cathy and Keith Hayes raised a chimpanzee named Viki with the explicit intent of teaching her to talk (Hayes & Hayes, 1951). Despite several years of effort, Viki learned to say only three words: *mama, papa,* and *cup.*

For nearly 20 years the thorough efforts and failure of the Hayeses to teach language to Viki discouraged others from trying to teach chimpanzees to talk. However, there has been a considerable resurgence of interest in teaching language to chimpanzees in recent years, stimulated in part by the innovative approach of Allen and Beatrice Gardner (Gardner & Gardner, 1969, 1975, 1978). Instead of trying to teach their chimpanzee Washoe to talk using vocal speech, they tried to teach her to communicate using American Sign Language. American Sign Language consists of manual gestures in place of words and is used by deaf people in North America. Chimpanzees are much more adept at making hand movements and gestures than at making the mouth, tongue, and lip movements required for the production of speech sounds. Washoe was a good learner. She learned to sign 132 words. Washoe's success suggests that earlier efforts to teach speech to chimpanzees may have failed not because of the inability of the chimpanzee to engage in language communication but because an inappropriate medium (vocalization) was used. Washoe held out the promise that given the appropriate medium for language, meaningful communication might still be established between chimpanzees and human beings.

Contemporary research on language in nonhuman primates is being conducted in two ways. Some investigators have continued to use the approach adopted by the Gardners in teaching American Sign Language to chimpanzees (for example, Fouts, 1972; Terrace, 1979; Terrace, Petitto, Sanders, & Bever, 1979) and gorillas (Patterson, 1978). Another approach has also stayed away from trying to teach chimpanzees vocalization. However, instead of adopting a human language that is in active use, such as sign language, the second approach has involved artificial language. One artificial language was developed and used by David Premack and his associates and consists of plastic forms of various shapes in place of words (Premack, 1971b, 1976). Figure 12.12 shows examples of the plastic symbols, which have a metal backing and are placed on a magnetized board in a vertical order to create sentences, as in Chinese. Another artificial language, developed by

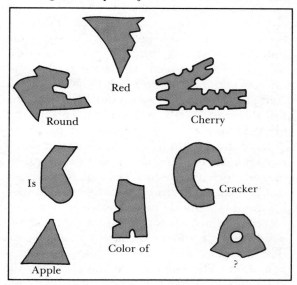

Figure 12.12. Examples of symbols in the artificial language developed by David Premack and his associates. *(From D. Premack, 1976.)*

Duane Rumbaugh and his colleagues at the Yerkes Primate Research Center, uses geometric shapes of various colors to represent words (Rumbaugh, 1977).

In investigations based on artificial languages, the context of the language training is often different than in attempts to teach sign language to chimpanzees. Sign-language training is usually conducted within the context of an established social relationship between the trainer and the chimpanzee. The chimpanzee may not be raised as a child in someone's family. However, it lives in a rich nonlaboratory environment and is cared for by a small number of people throughout the day, each of whom is adept at sign language. Every effort is made to engage the chimpanzee in active conversation (through signing) during its waking hours. Thus, the language training is a part of the subject's "natural" experiences. New signs are learned during games, in the course of getting dressed or undressed, or when going from place to place. Organized training sessions are also held. However, the social relationship between the trainer and the subject is used to encourage the signing behavior, rather than explicit reinforcers such as candy, cookies, or drinks. The intent is to teach language to the chimpanzee in the way that children presumably learn to talk during the normal course of interacting with parents and siblings.

In contrast to the efforts to create a naturalistic context for the training of sign language, investigators using artificial languages usually conduct language training in a more confined laboratory situation with the use of explicit reinforcers. In the Yerkes project, for example, the word symbols appear on keys of a keyboard (like a typewriter,) which is hooked up to a computer. The chimpanzee can "talk" to the computer and make various requests. The computer in turn communicates with the chimpanzee with symbols presented on a display console. This arrangement is very different from the type of social interaction in which children typically learn language. However, the computer communication method makes it much easier to obtain a permanent record of all the language responses of the subject. These responses can be automatically recorded for later analysis.

The considerable effort that has been devoted to teaching language to nonhuman primates has yielded at least one undisputed result. It is clear that chimpanzees and gorillas can learn to use arbitrary stimuli (manual gestures, plastic objects, or colored geometric shapes) as symbols for things and relations in their environment. Nonhuman primates are capable of learning a vocabulary well in excess of 100 words. Washoe's vocabulary after 51 months of training, in the order in which she first signed each word (Gardner & Gardner, 1975), is presented by way of example.

Come-gimme	Open
More	Tickle (touch)
Up	Go
Sweet	Out

Hurry	Dr. G.
Listen (hear)	Naomi
Toothbrush	Fruit (apple)
Drink	Comb
Hurt	Dirty
Sorry	String
Funny	Tree
Please	Light
Food-eat	Red
Flower	Hammer
Blanket (cover)	White
Dog	We
You	Meat
Wiper (napkin)	Smoke
In	Chair
Brush (rub)	Leaf
Hat	Enough
Me	Bug
Shoes	Ride
Roger	Cow
Smell	No
Good	Green
Washoe	Cheese
Pants	Black
Clothes	Berry (strawberry)
Cat	Spoon
Key	Window
Baby	Grass
Clean	Climb
Catch	Car
Down	Spin
Look	Yours
Susan	Kiss
Book	Can't
Oil	Hand
Mine	Tomato
Bed	Cucumber (green slices)
Banana	Dennis
Hug	Ron
Bird	Bite
Pencil (write)	Pipe
Mrs. G.	Cry
Quiet	Time
Greg	Pin
Help	Purse
Wende	Knife

Lollipop

Water

Woman

Different

Same

Larry

Man

House

Run

Smile

Hose

Stamp (letter)

Airplane

Telephone

Hot (warm)

Fork

Mirror

Cereal

Swallow

Hole

Butterfly

Lock

Linn

Ice (cold)

Floor

Good-by

Nut

Want (hunger)

There

Don

Bath

Who

Although it is agreed that nonhuman primates can learn a vocabulary, language is more than just a collection of words. In addition to a vocabulary, language involves arrangement of words in sequence according to certain rules set forth by the grammar of the language. Hence, a critical issue in teaching language to nonhuman primates is whether they can learn to construct word sequences on the basis of grammatical rules. There is considerable dispute about this. The smallest sequence of words possible is two words. However, the utterance of a pair of words does not prove that the subject is using grammar to create the sequence. One incident that has been the subject of controversy occurred when the chimp Washoe saw a swan in the water. She had never been exposed to a swan before. When asked "What is that?," she replied "Water bird." In this sequence was Washoe using "water" as an adjective to specify the kind of bird she saw? Perhaps she was. However, on the basis of just this much data an equally plausible interpretation is that she signed "water" because she saw the water and "bird" because she saw a bird. That is, she may have signed "water bird" as two independent words rather than as an utterance of two words related to each other as adjective and noun (Terrace et al., 1979).

Difficulties of interpretation may also arise with words arranged in a sentence. Consider the following sentence that could have been made by a chimpanzee in the Yerkes project: "Please machine make music." If the subject pressed the appropriate symbols in the appropriate order on the computer keyboard, the machine complied and made music for the chimpanzee. However, pressing those keys in that order does not prove that the subject could construct a sentence. The chimpanzee may have just memorized a sequence of symbols to get reinforced. If the chimpanzee is using grammatical rules, then on other occasions it should be able to use a variety of other words in place of each of the words in the original sentence. Furthermore, these substitutions should be appropriate to the context in which they are made. The chimpanzee should be able to use the grammatical structure of "Please machine make music" to make up sentences such as "Please Peter make music" when Peter is there, "Please machine stop music" if the music has been playing for a while, or "Please machine make cookie" when it is hungry. An analysis of the verbal behavior of Lana, the most famous of the chimpanzees in the Yerkes project, indicates that she did not learn such a flexible use of grammar to create new sentences. Rather, Lana appeared to have learned a set of stock sentences (such as "Please machine make music"), which she used repeatedly, changing only one or two of the words to suit the occasion (Thompson & Church, 1980). Thus, in the sentence "Please machine make music," she rarely changed any words except the last. By changing the last word, she could use the same stock sentence to ask the machine to show a movie, show slides, turn on the television, open the door, or open the window. This kind of behavior does not require knowledge of the grammatical relations among the first three words of the sentence. To press *please*, *machine*, and *make* in that order, the chimpanzee does not have to know, for example, that *machine* is the subject of the sentence and *make* is the verb.

Questions have also been raised about the sentence-forming abilities of chimpanzees taught sign language. Terrace and his associates have analyzed instances in which their chimpanzee Nim spontaneously made more than one sign in a row to see whether these sign combinations provided evidence for grammatical structure (see Terrace, 1979; Terrace et al., 1979). Several aspects of this analysis indicated that the sign combinations were not governed by the kinds of grammatical rules that seem to govern early speech in children. First, a careful study of videotape recordings of Nim with his teachers showed that many sequences of signs were not spontaneous but were repetitions of signs the teacher had recently made. If in fact Nim was just imitating his teachers, his sign sequences cannot be interpreted as evidence of sentence construction. Another aspect of Nim's performance that suggests he was not learning language the way a child learns is that the average number of signs he made in a sequence never increased beyond two. In contrast, once children who are learning to speak or to sign (if they are deaf) begin to make utterances of more than one word, the average length of their utterances increases rapidly. In addition, the maximum length of their utterances is close to the average length. Thus, a child who says two words at a time on the average will not make utterances that are more than 3–7 words long. Such results were not observed with Nim. Even when he signed two words in sequence on the average, occasionally he made utterances with as many as 16 signs. However, his longer utterances did not add meaningful information to his shorter sign sequences. Rather, they often included repetitions. For example, his most frequent four-sign combination was "eat drink eat drink." From such evidence Terrace and his associates concluded that their chimpanzee did not learn to use language despite the fact that he learned a vocabulary of well over 100 words.

The evidence obtained with the chimpanzee Nim indicates that he did not learn to construct sentences in about three and a half years of extensive training. What this implies for the issue of language in chimpanzees is a subject of heated debate. Terrace and his colleagues claim that the evidence that has been provided on the linguistic behavior of other nonhuman primates also does not demonstrate conclusively that these subjects were able to construct grammatical word combinations. However, this charge is contested by other investigators. Thus, the issue of language in nonhuman primates remains very much unresolved. We can expect that future discussions will help define what constitutes conclusive evidence of language in chimpanzees and that future investigations will involve more stringent documentation and analysis of results. It will be exciting to see how these developments ultimately resolve the issue of language in nonhuman animals.

Concluding comments

Research on animal cognition has highlighted many aspects of animal behavior that cannot be directly attributed to the stimuli subjects experience at the time of their actions. These responses appear to be guided by internal representations of various aspects of past events and experiences. Internal representations can involve relatively simple events, such as conditioned and unconditioned stimuli. They may also involve the encoding of serial patterns or complex concepts that may enable certain species to engage in language. How these internal representations influence behavior depends a great deal on memory mechanisms that govern their retention and accessibility.

Glossary

Accidental reinforcement—An instance in which the delivery of a reinforcer happens to coincide with a particular response even though that response was not responsible for the reinforcer.

Acquired drive—A source of motivation for instrumental behavior caused by the presentation of a stimulus that was previously conditioned with a primary, or unconditioned, reinforcer.

Adaptation—Evolutionary change that makes members of a species better able to cope with environmental challenges.

Adjunctive behavior—See **Schedule-induced adjunctive behavior**.

Adventitious reinforcement—Same as **Accidental reinforcement**.

Affective after-reaction—Emotions experienced after the termination of a biologically significant event. These emotions are typically opposite those experienced during the event.

Afferent neuron—A neuron that transmits messages from sense organs to the central nervous system. Same as **Sensory neuron**.

Amnesia—Loss of memory.

Animal cognition—The use of an internal representation or code as a basis for action.

Anxiety conservation—A theoretical idea according to which well-learned avoidance responses occur so quickly in discriminated avoidance procedures that the signal for the aversive stimulus is terminated before conditioned fear is elicited by the signal, thereby protecting the conditioned fear response from extinction.

"a" process—Same as **Primary process**.

Asymptote—The final and stable level of performance that is produced by a particular training procedure. Once the asymptote has been reached, additional training trials do not produce further changes in behavior.

Autoshaping—Same as **Sign tracking**.

Aversive stimulus—An unpleasant or noxious stimulus.

Avoidance — An instrumental-conditioning procedure in which the instrumental response prevents the future delivery of an aversive stimulus.

Avoidance trial—A trial on which the avoidance response occurs and prevents the delivery of the aversive unconditioned stimulus.

Backward conditioning—A classical-conditioning procedure in which the conditioned stimulus is presented *after* the unconditioned stimulus on each conditioning trial.

Behavioral baseline—The stable rate or pattern of operant behavior that is obtained after extensive exposure to a particular set of experimental conditions. The term is used mainly in connection with experiments that involve continuous recording of instrumental behavior.

Behavioral contrast—See **Positive behavioral contrast**.

Behavioral homeostasis—A balanced and stable distribution of the subject's activities. Deviations from this balanced state cause a redistribution of responses to reinstitute a stable state.

Behavioral psychology—An aspect of psychology that focuses on observable responses of organisms investigated with the methods of natural science.

Belongingness—A theoretical idea originally proposed by Thorndike according to which, because of the subject's evolutionary history, certain responses are more easily modified by certain reinforcers in instrumental conditioning than other responses are. For rapid instrumental conditioning, the response has to "belong with," or be appropriate to, the reinforcer used.

Biological drive—A source of motivation for instrumental behavior caused by a deviation from biological homeostasis.

Biological homeostasis—A state of the organism in which all physiological systems are in proper balance. Deviations from this state stimulate adjustments that return the subject to the balanced state.

Blocking effect—Interference with the conditioning of a novel stimulus by the presence of a previously conditioned stimulus.

"b" process—Same as **Opponent process**.

Cartesian—Referring to the ideas of the French philosopher René Descartes.

Cartesian dualism—See **Dualism**.

Central emotional state—The general state of the nervous system assumed to be produced by the presentation of a classically conditioned stimulus.

CER—Abbreviation for **Conditioned emotional response**.

Chained schedule of reinforcement—A procedure in which subjects have to make a series of responses to obtain primary reinforcement. Each response in the chain occurs in the presence of a particular stimulus, and the performance of each response produces the stimulus for the next response in the chain. Only the last response in the series results in delivery of the primary reinforcer. Each stimulus in the series serves as a secondary reinforcer for the response that produced it and as a discriminative stimulus for the next response in the series.

Change-over delay—A procedure used with concurrent schedules of reinforcement that prevents the delivery of reward for a short time after the subject switches from responding on one of the components of the concurrent schedule to responding on another component. This procedure prevents reinforcement of switching behavior per se.

Circular explanation—An explanation in which the facts to be accounted for are used as part of the explanation.

Classical conditioning—Learning that results from presentation of a conditioned stimulus in conjunction with an unconditioned stimulus independent of the ongoing activities of the organism.

COD—Abbreviation for **Change-over delay**.

Cognition—See **Animal cognition**.

Compensatory response—A response that is opposite the reaction elicited by the unconditioned stimulus and therefore compensates for this reaction.

Compound-stimulus test—A test procedure that identifies a stimulus as a conditioned inhibitor if that stimulus reduces the responding elicited by a conditioned excitatory stimulus.

Concurrent chained schedule of reinforcement—A complex procedure in which the subject is permitted to choose which of several simple reinforcement schedules will be in effect. Once a choice has been made, the rejected alternatives become unavailable for a certain amount of time.

Concurrent-measurement experiments—Experiments in which classically and instrumentally conditioned responses are measured at the same time.

Concurrent schedule of reinforcement—A complex procedure in which the subject can obtain reinforcement by satisfying the requirements of any one of two or more simple reinforcement schedules that are available simultaneously. Concurrent schedules allow for the measurement of choice among simple schedule alternatives.

Conditional or **conditioned response**—The response that is learned to the conditioned stimulus during classical conditioning.

Conditional or **conditioned stimulus**—A stimulus that initially does not elicit a particular response but comes to do so as a result of being presented repeatedly in conjunction with an unconditioned stimulus.

Conditioned emotional response—Suppression of food-rewarded instrumental behavior caused by the presentation of a stimulus conditioned with shock.

Conditioned reinforcer—A stimulus that becomes an effective reinforcer because of a conditioning history with a primary, or unconditioned, reinforcer.

Conditioned suppression—Same as **Conditioned emotional response**.

Conditioning trial—A single training episode. In classical conditioning this usually consists of a pairing of the conditioned stimulus with the unconditioned stimulus.

Consolidation—See **Memory consolidation**.

Consummatory-response theory—A theory according to which the responses involved in consuming a reinforcer, such as a pellet of food, are entirely responsible for its reinforcing effects. The nourishment provided by the food is assumed to be unimportant in reinforcing instrumental behavior.

Contiguity—The simultaneous or almost simultaneous occurrence of two or more events.

Contingency between the conditioned and unconditioned stimuli—The probability that the unconditioned stimulus will be presented with the conditioned stimulus, relative to the probability that it will be presented in the absence of the conditioned stimulus.

Contingency between the instrumental response and the reinforcer—The probability that the reinforcer will be presented when the response is performed, relative to the probability of reinforcement in the absence of the response.

Continuous reinforcement schedule—A schedule in which every occurrence of the instrumental response produces the reinforcer.

Contraprepared—Having an evolutionary history that is contrary to or incompatible with a particular learning task, making it particularly difficult (if not impossible) for the subject to learn the task.

Contrast—See **Positive behavioral contrast**.

Correlation between the instrumental response and the reinforcer—The relation between the response and the reinforcer as specified by the schedule of reinforcement. The relation may be characterized by the feedback function or the conditional probabilities between the response and the reinforcer.

Counterconditioning—A conditioning procedure that reverses the organism's previous response to a stimulus. For example, an animal may be conditioned to approach a stimulus that initially elicits withdrawal reactions.

CR—Abbreviation for **Conditioned response**.

CRF—Abbreviation for **Continuous reinforcement**.

CS—Abbreviation for **Conditioned stimulus**.

CS-preexposure effect—Interference with conditioning produced by repeated exposures of the subject to the conditioned stimulus before the conditioning trials.

CS-saturation hypothesis—A theoretical idea according to which there is a limit to how strongly a conditioned stimulus (CS) can become conditioned. As conditioning proceeds, the conditioned stimulus comes closer and closer to this limit, resulting in progressively smaller increases in the conditioned response.

CS-US interval—Same as **Interstimulus interval**.

Cumulative record—A graphical representation (usually made by a cumulative recorder) of the cumulative number of occurrences of a particular response as a function of the passage of time. The horizontal distance on the record represents the passage of time, the vertical distance represents the total number of responses that have occurred up to a particular moment, and the slope represents the rate of responding.

Cumulative recorder—An automatic event recorder that records occurrences of a particular response cumulatively as a function of the passage of time.

Delayed matching to sample—A procedure in which subjects are reinforced for responding to a test stimulus that is the same as a previously presented sample stimulus.

Deprivation—The procedure of denying access to certain stimuli or needed substances, such as food or water.

Deprivation hypothesis—The theoretical idea that any response can serve as a reinforcer if the subject is prevented from performing the response as often as it would if given unlimited opportunity.

Determinism—A philosophy according to which every aspect of behavior is governed by discoverable laws of nature.

Differential inhibition—A classical-conditioning procedure in which on some trials one stimulus (the CS+) is paired with the unconditioned stimulus and on other trials another stimulus (the CS−) is presented without the unconditioned stimulus. As a result of this procedure, the CS+ comes to elicit a conditioned response and the CS− comes to inhibit this response.

Differential reinforcement of high rates—A reinforcement schedule in which a response is reinforced only if it occurs *less than* a specified amount of time after the preceding response.

Differential reinforcement of low rates—A reinforcement schedule in which a response is reinforced only if it occurs *more than* a specified amount of time after the preceding response.

Differential reinforcement of other behavior—An instrumental-conditioning procedure in which a positive reinforcer is periodically delivered only if the subject fails to perform a particular response.

Differential responding—Responding differently in the presence of different stimuli. Differential responding may involve making different responses or the same response at different rates in the presence of the various stimuli.

Disappointment—A hypothetical emotional state that is presumably elicited by classically conditioned stimuli that signal the absence or removal of a positive reinforcer, such as food.

Discriminated avoidance—An avoidance-conditioning procedure in which occurrences of the aversive stimulus are signaled by a conditioned stimulus. Responding during the conditioned stimulus terminates the CS and prevents the delivery of the aversive unconditioned stimulus.

Discrimination hypothesis—A theoretical idea according to which the speed of extinction of instrumental behavior depends on how easily the subjects detect introduction of the extinction procedure.

Discrimination training procedure—See **Differential inhibition** and **Stimulus-discrimination procedure in instrumental conditioning**.

Discriminative punishment—A procedure in which responding is punished in the presence of a particular stimulus and is not punished in the absence of that stimulus.

Discriminative stimulus—A stimulus that controls the performance of instrumental behavior because it signals the availability (or nonavailability) of reinforcement.

Dishabituation—Recovery of a habituated response as a result of presentation of a strong extraneous stimulus.

Disinhibition—Recovery of a partly extinguished conditioned response as a result of presentation of a novel stimulus.

DRH—Abbreviation for **Differential reinforcement of high rates**.

Drive states—See **Acquired drive** and **Biological drive**.

DRL—Abbreviation for **Differential reinforcement of low rates**.

Drug tolerance—Reduction in the effectiveness of a drug that may occur with repeated use of the drug.

Dualism—A view of behavior according to which actions can be separated into two categories: voluntary behavior controlled by the mind and involuntary behavior controlled by reflex mechanisms.

Efferent neuron—A neuron that transmits impulses to muscles. Same as **Motor neuron**.

Empiricism—A philosophy according to which all ideas in the mind arise from experience.

Errorless discrimination procedure—A procedure devised by Terrace in which subjects hardly ever respond to the S−. During initial phases of discrimination training, the S− is presented only briefly and at a low intensity, so that the subject does not respond to it. The duration and intensity of the S− are then gradually increased. If this increase is conducted in small enough steps, subjects rarely if ever respond to the S−.

Escape—An instrumental conditioning procedure in which the instrumental response terminates an aversive stimulus.

Escape trial—A type of trial during avoidance training in which the required avoidance response is not made and the aversive unconditioned stimulus is presented. Performance of the instrumental response during the aversive stimulus results in termination of the aversive stimulus. Thus, the organism is able to escape from the aversive stimulus.

Evolution through natural selection—Gradual change in the characteristics of a species because individuals with certain features are more likely to leave offspring than individuals that do not have these features.

Excitatory conditioning—A type of classical conditioning in which the conditioned stimulus becomes a signal for presentation of the unconditioned stimulus.

Excitatory stimulus-generalization gradient—A gradient of responding that is observed when subjects are tested with the S+ from a discrimination procedure and with stimuli that increasingly differ from the S+. The highest level of responding occurs to stimuli similar to the S+, and progressively less responding occurs to stimuli that increasingly differ from the S+. Thus, the gradient has an inverted-U shape.

Exteroceptive stimulus—A stimulus, such as a light or tone, that arises from events outside the organism. (Compare with **Proprioceptive stimulus**.)

Extinction—Reduction of a learned response that occurs because the conditioned stimulus is no longer paired with the unconditioned stimulus (in classical conditioning) or because the response is no longer reinforced (in instrumental conditioning). Also, the procedure of withdrawing reinforcement for a response.

Fatigue—A temporary decrease in behavior caused by repeated or excessive use of the muscles involved in the behavior.

Fear—A hypothetical emotional state that presumably occurs when either an unconditioned aversive stimulus or a stimulus that was previously conditioned with an aversive event is presented.

Feedback function—The relation between rates of responding and rates of reinforcement on a particular reinforcement schedule.

Feedback stimulus—A stimulus that results from the performance of a response.

FI—Abbreviation for **Fixed-interval schedule**.

Fixed action pattern—An innate elicited behavior that is not governed by feedback stimuli.

Fixed-interval scallop—The gradually increasing rate of responding that occurs between successive reinforcements on a fixed-interval schedule.

Fixed-interval schedule—A reinforcement schedule in which reinforcement is delivered for the first response that occurs after a fixed amount of time from the last reinforcer.

Fixed-ratio schedule—A reinforcement schedule in which a fixed number of responses have to occur in order for the next response to be reinforced.

Flooding—A procedure for extinguishing avoidance behavior that consists in presenting the conditioned stimulus while the subject is prevented from making the avoidance response.

Forgetting—A reduction of a learned response that occurs because of the passage of time, not because of particular experiences.

FR—Abbreviation for **Fixed-ratio schedule**.

Fractional anticipatory goal response—A theoretical entity or response that, according to the $r_g = s_g$ mechanism, becomes classically conditioned to the stimuli that are experienced just before the performance of a reinforced instrumental response.

Free-operant avoidance—Same as **Nondiscriminated avoidance**.

Free-operant baseline—Same as **Operant level**.

Frustration—An aversive emotional reaction that results from the unexpected absence of reinforcement.

Habituation—A progressive decrease in the vigor of elicited behavior that may occur with repeated presentations of the eliciting stimulus.

Habituation process—A neural mechanism activated by repetitions of a stimulus that reduces the magnitude of responses elicited by the stimulus.

Hedonism—A philosophy according to which the actions of organisms are determined entirely by the pursuit of pleasure and the avoidance of pain.

Higher-order conditioning—A procedure in which a previously conditioned stimulus (CS_1) is used to condition a new stimulus (CS_2).

Homeostasis—See **Behavioral homeostasis** and **Biological homeostasis**.

Hope—A hypothetical emotional state that is presumably elicited by classically conditioned stimuli that signal the presentation of a positive reinforcer, such as food.

Incentive motivation—Motivation for instrumental behavior created by the sensory properties of a reinforcer.

Ingestional neophobia—A fear or reluctance to eat or drink novel substances or to eat or drink in unfamiliar circumstances.

Inhibitory conditioning—A type of classical conditioning in which the conditioned stimulus becomes a signal for the absence of the unconditioned stimulus.

Inhibitory stimulus-generalization gradient—A gradient of responding observed when subjects are tested with the S− from a discrimination procedure and with stimuli that increasingly differ from the S−. The lowest level of responding occurs to stimuli similar to the S−, and progressively more responding occurs to stimuli that increasingly differ from S−. Thus, the gradient has a U shape.

Instinctive drift—A gradual drift of instrumental behavior away from the responses required for reinforcement to instinctive responses related to the reinforcer and other stimuli in the experimental situation.

Instrumental behavior—An activity that occurs because it is effective in producing certain consequences.

Instrumental contingency—The relation between an instrumental response and the events (such as reinforcers) that it produces. (See also **Contingency between the instrumental response and the reinforcer**.)

Interim responses—Responses that increase in

frequency after the delivery of a reinforcer and then decline as the next reinforcer is due to be presented in a procedure that involves periodic presentations of the reinforcer.

Intermittent reinforcement schedule—A schedule in which only some of the occurrences of the instrumental response are reinforced. The instrumental response is reinforced occasionally, or intermittently.

Internal representation—The form in which information is held in memory—the mental record, for example, of some aspect of the environment.

Interneuron—A neuron in the spinal cord that transmits impulses from afferent (or sensory) to efferent (or motor) neurons.

Interresponse time—The interval between successive responses.

Interstimulus interval—The amount of time that elapses between the presentation of the conditioned stimulus and the unconditioned stimulus during a classical-conditioning trial.

Intertrial interval—The amount of time that elapses between two successive trials.

Interval schedule—A reinforcement schedule in which a response is reinforced only if it occurs more than a set amount of time after the last reinforcement.

Intracranial self-stimulation—Performance of an instrumental response that is reinforced by brief pulses of current passed through an electrode implanted in any one of certain areas of the animal's brain.

Intradimensional discrimination—A discrimination between stimuli that differ in only one stimulus characteristic, such as color, brightness, or pitch.

Introspection—A method of obtaining information about behavior that is based on reflecting on one's own reactions, motivations, and reasons for doing something.

Irradiation of excitation—A theoretical idea proposed by Pavlov according to which when a CS is presented and paired with reinforcement, excitation occurs in the brain locus corresponding to the CS, and this excitation radiates to adjacent brain locations, in much the same way that circular waves radiate from the point of contact when a pebble is tossed into a calm lake.

IRT—Abbreviation for **Interresponse time**.

Kinesis—An instance in which a stimulus produces a change in the speed of movement irrespective of the direction of the movement.

Latency of the conditioned response—The amount of time that elapses between presentation of the conditioned stimulus and occurrence of the conditioned response.

Latency of the running response—The amount of time a subject waits before leaving the start box of a runway after the start-box door is lifted.

Latent-inhibition effect—Same as **CS-preexposure effect.**

Law of effect—A rule for instrumental behavior proposed by Thorndike according to which if a response in the presence of a stimulus is followed by a satisfying event, the association between the stimulus and the response is strengthened; if the response is followed by an annoying event, the association is weakened.

Learned-helplessness effect—An interference with the learning of new instrumental responses, produced by exposure to inescapable and unavoidable aversive stimulation.

Learned-helplessness hypothesis—A theoretical idea according to which during exposure to inescapable and unavoidable aversive stimulation, subjects learn that their behavior does not control environmental events.

Learning—An enduring change in the neural mechanisms of behavior that results from experience with environmental events.

Learning set—A strategy acquired during the course of learning to solve a variety of problems that facilitates the learning of the appropriate responses in new problems.

Limited hold—A restriction on how long reinforcement remains available. In order for a response to be reinforced, it has to occur during the limited-hold period.

Long-delay conditioning—A classical-conditioning procedure in which the conditioned stimulus is presented a long time before the unconditioned stimulus on each conditioning trial.

Long-term memory—A theoretical term used to characterize instances in which a particular experience has a long-lasting effect on the actions of the organism.

Magazine training—A preliminary stage of instrumental conditioning in which a stimulus is repeatedly paired with the reward to enable the subject to learn to go and get the reward when it is presented. The sound of the food-delivery device, for example, may be repeatedly paired with food so that the animal will learn to go to the food cup when the food is delivered.

Matching law—A rule for instrumental behavior proposed by Herrnstein according to which the relative rate of response on a particular alternative equals the relative rate of reinforcement for that response alternative.

Maturation—A change in behavior caused by physical or physiological development of the organism in the absence of particular experiences with environmental events.

Maximizing hypothesis—A theoretical idea according to which subjects in a choice situation distribute their responses so as to receive the maximum frequency of reinforcement for the number of responses they perform.

Memory—A theoretical term used to characterize instances in which subjects' current behavior is determined by some aspect of their previous experience.

Memory consolidation—The establishment of a memory in relatively permanent form, or the transfer of information from short-term to long-term memory.

Monotonic sequence—A sequence in which all elements after the first are either less than or more than the preceding elements.

Motor neuron—Same as **Efferent neuron**.

Multiple schedule of reinforcement—A procedure in which different reinforcement schedules are in effect in the presence of different stimuli presented in succession. Generally, each stimulus comes to evoke a pattern of responding that corresponds to whatever reinforcement schedule is in effect in the presence of that stimulus.

Nativism—A philosophy according to which human beings are born with innate ideas.

Natural selection—A process that makes it more likely for individuals with certain features to leave offspring than individuals lacking these features.

Necessity—A relation between two events such that one of the events occurs only when the other event has occurred.

Negative contingency (in classical conditioning)—A relation between the conditioned and unconditioned stimuli such that the unconditioned stimulus is more likely to occur without the conditioned stimulus than with it.

Negative contingency (in instrumental conditioning)—A relation between the instrumental response and the reinforcer such that the response prevents or terminates presentation of the reinforcer. See **Avoidance** and **Escape**.

Negative law of effect—A theoretical idea according to which punishment weakens instrumental behavior in a manner that is comparable but opposite to the effects of positive reinforcement.

Negative punishment—An instrumental-conditioning procedure in which there is a negative contingency between the instrumental response and a rewarding stimulus. If the subject responds, the rewarding stimulus is withheld; if the subject fails to perform the instrumental response, the rewarding stimulus is presented.

Negative reinforcement—An instrumental-conditioning procedure in which there is a negative contingency between the instrumental response and an aversive stimulus. If the instrumental response is performed, the aversive stimulus is terminated or prevented from occurring; if the instrumental response is not performed, the aversive stimulus is presented.

Negative reinforcer—An aversive stimulus, such as shock or loud noise.

Negative sign tracking—Movement away from a stimulus that signals an aversive event, such as a brief shock or the unavailability of positive reinforcers.

Neophobia—Fear of novel stimuli.

Nondiscriminated avoidance—An avoidance-conditioning procedure in which occurrences of the aversive stimulus are not signaled by an external stimulus. In the absence of avoidance behavior, the aversive stimulus is presented periodically. Each occurrence of the avoidance response creates a certain amount of time without aversive stimulation.

Nonmonotonic sequence—A sequence in which some elements are greater than the preceding elements and some are smaller.

Nonsense syllable—A three-letter combination (a consonant followed by a vowel and another consonant) that has no meaning.

Omission control procedure—A procedure in which the unconditioned stimulus is presented after the conditioned stimulus (CS) only if the subject does not make the conditioned response during the CS. If the subject makes the conditioned response during the CS, the unconditioned stimulus is not presented on that trial.

Omission training—An instrumental-conditioning procedure in which the instrumental response prevents the delivery of a rewarding stimulus.

One-way avoidance—An avoidance-conditioning procedure in which the required instrumental response is always to cross from one side of an experimental chamber to the other in the same direction.

Operant—A response that is defined by the effect it produces in the environment. Examples include pressing a lever and opening a door. Any sequence of movements that depresses the lever or opens the door constitutes that particular operant.

Operant level—The rate of occurrence of an operant response before any experimental manipulation is introduced.

Opponent process—A compensatory mechanism that occurs in response to the primary process elicited by biologically significant events. (Sometimes also called the "*b* process.") The opponent process causes physiological and behavioral changes that are opposite those caused by the primary process.

Orienting response—An unspecified reflex or set of responses which is elicited by a novel stimulus (or a change in a familiar stimulus) and which habituates with repetitions of the eliciting event.

Overshadowing—Interference with the conditioning of a stimulus because of the simultaneous presence of another stimulus that is easier to condition.

Pairing hypothesis—A theoretical idea according to which the mere presence of a stimulus when a response is reinforced is sufficient for that stimulus to gain control over the behavior.

Partial-reinforcement extinction effect—The fact that subjects continue to perform an instrumental response much longer in extinction after partial (intermittent) reinforcement training than after continuous reinforcement training.

Partial reinforcement schedule—Same as **Intermittent reinforcement schedule.**

Peak shift—A displacement of the highest rate of responding in a stimulus-generalization gradient away from the S+ in a direction opposite the S− after intradimensional discrimination training.

Performance—An organism's activities at a particular time.

Phobia—A strong irrational fear.

Positive behavioral contrast—An increase in instrumental responding that occurs during an unchanged reinforcement component of a multiple schedule when reinforcement becomes unavailable in another component of the multiple schedule.

Positive contingency (in classical conditioning)—A relation between the conditioned and unconditioned stimuli such that the unconditioned stimulus is more likely to occur with the conditioned stimulus than without it.

Positive punishment—An instrumental-conditioning procedure in which there is a positive contingency between the instrumental response and an aversive stimulus. If the subject performs the instrumental response, it receives the aversive stimulus; if the subject does not perform the instrumental response, it does not receive the aversive stimulus.

Positive reinforcement—An instrumental-conditioning procedure in which there is a positive contingency between the instrumental response and a rewarding stimulus. If the subject performs the response, it receives the rewarding stimulus; if the subject does not perform the response, it does not receive the rewarding stimulus.

Positive reinforcer—A rewarding stimulus, such as food or water.

Postreinforcement pause—A pause in responding that typically occurs after the delivery of the reinforcer on fixed-ratio and fixed-interval schedules of reinforcement.

Premack's reinforcement principle—Given two responses arranged in an operant-conditioning procedure, the more probable response will reinforce the less probable behavior; the less probable response will not reinforce the more probable behavior.

Preparatory response—A response that enables the organism to deal more effectively and rapidly with the forthcoming presentation of the unconditioned stimulus so that the unconditioned stimulus causes less disruption in the state of the organism.

Prepared—Having an evolutionary history that is consonant or compatible with a particular learning task, enabling the subject to learn the task especially rapidly.

Preparedness—The extent to which the subject's evolutionary history makes it easy or difficult to learn a particular task.

PRF—Abbreviation for **Partial reinforcement**.

Primary motivation—Motivation for instrumental behavior created by a drive state (either a biological drive or an acquired drive).

Primary process—The process that is initially elicited by a biologically significant stimulus. (Sometimes also called the "*a* process.")

Primary reinforcer—Same as **Unconditioned reinforcer**.

Priming—Activation of some information in short-term memory.

Principle of transsituationality—A theoretical idea according to which if a stimulus is effective in strengthening (reinforcing) certain responses in one situation, it will also be effective in strengthening other kinds of responses in other situations.

Proactive interference—Disruption of memory by exposure to stimuli before the event to be remembered.

Proprioceptive stimulus—An internal response-feedback stimulus that arises from the movement of muscles and/or joints. (Compare with **Exteroceptive stimulus**.)

Psychic secretion—The term originally used by Pavlov to refer to the salivation he observed before the presentation of food when experienced dogs were brought into the experimental situation.

Punisher—Same as **Negative reinforcer** or **Aversive stimulus**.

Punishment—An instrumental-conditioning procedure that results in a decrease in the future probability of the instrumental response. (See also **Positive punishment** and **Negative punishment**.)

Radial maze—A maze that consists of a central area from which alleys extend like spokes of a wheel.

Random control procedure—A procedure in which the conditioned and unconditioned stimuli are presented at random times with respect to each other.

Ratio run—The high and invariant rate of responding observed after the postreinforcement pause on fixed-ratio reinforcement schedules. The ratio run ends when the necessary number of responses has been performed and the subject is reinforced.

Ratio schedule—A reinforcement schedule in which reinforcement depends only on the number of responses the subject performs, irrespective of when these responses occur.

Reflex—A mechanism whereby a specific environmental event elicits a specific response.

Reflex arc—Neural structures, consisting of the efferent (sensory) neuron, interneuron, and afferent (motor) neuron, that enable a stimulus to elicit a reflex response.

Rehearsal—A theoretical process whereby some information is maintained in an active state, available to influence behavior or the processing of other information.

Reinforcement—An instrumental-conditioning procedure that results in an increase in the future probability of the instrumental response. See also **Positive reinforcement** and **Negative reinforcement**.

Reinforcer—A rewarding or aversive stimulus. If the stimulus is rewarding, it is called a positive reinforcer; if aversive, it is called a negative reinforcer.

Relational learning—Learning to respond differentially to two stimuli on the basis of a comparison or relation between the stimuli rather than on the basis of the individual features of each stimulus.

Relative rate of reinforcement—The rate of reinforcement earned with one response alternative divided by the sum of the rates of reinforcement earned with all available response alternatives.

Relative rate of response—The rate of response on one response alternative divided by the sum of the response rates on all available response alternatives.

Releasing stimulus—Same as **Sign stimulus**.

Relief—A hypothetical emotional state that is presumably elicited by classically conditioned stimuli that signal the absence or removal of an aversive stimulus, such as shock.

Reminder treatment—A procedure that facilitates the recovery of information from long-term memory.

Representation—See **Internal representation**.

Response feedback stimulus—Same as **Feedback stimulus**.

Response prevention—Same as **Flooding**.

Response-rate schedule—A reinforcement schedule in which a response is reinforced depending on how soon that response is made after the previous occurrence of the behavior.

Retardation-of-acquisition test—A test procedure that identifies a stimulus as a conditioned inhibitor if that stimulus is slower to acquire excitatory properties than a comparison stimulus.

Retrieval—Recovery of information from long-term memory.

Retrieval-generated priming—Activation of some information (such as a characteristic of a US) in short-term memory because of exposure to an associated piece of information (such as a CS that had been conditioned with the US).

Retroactive interference—Disruption of memory by exposure to stimuli after the event to be remembered.

Retrograde amnesia—A gradient of memory loss going back in time from the occurrence of a major injury or physiological disturbance. Amnesia is greatest for events that took place closest to the time of injury.

r_g—Abbreviation for **Fractional anticipatory goal response**.

R-S interval—The interval between the occurrence of an avoidance response and the next scheduled presentation of the aversive stimulus in a nondiscriminated avoidance procedure.

Running speed—How fast (in feet per second, for example) subjects move in a runway.

Running time—The amount of time subjects

take to run from the start box to the goal box in a runway.

Runway—An alley with a start box at one end and a goal box at the other. Animals are placed in the start box at the start of a trial and allowed to run to the goal box.

S+—A discriminative stimulus that evokes instrumental behavior because it signals the availability of reinforcement.

S−—A discriminative stimulus that suppresses instrumental behavior because it signals the nonavailability of reinforcement.

S^D—Same as **S+**.

S$^\Delta$—Same as **S−**.

Safe compartment—The compartment of a one-way avoidance apparatus in which shock is never delivered. Subjects have to enter this compartment to avoid or escape shock.

Satiation—Providing so much access to a stimulus or needed substance (such as food or water) that the subject no longer seeks to contact or ingest it.

Schedule-induced adjunctive behavior—Responses such as drinking, gnawing, biting, or attack that develop with prolonged exposure to intermittent reinforcement schedules even though these responses do not influence the occurrence of reinforcement.

Schedule-induced polydipsia—The excessive drinking of water that is observed if subjects are periodically given small amounts of food.

Schedule of reinforcement—A program, or rule, that determines how and when the occurrence of a response will be followed by delivery of the reinforcer.

Secondary reinforcer—Same as **Conditioned reinforcer**.

Second-order schedule of reinforcement—A procedure that consists of a subordinate schedule embedded in a master schedule. Completions of the subordinate schedule are counted as "responses" in determining whether the master schedule has been satisfied. Satisfaction of the master schedule results in delivery of the primary reinforcer.

Each completion of the subordinate schedule results in delivery of a secondary reinforcer.

Self-generated priming—Activation of some information (such as a characteristic of a stimulus) in short-term memory because of exposure to that piece of information.

Sensitization—A progressive increase in the vigor of elicited behavior that results from repeated presentations of the eliciting stimulus.

Sensitization process—A neural mechanism that increases the magnitude of responses elicited by a stimulus.

Sensory adaptation—A temporary reduction in the sensitivity of sense organs caused by repeated or excessive stimulation.

Sensory neuron—Same as **Afferent neuron**.

Sensory preconditioning—A procedure in which one biologically weak stimulus (CS_2) is first repeatedly paired with another biologically weak stimulus (CS_1). CS_1 is then conditioned with an unconditioned stimulus. In a later test trial CS_2 is also found to elicit the conditioned response even though CS_2 was never directly paired with the unconditioned stimulus.

s_g—Response feedback stimuli from the fractional anticipatory goal response.

Shaping by successive approximations—Reinforcement of successive approximations to a desired instrumental response.

Shock compartment—The compartment of a one-way avoidance apparatus in which shock is delivered if the subject does not perform the avoidance response.

Short-delayed conditioning—A classical-conditioning procedure in which the conditioned stimulus is initiated shortly before the unconditioned stimulus on each conditioning trial.

Short-term memory—A theoretical term used to characterize instances in which a particular experience has only a short-lasting effect on the future actions of the organism.

Shuttle avoidance—A type of avoidance-conditioning procedure in which the required instrumental response consists in going back and forth (shuttling) between two sides of an experimental apparatus.

Sidman avoidance—Same as **Nondiscriminated** or **Free-operant avoidance**.

Signaled avoidance—Same as **Discriminated avoidance**.

Sign stimulus—A specific feature of an object or animal that elicits a particular innate response by another organism.

Sign tracking—Movement toward and possibly contact with a stimulus that signals the availability of food. (See also **Negative sign tracking**.)

Simultaneous conditioning—A classical-conditioning procedure in which the conditioned stimulus is presented simultaneously with the unconditioned stimulus on each conditioning trial.

Simultaneous matching to sample—A procedure in which subjects are reinforced for responding to a test stimulus that is the same as a sample stimulus presented at the same time.

Skinner box—A small experimental chamber provided with something that the subject can repeatedly manipulate, such as a response lever. Thus, the subject can repeatedly perform a particular response without being removed from the experimental situation. The chamber usually also has a mechanism that can deliver a reward, such as a pellet of food.

Spatial memory—Memory for locations in space.

Species-specific defense reactions—Innate responses animals perform when they experience aversive stimulation. The responses may involve freezing, fleeing, or fighting.

Spontaneous recovery—Recovery in the magnitude of a response produced by a period of rest after habituation or extinction.

S-R learning—The learning of an association between a stimulus and a response, with the result that the stimulus comes to elicit the response.

S-R system—The shortest neural pathway that connects the sense organs stimulated by an eliciting stimulus and the muscles involved in making the elicited response.

SSDR—Abbreviation for **Species-specific defense reaction**.

S-S interval—The interval between successive presentations of the aversive stimulus in a nondiscriminated avoidance procedure when the avoidance response is not performed.

S-S learning—The learning of an association between two stimuli, with the result that exposure to one of the stimuli comes to activate a representation, or "mental image," of the other stimulus.

Standard pattern of affective dynamics—A pattern of emotional changes specified by the opponent process theory of motivation that is frequently observed when a novel, biologically significant event is presented.

Startle response—A sudden jump or tensing of the muscles that may occur when an unexpected stimulus is presented.

State system—Neural structures that determine the general level of responsiveness, or readiness to respond, of the organism.

Stimulus belongingness—Same as **Stimulus relevance**.

Stimulus discrimination—Differential responding in the presence of two or more stimuli.

Stimulus-discrimination procedure (in classical conditioning)—Same procedure as **Differential inhibition**.

Stimulus-discrimination procedure (in instrumental conditioning)—A procedure in which reinforcement for responding is available whenever one stimulus (the S+, or S^D) is present, and reinforcement for responding is not available whenever another stimulus (the S−, or S^Δ) is present.

Stimulus generalization—The occurrence of behavior learned through habituation or conditioning in the presence of stimuli that are different from the stimuli used during training.

Stimulus-generalization gradient—A gradient of responding that may be observed if subjects are tested with stimuli that increasingly differ from the stimulus that was present during training. (See also **Excitatory stimulus-generalization gradient** and **Inhibitory stimulus-generalization gradient**.)

Stimulus relevance—The observation that learning occurs much more rapidly with certain combinations of conditioned and unconditioned stimuli (such as tastes and sickness) than with other stimulus combinations (such as tastes and shock).

Stimulus substitution—A theoretical idea according to which the outcome of classical conditioning is that organisms come to respond to the conditioned stimulus in much the same way that they respond to the unconditioned stimulus.

Sufficiency—A relation between two events such that one of the events occurs every time the other event occurs, but the first event also occurs by itself sometimes.

Supernormal stimulus—An artificially enlarged or exaggerated sign stimulus.

Superstition experiment—An experiment in which a reinforcer is periodically delivered independently of the subject's activities, and particular responses are learned even though these responses do not influence presentations of the reinforcer.

Superstitious behavior—Behavior that increases in frequency because of accidental pairings of the delivery of a reinforcer with occurrences of the behavior.

Systematic desensitization—A method of behavior therapy used to eliminate debilitating fears.

Taxis—An instance in which a stimulus causes movements toward or away from the eliciting stimulus.

Temporal contiguity—Same as **Contiguity**.

Temporal relation between the response and the reinforcer—The time between the reinforcer and the response.

Terminal responses—Responses that are much more likely to occur at the end of the interval between successive reinforcements than at other times in a procedure that involves periodic presentations of a reinforcer.

Test trial—A trial in which the conditioned stimulus is presented without the unconditioned stimulus. This allows measurement of the conditioned response in the absence of the unconditioned response.

T maze—An alley constructed in the shape of a T, with the start box at the end of the longest stem of the maze and goal boxes at the ends of the other stems. After leaving the start box, the subject has a choice of entering the right or left goal box.

Token economy—A system in which subjects can earn tokens by performing specified desirable behaviors. Tokens can then be exchanged for various goods and services the subject chooses.

Tolerance—See **Drug tolerance**.

Trace conditioning—A classical-conditioning procedure in which the unconditioned stimulus is presented after the conditioned stimulus has been terminated on each conditioning trial.

Trace decay—A theoretical idea according to which exposure to a stimulus produces changes in the nervous system that gradually decrease after the stimulus has been terminated.

Trace interval—The interval between the end of the conditioned stimulus and the start of the unconditioned stimulus in trace-conditioning trials.

Transfer-of-control experiment—An experiment that assesses the effects of a classically conditioned stimulus (CS) on the performance of instrumental behavior. The CS and the instrumental behavior are first conditioned in independent phases of the experiment. The effects of the CS on instrumental behavior are then determined in a transfer phase.

Transposition—Responding differentially to two stimuli on the basis of a comparison or relation between the two stimuli rather than on the basis of the individual features of each stimulus.

Transsituationality—See **Principle of trans-situationality**.

Unconditional or **unconditioned response**—A response that occurs to a stimulus in the absence of training.

Unconditional or **unconditioned stimulus**—A stimulus that elicits a particular response in the absence of training.

Unconditioned reinforcer—A stimulus that is an effective reinforcer in the absence of training.

Unprepared—Having an evolutionary history that is unrelated to the learning task at hand, so that the subject's evolutionary history neither facilitates nor hinders learning of the task.

UR—Abbreviation for **Unconditioned response**.

US—Abbreviation for **Unconditioned stimulus**.

US-preexposure effect—Interference with conditioning produced by repeated exposures of the subject to the unconditioned stimulus before the conditioning trials.

US-reduction hypothesis—A theoretical idea according to which the effectiveness of the unconditioned stimulus (US) becomes gradually reduced as conditioning proceeds, with the result that smaller increases in the conditioned response occur.

US representation—The hypothesized image or memory that organisms have of the unconditioned stimulus.

Variable-interval schedule—A reinforcement schedule in which reinforcement is provided for the first response that occurs after a variable amount of time from the last reinforcement.

Variable-ratio schedule—A reinforcement schedule in which a variable number of responses have to occur in order for the next response to be reinforced.

VI—Abbreviation for **Variable-interval schedule**.

VR—Abbreviation for **Variable-ratio schedule**.

Win-stay, lose-shift strategy—A strategy that helps solve a two-choice discrimination problem. If the reinforcer is obtained for the first stimulus chosen, staying with that stimulus on future trials will continue to yield reinforcers. If the reinforcer is not obtained for the first stimulus chosen, shifting to the other stimulus on future trials will yield reinforcers.

Working memory—Same as **Short-term memory**.

Zero contingency (in classical conditioning)—A relation between the conditioned and unconditioned stimuli such that the unconditioned stimulus is equally likely to occur with and without the conditioned stimulus.

References

Adams, G. P. On the negative and positive phototropism of the earthworm *Allolobophora foetida* as determined by light of different intensities. *American Journal of Physiology*, 1903, *9*, 26–34.

Allison, J. Contrast, induction, facilitation, suppression, and conservation. *Journal of the Experimental Analysis of Behavior*, 1976, *25*, 185–198.

Alloy, L. B., & Seligman, M. E. P. On the cognitive component of learned helplessness and depression. In G. H. Bower (Ed.), *The psychology of learning and motivation* (Vol. 13). New York: Academic Press, 1979.

Amsel, A. The role of frustrative nonreward in noncontinuous reward situations. *Psychological Bulletin*, 1958, *55*, 102–119.

Amsel, A. Partial reinforcement effects on vigor and persistence. In K. W. Spence & J. T. Spence (Eds.), *The psychology of learning and motivation* (Vol. 1). New York: Academic Press, 1967.

Amsel, A. Inhibition and mediation in classical, Pavlovian, and instrumental conditioning. In R. A. Boakes & M. S. Halliday (Eds.), *Inhibition and learning*. London: Academic Press, 1972.

Amsel, A. The ontogeny of appetitive learning and persistence in the rat. In N. E. Spear & B. A. Campbell (Eds.), *Ontogeny of learning and memory*. Hillsdale, N.J.: Lawrence Erlbaum, 1979.

Amsel, A., Rashotte, M. E., & MacKinnon, J. R. Partial reinforcement effects within subject and between subjects. *Psychological Monographs*, 1966, *80* (20, Whole No. 628).

Anderson, D. C., Crowell, C. R., Cunningham, C. L., & Lupo, J. V. Behavior during shock exposure as a determinant of subsequent interference with shuttle box escape-avoidance learning in the rat. *Journal of Experimental Psychology: Animal Behavior Processes*, 1979, *5*, 243–257.

Anger, D. The role of temporal discrimination in the reinforcement of Sidman avoidance behavior. *Journal of the Experimental Analysis of Behavior*, 1963, *6*, 477–506.

Anisman, H., de Catanzaro, D., & Remington, G. Escape performance following exposure to inescapable shock: Deficits in motor response maintenance. *Journal of Experimental Psychology: Animal Behavior Processes*, 1978, *4*, 197–218.

Annable, A., & Wearden, J. H. Grooming movements as operants in the rat. *Journal of the Experimental Analysis of Behavior*, 1979, *32*, 297–304.

Azrin, N. H. Some effects of two intermittent schedules of immediate and non-immediate punishment. *Journal of Psychology*, 1956, *42*, 3–21.

Azrin, N. H. Some effects of noise on human behavior. *Journal of the Experimental Analysis of Behavior*, 1958, *1*, 183–200.

Azrin, N. H. Punishment and recovery during fixed ratio performance. *Journal of the Experimental Analysis of Behavior*, 1959, *2*, 301–305.

Azrin, N. H. Effects of punishment intensity during variable-interval reinforcement. *Journal of the Experimental Analysis of Behavior*, 1960, *3*, 123–142.

Azrin, N. H., & Foxx, R. M. *Toilet training in less than a day*. New York: Simon & Schuster, 1974.

Azrin, N. H., & Hake, D. F. Positive conditioned suppression: Conditioned suppression using positive reinforcers as the unconditioned stimuli. *Journal of the Experimental Analysis of Behavior*, 1969, *12*, 167–173.

Azrin, N. H., Hake, D. F., Holz, W. C., & Hutchinson, R. R. Motivational aspects of escape from punishment. *Journal of the Experimental Analysis of Behavior*, 1965, *8*, 31–44.

Azrin, N. H., & Holz, W. C. Punishment during fixed-interval reinforcement. *Journal of the Experimental Analysis of Behavior*, 1961, *4*, 343–347.

Azrin, N. H., & Holz, W. C. Punishment. In W. K. Honig (Ed.), *Operant behavior: Areas of research and application.* New York: Appleton-Century-Crofts, 1966.

Azrin, N. H., Holz, W. C., & Hake, D. F. Fixed-ratio punishment. *Journal of the Experimental Analysis of Behavior*, 1963, *6*, 141–148.

Azrin, N. H., Hutchinson, R. R., & Hake, D. F. Extinction-induced aggression. *Journal of the Experimental Analysis of Behavior*, 1966, *9*, 191–204.

Baerends, G. P. The ethological analysis of fish behavior. In M. E. Brown (Ed.), *The physiology of fishes.* New York: Academic Press, 1957.

Bandura, A. *Principles of behavior modification.* New York: Holt, Rinehart & Winston, 1969.

Barker, L. M., Best, M. R., & Domjan, M. (Eds.). *Learning mechanisms in food selection.* Waco, Texas: Baylor University Press, 1977.

Baron, A. Delayed punishment of a runway response. *Journal of Comparative and Physiological Psychology*, 1965, *60*, 131–134.

Baum, M. Extinction of avoidance response following response prevention: Some parametric investigations. *Canadian Journal of Psychology*, 1969, *23*, 1–10.

Baum, M. Extinction of avoidance responding through response prevention (flooding). *Psychological Bulletin*, 1970, *74*, 276–284.

Baum, W. M. Time allocation in human vigilance. *Journal of the Experimental Analysis of Behavior*, 1975, *23*, 45–53.

Beatty, W. W., & Shavalia, D. A. Rat spatial memory: Resistance to retroactive interference at long retention intervals. *Animal Learning and Behavior*, 1980, *8*, 550–552. (a)

Beatty, W. W., & Shavalia, D. A. Spatial memory in rats: Time course of working memory and effects of anesthetics. *Behavioral and Neural Biology*, 1980, *28*, 454–462. (b)

Bechterev, V. M. *La psychologie objective.* Paris: Alcan, 1913.

Benedict, J. O., & Ayres, J. J. B. Factors affecting conditioning in the truly random control procedure in the rat. *Journal of Comparative and Physiological Psychology*, 1972, *78*, 323–330.

Bernstein, I. L. Learned taste aversions in children receiving chemotherapy. *Science*, 1978, *200*, 1302–1303.

Bernstein, I. L., & Webster, M. M. Learned taste aversions in humans. *Physiology and Behavior*, 1980, *25*, 363–366.

Best, M. R. Conditioned and latent inhibition in taste-aversion learning: Clarifying the role of learned safety. *Journal of Experimental Psychology: Animal Behavior Processes*, 1975, *1*, 97–113.

Best, M. R., & Gemberling, G. A. The role of short-term processes in the CS preexposure effect and the delay of reinforcement gradient in long-delay taste-aversion learning. *Journal of Experimental Psychology: Animal Behavior Processes*, 1977, *3*, 253–263.

Best, P. J., Best, M. R., & Henggeler, S. The contribution of environmental noningestive cues in conditioning with aversive internal consequences. In L. M. Barker, M. R. Best, & M. Domjan (Eds.), *Learning mechanisms in food selection.* Waco, Texas: Baylor University Press, 1977.

Bindra, D. The interrelated mechanisms of reinforcement and motivation and the nature of their influence on response. In W. J. Arnold & D. Levine (Eds.), *Nebraska Symposium on Motivation* (Vol. 17). Lincoln: University of Nebraska Press, 1969.

Bindra, D. A motivational view of learning, performance, and behavior modification. *Psychological Review*, 1974, *81*, 199–213.

Bitterman, M. E. Classical conditioning in the goldfish as a function of the CS-US interval. *Journal of Comparative and Physiological Psychology*, 1964, *58*, 359–366.

Bitterman, M. E. The comparative analysis of learning. *Science*, 1975, *188*, 699–709.

Black, A. H. Autonomic aversive conditioning in infrahuman subjects. In F. R. Brush (Ed.), *Aversive conditioning and learning.* New York: Academic Press, 1971.

Black, A. H. Comments on "Learned helplessness: Theory and evidence" by Maier and Seligman. *Journal of Experimental Psychology: General*, 1977, *106*, 41–43.

Black, R. W. Incentive motivation and the parameters of reward in instrumental conditioning. In W. J. Arnold & D. Levine (Eds.), *Nebraska Symposium on Motivation* (Vol. 17). Lincoln: University of Nebraska Press, 1969.

Blackman, D. Conditioned suppression and the effects of classical conditioning on operant behavior. In W. K. Honig & J. E. R. Staddon (Eds.), *Handbook of operant behavior.* Englewood Cliffs, N.J.: Prentice-Hall, 1977.

Blakemore, C., & Cooper, G. F. Development of the brain depends on visual environment. *Science*, 1970, *228*, 477–478.

Blough, D. S. Delayed matching in the pigeon.

Journal of the Experimental Analysis of Behavior, 1959, *2,* 151–160.

Boakes, R. A., & Halliday, M. S. (Eds.). *Inhibition and learning.* London: Academic Press, 1972.

Boakes, R. A., Poli, M., Lockwood, M. J., & Goodall, G. A study of misbehavior: Token reinforcement in the rat. *Journal of the Experimental Analysis of Behavior,* 1978, *29,* 115–134.

Boice, R. Domestication. *Psychological Bulletin,* 1973, *80,* 215–230.

Boice, R. Burrows of wild and albino rats: Effects of domestication, outdoor raising, age, experience, and maternal state. *Journal of Comparative and Physiological Psychology,* 1977, *91,* 649–661.

Boland, F. J., Mellor, C. S., & Revusky, S. Chemical aversion treatment of alcoholism: Lithium as the aversive agent. *Behaviour Research and Therapy,* 1978, *16,* 401–409.

Bolles, R. C. Avoidance and escape learning: Simultaneous acquisition of different responses. *Journal of Comparative and Physiological Psychology,* 1969, *68,* 355–358.

Bolles, R. C. Species-specific defense reactions and avoidance learning. *Psychological Review,* 1970, *71,* 32–48.

Bolles, R. C. Species-specific defense reaction. In F. R. Brush (Ed.), *Aversive conditioning and learning.* New York: Academic Press, 1971.

Bolles, R. C. The avoidance learning problem. In G. H. Bower (Ed.), *The psychology of learning and motivation* (Vol. 6). New York: Academic Press, 1972.

Bolles, R. C., & Grossen, N. E. Effects of an informational stimulus on the acquisition of avoidance behavior in rats. *Journal of Comparative and Physiological Psychology,* 1969, *68,* 90–99.

Bolles, R. C., Stokes, L. W., & Younger, M. S. Does CS termination reinforce avoidance behavior? *Journal of Comparative and Physiological Psychology,* 1966, *62,* 201–207.

Bouton, M. E., & Bolles, R. C. The role of conditioned contextual stimuli in reinstatement of extinguished fear. *Journal of Experimental Psychology: Animal Behavior Processes,* 1979, *5,* 368–378.

Brady, J. P., & Lind, D. L. Experimental analysis of hysterical blindness: Operant conditioning techniques. *Archives of General Psychiatry,* 1961, *4,* 331–339.

Breland, K., & Breland, M. The misbehavior of organisms. *American Psychologist,* 1961, *16,* 681–684.

Brener, J., & Goesling, W. J. Avoidance conditioning of activity and immobility in rats. *Journal of Comparative and Physiological Psychology,* 1970, *70,* 276–280.

Brogden, W. J., Lipman, E. A., & Culler, E. The role of incentive in conditioning and extinction. *American Journal of Psychology,* 1938, *51,* 109–117.

Brown, J. S., & Jacobs, A. The role of fear in the motivation and acquisition of responses. *Journal of Experimental Psychology,* 1949, *39,* 747–759.

Brown, P. L. & Jenkins, H. M. Auto-shaping the pigeons's key peck. *Journal of the Experimental Analysis of Behavior,* 1968, *11,* 1–8.

Brownstein, A. Predicting instrumental performance from independent rates of contingent responses in a choice situation. *Journal of Experimental Psychology,* 1962, *63,* 29–31.

Bull, J. A., III. An interaction between appetitive Pavlovian CS's and instrumental avoidance responding. *Learning and Motivation,* 1970, *1,* 18–26.

Bull, J. A., III, & Overmier, J. B. Additive and subtractive properties of excitation and inhibition. *Journal of Comparative and Physiological Psychology,* 1968, *66,* 511–514.

Burkhard, B. Preference and response substitutability with maximization of behavioral value. In M. Commons, R. J. Herrnstein, & H. Rachlin (Eds.), *Quantitative analysis of behavior* (Vol. 2). Cambridge, Mass.: Ballinger, 1981.

Burkhard, B., Rachlin, H., & Schrader, S. Reinforcement and punishment in a closed system. *Learning and Motivation,* 1978, *9,* 392–410.

Burkhardt, P. E., & Ayres, J. J. B. CS and US duration effects in one-trial simultaneous conditioning as assessed by conditioned suppression of licking in rats. *Animal Learning and Behavior,* 1978, *6,* 225–230.

Caggiula, A. R., & Hoebel, B. G. "Copulation-reward" site in the posterior hypothalamus. *Science,* 1966, *153,* 1284–1285.

Camp, D. S., Raymond, G. A., & Church, R. M. Temporal relationship between response and punishment. *Journal of Experimental Psychology,* 1967, *74,* 114–123.

Campbell, B. A., & Church, R. M. (Eds.). *Punishment and aversive behavior.* New York: Appleton-Century-Crofts, 1969.

Campbell, B. A., & Randall, P. K. The effect of reinstatement stimulus conditions on the maintenance of long-term memory. *Developmental Psychobiology,* 1976, *9,* 325–333.

Campbell, H. J. Pleasure-seeking brains: Artificial tickles, natural joys of thought. *Smithsonian,* October 1971, pp. 14–23.

Capaldi, E. J. A sequential hypothesis of instrumental learning. In K. W. Spence & J. T. Spence (Eds.), *The psychology of learning and motivation* (Vol. 1). New York: Academic Press, 1967.

Capaldi, E. J.   Memory and learning: A sequential viewpoint. In W. K. Honig & P. H. R. James (Eds.), *Animal memory*. New York: Academic Press, 1971.

Capaldi, E. J., & Molina, P.   Element discriminability as a determinant of serial-pattern learning. *Animal Learning and Behavior*, 1979, *7*, 318–322.

Capaldi, E. J., Verry, D. R., & Davidson, T. L.   Why rule encoding by animals in serial learning remains to be established. *Animal Learning and Memory*, 1980, *8*, 691–692.

Catania, A. C.   Concurrent performances: A baseline for the study of reinforcement magnitude. *Journal of the Experimental Analysis of Behavior*, 1963, *6*, 299–300.

Cerletti, U., & Bini, L.   Electric shock treatment. *Bollettino ed atti della Accademia medica di Roma*, 1938, *64*, 36.

Chomsky, N.   *Language and mind*. New York: Harcourt Brace Jovanovich, 1972.

Chung, S.-H.   Effects of delayed reinforcement in a concurrent situation. *Journal of the Experimental Analysis of Behavior*, 1965, *8*, 439–444.

Chung, S.-H., & Herrnstein, R. J.   Choice and delay of reinforcement. *Journal of the Experimental Analysis of Behavior*, 1967, *10*, 67–74.

Church, R. M.   The varied effects of punishment on behavior. *Psychological Review*, 1963, *70*, 369–402.

Church, R. M.   Response suppression. In B. A. Campbell & R. M. Church (Eds.), *Punishment and aversive behavior*. New York: Appleton-Century-Crofts, 1969.

Church, R. M., & Raymond, G. A.   Influence of the schedule of positive reinforcement on punished behavior. *Journal of Comparative and Physiological Psychology*, 1967, *63*, 329–332.

Church, R. M., Wooten, C. L., & Matthews, T. J.   Discriminative punishment and the conditioned emotional response. *Learning and Motivation*, 1970, *1*, 1–17.

Cicala, G. A., & Owen, J. W.   Warning signal termination and a feedback signal may not serve the same function. *Learning and Motivation*, 1976, *7*, 356–367.

Cohen, L. B.   Habituation of infant visual attention. In T. J. Tighe & R. N. Leaton (Eds.), *Habituation: Perspectives from child development, animal behavior, and neurophysiology*. Hillsdale, N.J.: Lawrence Erlbaum, 1976.

Coleman, S. R.   Consequences of response-contingent change in unconditioned stimulus intensity upon the rabbit (*Oryctolagus cuniculus*) nictitating membrane response. *Journal of Comparative and Physiological Psychology*, 1975, *88*, 591–595.

Coleman, S. R., & Gormezano, I.   Classical conditioning and the "Law of Effect": Historical and empirical assessment. *Behaviorism*, 1979, *7*, 1–33.

Conger, R., & Killeen, P.   Use of concurrent operants in small group research. *Pacific Sociological Review*, 1974, *17*, 399–416.

Coons, E. E., & Miller, N. E.   Conflict vs. consolidation of memory traces to explain "retrograde amnesia" produced by ECS. *Journal of Comparative and Physiological Psychology*, 1960, *53*, 524–531.

Coulter, X., Riccio, D. C., & Page, H. A.   Effects of blocking an instrumental avoidance response: Facilitated extinction but persistence of "fear." *Journal of Comparative and Physiological Psychology*, 1969, *68*, 377–381.

Crozier, W. J., & Navez, A. E.   The geotropic orientation of gastropods. *Journal of General Physiology*, 1930, *3*, 3–37.

Culler, E. A.   Recent advances in some concepts of conditioning. *Psychological Review*, 1938, *45*, 134–153.

D'Amato, M. R.   Delayed matching and short-term memory in monkeys. In G. H. Bower (Ed.), *The psychology of learning and motivation* (Vol. 7). New York: Academic Press, 1973.

D'Amato, M. R., Fazzaro, J., & Etkin, M.   Anticipatory responding and avoidance discrimination as factors in avoidance conditioning. *Journal of Comparative and Physiological Psychology*, 1968, *77*, 41–47.

Dammond, K. R.   The effects of temporal contiguity, necessity, and sufficiency on children's causal inferences. Unpublished doctoral dissertation, State University of New York at Stony Brook, 1978.

Dardano, J. F., & Sauerbrunn, D.   An aversive stimulus as a correlated block counter in FR performance. *Journal of the Experimental Analysis of Behavior*, 1964, *7*, 37–43.

Davis, H.   Conditioned suppression: A survey of the literature. *Psychonomic Monograph Supplements*, 1968, *2* (14, Whole No. 30), 283–291.

Davis, H., & Kreuter, C.   Conditioned suppression of an avoidance response by a stimulus paired with food. *Journal of the Experimental Analysis of Behavior*, 1972, *17*, 277–285.

Davis, M.   Effects of interstimulus interval length and variability on startle-response habituation in the rat. *Journal of Comparative and Physiological Psychology*, 1970, *72*, 177–192.

Davis, M.   Sensitization of the rat startle response by noise. *Journal of Comparative and Physiological Psychology*, 1974, *87*, 571–581.

Decke, E.   Effects of taste on the eating behavior of obese and normal persons. Cited in S. Schacter,

Emotion, obesity, and crime. New York: Academic Press, 1971.

Delprato, D. J. Extinction of one-way avoidance and delayed warning signal termination. *Journal of Experimental Psychology,* 1969, *80,* 192–193.

Denny, M. R. Relaxation theory and experiments. In F. R. Brush (Ed.), *Aversive conditioning and learning.* New York: Academic Press, 1971.

Desiderato, O. Generalization of excitation and inhibition in control of avoidance responding by Pavlovian CS's in dogs. *Journal of Comparative and Physiological Psychology,* 1969, *68,* 611–616.

Deutsch, J. A. *The structural basis of behavior.* Chicago: University of Chicago Press, 1960.

Deutsch, R. Conditioned hypoglycemia: A mechanism for saccharin-induced sensitivity to insulin in the rat. *Journal of Comparative and Physiological Psychology,* 1974, *86,* 350–358.

deVilliers, P. A. The law of effect and avoidance: A quantitative relationship between response rate and shock-frequency reduction. *Journal of the Experimental Analysis of Behavior,* 1974, *21,* 223–235.

Deweer, B., Sara, S. J., & Hars, B. Contextual cues and memory retrieval in rats: Alleviation of forgetting by a pretest exposure to background stimuli. *Animal Learning and Behavior,* 1980, *8,* 265–272.

Dinsmoor, J. A. A discrimination based on punishment. *Quarterly Journal of Experimental Psychology,* 1952, *4,* 27–45.

Dinsmoor, J. A. Punishment: I. The avoidance hypothesis. *Psychological Review,* 1954, *61,* 34–46.

Dinsmoor, J. A. Variable-interval escape from stimuli accompanied by shocks. *Journal of the Experimental Analysis of Behavior,* 1962, *5,* 41–48.

Dinsmoor, J. A. Escape, avoidance, punishment: Where do we stand? *Journal of the Experimental Analysis of Behavior,* 1977, *28,* 83–95.

Dinsmoor, J. A., & Sears, G. W. Control of avoidance by a response-produced stimulus. *Learning and Motivation,* 1973, *4,* 284–293.

Dobrzecka, C., Szwejkowska, G., & Konorski, J. Qualitative versus directional cues in two forms of differentiation. *Science,* 1966, *153,* 87–89.

Domjan, M. Determinants of the enhancement of flavored-water intake by prior exposure. *Journal of Experimental Psychology: Animal Behavior Processes,* 1976, *2,* 17–27.

Domjan, M. Selective suppression of drinking during a limited period following aversive drug treatment in rats. *Journal of Experimental Psychology: Animal Behavior Processes,* 1977, *3,* 66–76.

Domjan, M. Ingestional aversion learning: Unique and general processes. In J. S. Rosenblatt, R. A. Hinde, C. Beer, & M. Busnel (Eds.), *Advances in the study of behavior* (Vol 11). New York: Academic Press, 1980.

Domjan, M., & Best, M. R. Paradoxical effects of proximal unconditioned stimulus preexposure: Interference with and conditioning of a taste aversion. *Journal of Experimental Psychology: Animal Behavior Processes,* 1977, *3,* 310–321.

Domjan, M., & Best, M. R. Interference with ingestional aversion learning produced by preexposure to the unconditioned stimulus: Associative and nonassociative aspects. *Learning and Motivation,* 1980, *11,* 522–537.

Domjan, M., & Wilson, N. E. Specificity of cue to consequence in aversion learning in the rat. *Psychonomic Science,* 1972, *26,* 143–145.

Donegan, N. H., & Wagner, A. R. Conditioned diminution and facilitation of the UCR: A sometimes-opponent-process interpretation. In I. Gormezano, W. F. Prokasy, & R. F. Thompson (Eds.), *Classical conditioning III: Behavioral, neurophysiological, and neurochemical studies in the rabbit.* Hillsdale, N.J.: Lawrence Erlbaum, 1981.

Duncan, C. P. The retroactive effect of electroshock on learning. *Journal of Comparative and Physiological Psychology,* 1949, *42,* 32–44.

Duncker, K. On problem solving. *Psychological Monographs,* 1945, *58* (Whole No. 270).

Dunham, P. J. Punishment: Method and theory. *Psychological Review,* 1971, *78,* 58–70.

Dunham, P. J. Some effects of punishment on unpunished responding. *Journal of the Experimental Analysis of Behavior,* 1972, *17,* 443–450.

Dunham, P. J. Changes in unpunished responding during response-contingent punishment. *Animal Learning and Behavior,* 1978, *6,* 174–180.

Dweck, C. S., & Wagner, A. R. Situational cues and correlation between conditioned stimulus and unconditioned stimulus as determinants of the conditioned emotional response. *Psychonomic Science,* 1970, *18,* 145–147.

Eibl-Eibesfeldt, I. *Ethology: The biology of behavior.* New York: Holt, Rinehart & Winston, 1970.

Elkins, R. L. Aversion therapy for alcoholism: Chemical, electrical, or verbal imaginary? *International Journal of the Addictions,* 1975, *10,* 157–209.

Ellison, G. D. Differential salivary conditioning to traces. *Journal of Comparative and Physiological Psychology,* 1964, *57,* 373–380.

Ellison, G. D., & Konorski, J. Separation of the salivary and motor responses in instrumental conditioning. *Science,* 1964, *146,* 1071–1072.

Engberg, L. A., Hansen, G., Welker, R. L., & Thomas, D. R. Acquisition of key-pecking via autoshaping as a function of prior experience:

"Learned laziness"? *Science*, 1972, *178*, 1002–1004.

Epstein, S. M.   Toward a unified theory of anxiety. In B. Maher (Ed.), *Progress in experimental personality research* (Vol. 4). New York: Academic Press, 1967.

Esplin, D. W., & Woodbury, D. M.   Spinal reflexes and seizure patterns in the two-toed sloth. *Science*, 1961, *133*, 1426–1427.

Estes, W. K.   Discriminative conditioning: I. A discriminative property of conditioned anticipation. *Journal of Experimental Psychology*, 1943, *32*, 150–155.

Estes, W. K.   An experimental study of punishment. *Psychological Monographs*, 1944, *57* (3, Whole No. 263).

Estes, W. K.   Discriminative conditioning: II. Effects of a Pavlovian conditioned stimulus upon a subsequently established operant response. *Journal of Experimental Psychology*, 1948, *38*, 173–177.

Estes, W. K.   Outline of a theory of punishment. In B. A. Campbell & R. M. Church (Eds.), *Punishment and aversive behavior*. New York: Appleton-Century-Crofts, 1969.

Estes, W. K., & Skinner, B. F.   Some quantitative properties of anxiety. *Journal of Experimental Psychology*, 1941, *29*, 390–400.

Falk, J. L.   Production of polydipsia in normal rats by an intermittent food schedule. *Science*, 1961, *133*, 195–196.

Falk, J. L.   The nature and determinants of adjunctive behavior. In R. M. Gilbert & J. D. Keehn (Eds.), *Schedule effects: Drug, drinking, and aggression*. Toronto: Addiction Research Foundation and University of Toronto Press, 1972.

Feldman, D. T., & Gordon, W. C.   The alleviation of short-term retention decrements with reactivation. *Learning and Motivation*, 1979, *10*, 198–210.

Ferster, C. B., & Skinner, B. F.   *Schedules of reinforcement*. New York: Appleton-Century-Crofts, 1957.

Flexner, J. B., Flexner, L. B., & Stellar, E.   Memory in mice as affected by intracerebral puromycin. *Science*, 1963, *141*, 57–59.

Flory, R.   Attack behavior as a function of minimum interfood interval. *Journal of the Experimental Analysis of Behavior*, 1969, *12*, 825–828.

Foree, D. D., & LoLordo, V. M.   Attention in the pigeon: The differential effects of food-getting vs. shock avoidance procedures. *Journal of Comparative and Physiological Psychology*, 1973, *85*, 551–558.

Foree, D. D., & LoLordo, V. M.   Stimulus-reinforcer interactions in the pigeon: The role of electric shock and the avoidance contingency.

Journal of Experimental Psychology: Animal Behavior Processes, 1975, *1*, 39–46.

Fouts, R.   Use of guidance in teaching sign language to a chimpanzee. *Journal of Comparative and Physiological Psychology*, 1972, *80*, 515–522.

Fox, L.   Effecting the use of efficient study habits. In R. Ulrich, T. Stachnik, & J. Mabry (Eds.), *Control of human behavior*. Glenview, Ill.: Scott, Foresman, 1966.

Foxx, R. M., & Azrin, N. H.   The elimination of autistic self-stimulatory behavior by overcorrection. *Journal of Applied Behavioral Analysis*, 1973, *6*, 1–14.

Fraenkel, F. D.   The role of response-punishment contingency in the suppression of a positively-reinforced operant. *Learning and Motivation*, 1975, *6*, 385–403.

Fraenkel, G. S., & Gunn, D. L.   *The orientation of animals* (2nd ed.). New York: Dover, 1961.

Gamzu, E. R., & Williams, D. R.   Classical conditioning of a complex skeletal act. *Science*, 1971, *171*, 923–925.

Gamzu, E. R., & Williams, D. R.   Associative factors underlying the pigeon's key pecking in autoshaping procedures. *Journal of the Experimental Analysis of Behavior*, 1973, *19*, 225–232.

Gantt, W. H.   Conditional or conditioned, reflex or response? *Conditioned Reflex*, 1966, *1*, 69–74.

Garb, J. J., & Stunkard, A. J.   Taste aversions in man. *American Journal of Psychiatry*, 1974, *131*, 1204–1207.

Garcia, J., Ervin, F. R., & Koelling, R. A.   Learning with prolonged delay of reinforcement. *Psychonomic Science*, 1966, *5*, 121–122.

Garcia, J., Hankins, W. G., & Rusiniak, K. W.   Behavioral regulation of the milieu interne in man and rat. *Science*, 1974, *185*, 824–831.

Garcia, J., & Koelling, R. A.   Relation of cue to consequence in avoidance learning. *Psychonomic Science*, 1966, *4*, 123–124.

Gardner, E. T., & Lewis, P.   Negative reinforcement with shock-frequency increase. *Journal of the Experimental Analysis of Behavior*, 1976, *25*, 3–14.

Gardner, R. A., & Gardner, B. T.   Teaching sign language to a chimpanzee. *Science*, 1969, *165*, 664–672.

Gardner, R. A., & Gardner, B. T.   Early signs of language in child and chimpanzee. *Science*, 1975, *187*, 752–753.

Gardner, R. A., & Gardner, B. T.   Comparative psychology and language acquisition. *Annals of the New York Academy of Science*, 1978, *309*, 37–76.

Gemberling, G. A., & Domjan, M.   Selective association in one-day-old rats: Taste-toxicosis and texture-shock aversion learning. *Journal of Comparative and Physiological Psychology*, in press.

Gentry, W. D. Fixed-ratio schedule-induced aggression. *Journal of the Experimental Analysis of Behavior*, 1968, *11*, 813–817.

Glickman, S. E., & Schiff, B. B. A biological theory of reinforcement. *Psychological Review*, 1967, *74*, 81–109.

Gold, P. E., Haycock, J. W., Macri, J., McGaugh, J. L. Retrograde amnesia and the "reminder effect": An alternative interpretation. *Science*, 1973, *180*, 1199–1201.

Gollub, L. R. The chaining of fixed-interval schedules. Unpublished doctoral dissertation, Harvard University, 1958.

Gollub, L. R. Conditioned reinforcement: Schedule effects. In W. K. Honig & J. E. R. Staddon (Eds.), *Handbook of operant behavior*. Englewood Cliffs, N.J.: Prentice-Hall, 1977.

Gonzalez, R. C., Gentry, G. V., & Bitterman, M. E. Relational discrimination of intermediate size in the chimpanzee. *Journal of Comparative and Physiological Psychology*, 1954, *47*, 385–388.

Gordon, W. C. Mechanisms for cue-induced retention enhancement. In N. E. Spear & R. R. Miller (Eds.), *Information processing in animals: Memory mechanisms*. Hillsdale, N.J.: Lawrence Erlbaum, 1981.

Gordon, W. C., Brennan, M. J., & Schlesinger, J. L. The interaction of memories in the rat: Effects on short-term retention performance. *Learning and Motivation*, 1976, *7*, 406–417.

Gordon, W. C., & Feldman, D. T. Reactivation-induced interference in a short-term retention paradigm. *Learning and Motivation*, 1978, *9*, 164–178.

Gordon, W. C., & Mowrer, R. R. An extinction trial as a reminder treatment following electroconvulsive shock. *Animal Learning and Behavior*, 1980, *8*, 363–367.

Gormezano, I. Classical conditioning. In J. B. Sidowski (Ed.), *Experimental methods and instrumentation in psychology*. New York: McGraw-Hill, 1966.

Gormezano, I., & Coleman, S. R. The law of Effect and CR contingent modification of the UCS. *Conditioned Reflex*, 1973, *8*, 41–56.

Gormezano, I., & Hiller, G. W. Omission training of the jaw-movement response of the rabbit to a water US. *Psychonomic Science*, 1972, *29*, 276–278.

Grant, D. S. Proactive interference in pigeon short-term memory. *Journal of Experimental Psychology: Animal Behavior Processes*, 1975, *1*, 207–220.

Grant, D. S. Effect of sample presentation time on long-delay matching in the pigeon. *Learning and Motivation*, 1976, *7*, 580–590.

Grant, D. S. Short-term memory in the pigeon. In N. E. Spear & R. R. Miller (Eds.), *Information processing in animals: Memory mechanisms*. Hillsdale, N.J.: Lawrence Erlbaum, 1981. (a)

Grant, D. S. Stimulus control of information processing in pigeon short-term memory. *Learning and Motivation*, 1981, *12*, 19–39. (b)

Grant, D. S., & Roberts, W. A. Trace interaction in pigeon short-term memory. *Journal of Experimental Psychology*, 1973, *101*, 21–29.

Grant, D. S., & Roberts, W. A. Sources of retroactive inhibition in pigeon short-term memory. *Journal of Experimental Psychology: Animal Behavior Processes*, 1976, *2*, 1–16.

Grice, G. R. The relation of secondary reinforcement to delayed reward in visual discrimination learning. *Journal of Experimental Psychology*, 1948, *38*, 1–16.

Griffin, D. R. *The question of animal awareness*. New York: Rockefeller University Press, 1976.

Grossberg, J. M. Successful behavior therapy in a case of speech phobia ("stage fright"). *Journal of Speech and Hearing Disorders*, 1965, *30*, 285–288.

Grossen, N. E., & Kelley, M. J. Species-specific behavior and acquisition of avoidance behavior in rats. *Journal of Comparative and Physiological Psychology*, 1972, *81*, 307–310.

Grossen, N. E., Kostansek, D. J., & Bolles, R. C. Effects of appetitive discriminative stimuli on avoidance behavior. *Journal of Experimental Psychology*, 1969, *81*, 340–343.

Groves, P. M., Lee, D., & Thompson, R. F. Effects of stimulus frequency and intensity on habituation and sensitization in acute spinal cat. *Physiology and Behavior*, 1969, *4*, 383–388.

Groves, P. M., & Thompson, R. F. Habituation: A dual-process theory. *Psychological Review*, 1970, *77*, 419–450.

Guha, D., Dutta, S. N., & Pradhan, S. N. Conditioning of gastric secretion by epinephrine in rats. *Proceedings of the Society for Experimental Biology and Medicine*, 1974, *147*, 817–819.

Guthrie, E. R. *The psychology of human conflict*. New York: Harper, 1938.

Guthrie, E. R. *The psychology of learning* (Rev. ed.). New York: Harper & Row, 1952.

Gutman, A., & Maier, S. F. Operant and Pavlovian factors in cross-response transfer of inhibitory stimulus control. *Learning and Motivation*, 1978, *9*, 231–254.

Guttman, N., & Kalish, H. I. Discriminability and stimulus generalization. *Journal of Experimental Psychology*, 1956, *51*, 79–88.

Hake, D. F., & Azrin, N. H. Conditioned punishment. *Journal of the Experimental Analysis of Behavior*, 1965, *8*, 279–293.

Hale, E. B., & Almquist, J. O. Relation of sexual behavior to germ cell output in farm animals. *Journal of Dairy Science*, Supplement, 1960, *43*, 145–149.

Hammond, L. J. Increased responding to CS− in differential CER. *Psychonomic Science*, 1966, *5*, 337–338.

Hammond, L. J. Retardation of fear acquisition by a previously inhibitory CS. *Journal of Comparative and Physiological Psychology*, 1968, *66*, 756–759.

Hankins, W. G., Rusiniak, K. W., & Garcia, J. Dissociation of odor and taste in shock-avoidance learning. *Behavioral Biology*, 1976, *18*, 345–358.

Hanson, H. M. Effects of discrimination training on stimulus generalization. *Journal of Experimental Psychology*, 1959, *58*, 321–333.

Harlow, H. F. The formation of learning sets. *Psychological Review*, 1949, *56*, 51–65.

Harlow, H. F. Age-mate or peer affectional system. In D. S. Lehrman, R. H. Hinde, & E. Shaw (Eds.), *Advances in the study of behavior* (Vol. 2). New York: Academic Press, 1969.

Haroutunian, V., & Riccio, D. C. Drug-induced "arousal" and the effectiveness of CS exposure in the reinstatement of memory. *Behavioral and Neural Biology*, 1979, *26*, 115–120.

Hart, B. L. Reflexive behavior. In G. Bermant (Ed.), *Perspectives in animal behavior*. Glenview, Ill.: Scott, Foresman, 1973.

Hayes, K. J., & Hayes, C. The intellectual development of a home-raised chimpanzee. *Proceedings of the American Philosophical Society*, 1951, *95*, 105–109.

Hearst, E. Stress-induced breakdown of an appetitive discrimination. *Journal of the Experimental Analysis of Behavior*, 1965, *8*, 135–146.

Hearst, E. Discrimination learning as the summation of excitation and inhibition. *Science*, 1968, *162*, 1303–1306.

Hearst, E. Excitation, inhibition, and discrimination learning. In N. J. Mackintosh & W. K. Honig (Eds.), *Fundamental issues in associative learning*. Halifax: Dalhousie University Press, 1969.

Hearst, E. Pavlovian conditioning and directed movements. In G. Bower (Ed.), *The psychology of learning and motivation* (Vol. 9). New York: Academic Press, 1975.

Hearst, E., & Franklin, S. R. Positive and negative relations between a signal and food: Approach-withdrawal behavior to the signal. *Journal of Experimental Psychology: Animal Behavior Processes*, 1977, *3*, 37–52.

Hearst, E., & Jenkins, H. M. *Sign-tracking: The stimulus-reinforcer relation and directed action*. Austin, Texas: Psychonomic Society, 1974.

Hearst, E., & Peterson, G. B. Transfer of conditioned excitation and inhibition from one operant response to another. *Journal of Experimental Psychology*, 1973, *99*, 360–368.

Hearst, E., & Sidman, M. Some behavioral effects of a concurrently positive and negative stimulus. *Journal of the Experimental Analysis of Behavior*, 1961, *4*, 251–256.

Hebb, D. O. The distinction between "classical" and "instrumental." *Canadian Journal of Psychology*, 1956, *10*, 165–166.

Heingartner, A., & Hall, J. V. Affective consequences in adults and children of repeated exposure to auditory stimuli. *Journal of Personality and Social Psychology*, 1974, *29*, 719–723.

Herberg, L. J. Seminal ejaculation following positively reinforcing electrical stimulation of the rat hypothalamus. *Journal of Comparative and Physiological Psychology*, 1963, *56*, 679–685.

Herman, L. M., & Gordon, J. A. Auditory delayed matching in the bottlenose dolphin. *Journal of the Experimental Analysis of Behavior*, 1974, *21*, 19–26.

Herman, R. L., & Azrin, N. H. Punishment by noise in an alternative response situation. *Journal of the Experimental Analysis of Behavior*, 1964, *7*, 185–188.

Herrnstein, R. J. Relative and absolute strength of response as a function of frequency of reinforcement. *Journal of the Experimental Analysis of Behavior*, 1961, *4*, 267–272.

Herrnstein, R. J. Superstition: A corollary of the principles of operant conditioning. In W. K. Honig (Ed.), *Operant behavior: Areas of research and application*. New York: Appleton-Century-Crofts, 1966.

Herrnstein, R. J. Method and theory in the study of avoidance. *Psychological Review*, 1969, *76*, 49–69.

Herrnstein, R. J. On the law of effect. *Journal of the Experimental Analysis of Behavior*, 1970, *13*, 243–266.

Herrnstein, R. J., & Hineline, P. N. Negative reinforcement as shock-frequency reduction. *Journal of the Experimental Analysis of Behavior*, 1966, *9*, 421–430.

Herrnstein, R. J., & Loveland, D. H. Complex visual concept in the pigeon. *Science*, 1964, *146*, 549–551.

Herrnstein, R. J., Loveland, D. H., & Cable, C. Natural concepts in pigeons. *Journal of Experimental Psychology: Animal Behavior Processes*, 1976, *2*, 285–301.

Heth, C. D., & Rescorla, R. A. Simultaneous and backward fear conditioning in the rat. *Journal of Comparative and Physiological Psychology*, 1973, *82*, 434–443.

Hilgard, E. R. The nature of the conditioned response: I. The case for and against stimulus substitution. *Psychological Review*, 1936, *43*, 366–385.

Hilgard, E. R., & Bower, G. H. *Theories of learning* (4th ed). Englewood Cliffs, N.J.: Prentice-Hall, 1975.

Hilgard, E. R., & Marquis, D. G. Acquisition, extinction, and retention of conditioned lid responses to light in dogs. *Journal of Comparative Psychology*, 1935, *19*, 29–58.

Hill, W. F. Effects of mere exposure on preferences in nonhuman mammals. *Psychological Bulletin*, 1978, *85*, 1177–1198.

Hinde, R. A. Factors governing the changes in strength of a partially inborn response, as shown by the mobbing behavior of the chaffinch *(Fringilla coelebs):* I. The nature of the response, and an examination of its course. *Proceedings of the Royal Society*, Series B, 1954, *142*, 306–331.

Hineline, P. N. Negative reinforcement without shock reduction. *Journal of the Experimental Analysis of Behavior*, 1970, *14*, 259–268.

Hineline, P. N. Negative reinforcement and avoidance. In W. K. Honig & J. E. R. Staddon (Eds.), *Handbook of operant behavior*. Englewood Cliffs, N.J.: Prentice-Hall, 1977.

Hiroto, D. S. Locus of control and learned helplessness. *Journal of Experimental Psychology*, 1974, *102*, 187–193.

Hoebel, B. G., & Teitelbaum, P. Hypothalamic control of feeding and self-stimulation. *Science*, 1962, *135*, 375–377.

Hoffman, H. S. The analysis of discriminated avoidance. In W. K. Honig (Ed.), *Operant behavior: Areas of research and application*. New York: Appleton-Century-Crofts, 1966.

Hoffman, H. S., & Fleshler, M. An apparatus for the measurement of the startle-response in the rat. *American Journal of Psychology*, 1964, *77*, 307–308.

Hoffman, H. S., & Solomon, R. L. An opponent-process theory of motivation: III. Some affective dynamics in imprinting. *Learning and Motivation*, 1974, *5*, 149–164.

Hogan, J. A. Responses in Pavlovian conditioning studies. *Science*, 1974, *186*, 156–157.

Holland, J. G., & Skinner, B. F. *The analysis of behavior*. New York: McGraw-Hill, 1961.

Holland, P. C. Conditioned stimulus as a determinant of the form of the Pavlovian conditioned response. *Journal of Experimental Psychology: Animal Behavior Processes*, 1977, *3*, 77–104.

Holland, P. C. Influence of visual conditioned stimulus characteristics on the form of Pavlovian appetitive conditioned responding in rats. *Journal of Experimental Psychology: Animal Behavior Processes*, 1980, *6*, 81–97.

Holland, P. C., & Rescorla, R. A. The effect of two ways of devaluing the unconditioned stimulus after first- and second-order appetitive conditioning. *Journal of Experimental Psychology: Animal Behavior Processes*, 1975, *1*, 355–363. (a)

Holland, P. C., & Rescorla, R. A. Second-order conditioning with food unconditioned stimulus. *Journal of Comparative and Physiological Psychology*, 1975, *88*, 459–467. (b)

Holland, P. C., & Straub, J. J. Differential effect of two ways of devaluing the unconditioned stimulus after Pavlovian appetitive conditioning. *Journal of Experimental Psychology: Animal Behavior Processes*, 1979, *5*, 65–78.

Holz, W. C., & Azrin, N. H. Discriminative properties of punishment. *Journal of the Experimental Analysis of Behavior*, 1961, *4*, 225–232.

Honig, W. K., Boneau, C. A., Burstein, K. R., & Pennypacker, H. S. Positive and negative generalization gradients obtained under equivalent training conditions. *Journal of Comparative and Physiological Psychology*, 1963, *56*, 111–116.

Honig, W. K., & James, P. H. R. (Eds.). *Animal memory*. New York: Academic Press, 1971.

Huesmann, L. R. (Ed.). Special issue: Learned helplessness as a model of depression. *Journal of Abnormal Psychology*, 1978, *87*, 1–198.

Hull, C. L. Knowledge and purpose as habit mechanisms. *Psychological Review*, 1930, *30*, 511–525.

Hull, C. L. Goal attraction and directing ideas conceived as habit phenomena. *Psychological Review*, 1931, *38*, 487–506.

Hull, C. L. *A behavior system*. New Haven, Conn.: Yale University Press, 1952.

Hulse, S. H. Cognitive structure and serial pattern learning by animals. In S. H. Hulse, H. Fowler, & W. K. Honig (Eds.), *Cognitive processes in animal behavior*. Hillsdale, N. J.: Lawrence Erlbaum, 1978.

Hulse, S. H. The case of the missing rule: Memory for reward vs. formal structure in serial-pattern learning by rats. *Animal Learning and Behavior*, 1980, *8*, 689–690.

Hulse, S. H., & Campbell, C. E. "Thinking ahead" in rat discrimination learning. *Animal Learning and Behavior*, 1975, *3*, 305–311.

Hulse, S. H., & Dorsky, N. P. Structural complexity

as a determinant of serial pattern learning. *Learning and Motivation*, 1977, *8*, 488–506.

Hulse, S. H., & Dorsky, N. P.   Serial pattern learning by rats: Transfer of a formally defined stimulus relationship and the significance of nonreinforcement. *Animal Learning and Behavior*, 1979, *7*, 211–220.

Hulse, S. H., Fowler, H., & Honig, W. K. (Eds.).   *Cognitive processes in animal behavior*. Hillsdale, N.J.: Lawrence Erlbaum, 1978.

Hume, D.   *An enquiry concerning human understanding*. Reprinted from the posthumous edition of 1777, L. A. Selby-Bigge (Ed.). Oxford: Clarendon Press, 1902.

Hunt, H. F., & Brady, J. V.   Some effects of punishment and intercurrent anxiety on a simple operant. *Journal of Comparative and Physiological Psychology*, 1955, *48*, 305–310.

Hunter, W. S.   The delayed reaction in animals and children. *Behavior Monographs*, 1913, *2*, serial #6.

Hursh, S. R., Navarick, D. J., & Fantino, E.   "Automaintenance": The role of reinforcement. *Journal of the Experimental Analysis of Behavior*, 1974, *21*, 117–124.

Hutchinson, R. R.   By-products of aversive control. In W. K. Honig & J. E. R. Staddon (Eds.), *Handbook of operant behavior*. Englewood Cliffs, N.J.: Prentice-Hall, 1977.

Hutchinson, R. R., Azrin, N. H., & Hake, D. F.   An automatic method for the study of aggression in squirrel monkeys. *Journal of the Experimental Analysis of Behavior*, 1966, *9*, 233–237.

Hutchinson, R. R., Azrin, N. H., & Hunt, G. M.   Attack produced by intermittent reinforcement of a concurrent operant response. *Journal of the Experimental Analysis of Behavior*, 1968, *11*, 489–495.

Hutt, P. J.   Rate of bar pressing as a function of quality and quantity of food reward. *Journal of Comparative and Physiological Psychology*, 1954, *47*, 235–239.

Israel, A. C., Devine, V. T., O'Dea, M. A., & Hamdi, M. E.   Effect of delayed conditioned stimulus termination on extinction of an avoidance response following differential termination conditions during acquisition. *Journal of Experimental Psychology*, 1974, *103*, 360–362.

Jackson, R. L., Alexander, J. H., & Maier, S. F.   Learned helplessness, inactivity, and associative deficits: Effects of inescapable shock on response choice escape learning. *Journal of Experimental Psychology: Animal Behavior Processes*, 1980, *6*, 1–20.

Jarrard, L. E., & Moise, S. L.   Short-term memory in the monkey. In L. E. Jarrard (Ed.), *Cognitive processes of nonhuman primates*. New York: Academic Press, 1971.

Jarvik, M. E., Goldfarb, T. L., & Carley, J. L.   Influence of interference on delayed matching in monkeys. *Journal of Experimental Psychology*, 1969, *81*, 1–6.

Jenkins, H. M.   Resistance to extinction when partial reinforcement is followed by regular reinforcement. *Journal of Experimental Psychology*, 1962, *64*, 441–450.

Jenkins, H. M.   Sensitivity of different response systems to stimulus-reinforcer and response-reinforcer relations. In H. Davis & H. M. B. Hurwitz (Eds.), *Operant-Pavlovian interactions*. Hillsdale, N.J.: Lawrence Erlbaum, 1977.

Jenkins, H. M.   Personal communication, 1980.

Jenkins, H. M., & Harrison, R. H.   Effects of discrimination training on auditory generalization. *Journal of Experimental Psychology*, 1960, *59*, 246–253.

Jenkins, H. M., & Harrison, R. H.   Generalization gradients of inhibition following auditory discrimination learning. *Journal of the Experimental Analysis of Behavior*, 1962, *5*, 435–441.

Jenkins, H. M., & Moore, B. R.   The form of the autoshaped response with food or water reinforcers. *Journal of the Experimental Analysis of Behavior*, 1973, *20*, 163–181.

Jones, F. R. H.   Photo-kinesis in the ammocoete larva of the brook lamprey. *Journal of Experimental Biology*, 1955, *32*, 492–503.

Jones, M. R.   Cognitive representations of serial patterns. In B. Kantowitz (Ed.), *Human information processing: Tutorials in performance and cognition*. Hillsdale, N.J.: Lawrence Erlbaum, 1974.

Kachanoff, R., Leveille, R., McClelland, J. P., & Wayner, M. J.   Schedule-induced behavior in humans. *Physiology and Behavior*, 1973, *11*, 395–398.

Kalat, J. W.   Taste salience depends on novelty, not concentration, in taste-aversion learning in the rat. *Journal of Comparative and Physiological Psychology*, 1974, *86*, 47–50.

Kamil, A. C.   Systematic foraging by a nectar-feeding bird, the amakihi *(Loxops virens)*. *Journal of Comparative and Physiological Psychology*, 1978, *92*, 388–396.

Kamin, L. J.   The effects of termination of the CS and avoidance of the US on avoidance learning. *Journal of Comparative and Physiological Psychology*, 1956, *49*, 420–424.

Kamin, L. J.   Temporal and intensity characteristics of the conditioned stimulus. In W. F. Prokasy (Ed.), *Classical conditioning*. New York: Appleton-Century-Crofts, 1965.

Kamin, L. J.   "Attention-like" processes in classical conditioning. In M. R. Jones (Ed.), *Miami Symposium on the Prediction of Behavior: Aversive stimu-*

lation. Miami: University of Miami Press, 1968.

Kamin, L. J. Predictability, surprise, attention, and conditioning. In B. A. Campbell & R. M. Church (Eds.), *Punishment and aversive behavior.* New York: Appleton-Century-Crofts, 1969.

Kamin, L. J., & Brimer, C. J. The effects of intensity of conditioned and unconditioned stimuli on a conditioned emotional response. *Canadian Journal of Psychology,* 1963, *17,* 194–198.

Kamin, L. J., Brimer, C. J., & Black, A. H. Conditioned suppression as a monitor of fear of the CS in the course of avoidance training. *Journal of Comparative and Physiological Psychology,* 1963, *56,* 497–501.

Kamin, L. J., & Schaub, R. E. Effects of conditioned stimulus intensity on the conditioned emotional response. *Journal of Comparative and Physiological Psychology,* 1963, *56,* 502–507.

Kandel, E. R. *Cellular basis of behavior: An introduction to behavioral neurobiology.* San Francisco: W. H. Freeman, 1976.

Karpicke, J., Christoph, G., Peterson, G., & Hearst, E. Signal location and positive versus negative conditioned suppression in the rat. *Journal of Experimental Psychology: Animal Behavior Processes,* 1977, *3,* 105–118.

Katzev, R. Extinguishing avoidance responses as a function of delayed warning signal termination. *Journal of Experimental Psychology,* 1967, *75,* 339–344.

Katzev, R. What is both necessary and sufficient to maintain avoidance responding in the shuttle box? *Quarterly Journal of Experimental Psychology,* 1972, *24,* 310–317.

Katzev, R. D., & Berman, J. S. Effect of exposure to conditioned stimulus and control of its termination in the extinction of avoidance behavior. *Journal of Comparative and Physiological Psychology,* 1974, *87,* 347–353.

Kazdin, A. E., & Bootzin, R. R. The token economy: An evaluative review. *Journal of Applied Behavior Analysis,* 1972, *5,* 343–372.

Keehn, J. D., & Nakkash, S. Effect of a signal contingent upon an avoidance response. *Nature,* 1959, *184,* 566–568.

Keith-Lucas, T., & Guttman, N. Robust single-trial delayed backward conditioning. *Journal of Comparative and Physiological Psychology,* 1975, *88,* 468–476.

Kelleher, R. T. Conditioned reinforcement in second-order schedules. *Journal of the Experimental Analysis of Behavior,* 1966, *9,* 475–485.

Keller, K. The role of elicited responding in behavioral contrast. *Journal of the Experimental Analysis of Behavior,* 1974, *21,* 249–257.

Kellogg, W. N. *The ape and the child.* New York: McGraw-Hill, 1933.

Kendler, T. S. An experimental investigation of transposition as a function of the difference between training and test stimuli. *Journal of Experimental Psychology,* 1950, *40,* 552–562.

Kintsch, W., & Witte, R. S. Concurrent conditioning of bar press and salivation responses. *Journal of Comparative and Physiological Psychology,* 1962, *52,* 963–968.

Klein, M., & Rilling, M. Generalization of free-operant avoidance behavior in pigeons. *Journal of the Experimental Analysis of Behavior,* 1974, *21,* 75–88.

Köhler, W. Simple structural functions in the chimpanzee and in the chicken. In W. D. Ellis (Ed.), *A source book of Gestalt psychology.* New York: Harcourt Brace Jovanovich, 1939.

Konorski, J. *Conditioned reflexes and neuron organization.* Cambridge: Cambridge University Press, 1948.

Konorski, J., & Miller, S. Méthode d'examen de l'analysateur moteur par les réactions salivomatrices. *Compte et Mémoires de la Société de Biologie,* 1930, *104,* 907–910.

Konorski, J., & Szwejkowska, G. Chronic extinction and restoration of conditioned reflexes: I. Extinction against the excitatory background. *Acta Biologiae Experimentalis,* 1950, *15,* 155–170.

Konorski, J., & Szwejkowska, G. Chronic extinction and restoration of conditioned reflexes: IV. The dependence of the course of extinction and restoration of conditioned reflexes on the "history" of the conditioned stimulus (The principle of the primacy of first training). *Acta Biologiae Experimentalis,* 1952, *16,* 95–113.

Korol, B., Sletten, I. W., & Brown, M. I. Conditioned physiological adaptation to anticholinergic drugs. *American Journal of Physiology,* 1966, *211,* 911–914.

Krane, R. V., & Wagner, A. R. Taste aversion learning with a delayed shock US: Implications for the "generality of the laws of learning." *Journal of Comparative and Physiological Psychology,* 1975, *88,* 882–889.

Kremer, E. F. The Rescorla-Wagner model: Losses in associative strength in compound conditioned stimuli. *Journal of Experimental Psychology: Animal Behavior Processes,* 1978, *4,* 22–36.

Kremer, E. F., & Kamin, L. J. The truly random control procedure: Associative or nonassociative effects in rats. *Journal of Comparative and Physiological Psychology,* 1971, *74,* 203–210.

Landford, A., Benson, L., & Weisman, R. G. Operant drinking and prediction of instrumental performance. *Psychonomic Science,* 1969, *16,* 166.

Lang, W. J., Brown, M. L., Gershon, S., & Korol, B. Classical and physiologic adaptive conditioned responses to anticholinergic drugs in conscious dogs. *International Journal of Neuropharmacology,* 1965, *5,* 311–315.

Lantz, A. Effect of number of trials, interstimulus interval, and dishabituation during CS habituation on subsequent conditioning in a CER paradigm. *Animal Learning and Behavior,* 1973, *4,* 273–278.

Lashley, K. S., & Wade, M. The Pavlovian theory of generalization. *Psychological Review,* 1946, *53,* 72–87.

Leaton, R. N. Long-term retention of the habituation of lick suppression and startle response produced by a single auditory stimulus. *Journal of Experimental Psychology: Animal Behavior Processes,* 1976, *2,* 248–259.

Leclerc, R., & Reberg, D. Sign-tracking in aversive conditioning. *Learning and Motivation,* 1980, *11,* 302–317.

Lehrman, D. S. Interaction between internal and external environments in the regulation of the reproductive cycle of the ring dove. In F. A. Beach (Ed.), *Sex and behavior.* New York: Wiley, 1965.

Lennenberg, E. H. *Biological foundations of language.* New York: Wiley, 1967.

Leon, G. R. *Case histories of deviant behavior: A social learning analysis.* Boston: Holbrook Press, 1974.

Lett, B. T. Taste potentiates color-sickness associations in pigeons and quail. *Animal Learning and Behavior,* 1980, *8,* 193–198.

Levis, D. J. Learned helplessness: A reply and alternative S-R interpretation. *Journal of Experimental Psychology: General,* 1976, *105,* 47–65.

Levitsky, D., & Collier, G. Schedule-induced wheel running. *Physiology and Behavior,* 1968, *3,* 571–573.

Lewis, D. J. Psychobiology of active and inactive memory. *Psychological Bulletin,* 1979, *86,* 1054–1083.

Linden, D. R. Attenuation and reestablishment of the CER by discriminated avoidance conditioning in rats. *Journal of Comparative and Physiological Psychology,* 1969, *69,* 573–578.

Lipsitt, L. P., & Kaye, H. Changes in neonatal response to optimizing and non-optimizing suckling stimulation. *Psychonomic Science,* 1965, *2,* 221–222.

Lockard, R. B. The albino rat: A defensible choice or a bad habit? *American Psychologist,* 1968, *23,* 734–742.

Logan, F. A. The Hull-Spence approach. In S. Koch (Ed.), *Psychology: A study of a science* (Vol. 2). New York: McGraw-Hill, 1959.

LoLordo, V. M. Facilitation of food-reinforced responding by a signal for response-independent food. *Journal of the Experimental Analysis of Behavior,* 1971, *15,* 49–55.

LoLordo, V. M. Selective assocations. In A. Dickinson & R. A. Boakes (Eds.), *Mechanisms of learning and motivation.* Hillsdale, N.J.: Lawrence Erlbaum, 1979.

LoLordo, V. M., & Furrow, D. R. Control by the auditory or the visual element of a compound discriminative stimulus: Effects of feedback. *Journal of the Experimental Analysis of Behavior,* 1976, *25,* 251–256.

LoLordo, V. M., McMillan, J. C., & Riley, A. L. The effects upon food-reinforced pecking and treadle-pressing of auditory and visual signals for response-independent food. *Learning and Motivation,* 1974, *5,* 24–41.

Lorenz, K., & Tinbergen, N. Taxis und Instinkthandlung in der Eirrollbewegung der Graugans: I. *Zeitschrift für Tierpsychologie,* 1939, *3,* 1–29.

Lovaas, O. I., & Newsom, C. D. Behavior modification with psychotic children. In H. Leitenberg (Ed.), *Handbook of behavior modification and behavior therapy.* Englewood Cliffs, N.J.: Prentice-Hall, 1976.

Lubow, R. E. Latent inhibition. *Psychological Bulletin,* 1973, *79,* 398–407.

Lubow, R. E. High-order concept formation in the pigeon. *Journal of the Experimental Analysis of Behavior,* 1974, *21,* 475–483.

Lubow, R. E., & Moore, A. U. Latent inhibition: The effect of nonreinforced preexposure to the conditioned stimulus. *Journal of Comparative and Physiological Psychology,* 1959, *52,* 415–419.

Lyon, D. O. Conditioned suppression: Operant variables and aversive control. *Psychological Record,* 1968, *18,* 317–338.

MacCorquodale, K., & Meehl, P. E. On the distinction between hypothetical constructs and intervening variables. *Psychological Review,* 1948, *55,* 97–105.

Mackintosh, J. J. Stimulus control: Attentional factors. In W. K. Honig & J. E. R. Staddon (Eds.), *Handbook of operant behavior.* Englewood Cliffs, N.J.: Prentice-Hall, 1977.

Mactutus, C. F., Riccio, D. C., & Ferek, J. M. Retrograde amnesia for old (reactivated) memory: Some anomalous characteristics. *Science,* 1979, *204,* 1319–1320.

Mahoney, W. J., & Ayres, J. J. B. One-trial simultaneous and backward conditioning as reflected in conditioned suppression of licking in rats. *Animal Learning and Behavior,* 1976, *4,* 357–362.

Maier, S. F. Failure to escape traumatic shock: Incompatible skeletal motor responses or learned helplessness? *Learning and Motivation,* 1970, *1,* 157–170.

Maier, S. F., Albin, R. W., & Testa, T. J. Failure to learn to escape in rats previously exposed to inescapable shock depends on the nature of the escape response. *Journal of Comparative and Physiological Psychology,* 1973, *85,* 581–592.

Maier, S. F., & Jackson, R. L. Learned helplessness: All of us were right (and wrong): Inescapable shock has multiple effects. In G. H. Bower (Ed.), *The psychology of learning and motivation* (Vol. 13). New York: Academic Press, 1979.

Maier, S. F., Rapaport, P., & Wheatley, K. L. Conditioned inhibition and the UCS-CS interval. *Animal Learning and Behavior,* 1976, *4,* 217–220.

Maier, S. F., & Seligman, M. E. P. Learned helplessness: Theory and evidence. *Journal of Experimental Psychology: General,* 1976, *105,* 3–46.

Maki, W. S. Pigeon's short-term memories for surprising vs. expected reinforcement and nonreinforcement. *Animal Learning and Behavior,* 1979, *7,* 31–37.

Maki, W. S., Brokofsky, S., & Berg, B. Spatial memory in rats: Resistance to retroactive interference. *Animal Learning and Behavior,* 1979, *7,* 25–30.

Maki, W. S., & Hegvik, D. K. Directed forgetting in pigeons. *Animal Learning and Behavior,* 1980, *8,* 561–566.

Maki, W. S., Moe, J. C., & Bierley, C. M. Short-term memory for stimuli, responses, and reinforcers. *Journal of Experimental Psychology: Animal Behavior Processes,* 1977, *3,* 156–177.

Malott, R. W., & Siddall, J. W. Acquisition of the people concept in pigeons. *Psychological Reports,* 1972, *31,* 3–13.

Marchant, H. G., III, Mis, F. W., & Moore, J. W. Conditioned inhibition of the rabbit's nictitating membrane response. *Journal of Experimental Psychology,* 1972, *95,* 408–411.

Margules, D. L., & Olds, J. Identical "feeding" and "rewarding" systems in the lateral hypothalamus of rats. *Science,* 1962, *135,* 374–375.

Marsh, G. Prediction of the peak shift in pigeons from gradients of excitation and inhibition. *Journal of Comparative and Physiological Psychology,* 1972, *81,* 262–266.

Martin, R. C., & Melvin, K. B. Fear responses of bobwhite quail *(Colinus virginianus)* to a model and a live red-tailed hawk *(Buetos jamaicensis). Psychologische Forschung: Zeitschrift für Psychologie und ihre Genzwissenschaften,* 1964, *27,* 323–336.

Masserman, J. H. *Principles of dynamic psychiatry.* Philadelphia: Saunders, 1946.

Mayer-Gross, W. Retrograde amnesia. *Lancet,* 1943, *2,* 603–605.

Mazur, J., & Wagner, A. R. An episodic model of associative learning. In M. Commons, R. Herrnstein, & A. R. Wagner (Eds.), *Quantitative analyses of behavior.* Vol. 3: *Acquisition.* Cambridge, Mass.: Ballinger, 1981.

McAllister, W. R., & McAllister, D. E. Behavioral measurement of fear. In F. R. Brush (Ed.), *Aversive conditioning and learning.* New York: Academic Press, 1971.

McGaugh, J. L., & Herz, M. J. *Memory consolidation.* San Francisco: Albion, 1972.

McGaugh, J. L., & Petrinovich, L. F. Effects of drugs on learning and memory. *International Review of Neurobiology,* 1965, *8,* 139–196.

McReynolds, W. T., & Coleman, J. Token economy: Patient and staff changes. *Behaviour Research and Therapy,* 1972, *10,* 29–34.

Medin, D. L., Roberts, W. A., & Davis, R. T. *Processes of animal memory.* Hillsdale, N.J.: Lawrence Erlbaum, 1976.

Meehl, P. E. On the circularity of the law of effect. *Psychological Bulletin,* 1950, *47,* 52–75.

Meltzer, D., & Brahlek, J. A. Conditioned suppression and conditioned enhancement with the same positive UCS: An effect of CS duration. *Journal of the Experimental Analysis of Behavior,* 1970, *13,* 67–73.

Mendelson, J. Lateral hypothalamic stimulation in satiated rats: The rewarding effects of self-induced drinking. *Science,* 1967, *157,* 1077–1079.

Mendelson, J., & Chillag, D. Schedule-induced air licking in rats. *Physiology and Behavior,* 1970, *5,* 535–537.

Meyer, V. Modifications of expectations in cases with obsessional rituals. *Behaviour Research and Therapy,* 1966, *4,* 273–280.

Michotte, A. *The perception of causality.* New York: Basic Books, 1963.

Miczek, K. A., & Grossman, S. Positive conditioned suppression: Effects of CS duration. *Journal of the Experimental Analysis of Behavior,* 1971, *15,* 243–247.

Milgram, N. W., Krames, L., & Alloway, T. M. (Eds.). *Food aversion learning.* New York: Plenum Press, 1977.

Miller, N. E. Studies of fear as an acquirable drive: I. Fear as motivation and fear-reduction as reinforcement in the learning of new responses. *Journal of Experimental Psychology,* 1948, *38,* 89–101.

Miller, N. E. Learnable drives and rewards. In S. S. Stevens (Ed.), *Handbook of experimental psychology.* New York: Wiley, 1951.

Miller, N. E. Learning resistance to pain and fear:

Effects of overlearning, exposure, and rewarded exposure in context. *Journal of Experimental Psychology*, 1960, *60*, 137–145.

Miller, N. E., & DeBold, R. C. Classically conditioned tongue-licking and operant bar-pressing recorded simultaneously in the rat. *Journal of Comparative and Physiological Psychology*, 1965, *59*, 109–111.

Miller, N. E., & Kessen, M. L. Reward effect of food via stomach fistula compared with those of food via mouth. *Journal of Comparative and Physiological Psychology*, 1952, *45*, 555–564.

Miller, R. R., & Springer, A. D. Amnesia, consolidation, and retrieval. *Psychological Review*, 1973, *80*, 69–79.

Milner, P. M. *Physiological psychology*. New York: Holt, Rinehart & Winston, 1970.

Milner, P. M. Theories of reinforcement, drive, and motivation. In L. L. Iverson, S. D. Iverson, & S. H. Snyder (Eds.), *Handbook of psychopharmacology* (Vol. 7). New York: Plenum Press, 1976.

Mineka, S. The role of fear in theories of avoidance learning, flooding, and extinction. *Psychological Bulletin*, 1979, *86*, 985–1010.

Mineka, S., & Gino, A. Dissociative effects of different types and amounts of nonreinforced CS exposure on avoidance extinction and the CER. *Learning and Motivation*, 1979, *10*, 141–160.

Mineka, S., & Gino, A. Dissociation between conditioned emotional response and extended avoidance performance. *Learning and Motivation*, 1980, *11*, 476–502.

Mineka, S., Suomi, S. J., & DeLizio, R. Multiple separations in adolescent monkeys: An opponent-process interpretation. *Journal of Experimental Psychology: General*, 1981, *110*, 56–85.

Misanin, J. R., Miller, R. R., & Lewis, D. J. Retrograde amnesia produced by electroconvulsive shock after reactivation of a consolidated memory trace. *Science*, 1968, *160*, 554–555.

Mogenson, G., & Cioe, J. Central reinforcement: A bridge between brain function and behavior. In W. K. Honig & J. E. R. Staddon (Eds.), *Handbook of operant behavior*. Englewood Cliffs, N.J.: Prentice-Hall, 1977.

Mogenson, G. J., & Huang, Y. H. The neurobiology of motivated behavior. In G. A. Kerkut & J. W. Phillis (Eds.), *Progress in neurobiology* (Vol. 1). Oxford: Pergamon Press, 1973.

Mogenson, G. J., & Kaplinsky, M. Brain self-stimulation and mechanisms of reinforcement. *Learning and Motivation*, 1970, *1*, 186–198.

Mogenson, G. J., & Morgan, C. W. Effects of induced drinking on self-stimulation of the lateral hypothalamus. *Experimental Brain Research*, 1967, *3*, 111–116.

Mogenson, G. J., & Stevenson, J. A. F. Drinking and self-stimulation with electrical stimulation of the lateral hypothalamus. *Physiology and Behavior*, 1966, *1*, 251–254.

Morris, R. G. M. Pavlovian conditioned inhibition of fear during shuttlebox avoidance behavior. *Learning and Motivation*, 1974, *5*, 424–447.

Morris, R. G. M. Preconditioning of reinforcing properties to an exteroceptive feedback stimulus. *Learning and Motivation*, 1975, *6*, 289–298.

Moscovitch, A., & LoLordo, V. M. Role of safety in the Pavlovian backward fear conditioning procedure. *Journal of Comparative and Physiological Psychology*, 1968, *66*, 673–678.

Mowrer, O. H. On the dual nature of learning: A reinterpretation of "conditioning" and "problem-solving." *Harvard Educational Review*, 1947, *17*, 102–150.

Mowrer, O. H. *Learning theory and behavior*. New York: Wiley, 1960.

Mowrer, O. H., & Lamoreaux, R. R. Avoidance conditioning and signal duration: A study of secondary motivation and reward. *Psychological Monographs*, 1942, *54* (Whole No. 247).

Nisbett, R. E. Determinants of food intake in human obesity. *Science*, 1968, *159*, 1254–1255.

Obal, F. The fundamentals of the central nervous system of vegetative homeostasis. *Acta Physiologica Academiae Scientiarum Hungaricae*, 1966, *30*, 15–29.

Olds, J. Runway and maze behavior controlled by basomedial forebrain stimulation in the rat. *Journal of Comparative and Physiological Psychology*, 1956, *49*, 507–512.

Olds, J. Effects of hunger and male sex hormone on self-stimulation of the brain. *Journal of Comparative and Physiological Psychology*, 1958, *51*, 320–324.

Olds, J., & Milner, P. Positive reinforcement produced by electrical stimulation of septal area and other regions of the rat brain. *Journal of Comparative and Physiological Psychology*, 1954, *47*, 419–427.

Olton, D. S. Characteristics of spatial memory. In S. H. Hulse, H. Fowler, & W. K. Honig (Eds.), *Cognitive processes in animal behavior*. Hillsdale, N.J.: Lawrence Erlbaum, 1978.

Olton, D. S. Mazes, maps, and memory. *American Psychologist*, 1979, *34*, 583–596.

Olton, D. S., Collison, C., & Werz, M. A. Spatial memory and radial arm maze performance of rats. *Learning and Motivation*, 1977, *8*, 289–314.

Olton, D. S., & Samuelson, R. J. Remembrance of

places passed: Spatial memory in rats. *Journal of Experimental Psychology: Animal Behavior Processes*, 1976, *2*, 97–116.

Ost, J. W. P., & Lauer, D. W.   Some investigations of salivary conditioning in the dog. In W. F. Prokasy (Ed.), *Classical conditioning*. New York: Appleton-Century-Crofts, 1965.

Overmier, J. B., Bull, J. A., & Pack, K.   On instrumental response interaction as explaining the influences of Pavlovian CSs upon avoidance behavior. *Learning and Motivation*, 1971, *2*, 103–112.

Overmier, J. B., & Lawry, J. A.   Pavlovian conditioning and the mediation of behavior. In G. H. Bower (Ed.), *The psychology of learning and motivation* (Vol. 13). New York: Academic Press, 1979.

Overmier, J. B., & Seligman, M. E. P.   Effects of inescapable shock upon subsequent escape and avoidance learning. *Journal of Comparative and Physiological Psychology*, 1967, *63*, 23–33.

Owen, J. W., Cicala, G. A., & Herdegen, R. T.   Fear inhibition and species specific defense reaction termination may contribute independently to avoidance learning. *Learning and Motivation*, 1978, *9*, 297–313.

Page, H. A.   The facilitation of experimental extinction by response prevention as a function of the acquisition of a new response. *Journal of Comparative and Physiological Psychology*, 1955, *48*, 14–16.

Patten, R. L., & Rudy, J. W.   The Sheffield omission of training procedure applied to the conditioning of the licking response in rats. *Psychonomic Science*, 1967, *8*, 463–464.

Patterson, F. G.   The gestures of a gorilla: Language acquisition in another pongid. *Brain and Language*, 1978, *5*, 56–71.

Pavlov, I. P.   *Conditioned reflexes* (G. V. Anrep, trans.). London: Oxford University Press, 1927.

Payne, A. P., & Swanson, H. H.   Agonistic behaviour between pairs of hamsters of the same and opposite sex in a neutral observation area. *Behaviour*, 1970, *36*, 259–269.

Pearce, J. M., Colwill, R. M., & Hall, G.   Instrumental conditioning of scratching in the laboratory rat. *Learning and Motivation*, 1978, *9*, 255–271.

Peden, B. F., Browne, M. P., & Hearst, E.   Persistent approaches to a signal for food despite food omission for approaching. *Journal of Experimental Psychology: Animal Behavior Processes*, 1977, *3*, 377–399.

Perkins, C. C., Jr.   The stimulus conditions which follow learned responses. *Psychological Review*, 1955, *62*, 341–348.

Perkins, C. C., Jr.   An analysis of the concept of reinforcement. *Psychological Review*, 1968, *75*, 155–172.

Perry, D. G., & Parke, R. D.   Punishment and alternative response training as determinants of response inhibition in children. *Genetic Psychology Monographs*, 1975, *91*, 257–279.

Peterson, G. B., Ackil, J. E., Frommer, G. P., & Hearst, E. S.   Conditioned approach and contact behavior toward signals for food and brain-stimulation reinforcement. *Science*, 1972, *177*, 1009–1011.

Peterson, N.   Effect of monochromatic rearing on the control of responding by wavelength. *Science*, 1962, *136*, 774–775.

Pfaffman, C.   The pleasures of sensation. *Psychological Review*, 1960, *67*, 253–268.

Phillips, A. G., & Mogenson, G. J.   Effects of taste on self-stimulation and induced drinking. *Journal of Comparative and Physiological Psychology*, 1968, *66*, 654–660.

Pickens, R., & Dougherty, J.   Conditioning the activity effects of drugs. In T. Thompson & C. Schuster (Eds.), *Stimulus properties of drugs*. New York: Appleton-Century-Crofts, 1971.

Postman, L.   Transfer, interference, and forgetting. In J. W. Kling & L. A. Riggs (Eds.), *Woodworth and Schlosberg's experimental psychology* (3rd ed.). New York: Holt, Rinehart & Winston, 1971.

Premack, A. J.   *Why chimps can read*. New York: Harper & Row, 1976.

Premack, D.   Predicting instrumental performance from the independent rate of the contingent response. *Journal of Experimental Psychology*, 1961, *61*, 163–171.

Premack, D.   Reversibility of the reinforcement relation. *Science*, 1962, *136*, 255–257.

Premack, D.   Prediction of the comparative reinforcement values of running and drinking. *Science*, 1963, *139*, 1062–1063.

Premack, D.   Reinforcement theory. In D. Levine (Ed.), *Nebraska Symposium on Motivation* (Vol. 13). Lincoln: University of Nebraska Press, 1965.

Premack, D.   Catching up with common sense, or two sides of a generalization: Reinforcement and punishment. In R. Glaser (Ed.), *The nature of reinforcement*. New York: Academic Press, 1971. (a)

Premack, D.   Language in chimpanzee? *Science*, 1971, *172*, 808–822. (b)

Premack, D.   *Intelligence in ape and man*. Hillsdale, N.J.: Lawrence Erlbaum, 1976.

Quartermain, D., McEwen, B. S., & Azmitia, E. C., Jr.   Amnesia produced by electroconvulsive shock or cycloheximide: Conditions for recovery. *Science*, 1970, *169*, 683–686.

Quinsey, V. L. Conditioned suppression with no CS-US contingency in the rat. *Canadian Journal of Psychology*, 1971, *25*, 69–82.

Rachlin, H. C. On the tautology of the matching law. *Journal of the Experimental Analysis of Behavior*, 1971, *15*, 249–251.

Rachlin, H. C., & Burkhard, B. The temporal triangle: Response substitution in instrumental conditioning. *Psychological Review*, 1978, *85*, 22–47.

Rachlin, H. C. & Green, L. Commitment, choice, and self-control. *Journal of the Experimental Analysis of Behavior*, 1972, *17*, 15–22.

Rachlin, H. C., Green, L., Kagel, J. H., & Battalio, R. C. Economic demand theory and studies of choice. In G. H. Bower (Ed.), *The psychology of learning and motivation* (Vol. 10). New York: Academic Press, 1976.

Rachlin, H. C., & Herrnstein, R. L. Hedonism revisted: On the negative law of effect. In B. A. Campbell & R. M. Church (Eds.), *Punishment and aversive behavior*. New York: Appleton-Century-Crofts, 1969.

Rachman, S., & Hodgson, R. J. *Obsessions and compulsions*. Englewood Cliffs, N.J.: Prentice-Hall, 1980.

Randich, A., & LoLordo, V. M. Associative and nonassociative theories of the UCS preexposure phenomenon: Implications for Pavlovian conditioning. *Psychological Bulletin*, 1979, *86*, 523–548.

Rashotte, M. E., Griffin, R. W., & Sisk, C. L. Second-order conditioning of the pigeon's keypeck. *Animal Learning and Behavior*, 1977, *5*, 25–38.

Razran, G. H. S. Conditioned withdrawal responses with shock as the conditioning stimulus in adult human subjects. *Psychological Bulletin*, 1934, *31*, 111–143.

Reberg, D. Compound tests for excitation in early acquisition and after prolonged extinction of conditioned suppression. *Learning and Motivation*, 1972, *3*, 246–258.

Reberg, D., & Black, A. H. Compound testing of individually conditioned stimuli as an index of excitatory and inhibitory properties. *Psychonomic Science*, 1969, *17*, 30–31.

Reberg, D., Innis, N. K., Mann, B., & Eizenga, C. "Superstitious" behavior resulting from periodic response-independent presentations of food or water. *Animal Behaviour*, 1978, *26*, 506–519.

Reberg, D., Mann, B., & Innis, N. K. Superstitious behavior for food and water in the rat. *Physiology and Behavior*, 1977, *19*, 803–806.

Rescorla, R. A. Inhibition of delay in Pavlovian fear conditioning. *Journal of Comparative and Physiological Psychology*, 1967, *64*, 114–120. (a)

Rescorla, R. A. Pavlovian conditioning and its proper control procedures. *Psychological Review*, 1967, *74*, 71–80. (b)

Rescorla, R. A. Pavlovian conditioned fear in Sidman avoidance learning. *Journal of Comparative and Physiological Psychology*, 1968, *65*, 55–60.

Rescorla, R. A. Conditioned inhibition of fear resulting from negative CS-US contingencies. *Journal of Comparative and Physiological Psychology*, 1969, *67*, 504–509. (a)

Rescorla, R. A. Pavlovian conditioned inhibition. *Psychological Bulletin*, 1969, *72*, 77–94. (b)

Rescorla, R. A. Effect of US habituation following conditioning. *Journal of Comparative and Physiological Psychology*, 1973, *82*, 137–143.

Rescorla, R. A. Effect of inflation of the unconditioned stimulus value following conditioning. *Journal of Comparative and Physiological Psychology*, 1974, *86*, 101–106.

Rescorla, R. A. Aspects of the reinforcer learned in second-order Pavlovian conditioning. *Journal of Experimental Psychology: Animal Behavior Processes*, 1979, *5*, 79–95.

Rescorla, R. A. *Pavlovian second-order conditioning*. Hillsdale, N.J.: Lawrence Erlbaum, 1980.

Rescorla, R. A., & Cunningham, C. L. The erasure of reinstatement. *Animal Learning and Behavior*, 1977, *5*, 386–394.

Rescorla, R. A., & Cunningham, C. L. Spatial contiguity facilitates Pavlovian second-order conditioning. *Journal of Experimental Psychology: Animal Behavior Processes*, 1979, *5*, 152–161.

Rescorla, R. A., & Furrow, D. R. Stimulus similarity as a determinant of Pavlovian conditioning. *Journal of Experimental Psychology: Animal Behavior Processes*, 1977, *3*, 203–215.

Rescorla, R. A., & Gillan, D. J. An analysis of the facilitative effect of similarity on second-order conditioning. *Journal of Experimental Psychology: Animal Behavior Processes*, 1980, *6*, 339–351.

Rescorla, R. A., & Heth, D. C. Reinstatement of fear to an extinguished conditioned stimulus. *Journal of Experimental Psychology: Animal Behavior Processes*, 1975, *1*, 88–96.

Rescorla, R. A., & LoLordo, V. M. Inhibition of avoidance behavior. *Journal of Comparative and Physiological Psychology*, 1965, *59*, 406–412.

Rescorla, R. A., & Solomon, R. L. Two-process learning theory: Relationships between Pavlovian conditioning and instrumental learning. *Psychological Review*, 1967, *74*, 151–182.

Rescorla, R. A., & Wagner, A. R. A theory of Pavlovian conditioning: Variations in the effectiveness of reinforcement and nonreinforcement. In A. H. Black & W. F. Prokasy (Eds.), *Classical condi-*

tioning II: Current research and theory. New York: Appleton-Century-Crofts, 1972.

Restle, F., & Brown, E. Organization of serial pattern learning. In G. H. Bower & J. T. Spence (Eds.), *The psychology of learning and motivation* (Vol. 4). New York: Academic Press, 1970.

Revusky, S. H., & Garcia, J. Learned associations over long delays. In G. H. Bower & J. T. Spence (Eds.), *The psychology of learning and motivation* (Vol. 4). New York: Academic Press, 1970.

Reynolds, G. S. Attention in the pigeon. *Journal of the Experimental Analysis of Behavior,* 1961, *4,* 203–208. (a)

Reynolds, G. S. Behavioral contrast. *Journal of the Experimental Analysis of Behavior,* 1961, *4,* 57–71. (b)

Reynolds, G. S. *A primer of operant conditioning.* Glenview, Ill.: Scott, Foresman, 1968.

Riccio, D. C., Hodges, L. A., & Randall, P. R. Retrograde amnesia produced by hypothermia in rats. *Journal of Comparative and Physiological Psychology,* 1968, *3,* 618–622.

Richter, C. P. Experimentally produced behavior reactions to food poisoning in wild and domesticated rats. *Annals of the New York Academy of Sciences,* 1953, *56,* 225–239.

Riegert, P. W. Humidity reactions of *Melanoplus birittatus* (Say) and *Camnula pellucida* (Scudd.) (Orthoptera, Acrididae): Reactions of normal grasshoppers. *Canadian Entomologist,* 1959, *91,* 35–40.

Rilling, M. Stimulus control and inhibitory processes. In W. K. Honig & J. E. R. Staddon (Eds.), *Handbook of operant behavior.* Englewood Cliffs, N.J.: Prentice-Hall, 1977.

Rilling, M., Kendrick, D. F., & Stonebraker, T. B. Stimulus control of forgetting: A behavioral analysis. In M. L. Commons, A. R. Wagner, & H. R. Herrnstein (Eds.), *Quantitative studies in operant behavior: Acquisition.* New York: Ballinger, 1981.

Rizley, R. C., & Rescorla, R. A. Associations in second-order conditioning and sensory preconditioning. *Journal of Comparative and Physiological Psychology,* 1972, *81,* 1–11.

Roberts, W. A., & Grant, D. S. Studies of short-term memory in the pigeon using the delayed matching to sample procedure. In D. L. Medin, W. A. Roberts, & R. T. Davis (Eds.), *Processes of animal memory.* Hillsdale, N.J.: Lawrence Erlbaum, 1976.

Roberts, W. A., & Grant, D. S. An analysis of light-induced retroactive inhibition in pigeon short-term memory. *Journal of Experimental Psychology: Animal Behavior Processes,* 1978, *4,* 219–236.

Ross, R. R. Positive and negative partial reinforcement effects carried through continuous reinforcement, changed motivation, and changed response. *Journal of Experimental Psychology,* 1964, *68,* 492–502.

Rovee, C. K., & Rovee, D. T. Conjugate reinforcement of infant exploratory behavior. *Journal of Experimental Child Psychology,* 1969, *8,* 33–39.

Rovee-Collier, C. K., Sullivan, M. W., Enright, M., Lucas, D., & Fagen, J. W. Reactivation of infant memory. *Science,* 1980, *208,* 1159–1161.

Rozin, P., & Kalat, J. W. Specific hungers and poison avoidance as adaptive specializations of learning. *Psychological Review,* 1971, *78,* 459–486.

Rumbaugh, D. M. (Ed.). *Language learning by a chimpanzee: The Lana project.* New York: Academic Press, 1977.

Russell, W. R., & Nathan, P. W. Traumatic amnesia. *Brain,* 1946, *69,* 280–300.

Rzoska, J. Bait shyness, a study in rat behaviour. *British Journal of Animal Behaviour,* 1953, *1,* 128–135.

Schachter, S. *Emotion, obesity, and crime.* New York: Academic Press, 1971. (a)

Schachter, S. Some extraordinary facts about obese humans and rats. *American Psychologist,* 1971, *26,* 129–144. (b)

Schiff, R., Smith, N., & Prochaska, J. Extinction of avoidance in rats as a function of duration and number of blocked trials. *Journal of Comparative and Physiological Psychology,* 1972, *81,* 356–359.

Schleidt, W. Reaktionen von Truthuhnern auf fliegende Raubvogel und Versuche zur Analyse ihrer AAM's. *Zeitschrift für Tierpsychologie,* 1961, *18,* 534–560. (a)

Schleidt, W. Über die Auslosung der Flucht vor Raubvogeln bei Truthuhnern. *Naturwissenschaften,* 1961, *48,* 141–142. (b)

Schlosberg, H. Conditioned responses in the white rat. *Journal of Genetic Psychology,* 1934, *45,* 303–335.

Schlosberg, H. Conditioned responses in the white rat: II. Conditioned responses based upon shock to the foreleg. *Journal of Genetic Psychology,* 1936, *49,* 107–138.

Schlosberg, H. The relationship between success and the laws of conditioning. *Psychological Review,* 1937, *44,* 379–394.

Schneider, A. M., Tyler, J., & Jinich, D. Recovery from retrograde amnesia: A learning process. *Science,* 1974, *184,* 87–88.

Schneiderman, N., Fuentes, I., & Gormezano, I. Acquisition and extinction of the classically conditioned eyelid response in the albino rabbit. *Science,* 1962, *136,* 650–652.

Schneiderman, N., & Gormezano, I. Conditioning of the nictitating membrane of the rabbit as a function of CS-US interval. *Journal of Comparative and Physiological Psychology,* 1964, *57,* 188–195.

Schreibman, L., & Lovaas, O. I. Overselective response to social stimuli by autistic children. *Journal of Abnormal Child Psychology, 1973, 1,* 152–168.

Schuster, R. H. A functional analysis of conditioned reinforcement. In D. P. Hendry (Ed.), *Conditioned reinforcement.* Homewood, Ill.: Dorsey Press, 1969.

Schuster, R. H., & Rachlin, H. Indifference between punishment and free shock: Evidence for the negative law of effect. *Journal of the Experimental Analysis of Behavior,* 1968, *11,* 777–786.

Schwartz, B. Positive and negative conditioned suppression in the pigeon: Effects of the locus and modality of the CS. *Learning and Motivation,* 1976, *7,* 86–100.

Schwartz, B., & Gamzu, E. Pavlovian control of operant behavior. In W. K. Honig & J. E. R. Staddon (Eds.), *Handbook of operant behavior.* Englewood Cliffs, N.J.: Prentice-Hall, 1977.

Schwartz, B., & Williams, D. R. The role of the response-reinforcer contingency in negative automaintenance. *Journal of the Experimental Analysis of Behavior,* 1972, *17,* 351–357.

Scobie, S. R. Interaction of an aversive Pavlovian conditioned stimulus with aversively and appetitively motivated operants in rats. *Journal of Comparative and Physiological Psychology,* 1972, *79,* 171–188.

Seligman, M. E. Γ. Chronic fear produced by unpredictable electric shock. *Journal of Comparative and Physiological Psychology,* 1968, *66,* 402–411.

Seligman, M. E. P. On the generality of the laws of learning. *Psychological Review,* 1970, *77,* 406–418.

Seligman, M. E. P. *Helplessness: On depression, development, and death.* San Francisco: W. H. Freeman, 1975.

Seligman, M. E. P., & Beagley, G. Learned helplessness in the rat. *Journal of Comparative and Physiological Psychology,* 1975, *88,* 534–541.

Seligman, M. E. P., & Binik, Y. M. The safety signal hypothesis. In H. Davis & H. M. B. Hurwitz (Eds.), *Operant-Pavlovian interactions.* Hillsdale, N.J.: Lawrence Erlbaum, 1977.

Seligman, M. E. P., & Maier, S. F. Failure to escape traumatic shock. *Journal of Experimental Psychology,* 1967, *74,* 1–9.

Seligman, M. E. P., & Meyer, B. Chronic fear and ulcers in rats as a function of the unpredictability of safety. *Journal of Comparative and Physiological Psychology,* 1970, *73,* 202–207.

Shapiro, M. M. Respondent salivary conditioning during operant lever pressing in dogs. *Science,* 1960, *132,* 619–620.

Shapiro, M. M. Salivary conditioning in dogs during fixed-interval reinforcement contingent upon lever pressing. *Journal of the Experimental Analysis of Behavior,* 1961, *4,* 361–364.

Shapiro, M. M. Temporal relationship between salivation and lever pressing with differential reinforcement of low rates. *Journal of Comparative and Physiological Psychology,* 1962, *55,* 567–571.

Sheffield, F. D. Avoidance training and the contiguity principle. *Journal of Comparative and Physiological Psychology,* 1948, *41,* 165–177.

Sheffield, F. D. Relation between classical conditioning and instrumental learning. In W. F. Prokasy (Ed.), *Classical conditioning.* New York: Appleton-Century-Crofts, 1965.

Sheffield, F. D., Roby, T. B., & Campbell, B. A. Drive reduction versus consummatory behavior as determinants of reinforcement. *Journal of Comparative and Physiological Psychology,* 1954, *47,* 349–354.

Sheffield, F. D., Wulff, J. J., & Backer, R. Reward value of copulation without sex drive reduction. *Journal of Comparative and Physiological Psychology,* 1951, *44,* 3–8.

Shettleworth, S. J. Reinforcement and the organization of behavior in golden hamsters: Hunger, environment, and food reinforcement. *Journal of Experimental Psychology: Animal Behavior Processes,* 1975, *1,* 56–87.

Shettleworth, S. J. Reinforcement and the organization of behavior in golden hamsters: Punishment of three action patterns. *Learning and Motivation,* 1978, *9,* 99–123.

Shimp, C. P. Probabilistically reinforced choice behavior in pigeons. *Journal of the Experimental Analysis of Behavior,* 1966, *9,* 443–455.

Shimp, C. P. Optimum behavior in free-operant experiments. *Psychological Review,* 1969, *76,* 97–112.

Sidman, M. Avoidance conditioning with brief shock and no exteroceptive warning signal. *Science,* 1953, *118,* 157–158. (a)

Sidman, M. Two temporal parameters of the maintenance of avoidance behavior by the white rat. *Journal of Comparative and Physiological Psychology,* 1953, *46,* 253–261. (b)

Sidman, M. Reduction of shock frequency as reinforcement for avoidance behavior. *Journal of the Experimental Analysis of Behavior,* 1962, *5,* 247–257.

Sidman, M. Avoidance behavior. In W. K. Honig (Ed.), *Operant behavior.* New York: Appleton-Century-Crofts, 1966.

Siegel, R. K., & Honig, W. K. Pigeon concept formation: Successive and simultaneous acquisition. *Journal of the Experimental Analysis of Behavior,* 1970, *13,* 385–390.

Siegel, S. Conditioning insulin effects. *Journal of Comparative and Physiological Psychology,* 1975, *89,* 189–199. (a)

Siegel, S. Evidence from rats that morphine tolerance is a learned response. *Journal of Comparative and Physiological Psychology,* 1975, *89,* 498–506. (b)

Siegel, S. Morphine analgesic tolerance: Its situation specificity supports a Pavlovian conditioning model. *Science,* 1976, *193,* 323–325.

Siegel, S. Morphine tolerance acquisition as an associative process. *Journal of Experimental Psychology: Animal Behavior Processes,* 1977, *3,* 1–13. (a)

Siegel, S. A Pavlovian conditioning analysis of morphine tolerance (and opiate dependence). In N. A. Krasnegor (Ed.), *Behavioral tolerance: Research and treatment implications.* National Institute for Drug Abuse, Monograph No. 18. Government Printing Office Stock No. 017-024-00699-8. Washington, D.C.: Government Printing Office, 1977. (b)

Siegel, S. Tolerance to the hyperthermic effect of morphine in the rat is a learned response. *Journal of Comparative and Physiological Psychology,* 1978, *92,* 1137–1149.

Siegel, S., & Domjan, M. Backward conditioning as an inhibitory procedure. *Learning and Motivation,* 1971, *2,* 1–11.

Siegel, S., Hinson, R. E., & Krank, M. D. The role of predrug signals in morphine analgesic tolerance: Support for a Pavlovian conditioning model of tolerance. *Journal of Experimental Psychology: Animal Behavior Processes,* 1978, *4,* 188–196.

Siegel, S., Hinson, R. E., & Krank, M. D. Pavlovian conditioning and heroin "overdose." Presented at the 20th annual meeting of the Psychonomic Society, Phoenix, Arizona, November 1979.

Siegler, R. S., & Liebert, R. M. Effects of contiguity, regularity, and age on children's causal inferences. *Developmental Psychology,* 1974, *10,* 574–579.

Simon, H. A., & Kotovsky, K. Human acquisition of concepts for sequential patterns. *Psychological Review,* 1963, *70,* 534–546.

Skinner, B. F. *The behavior of organisms.* New York: Appleton-Century-Crofts, 1938.

Skinner, B. F. "Superstition" in the pigeon. *Journal of Experimental Psychology,* 1948, *38,* 168–172.

Skinner, B. F. Are theories of learning necessary? *Psychological Review,* 1950, *57,* 193–216.

Skinner, B. F. *Science and human behavior.* New York: Macmillan, 1953.

Skinner, B. F. *About behaviorism.* New York: Knopf, 1974.

Skinner, B. F., & Morse, W. H. Concurrent activity under fixed-interval reinforcement. *Journal of Comparative and Physiological Psychology,* 1957, *50,* 279–281.

Slamecka, N. J., & Ceraso, J. Retroactive and proactive inhibition of verbal learning. *Psychological Bulletin,* 1960, *57,* 449–475.

Smith, J. C., & Roll, D. L. Trace conditioning with X-rays as an aversive stimulus. *Psychonomic Science,* 1967, *9,* 11–12.

Smith, M. C., Coleman, S. R., & Gormezano, I. Classical conditioning of the rabbit's nictitating membrane response at backward, simultaneous, and forward CS-US intervals. *Journal of Comparative and Physiological Psychology,* 1969, *69,* 226–231.

Sokolov, E. N. *Perception and the conditioned reflex.* Oxford and New York: Pergamon Press, 1963.

Sokolov, E. N., & Vinogradova, O. S. (Eds.). *Neuronal mechanisms of the orienting reflex.* Hillsdale, N.J.: Lawrence Erlbaum, 1975.

Solomon, R. L. Punishment. *American Psychologist,* 1964, *19,* 239–253.

Solomon, R. L. An opponent-process theory of acquired motivation: The affective dynamics of addiction. In J. D. Maser & M. E. P. Seligman (Eds.), *Psychopathology: Experimental models.* San Francisco: W. H. Freeman, 1977.

Solomon, R. L. The opponent-process theory of acquired motivation: The costs of pleasure and the benefits of pain. *American Psychologist,* 1980, *35,* 691–712.

Solomon, R. L., & Corbit, J. D. An opponent-process theory of motivation: II. Cigarette addiction. *Journal of Abnormal Psychology,* 1973, *81,* 158–171.

Solomon, R. L., & Corbit, J. D. An opponent-process theory of motivation: I. The temporal dynamics of affect. *Psychological Review,* 1974, *81,* 119–145.

Solomon, R. L., Kamin, L. J., & Wynne, L. C. Traumatic avoidance learning: The outcomes of several extinction procedures with dogs. *Journal of Abnormal and Social Psychology,* 1953, *48,* 291–302.

Solomon, R. L., & Wynne, L. C. Traumatic avoidance learning: Acquisition in normal dogs. *Psychological Monographs,* 1953, *67* (Whole No. 354).

Solomon, R. L., & Wynne, L. C. Traumatic avoidance learning: The principles of anxiety conservation and partial irreversibility. *Psychological Review,* 1954, *61,* 353–385.

Spear, N. E. Forgetting as retrieval failure. In W. K. Honig & P. H. R. James (Eds.), *Animal Memory.* New York: Academic Press, 1971.

Spear, N. E.   Retrieval of memory in animals. *Psychological Review*, 1973, *80*, 163–194.

Spear, N. E.   Retrieval of memories: a psychobiological approach. In W. K. Estes (Ed.), *Handbook of learning and cognitive processes* (Vol. 4). Hillsdale, N.J.: Lawrence Earlbaum, 1976.

Spear, N. E.   *The processing of memories: Forgetting and retention.* Hillsdale, N.J.: Lawrence Erlbaum, 1978.

Spear, N. E., & Miller, R. R. (Eds.).   *Information processing in animals: Memory mechanisms.* Hillsdale, N.J.: Lawrence Erlbaum, 1981.

Spence, K. W.   The nature of discrimination learning in animals. *Psychological Review*, 1936, *43*, 427–449.

Spence, K. W.   The differential response in animals to stimuli varying within a single dimension. *Psychological Review*, 1937, *44*, 430–444.

Spence, K. W.   *Behavior theory and conditioning.* New Haven, Conn.: Yale University Press, 1956.

Staddon, J. E. R.   Regulation, time allocation, and schedule constraint: A commentary on "Conservation in behavior." Presented in the symposium Response Strength (J. A. Nevin, Chair) at the meeting of the American Psychological Association, Washington, D. C., 1976.

Staddon, J. E. R., & Simmelhag, V. L.   The "superstition" experiment: A reexamination of its implications for the principles of adaptive behavior. *Psychological Review*, 1971, *78*, 3–43.

Starr, M. D.   An opponent-process theory of motivation: VI. Time and intensity variables in the development of separation-induced distress calling in ducklings. *Journal of Experimental Psychology: Animal Behavior Processes*, 1978, *4*, 338–355.

Starr, M. D., & Mineka, S.   Determinants of fear over the course of avoidance learning. *Learning and Motivation*, 1977, *8*, 332–350.

Steinert, P., Fallon, D., & Wallace, J.   Matching to sample in goldfish *(Carassuis auratus). Bulletin of the Psychonomic Society*, 1976, *8*, 265.

Stiers, M., & Silberberg, A.   Lever-contact responses in rats: Automaintenance with and without a negative response-reinforcer dependency. *Journal of the Experimental Analysis of Behavior*, 1974, *22*, 497–506.

Stuart, R. B., & Davis, B.   *Slim chance in a fat world: Behavioral control of obesity.* Champaign, Ill.: Research Press, 1972.

Stunkard, A. J., & Mahoney, M. J.   Behavioral treatment of eating disorders. In H. Leitenberg (Ed.), *Handbook of behavior modification and behavior therapy.* Englewood Cliffs, N.J.: Prentice-Hall, 1976.

Sutherland, N. S., & Mackintosh, M. J.   *Mechanisms of animal discrimination learning.* New York and London: Academic Press, 1971.

Suzuki, S., Augerinos, G., & Black, A. H.   Stimulus control of spatial behavior on the eight-arm maze in rats. *Learning and Motivation*, 1980, *11*, 1–18.

Terrace, H. S.   Wavelength generalization after discrimination learning with and without errors. *Science*, 1964, *144*, 78–80.

Terrace, H. S.   Discrimination learning and inhibition. *Science*, 1966, *154*, 1677–1680. (a)

Terrace, H. S.   Stimulus control. In W. K. Honig (Ed.), *Operant behavior: Areas of research and application.* New York: Appleton-Century-Crofts, 1966. (b)

Terrace, H. S.   By-products of discrimination learning. In G. H. Bower (Ed.), *The psychology of learning and motivation* (Vol. 5). New York: Academic Press, 1972.

Terrace, H. S.   *Nim.* New York: Knopf, 1979.

Terrace, H. S., Petitto, L. A., Sanders, R. J., & Bever, T. G.   Can an ape create a sentence? *Science*, 1979, *206*, 891–1201.

Terry, W. S.   Effects of priming unconditioned stimulus representation in short-term memory on Pavlovian conditioning. *Journal of Experimental Psychology: Animal Behavior Processes*, 1976, *2*, 354–369.

Terry, W. S., & Wagner, A. R.   Short-term memory for "surprising" versus "expected" unconditioned stimuli in Pavlovian conditioning. *Journal of Experimental Psychology: Animal Behavior Processes*, 1975, *1*, 122–133.

Testa, T. J.   Causal relationships and the acquisition of avoidance responses. *Psychological Review*, 1974, *81*, 491–505.

Theios, J.   The partial reinforcement effect sustained through blocks of continuous reinforcement. *Journal of Experimental Psychology*, 1962, *64*, 1–6.

Thomas, D. R., Mariner, R. W., & Sherry, G.   Role of preexperimental experience in the development of stimulus control. *Journal of Experimental Psychology*, 1969, *79*, 375–376.

Thomas, J. R.   Fixed ratio punishment by timeout of concurrent variable-interval behavior. *Journal of the Experimental Analysis of Behavior*, 1968, *11*, 609–616.

Thompson, C. R., & Church, R. M.   An explanation of the language of a chimpanzee. *Science*, 1980, *208*, 313–314.

Thompson, R. F., Groves, P. M., Teyler, T. J., & Roemer, R. A.   A dual-process theory of habituation: Theory and behavior. In H. V. S. Peeke & M. J. Herz (Eds.), *Habituation.* New York: Academic Press, 1973.

Thompson, R. F., & Spencer, W. A.   Habituation: A

model phenomenon for the study of neuronal substrates of behavior. *Psychological Review*, 1966, *73*, 16–43.

Thorndike, E. L. Animal intelligence: An experimental study of the association processes in animals. *Psychological Review Monograph*, 1898, *2* (Whole No. 8).

Thorndike, E. L. *Animal intelligence: Experimental studies*. New York: Macmillan, 1911.

Thorndike, E. L. *Human learning*. New York: Century, 1931.

Thorndike, E. L. *The fundamentals of learning*. New York: Teachers College, Columbia University, 1932.

Timberlake, W. The functional organization of appetitive behavior: Behavior systems and learning. In M. D. Zeiler & P. Harzem (Eds.), *Advances in analysis of behavior*. Vol 3: *Biological factors in learning*. Chichester: Wiley, 1980. (a)

Timberlake, W. Personal communication, 1980. (b)

Timberlake, W., & Allison, J. Response deprivation: An empirical approach to instrumental performance. *Psychological Review*, 1974, *81*, 146–164.

Timberlake, W., & Grant, D. L. Auto-shaping in rats to the presentation of another rat predicting food. *Science*, 1975, *190*, 690–692.

Tinbergen, N. *The study of instinct*. Oxford: Clarendon Press, 1951.

Tinbergen, N. The behavior of the stickleback. *Scientific American*, 1952, *187* (6), 22–26.

Tinbergen, N. *The herring gull's world*. New York: Basic Books, 1960.

Tinbergen, N., & Perdeck, A. C. On the stimulus situation releasing the begging response in the newly hatched herring gull chick *(Larus argentatus argentatus Pont.)*. *Behaviour*, 1950, *3*, 1–39.

Tolman, E. C. *Purposive behavior in animals and men*. New York: Appleton-Century-Crofts, 1932.

Tolman, E. C. The determiners of behavior at a choice point. *Psychological Review*, 1938, *45*, 1–41.

Tolman, E. C., Ritchie, B. F., & Kalish, D. Studies in spatial learning: II. Place learning versus response learning. *Journal of Experimental Psychology*, 1946, *36*, 221–229.

Tolstoy, L. N. *War and peace* (R. E. Hardmondsworth, trans.). Middlesex, England: Penguin Books, 1957.

Trapold, M. A., & Winokur, S. Transfer from classical conditioning to acquisition, extinction, and stimulus generalization of a positively reinforced instrumental response. *Journal of Experimental Psychology*, 1967, *73*, 517–525.

Twitmyer, E. B. A study of the knee jerk. *Journal of Experimental Psychology*, 1974, *103*, 1047–1066.

Ulrich, R. E., Hutchinson, R. R., & Azrin, N. H. Pain-elicited aggression. *Psychological Record*, 1965, *15*, 111–126.

Underwood, B. J. Interference and forgetting. *Psychological Review*, 1957, *64*, 49–60.

Villareal, J. *Schedule-induced pica*. Paper presented at the meeting of the Eastern Psychological Association, Boston, 1967.

Wagner, A. R. Priming in STM: An information processing mechanism for self-generated or retrieval-generated depression in performance. In T. J. Tighe & R. N. Leaton (Eds.), *Habituation: Perspectives from child development, animal behavior, and neurophysiology*. Hillsdale, N.J.: Lawrence Erlbaum, 1976.

Wagner, A. R. Expectancies and the priming of STM. In S. H. Hulse, H. Fowler, & W. K. Honig (Eds.), *Cognitive processes in animal behavior*. Hillsdale, N.J.: Lawrence Erlbaum, 1978.

Wagner, A. R. Habituation and memory. In A. Dickinson & R. A. Boakes (Eds.), *Mechanisms of learning and motivation: A memorial to Jerzy Konorski*. Hillsdale, N.J.: Lawrence Erlbaum, 1979.

Wagner, A. R. SOP: A model of automatic memory processing in animal behavior. In N. E. Spear & R. R. Miller (Eds.), *Information processing in animals: Memory mechanisms*. Hillsdale, N.J.: Lawrence Erlbaum, 1981.

Wagner, A. R., Logan, F. A., Haberlandt, K., & Price, T. Stimulus selection in animal discrimination learning. *Journal of Experimental Psychology*, 1968, *76*, 171–180.

Wagner, A. R., & Rescorla, R. A. Inhibition in Pavlovian conditioning: Application of a theory. In R. A. Boakes & M. S. Halliday (Eds.), *Inhibition and learning*. London: Academic Press, 1972.

Wallace, J., Steinert, P. A., Scobie, S. R., & Spear, N. E. Stimulus modality and short-term memory in rats. *Animal Learning and Behavior*, 1980, *8*, 10–16.

Wallace, M., Singer, G., Wayner, M. J., & Cook, P. Adjunctive behavior in humans during game playing. *Physiology and Behavior*, 1975, *14*, 651–654.

Walter, H. E. The reaction of planarians to light. *Journal of Experimental Zoology*, 1907, *5*, 35–162.

Walters, G. C., & Grusec, J. F. *Punishment*. San Francisco: W. H. Freeman, 1977.

Wasserman, E. A. Pavlovian conditioning with heat reinforcement produces stimulus-directed pecking in chicks. *Science*, 1973, *181*, 875–877.

Wasserman, E. A. Responses in Pavlovian conditioning studies (reply to Hogan). *Science*, 1974, *186*, 157.

Wasserman, E. A., Franklin, S. R., & Hearst,

E. Pavlovian appetitive contingencies and approach versus withdrawal to conditioned stimuli in pigeons. *Journal of Comparative and Physiological Psychology,* 1974, *86,* 616–627.

Watson, J. B. Psychology as the behaviorist views it. *Psychological Review,* 1913, *20,* 158–177.

Watson, J. B. *Behaviorism.* New York: W. W. Norton, 1924.

Webster, B. Man and bird dance together to preserve species. *New York Times,* March 25, 1980, p. C1.

Weinberger, N. Effect of detainment on extinction of avoidance responses. *Journal of Comparative and Physiological Psychology,* 1965, *60,* 135–138.

Weisman, R. G., & Litner, J. S. The course of Pavlovian excitation and inhibition of fear in rats. *Journal of Comparative and Physiological Psychology,* 1969, *69,* 667–672.

Weisman, R. G., & Litner, J. S. The role of Pavlovian events in avoidance training. In R. A. Boakes & M. S. Halliday (Eds.), *Inhibition and learning.* London: Academic Press, 1972.

Weisman, R. G., & Premack, D. Reinforcement and punishment produced by the same response depending upon the probability relation between the instrumental and contingent responses. Paper presented at the meeting of the Psychonomic Society, St. Louis, 1966.

Weiss, J. M. Somatic effects of predictable and unpredictable shock. *Psychosomatic Medicine,* 1970, *32,* 397–409.

Weiss, J. M. Effects of coping behavior in different warning signal conditions on stress pathology in rats. *Journal of Comparative and Physiological Psychology,* 1971, *77,* 1–13.

Weiss-Fogh, T. An aerodynamic sense organ stimulating and regulating flight in locusts. *Nature,* 1949, *164,* 873–874.

Welsh, J. H. Light intensity and the extent of activity of locomotor muscles as opposed to cilia. *Biological Bulletin,* 1933, *65,* 168–174.

Wessells, M. G. The effects of reinforcement upon the prepecking behaviors of pigeons in the autoshaping experiment. *Journal of the Experimental Analysis of Behavior,* 1974, *21,* 125–144.

Whitlow, J. W. Short-term memory in habituation and dishabituation. *Journal of Experimental Psychology: Animal Behavior Processes,* 1975, *1,* 189–206.

Wigglesworth, V. B., & Gillett, J. D. The function of the antennae of *Rhodnius prolixus* (Hemiptera) and the mechanisms of orientation to the host. *Journal of Experimental Biology,* 1934, *11,* 120–139.

Wilcoxon, H. C., Dragoin, W. B., & Kral, P. A. Illness-induced aversions in rat and quail: Relative salience of visual and gustatory cues. *Science,* 1971, *171,* 826–828.

Williams, D. R. Classical conditioning and incentive motivation. In W. F. Prokasy (Ed.), *Classical conditioning.* New York: Appleton-Century-Crofts, 1965.

Williams, D. R., & Williams, H. Automaintenance in the pigeon: Sustained pecking despite contingent non-reinforcement. *Journal of the Experimental Analysis of Behavior,* 1969, *12,* 511–520.

Wolfe, J. B. The effect of delayed reward upon learning in the white rat. *Journal of Comparative and Physiological Psychology,* 1934, *17,* 1–21.

Wolpe, J. Isolation of a conditioning procedure as the crucial psychotherapeutic factor: A case study. *Journal of Nervous and Mental Disease,* 1962, *134,* 316–329.

Woodworth, R. S., & Schlosberg, H. *Experimental psychology.* New York: Holt, Rinehart & Winston, 1954.

Worsham, R. W., & D'Amato, M. R. Ambient light, white noise, and monkey vocalization as sources of interference in visual short-term memory of monkeys. *Journal of Experimental Psychology,* 1973, *99,* 99–105.

Yerkes, R. M., & Morgulis, S. The method of Pavlov in animal psychology. *Psychological Bulletin,* 1909, *6,* 257–273.

Zajonc, R. B. Attitudinal effects of mere exposure. *Journal of Personality and Social Psychology,* Monograph Supplement, 1968, *9* (No. 2, Part 2), 1–27.

Zener, K. The significance of behavior accompanying conditioned salivary secretion for theories of the conditioned response. *American Journal of Psychology,* 1937, *50,* 384–403.

Zentall, T., & Hogan, D. Abstract concept learning in the pigeon. *Journal of Experimental Psychology,* 1974, *102,* 393–398.

Zimney, G. H., & Kienstra, R. A. Orienting and defensive responses to electric shock. *Psychophysiology,* 1967, *3,* 351–362.

Zimney, G. H., & Miller, F. L. Orienting and adaptive cardiovascular responses to heat and cold. *Psychophysiology,* 1966, *3,* 81–92.

Zimney, G. H., & Schwabe, L. W. Stimulus change and habituation of the orienting response. *Psychophysiology,* 1965, *2,* 103–115.

Zoladek, L., & Roberts, W. A. The sensory basis of spatial memory in the rat. *Animal Learning and Behavior,* 1978, *6,* 77–81.

Name Index

Ackil, J. F., 105
Adams, G. P., 29
Albin, R. W., 135
Alexander, J. H., 136
Allison, J., 186, 187
Alloway, T. M., 64
Alloy, L. B., 135
Almquist, J. O., 47
Amsel, A., 62, 165, 281, 283
Anderson, D. C., 136
Anger, D., 253
Anisman, H., 136
Annable, A., 138
Aristotle, 8
Augerinos, G., 315
Ayres, J. J. B., 67, 69
Azmita, N. H., 322
Azrin, N. H., 133, 163, 188, 259–265, 268, 271, 293

Backer, R., 177
Baerends, G. P., 29
Bandura, A., 84
Barker, L. M., 64
Baron, A., 261
Battalio, R. C., 159
Baum, M., 246, 247
Baum, W. M., 156
Beagley, G., 135
Beatty, W. W., 316, 317
Bechterev, V. M., 238
Begin, M., 20
Bell, C., 9
Benedict, J. O., 69
Benson, L., 187

Berg, B., 317
Berman, J. S., 247
Bernstein, I. L., 65
Best, M. R. , 64, 75, 76, 90, 92, 325
Best, P., 92
Bever, T. G., 333, 335, 336
Bierley, C. M., 313
Bindra, D., 180, 306
Bini, L., 319
Binik, Y. M., 75
Bitterman, M. E., 14, 67, 220
Black, A. H., 77, 136, 244, 284, 286, 315
Black, R. W., 177
Blackman, D., 291
Blakemore, C., 14
Blough, D. S., 311
Boakes, R. A., 71, 138
Boice, R., 15, 16
Bolles, R. C., 61, 107, 248–250, 255–257, 291
Boneau, C. A., 213
Bootzin, R. R., 235
Bouton, M. E., 107
Bower, G. H., 122
Brady, J. P., 152
Brady, J. V., 188
Brahlek, J. A., 293
Breland, K., 138
Breland, M., 138
Brener, J., 258
Brennan, M. J., 317
Brimer, C. J., 60, 90, 244
Brogden, W. J., 238–241

Brokofsky, S., 317
Brown, E., 326
Brown, J. S., 242–243
Brown, M. L., 110
Brown, P. L., 62
Brown, T., 8
Browne, M. P., 275, 276
Brownstein, A., 187
Bull, J. A. III, 291, 292
Burkhard, B., 187, 188, 189, 190, 269
Burkhardt, P. E., 67
Burstein, K. R., 213

Cable, C., 331, 332
Caggiula, A. R., 179
Camp, D. S., 260, 261
Campbell, B. A., 177, 259, 323
Campbell, C. E., 327
Campbell, H. J., 179, 180
Capaldi, E. J., 166, 329, 330
Carley, J. L., 317, 318
Catania, A. C., 157
Catanzaro, D., 136
Cattel, J., 123
Ceraso, J., 317
Cerletti, U., 319
Chillag, D., 188
Chomsky, N., 332
Christoph, G., 296, 297
Chung, S-H., 157
Church, R. M, 259, 260, 261, 263, 270, 335
Cicala, G. A., 255

Cioe, J., 179
Cohen, L. B., 304
Coleman, J., 235, 265
Coleman, R. R., 67
Coleman, S. R., 274, 277
Collier, G., 188
Collison, C., 315, 316
Colwill, R. M., 138
Conger, R., 156
Cook, P., 189
Coolidge, C., 47
Coons, E. E., 320
Cooper, G. F., 14
Corbit, J. D., 49, 50, 51
Coulter, X., 247
Crowell, C. R., 136
Crozier, W. J., 29
Culler, E. A., 108, 238–241
Cunningham, C. L., 93, 107, 136

D'Amato, M. R., 218, 255, 311, 313
Dammond, K. R., 174
Dardano, J. F., 263
Darwin, C., 10, 11, 12, 122, 193
Davidson, T. L., 330
Davis, B., 227
Davis, H., 291
Davis, M., 36, 37, 45, 49
Davis, R. T., 308
DeBold, R. C., 284, 285
deCatanzaro, D., 136
Decke, E., 178
DeLizio, R., 52
Delprato, D. J., 243
Denny, M. R., 254
Descartes, R., 6–12
Desiderato, O., 291
Deutsch, J. A., 180
deVilliers, P. A., 255
Devine, V. T., 243
Deweer, B., 323
Dinsmoor, J. A., 243, 255, 264, 267
Dobrzecka, C., 223, 224
Domjan, M., 43, 44, 61, 64, 68, 90, 92, 325
Donegan, N. H., 326
Dorsky, N. P., 327–329
Dougherty, J., 110
Dragoin, W. B., 94
Duncan, C. P., 320
Duncker, K., 174
Dunham, P. J., 266, 270

Dutta, S. N., 109
Dweck, C. S., 74

Ebbinghaus, H., 8, 10
Edmonds, R. R., 173
Eibl-Eibesfeldt, I., 27
Eizenga, C., 192
Elkins, R. L., 84
Ellison, G. D., 68, 286
Engberg, L. A., 137
Enright, M., 323
Epstein, S. M., 52
Ervin, F. R., 64
Esplin, S. M., 23
Estes, W. K., 60, 259, 266, 267, 291
Etkin, M., 255

Fagen, J. W., 323
Falk, J. L., 188, 190
Fallon, D., 311, 312
Fantino, E., 275
Fazzaro, J., 255
Feldman, D. T., 317, 323
Ferek, J. M., 323
Ferster, C. B., 144
Fleshler, M., 37
Flexner, J. B., 320
Flexner, L. B., 320
Flory, R., 190
Foree, D. D., 222, 223
Fouts, R., 333
Fowler, H., 303
Fox, L., 226
Foxx, R. M., 133, 259
Fraenkel, F. D., 260
Fraenkel, G. S., 28
Franklin, S. R., 75
Frommer, G. P., 105
Fuentes, I., 61
Furrow, D. R., 93, 222

Gamzu, E. R., 63, 294, 295
Gantt, W. H., 58
Garb, J. J., 65, 92
Garcia, J., 64, 91–94
Gardner, B. T., 333, 334
Gardner, E. T., 256
Gardner, R. A., 333, 334
Gemberling, G. A., 90, 92, 325
Gentry, G. V., 220
Gentry, W. D., 188
Gershon, S., 110
Gillan, D. J., 93
Gillett, J. D., 29

Gino, A., 245, 247, 255
Glickman, S. E., 180
Glisson, F., 9
Goesling, W. J., 258
Gold, P. E., 322
Goldfarb, T. L., 317, 318
Gollub, L. R., 231, 233–235
Gonzalez, R. C., 220
Goodall, G., 138
Gordon, J. A., 311
Gordon, W. C., 317, 321–323
Gormezano, I., 59, 61, 67, 274, 275
Grant, D. L., 112,
Grant, D. S., 311, 312, 313, 317, 318
Green, L., 159, 161
Grice, G. R., 145
Griffin, D. R., 303
Griffin, R. W., 108
Grossberg, J. M., 248
Grossen, N. E., 255, 258, 291, 292
Grossman, S., 293
Groves, P. M., 38, 40, 45, 48, 49
Grusec, J. F., 260
Guha, D., 109
Gunn, D. L., 28
Guthrie, E. R., 123, 125, 203
Gutman, A., 291
Guttman, N., 68, 200

Haberlandt, K., 210, 211
Hake, D. F., 163, 259, 260, 262, 271, 293
Hale, E. B., 47
Hall, G., 44
Hall, J. V., 138
Halliday, M. S., 71
Hamdi, M. E., 243
Hammond, L. J., 75, 76, 291
Hankins, W. G., 92
Hansen, G., 137, 217
Hanson, H. M., 216, 217
Harlow, H. F., 14, 133, 134
Haroutunian, V., 323
Harrison, R. H., 208–210, 225
Hars, B., 323
Hart, B. L., 23
Hawthorne, N., 82
Haycock, J. W., 322
Hayes, C., 332
Hayes, K. J., 332
Hearst, E., 62, 63, 75, 105, 220, 271, 275, 276, 291, 296, 297
Hebb, D. O., 274

Hegvik, D. K. , 313
Heingartner, A. , 44
Henggeler, S. , 92
Herberg, L. J. , 179
Herdegen, R. T. , 255
Herman, L. M. , 311, 360
Herman, R. L. , 263, 264
Herrnstein, R. J. , 155–157, 170, 171, 176, 253, 255, 256, 268, 330–332
Herz, M. J. , 308, 320
Heth, D. C. , 67, 107
Hilgard, E. R. , 78, 105, 122
Hill, W. F. , 44
Hiller, G. W. , 275
Hinde, R. A. , 37, 38
Hineline, P. N. , 252, 253, 255, 256
Hinson, R. E. , 111
Hiroto, D. S. , 136
Hobbes, T. , 7, 11
Hodges, L. A. , 320
Hodgson, R. J. , 243, 248
Hoebel, B. G. , 179
Hoffman, H. S. , 37, 49, 52, 240
Hogan, D. , 331
Hogan, J. A. , 114
Holland, J. G. , 215
Holland, P. C. , 107, 108, 113, 306, 307
Holz, W. C. 259–265, 268, 271
Honig, W. K. , 213, 214, 303, 308, 331
Huang, Y. H. , 180
Huesman, L. R. , 136
Hull, C. L. , 123, 126, 127, 130, 131, 176, 202, 203, 279
Hulse, S. H. , 303, 327–330
Hume, D. , 173, 174
Hunt, H. F. , 188
Hunter, W. S. , 309, 310
Hursh, S. R. , 275
Hutchinson, R. R. , 163, 188, 271
Hutt, P. J. , 141

Innis, N. K. , 192
Israel, A. C. , 243

Jackson, R. L. , 135, 136
Jacobs, A. , 242–243
James, P. H. R. , 308
James, W. , 123
Jarrad, L. E. , 311
Jarvik, M. E. , 317, 318
Jenkins, H. M. , 62, 63, 105, 165,

208–210, 225, 276
Jinich, D. , 322
Jones, F. R. H. , 29
Jones, M. R. , 326

Kachanoff, R. , 189
Kagel, J. H. , 159
Kalat, J. W. , 64, 90, 93
Kalish, D. , 126, 127
Kalish, H. I. , 200
Kamil, A. C. , 314
Kamin, L. J. , 60, 68, 69, 90, 95, 96, 225, 244, 248, 255, 256
Kandel, E. R. , 45
Kantorovich, N. V. , 84
Kaplinsky, M. , 180
Karpicke, J. , 296, 297
Katzev, R. , 243, 247
Kaye, H. , 36
Kazdin, A. E. , 235
Keehn, J. D. , 255
Keith-Lucas, T. , 68
Kelleher, R. T. , 229, 230
Keller, K. , 295, 296
Kelley, M. J. , 258
Kellogg, L. , 332
Kellogg, W. N. , 332
Kendler, T. S. , 220
Kendrick, D. F. , 313
Kessen, M. L. , 178
Kienstra, R. A. , 42
Killeen, P. , 156
Kintsch, W. , 285
Klein, M. , 220
Koelling, R. A. , 64, 91, 92, 93
Köhler, W. , 217, 218
Kohts, N. , 332
Konorski, J. , 57, 79, 223, 224, 286, 293
Korol, B. , 110
Kostansek, D. J. , 291
Kotovsky, K. , 326
Kral, P. A. , 94
Krames, L. , 64
Krane, R. V. , 92
Krank, M. D. , 111
Kremer, E. F. , 68, 100
Kreuter, C. , 291

LaMaze, F. , 89
Lamoreaux, R. R. , 238, 258
Landford, A. , 187
Lang, W. J. , 110
Lantz, A. , 90
Lashley, K. S. , 202, 205

Lauer, D. W. , 67
Lawry, J. A. , 292, 300, 301
Leaton, R. N. , 45, 46, 47
Leclerc, R. , 292
Lehrman, D. S. , 30, 31
Lennenberg, E. H. , 332
Leon, G. R. , 343
Lett, B. T. , 94
Leveille, R. , 189
Levis, D. J. , 136
Levitsky, D. , 188
Lewis, D. J. , 321, 323
Lewis, P. , 256
Liebert, R. M. , 174
Lind, D. L. , 152
Linden, D. R. , 245
Lipman, E. A. , 238–241
Lipsitt, L. P. , 36
Litner, J. S. , 255, 291
Lockard, R. B. , 15
Locke, J. , 7, 11
Lockwood, M. J. , 138
Logan, F. A. , 210, 211, 287
LoLordo, V. M. , 68, 71, 73, 90, 93, 222–223, 225, 291, 292
Lorenz, K. , 29
Lovaas, O. I. , 97, 272
Loveland, D. H. , 330, 331, 332
Lubow, R. E. , 90, 330
Lucas, D. , 323
Lupo, J. V. , 136
Lyon, D. O. , 291

MacCorquodale, K. , 287
MacKinnon, J. R. , 283
Mackintosh, N. J. , 225, 226
Macri, J. , 322
Mactutus, C. F. , 323
Magendie, F. , 9
Mahoney, M. J. , 67
Mahoney, W. J. , 226
Maier, S. F. , 68, 134–136, 291
Maki, W. S. , 313, 314, 315, 316, 317
Malott, R. W. , 331
Mann, B. , 192
Marchant, H. G. , 72
Margules, D. L. , 180
Mariner, R. W. , 210
Marquis, D. G. , 78
Marsh, G. , 220
Martin, R. C. , 44
Masserman, J. H. , 259
Matthews, T. J. , 270
Mayer-Gross, W. , 320

Mazur, J., 326
McAllister, D. E., 243
McAllister, W. R., 243
McClelland, J. P., 189
McEwen, B. S., 322
McGaugh, J. L., 308, 320, 322
McMillan, J. C., 292
McReynolds, W. T., 235
Medin, D. L., 308
Meehl, P. E., 175, 287
Mellor, C. S., 84
Meltzer, D., 293
Melvin, K. B., 44
Mendelson, J., 180, 188
Meyer, B., 75
Meyer, V., 248
Michotte, A., 174
Miczek, K. A., 293
Milgram, N. W., 64
Miller, F. L., 42
Miller, N. E., 178, 241, 242, 260, 284, 285, 320
Miller, R. R., 308, 321, 323
Miller, S., 293
Milner, P. M., 178–181
Mineka, S., 52, 244, 245, 247, 255
Mis, F. W., 72
Misanin, J. R., 323
Moe, J. C., 313
Mogenson, G., 179, 180
Moise, S. L., 311
Molina, P., 329, 330
Moore, A. U., 90
Moore, B. R., 105
Moore, J. W., 72
Morgan, C. W., 179, 180
Morgulis, S., 57
Morris, R. G. M., 255
Morse, W. H., 170, 171, 189
Moscovitch, A., 68, 71
Mowrer, O. H., 238, 241, 258, 288, 289
Mowrer, R. R., 322, 323

Nakkash, S., 255
Nathan, P. W., 319
Navarik, D. J., 275
Navez, A. E., 29
Newsom, C. D., 97, 272
Nisbett, R. E., 178

Obal, F., 109
O'Dea, M. A., 243
Olds, J., 178, 179, 180

Olton, D. S., 314, 315, 316
Ost, J. W. P., 67
Overmier, J. B., 134, 135, 291, 292, 300, 301
Owen, J. W., 255

Pack, K., 292
Page, H. A., 247
Parke, R. D., 264
Patten, R. L., 275
Patterson, F. G., 333
Pavlov, I. P., 9, 10, 55–59, 62, 67, 68, 71, 72, 77–79, 86–89, 104, 107, 199, 201, 202, 225, 228, 238
Payne, A. P., 30
Pearce, J. M., 138
Peden, B. F., 275, 276
Pennypacker, H. S., 213
Perdeck, A. C., 25
Perkins, C. C. Jr., 274
Perry, D. G., 264
Peterson, G., 296, 297
Peterson, G. B., 105, 113
Peterson, N., 205
Petitto, L. A., 333, 335, 336
Petrinovich, L. F. 320
Pfaffman, C., 180
Pfautz, 325, 326
Phillips, A. G., 180
Pickens, R., 110
Poli, M., 138
Postman, L., 317
Pradhan, S. N., 109
Premack, A. J., 332
Premack, D., 181–187, 268, 269, 330, 332, 333
Price, T., 210, 211
Prochaska, J., 246, 247

Quartermain, D., 322
Quinsey, V. L., 69

Rachlin, H., 157, 159, 161, 188, 189, 190, 268, 269
Rachman, S., 243, 248
Randall, P., 320, 323
Randlich, A., 90
Rapaport, P., 68
Rashotte, M. E., 108, 283
Raymond, G. A., 260, 261, 263
Razran, G. H. S., 84
Reberg, D., 77, 79, 192, 292
Remington, G., 136
Rescorla, R. A., 67, 68, 70–74,

76, 79, 88, 93, 95, 97–103, 106–108, 113, 255, 284, 286, 288, 291, 307
Restle, F., 326
Revusky, S. H., 64, 84
Reynolds, G. S., 150, 151, 172, 197, 198, 294, 296
Riccio, D. C., 247, 320, 323
Richter, C. P., 64
Riegert, P. W., 28
Riley, A. L., 292
Rilling, M., 216, 220, 313
Ritchie, B. F., 126, 127
Rizley, R. C., 107
Roberts, W. A., 308, 311, 312, 315, 317, 318, 319
Roby, T. B., 177
Roemer, R. A., 38
Roll, D. L., 64, 65
Ross, R. R., 283
Rovee, C. K., 118
Rovee, D. T., 118
Rovee-Collier, C. K., 323
Rozin, P., 64, 93
Rudolph, R., 225
Rudy, J. W., 275
Rumbaugh, D. M., 333
Rusinak, K. W., 92
Russell, W. R., 319
Rzoska, J., 64

Sadat, A., 20
Samuelson, R. S., 314, 315, 316
Sanders, R. J., 333, 335, 336
Sara, S. J., 323
Sauerbrunn, D., 263
Schachter, S., 163, 178
Schaub, R. E., 90
Schiff, B. B., 180
Schiff, R., 246, 247
Schleidt, W., 44
Schlesinger, J. L., 317
Schlosberg, H., 153, 238, 274
Schneider, A. M., 322
Schneiderman, N., 61, 67
Schrader, S., 269
Schreibman, L., 97
Schuster, R. H., 231, 268
Schwabe, L. W., 42
Schwartz, B., 276, 292–296
Scobie, S. R., 292, 312
Sears, G. W., 255
Sechenov, I. M., 9, 10
Seligman, M. E. P., 75, 134–139
Shakespeare, W., 82, 173

Shapiro, M. M., 284, 285
Shavalia, D. A., 316, 317
Sheffield, F. D., 177, 180, 245, 275
Sherry, G., 210
Shettleworth, S. J., 138, 266
Shimp, C. P., 158
Siddall, J. W., 331
Sidman, M., 250–256, 271
Siegel, R. K., 331
Siegel, S., 68, 109, 110, 111
Siegler, R. S., 174
Silberberg, A., 275
Simmelhag, V. L., 191–194
Simon, H. A., 326
Singer, G., 189
Sisk, C. L., 108
Skinner, B. F., 60, 121, 127, 129, 130, 131, 144, 169–171, 176, 189, 191, 215, 259, 266
Slamecka, N. J., 317
Sletten, I. W., 110
Smith, J., 130
Smith, J. C., 64, 65
Smith, M. C., 67, 68
Smith, N., 246, 247
Sokolov, E. N., 42, 43
Solomon, R. L., 49–53, 244, 245, 259, 284, 286, 288
Spear, N. E., 308, 312, 320, 321, 323
Spence, K. W., 126, 202, 212, 218–221, 279
Spencer, W. A., 46, 47
Springer, A. D., 321
Staddon, J. E. R., 189, 191–194
Starr, M. D., 52, 245
Steinert, P. A., 311, 312
Stellar, E., 320
Stevenson, J. A. F., 180
Stiers, M., 275
Stokes, L. W., 248, 249, 250, 256
Stonebraker, T. B., 313
Straub, J. J., 107
Stuart, R. B., 227
Stunkard, A. J., 65, 92, 226

Sullivan, M. W., 323
Suomi, S. J., 52
Sutherland, N. S., 225
Suzuki, S., 315
Suzuki, Shinicki, 139
Swammerdam, J., 9
Swanson, H. H., 30
Szwejkowska, G., 79, 223, 224

Teitelbaum, P., 179
Terrace, H. S., 210, 214–216, 333, 335, 336
Terry, W. S., 90, 313, 325
Testa, T. J., 93, 135
Teyler, T. J., 38
Theios, J., 165
Thomas, D. R., 137, 210
Thomas, J. R., 259
Thompson, R. F., 38, 40, 45, 48, 49
Thorndike, E. L., 122–126, 130, 137, 159, 168, 175, 176, 203, 259, 268, 279
Timberlake, W., 112, 113, 186, 187
Tinbergen, N., 25, 26, 30, 32, 33, 44
Tolman, E. C., 123, 125, 127, 129, 131, 153, 303
Tolstoy, L. N., 82, 173
Trapold, M. A., 281
Twitmyer, E. B., 56
Tyler, J., 322

Ulrich, R. E., 271
Underwood, B. J., 317

Van Houten, R., 225
Verry, D. R., 330
Villareal, J., 188
Vinogradova, O. S., 42
Voegtlin, W. L., 84

Wade, M., 202, 205
Wagner, A. R., 43, 47, 72, 74, 92, 95, 97–103, 113, 210, 211, 213, 313, 324, 325, 326

Wallace, J., 312
Wallace, M., 189
Walter, H. E., 28
Walters, G. C., 259
Wasserman, E. A., 75, 114
Watson, J. B., 11, 18
Wayner, M. J., 189
Wearden, J. H., 138
Webster, B., 31
Webster, M. M., 65
Weinberger, N., 247
Weisman, R. G., 187, 255, 269, 291
Weiss, J. M., 75
Weiss-Fogh, T., 29
Welker, R. L., 137
Welsh, J. H., 28
Werz, M. A., 315, 316
Wessells, M. G., 275
Wheatley, K. L., 68
Whitlow, J. W., 325
Wigglesworth, V. B., 29
Wilcoxon, H. C., 94
Williams, D. R., 63, 68, 275, 276, 284–287
Williams, H., 275
Wilson, N. E., 92
Winokur, S., 281
Witte, R. S., 285
Wolfe, J. B., 145
Wolpe, J., 83
Woodbury, D. M., 23
Woodworth, R. S., 153
Wooten, C. L., 270
Worsham, R. W., 318
Wulff, J. J., 177
Wynne, L. C., 244, 245

Yerkes, R. M., 57
Younger, M. S., 248, 250, 256

Zajonc, R. B., 44
Zener, K., 105
Zentall, T., 331
Zimney, G. H., 42
Zoladek, L., 315

Subject Index

Accidental reinforcement, 153–154, 170–171, 188, 192–193, 274–276
Acquired drive, 242–243 (*see also* Fear conditioning)
Acquisition:
  in classical conditioning, 94–103 (*see also* Classical conditioning)
  in instrumental conditioning, 123–124, 171 (*see also* Learning; Shaping)
Activity, 133
Adaptation, *see* Evolution
Adaptation phase, 50
Adjunctive behavior, 188–192
Adventitious reinforcement, *see* Accidental reinforcement
Advertising, 177
Affective after-reaction, 50–53
Afferent neuron, 22
Aggression, 25–26, 30, 163–164, 188–189, 215, 257, 270–271 (*see also* Frustration)
  schedule-induced, 188, 190
Agoraphobia, 83
Alarm response, 44–45
Alcohol, 52–53
  aversion to, 84 (*see also* Aversion learning; Taste aversion)
Amakihi, in research, 314
American Sign Language, 333–336
Amnesia, 319–323

Amphetamine, 52–53, 110
Analgesia, 111
Anesthesia, 320–321
Animals, use of in research, 14–16
Animal behavior, relevance of, to human behavior, 16–17
Animal cognition, *see* Cognition in animal behavior
Animal intelligence, 122, 332
Animal spirits, 9
Anticholinergic drugs, 110
Anticipatory frustration, *see* Frustration, theory of
Anticipatory salivation, *see* Salivary conditioning
Anxiety, 75, 243
Anxiety conservation, 245
Apparatus, types of:
  eyeblink conditioning in rabbits, 59
  key pecking in pigeons, 4
  lever pressing in rats, 127–128
  radial maze, 314
  running wheel, 182, 183, 238
  runway, 123
  salivary conditioning in dogs, 57
  shuttle box, 240
  sign tracking in pigeons, 63
  stabilimeter, 36–37
  T maze, 124
  Wisconsin General Test Apparatus, 133, 134
  + maze, 126

a process, 50–51
Arbitrary operant, 130
Arousal, 23, 40, 180
Associations, 8–9, 11, 68–69, 113, 122–123, 176, 203, 324–325 (*see also* S-R learning; S-S learning)
  of CS and US, 68
  and learning to learn, 133–134
  mechanisms of, 94–103
  of stimulus and response, 122–127
Associative strength, 94, 102–103, 113
  in inhibition, 102–103
  measurement of, 99
  and Rescorla/Wagner model, 99–103
Asympote, 94, 98, 102–103
Attention, *see* Selective attention
Autism, 97, 272
Autoshaping, *see* Sign tracking
Aversion learning, 84, 91–93, 103 (*see also* Avoidance behavior; Taste-aversion learning)
Aversion therapy, 84
Aversive control, *see* Avoidance; Escape; Punishment
Aversive stimulus, 117, 119, 120, 135, 237, 259, 277 (*see also* Negative reinforcer)
Avoidance behavior, 120, 215, 222, 223, 237–258, 259, 288–291, 300, 320, 322

Avoidance behavior (*continued*)
  and acquired-drive
    experiments, 242–243
  asymptotic level of, 245
  and classical conditioning,
    238–239, 241, 242
  and concurrent measurement
    of fear, 243–245
  conditioned-inhibition
    reinforcement of, 254–256,
    258
  contingency, 241
  and discriminated avoidance
    procedures, 239–251, 256
  experimental analysis of,
    242–253
  extinction of, 239, 241,
    245–248
  history of, 238–240
  and nondiscriminated
    avoidance procedures,
    250–255
  positive reinforcement of,
    253–256, 258
  and punishment, 250,
    256–258
  relaxation theory of, 254, 258
  safety-signal theory of,
    254–255
  and shock-frequency
    reduction, 255–256, 258
  and species-specific defense
    reactions, 256–258
  two-process theory of,
    241–255, 258, 267
Avoidance theory of
    punishment, 267–268
Avoidance trial, 239–240

Background stimuli, *see*
    Contextual cues
Backward conditioning, 66–71
Bar pressing, *see* Lever pressing
Behavioral approach, history of,
    6–12
Behavioral baseline, 130–131
  and multiple-response
    measures, 188–193
  and response probability,
    182–186
Behavioral contrast, 294–296
Behavioral drift, 172
Behavioral psychology, 3–12,
    17–20, 303
Behavioral unit, 129–130

Behaviorism, 18–21
Belongingness, 137–139,
    191–193 (*see also* CS-US
    relevance)
Bidirectional response systems,
    74–76, 79, 130
Biofeedback, 17
Biological drive or need,
    176–177
Biological strength of CS and
    US, 87–89
Biting, 271
Blocking effect, 95–97, 99–100,
    306–308, 326
Blocking of avoidance
    responding, 245–248
Bloodsucker, in research, 29
Blood sugar, 81
Body cooling, *see* Hypothermia
b process, 50, 51
Brain stimulation, 178–181
Brooding, 26

Caffeine, 53
Cat, in research, 27, 122, 123,
    125, 137
Causality, 172–174
Central emotional state,
    288–293, 298, 300–302
Central nervous system, 9, 180
Chaffinches, in research, 37–38,
    42, 48
Chained schedule of
    reinforcement, 231–235 (*see
    also* Concurrent chained
    schedules)
Chains of responses, *see*
    Response chains
Change-over delay, 154
Chemotherapy, 65
Chickens, 114, 217, 218
Childbirth, 89
Children, 23–25, 35–36, 81–82,
    97, 118–120, 133, 137, 140,
    196–197, 204, 227, 228,
    234, 265, 271, 304, 334, 336
  in research, 174, 182, 259,
    264, 269
Chimpanzee, in research, 330,
    332–336
Choice behavior, 124, 126,
    152–163, 217–221, 231,
    263–264, 310–319
Choice link of concurrent-
    chained schedule, 160, 162

Cichlid, in research, 29, 257
Circular explanation, 3, 175,
    177
Citric acid, 141
Clasping reflex, 23
Classical conditioning, 55–115
    (*see also* Inhibitory
    conditioning; Interaction
    between classical and
    instrumental conditioning)
  and avoidance learning, 238,
    239, 241, 242
  basic paradigm of, 58
  cognitive aspects of, 305–308
  control procedures for, 68–69
  excitatory conditioning
    procedures, 65–68
  experimental situations,
    59–65
  extinction of, 77–80
  history of, 56–58
  inhibitory, 71–77
  laboratory examples of, 59–65
  and learning, 55–56
  mechanisms of, 86–115
  nonlaboratory examples of,
    80–84
  and psychotherapy, 83–84
  and rehearsal theory, 325–326
  role of instrumental
    reinforcement in, 274–278
  and signal relations, 69–71
  and stimulus control of
    instrumental behavior, 197,
    202–203
Cocoon spinning, 27–28
COD, 154
Cognition, 4, 5, 180, 303, 304
Cognition in animal behavior,
    303–336
  and classical conditioning,
    305–308
  concept formation in animals,
    330–332
  definition of, 304
  interrelations of learning and
    memory, 323–326
  and memory mechanisms,
    308–323
  serial-pattern learning,
    326–330
  teaching language to
    chimpanzees, 332–336
Compensatory-response model,
    109–111, 112–113

Complex behavior, as elicited behavior, 31–33
Compound stimulus, 77–79, 221–227 (*see also* Selective attention)
Concept formation in animals, 330–332
Concurrent chained schedules, 159–163, 268
Concurrent measurement of instrumental and classically conditioned responses, 243–245, 284–288, 302
Concurrent schedules, 152–159 (*see also* Concurrent chained schedules)
Conditioned emotional response, *see* Conditioned suppression
Conditioned emotional-response theory of punishment, 266–267
Conditioned excitation, *see* Excitation
Conditioned inhibition, *see* Inhibitory conditioning
Conditioned reinforcer, 145 (*see also* Secondary reinforcer)
Conditioned response:
  compensatory response model of, 109–111
  definition of, 58
  as a function of the CS, 111–113
  as a function of the US, 104–108, 112–113
  as indicator of associations, 113–114
  as interaction of conditioned and innate processes, 114–115
  measurement of, 66–67
  preparatory response model of, 108–109
  stimulus substitution model of, 104–108
Conditioned salivation, *see* Salivary conditioning
Conditioned stimulus:
  definition of, 58
  and form of the conditioned response, 111–113
  identification of, 86–89
  intensity of, 90
  in magazine training, 128
  novelty of, 89–90

Conditioned stimulus (*continued*)
  preexposure or familiarity, 90, 111, 325–326
  relevance to US, 90–94
  signal relations to US, 69–71
  similarity to US, 93–94
  and stimulus control of instrumental behavior, 197, 202–203
Conditioned suppression, 60–62, 76–77, 95, 106–107, 131, 244, 266–267, 289, 291 (*see also* Fear conditioning)
  and behavioral-baseline technique, 130–131
  and blocking effect, 95–97
  and US devaluation, 106–107
Conditioning, *see* Avoidance; Classical conditioning; Counterconditioning; Escape; Higher-order conditioning; Instrumental behavior; Learning; Punishment; Second-order conditioning; Sensory preconditioning
Conditioning trial, 65, 94
Conflict, 125, 259, 263, 282
Consciousness, 303–304
Conservation hypothesis of reinforcement, 187–188
Consolidation, *see* Memory consolidation
Constraints on learning, 21, 90–94, 137–140, 191–193, 222–225, 256–258
Consummatory responses, 168–169, 177, 179–181
Contextual cues, 73–74, 102–103, 196, 210, 325–326
Contiguity, spatial, 174
Contiguity, temporal, 8
  and causality perception, 173–174
  response-reinforcer, 169–174
  stimulus-response, 125, 203
Contingency:
  in avoidance conditioning, 241
  in classical conditioning, 70–71, 80
  in instrumental conditioning, 117–121, 172, 186, 190, 192, 193, 202, 206–261
  positive, 70, 118–119, 121

Continuous reinforcement, 145–146, 164–169, 282–283
Contrapreparedness, 140
Control procedures:
  omission control, 274–277
  random control, 68–69, 76
Coolidge effect, 47
Cord or chain pulling, 232–234, 296–297
Correlation between response and reinforcer, 169–172 (*see also* Contingency, in instrumental conditioning)
Counterconditioning, 84, 88–89
Courtship, 25–26, 30–33
CR, *see* Conditioned response
Crane, whooping, 31
Crop milk, 31
CS, *see* Conditioned stimulus
CS-preexposure effect, 90, 111, 325, 326
CS-saturation hypothesis, 94–95
CS termination and avoidance behavior, 243, 248–250
CS-US interval, 64–68
CS-US relevance, 90–94, 137
CS-US similarity, 93–94
Cue-consequence specificity, *see* CS-US relevance
Cumulative recorder, 128, 129
Curiosity, 177

Delayed conditioning, 66–69
Delayed matching to sample, 310–313, 317–319
Depression, 53, 136
Deprivation, 126, 132, 133, 169, 176, 181–183, 185
  and motivation, 132
  of reinforcing response, 186–188
Deprivation hypothesis, 186–188
Desensitization, *see* Systematic desensitization
Determinism, 18–20
Dieting, 161–163
Differential inhibition, 73
Differential reinforcement, 120, 152, 284 (*see also* Stimulus discrimination)
Differential responding, *see* Stimulus control of instrumental behavior; Stimulus discrimination
Digestion, 56–57, 65, 80–81

Dinitrophenol, 109
Disappointment, 289, 290
Discrimination, *see* Stimulus control; stimulus discrimination
Discriminated avoidance, 239–251, 255–256
Discrimination hypothesis, 165
Discriminative punishment, 264–265, 270
Discriminative stimulus, 206, 210–211, 227–228, 232, 234, 254, 298–299, 300–302, 329–330 (*see also* S+; S−; Stimulus discrimination)
in punishment, 264–265, 270
Dishabituation, 48, 78
Disinhibition, 78–79, 80
Dogs, in research, 23, 49–51, 57–58, 135, 204, 223–224, 245, 274–275, 284–287, 300, 309–310
Dolphins, in research, 311
Domestication, 15–16
Doves, in research, 30–31
DRH, 152
Drinking, 43–44, 64–65, 91–92, 109, 177–190 passim, 266, 269
Drive induction, 180
Drive reduction, 126, 176–181
Drive state, 176–180
DRL, 152
DRO, 120
Drug addiction, 52–53
Drug tolerance:
classical-conditioning theory of, 109–111
opponent-process theory of, 53
Dualism, 6–7
Dual process theory of habituation, 40–42, 47
Ducks, in research, 205

Earthworms, 29
Eating, 177–186, 190, 192, 226–227
Economic theory, 189–191, 269–270
ECS, *see* Electroconvulsive shock
Efferent neuron, 22
Electroconvulsive shock, 319–323
Elicited behavior (*see also* Conditioned response;

Elicited behavior (*continued*)
Reflexive behavior; Unconditioned response):
and complex response sequences, 31–33
and eliciting stimuli, 25–27
and internal states, 30–31
role of feedback stimuli, 27–30
Eliciting stimulus, 25–29 (*see also* Conditioned stimulus; Unconditioned stimulus)
Emitted behavior, 121
Emotional behavior, 5, 16, 49–53, 82–83, 188, 267 (*see also* Aggression; Conditioned suppression; Fear; Fear conditioning; Frustration)
Emotional state, *see* Central emotional state
Empiricism, 7, 8, 11
Epinephrine, 109
Errorless discrimination training, 214–216
Escape, 44–45, 119–125, 135–138, 215, 240, 242, 248–250, 268, 270–271 (*see also* Negative reinforcement)
Escape trial, 240
Estrogen, 31
Evolution, 10–11, 14, 138, 140, 178, 193, 223
Evolutionary model of behavior, 192–193
Excitation:
in classical conditioning, 59–68, 341
in inhibitory conditioning procedures, 72–74
in instrumental conditioning, 212–214, 216, 218
in tests of inhibitory conditioning, 75–77
Excitatory stimulus-generalization gradient, 212–221 (*see also* Stimulus-generalization gradient)
Expectancy, 103, 113, 114, 126–127, 165–166, 279, 280, 282, 284
Expectation, 98
Explanation, circular, 3, 175, 177
Extension reflex, 23
Exteroceptive stimulus, 341
Extinction, as test of secondary reinforcement, 228–229

Extinction of avoidance behavior, 239, 241, 245–248
Extinction of classical conditioning, 77–80
and avoidance behavior, 239, 241, 245, 247
interpretations of, 79–80
relation to habituation, 78–79
Extinction of the fractional anticipatory goal response, 280–281
Extinction of instrumental conditioning, 163–167, 170, 171, 272, 282, 283, 329
definition of, 163
determinants of, 164–165
effects of, 163–164
and positive behavioral contrast, 294–296
theories of, 165–167
Extinction of long-term habituation, 325
Extinction trial, 322–323
Eyeblink conditioning, 60, 62, 64, 76–77, 103, 105, 326

Fading procedures, 214–215
Fatigue, 13, 39–40, 53
Fear, 60, 75, 82–84, 125, 242–248, 255, 267, 289–290, 300–301
Fear conditioning, 60–62, 64, 67–68, 76–77, 88, 103, 107–108, 241, 253, 257 (*see also* Conditioned suppression)
Fear reduction, 241–253
Feedback function, 158–159, 169, 187
Feedback stimulus, 27–30, 228, 231, 254–258, 279–282
FI, *see* Fixed-interval schedule of reinforcement
Finger-withdrawal response, 238
Fish, 29
Fixed action pattern, 27–28, 30
Fixed-interval scallop, 148–149, 230, 233, 263, 284–285
Fixed-interval schedules, 146–151, 170–171, 190–191, 207, 229–230, 262–263, 284–286
Fixed-ratio schedules, 146–147, 150, 160, 162, 186, 229–233, 262–263, 286–287

Fixed-time schedules, 169–172
Flatworms, 28
Flexion reflex, 23
Flight, 257
Flooding, 246–247, 254
Food-aversion learning, 65, 92, 107 (*see also* Taste-aversion learning)
Food selection, 43–44, 65, 92
Foraging, 314
Forgetting, 78, 313
FR, *see* Fixed-ratio schedules
Fractional anticipatory frustration response, 282–283
Fractional anticipatory goal response, 279, 280 (*see also* r_g-s_g mechanism)
Free-operant avoidance, *see* Nondiscriminated avoidance
Free-operant baseline, 130–132
Free will, 18–20, 304
Freezing, 61, 257–258, 266–267
Frustration, 63, 163–164, 282–283
    theory of, 165–167, 281–284
Frustrative aggression, 163–164

Galvanic skin response, 42
Generalization, *see* Stimulus generalization
Goal box, 123–127
Goal-directed behavior, 5, 117 (*see also* Instrumental behavior)
Goldfish, 311
Goose, greylag, in research, 29–30
Gorilla, 334
Grammar, 335–336
Grasshopper, 28
Grief reaction, 52
Group-statistical approach, 131
GSR, *see* Galvanic skin response
Guinea pigs, in research, 238–239, 266

Habit strength, 126
Habituation, 35–54
    adaptiveness of, 38–39
    of alarm and escape in birds, 44–45
    and classical conditioning, 90
    comparison to extinction, 78–79

Habituation (*continued*)
    dual-process theory of, 39–42
    of ingestional neophobia, 43–44
    and memory mechanisms, 323–326
    of mobbing, 37–38
    of the orienting response, 42–43
    process, 40–42
    and punishment effects, 260, 270
    rehearsal theory of, 323–325
    response-comparator model of, 43
    of the startle response, 36–37
    stimulus frequency effects on, 48–49
    stimulus intensity effects on, 48–49
    stimulus specificity of, 47–48
    of the sucking reflex, 35–36
    time course of, 45–47, 325, 326
    and US representation, 107, 307
Hamster, in research, 30
Head-turning reflex, 23–24
Heart rate, 74
Heat response, 114
Hedonism, 8, 11, 342
Helplessness, *see* Learned helplessness
Heroin, 52–53, 111
Herring gull, in research, 25, 26
Higher-order conditioning, 87–88, 93, 107–108, 306–308
Homeostasis:
    behavioral, 181–191, 269–270
    biological, 176–177, 181
Honeycreeper, in research, 314
Hope, 289–290, 300–301
Hormones, and behavior, 30–31
Human development, 137
Humans, in research, 136–137, 152, 156, 174, 190, 238, 263–264, 271, 326
Hunger, 126–127, 132, 177
Hypothermia, 320–321, 323
Hypothetical construct, 287
Hysterical blindness, 152

Image, *see* Representation

Incentive motivation, 177–178, 180
Incubation, 26, 31
Individual-subject approach, 131
Infants, human, *see* Children
Ingestional aversion, 94
Ingestional neophobia, 43–44
Inhibition, 9, 13, 267
Inhibition of delay, 68
Inhibitory conditioning, 68, 71–77, 326
    and extinction, 79
    of fear, 75, 254–258
    and reinforcement of avoidance, 254–258
    procedures, 72–74
    Rescorla/Wagner model of, 102–103
    and stimulus control, 212–218
Inhibitory stimulus-generalization gradient, 212–214, 218–221
Innate behavior, 21–34
    interactions with learning, 21, 114–115, 138–140, 191–193, 256–258
Instinctive drift, 138, 191, 193
Instrumental behavior (*see also* Avoidance; Escape; Interactions between classical and instrumental conditioning; Punishment)
    cognitive aspects of, 135–137, 218, 220–221, 305
    compared to classically conditioned behavior, 116, 121
    and consequences, 121–122
    definition of, 116
    as a determinant of stimulus control, 223–225
    foundations of, 116–142
    importance of, 116–117
    measurement of, 123–124, 127–129
    reinforcement of, 168–194
    and schedules of reinforcement, 143–167
    secondary reinforcement of, 227–235
    stimulus control of, 195–227
    and the study of learning, 123–127
Instrumental conditioning, *see* Instrumental behavior

Instrumental contingency,
117–120
Instrument response, *see*
Instrumental behavior
Insulin, 81, 110
Interaction between classical and
instrumental conditioning,
273–302
behavioral contrast, 294–296
concurrent measurement,
284–288, 302
discriminative-stimulus
properties of classically
conditioned states, 297–302
modern two-process theory,
287–291, 302
response interactions,
292–297, 302
r_g-s_g mechanism, 278–284,
286–288, 302
role of instrumental
reinforcement in classical
conditioning, 274–278
Interim response, 192–193
Intermediate choice problem,
220–221
Intermittent reinforcement
schedule, (*see* Partial
reinforcement)
Internal states, 30–31
International Crane Foundation,
31
Interneuron, 22
Interresponse time, 152
Interstimulus interval, *see* CS-US
interval
Intertrial interval, 66
Interval schedules,
147–151, 159, 172 (*see also*
Concurrent schedule)
Intercranial self-stimulation,
178–181
Intradimensinal discrimination
training, 216–221
Introspection, 2
Involuntary behavior, 6–7
Irradiation of excitation,
201–202
IRT, 152

Jumping, 119

Kinesis, 28–29
King Lear, 173
Knee-jerk reflex, 27

Lamaze method, 89
Lamprey, in research, 28–29
Language, 138, 140, 330,
332–336
Lashley-Wade hypothesis, 202,
205
Latency, 67, 124
Latent inhibition, 90, 111,
325–326
Law of effect, 122–123, 125,
159, 203 (*see also* Negative
law of effect)
Learned helplessness, 134–137,
172–173, 305
Learning, 12–14 (*see also*
Classical conditioning;
Instrumental behavior; S-R
learning; S-S learning)
curve, 94–95
definition of, 12
of language, 332–336
to learn, 133–134
and memory, 309, 323–326
and other processes, 13–14
and performance, 13, 113,
127, 144
serial pattern, 326–330
set, 134
theories of, 123–127
Leg flexion, 46
Lever pressing, 61–62, 75,
118–120, 127–133, 137, 141,
146–147, 153, 175, 178,
181–185, 188, 195, 210,
227–228, 232–234, 240,
243–244, 251–256 passim,
260–269 passim, 284–291
passim, 296
Licking, 284–285
Limbic system, 178–180
Limited hold, 149–150
Lithium, 109
Locust, 29
Long-delayed conditioning,
66–69
Long-delayed taste-aversion
learning, 64–65
Long-term memory, 310, 321,
324
Love and attachment, 51–52

Magazine training, 128
Matching law, 154–159
Maturation, 13
Maximizing, 157–159, 189–190

Memory, 166, 304, 308–323,
329–330, 335–336,
consolidation, 320–321
definition of, 309, 344
disruption and facilitation of,
317–323
interrelations with learning,
309, 323–326
long-term, 310
reactivation, 321–323
retrieval, 321, 324
short-term, 309–317
spatial, 314–317
stimulus control of, 313
Mental retardation, 235
Mere-exposure effect, 44
Milk-letdown reflex, 81–82
Mind, 6–9
Mobbing, 37–38, 42, 48, 257
Modern two-process theory,
287–291, 302
Momentary probability of
response, 185–186
Monkeys, in research, 133–134,
188, 271, 311, 313, 317,
330–336
Monotonic sequence, 327–330
Morphine, 111
Motivation, 2, 3, 5, 132–133,
176–181, 185, 280–281,
284, 288–290, 298
opponent-process theory of,
49–53
Motivational state, 267
Motor nerve, 9
Motor neuron, 22
Musical training, 139

Nativism, 7, 11
Natural selection, 10
Nausea, 84
Necessity, 174
Negative contingency, 71, 73–74,
79, 119–121
Negative law of effect, 268–270
Negative punishment, *see*
Punishment
Negative reinforcement,
118–121, 140, 241, 243, 245,
248, 253, 255, 257, 268,
289–291
Negative sign tracking, 292, 297
Neophobia, 43–44
Nest building, 30, 32
Neural conduction, 9

Neuron, 22
Nicotine, 52, 53
Nictitating-membrane response, 277
Nobel prize, 20, 56
Nondiscriminated avoidance, 250–255, 300–301
Nonlinguistic behavior, 16
Nonmonotonic sequence, 327–330
Nonsense syllable, 8
Novelty, 43–45, 79–80, 89–90, 325–326 (*see also* Surprise)
Nursing, 24–25 (*see also* Sucking)

Obesity, 178, 226–227
Obsessive-compulsive behavior, 243, 248
Odor trails, 315
Omission control procedure, 274–277
Omission training, 120
One-way avoidance procedure, 241, 246, 322
Operant, 129–130
Operant behavior, 127–131, 144 (*see also* Instrumental behavior)
Operant level, 130–131
Opiates, 52–53, 111
Opponent-process theory of motivation, 49–54, 254
Orienting response, 42–43
Overcorrection, 259
Overshadowing, 225–226

Pairing hypothesis of stimulus control, 202–203, 211
Parental behavior, 23–25
Partial reinforcement, 145–167, 188, 193, 210–211, 282–283 (*see also* Frustration theory; Sequential theory)
    extinction effect of, 164–167, 281–283
Pattern learning, *see* Serial pattern learning
Peak-shift effect, 215–219
Pecking, 4, 62–63, 105, 109, 114, 130, 137, 150–155 passim, 160–163, 169–172, 191–193, 197–200, 205, 208–217 passim, 225, 229–231, 262, 265, 292–296, 310–312, 330
Performance, 13, 99, 113, 127, 144

Phobias, 83–84, 125, 243, 248
Phototaxis, 29
Phylogeny, 179
Pigeons, in research, 4, 62–63, 75, 93, 105, 109, 130, 150–155 passim, 159–163 passim, 169–172, 188, 191, 193, 197–202, 208–217 passim, 222, 225, 229–231, 262, 265, 275–276, 292–296, 310–312, 318, 330–332
Pigs, in research, 138
Pineal gland, 6, 7, 9
Pituitary gland, 31
Poisoning, 65, 107, 307
Positive behavioral contrast, 294–296
Positive contingency, 70, 118–119, 121
Positive punishment, *see* Punishment
Positive reinforcement, 117–121, 197, 258, 275, 280–281, 284, 289–290 (*see also* Reinforcement)
    of avoidance behavior, 253–256, 258
Postreinforcement pause, 147, 149, 263
Praise, 144
PRE, *see* Partial reinforcement, extinction effect of
Predator, 62, 237
Predictability, 69–71, 75
Predictive value, 69–71, 103, 210–212 (*see also* Blocking; Contingency, Redundancy; Surprise)
Preexposure effects, *see* CS-preexposure effect; US-preexposure effect
Pregnancy, 174
Premack principle, 181
Premack's theory of punishment, 268–270
Premack's theory of reinforcement, 181–186
Preparatory-response model, 108–109, 112–113
Preparedness, 138–140, 191
PRF, *see* Partial reinforcement
Primary motivation, 177–178
Primary process, 50–53
Priming, 324–326
Proactive interference, 317–319

Probability of response, 130, 182–186
Procrastination, 149
Programmed instruction, 215
Prolactin, 31
Proprioceptive stimuli, 27, 145, 254, 256, 267
Psychic secretion, 58
Psychoactive drugs, 52–53
Psychosomatic illness, 75
Psychotherapy, 17, 83–84
Psychotic behavior, 190
Punishment, 119, 121, 256, 257, 259–272
    applications of, 264–265, 270–272
    and availability of alternate responses, 263–264
    in avoidance conditioning, 256–258
    delay of, 261, 270
    discriminative stimulus for, 264–266
    intensity of, 260
    negative, 118–121, 259, 274–277
    positive, 118–121
    response-contingent vs. response-independent, 260–261, 267
    and response reallocation, 266
    schedules of, 261–263
    side effects of, 270–271
    as signal for positive reinforcement, 265–266
    theories of, 266–270
Puzzle box, 122, 123, 125, 137, 138

Quail, 44, 94

Rabbits, in research, 59–60, 277, 326
Raccoons, in research, 138, 309–310
Radial maze, 314–316
Radiation exposure, 64, 91–92
Random control procedure, 68–69, 76
Ratio run, 147, 149, 263
Ratio schedules, 146–147, 150–151, 158–159, 172 (*see also* Continuous reinforcement; Fixed-ratio schedules; Variable ratio schedules)

Ratio strain, 147
Rats, in research, 36–37, 43–44, 60–62, 75–77, 91–95, 112–113, 118–133 passim, 140–147 passim, 175, 177–182, 185, 188, 195, 210, 232–233, 240, 242–243, 246, 251–257 passim, 260, 264–269 passim, 280, 284, 291, 296–297, 309, 316, 326–329
Reactivation, *see* Remainder treatments
Reallocation of behavior, 186–191, 266, 270
Rearing, 258
Redundancy, stimulus, 96–97
Reflex, 6, 9–10, 22–25
Reflex arc, 9, 22, 40
Reflexive behavior, 5, 11, 23–25 (*see also* Conditioned response; Eyeblink conditioning; Unconditioned response)
Regurgitation, 25, 31
Rehearsal, 324–326
Reinforcement, 119–121, 124–126, 130, 132, 168–194, 274 (*see also* Negative reinforcement; Positive reinforcement; Schedules of reinforcement; Secondary reinforcement)
and behavioral homeostasis, 181–191
and biological motivation, 176–181
and brain stimulation, 178–181
in classical conditioning, 274–278
delay of, 144–145, 157, 161, 162, 169, 228
and the deprivation hypothesis, 186
multiple-response approaches to, 188–193
multiple schedules of, 206–208, 294–296
Premack's theory of, 181–186
quality and quantity of, 140–141, 157, 161, 162, 327
rate of, 154
and response probability, 184–185

Reinforcement (*continued*)
and response selection, 191–193
theories and experimental analysis of, 168–194
and time reallocation, 187–191
type of, and stimulus control, 222–223
value of, 157
Reinstatement, *see* Reminder treatments
Relational learning, 218, 220–221, 305
Relative rate of reinforcement, 154–155, 159
Relative rate of response, 154–157
Relaxation, 84, 89
Relaxation theory of avoidance, 254, 258
Releasing stimulus, 25–26
Relevance, *see* Belongingness; Stimulus relevance
Relief, 289, 290
Reminder treatments, 321–323
Representation, 304–309, 336
definition of, 304
of first-order conditioned stimulus, 107–108
of the unconditioned stimulus, 106–107, 307–308
Reproductive behavior, 30–33
Rescorla/Wagner model, 97–103
Respiration, 74
Respiratory-occlusion reflex, 24–25
Response blocking, 245–248
Response chains, 31–33, 315–316 (*see also* Chained schedule of reinforcement)
Response choice, *see* Choice behavior
Response-comparator model, 43
Response feedback stimulus, *see* Feedback stimulus
Response-independent schedule of punishment, 260–261
Response-independent schedule of reinforcement, 169–171, 186, 189, 191–193
Response probability, *see* Probability of response
Response rate, 112, 130, 151–152

Response reallocation, *see* Reallocation of behavior; Time allocation
Response/reinforcer contingency, 121, 172, 186, 190–193, 202, 260–261
Response selection, 193
Response value, 184–187, 268–270
Retardation-of-acquisition test, 76–77, 79
Retrieval, 321, 324
Retroactive interference, 317–319
Retrograde amnesia, 319–321
r_f, *see* Frustration theory
r_g-s_g mechanism, 278–284, 286–288, 302
and frustration theory, 281–284
and positive reinforcement, 278–281
Ring dove, in research, 30–31
Rotational stimulation, 107
R-S interval, 251–253
Running, 119, 126, 175, 182–183, 188, 281–283, 327–330 (*see also* Running wheel; Runway)
speed, 123–124
time, 123–124
Running wheel, 182–183, 188, 238, 249–250, 256–258, 266, 269
Runway, 119, 123, 126–127, 130, 175, 281–283, 327

S+, 205–227 passim, 280–281, 298–302, 329
S^D, 205
S−, 205–224 passim, 329
S^Δ, 205
Saccharin, 43–44, 64, 81, 87, 141, 177, 180
Safe compartment, 241, 246
Safety-signal hypothesis, 75
Safety-signal theory of avoidance, 254–258
Salience, 99, 203, 231
Salivary conditioning, 56–58, 62, 64, 68, 87, 103, 105, 109, 274–275, 284–287, 306, 309
Satiation, 107, 132, 179
Scallop, *see* Fixed-interval scallop
Schedule-induced adjunctive behavior, 188–192

Schedule-induced aggression, 188–190
Schedule-induced polydipsia, 188, 190
Schedules of punishment, 261–263
Schedules of reinforcement, 143–169, 348
  and central emotional states, 289–290
  chained, 231–235
  concurrent, 152–159
  concurrent chained, 159–163
  definition of, 143
  extinction, 163–167
  multiple, 229–231
  and punishment, 263
  response-rate, 151–152
  second-order, 229–231
  simple, 145–151, 156–157
Scratching, 137–138
Secondary reinforcement, 145, 169, 196, 227–235
  application in token economies, 235
  and chained schedules, 231–235
  extinction, test of, 228–229
  functions of, 227–228, 232
  and second-order schedules, 229–231
Second-order conditioning, 88, 93, 107–108, 306–308
Second-order schedule of reinforcement, 229–231
Selective attention, 95–100, 210–212, 221–226
Self-control, 149, 161–163, 226–227
Self-injurious behavior, 272
Self-stimulation, *see* Intracranial self-stimulation
Sensitization, 34–54, 80
  adaptiveness of, 38–39
  of ingestional neophobia, 44
  mechanisms of, 40–42
  of mobbing, 37–38
  process, 40–42
  of the startle response, 36–37
  stimulus-frequency effects on, 48–49
  stimulus-intensity effects on, 48–49
  stimulus-specificity of, 47–48
  of the sucking reflex, 35–36
  time course of, 45

Sensory adaptation, 39–40
Sensory nerve, 9
Sensory neuron, 22
Sensory preconditioning, 88
Septal area, 178
Sequential theory, 166–167, 329–330
Serial-pattern learning, 326–330
Sexual-aversion conditioning, 89
Sexual behavior, 9, 47, 82, 132, 174, 177, 179, 184–185 (*see also* Reproductive behavior)
s_f, *see* Frustration theory
s_g, *see* r_g-s_g mechanism
Shaping, 128, 133, 144
Shock compartment, 241
Shock-frequency reduction, 255–256, 258
Shoelace tying, 234
Short-delayed conditioning, 66–69, 80
Short-term memory, 309–317, 320, 323–326
Shuttle avoidance, 240
Shuttle box, 240
Shuttle response, 240, 244, 247, 249, 250, 254, 292, 298–301
Sickness, 64–65, 75, 81, 91–92, 107
Sidman avoidance, *see* Nondiscriminated avoidance
Signal detection, 156
Signaled avoidance, *see* Discriminated avoidance
Signal relations, 69–72, 86, 231
Signal value in instrumental conditioning, *see* Secondary reinforcement; Stimulus control of instrumental behavior
Sign language, *see* American Sign Language
Sign learning, 126–127
Sign stimulus, 25–27
Sign tracking, 62–64, 68, 75, 82, 87, 108–109, 191–193, 275–276, 292–297
Simple schedules of reinforcement, 145–151, 156–157, 164
Simultaneous conditioning, 66–69
Simultaneous matching to sample, 311
Situational cues, *see* Contextual cues

Skinner box, 127–131, 144, 153, 163–164, 175, 197, 210, 227, 240
Skydiving, 52
Sloth, in research, 23
Snail, in research, 29
Sniffing, 130
Social responsibility, 19–20
SOP model, 326
Soul, 7
Spatial memory, 313–317
Species-specific defense reactions, 61, 256–258
Spence's theory of discrimination learning, 212–214, 218–221
Spider, in research, 27–28
Spontaneous recovery, 46, 78, 163, 325
S-R learning, 122–127, 133–134, 203, 305, 308
S-R system, 40–42
S-R theories of reinforcement, 124–127
S-S interval, 251
S-S learning, 106–108, 113–114, 305–308
SSDR, *see* Species-specific defense reactions
Stabilimeter, 36–37
Standard pattern of affective dynamics, 49–51
Start box, 123–127
Startle response, 36–37, 41–42, 45–48
State system, 40–42
Stickleback, 25–26, 32–33
Stimulus:
  compound, 77, 79, 221–226
  intensity of, 10, 90–91, 225, 259–260, 270, 276
  salience, 99, 203, 231
Stimulus belongingness, *see* Stimulus relevance
Stimulus control of instrumental behavior, 195–227, 264–265, 282 (*see also* Chained schedules; Multiple schedules; Stimulus discrimination; Stimulus generalization)
  applications to self-control, 226–227
  control by component stimuli, 221–226
  effects of past experience on, 205–212

Stimulus control of instrumental behavior (*continued*)
as a function of the reinforcer, 222–223, 225
as a function of the response, 223–225
measurement of, 198–201
and the pairing hypothesis, 202–203
and the subject's perspective, 203–204
Stimulus control of memory, 313
Stimulus discrimination, 198, 205–226, 280, 294, 298–299, 331
and chained schedules, 231–235
and concept formation, 331
control by component stimuli, 221–226
effects on stimulus control, 208–210
errorless discrimination training, 214–216
intradimensional discrimination training, 216–221
and multiple schedules, 206–208
procedures, 205–208, 214–215
and signal value, 210–212
Spence's theory of, 212–214, 218–221
Stimulus generalization, 47–48, 199–202, 212–214, 218–221, 330
theories of, 201–202
Stimulus-generalization gradient, 200–202, 205, 208–221
as measure of stimulus control, 200–201, 208
Stimulus relevance, 90–93, 222–223
Stimulus-response association, *see* S-R learning
Stimulus-response contiguity, *see* Contiguity, temporal
Stimulus-response theories of learning, 124–127
Stimulus substitution, 104–108, 112–113, 241, 279, 305
Stress, 75
Studying, 226
Submaxillary gland, 57

Successive approximations, 128
Sucking, 23–25, 28, 35–36, 41, 81–82
Sufficiency, 174
Supernormal stimulus, 26–27
Superstition experiment, 169–174, 176, 186, 191–193
Suppression ratio, 61–62, 260
Surprise, 96–103, 313 (*see also* Rehearsal theory)
Swimming, 29, 32–33, 176, 257
Systematic desensitization, 83–84

Tabula rasa, 7
Taste, 43–44, 64–65, 68, 75–76, 81, 84, 87, 91–94, 140, 178, 180
Taste-aversion learning, 64–65, 68, 84, 87, 91–93, 140
Taste preference, 75
Taxis, 29
Temporal contiguity, *see* Contiguity
Temporal cues, 253, 256
Terminal response, 192, 193
Territoriality, 25–26
Test trials, 67
Thermotaxis, 29
Thigmotaxis, 258
Thinking, *see* Cognition
Thrushes, in research, 26
Time allocation, 184, 186–191, 266
Time out, 259
T-maze, 124, 126–127, 144, 153
Toilet training, 133
Token economy, 235
Tolerance, *see* Drug tolerance
Toxicosis, *see* Poisoning
Trace conditioning, 66–69
Trace-decay hypothesis, 312–313
Trace interval, 66, 68
Transfer-of-control experiments, 290–294, 296–302
Transposition, 218–221
Transsituationality, principle of, 175
Treadle press, 222–223
Trial-and-error learning, 122–123
Turkey, in research, 44
Two-process theory, *see* Modern two-process theory; Two-process theory of avoidance; r_g-s_g mechanism

Two-process theory of avoidance, 241–255, 258, 267

Ulcers, 75
Ultrasound, 203–204
Unconditioned response, 58
Unconditioned stimulus:
definition of, 58
devaluation of, 107–108, 307–308
identification of, 86–89
intensity of, 90
novelty of, 89–90, 325–326
relevance to CS, 90–93
representation of, 106–108, 307–308
similarity to CS, 93–94
surprising, 96–103
Unpreparedness, 140
UR, *see* Unconditioned response
US, *see* Unconditioned stimulus
US escape, 248–250
US-preexposure effect, 89–90, 325–326
US-reduction hypothesis, 95–97

Value, 157, 184–187, 268–270
Variable-interval schedule, 146–160, 172, 188, 197, 232, 233, 244, 260–265, 292–295
Variable-ratio schedules, 147, 150, 151, 172, 207
VI, *see* Variable-interval schedules
Violin playing, 139
Voluntary behavior, 6–8, 10, 121, 303, 304
Vomiting, 84
VR, *see* Variable-ratio schedules

War and Peace, 173
Whooping crane, 31
Win-stay, lose-shift strategy, 134
Wisconsin General Test Apparatus, 133–134
Woodlouse, in research, 28
Working memory, 309–317

X rays, 64–65

Yawning, 137–138
Yoking procedure, 135, 150, 172

Zero contingency, 70–71